T0235957

Lecture Notes of the Institute for Computer Sciences, Social Informatics and Telecommunications Engineering 170

More information about this series at http://www.springer.com/series/8197

Benny Mandler · Johann Marquez-Barja
Miguel Elias Mitre Campista · Dagmar Cagáňová
Hakima Chaouchi · Sherali Zeadally
Mohamad Badra · Stefano Giordano
Maria Fazio · Andrey Somov
Radu-Laurentiu Vieriu (Eds.)

Internet of Things

IoT Infrastructures

Second International Summit, IoT 360° 2015
Rome, Italy, October 27–29, 2015
Revised Selected Papers, Part II

Springer

Editors

Benny Mandler
IBM Research
Haifa, Israel

Johann Marquez-Barja
CONNECT Centre, Trinity College
University of Dublin
Dublin, Ireland

Miguel Elias Mitre Campista
GTA/PEE-COPPE/DEL-Poli
Universidade Federal do Rio de Janeiro
  (UFRJ)
Rio de Janeiro, Brazil

Dagmar Cagáňová
Faculty of Materials Science
  and Technology in Trnava
Slovak University of Technology
  in Bratislava
Trnava, Slovakia

Hakima Chaouchi
Institut Télécom SudParis
Evry, France

Sherali Zeadally
College of Communication and Information
University of Kentucky
Lexington, KY, USA

Mohamad Badra
College of Technological Innovation
Zayed University
Dubai, United Arab Emirates

Stefano Giordano
University of Pisa
Pisa, Holy See (Vatican City State)

Maria Fazio
DICIEAMA Department
University of Messina
Messina, Italy

Andrey Somov
CREATE-NET
Trento, Italy

Radu-Laurentiu Vieriu
University of Trento
Trento, Italy

ISSN 1867-8211 ISSN 1867-822X (electronic)
Lecture Notes of the Institute for Computer Sciences, Social Informatics
and Telecommunications Engineering
ISBN 978-3-319-47074-0 ISBN 978-3-319-47075-7 (eBook)
DOI 10.1007/978-3-319-47075-7

Library of Congress Control Number: 2016954126

Printed on acid-free paper

This Springer imprint is published by Springer Nature
The registered company is Springer International Publishing AG
The registered company address is: Gewerbestrasse 11, 6330 Cham, Switzerland

SaSeIoT 2015

Preface

The Second EAI International Conference on Safety and Security in Internet of Things (SaSeIoT' 2015) was held in Rome, Italy, during October 26–27, 2015, as a collocated event of the IoT 360° Summit 2015.

This international conference attracted submissions from various countries. Each paper went through a rigorous peer-review process, with each submission receiving multiple reviews from the members of the Technical Program Committee. We could only select a few of the highest-quality papers for inclusion in the final program.

The accepted papers, which focus on security and privacy issues, provide great insight into the latest research findings in the area of the Internet of Things. In addition to the technical papers, the workshop program also included two keynote speeches. The first keynote entitled "Contract-Based Design Tailored to Safety Issues for Cyber-physical Systems" was delivered by Dr. Daniela Cancila. The second keynote entitled "Security and Privacy in IoT" was delivered by Dr. Hakima Chaouchi.

We would like to thank all the people who worked hard to make this conference a real success. First and foremost, we thank all authors who submitted their papers for consideration for this conference as well as all Technical Program Committee members for providing rigorous, timely reviews. We would also like to thank the European Alliance for Innovation (EAI) for its sponsorship. Finally, we express our gratitude to Kristina Lukáčová for her continuous administrative support throughout the preparation of this conference.

Hakima Chaouchi
Sherali Zeadally

CYCLONE 2015

Preface

The First EAI International Conference on Cyber Physical Systems, IoT and Sensors Networks (CYCLONE 2015) was held in Rome, Italy, on October 26, 2015, as a collocated event of the IoT 360° Summit 2015.

The conference was an incredible first step on the way to becoming a benchmark in the multidisciplinary fields of CPS, IoT, and sensor networks. The technologies originating from the areas of sensing, networking, control, and processing are enablers for exciting new opportunities for researchers, engineers, and business people to innovate in meaningful ways. And that is who CYCLONE 2015 was created for – the goal was to bring all of these different parties together to share ideas and visions.

It was our great pleasure to host prominent keynote speakers, and authors of all the excellent accepted papers, courtesy of the passionate and dedicated Program Committee members, to whom we would like to extend our warmest thanks. Lastly, this event could not happen without the support of EAI and Kristina Lukáčová, the event manager, who organized CYCLONE 2015 with great effort and expertise; and we wish to extend our sincere gratitude to both.

GOODTECHS 2015

Preface

The GOODTECHS 2015 Conference was the first edition of a conference that aims to become a point of attraction for researchers in the area and it was held in the beautiful city of Rome, a worldwide renowned historical, academic and cultural center. In GOODTECHS we were interested in experiences with the design, implementation, deployment, operation, and evaluation of smart objects and technologies for social good. Clearly, we were not considering only the so-called first world as the scenario for this evolution; we also referred to those areas where ICT is currently less widespread, hoping that it may represent a societal development opportunity rather than a source for further divide.

It was our honor to have prominent international scholars as speakers. The conference program included technical papers selected through peer reviews by the Technical Program Committee members and keynote speakers who provided even more insight into this area. We would like to thank the EAI for the support and all the members of the conference committees and the reviewers for their dedicated and passionate work. None of this would happen without the support and curiosity of the authors who sent their papers to this first event. Finally, we would like to encourage current and future authors to continue working in this direction and to participate in forums like this conference so as to exchange knowledge and experiences and to make ICT actually helpful to society.

Ombretta Gaggi
Pietro Manzoni
Claudio Palazzi

CN4IoT 2015

Preface

The First International Conference on Cloud, Networking for IoT systems (CN4IoT) was held in Rome, Italy, during October 26–27, 2015, as a collocated event of the IoT 360° Summit 2015.

CN4IoT 2015 was conceived to analyze limits and/or advantages in the exploitation of existing solutions developed for cloud, networking, and IoT, and to foster new, original, and innovative contributions. We strongly believe that it is time to link cloud, networking, and IoTs. Nowadays, ICT researchers are looking to improve networking, for example, to effectively improve the quality of life of citizens in smart city scenarios using IoT devices, and to put everything in place trying to improve the experience of common users. There are masses of users who like to use the cloud but it has to be easy to use and it must have a positive impact on their lives. Before, the cloud was an issue only ICT researchers were concerned with. Today, many people are trying to involve professionals in their activities, such as lawyers, doctors, engineers, and so on. They use services like cloud services, small things, and say, "It's amazing, that we can interact with each other, write in the same document, we can make progress in our work and make the workflow better." The workflow has changed. We realize this, and we try to move forward. It is a challenge but it is also time to change how we think, and we are first in the row.

It was our honor to have invited prominent and valuable ICT worldwide experts as keynote speakers. The conference program comprised technical papers selected through peer reviews by the Technical Program Committee members and invited talks. SDWN 2015 would not have been realized without the help and dedication of our conference manager, Kristina Lukáčová, from the European Alliance for Innovation (EAI). We would like to thank the conference committees and the reviewers for their dedicated and passionate work. None of this would have happened without the support and curiosity of the authors who sent their papers to this first edition of CN4IoT.

HealthyIoT 2015

Preface

The Second EAI International Conference on IoT Technologies for Health Care (HealthyIoT 2015) was held in Rome, Italy, during October 26–27, 2015, as a collocated event of the IoT 360° Summit 2015.

Internet of Things (IoT) devices are becoming more powerful every year, and there is an immense amount of information flowing between them in the cloud. By applying the concept of IoT to the health-care sector, it is possible to collect, store, and analyze physiological data and to provide new medical services for citizens based on a constant monitoring and early detection of dangerous situations. IoT offers greater opportunities in the field of health care, allowing for a wider access, a better quality, and a lower cost of health care.

When combining the power of IoT devices and physiological sensors, as well as cloud technology that enables us to work with data in new exciting ways, we can introduce the concept of pervasive health-care systems that provide new health services for chronically ill patients, for people with specific diseases or disorders, and for individuals switching to a healthier lifestyle. The HealthyIoT 2015 workshop produced valuable insights on how the IoT systems, together with new cloud computing and big data capabilities, can help patients, caregivers, and medical personnel to envisage new, value-added health-care solutions for the future.

We wish to extend our great thanks to all the members of the Program Committee for their rigorous effort, dedication, and critical eye. We would also like to thank all of the contributing authors, whose great passion and expertise have produced deep insight into the applications of IoT for health care. Finally, we would like to thank EAI for their support, and Kristina Lukáčová for managing HealthyIoT 2015 with great skill and enthusiasm.

IoTaaS 2015

Preface

It gives us a great pleasure to welcome you to the proceedings of the Second EAI International Conference on IoT as a Service (IoTaaS 2015) held in the beautiful city of Rome, as a part of IoT360, the international summit on Internet of Things. We plan this event as a melting point for researchers, engineers, and business people to meet and exchange ideas and information. IoTaaS is an international venue for publishing innovative and cutting-edge results on the convergence of next-generation technologies and methodologies reshaping our way of living. This conference focuses on the Internet of Things (IoT) in general and in particular on providing innovative and enabling capabilities "as a service." The cloud serves as the central focal point for consumption and delivery of such technologies and applications.

As we are striding into the era of IoT, a key question is how we make the most of IoT for all stakeholders, including platform providers, IoT application developers, end-users, large and small organizations (such as city councils, enterprises) that wish to provide better service, and manufacturers of smart devices. The amount of smart devices immersed in everyday life, from manufacturing to clothing, is growing every day in terms of power, processing, and network connectivity. The sheer size and variety of contextual data that they produce, along with the actions they can take on their environment, is enormous. It remains to be answered how all this potential will come to bear; the Second International Conference on IoT as a Service (IoTaaS 2015) aimed to contribute to the discussion on the challenges posed by these trends.

The conference program comprised technical papers selected through peer reviews by the Technical Program Committee members, invited talks, industrial presentations, and a demo session. We received many good papers. These papers went through a rigorous review process for the selection of papers for the program. The selected papers cover a wide spectrum of topics related to IoTaaS. We had papers on architectures for the IoT, security and privacy, semantics, and testing. Additionally, we were honored to have two prominent keynote speakers: Gabi Zodik from IBM Research discussing "Future Directions in Mobile, IoT and Wearable Enterprise Computing"; and Alfeo Pareschi from Axiros, discussing "IoT Platforms: Security, Identity Management, Ontologies and Interoperability." Finally we were honored to have an invited talk by Afonso Ferreira from the European Commission, who provided the commission's point of view on IoT research and innovation in the European Commission. We believe that this strong program laid a concrete foundation for this conference for years to come.

We would like to thank the EAI for their initiative and support and all the members of the conference committees and the reviewers for their dedicated and passionate work. None of this could happen without the support and curiosity of the authors who sent their papers to this event.

Benny Mandler
Kostas Magoutis

MobilityIoT 2015

Preface

A wide selection of cutting-edge and insightful research papers were presented at the Second EAI International Conference on Mobility in IoT 2015.

The 2015 conference was an IoT co-located event that took place in Rome, Italy, during October 26–27 2015, forming one of the main conferences within the IoT 360 Summit organized by the European Alliance for Innovation, in Trento, Italy, and the European Alliance for Innovation in Slovakia.

The Mobility in IoT 2015 conference was organized by the Faculty of Materials Science and Technology (MTF STU) in Trnava, Institute of Industrial Engineering and Management, in collaboration with the European Alliance for Innovation in Slovakia, and its partner, the European Alliance for Innovation, in Trento, Italy.

It was a great satisfaction to have the opportunity to welcome and meet individuals from around the world, all of whom share a common interest in the area of mobility in IoT. In particular, the organizers would like to thank the presenters, who showcased their latest research, and the audience members, who added to active discussions and debate regarding the recent developments and the outlook for the future for the field.

The goal of the EAI International Conference on Mobility in IoT 2015 was to provide a platform for the cross-fertilization of ideas and to present cutting-edge innovation and technologies for sustainable solutions to the mobility agenda. The focus of the conference reflected the EU thematic priorities for research and innovation to improve the quality of life of citizens and make cities more sustainable with less impact on the environment. The conference presented participants with a unique opportunity to engage with different stakeholders from across Europe and around the world. In doing so, the conference offered an ideal platform to empower the triple helix of university research, industry, and government, while also providing innovative opportunities focusing on the growth and development of mobility in IoT.

A total of 13 research papers are featured in this publication, with contributions by researchers from across Europe and around the world. The publication includes articles that were written and presented by authors from nine countries, including Poland, the Czech Republic, Serbia, Italy, South Korea, Germany, Colombia, India, and Slovakia.

Among the papers presented at the conference were these presented by the conference keynote speakers, Prof. Milan Dado, the Dean of the Faculty of Electronics, TU Zilina, Slovakia, and a coordinator of the project ERA Chair H2020, who discussed the "Internet of Things as Advanced Technology to Support Mobility and Intelligent

Transport," Jaroslav Holeček, vice-president of the Slovak Automotive Industry Association (ZAP), who discussed the topic of "Innovation as Basic Prerequisite of Competitiveness of Automotive Industry in Slovakia," Prof. George Teodorescu, from the International Institute for Integral Innovation, Köln, Germany who presented the topic of "i-WALK, a Different Approach to Urban Mobility," Prof. Dušan Petráš, of the Slovak University of Technology in Bratislava, Slovakia, former vice-rector of STU and former dean of the Faculty of Civil Engineering, who gave a talk on the topic "Smart Cities — Energy-Efficient and Environmentally Friendly Housing," and Dr. Predrag K. Nikolic, Associate Professor at the Faculty of Digital Production, EDUCONS University, Serbia, and visiting professor at the Bergen Academy of Art and Design, Norway, as well as Shenzhen School of Industrial Design, China, who presented the topic of "Multimodal Interactions: Embedding New Meanings to Known Forms and Objects."

The participants were particularly impressed by the wide range of innovative research solutions presented during the conference. As a result, the papers included here, in our opinion, accurately reflect the diversity of content and rapidly developing nature of the IoT agenda. The research not only illustrates the current state of the art in the field but it also helps to contribute to defining the future thematic areas of debate.

In conclusion, the Scientific Committee members and organizers would like to express their sincere thanks to all the authors and audience members who attended the conference in Rome, Italy, and also the authors, who contributed to the creation of this Mobility in IoT publication.

Dagmar Cagáňová
Jana Šujanová

S-Cube 2015

Preface

This volume contains the proceedings of S-Cube 2015, the 6th International Conference on Sensor Systems and Software. The conference took place in Rome, Italy, during October 26–27, 2015. The aim of the conference was to provide a forum in which researchers and practitioners from academia and industry, as well as the "makers," may work together in order to present and debate the different innovative solutions and applications in sensing systems and associated software.

This year the conference was organized in conjunction with the IoT360 Summit and was focused on the Internet of Things (IoT) paradigm. The reason for choosing this topic is that the IoT has slowly but steadily and increasingly permitted what researchers and engineers study and build. "Sensing systems" and "software" play a crucial role for the emerging world of the IoT.

S-Cube received a total of 28 paper submissions of which ten were selected for full publication and presentation. Apart from full papers, six short papers and four invited contributions are published and were presented during the conference. Paper submissions were received from 14 different countries from all over the world. The selection process involved over 90 reviews with all papers being evaluated by at least three independent reviewers. In addition, the reviews were discussed off-line by the chairs and the Technical Program Committee, prior to making final decisions. The final program covered a wide range of topics, which were grouped into six sessions: Sensors, Experimentation and Prototyping, IoT and Cyber Physical Systems, Software, Self-x and Smart Methods, and Evaluation and Analysis.

The conference program included other elements in addition to the presentation of research papers. Two keynotes were given by Andrew Markham, Lecturer in Software Engineering at the University of Oxford, UK, and Fahim Kawsar, Head of IoT Research at Alcatel Lucent Bell Laboratories, Belgium. Dr. Markham and Dr. Kawsar spoke about "Structural Monitoring" and "Innovative Human Centered IoT Systems," respectively.

We would like to thank all authors for their contributions to this volume and in particular the reviewers for their hard work that significantly helped to improve the initial submissions and made our work easier when selecting the papers. We would like to also thank all the volunteers who shared their talent, dedication, and time for the workshop arrangements and for preparing these proceedings.

Andrey Somov
David Boyle

InterIoT 2015

Preface

It is our real pleasure to welcome you to the proceedings of the First EAI International Conference on Interoperability in IoT held in the amazing city of Rome, Italy. Colocated with the IoT360 summit and taking advantage of its attractiveness, InterIoT 2015 offered an exciting technical program consisting of a keynote speech, invited talks, and technical sessions that presented original and fundamental research advances in all aspects of interoperability of these heterogeneous IoT platforms. Indeed, IoT products are now hitting the market across a large variety of segments. Often driven by the fear of "falling behind", small and large companies push their engineering teams to produce solutions quickly. The result is that the market is highly fragmented: A large number of non-interoperable solutions are being installed, eventually leading to increased costs, inefficiencies, customer frustration, and a rate of adoption of the IoT that is much slower than that touted by analysts. The market is now at a state where we ought to think about interoperability. Interoperability appears to a major and new challenge.

The goal of InterIoT is to bring together practicing engineers and advanced researchers to share information on the state of the art around interoperability in the IoT, analyze what is needed, and identify the work that lies ahead to increase the number of interoperable IoT products.

We received high-quality submissions from all parts of the world. After a rigorous review process, eight regular and invited papers were included in the technical program. The program also featured a keynote addressed by Prof. Carsten Bormann from Universität Bremen, Germany.

We would like to thank the Technical Program Committee chair Dr. Thomas Watteyne, who did a remarkable job in the establishment of the technical program. The conference would not have been possible without his help or that of all the TPC members, publicity chair, and external reviewers, who volunteered their time and professional expertise. We would like to take this opportunity to thank all of them for their help. We would also like to thank all the authors for contributing their quality work, and our sponsors and partners for their support, including CREATE-NET and EAI. We received excellent and support from our sponsors, especially from Kristina Lukáčová who managed the conference organization. Sincere and dedicated thanks to her.

Finally, we hope you enjoy the proceedings.

Nathalie Mitton
Thomas Noel

SDWNCT 2015

Preface

The Second EAI International Conference on Software Defined and Virtualized Future Wireless Networks and Cognitive Technologies (SDWNCT 2015) was held in Rome, Italy, on October 26, 2015, as a collocated event of the IoT 360° Summit 2015. SDWNCT aims to explore new design spaces, new challenges and solutions, as well as new applications and services of software-defined virtualized future mobile and wireless networks. At the same time, it targets enthusiastic researchers and practitioners from AI and IoT-related areas sharing the common goal of addressing the challenges posed by the Cognitive aspect of IoT by using new or leveraging existing Artificial Intelligence techniques. All this to bring to the community original and inspiring research contributions from technology experts, designers, researchers, and architects in academia and industry.

It was our honor to have invited prominent scholars as keynote speakers. The conference program comprised technical papers selected through peer reviews by the Technical Program Committee members, invited talks, special sessions, and a demo session. Putting together a workshop of the scope and caliber of SDWN was a challenging and exciting undertaking. We are very grateful for the contributions of each of the members of the Technical Program Committee in selecting the best out of all outstanding work submitted. SDWNCT 2015 would not have been a reality without the help and dedication of our conference manager, Kristina Lukáčová, from the European Alliance for Innovation (EAI), who worked with us and the Technical Program Committee chairs. As Organizing Committee, we hope you enjoy the procedings of SDWNCT 2015 and the IoT 360° Summit 2015, which includes high-quality and exciting research work in SDN and Cognitive Technologies applied to future services in IoT.

Bruno Astuto
Athanasios V. Vasilakos
Frederik Santens
Radu-Laurențiu Vieriu

SaSeIoT 2015

Organization

Steering Committee

Steering Committee Chair

Imrich Chlamtac   Create-Net, EAI, Italy

Steering Committee Members

Hakima Chaouchi   EIT ICT Labs, Institut Mines Telecom-Telecom Sud
                             Paris, France

Organizing Committee

General Chair

Hakima Chaouchi   EIT ICT Labs, Institut Mines Telecom-Telecom Sud
                             Paris, France

Technical Program Chair

Sherali Zeadally   University of Kentucky, USA

Web Chair

Sandrine Bourger   Telecom Sud Paris, France

Workshop Chairs

Anis Laouiti   Telecom Sud Paris, France
Thomas Bourgeau   UPMC, France

Publicity Chairs

Scott Fowler   Linkoping University, Sweden
Wendong Xiao   University of Science and Technology Beijing, China
Mauro Fonseca   Federal Technological University of Paraná, Brazil

Publication Chair

Mohamad Badra   Zayed University, UAE

Conference Manager

Kristina Lukáčová   European Alliance for Innovation, Slovakia

Technical Program Committee

Sergey Andreev	Tampere University, Finland
Cristina Alcaraz	University of Malaga, Spain
Ioannis Anagnostopoulos	University of Thessaly, Greece
Mohamad Badra	Zayed University, UAE
Zubair Baig	Edith Cowan University, Australia
Zorica Bogdanovic	University of Belgrade, Serbia
Thomas Bourgeau	Paris VI University, France
Patrick Capolsini	University of French Polynesia, Tahiti
Ashok Chandra	Indian Institute of Technology Bombay, India
Naveen Chilamkurti	La Trobe University, Australia
Ernesto Exposito	LAAS-CNRS, University of Toulouse, France
Scott Fowler	Linkoping University, Sweden
Alban Gabillon	University of French Polynesia, Tahiti
Zeynep Gurkas Aydin	Istanbul University, Turkey
Jassim Happa	Oxford University, UK
Debiao He	Wuhan University, China
Leila Ismail	United Arab Emirates University, UAE
Arshad Jhumka	Warwick University, UK
Muhammad Khan	King Saud University, Saudi Arabia
Dong-Seong Kim	University of Canterbury, New Zealand
Anis Laouiti	Telcom Sud Paris, France
Albert Levi	Sabanci University, Turkey
Toktam Mahmoodi	King's College, UK
Gregorio Martinez	University of Murcia, Spain
Hassnaa Moustafa	Intel Corporation, USA
Rajarajan Muttukrishnan	City University, UK
Farid Naït-Abdesselam	Paris Descartes University, France
Jalel Othman	University of Paris 13, France
Lotfi Othmane	Fraunhofer Institute for Secure Information Technology (SIT), Germany
Damith Ranasinghe	University of Adelaide, Australia
Sushmita Ruj	Indian Statistical Institute, India
Giovanni Russello	University of Auckland, New Zealand
Khaled Salah	Khalifa University, UAE
Nishanth Sastry	King's College, UK
Faisal Shaikh	Mehran University of Engineering and Technology, Pakistan

CYCLONE 2015

Organization

Steering Committee

Steering Committee Chair

Imrich Chlamtac | CREATE-NET, Italy

Steering Committee Members

Periklis Chatzimisios | Alexander TEI of Thessaloniki, Greece
Stefano Giordano | University of Pisa, Italy

Organizing Committee

General Co-chairs

Stefano Giordano | University of Pisa, Italy
Periklis Chatzimisios | Alexander TEI of Thessaloniki, Greece

Technical Program Co-chairs

Honggang Wang | UMass Dartmouth, USA
Athanasios C. Iossifides | Alexander TEI of Thessaloniki, Greece
Gennaro Boggia | Politecnico di Barri, Italy

Publicity and Social Media Chairs

Daniele Mazzei | Research Center E. Piaggio, Univerity of Pisa, Italy
Alessio Botta | Università degli Studi di Napoli Federico II, Italy
Syed Zaidi | University of Leeds, UK

Workshops Chair

Kan Zheng | Beijing University of Posts and Telecommunications China

Special Session Chair

Toktam Mahmoodi | King's College London, UK

Sponsorship and Exhibits Chair

Luca Foschini | University of Bologna, Italy

Panels Chair

Giuliano Manara   University of Pisa, Italy

Tutorial Chair

Charalabos Skianis   University of the Aegean, Greece

Demos Chair

Davide Adami   CNIT, Italy

Posters and PhD Track Chair

Christian Callegari   University of Pisa, Italy

Local Chair

Michele Pegano   University of Pisa, Italy
Raffaele Giaffreda   CREATE-NET, Italy

Web Chair

Christos Klisiaris   Alexander TEI of Thessaloniki, Greece

GOODTECHS 2015

Organization

Steering Committee

Steering Committee Chair

Imrich Chlamtac   Create-Net Trento, Italy

General Co-chairs

Ombretta Gaggi   Università degli Studi di Padova, Italy
Pietro Manzoni   Universitat Politècnica de València, Spain
Claudio Palazzi   Università degli Studi di Padova, Italy

Organizing Committee

Technical Program Committee Chair

Armir Bujari   Università degli Studi di Padova, Italy

Workshops Chair

Priscila Solis   University of Brasilia, Brazil

Publications Chair

Johann M. Marquez-Barja   CONNECT, Trinity College Dublin, Ireland

Web Chair

Carlos Calafate   Universitat Politècnica de València, Spain

Publicity and Social Media Chair

Carlos Calafate   Universitat Politècnica de València, Spain

Conference Manager

Kristina Lukáčová   European Alliance for Innovation

Program Committee

Antonella Molinari   Università Mediterranea di Reggio Calabria, Italia
Antonio Jara   HES SO University of Applied Sciences Western
                                    Switzerland

CN4IoT 2015

Organization

Steering Committee

Steering Committee Chair

Imrich Chlamtac   CREATE-NET, Italy

Steering Committee Members

Antonio Celesti   University of Messina, Italy
Burak Kantarci   Clarkson University, NY, USA
Georgiana Copil   TU Vienna, Austria
Schahram Dustdar   TU Vienna, Austria
Alex Galis   UCL, UK
Fahim Kawsar   Bell Labs, Belgium
Prem Prakash Jayaraman   CSIRO, Digital Productivity Flagship, Australia
Rajiv Ranjan   CSIRO, Digital Productivity Flagship, Australia
Massimo Villari   University of Messina, Italy
Joe Weinman   IEEE Intercloud Testbed, Telx, USA

Organizing Committee

General Chairs

Massimo Villari   University of Messina, Italy

Technical Program Committee Chair

Schahram Dustdar   TU Vienna, Austria
Alex Galis   UCL, UK
Fahim Kawsar   Bell Labs, Belgium

Publication Chair

Maria Fazio   University of Messina, Italy

Publicity Chair

Luca Foschini   University of Bologna, Italy

Conference Manager

Kristina Lukáčová   European Alliance for Innovation, Slovakia

Technical Program Committee

Dana Petcu	West University of Timisoara, Romania
Sourav Bhattacharya	Bell Labs
Kaori Fujinami	Tokyo University of Agriculture and Technology, Japan
Takuro Yonezawa	Keio University, Japan
Akhil Mathur	Bell Laboratories, Ireland
Artemis Voulkidis	Synelixis Solutions Ltd., Greece
Roberto Riggio	Create-net, Italy
Kashinath Basu	Oxford Brokes University, UK
Antonio Skarmeta	Universidad de Murcia, Spain
Flavio de Oliveira Silva	Federal University of Uberlandia, Brazil
Rajiv Ranjan	CSIRO, Australia
Antonio Manzalini	Telecom Italia, Italy
Lefteris Mamates	University of Macedonia, Macedonia
Jaime Lloret	Universidad Politecnica de Valencia, Spain
Slawomir Kuklinski	Orange Labs, Poland
Imen Grida Ban Yahia	Orange Labs, France
Stefano Giordano	Università di Pisa, Italy
Gabi Dreo Rodosek	Universität der Bundeswehr München, Germany
José de Souza	Federal University of Ceará, Brazil
Stuart Clayman	University College London, UK
Walter Cerroni	University of Bologna, Italy
David Breitgand	IBM Haifa Research Lab, Israel
Sergio Beker	DoCoMo, Germany
Rui Aguiar	University of Aveiro, Portugal
Antonio Celesti	University of Messina, Italy
Burak Kantarci	Clarkson University, NY, USA
Georgiana Copil	TU Vienna, Austria
Schahram Dustdar	TU Vienna, Austria
Alex Galis	UCL, UK
Fahim Kawsar	Bell Labs, Belgium
Prem Prakash Jayaraman	CSIRO, Digital Productivity Flagship, Australia
Rajiv Ranjan	CSIRO, Digital Productivity Flagship, Australia
Massimo Villari	University of Messina, Italy
Joe Weinman	IEEE Intercloud Testbed, Telx, USA
Maria Fazio	University of Messina, Italy
Luca Foschini	University of Bologna, Italy
Surya Nepal	CSIRO, Australia
Danilo Ardagna	Politecnico di Milano, Italy

HealthyIoT 2015

Organization

Steering Committee

Steering Committee Chair

Imrich Chlamtac   Create-Net, EAI, Italy

Steering Committee Members

Joel J.P.C. Rodrigues   Instituto de Telecomunicações, University of Beira
                                       Interior, Portugal

Antonio J. Jara   Institute of Information Systems, University of Applied
                                       Sciences Western Switzerland (HES-SO),
                                       Switzerland

Shoumen Palit Austin Datta   Massachusetts Institute of Technology; Industrial
                                       Internet Consortium, USA

Organizing Committee

General Chair

Antonio J. Jara   Institute of Information Systems, University of Applied
                                       Sciences Western Switzerland (HES-SO),
                                       Switzerland

Technical Program Chair

Diego Gachet   Universidad Europea de Madrid, Spain

Sponsorship and Exhibit Chair

Andrej Kos   University of Ljubljana, Slovenia

Publication Chair

Mohamad Badra   Zayed University, UAE

Publicity Co-chairs

Mauro Fonseca   Federal Technological University of Paraná, Brazil
Scott Fowler   Linkoping University, Sweden
Wendong Xiao   University of Science and Technology Beijing, China

Web Chair

Ramon Alcarria   Universidad Politecnica de Madrid, Spain

Local Chair

Raffaele Giaffreda   CREATE-NET, Italy

Conference Manager

Kristina Lukáčová   European Alliance for Innovation, Slovakia

Technical Program Committee

Mobyen Ahmed   Mälardalen University, Sweden
Manuel de Buenaga   Universidad Europea Madrid, Spain
Maria José Busto   Universidad Europea Madrid, Spain
Malconlm Clarke   Brunel University, UK
Ramiro Delgado   Army Forces University, Ecuador
Silvia Gabrielli   Create-net, Italy
Jesús Favela   Cicese, Mexico
Emad Felemban   Umm Al-Qura University, Saudi Arabia
Rubén García   Universidad de las Palmas de Gran Canaria, Spain
Alan Jovic   University of Zagreb, Croatia
Faisal Karim   Meharn University, Pakistan
Ahsank Khandoker   University of Melbourne, Australia
Carlos Lisboa Bento   Universidade de Coimbra, Portugal
Kunal Mankodiya   University of Rhode Island, USA
Venet Osmani   Create-Net, Italy
Enrique Puertas   Universidad Europea Madrid, Spain
Marcela Rodríguez   Universidad Autónoma de Baja California, Mexico
Liane Rockenbach Tarouco   Federal University of Rio Grande do Sul, Brazil
Emilija Stojmenova   University of Ljubljana, Slovenia
Jun Suzuki   University of Massachusetts, USA
Yunchuan Sun   Beijing Normal University, China
Christopher Thuemmler   Edinburgh Napier University, UK
Tonny Velin   AnswareTech, Spain

IoTaaS 2015

Organization

Steering Committee

General Chair

Benny Mandler   IBM Research — Haifa, Israel

Program Chair

Kostas Magoutis   University of Ioannina and ICS-FORTH, Greece

Publicity Chair

George Baryannis   ICS-FORTH, Greece

Local Chair

Raffaele Giaffreda   CREATE-NET, Italy

Conference Manager

Kristina Lukáčová   European Alliance for Innovation, Slovakia

Program Committee Members

Iacopo Carreras	U-Hopper, Italy
Eliezer Dekel	IBM, Israel
Sarunas Girdzijauskas	Royal Institute of Technology, Sweden
Vincenzo Gulisano	Chalmers University of Technology, Sweden
Kostas Magoutis	University of Ioannina and ICS-FORTH, Greece
Benny Mandler	IBM, Israel
Dana Petcu	West University of Timisoara, Romania
Joachim Posegga	University of Passau, Germany
Hong-Linh Truong	TU Vienna, Austria
Apostolos Zarras	University of Ioannina, Greece

MobilityIoT 2015

Organization

Steering Committee

Steering Committee Chairs

Imrich Chlamtac

General Chair

Dagmar Cagáňová

Organizing Committee

Dagmar Cagáňová
Paul Woolliscroft
Daynier Rolando Delgado Sobrino
Tibor Zvonár
Raffaele Giaffreda
Kristína Lukáčová

Technical Program Chairs

Milan Dado
Michal Balog
Jana Šujanová
Jaroslav Holeček
Dušan Petráš
Miloš Čambál
Daniela Špirková
Edita Hekelová
Soňa Ferenčíková
Jozef Hvorecký
Dagmar Cagáňová
Miloš Čambál
Neven Vrček
Daynier Rolando Delgado Sobrino
Paul Woolliscroft
Cristian-Gyözö Haba

Dorin Dumitru Lucache
Eduardo Tome
Florinda Matos
Predrag K. Nikolic
Krzysztof Witkowski
Peter Bindzár
Sebastian Saniuk
Tibor Zvonár
Martin Straka
Petr Štěpánek
Giovanni Del Galdo
Thomas Sporer
Konrad Osterwalder
Frank T. Anbari
Ladislav Janoušek
Michael Stankosky

Pawel Sobcyak
Marek Walancik
Joanna Kurowska Pysz
Thomas Palatin
Walter Mayrhofer
Ullas Ehrlich
Nikolay Madzharov
Ettore Bolisani
Ilpo Pohjola
Enrico Scarso
Jose Maria Viedma Marti
Malgorzata Zieba
Atul Borade

Shawn Chen
Małgorzata Zięba
Florian Marcel Nuta
Sergey Zapryagaev
Janusz K. Grabara
Giorgos Cristonakis
Emanuel-Stefan Marinescu
Yhing Sawheny
John Kelly
Abdul Dewale Mohammed
Gabriela Koľveková
Roswitha Wiedenhofer

Local Chair

Raffaele Giaffreda

S-CUBE 2015

Organization

Steering Committee

Steering Committee Chair

Imrich Chlamtac   Create-Net, Italy

Organizing Committee

General Chair

Andrey Somov   CREATE-NET, Italy

Technical Program Committee Chair

David Boyle   Imperial College London, UK

Publicity Chair

Salil Kanhere   University of New South Wales, Australia

Web Chair

Swaytha Sasidharan   CREATE-NET/University of Trento, Italy

Conference Manager

Kristina Lukáčová   European Alliance for Innovation, Slovakia

Technical Program Committee

Alexander Baranov	MATI-Russian State Technological University, Russia
Iain Bate	University of York, UK
Stefano Basagni	Northeastern University, USA
Carlo Alberto Boano	TU Graz, Austria
Matteo Ceriotti	University of Duisburg-Essen, Germany
Jason O. Hallstrom	Florida Atlantic University, USA
Salil Kanhere	University of New South Wales, Australia

InterIoT 2015

Organization

Steering Committee

Steering Committee Chair

Imrich Chlamtac　　　　　　　CREATE-NET, Italy

Organizing Committee

General Chairs

Nathalie Mitton　　　　　　　Inria, France
Thomas Noel　　　　　　　　University of Strasbourg, France

Program Chair

Thomas Watteyne　　　　　　Inria, France

Web, Publicity, and Publications Chair

Miguel Elias M. Campista　　UFRJ, Brazil

Conference Manager

Kristina Lukáčová　　　　　　European Alliance for Innovation, Slovakia

Technical Program Committee

Animesh Pathak　　　　　　Inria, France
Antonella Molinaro　　　　　UNIRC, Italy
Antonio Puliafito　　　　　　Messina University, Italy
Cedric Adjih　　　　　　　　Inria, France
Cesar Viho　　　　　　　　　Université Rennes 1, France
Edgar Chavez　　　　　　　Cicese, Mexico
Emery Jou　　　　　　　　　Institute for Information Industry, Taiwan
Fumio Teraoka　　　　　　　Keio University, Japan
Giancarlo Fortino　　　　　　University of Calabria, Italy
Gregor Schiele　　　　　　　Dusseldorf University, Germany
Ines Robles　　　　　　　　Ericsson, Finland
Ivan Mezei　　　　　　　　　Novi Sad University, Serbia
John Soldatos　　　　　　　AIT, Greece
Konrad Wrona　　　　　　　NATO, The Netherlands

SDWNCT 2015

Organization

Steering Committee

Steering Committee Chair

Imrich Chlamtac   CREATE-NET, Italy

Steering Committee Members

Bruno Astuto   GE Global Research Center, Brazil
Frederik Santens   Imtech ICT Belgium, Belgium
Ramanathan Subramanian Advanced Digital Sciences Center, Singapore
Athanasios V. Vasilakos   University of Western Macedonia, Greece

Organizing Committee

General Chairs

Bruno Astuto   GE Global Research Center, Brazil
Athanasios V. Vasilakos   Lulea University of Technology, Sweden
Frederik Santens   Imtech ICT Belgium, Belgium
Radu-Laurentiu Vieriu   University of Trento, Italy

Technical Program Chair

Christian Esteve   UNICAMP, Brazil
 Rothenberg
Artur Arsenio   Universidade da Beira Interior/YDreams
           Robotics CEO, Portugal
Erik Mannens   MMLab/iMinds-UGent, Belgium

Web and Publicity Chair

Mateus Silva Santos   University of Campinas, Brazil
Larissa Romualdo Suzuki UCL/Imperial College, UK
Stanislau Semeniuta   University of Trento, Italy

Workshop Chair

Amir H. Moin   Fortiss, An-Institut Technische Universität, München,
           Germany

Local Chair

Raffaele Giaffreda   CREATE-NET, Italy

Conference Manager

Kristina Lukáčová   European Alliance for Innovation, Slovakia

Technical Program Committee

Xiaobo Long	ONF Wireless and Mobile Working Group, USA
Hui Ni	Huawei, USA
Xin Wu	Big Switch, USA
Junaid Qadir	National University of Sciences and Technology (NUST), Pakistan
Luis Contreras	Telefónica I+D, Spain
Giancarlo Fortino	University of Calabria, Italy
Miguel Elias Campista	Federal University of Rio de Janeiro, Brazil
Jose Ferreira de Rezende	Federal University of Rio de Janeiro, Brazil
Wolfgang Kellerer	Technische Universität München (TUM), Germany
Giuseppe Carella	TU Berlin, Germany
Mateus Silva Santos	Ericsson Research, Brazil
Nuno Garcia	Beira Interior University, Portugal
Neeli R. Prasad	Aalborg University, Denmark
Nik Bessis	University of Derby, UK
Wesley De Neve	MMLab/iMinds-UGent, Belgium
Ruben Verborgh	MMLab/iMinds-UGent, Belgium
Simon Mayer	ETH Zürich - Distributed Systems Group, Switzerland
S. Shyam Sundar	The Pennsylvania State University, USA
Alice Ruggeri	University of Turin, Italy
Alessio Antonini	University of Turin, Italy
Luigi Di Caro	University of Turin, Italy

Contents – Part II

Mobility IoT

S-CUBE

InterIoT

SDWNCT

Contents – Part I

GOODTECHS

CN4IoT

HealthyIoT

IoTaaS

Managing Connected Smart Objects

Alan McGibney[(⊠)], Alejandro Esquiva Rodriguez,
Oliva Brickley, and Susan Rea

Nimbus Centre, Rossa Avenue, Bishopstown, Cork, Ireland
{alan.mcgibney, oliva.brickley, susan.rea}@cit.ie,
a.esquiva-rodraguez@mycit.ie

Abstract. This paper provides an initial architecture specification of a management framework to address the challenges associated with the robustness and reliability of large scale IoT systems, specifically through mechanisms for orchestration of resources for reliability and dependability supported by IoT functional virtualization.

Keywords: IoT management · Architecture · Software defined networking

1 Introduction

The Internet of Things (IoT) domain continues to grow rapidly and the numbers of devices, interfaces, operating environments, applications and services has exploded making the need for integration and management of intelligent devices and data more critical if efficiencies of scale are to be achieved within IoT ecosystems. The IERC in [1] explore three macro challenges that have been identified in relation to the evolution of IoT - namely: billions of devices, IOT management for robustness and reliability, and thirdly intelligent reasoning over IoT data. Forecasts tell us that by 2020 there will be in excess of 50 billion devices connected to the Internet generating massive volumes of data that must be delivered on time, in the correct format and to the appropriate end-user in order to deliver sustainable services, this drives the need for robust IoT management and the ability to transform raw data streams into actionable knowledge. This paper focuses on the IoT management for robustness and reliability macro challenge and specifically the sub-challenges of (i) orchestration of resources for reliability and dependability, and (ii) IoT functional virtualization. Resource orchestration relates to the ability to evaluate dependencies between sensing requirements, networking and physical resources and their relationship to QoE and reliability and the overlaying application. Functional virtualization offers the ability to decouple applications from the underlying physical infrastructure and can support multi-tenant applications. This paper will provide the initial specification of an architecture (utilizing the IoT-A reference architecture as a basis) to support seamless interaction between IoT applications and connected smart objects (things, people, and products) through the realization of a framework, based on the software defined networking (SDN) principles, which bridges the digital and physical system components. This will result in the specification of reference architecture for infrastructure (embedded and mobile devices) management within IoT ecosystems where the orchestration of resources and

B. Mandler et al. (Eds.): IoT 360° 2015, Part II, LNICST 170, pp. 3–9, 2016.
DOI: 10.1007/978-3-319-47075-7_1

virtualization is addressed through SDN partitioning using physical and virtual partitioning to create a service management framework for sustainable service delivery.

2   Current Approaches to Smart Object Management

The integration of smart objects into IoT platforms typically focus on providing a data-centric mechanism for IoT services. This involves data being published remotely (either directly or via an Internet bridge), stored in a data warehouse and published to third party cloud platforms. This supports the development of content rich applications; however the impact these applications have on the underlying infrastructure is only loosely coupled. With the upsurge of connected devices, there is an ever increasing need to provide a set of autonomous management functions that integrate configuration, operation, administration, security, and maintenance of all elements of the IoT network. The dynamic grouping and autonomous management of smart objects expected by IoT applications means that traditional network management is not directly transferable in cases where manual configuration and tuning is often required by network administrators.

2.1   Software Defined Networking for IoT Infrastructures

SDN brings with it the opportunity to separate the control plane from the data plane, centralize the logical network control and abstract the underlying physical infrastructure from the applications and services being executed in the network [2]. The control plane is the core element in a SDN infrastructure and is defined as a set of software controllers that provide the network forwarding function and lies between the physical devices at one end and the applications/services at the other. Abstracting the entire underlying infrastructure in virtual entities makes it possible to create different network applications which accomplish the needs and requirements of different IoT applications, using the same infrastructure. Different IoT marketplaces have been appearing over recent years, which use virtualization of the network and the virtualization of the smart objects to provide end-to-end services without considering the characteristics or state of the network and their components. From the end-user view, the underlying infrastructure should be considered as an autonomous system which works as expected and is managed by itself. The translation of application requirements to the underlying infrastructure can be achieved by the generation of policies, which will provide a set of rules to meet application specifications. In terms of SDN this task is handling by the North Bound API. There are several policy-based languages (Procera, Frenetic, FML and Nettle) which build a policy layer on top of existing controllers and are responsible for converting high-level policies to flow constraints that are be used by the controller. However, these policy-based languages are standalone and provide compatibility only with the South Bound API standard OpenFlow. A common alternative for the North Bound API are RESTFul APIs which are simple and straightforward for developers, but often do not support the metadata necessary for programing automation [3]. Currently, for the North Bound API there is no standard approach defined, and the existing solutions do not accommodate the needs of general IoT ecosystems resulting in static, application specific APIs. In enterprise networking SDN has been promoted as a solution to manage large-scale distributed networks and brings with it scalability and reliability making it an attractive solution to manage, coordinate and optimize the use of resources in diverse IoT infrastructures. Key performance indicators at the control plane are managing scalability and guaranteeing reliability and to do this the deployment of multiple distributed controllers is required. Control partitioning is driven by horizontal or vertical partitioning in order to subdivide the physical infrastructure into multiple domains. Hand-in-hand with this is the need to identify where to place controllers and how many controllers are required when dimensioning the network. Approaches to distributed control partitioning include Onix [4], DevoFlow [5], HyperFlow [6]. These SDN technologies are designed based on assigning fixed partitions over a rigid infrastructure with static controller assignment per partition where the network infrastructure is considered to be composed of typically wired switches, routers and high end servers. However, in IoT infrastructures such networking infrastructure will not be the norm and physical devices will be dispersed over a significantly more loosely coupled heterogeneous environment. The complementary problem of controller placement and quantity has been explored in [7, 8] and their findings surmise that no generalization can be drawn on the numbers and placement of controllers that is applicable to all networks. Placement depends on the network topography and performance metrics defined by service level agreements (SLAs) that need to be met based on delay, bandwidth, and reliability for example. SDN Controller communications is driven by one of three communications interfaces, namely the northbound, southbound and east-west bound interfaces. OpenFlow is the protocol that is most widely accepted as de facto when implementing SDN solutions for the southbound communications interface and on the northbound interface REST APIs are proving popular choice among vendors. The east-west bound interface while being accepted as being needed to support inter-controller communications between partitions or federations of devices is not currently supported by any standard or established protocol and is as such the most immature among the available interfaces in SDN implementations but is critical in order to manage federations of SDN domains.

3   Proposed Management Framework

IoT-A [9] was developed to define the basic IoT domain concepts and the functional components of the reference architecture. Furthermore, IoT-A encapsulates a set of models to establish a common understanding of the IoT domain such as a Domain Model to identify entities, resources and services that are important actors of the IoT scenario, and an Information Model which specifies how the information will be modelled. Utilizing a direct instance of the IoT-A reference architecture as a basis, we have created the initial specification of an architecture to support the management of connected smart objects. An abstract representation of the framework is provided by the functional model that defines IoT-A. The functional model is composed of several functionality groups (FGs) which provide the functionalities for interacting with the instances of these concepts or managing the information related to the concepts.

Figure 1 shows our functional model instanced by the IoT-A. Each FG is composed of different functional modules (FMs).

The *Management FG* encapsulates the control and maintenance modules of the framework, providing tools to assess the performance of smart object networks in terms of resources constraints, throughput, connectivity etc. The *Service Organisation FG* maintains a domain registry including a semantic model of smart object(s) and partitions. The *IoT Process Management* provides the network operating system that is responsible for generating, mediating and invoking service policies between applications and smart objects. The *Virtual Entity* and *IoT Service FGs* provide capabilities to represent the current state of resources, conflict resolution between service requirements and a set of services to monitor and maintain system stability. The *Communication FG* provides an abstraction from the various interfaces required to form a communications backbone for the components of the framework. This component is logically located in the smart object, with the aim to provide common APIs for

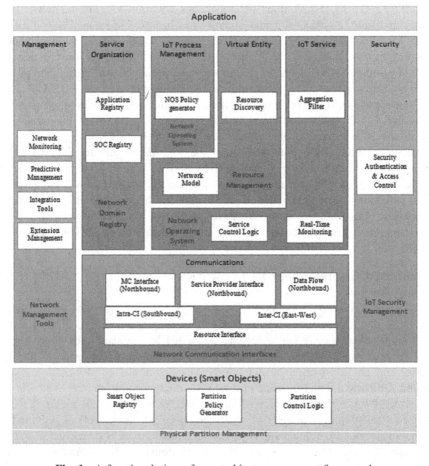

Fig. 1. A functional view of smart object management framework.

exploiting resources, manage network services and handle inconsistence issues. The *Device FG* is not included in the mapping of functional Unified Requirements of the IoT-A while it needs to be considered when devising a concrete IoT system. However from an infrastructure management perspective, the *Device FG* plays an important role, as the devices need to host common functional blocks to enable autonomous management between smart objects. From an implementation perspective the type of device will dictate the level of sophistication of the controllers deployed on them. A key aspect to the proposed management framework is to ability to dynamically partition the infrastructure to meet IoT application needs. Figure 2 provides a high level functional view of the proposed partitioning mechanism. It is composed of a number of functional blocks that from one side allow for the dynamic partitioning of physical infrastructures and from another derive a virtual overlay to service IoT applications.

A number of context-aware smart controllers are required to coordinate and optimize the use of physical resources. A key component is the development of a Master Controller (MC) which is responsible for the discovery, classification and registration of smart objects within the management framework. Thus, the MC will act as the initial mediator between applications and the supporting physical infrastructure. The MC will utilize existing approaches for the classification, registration and discovery of smart objects. It is assumed that each smart object has a remotely configured Smart Object Controller (SOC). This concept will enable smart object bootstrapping where they connect and register with the resource repository. To realize a SOC requires the following base functionality, RESTful service interface to consume and process RESTful requests, object interface (for control of physical devices), information model and embedded management functionality. The use of the reference framework specification will ensure implementation is consistent however the execution environment may result

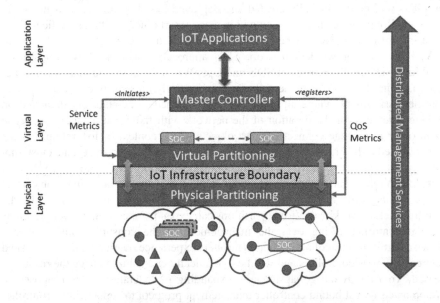

Fig. 2. IoT infrastructure partitioning

in a number of SOC types. From an IoT system management perspective, EU FP7 project *iCore* provides a base framework for the representation, registration, composition and discovery of virtual entities to support multiple IoT applications over the same infrastructure. Similarly EU FP7 project *OpenIoT* provides mechanisms for context-aware ranking of smart objects to establish relevance to application needs; it is acknowledged that many middleware platforms provide basic search capabilities (proximity and data type) focus and as such should be leveraged by the proposed framework.

To distribute the management functionality requires the creation of localized controllers that can proactively partition the physical infrastructure to meet varying QoS demands. The formation of these **physical partitions** in highly-dynamic IoT environments is analogous to clustering mechanisms used in MANETs. Within this domain a number of works have been proposed for clustering, each using various factors to drive the election of a device as a cluster head (CH). The factors utilized include the degree of the nodes (the number of neighbors that a node has), node mobility and node energy. In addition there exist approaches that target the combination of these factors as weighted metrics to optimize the selection of the cluster head. The challenge is to maintain the stability of the network once the cluster head has been elected, it is impacted by mobility of devices, resource depletion, connectivity etc. This challenge is exacerbated further in IoT systems where a number of virtual overlays driven by service level agreements are formed and rely on the stability of the underlying physical infrastructure. Therefore it is proposed to extend these metrics to incorporate the current context (how the smart objects are being used, what they are being used for, and the resources available, smart object/service priority and current SLAs being supported).

Virtual Partitioning will create an elastic overlay that collapses or expands depending on the current context and workload. Unlike existing SDN implementations, controllers will be dynamically created and deployed based current context including new and existing service requests and will manage smart objects within specific regions of the infrastructures. Neither enterprise wired SDN solutions such as OniX, Devo-FloW, FlowVisor or wireless network SDN approaches such as TinySDN, Sensor OpenFlow, SDWN, UbiFlow, CellSDN and OpenWireless consider dynamic controller creation, assignment or deployment. These solutions rely on proactive partitioning and controller assignment, where all controllers are assumed to be statically deployed on permanent devices for the duration of the network with fixed end devices. We argue that in order to manage connected smart objects in the context of IoT relying on the need for fixed infrastructure to manage scalability is not appropriate and clustering devices must be reactive based on current context. Smart Object Controllers (SOC) are software modules that are assigned and deployed on appropriate smart objects at specific instances of time and can be moved, split or consumed at will, driven by the IoT infrastructure workload. Virtual partitions can expand and consume other partitions with the controller taking over the management of the consumed smart objects. Likewise partitions can collapse when controllers experience overload and need to shed resources and new controllers and will be dynamically created to manage the resources released. To support the collapsing and expanding of federations it is proposed to develop an east-west bound controller management protocol to support inter-controller communications and will leverage existing protocols such as OpenFlow, BGP, EIGRP and will be used for partition maintenance and stabilization. The primary focus for this framework is context driven partitioning and dynamic controller creation/assignment rather than flow management. To enable flow management, load balancing, mobility and handover management the framework will adopt concepts from SDN wireless solutions such as UbiFloW (which has been designed for urban scale software defined IoT networking and uses distributed hash tables to support mobility and network calculus for flow management), CellSDN, which targets policies for cellular applications that are driven by subscriber needs, instead of physical locations, Sensor Flow targets SDN over WSNs and OpenWireless which looks at handover for high rate video stream between networks. A critical consideration is the impact the formation of virtual partitions will have on the physical infrastructure; this is represented as the IoT infrastructure boundary in Fig. 2, this requires cross-layer collaboration among smart object controllers to ensure firstly, the physical infrastructure can support IoT services and secondly, the virtual partitioning of smart objects does not to detrimentally impact the stability of the supporting infrastructure.

This paper provides a functional specification of a management framework based on the IoT-A reference architecture that aims to ensure the impact of multi-tenant IoT applications has on the stability and robustness of the supporting physical infrastructure is taken into account during development. Future work includes the realization of a concrete instance of the reference architecture and the development of novel methodologies using concepts of SDN to manage the boundary between the physical and virtual partitions that support future dynamic and scalable IoT applications.

References

1. Vermesan, O., Friss, P.: Building the Hyperconnected Society - IoT Research and Innovation Value Chains, Ecosystems and Markets. River Publishers, Aalborg (2015). ISBN 978-87-93237-99-5
2. Jarraya, Y., Madi, T., Debbabi, M.: A survey and a layered taxonomy of software-defined networking. IEEE Commun. Surv. Tutor. **16**(4), 1955–1980 (2014)
3. Dmitry, N., Sneps-Sneppe, M.: Metadata in SDN API (2015). arXiv preprint: arXiv:1503. 06630
4. Koponen, T., Casado, M., Gude, N., Stribling, J., Poutievski, L., Zhu, M., Ramanathan, R., Iwata, Y., Inoue, H., Hama, T., Shenker, S.: Onix: a distributed control platform for large-scale production networks. In: USENIX OSDI (2010)
5. Curtis, A.R., et al.: Devoflow: scaling flow management for high-performance networks. In: ACM SIGCOMM (2011)
6. Tootoonchian, A., Ganjali, Y.: HyperFlow: a distributed control plane for OpenFlow. In: INM/WREN (2010)
7. Heller, B., Sherwood, R., McKeown, N.: The controller placement problem. In: HotSDN (2012)
8. Hu, Y., et al.: On the placement of controllers in software-defined networks. China Univ. Posts Telecommun. **19**(S2), 92–171 (2012)
9. Bassi, A., et al.: Enabling Things to Talk, Designing IoT Solutions With the IoT Architectural Reference Model. Springer, Heidelberg (2013). ISBN 978-3-642-40402-3

Configurable Role Based Concrete Architecture Layers: Constituting Business Process Aware Internet-of-Things Services' Reference Architecture

Vikas S. Shah[✉]

Wipro Technologies, Connected Enterprise Services, East Brunswick, NJ, USA
vikas.shah@wipro.com

Abstract. Internet-of-Things (IoT) services offer a great potential in many different enterprise application areas for improving efficiency gains to completely new business processes (BPs). However, due to diversified nature of the devices involved and uncertainty of business objectives associated when structuring BP aware IoT services, significant concerns of standardizations still have to be overcome. In this paper, we identified and integrated contexts of BPs to IoT services by means of role-centric view in order to define BP aware IoT services' reference architecture. Configurable role based approach and model enables a systematic credentials and reuse of standardized IoT services in layers, while allowing participants of IoT services' reference architecture to understand and imply possible variations. It is proposing a configurable role based concrete architecture layers incorporating topographies for capturing resources, data, and physical objects involved to IoT services. The methodology is validated with a case study of commercial surveillance camera and security alarm systems.

Keywords: Business processes (BPs) · Configurable · Integration · Internet-of-Things (IoT) · Reference architecture · Role based

1 Introduction

The next wave in the era of IoT services will be outside the realm of the traditional automation paradigms, many of the objects that surround us will be in adherence to BPs in one form or another. BP modeling specializes on describing how activities interact and relate with services rendered for IoT while supporting the operation of the business. The representation of an enterprise and its BPs have been the focus of research in past years and significant work has been done on developing BP modeling concepts, methodologies and ontologies [1–3]. Recently, various attempts and analysis have been performed to synergies between BPs and the specification of IoT service modeling [4, 5].

In order to integrate IoT resources into BPs, it is therefore necessary to establish principles and reference architecture for service-enable IoT resources, example, utility device's monitoring services that are accurately structured, composited, and mapped to interact with the billing and payment BPs. Using a service-based approach offers the additional advantage of hiding the heterogeneity of IoT device and associated

© ICST Institute for Computer Sciences, Social Informatics and Telecommunications Engineering 2016
B. Mandler et al. (Eds.): IoT 360° 2015, Part II, LNICST 170, pp. 10–19, 2016.
DOI: 10.1007/978-3-319-47075-7_2

information model from the BP orchestration. However, it results in the generation of enormous amounts of concrete relationship between IoT services and BPs. The relationship information have to be stored, processed, and presented in a seamless, efficient, and easily interpretable form. This model will consist of set of IoT services that are commodities and delivered in a standardized manner.

Inherently, it needs to be based on actual events that are either detected directly or by anticipated real-time behavioral analysis of the IoT services. Such events can occur at any time in the correlations of the BP activities [4]. Modelling such events into an IoT service is cumbersome, as they would have to be included into all possible BP activities. It leads to an additional complexity and making it more difficult to understand the modelled BP. Secondly, how to react on a single event can depend on the context of BP. A simple critical example is the smoke detecting device that recognizes a sharp rise in temperature then the nearest rescue team needs to be notified.

Modeling BP involves capturing the structure of enterprise's business objects and their relationships to correctly enumerate corresponding activities associated with the business object [2, 6]. A business object exhibits different role according to the relationships that it has at a given time. Currently, due to the uncertainty in the behavior of such business object, integrating IoT services into BPs requires a lot of engineering, deployment, configuration within middleware, and enablement of custom development. Every new IoT resource and installation requires significant effort. A major shortcoming of existing approaches to configurable BP modeling in the context of IoT services is the lack of mechanisms for standardizing and capturing categories of variability beyond the control flow perspective of business objects.

In this paper, we proposed configurable role based concrete architecture layers to streamline and classify IoT services and associated compositions. The key contribution is to place reference architecture for IoT services in the context of enterprise-grade BPs to support a range of variations in the way roles and business objects are associated to BP activities. It provides a framework and a platform to introduce and configure role models that can relate IoT services in association with the activities of BPs. Section 2 represents our analysis to indicate the significance of roles in BP aware IoT services. Section 3 describes the potential variability requirements of IoT services and desired configurability paradigms. Section 4 presents our approach to structure role based layered architecture to constitute BP aware IoT reference architecture, whereas, Sect. 5 provides a real case study performed and our observations. Section 6 concludes our findings and discusses future evolvement.

2   Implications of Roles in BP Aware IoT Services

Role-based modeling allows roles to focus on BP activities and their own parts of work. The role models are required to negotiate with each other in order to associate with the IoT services. Due to the collaborative nature of role-based modeling, negotiations among roles have a crucial impact on the overall BP. Typically, roles differs from each other based on the differences in their behavioral characteristics of responsibilities as well as method of negotiation. We have analyzed significance of roles and their categories in BP aware IoT services.

The concept of role is used in various different methodologies. As indicated in [3, 6], Kristiansen has proposed to set role properties, which are commonly regarded as a conceptual basis for defining roles. In BP modeling, there are also approaches based on role modeling such as Role Interaction Networks (RIN) and Role Activity Diagrams (RAD). Here, roles are considered as sets of ordered interactions. Role activities describe the interaction between pairs of roles, from a driving to a target role. However, these approaches do not fully depict context of IoT services and describe relationships or separate other concerns of IoT services.

IoT service delegation is often defined as a mechanism of all or a subset of roles to one or more other business objects including the physical devices that participate in BP activities [7–9]. No business object can delegate the defined role. However, in many cases, a business object may want to delegate some missions from specified role. In most cases, when IoT services are involved, IoT service to role delegation is needed. For example, if the satellite transmission of dedicated radio frequency is distressed due to signal to noise ratio, it must delegate to other radio frequency based on the defined role rather than based on business object (satellite). For instance, IoT services "evaluating the conditions of the quality of transmission" and "preparing the diversification to receive and/or transmit the information stream" can be delegated to the channels associated with the other radio frequencies pertaining to the role.

The analysis also indicates that the rules must be defined and configured [10], as there are constraints required to be imposed on the roles to IoT services delegation associated with the BP activity. In the presented scenario, not all dedicated radio frequencies can be utilized for the particular purpose in context or information stream that needs to be transmitted.

IoT service to role delegation allows precisely specifying and emulating anticipated physical behavior in the context of the BP activity. A role defines a set of extrinsic properties and behavior necessary to realize its participating IoT services. Roles can be

Table 1. Primary categories of role models for IoT services.

Type of role model	Example context of IoT service	Areas of implication
Representative	Specifying serial number and version of IoT device	IoT service binding and presentation
Observatory	Logical tracing of the physical IoT resource	IoT service's service level agreement (SLA) association and monitoring
Associative	Update states of multiple IoT devices to perform an activity	Multifaceted characterization of IoT services operations
Collaborative	Integrating platform or system feature capabilities to IoT service	Cross-functionality of IoT service operations
Operative	Defining actions and alternatives in the course of state change of IoT device	IoT service operations' action associated with BP activities
Executive	Decision to terminate or instantiate IoT service session	IoT service execution and transition
Enumerative	Listing states of IoT device to the IoT service variable	IoT service parameters and validation

constrained in the context of IoT services. A constraint asserts conditions between the roles and IoT services that can be expressed informally or formally. Binding the roles with the IoT services depicts the classification and association in the context of specific BP activity or set of BP activities. We have identified 7 different primary categories of role models that can be utilized for IoT services. Table 1 provides the type of role models identified, example context of IoT service, and their areas of implication.

A configurable IoT service to role model is needed to provide multiple forms of delegations and to enable flexible role model association with IoT service. We defined configurability paradigms as a mechanism that allows an IoT service to participate in various BP activities with different objectives.

3   Variability of IoT Services and Configurability Paradigms

In principle, the variability of the IoT services can be depicted independently of the BPs by means of a set of IoT resource facts that form the space of IoT resource's logical states. IoT resource fact is a set of variables and their responsibilities representing a feature of the IoT service operations, example, performing a video recording of the installed surveillance camera to particular zone of construction site. The surveillance camera can be physically enabled or disabled. The Boolean variable to enable surveillance camera and zone are the IoT resource facts in above example.

IoT service operations can group IoT resource facts according to their content and required actions. All facts of the same IoT resource can be set at once by identifying the corresponding logical states and their transitioning. Interdependencies between these states can specify a partial order in which the IoT service operations should be posed in association with any of the role model identified in Sect. 2 Table 1.

The configuration expression of role model associated with the IoT service can then be conditionally dependent on such IoT resource facts. For example, the *operative role model* associated with the IoT service in which the video recording is performed must be set to allowed when the corresponding fact of installed surveillance camera is set to enabled, while it must be blocked or hidden when the fact is set to disabled. Such a configuration expression might also be dependent on a combination of multiple IoT resource facts. The facts can be combined in propositional logic within the configuration expression of role model that captures their interplay. It is then possible to ensure that a single instance of role model will never have two configuration values at the same time (example: blocked and hidden).

Additional constraints when associating instance of role model with IoT service can be specified in the configuration expression in the form of either through specifying maximum value, minimum value, or range of values to the facts. In the example of satellite radio frequency transmission in Sect. 2, type of information stream that is required to transmit can be constrained for specified range of satellite radio frequency.

During the modeling of roles for IoT services, we adapted and implied four distinct methods to identify configurability paradigms, each having its own application areas as detailed in [5]. Following is the list of methods and their overview.

- Design: The type of configurability paradigms is for handling anticipated changes in the IoT services, where supporting operations can be defined at design-time in considerations of the IoT resource facts.
- Deviation: It is for handling the occasional unforeseen behavior of IoT service operations, where differences with the expected behavior are minimal.
- Under-specification: It is for handling anticipated changes in the IoT service operations, where IoT resource facts cannot be defined at design-time due to the final state is not known in advance or is not generally applicable.
- Change: It is either for handling occasional unforeseen behavior, where differences require BP adaptations, or for handling permanent unforeseen behavior.

Each method provides insight of the correlations between the associated role model and IoT service. The role model specification and corresponding configuration expression participates to construct BP aware IoT services in the form of IoT services' metadata. They also ensure the anticipated completeness of IoT service for the BP activity in consideration. Based on the above methods, we distinguished 5 types of configuration expressions that can be leveraged to the role models identified in Sect. 2 Table 1 and corresponding IoT resource facts. Table 2 presents the types of configuration expressions of role models, the respective type of role models on which they can imply to, and example context of IoT resource facts.

Table 2. Types of configuration expression of role model associated with IoT service.

Configuration expression type	Role model type(s)	Example context of IoT resource facts
Reactive	Executive and operative	Setting lower and upper limits for voltage control
Proactive	Observatory, associative, collaborative, and enumerative	Configure specific system alert type for particular state of machine
Conjugative	All	Setting voltage control limit for particular state of the machine
Predictive	Observatory and enumerative	Setting valid states of machine for the specified timeframe
Conductive	Executive, operative, and associative	Allocate action type of "switch-off" for the particular state of machine

4   Deriving Role-Based Architecture Layers: BP Aware IoT Services

IoT services' reference architecture provides a generic solution that needs to be individualized to fit a specific set of BPs. An IoT service is anticipated to integrate multiple elements that are distributed across several enterprises and communicate with each other, at least partially, by using underline protocols and standards. Furthermore, the IoT services to be operated and maintained throughout the whole lifecycle of the enterprise and corresponding BPs. If BP activities are facilitated by an enterprise, the efforts expected from the IoT service providers can be streamlined and derived, thereby enabling the entry of new requirements and new enterprise elements to the emerging ecosystem effectively through the established reference architecture.

For this reason, the reference architecture shall provide support throughout all the lifecycle phases of the IoT services. These phases can be derived in the perception of delegations of role models and IoT services. It must enable IoT services to support associating the configuration expression of role model necessary to meet the completeness of IoT services in the context of BP activities. In the reference architecture, the difference is made between the processes dealing with the design, development, and deployment of the IoT services (that is, strategy, system, information, infrastructure, and product related events associated with the IoT resources and their facts) and their core operations, which include the anticipated groups of fulfillment and assurance of BP activities. Following principles of service oriented architecture [11–13], we defined discrete IoT services' reference architecture layers by means of specifying delegations of role model and IoT service.

Figure 1 provides the layers of reference architecture and corresponding responsibilities. Each layer reveals and factorizes correlations between role model and IoT service to depict the concrete architecture for a specific set of BP activities.

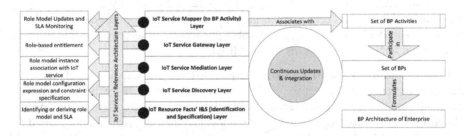

Fig. 1. Layers of BP aware IoT services' reference architecture

IoT Resource Facts' I&S (Identification and Specification) Layer: It is the foremost and initial layer to recognize IoT resource facts including paradigms of physical objects involved. The example facts that can be captured are installation zone, version, and status of security alarm device. The layer is also responsible to either identifying or deriving (if already exists) role model and SLA (service level agreement) specification in association with the IoT resources' facts. In the specific example, observatory role model can be recognized with the zone to monitor any deviation in status of security alarm device.

IoT Service Discovery Layer: Discovery layer is to define and model granularity of the IoT service. It includes modeling service output, service type, service level metadata, and the geographic area for which the service is provided. The representation of the service specification will also be linked to the service description during the modeling. Role model configuration expression and constraint specification in adherence to identified facts are the responsibilities of this layer. For instance, IoT service model to manage security alarm device requires to express and designate security alarm observatory role derived from observatory role model with the firmly defined status values (example: it can either be away, stay, bypass, not ready, ready, alarm, and check, however, can't be anything else than the specified values).

IoT Service Mediation Layer: Actual composition of the IoT services and definition of the corresponding operation are the primary responsibilities of the layer. IoT services can be invoked either in a synchronous way by responding to service requests or in an asynchronous way by sending notifications according to subscriptions previously made through the service. Service registry is being utilized to register resource history and metadata associated with IoT service operations. Role model instance association with IoT service model and specification are also integral part of service mediation layer. It actually provides reusability across multiple BP activities by differentiating IoT services in presence of type of role model associated with it. The IoT service to manage security alarm device can be associated with observatory role model as well as operative role model, however, the purpose of the IoT service changes and respective model, instance, and utilization differs (as indicated in the case study of Sect. 5).

IoT Service Gateway Layer: IoT service gateway responsible, at the very minimum, for enabling the secure connectivity between the short range IoT resources, sensing and actuating devices, and other services of the enterprise and/or BPs. It may also implement security-related functions as well as perform run-time discovery and validity of the devices and their services. Role-based entitlement and enforcing security policies are also the accountabilities of this layer. The policies for security alarm observatory role can be defined and checked to ensure that the right level of access to the manage security alarm device IoT service is available including any security protocol (such as token based authentication) needs to be utilized.

IoT Service Mapper (to BP Activity) Layer: IoT service mapping to BP activities that complements the capabilities of BP aware IoT service. It establishes common understanding between the IoT services utilization with respective to the identified and placed BPs. Continuous update to the role model and their desired variations based on BP activity and SLA monitoring are the critical aspect of the functionalities of this layer. The manage security alarm device IoT service with associated security alarm observatory role can be utilized within the BP activity of inventory check pertaining to billing and payment BP.

5 Case Study and Observations: Security Alarm System and Surveillance Camera

For the initial proof-of-concept, we considered first level primary BPs for the enterprise offering commercial security alarm system and surveillance camera to their customers. Following are the four initial BPs modeled for various desired activities to manage integrated security products along with accessible commercial monitoring services option. For each of the four selected BPs, we then identified all the differences among the associated requirements and activities variants. Based on this information, we created a single multifaceted BP model for each BP that incorporates all the BP activities and respective ordinary runtime choices using IBM WebSphere Process Server's process modeling capabilities [2]. Following are the four BPs.

- **Prospect and Quote to Order**: It is a BP to approach the prospect and generate the quotation based on the required integrated security products by the customers. It also validates the legitimacy of customer, product, and location.
- **Installation and Activation**: This BP is to procure material, establish physical equipment and agent support, initial system level updates and setup, customer approval, and closing of an order.
- **Provisioning and Monitoring**: It is the subsequent BP to installation and activation to offer monitoring and surveillance of activities based on installed products. However, it is independent of installation and activation process as customer has option to subscribe or degrade levels of provisioning.
- **Billing and Payment**: The BP is to introduce automation to trigger invoicing and online payment based on the utilization of the installed and activated products as well as subscribed provisioning levels. It also addressed non-payment through termination of provisioning and initiating collections.

The IoT solution architecture is derived from the presented reference architecture and the role model variants for acknowledging the utilization of IoT services in daily practice. We modeled IoT resources facts of all versions of the surveillance camera and security alarm products that are either deployed or under deployment to the customers. Each layer of the reference architecture is disseminated, for example, IoT Resource Facts' I&S layer considers the properties of security alarms such as zone that observatory role has to monitor for billing and payment BP.

We have logically categorized and build the information model that carries 146 IoT resources facts. Eventually, the analysis to model IoT services has been performed and 17 IoT services are being deployed in the production environment using IBM integration bus features [12]. As part of a BP definition, a process designer defines BP activities that describe the high-level interfaces and business objects to an IoT service in association with configured role model.

The total number of mapped (to the identified BP activities) differentiated IoT services with the variant role model association is 64. It indicates the factor of reuse is significantly higher (1:4 and 276 %) than legacy methodologies and existing approaches. Table 3 provides an example of differentiated IoT service for managing security alarm device in the context of diversified BP activities of different BPs.

Table 3. Differentiated IoT services example for *managing security alarm device* and its utilization.

Reference architecture paradigms	Provisioning and monitoring BP	Billing and Payment BP
Associated BP activity	Create alert	Create invoice
Number of IoT resource facts participated	7	4
Role model type	Operative	Observatory
Configuration expression type	Conductive	Predictive
IoT service operation responsibility	Identify provisioning level subscribed and compute the severity of alert	Identify provisioning level subscribed and compute the associated pricing

During the modeling as well as deployment of the IoT services, we have observed certain subjective advantages and challenges. Following list describes the primary findings when constituting BP aware IoT services utilizing configurable role-based architecture layers that BP architect can take into consideration.

- When modeling IoT service and their variants in terms of role association, we have to decide which information flow or control flow alternatives are subject to configuration and which ones shall be common across BP activities.
- When defining relevant constraints for a set of IoT resource facts within the configuration expression of role model, the architecture usually does not only refer to one type of constraint, however, to increase the correctness of the operations, different constraint types must be considered.
- To combine several options to configure a specific role model variant, the IoT services' solution architecture derived from reference architecture must decide how to group IoT resource facts to the operations. Thereby aspects such as maintainability as well as extendibility have to be considered. The resolution and judgement between coarse-grained versus fine-grained also must have to be implied when deriving as well as delegating IoT services with role models.
- If different facts pertaining to different IoT resources shall be applied conjointly to the IoT service due to semantical dependencies then architecture may explicitly define an implication constraint between them. Implication constraints are always directed to the configuration expression of the dedicated role model for the specific IoT service.

6 Conclusion and Future Work

This paper has presented the fundamental concepts towards generating BP aware IoT services' reference architecture framework by means of configurable role-based architecture layers. It relies on specifying role models and corresponding configuration expression in association with IoT services to consistently utilize them into the identified BP activities. Furthermore, the IoT services' reference architecture provides the principles to guide the definition of the IoT services. Essentially, it is an effort to streamline and standardize building and deploying IoT services with variations in the dilemma of enterprise-grade BPs.

The case study of integrated security products indicates the advantages and potential challenges that needs to be overcome during the deployment of the IoT services. The results are encouraging considering the consistency, reusability, maintainability, and variability being accomplished across the enterprise. The present effort is to formalize and imply constraint specification with the configuration expression pertaining to the identified categories of role model across enterprise. Subsequent research interest is to extend the dynamicity as well as many-to-many relationship between the role models and IoT services.

References

1. La Rosa, M., et al.: Configurable multi-perspective business process models. Inf. Syst. **36**(2), 313–340 (2011)
2. Pillai, U., et al.: Business Process Management Deployment Guide Using IBM Business Process Manager V8.5. IBM Redbooks, January 2014. ISBN 0738438944
3. Ertugrul, A.M., Demirors, O.: An exploratory study on role-based collaborative business process modeling approaches. In: Proceedings of the 7th International Conference on Subject-Oriented Business Process Management, S-BPM ONE 2015, NY, USA, p. 14 (2015)
4. Haller, S., Magerkurth, C.: The real-time enterprise: IoT-enabled business processes. In: IETF IAB Workshop on Interconnecting Smart Objects, March 2011
5. Ferreira, P., Martinho, R., Domingos, D.: IoT-aware business processes for logistics: limitations of current approaches. In: INForum 2010 – II, pp. 611–622 (2010)
6. Caetano, A., et al.: A role-based framework for business process modeling. In: IEEE Proceedings of the 38th Hawaii International Conference on System Sciences, January 2005
7. Bauer, M., et al.: IoT reference architecture. In: Bassi, A., et al. (eds.) Enabling Things to Talk, pp. 165–210. Springer, Heidelberg (2013). doi:10.1007/978-3-642-40403-0_8
8. Thoma, M., Meyer, S., Sperner, K., Meissner, S., Braun, T.: On IoT-services: survey, classification and enterprise integration. In: 2012 IEEE International Conference on Green Computing and Communications (GreenCom), pp. 257–260, November 2012
9. Guo, B., et al.: Opportunistic IoT: exploring the harmonious interaction between human and the Internet of Things. J. Netw. Comput. Appl. **36**(6), 1531–1539 (2013). doi:10.1016/j.jnca. 2012.12.028
10. Elkhodr, M., Shahrestani, S., Cheung, H.: The Internet of Things: vision & challenges. In: IEEE 2013 TENCON Spring Conference, pp. 218–222, April 2013
11. Zhou, Z., et al.: CPS track report: 2nd track on cyber physical society with SOA, BPM and sensor networks. In: 2012 IEEE 21st International Workshop on Enabling Technologies: Infrastructure for Collaborative Enterprises (WETICE), pp. 25–27, June 2012
12. Howes, A.J., Wong, G.: Integrating IBM Business Process Manager Standard with synchronous and asynchronous applications using IBM Integration Bus V9. IBM DeveloperWorks, July 2013
13. Espinha, T., Zaidman, A., Gross, H.-G.: Understanding the runtime topology of SOA systems. In: IEEE 19th Working Conference on Reverse Engineering (WCRE), pp. 87–196, October 2012

Lightweight Device Task Actuation Framework as IoT Test Platform

Dhiman Chattopadhyay$^{(\boxtimes)}$, Abinash Samantaray, and Hari Raghav

Innovation Lab, Tata Consultancy Services, Kolkata, India
{dhiman.chattopadhyay,abinash.samantaray,hariraghav.1}@tcs.com

Abstract. Popular test automation frameworks target the enterprise application testing but there is scarcity of test automation framework for device applications, especially for IoT domain. IoT testing paradigm throws a new set of challenges involving device integration, protocol adapters, task actuation, data integrity, security and non functional requirements. In this paper, we propose a scalable, lightweight device task actuation framework for IoT testing based on TCS Connected Universe Platform Device Management enabler. This framework can execute test suite on multiple remote devices spread across geographies and then show the results on the IoT tester's screen. Moreover it has the ability to gather runtime device statistics during test execution, thus can do dynamic health check for IoT devices deployed on field.

Keywords: TCUP · DM · DTAF · ITP · LWM2M · CoAP · REST · IoT

1 Introduction

The important consideration in case of a software testing are safety, reliability, resilience, availability and security. Legacy Test Automation frameworks [1, 2] are web based tool to execute test suite without manual intervention and monitoring. There are tools [3] to automate enterprise application testing where applications deal with predominantly human generated data. Such tools deal with UI testing and as well as functional testing of enterprise application with predefined set of inputs and arrive at pass fail decision in comparison with reference results. With the arrival of era of Internet of Things (IoT) devices are set to take the driver seat in terms of data generation, acquisition, transfer and task actuation. IoT solution testing involves validation of functionality, security, actuation and benchmarking for testing the reliability, security, stability and performance of IoT solution. The IoT devices vary in hardware type ranging from constrained embedded microcontrollers like Arduino and mbed platform to more resourceful gateways like RaspberryPi, Intel Galileo, Edison, Beagle Bone etc. and even smart-phones can act as a gateway. But the commonality among the edge devices is the ability to acquire, communicate and compute. As the importance of device application is paramount in IoT application it has become necessary to rigorously test the device applications before field deployment. There are popular

© ICST Institute for Computer Sciences, Social Informatics and Telecommunications Engineering 2016
B. Mandler et al. (Eds.): IoT 360° 2015, Part II, LNICST 170, pp. 20–27, 2016.
DOI: 10.1007/978-3-319-47075-7_3

commercial and open source test automation tools like Winrunner, Selenium widely used in web application test automation. But there is a void in the availability of test automation framework for IoT applications dealing with machine generated data and task actuation. There are popular mobile test automation framework like Sikuli, Robot, Monkeyrunner for mobile app testing but those are not portable on constrained devices for IoT application testing. The reason of unavailability of such test automation support in IoT domain is due to resource constraints of the device under test (DUT) as aforesaid tools use resource hungry protocols requiring large amount of resources like CPU, memory, power and bandwidth. Presently the testing of device applications is done at a central site before field deployment. Engineers execute the test suite and collect the results from tests running on individual devices. Manual testing of device application involves tedious manual intervention and constant monitoring.

2   TCUP Overview

TCS Connected Universe Platform (TCUP) [4,5] is an IoT PAAS offering that includes Device Management (DM), Message Router service, Sensor observation service (SOS), Data Analytics service and Complex Event Processing service. TCUP is a cloud based multitenant Platform-as-a-Service (PaaS) offering that makes it easy to develop, deploy and administer M2M or IoT applications. TCUP consists of a set of RESTful modules exposing web services, device agents and web portal that are specifically designed for application developers to create highly scalable and intelligent analytics driven applications that make use of sensors and devices. TCUP can be hosted on private cloud like Openstack or public cloud like AWS or Azure. Figure 1 depicts a high level overview of TCUP. TCUP also serves as a horizontal IoT application management platform where vertical domain specific services can be hosted with which corresponding device agents can interact, generated events can be stored, analyzed and finally some action can be triggered based on the application decision logic.

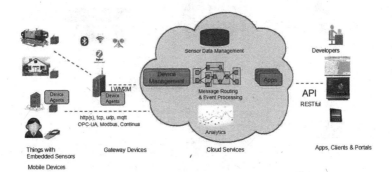

Fig. 1. TCUP modular overview

3   Device Management Concept

TCUP platform has a Device Management (DM) module which allows remote monitoring of devices and sensors, monitor health and connectivity status of devices, observe devices and their resources send commands to devices. TCUP supports the OMA LightweightM2M(LWM2M) standard [6] which uses underlying protocol CoAP [7]. The choice of CoAP over HTTP in IoT is gaining impetus as it is less resource hungry in terms of CPU load, memory footprint and bandwidth usage and energy consumption [8]. LWM2M follows Client-Server architecture where the Device hosts the LWM2M client and the DM server hosts the LWM2M server. LWM2M uses the Constrained Application Protocol (CoAP) with UDP bindings for transport. Each property of a device is modeled as a CoAP resources and similar resources are clubbed under one LWM2M objects for logical grouping. For e.g. location related resources like latitude, longitude and altitude resources are grouped together under location object.Multiple DM clients' resources form a hierarchic tree at DM server side and DM Server can access each device through CoAP resources URIs. DM server maintains the mapping between device endpoints and their IP along with their corresponding resource sub-tree structure and IP gets updated during periodic registration update by devices. LWM2M protocol stack with CoAP-HTTP bidirectional proxy forms the core engine of DM module. The DM service layer atop provides a RESTful interface which can be consumed by DM portal or other third party application. Following Fig. 2 depicts an high level architecture of DM service module. The notifications on any observable resources are automatically posted by DM agents to DM server. The observed data may be consumed by any application through Message Router (MR) module like posting the observation data to TCUP Sensor Data Management module. For scalability and high availability server clusters can be formed with UDP load-balancer for LWM2M core and HTTP load-balancer for DM service.

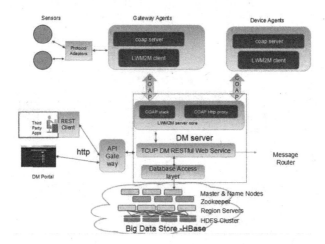

Fig. 2. TCUP DM service high level architecture

Access control list (ACL) defines permissible operation on a resource. API gateway authorise and authicates every call based API key passed with service call. Device data is stored in a NoSQL database (HBase). Every device resource is either static (like make, IMEI etc.), dynamic (like sensor value, CPU load etc.) or editable (like device description). If DM resource is observable then events for that observable resource can be subscribed by DM user through RESTful interface of DM service in order to receive automatic notification if there is any change in the resource value. This feature is useful to get automatic notification every time a sensor value changes or some events occur.

4   Device Task Actuation Framework High Level Overview

TCUP Device Task Actuation Framework (DTAF) as IoT Test Platform (ITP) is a cloud based solution on TCUP PAAS offering which facilitates the tester to remotely execute IoT test applications on multiple devices and get the results. ITP also enables the tester to view runtime device data varying CPU load or RAM usage and as well as sensor values during test execution. In case of DTAF device agent runs on DUT and works as test controller. High level overview of lightweight device test automation framework is shown in Fig. 3. Tester can launch test applications on remote DUTs from any device and get test results after test completion.

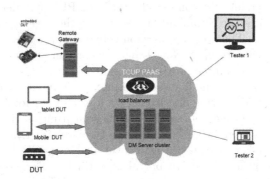

Fig. 3. Device task actuation framework overview

The device agent is modeled as a group of RESTful CoAP resources which represent static or dynamic device parameters, configurations and actions. First device needs to commission itself with TCUP DM server which is initiated by the DM agent registration with DM server, henceforth device can be managed through TCUP. Java implementation of device agent architecture is shown in the Fig. 4. DM agent includes CoAP resource class for every resource where every individual resources can have GET and PUT handlers depending on read/write

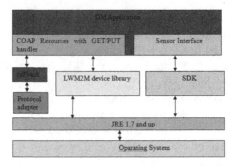

Fig. 4. Device agent highlevel architecture

access control list. Protocol adapters enable agent to communicate with sensors over various protocols. The sensory resources also invokes OS specific sensor interface API to acquire sensor data. Test launcher is defined as a CoAP resource in DM agent with CoAP GET/PUT handlers which serves test launching request coming from the DM server end.

4.1 Test Execution Process in DTAF ITP

As tester fires a test from portal the DM Server (DMS) gets test command through DM Rest API call from test portal, a consumer of DM services. DM service translates command from Http to CoAP and send that to DMC over CoAP protocol. DMC works as test controller and has a resource "launcher" with GET PUT handlers. Receiving test command launcher's PUT handler invokes a callback that autheticates the command and then fires the specific preinstalled test application on device. Then test application gets test parameters from DMC and performs execution accordingly. Now Device agent can get runtime data from test application over any inter process communication (IPC) mechanism available for DUT's OS like a domain socket in Linux or an intent broadcast receiver mechanism in Android. During test execution user can opt for subscribing runtime data from DUT through portal and can view the runtime device parameters along with sensor data on TCUP Sensor Data Explorer (SDE), a HTML5 based visualizer. DMC sends test result to DMS over CoAP and DMS does the CoAP to HTTP translation and sends to portal over HTTP. Then portal shows the result. The interaction between different modules of DTAF is explained with a Fig. 5a.

Device agent accepts commands from DMS, controls test execution, gathers dynamic device data, aggregates generated result and send back the result to DMS. If test nature requires a pass-fail decision then generated result is compared against stored golden reference either at device side or at server side. Transfer of result set at server for comparison involves more bandwidth usage whereas comparison at device side loads device computation resource. So the choice of place of decision making requires a trade off between device hardware capacity and bandwidth availability. Following sequence diagram in Fig. 5b depicts the aforesaid message flow between DTAF entities.

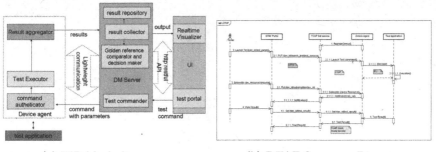

(a) ITP block diagram   (b) DTAF Sequence Diagram

Fig. 5. DTAF message flow

5 Prototype Implementation and Results

Tester first runs device agent i.e. DM client (DMC) on Device under test (DUT) and registers it in TCUP. He logs into ITP portal to see list of DUTs registered by him and he selects a particular device and view the details of the selected device. As the tester clicks on the launch button against test name from action tab test starts running on the DUT. The result button and launch button will be disabled during test execution. During execution a tester can opt to see dynamic resources (like sensor)on a live graph on SDE by subscribing the resource through portal, live graph runs until tester opts out by unsubscribing the resource. Once the test is finished the test result can be seen by clicking on result button against the test. Figure 6a shows a screenshot of a test result by running a sample benchmark test on device while Fig. 6 shows live graph in TCUT DTAF ITP portal. This sample test is based on open source benchmark algorithm like Wheatstone, Dhrystone, Linpack etc.

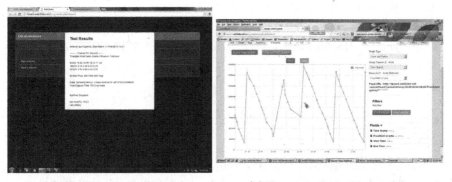

(a) Test Result on Portal   (b) Dynamic Data Live stream

Fig. 6. Screenshots from ITP prototype

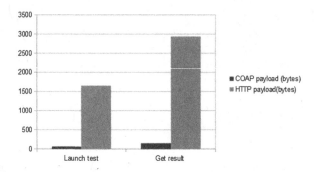

Fig. 7. Bandwidth savings

5.1 Bandwidth Usage and Performance Measurement

Less bandwidth is used by CoAP based DTAF framework against a HTTP based mobile test automation framework. Average bandwidth usage by DTAF over 100 iterations shows the improvement in bandwidth consumption in Fig. 7. Although bandwidth is getting cheaper with time, the traffic reduction continues to be an important consideration due to huge number of devices. From results it is evident that CoAP payload uses hundred times less bandwidth than HTTP to transmit the same information.

We have measured performance of our test automation framework through load testing using Apache JMeter. The performance test setup comprised of the following hardware configuration: 1. Phoenix 4.2.2 plus HBASE 0.98 cluster running on HDFS with 1 zookeper, 1 hbase master and 3 region servers, all with 1 core, 2 GB RAM Ubuntu VMs on Openstack cloud 2. DM Service, developed using Spring v4, running on Apache Tomcat 7.47 on a Intel Core i5, 4 GB RAM machine with 32 bit Windows 7. DM Server is allocated 268MB of Memory. 3. Internet Connectivity with 100 Mbps backbone for server and 3G for devices The result is given below in Table 1.

Table 1. Performance measurement: concurrent request/second

Throughput per sec	100	500	1000
Query result (GET)	45	43	42
Launch application (PUT)	87	85	83

Study of results reveals that the performance in launching test is better than querying the result. The reason is launching application involves passing on a JSON payload comprising of test name and parameters whereas result query returns a large payload which internally gets sliced into multiple chunks handled by CoAP block mode transfer protocol. Also DM's underlying database is HBase where read has more latency than write operation [9]. It is evident from result that throughput remains nearly constant despite increasing number of concurrent request handled by DM server, so the complexity of test launching is O(1) independent of individual test application's complexity. This behaviours is expected as one TCUP DM server has capacity to handle 10000 request per second, although performance measurement with further increase in load is a subject of our future scope of work. To serve load more than 10000 request per second would require server cluster with load balancer.

6   Conclusion

DTAF based ITP uses Lightweight M2M protocol to make this framework a suitable candidate for IoT device application test automation. The runtime data collection feature during execution enables hardware behaviour test for sensor intensive gaming consoles. ITP can be utilized to run resident device health check and security verification script during device idle time. The device task actuation framework can be leveraged to design smart home or smart automative solution [10]. For e.g. this framework can be used for contextual actuation of a remote media controller to control a home entertainment device. Controlling of device side actuation poses a new security threat that generates the need of lightweight authentication and authorization of device commands which will be our new area of research.

References

1. Wang, F., Du, W.: A test automation framework based on WEB. In: 2012 IEEE/ACIS 11th International Conference on Computer and Information Science (ICIS), pp. 683–687, 30 May 2012–1 June 2012
2. Fu, L.L., Dai, J.Q., Liu, J.H.: Auto test solution for web application. Inf. Techonl. 4(39), 23 (2010)
3. Wu, Y.: Automation testing framework for web base on web base on selenium. Inf. Techonl. 9, 187–188 (2011)
4. Misra, P., et al.: A computing platform for development and deployment of sensor data based applications and services. Patent No. WO2013072925 A2
5. http://www.tcs.com/SiteCollectionDocuments/Brochures/Innovation-Brochure-TC S-Connected-Universe-Platform-1014-1.pdf
6. http://technical.openmobilealliance.org/Technical/technical-information/release-pr ogram/current-releases/oma-lightweightm2m-v1-0
7. Shelby, Z.: Constrained Application Protocol (CoAP) RFC6690. http://tools.ietf. org/html/rfc6690z
8. Sammarco, C., Iera, A.: Improving service management in the internet of things. MDPI Sens. 12(9), 11888–11909 (2012)
9. http://planetcassandra.org/nosql-performance-benchmarks
10. Ghose, A., et al.: Internet of Things application development. Patent No. EP2806356 A1

Networked Smart Objects: Moving Data Processing Closer to the Source

Alessandra Rizzardi[1]([⊠]), Daniele Miorandi[2], Sabrina Sicari[1],
Cinzia Cappiello[3], and Alberto Coen-Porisini[1]

[1] Universita' degli Studi dell'Insubria, Via Mazzini 5, 21100 Varese, Italy
{alessandra.rizzardi,sabrina.sicari,alberto.coenporisini}@uninsubria.it
[2] CREATE-NET, Via alla Cascata 56/D, 38123 Trento, Italy
daniele.miorandi@create-net.org
[3] Politecnico di Milano, Piazza Leonardo da Vinci 32, 20133 Milano, Italy
cinzia.cappiello@polimi.it

Abstract. The satisfaction of security and data quality requirements
plays a fundamental role in the Internet of Things (IoT) scenario. Such
a dynamic environment requires the adoption of heterogeneous technologies to provide customized services in various application domains and
both security threats and data quality issues need to be addresses in
order to guarantee an effective and efficient data management. In this
paper, a lightweight and cross-domain prototype of distributed architecture for IoT is presented and evaluated by means of open data provided
by different sources. We show how users can access different types of data
by changing security and quality requirements.

Keywords: Internet of Things · Security · Data quality · Middleware ·
Prototype

1 Introduction

The term "Internet of Things" (IoT) [1] is becoming widely used for broadly
defining a future in which objects equipped with sensing and actuation capabilities get connected to a global networked infrastructure. An IoT system can be
depicted as a collection of smart devices which interact on a collaborative basis
to fulfill a common goal, acquiring data from and acting upon the environment
they are in. Security, privacy and data quality represent critical requirements,
which can hinder the large scale adoption of IoT services. Furthermore, IoT
deployments are characterized by a large heterogeneity in terms of adopted technologies; some deployments may include a large number of devices, leading to
scalability issues to be faced. The most crucial challenge in building an IoT system lies in the lack of common and standardised software framework. To fill this
gap, the adoption of Service Oriented Architectures (SOA) and Service-oriented
Communications technologies [2,3] in IoT is shared by the majority of scientific community, but the state of the art is mostly limited to starting research

© ICST Institute for Computer Sciences, Social Informatics and Telecommunications Engineering 2016
B. Mandler et al. (Eds.): IoT 360° 2015, Part II, LNICST 170, pp. 28–35, 2016.
DOI: 10.1007/978-3-319-47075-7_4

activities[1]. Furthermore, several middleware layers are employed to enforce the integration and the security of devices and data within the same information network [4–6]. Several related scenarios have been encompassed in related EU projects, such as: FP7 COMPOSE (Collaborative Open Market to Place Objects at your Service), iCORE, IoT.EST (Internet of Things Environment for Service Creation and Testing), Ebbits, uTRUSTit, Butler[2].

Besides security and privacy, also data quality has to be addressed. In [7], authors claim the need of control over data sources to ensure their validity, information accuracy and credibility. Accuracy, timeliness and the trustworthiness are instead the dimensions considered in [8]: anomaly detection techniques are widely employed to remove noises and inaccurate data in order to improve data quality. Besides temporal aspects (i.e., currency) and data validity, another important dimension is availability [9]. Authors defined new metrics for the cited quality dimensions in the IoT environment and evaluate the quality of the real world data available on an open IoT platform called Cosm. They have shown that data quality problems are frequent and they should be solved or at least users should be aware of the poor quality of the used data sources.

In order to address these issues, we propose a flexible and distributed IoT architecture based on the idea of bringing processing, security and data qualification closer to the actual data sources. In a previous work [10], we presented a security-and quality-aware system architecture for IoT, based on the concept of the Networked Smart objects (NOS), which are computationally powerful smart nodes aiming to create a distributed storage in order to handle the data acquired from large-scale IoT deployments. In order to ease the development of applications and the management of the system, a middleware has been designed and prototyped. It includes features for users and applications to dynamically specify the minimal level of security and data quality suitable for their own purpose. The distributed architecture automates the deployment of adequate filters for ensuring that only qualified data are passed over to the actual service. The prototype is evaluated connecting real-time open data services to a simple visualization dashboard. The main innovative contribution lies in the implementation of a highly modular and lightweight architecture for the NOS, able to (i) provide proper interfaces with heterogeneous data sources (ii) automatically evaluate the security and quality of the received data, and (iii) provide standardized interfaces and data models for applications/services to access qualified IoT information, where raw data is enriched with metadata specifying their security and quality levels.

2 Architecture

In the IoT system we identified two main entities: (i) the nodes, which are the sources of the data and can be represented by heterogeneous devices (RFID,

---

[1] www.hcilab.org/projects/perci/index.htm, cs.adelaide.edu.au/peertrack.

[2] iot-at-work.eu, iot-icore.eu, ict-iotest.eu/iotest, www.ebbits-project.eu, www.utrustit.eu, www.iot-butler.eu/.

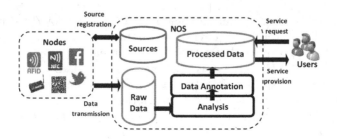

Fig. 1. System architecture

NFC, WSN, actuators, social networks); (ii) the users, who interact with the IoT system by requesting some information by means of services. In order to handle such a huge amount of data closer to the sources and better satisfy the users service requests (in terms of quality and reliability), the NOS layer is introduced (Fig. 1) [10]. NOSs are networked smart nodes without strict constraints in terms of energy and computational capabilities. They include self-organizing features and can be deployed where and when needed, in a distributed manner; through their interface with enterprise platforms and IoT enabling technologies, they can be used to enrich software platforms, making them able to interact with the physical world following the adopted rules. NOSs collect the data provided by different sources, which can be registered and no registered. Registered sources may specify an encryption scheme for their interactions with NOSs. Since the received data are of different types and formats, NOSs initially put them in the storage unit named *Raw Data* and elaborate them according to the two-phases named *Analysis* and *Data Annotation*, in order to obtain a uniform representation.

Firstly, the data are analyzed (*Analysis* phase) in terms of security and data quality. As regards security [11], if the data source is a registered one, the information access requires the authentication of the source and the decryption of the data; therefore, the system preserves indeed complete knowledge, including encryption scheme, used key etc. Each encryption schema (ECC, RSA, PKI) has associated a score in the range [0:10], established by the system administrator, who, according to the required security levels, defines the score assignment rules. Then, a score is assigned to: authentication, confidentiality, integrity and privacy. For registered sources: (i) *confidentiality* and *privacy* are evaluated assigning a score to the encryption schema (based on the robustness of the used encryption technique and of the adopted key distribution schema); (ii) *integrity* is checked and a score is given (0 for a violated and 2 for a unviolated data); (iii) *authentication* is set to 1. For non registered sources confidentiality, privacy and authentication are set to 0, while integrity is set to 1. Note that some registered sources may use neither authentication credentials nor encryption. Further, for unregistered/unknown sources no information may be available, therefore the scores have associated a low value. As regards data quality assessment, a score in the range [0:10] is assigned to timeliness, completeness, accuracy and precision levels [12,13]. *Timeliness* is conceived as the temporal validity of data and is calculated on the basis of the freshness (currency) of data and on the frequency of changes (volatiliy), as in Eq. 1.

$$Timeliness = \max\left(1 - \frac{Currency}{Volatility}, 0\right), \tag{1}$$

where currency can be defined as the interval from the time when the value was sampled to the time instant at which data are sent to NOS. Volatility is a static information which indicates the amount of time units (seconds) during which data remain valid; it is usually associated with the type of phenomena that the system monitors and depends on the change frequency. *Completeness* is calculated as the ratio between the numbers of collected values and the number of expected values. *Accuracy* is usually defined as the degree of conformity of a measured quantity to its actual (i.e., true) value; it is also related to *precision*, which is the degree to which further measurement or calculations show the same or similar results. Formally, accuracy can be defined as the error expressed by the difference between the mean of the measurements v_n and a reference value v_{ref}. The measure is considered accurate if such difference is smaller than the acceptable measurement error ϵ_{acc}. Precision is often characterized in terms of the standard deviation of the measured values: the smaller the standard deviation, the higher the precision. For this reason, a measure can be considered precise if the reciprocal of variance is smaller than ϵ_{prec}. Note that in case of streaming data such metrics have to be calculated periodically on data samples in order to detect quality changes over time and also to gather information about the trustworthiness of the source. The choice to provide a score for each security and data quality requirement makes such a solution flexible for smart integration in different application scenarios. Finally, *Data Annotation* phase represents the information obtained from *Analysis* phase according to a specified format [10] and includes also a semantic description of the data content: the data are annotated with a set of metadata (a score for each security and quality level). The annotated data are stored in the storage unit named *Processed Data*.

3   Prototype

In this section we describe a lightweight data management and service middleware platform consisting of distributed NOSs. The proposed prototype is based on the architecture described in Sect. 2 and its main features are:

- *Data acquisition and analysis:* the middleware is modelled in order to manage registered and no registered sources, characterized by different security communication schemas and providing diverse quality levels for their data.
- *Unified data representation:* the middleware addresses the need of an uniform representation for the data by providing a format for annotating data once they are processed by the NOS layer.

- *Standardised design:* in order to deal with heterogeneous services, the middleware consists of a set of lightweight modules and interfaces working in a non-blocking manner through distributed NOS devices, aiming to perform data analysis, discovery, and query.
- *Reconfigurability:* since the existing IoT deployments are conceived for very specific applications and thus hardly reconfigurable, the middleware supports dynamic reconfiguration capabilities and can be remote orchestrated through internet/intranet settings, which are based on open standards.

More in details, the prototypical implementation of NOS has been realized by means of *Node.JS* platform[3] and *MongoDB*[4] for storage management. The code is released openly[5]. Modules interact among themselves through *RESTful* services. They can be distinguished in: node interfaces, processing modules, and service interfaces. The node interfaces manage the sources registrations, receive the data from the external sources, and insert them in the storage of *Raw Data*. The processing modules are in charge of performing *Analysis* and *Data Annotation* phases. Finally, the service interfaces publish the *RESTful* services and web pages to which users or external applications can interact at any time.

Note that, a great advantage of such an implementation is that it is possible to add new modules or duplicate the existing ones since they are able to work in a parallel (non-blocking) manner or to define new functionalities or removing the active ones. The exploitation of *MongoDB*, which is a no-relational database (i.e., NoSQL), consent to the data model to evolve dynamically; in fact, data are handled as document in *JSON* format, which is a lightweight data-interchange format and is both easy for humans to read and write and easy for machines to parse and generate. Hence, such an implementation is independent both from the data model and the application domain. In a production setting the usage of *MongoDB* would be more likely replaced by a message queueing system providing durability guarantees (e.g., Apache Kafka[6]) and a stream processing framework (e.g., Apache Storm[7]) implementing the analysis and data annotation tasks.

4   Application Case Study

In order to verify the behavior of the presented middleware platform, a set of open data are exploited as sources for running the system. These are obtained in real time from six sensors at the meteorological station of the city of Campodenno (Trentino, Italy). The measures, referred to temperature, humidity, wind, energy consumption, air quality, are retrieved in *JSON* format, which is compliant with *MongoDB*, through *GET* requests. Furthermore, also the data in the storages are stored in *JSON* format.

---

[3] nodejs.org/.

[4] www.mongodb.org/.

[5] bitbucket.org/alessandrarizzardi/nos.

[6] kafka.apache.org/.

[7] storm.apache.org/.

The experimental setup includes: a Raspberry Pi on which NOS platform is installed; a laptop, which emulates the behavior of several nodes which send the data; a set of user devices, which access the provided service. As just said, the Raspberry Pi executes NOS functionalities and communicates with the nodes running on the laptop. The data analyzed by NOS are accessible through a RESTful service and can be interpreted by various applications (web services, desktop applications, mobile applications). Users can connect to a public IP address by means of their computers, tablets or smartphones, in order to visualize on their browser the gathered data, dinamically filtering them on the basis of the required security and quality levels, in terms of confidentiality, integrity, privacy, authentication, completeness, timeliness, accuracy, and precision, respectively, through the sliders provided by the web service itself, as shown in Fig. 2. Since meteorological data are obtained from six different sources, we assign to them the security and quality scores through an analysis of the incoming data, as specified in Table 1.

Table 1. Source parameters

Parameters	Source 1	Source 2	Source 3	Source 4	Source 5	Source 6
Authentication	1	1	0	1	0	0
Security schema score	10	6	0	2	0	0
Privacy schema score	10	6	0	2	0	0
Timeliness	9	8	6	3	9	7
Completeness	9	10	8	6	7	10
Accuracy	9	7	5	6	7	10
Precision	9	8	4	5	8	9

Figure 2(a) shows in the graph the data of wind speed (in Km/h) and humidity (in %) processed by NOS without any filters of security or quality; in fact all the sliders are set to 0, therefore the data provided by all the sources are displayed to the requesting user. Whereas, in Fig. 2(b) both filters on security and quality are applied: the data, shown in the graph, are obtained from authenticated sources (the parameter related to the authentication is set to 1), for which the robustness of the encryption algorithm has a score equal or higher than 2; while the data quality parameters have to be equal or higher than 4. We remark that, in this case, the web service provides less data with respect to Fig. 2(a).

We remark that this represents only an example of NOS application in a context which has to deal with data received in real time. Other possible applications are: the management of smart home and/or buildings from an energy consumption point of view; the analysis of business activities in real time; the retailing experiences; the search for restaurants or other places related to tourism experiences; all the domains which require an asynchronous data analysis in order to take strategic decisions. In fact, from an application standpoint, the acquisition

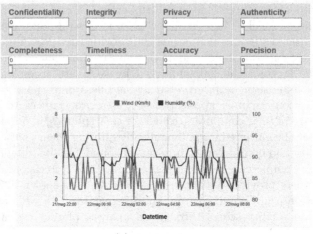

(a) No_Filters

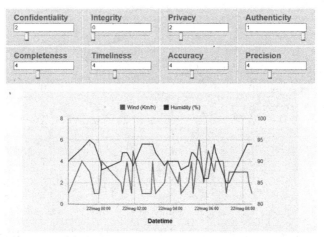

(b) Security_and_Quality_Filters

Fig. 2. Results

and management of data in real time represent critical issues also regarding user satisfaction and market expansion of specific categories of services.

5 Conclusions

In this paper, a distributed IoT middleware, named NOS, has been designed and prototyped. Since security, privacy and data quality have been identified as critical requirements for the large scale adoption of IoT applications, NOS aims to create a distributed storage for handling IoT data along with their security and data qualification closer to the actual data sources. The analyzed data are then provided in real time to users, which are aware of the levels of security, privacy and quality of the data themselves. The prototype has been implemented with a highly modular and lightweight design, and NOS finally runs on a Raspberry Pi. Also an example of application case study is presented, in order to clarify the functionalities of NOS and its dynamic structure. In the future, we are planning to evaluate the robustness of the NOS architecture in a real IoT scenario, exploiting sensitive data and applying a new defined secure score algorithm.

References

1. Miorandi, D., Sicari, S., De Pellegrini, F., Chlamtac, I.: Survey internet of things: vision, applications and research challenges. Ad Hoc Netw. **10**(7), 1497–1516 (2012)
2. Papazoglou, M., Traverso, P., Dustdar, S., Leymann, F.: Service-oriented computing: state of the art and research challenges. Computer **40**(11), 38–45 (2007)
3. Yu, Q., Liu, X., Bouguettaya, A., Medjahed, B.: Deploying and managing web services: issues, solutions, and directions. VLDB J. **17**(3), 537–572 (2008)
4. Conzon, D., Bolognesi, T., Brizzi, P., Lotito, A., Tomasi, R., Spirito, M.: The virtus middleware: an XMPP based architecture for secure IoT communications. In: 2012 21st International Conference on Computer Communications and Networks, ICCCN 2012, Munich, Germany, pp. 1–6, July 2012
5. Gòmez-Goiri, A., Orduna, P., Diego, J., de Ipina, D.L.: Otsopack: lightweight semantic framework for interoperable ambient intelligence applications. Comput. Hum. Behav. **30**, 460–467 (2014)
6. Liu, C.H., Yang, B., Liu, T.: Efficient naming, addressing and profile services in internet-of-things sensory environments. Ad Hoc Netw. **18**, 85–101 (2013)
7. Guo, B., Zhang, D., Wang, Z., Yu, Z., Zhou, X.: Opportunistic IoT: exploring the harmonious interaction between human and the internet of things. J. Netw. Comput. Appl. **36**(6), 1531–1539 (2013)
8. Metzger, A., Chi, C.-H., Engel, Y., Marconi, A.: Research challenges on online service quality prediction for proactive adaptation. In: 2012 Workshop on European Software Services and Systems Research - Results and Challenges (S-Cube), pp. 51–57, June 2012
9. Li, F., Nastic, S., Dustdar, S.: Data quality observation in pervasive environments. In: Proceedings of the 2012 IEEE 15th International Conference on Computational Science and Engineering, pp. 602–609. IEEE Computer Society (2012)
10. Sicari, S., Cappiello, C., Pellegrini, D., Miorandi, D., Coen-Porisini, A.: A security- and quality-aware system architecture for internet of things. Inf. Syst. Front. **18**(4), 665–677 (2016)
11. Sicari, S., Rizzardi, A., Grieco, L.A., Coen-Porisini, A.: Security, privacy and trust in internet of things: the road ahead. Comput. Netw. **76**, 146–164 (2015)
12. Cappiello, C., Schreiber, F.A.: Quality- and energy-aware data compression by aggregation in WSN data streams. In: Proceedings of the 2009 IEEE International Conference on Pervasive Computing, Communications, pp. 1–6. IEEE Computer Society, Washington, DC, USA (2009)
13. Klein, A., Lehner, W.: Representing data quality in sensor data streaming environments. J. Data Inf. Qual. **1**(2), 10:1–10:28 (2009)

Automated Workflow Formation for IoT Analytics: A Case Study

Tanushyam Chattopadhyay[✉], Avik Ghose, Arijit Mukherjee, Santa Maiti, and Arpan Pal

Innovation Labs, Tata Consultancy Services, Kolkata, India
{t.chattopadhyay,avik.ghose,mukherjee.arijit, santa.maiti,arpan.pal}@tcs.com

Abstract. The rapid deployment of sensors across the world in various sectors has fuelled a growing demand of smart applications and services that can leverage this boom of Internet of Things (IoT). However, developing analytical applications for IoT is a difficult process as applications tend to be cross-domain and there are close relationships with the physical world. It is unreasonable to imagine that the application developers will possess all relevant skills and knowledge related to the domain, physical world, signal processing and deployment infrastructure. This paper presents an method that assists the IoT application developer by (i) providing an annotated repository of algorithms, (ii) recommending algorithms depending on the signal type to reduce the effort required from a signal processing expert, and (iii) providing a framework to execute the IoT application thereby reducing the development cost and time by capturing the knowledge of experts in models. We have evaluated our method by comparing the accuracy for a typical IoT application obtained by using the algorithms used by signal processing experts against the algorithms recommended by our method.

Keywords: Model driven development · IoT analytics · Automated work flow creation

1 Introduction

The importance of *not-so-distant-future* sensor-based intelligent and ubiquitous systems has been apparent during the past few years when global technology giants have all underlined the potential of the "Internet of Things (IoT)". The technology is capable of creating a vast network of smart devices and connected things to an unprecedented extent and enhance solutions and services in multiple domains such as healthcare, energy & utilities, transportation etc. and also delve into the development of cross-domain solutions and services. However, developing IoT applications is inherently difficult due to the requirement of cross domain and cross technology knowledge. This poses requirements for technical experts who charge heavily for their time, thereby increasing product costs. The primary motivation of this work is to reduce the dependency on the availability of such

© ICST Institute for Computer Sciences, Social Informatics and Telecommunications Engineering 2016
B. Mandler et al. (Eds.): IoT 360° 2015, Part II, LNICST 170, pp. 36–43, 2016.
DOI: 10.1007/978-3-319-47075-7_5

niche skilled workers and automate the process of application development by using knowledge models covering the aforesaid aspects. Working towards this vision, we have created a framework that is capable of recommending suitable algorithms for sensor signal processing once the application goal is defined. We have also constructed a knowledge-base and associated libraries for extracting a super set of features that can be used in any signal processing work-flow in order to automatically select the most suitable set of features for classification. We make an hypothesis that feature extraction and selection methods depend on the sensor signal class and the classification goal. This is the step we have automated at the first level, this is because this step is intutive and knowledge driven, requiring maximum time of the domain and algorithm experts.

Traditionally IoT applications [1,2] involves four steps namely (i) sensor integration, (ii) sensor data collection, (iii) data storage, and (iv) data analysis. Existing platform as services (PaaS) for IoT like Google App Engine, Heroku doesn't support any specialized services for IoT application development. [3,4] proposes an integrated application development platform but no work flow automation tool is provided. We found only two prior works that tries to bring in automation. In [5], authors have used a database that stores prior performance and complexity of different algorithms. They have initially converted raw data into a set of features that can be mined and then used in automatic selection of appropriate algorithms based on the problem data set. However, the proposed method has no means to capture the various levels of knowledge. Also they do not provide means to define the goal or the sensors to be used. In [6], authors have presented a survey which provides useful insights regarding automation of the outlier removal process if the data type can be properly classified.

We illustrate our work by automating an example work-flow for computing heart-rate (HR) using Photo Plethysmograph (PPG). This is a well researched topic and we have chosen to compare our results against [11]. We study the features used by this approach and then try to reason out the same using knowledge driven method, this is illustrated in Sect. 2.

The proposed system consists of a designer interface, an algorithm repository and a execution framework. The designer interface allows users to author application work-flows using a web-based interactive Graphical User Interface (GUI). The algorithm repository is a crowd-sourced repository of algorithms which are designed and implemented by researchers, domain experts and analysts using a common set of languages and a common interface. The execution framework provides the spinal cord for such design. The framework is detailed in Sect. 2.2.

2   Proposed Method

The generic signal processing work flow involves the steps as shown in Fig. 1.

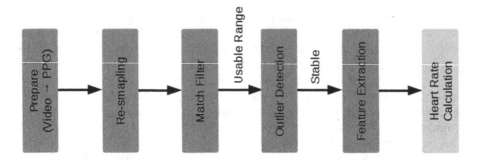

Fig. 1. High level workflow for IoT signal processing

2.1 Work-Flow Design

Prepare: The first phase of our work flow is prepare. In this phase the input video is converted into PPG. As discussed, we have used the method described in [10]. This paper takes only the red component of the RGB video obtained from mobile camera. Then the video is cropped from the central region and an average of 'R' component for all the pixels within the region of interest is computed. This is reported as a single sample of the PPG time-series.

Re-sampling: This module is required when the input sample rate of the input varies over time or varies for different devices. This is also required for predicting the result more precisely. For example if we capture video at 30 Frames per Second (FPS), each sample represents almost 2 heart beats per minute on the other hand if we sample at 15 FPS, each sample point is equivalent to 4 heart beats per minute. Thus sample rate is also indicative for the precision level of the outcome. We capture this expected sample rate information from the question like "what is the expected accuracy level for this application". Once the precision requirement is finalized by the developer, we translate it to the required sample rate. Simple re-sampling algorithms are used to re-sample the input signal to the required sample rate.

Matched Filter: Match filter is required to truncate the signal using the domain knowledge. This parameters are obtained from the question "What is the possible range of heart rate?" to be answered by the developer. Any one having the domain knowledge gives this input to be within the range of 50 to 180 (normal). In this use case the specific range of heart beat allows to truncate the frequency range and also to estimate the periodicity of the time domain signal.

Outlier Detection: Outlier detection is an important module in this work-flow as it helps to remove the undesired part of the signal and thus reduce the execution time. Moreover the frequency response of the signal after removing the

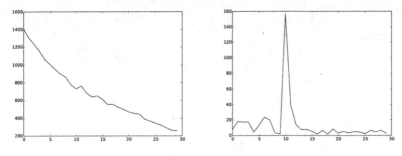

(a) FFT of the signal before noise cleaning

(b) FFT of the signal after noise cleaning

Fig. 2. Comparison of FFT with and without noise cleaning

outlier is more informative. In the Fig. 2a shows the frequency response of the signal before outlier removal and the Fig. 2b represents the FFT (Fast Fourier Transform) of the input signal after removing the outlier. Our outlier detection module takes the knowledge that there should be a consistency of the signal over time as there is a periodicity in the signal. Outlier removal involves two sub-steps namely (i) estimation of window length, and (ii) outlier removal.

In the proposed method the pseudo code for window estimation is like:

- Compute the valid range of the periodicity or wavelength from the input given in match filter
- Vary the window size within this range (say here it is 10 to 45 for a 30 FPS video)
- Compute the KL distance (d_i) between the time domain signature of two consecutive i and $(i+1)^{th}$ windows
- Find the i for which d_i = minimum of $d_i \forall i$
- Repeat this for all samples in the signal and get the different window size for the signal and store it in a buffer

The next step is to compute the statistical moment variance for each window. We are not considering mean as mean value of the signal over a window may vary over time. This is a property of PPG signal. So we have considered only the difference between the variance of the time domain values over windows. We also applied a threshold based approach to remove the outlier. In the Fig. 3a we have shown the first order difference of variance over time.

Feature Extraction: We have constructed a super set of features those are usually used in signal processing. Our feature set considers the different features used in signal processing. We have initially reduces the feature set depending on the type of the signal as shown in Table 1. As we know that the input signal for this use case is stationary and periodic in nature we have used FFT as the frequency domain feature and the time domain features are described below: We have already defined the method of window selection.

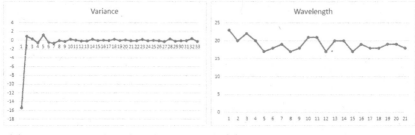

(a) Difference of Variance over cycles   (b) Time Domain Detected cycles

Fig. 3. Variance over cycles and periods

Table 1. Recommended features depending on the signal type

Type	Type	Recommended feature
Periodic	Stationary	FFT and time domain peaks
Periodic	Non-stationary	DWT, and envelope
Aperiodic	Linear	STFT and DWT
Aperiodic	Non-linear	Time delay embedding and recurrence plot

– Compute the k number of local peaks with top k amplitudes for each window.
– Let $px_{i,j}$ and $py_{i,j}$ represents the sample number and the corresponding amplitude respectively for the jth peak of the ith window.
– Compute the ratio of $px_{i,j}$ and $px_{i+1,j}$ for all i and j values and let it be feature f_1.
– Compute the ratio of $py_{i,j}$ and $py_{i+1,j}$ for all i and j values and let it be feature f_2.
– Compute the difference of $px_{i,j}$ and $px_{i+1,j}$ for all i and j values and let it be feature f_3.
– Compute the difference of $py_{i,j}$ and $py_{i+1,j}$ for all i and j values and let it be feature f_4.

Now we observe that the for PPG signal f_3 is consistent over time. From the ontology as we have defined earlier, it is a mandatory feature for this use case. So we have not considered other features in this use case and used only f_3 for heart rate computation. Similarly we get the heart rate from the FFT of the signal, too. In our experiment we have used k = 3. Thus we get 3 time domain values and one frequency domain value as expected heart rate. Finally we have taken an average of these four values to compute the final heart rate.

2.2   Execution Framework

The execution framework provides a method to build and execute the code generated using the work-flow execution. The execution framework performs the following tasks.

- Build the algorithm code for target platform
- Generate models for target platform code. These can be statistical or mathematical models as standard model files
- Generate the application code for target platform using work-flow logic
- Deploy the code on target platform using Open Systems Gateways Interconnect (OSGI) standards
- Run the code and generate results on user request

The execution model for portable platforms has been discussed in [12], which our work re-uses to implement the execution model and takes the framework beyond phones to other embedded gateway platforms. The execution framework is details in Fig. 4.

The framework provides skeleton for parameter passing, returning results and function sequencing using a simple construct of data structures and function references. All functions in-take a generic set of parameters which are converted to specifics inside the implementations. The functions can be chained or branched. So, the framework interface is a composite design pattern which combines both facade, strategy and adapter design pattern. The function flow follows a hybrid between pipe design pattern and the decorator design pattern, allowing both stage-wise refinement as well as same step improvement. The code for the final application is generated by following this framework by the code-generation engine which picks algorithms from the design work-flow and stitches them together into the framework.

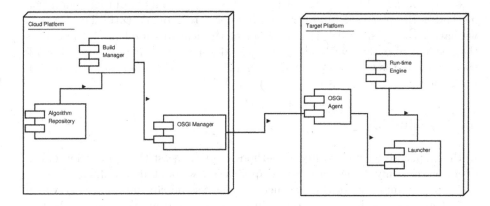

Fig. 4. Execution framework overview

3   Results and Discussions

We have used the feature recommended by our work-flow and also used our recommended windowing method to generate the code for [10]. The code was generated using our execution framework for Android phones and the generated C code was integrated into the phone using Java Native Interface (JNI).

We tested the accuracy against our captured data that comprises of 316 PPG readings captured using different mobile devices like Samsung S-Duos, iPhone 4, Intel Xolo, Sony Xperia, and LG Nexus 4. We are going to describe the method in terms of two aspects (i) accuracy of the proposed automated work flow generation and (ii) reduction in development time using our proposed work. We have evaluated our result against the state of the art method described in [10] and we have found that our proposed method which uses automatically generated feature set produces almost same result. The comparison with ground truth and state of the art work as reported in [10] is presented in Table 2. It is evident from the table that the predicted feature set works with almost same accuracy.

Table 2. Comparison of the accuracy obtained by purposed tool generated algorithm workflow and manual human programmed workflow

User	1	2	3	4	5	6	7	8
Actual heart rate	54	66	84	106	80	105	105	80
Heart rate in [10]	53	63	84	98	88	102	104	81
Heart rate in present	54	65	84	98	89	101	104	80

The results described in Table 2 shows that our result is quite compliant with the ground truth. Here all heart rates reported are the rates per minute. The noise in some signal that were not detected in our automated outlier generation method is the reason behind error with respect to ground truth. The features we have used in this work is a superset of the features used in [10] and thus the result is also close with this work. The development time for the [10] work was three months to develop the algorithm chain. On the other hand the similar workflow was generated using our tool is 3 days only.

4   Conclusion

In this paper we have presented a method that can assist the application developer to write any signal processing application without details knowledge on signal processing or algorithm. He needs to have some domain knowledge which is captured to populate an ontology in a question and answer manner. In this paper we are also claiming that the feature set to be used does not depend on the type of sensor and instead it is dependent on the type of the signal. We have also proposed a super set of possible features that are to be processed for any stationary signal. Dimensionality of the feature can be reduced either by giving the ground truth as the input for feature optimizer like MIC. Otherwise the domain knowledge is captured by question and answer based manner from the developer as we did it in this use case. Finally we have shown that the results obtained by automatic feature selection is producing the result which is at per with the manually selected features. So this work will help the future researchers of signal processing application developers in IoT. We have also shown this on a simple use case but can try on complicated problems like [13,14].

References

1. Gubbi, J., et al.: Inter-net of Things (IoT): a vision, architectural elements, and future directions. Elsevier J. Future Gener. Comput. Syst. **29**, 1645–1660 (2013)
2. Balamurali, P., et al.: Software platforms for internet of things M2M. J. Indian Inst. Sci. Multidiscip. Rev. J. **93**(3), 487–498 (2013). ISSN 0970-4140 Coden-JIISAD
3. Pal, A., et al.: Model driven development for internet of things: towards easingthe concerns of application developers. In: International Conference on IoT as a Service, IoT360 Summit, Rome (2014)
4. Misra, P., et al.: A computing platform for development and deployment of sensor data based applications and services. Patent No. WO2013072925 A2
5. Automatic mapping from data TP preprocessing algorithms. US Patent No WO2002073529
6. Gupta, M., Gao, J., Aggarwal, C.C., Han, J.: Outlier detection for temporal data: a surve. IEEE Trans. Knowl. Data Eng. **25**(1), 1–20 (2014)
7. Sackner, M.A., Inman, D.M.: Method and system for extracting cardiac parameters from plethysmographic signals. US Patent Number: 6783498, 31 August 2004
8. Wieringa, F.P., et al.: Contactless multiple wavelength photoplethysmographic imaging: a first step towards SpO2 camera technology. Ann. Biomed. Eng. **33**(8), 1034–1041 (2005)
9. Humphreys, K., et al.: Noncontact simultaneous dual wavelength photoplethysmography: a further step toward noncontact pulse oximetry. Rev. Sci. Instrum. **78**(4), 044304 (2007)
10. Pal, A., et al.: A robust heart rate detection using smart-phone video. In: Proceedings of 3rd ACM MobiHoc Workshop on Pervasive Wireless Healthcare. ACM (2013)
11. Banerjee, R., et al.: PhotoECG: Photoplethysmography to estimate ECG parameters. In: ICASSP 2014
12. Ghose, A., et al.: Design insights for a mobile based sensor application framework: for aiding platform independent algorithm design. In: IPSN 2015
13. Chattopadhyay, T., et al.: Recognition of channel logos from streamed videos for value added services in connected TV. In: IEEE International Conference on Consumer Electronics (ICCE) (2011)
14. Ghosh, H., et al.: Multimodal indexing of multilingual news video. Int. J. Digit. Multimedia Broadcast. (2010)

On Integrating Heterogeneous Locating Services

Hiroki Takatsuka[✉], Sachio Saiki, Shinsuke Matsumoto,
and Masahide Nakamura

Graduate School of System Informatics, Kobe University, Kobe, Japan
tktk@ws.cs.kobe-u.ac.jp, sachio@carp.kobe-u.ac.jp,
{shinsuke,masa-n}@cs.kobe-u.ac.jp

Abstract. This paper presents a unified locating service, KULOCS, which horizontally integrates the existing heterogeneous locating services. Focusing on technology-independent elements [when], [where] and [who] in querying locations of objects, KULOCS integrates data and operations of the existing services. In the data integration, we propose a method where the time representation, the locations, the namespace of user are consolidated by Unix time, the location labels and the alias table, respectively. We then propose KULOCS-API that integrates operations by all possible combinations of [when], [where] and [who]. Since KULOCS works as a seamless façade to the underlying locating services, clients can consume location information easily and efficiently, without knowing concrete services actually locating target objects. Also, we examine feasibility of two practical value-added services with KULOCS.

Keywords: Locating service · Indoor positioning system · Location information · Web services · Location-aware service

1 Introduction

Smart coupling of IoT, positioning systems and cloud technologies enables an extensible infrastructure to acquire and manage *locations* of users and objects. Nowadays, every smartphone is equipped with GPS. Also, various GPS modules for IoT appear on the market (e.g., [4]). The emerging *indoor positioning systems (IPS)* can locate users even inside buildings or underground, where GPS cannot cover. The enabling technologies of IPS include Wi-Fi [6], Bluetooth beacons [10], RFID [12], IMES [11]. Gathering such indoor/outdoor location information in the cloud would create a variety of location-based services and applications.

The location information gathered in the cloud should be provided *as a service*, so that client applications can easily consume the locations via API, without knowing implementation details of underlying positioning systems. We call such a cloud service *locating service* in this paper. In fact, several practical services come onto market recently. They include Swarm [7], Glympse [1], Pathshare [5], and IndoorAtlas [2]. Although features and operation policies vary from one to another, the basic idea is to use the cloud for exchanging or sharing location

© ICST Institute for Computer Sciences, Social Informatics and Telecommunications Engineering 2016
B. Mandler et al. (Eds.): IoT 360° 2015, Part II, LNICST 170, pp. 44–52, 2016.
DOI: 10.1007/978-3-319-47075-7_6

information acquired by a certain positioning system. Most services provide API for developers.

Basically, there is no compatibility among different locating services and API, since they are individually developed and operated. Each service is tightly coupled with the underlying positioning system. For example, Glympse assumes to use GPS information collected by smartphones, while IndoorAtlas use a magnetic field to locate the position inside a building. Thus, Glympse cannot directly use the data of IndoorAtlas, and vice versa. In order to cover both indoor and outdoor locations, one may want to *integrate* these two services. However, the lack of compatibility forces the application developer to use different API, and to perform expensive data integration within the application.

Figure 1 shows the conventional architecture to integrate the existing locating services. Let us assume an application, say "where-are-you?", with which a user A queries the location of another mobile user B. The user B is either inside or outside of any building, and is supposed to be located by a certain locating service. Then, "where-are-you?" executed by A invokes different API for all possible locating services, in order to find B. Although A's the query "Where is B?" is essentially simple, the application has to know how to query and interpret the location for individual locating services, respectively. This makes the application quite complex, low-performance, and non-scalable.

To cope with the problem, we propose in this paper a unified locating service, called *KULOCS (Kobe-university Unified LOCating Service)*. KULOCS horizontally integrates the existing heterogeneous locating services, and provides an abstraction layer between the applications and the locating services. To make location queries compatible among many locating services, we design KULOCS with three technology-independent elements [when], [where] and [who].

Based on the three elements, KULOCS integrates data and operations of the heterogeneous locating services. In the data integration, we propose a

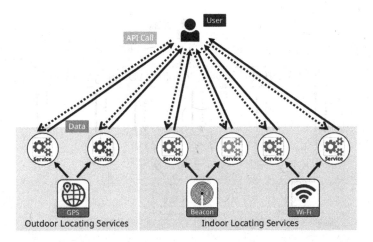

Fig. 1. Conventional architecture to integrate locating services

method that different representation of time, heterogeneous locations and different namespace of a user are consolidated by *Unix time, location labels* and *alias table*, respectively. The location labels consist of local label and global label, which abstract concrete coordinates of IPS and GPS, respectively. A user of KULOCS queries every location by a label, whereas KULOCS internally converts the label to specific representation for individual locating services.

For the operation integration, we propose KULOCS-API, which integrates heterogeneous operations by possible combinations of [when], [where] and [who]. The API is deployed as Web service, so that applications on various platforms can easily consume KULOCS. For example, the query "Where is B?" of "where-are-you?" is simply implemented by `http://kulocs/where?user=B&time=now`. For this, the application needs not to know how B is located by which service. Thus, the application can consume location information quite easily and efficiently.

To show the practical feasibility of KULOCS, we examine two practical value-added services with KULOCS. One example is Seamless Locating Service, which allows a user to locate a mobile object in either indoor or outdoor space. The another example is Personalized Location-Aware Service. A user can create and customize own location-aware services by associating a location and an action. We discuss how these two services can be implemented by KULOCS.

2   KULOCS (Kobe-University Unified Locating Service)

2.1   Overview

We propose *KULOCS (Kobe-university Unified LOCating Service)* in this section. Figure 2 shows its architecture. KULOCS works as a *façade* of the heterogeneous locating services. It provides the unified interface (KULOCS-API) for a user, by which the user can access to different locating services seamlessly,

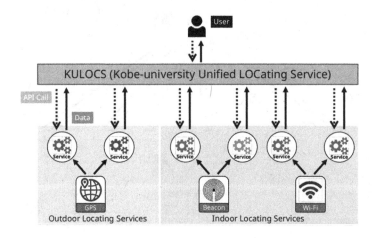

Fig. 2. Architecture of KULOCS

without being aware of the difference of individual services. Since KULOCS is an abstract layer that integrates heterogeneous locating services, we have to achieve the followings:

Data Integration: Individual locating services represent location information in different ways. Hence, KULOCS must exploit unified location data representation that is independent of any specific service or positioning system.

Operation Integration: Also, individual locating services exhibit own operations in terms of API, which vary from a service to another. KULOCS needs to integrate them and provide generic API (i.e., KULOCS-API) to a user.

Our key idea to achieve the above integration is to focus the following technology-independent elements necessary for any services to locate an object:

When: Represent the date and time when the target object exists.
Where: Represent the location where the target object exists.
Who: Represent the identity of the target object.

KULOCS is designed to accept *generic* location queries based on possible combinations of the above three elements. KULOCS then translates the generic query to service-specific queries for individual services.

2.2 Data Integration

We here describe how to integrate location data of heterogeneous locating services. To help understanding, let us consider the following data records.

- **L1:** {time:2015-06-21T08:50:12+0900, user:tktk, location: {latitude: 35.4313, longitude:135.147, address:"1-1 Rokkodai Nada Kobe Japan"}}
- **L2:** Takatsuka is now in (3.0, 4.5, 0.5) from entrance of ShopABC.
- **L3:** Mon Jun 29 15:49:34 CEST 2015, Object123, KobeUniv.Lab.S101

L1 describes a location of user tktk by a geographic coordinate, where we imagine the data is taken by a GPS-based service. L2 would be obtained by a fine-resolution IPS, which represents the current position of Takatsuka by 3D offset from a reference point. L3 describes that Object123 is in room S101 of our laboratory, which may be located by a certain zone-based IPS. Note that L1, L2 and L3 respectively use different time representation (and time zone).

To integrate these heterogeneous locations, we consider the elements [when], [where], [who]. As for [when], it is easy to introduce the common representation with the *Unix time stamp*, which is the number of seconds elapsed from January 1st, 1970 at UTC. KULOCS deals with any time information by Unix time.

As for [where], there are many ways and different granularity levels to represent a location. The GPS coordinate looks generic representation that can describe exact locations. However, it is too detailed for a user to specify it as a parameter of location queries. Also, the GPS coordinate is not useful for indoor locations, which are often relative coordinates from the reference point.

To compromise different granularity levels and various use cases, we propose to represent every location by a *location label*. A location label is a unique string that is bound for a location information. Just for convenience, we introduce two kinds of labels: *local label* and *global label*. The local label is a string, written in `position@building`, to be used to represent an indoor location. In the string, `building` represents the ID of a building, and `position` represents the name of the position in the building. For example, a local label `casher@ShopABC` is used to refer to the location in L2. On the other hand, the global label is a string without `@`, to be used to represent an outdoor location. For example, we can bind a global label `kobe_univ` to the location in L1.

Thus, KULOCS represents every location by a location label. It internally maintains binding between a label and actual location information with the *location table* shown in Table 1. We assume that the location labels are registered in the table by users in a crowd-sourcing fashion, and shared among the users.

Finally, as for [who], since every locating service has different namespace for users and objects, KULOCS has an *alias table*, which consolidates different IDs for the same user (or object) into a single unique ID. For example, let us recall L1, L2 and L3, and suppose that all of tktk in L1, Takatsuka in L2, and Object123 in L3 refer to the same person "hiroki". Then, the alias table contains an element: `{"id":"hiroki", "alias":{"L1":"tktk", "L2":"Takatsuka", "L3":"Object123"}}`. With this information, KULOCS converts the representative name `hiroki` into a real user id when querying each of locating services. The integration of IDs can be also implemented with *common identity services* (e.g., OpenID [3]). However, it is beyond this paper.

Based on the above design principle, KULOCS unifies L1, L2 and L3 as shown in Table 2. Through KULOCS, the location data from any locating service is unified into the abstract location data with [when], [where] and [who].

Table 1. Location table of KULOCS

Loc. label (PK)	Service	Actual location info.
`kobe_univ`	gps01	`{latitude: 35.4313, longitude:135.147, address:"1-1 Rokkodai Nada Kobe Japan"}`
`casher@ShopABC`	ips01	ShopABC, (3.0, 4.5, 0.5)
`S101@kobe_univ`	ips02	KobeUniv.Lab.S101

Table 2. Data integration of L1, L2 and L3

Data ID	When/time	Where/location	Who/ID
L1	1434869412	`kobe_univ`	`hiroki`
L2	1435592713	`casher@ShopABC`	`hiroki`
L3	1435585774	`S101@kobe_univ`	`hiroki`

2.3 Operation Integration

We then propose KULOCS-API, which integrates heterogeneous operations of the existing locating services. Basically, KULOCS-API is the interface for querying KULOCS about a location of a mobile user (or object). The way of the query must be technology-neutral and independent of any specific locating services. Therefore, we again focus on the elements of [when], [where] and [who].

Table 3. List of methods in KULOCS-API

Method	Description
when(location, id)	Returns the latest time when the object is in the location.
where(time, id)	Returns the location where the object exists in the time.
who(time, location)	Returns all objects who exist in the location in the time.
whenwhere(id)	Returns a list of [time, location] where the given object exists.
whenwho(location)	Returns a list of [time, id] that exist in the given location.
wherewho(time)	Returns a list of [location, id] are located within the given time.

According to the possible combinations of the three elements, we derived six methods for KULOCS-API, as shown in Table 3. For example, where(time, id) is for asking [where] based on known time (i.e., [when]) and id (i.e., [who]). Thus, a user can invoke where(NOW, B) to know "Where is B (now)?". To achieve programmable interoperability, we publish KULOCS-API as a Web service, and deploy it in a cloud. For example, the method invocation where(NOW, B) can be performed in REST format http://kulocs/where?time=NOW&id=B.

Once a method of KULOCS-API is invoked, KULOCS internally *converts* the method invocation into an appropriate API call for each locating service (see Fig. 2). For the purpose of the method conversion, KULOCS manages the *service database*. Figure 3 shows the ER diagram of the service database.

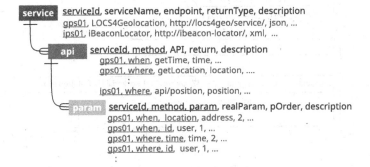

Fig. 3. ER diagram of KULOCS service database

The service database has three entities: service, api and param. The *service* entity manages master information of all the underlying locating services. The information includes a name, an endpoint of the service, a type of the return value. In Fig. 3, we can see that there are two locating services (LOCS4Geolocation, iBeaconLocator) registered. For each service, the *api* entity manages the mapping from the six methods of KULOCS-API to actual API in the service. In Fig. 3, we can see that where() method is mapped into getLocation() for gps01 (i.e., LOCS4Geolocation). The *param* entity manages the mapping and order of parameters within every method of KULOCS-API and the ones within the actual API call. For example, we can see, in Fig. 3, that time and id parameters of where(time, id) method are respectively passed to time and user parameters of getLocation(user, time) of gps01. Thus, the method can be converted.

Figure 4 shows a sequence diagram, where the user executes where(NOW, B) of KULOCS-API. In this scenario, KULOCS first finds a service gps01 from the service DB, and then identifies getLocation() API and its parameters user and time. Next, KULOCS looks up the alias table to convert the id of "B" into the local name "tktk" within gps01. Next, it invokes getLocation() of LOCS4Geolocation service with tktk and the current time, to locate tktk. Finally, the obtained location information is converted into a location label with the location table. Finally, the label kobe_univ is returned to the user, as the answer of where(NOW, B). Similarly, KULOCS can invoke other locating services for where(NOW, B). However, the sequences are omitted due to limited space.

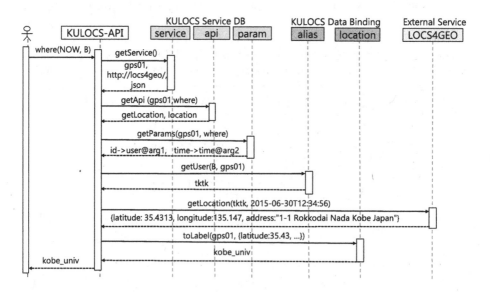

Fig. 4. Sequence diagram of KULOCS-API, in which where(NOW, B) is executed

2.4 Implementation

We are currently implementing KULOCS as a Java Web service. The implementation details and evaluation are left for our future publications. We are also interested in pragmatic issues, including security and privacy policies in location-based services. These are also planed for our future research.

3 Creating Value-Added Services with KULOCS

The proposed KULOCS unifies heterogeneous locating services, seamlessly. We examine here two practical services enabled by KULOCS.

Seamless Locating Service: For a given ID of a registered mobile user, this service locates the user regardless the user is in indoor or outdoor place. Although this service uses all possible locating services, there is no need to take care of proprietary communications, thanking KULOCS.

Personalized Location-Aware Service: KULOCS allows a user to easily evaluate *location context*, which returns true when the user come to a pre-registered location. Binding a location context and a certain action implements a *location-aware service*. If a system allows the user to register favorite locations and binding rules, it implements *personalized location-aware services*. For example, when the user gets close to home, the lights are turned on. When the user sits on a sofa in a living room, a music is automatically played back.

4 Related Work

Ficco et al. [9] proposed a hybrid location system, which combines wireless fingerprinting technologies for indoor positioning together with GPS-based positioning for outdoor localization. As a user moves to different places, the system autonomously switches to available positioning method supported by the mobile device and the surrounding environment. This study mainly focuses on the switching mechanism in the mobile clients. Thus, the difference is that they try to integrate different positioning systems within client side, which relies on the capability of the device. On the other hand, we try to integrate them within the server side, which does not rely on any capability of clients.

Ahn and Nah [8] proposed a web service framework based on service-oriented architecture, called *LOCA*. It discovers best-available Web services based on client location information and preference. Thus, a client can dynamically find, integrate and consume Web service available in the current location. The difference is that LOCA provides a location-based service discovery, while KULOCS provides a location query portal for any location-based services. In this sense, LOCA can exploit KULOCS for more extensive location management.

Acknowledgements. This research was partially supported by the Japan Ministry of Education, Science, Sports, and Culture [Grant-in-Aid for Scientific Research (B) (Nos. 26280115, 15H02701), Young Scientists (B) (No. 26730155), and Challenging Exploratory Research (15K12020)].

References

1. Glympse. https://www.glympse.com/
2. IndoorAtlas. https://www.indooratlas.com/
3. OpenID. http://openid.net/specs/openid-connect-core-1_0.html
4. OriginGPS. http://www.origingps.com/
5. Pathshare. https://pathsha.re/
6. Skyhook. http://www.skyhookwireless.com/
7. Swarm by foursquare. https://www.swarmapp.com/
8. Ahn, C., Nah, Y.: Design of location-based web service framework for context-aware applications in ubiquitous environments. In: 2010 IEEE International Conference on Sensor Networks, Ubiquitous, and Trustworthy Computing, pp. 426–433
9. Ficco, M., Palmieri, F., Castiglione, A.: Hybrid indoor and outdoor location services for new generation mobile terminals. Pers. Ubiquit. Comput. **18**(2), 271–285 (2014)
10. Kohne, M., Sieck, J.: Location-based services with ibeacon technology. In: 2014 2nd International Conference on Artificial Intelligence, Modelling and Simulation, pp. 315–321
11. Manandhar, D., Torimoto, H.: Opening up indoors: Japan's indoor messaging system, IMES (2011). http://gpsworld.com/wirelessindoor-positioningopening-up-indoors-11603/
12. Ting, S., Kwok, S.K., Tsang, A.H., Ho, G.T.: The study on using passive RFID tags for indoor positioning. Int. J. Eng. Bus. Manag. **3**, 9–15 (2011)

A Semantic Algorithm Repository and Workflow Designer Tool: Signal Processing Use Case

Sounak Dey[✉], Dibyanshu Jaiswal, Himadri Sekhar Paul,
and Arijit Mukherjee

Innovation Lab, TCS, Kolkata, India
{sounak.d,dibyanshu.jaiswal,himadrisekhar.paul,mukherjee.arijit}@tcs.com

Abstract. Recently major emphasis is exerted on development of effective tools and techniques for enriching IoT development environment. Typically an IoT application, for example a health monitoring application, not only requires domain knowledge of a programmer, but also similar knowledge from a medical practitioner, a sensor manufacturer, an infrastructure manager, etc. Such involvement of several experts makes the development process complex, resulting in escalation of time and cost of the effort. Model Driven Development (MDD) has been proposed as a development technique where such problem can be mitigated. This paper presents a system based on the MDD paradigm. As a part of the system, we present a work-flow designer framework, a visual drag and drop interface, where a developer can stitch various functional models recommended from a well-organized, annotated and crowd-sourced semantic repository of algorithms (from various domains), named as Algopedia, to quickly build a semantic workflow and in turn an end to end IoT application.

Keywords: Algorithm ontology · Algorithm repository · Semantic workflow · Workflow design · Signal processing · Model driven development

1 Introduction

As we are progressing towards the age of Internet of Things (IoT), the number of deployed connected objects across the world are increasing tremendously and is predicted to reach a count of 4.9 billion today to about 25 billion by 2020 [7]. As a consequence, an avalanche of data is hitting our servers, gateways everyday, every moment. But mere capturing such data does not make much sense unless one can analyze and find useful insights from such data and use them in IoT based applications to solve different use cases in domains like healthcare, education, transportation etc. Compared to traditional IT systems, developing such analytical applications for IoT is a difficult process as dependencies exist on a very diverse set of skills like knowledge of sensor/things, signal processing on sensor observation, knowledge of algorithms for analyzing such data, finding semantics of data etc. This requires involvment of experts of sensor, algorithm, infrastructure, programming, knowledge modelling, domain etc. Clearly,

© ICST Institute for Computer Sciences, Social Informatics and Telecommunications Engineering 2016
B. Mandler et al. (Eds.): IoT 360° 2015, Part II, LNICST 170, pp. 53–61, 2016.
DOI: 10.1007/978-3-319-47075-7_7

this process involves too many stakeholders and requires application developer to know each subject to some depth. Practically this slows down the process of development.

A Model-Driven-Development (MDD) paradigm for IoT application development is one interesting approach which advocates separation of concerns among different stakeholders by introducing re-usable metamodels for IoT system and then automating the development process by stitching required models relevant to a solution; thus augmenting capability of developer and minimizing development time. This also enhances reusability of models. Pal et al. in [15] proposed a concept for MDD by creating metamodels for sensors/things, algorithms, infrastructure, domain etc. Based on that cenceptual metamodels, we have created a framework for quick application development in IoT domain. The framework consists of 1. a tool for creating and editing semantic algorithm repository and 2. a recommendation based workflow generation and execution tool. The second tool helps stitching the recommended algorithms (created using first tool) for a paticular IoT use case. In this paper, these two key developments for MDD for IoT has been discussed in details using one example of sensor signal processing use case. The rationale behind choosing a sensor signal processing use case are: (i) most IoT applications are expected to process signals received from sensors, and (ii) usefulness of semantic repository and workflow generation tool can be best exhibited by this use case as it involves many substeps like sampling, signal extracting, feature selection etc.

Following section discusses other relevant works in this field. In Sects. 3 and 4, detailed architechture of the system and its working is explained respectively while in Sect. 5 we conclude with future works.

2   Relevant Works

There are many works related to algorithm repositories and workflow designer tools. We found that most of the algorithm repositories come with a workflow designer tool associated with them; but vice versa is not always true. Algorithmia [8] is a work that falls in first category. It comes with a tool for submission of new algorithms but it lacks depth in terms of variety and count. Also it does not recommend algorithms while creating a workflow. Caiman [16] is an online algorithm repository with very limited set of image processing algorithms focussed only for cancer research. Stony Brook Algorithm repository [17] is a very comprehensive algorithm repository but it does not facilitate creation of workflow. There is an algorithm ontology called OpenTox [2] targeted to create models for detecting chemical toxicity; this can be externally connected to our ontology to enrich it, but its structure is not exhaustive and generic enough to accomodate various types of algorithms used in IoT domain.

On the second category of works, Galaxy [10] is a genome data based workflow creation and execution system but it has its proprietary execution platform thus restricting variety in workflow designing. Wotkit [9] is another online tool which helps user add sensor, capture and visualize data and create custom IoT application based on widgets exposed as REST APIs, but does not allow any features like processing and analysis of data. There are some cloud based IoT application development frameworks like Axeda [3], BlueMix [1], ThingWorx [5] etc. which have features like device management and configuration, cloud application development, connectivity service provisioning and management; but they lack in standard algorithm repository and semantic search and recommendation during workflow designing. In the next section, overall architechture of the system is presented.

3   System Architechture

As shown in Fig. 1, the system has three main components: 1. Algopedia: an annotated algorithm repository. 2. Web Based UI for creating/modifying Algopedia. 3. A web based workflow designing and execution tool.

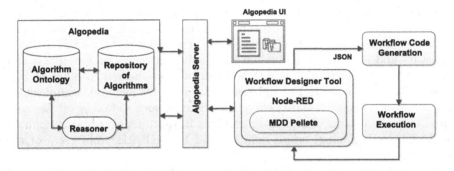

Fig. 1. Architecture diagram

3.1   Algopedia

Algopedia consists of three distinct parts: an algorithm ontology, a repository and a reasoner module. The core ontology structure has been created using Protege 4.0 [4]. Basic algorithm classes like Machine Learning, Statistical Analysis, Filtering etc. and their subclasses are captured here. Other related entities like *Features, SignalType* etc. are also defined here along with associated rules, restrictions and annotations (refer Fig. 2). This ontology contains pseudocodes associated with algorithm classes. The structure and elements of this ontology provides the basic model for algorithms. This core ontology can be enriched with more algorithm classes, relations and annotations by mining relevant information from web and by crowd sourcing from algorithm domain experts.

Based on the algorithm models in this ontology and following the pseudocodes therein, a repository of implemented working code is created. Any coder who

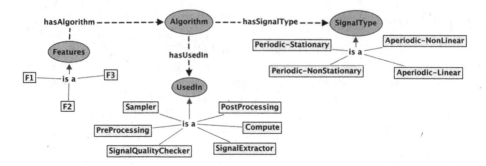

Fig. 2. Relations and entities around algorithm class

have implemented a code instance following an algorithm pseudocode can submit his/her work in this repository with proper annotations. To elaborate, algorithm class *Filter* and its subclass *BandPassFilter* are created by algorithm domain expert and is stored in Algopedia ontology along with their respective pseudocodes. If somebody implements a *bandpassfilter.c* based on *BandPass-Filter* pseudocode then that particular code implementation goes to algorithm repository and stays as an individual (also called instance) of *BandPassFilter* class. Same *BandPassFilter* pseudocode can be implemented in different languages (like C, R, Java etc.) by different coder with different code complexities; the repository can accomodate each of them and all such instances will be associated with the class of *BandPassFilter*. This instance repository can again be enriched by web mining, crowd-sourcing and by feedbacks from users of the instances.

The reasoner module in Algopedia works both on algorithm ontology and repository. This module 1. validate correctness of ontology and repository after a new entry is made or after a round of enrichment via web/experts/coders and 2. can recommend a set of ranked algorithms most suitable for given criteria like signal type, feature type etc.

3.2 Web Based User Interface (UI)

Purpose of this web based user interface is to allow algorithm code writers to submit their instance of an algorithm implementation in Algopedia repository along with relevant annotation and metadata like author name, library dependencies, compiler version, input/output parameter details etc. This user interface can also be used to edit/modify aforesaid details of instances those are already there in the repository. Figure 3 shows a snapshot of this UI. The UI submits and fetches data from algorithm repository using REST APIs. This user interface is dynamically bound with the underlying Algopedia ontology. This means: the right panel in (Fig. 3) is created dynamically as per properties defined in ontology. If a property of an Algorithm class changed or a new property is added, then the changes automatically reflects back in UI as a text box or combo box (depending on the

Fig. 3. Algopedia user interface

nature of the property). This is achieved without any re-coding done at user interface end. To and fro of data from repository to UI is carried in the form of JSON and the structure of JSON along with some annotations dictates how the user interface will looks.

3.3 Workflow Designing and Execution Tool

To use algorithm instances for practical problems, a customised workflow generation tool based on Node-RED [6] is used. This has a web based user interface where developers can drag and drop nodes, select their choice of algorithm instances (based on recommendation) and can stitch them to complete a workflow. Once completed and deployed the workflow is converted into JSON structure, using which "Workflow Code Generation" block creates an executable code. This can be executed in a local execution platform when supplied with proper data.

In following section, a detail description of how the system works is explained using a signal processing domain use case.

4   Detail Description of Working of System

We have already mentioned that algorithm developers from various domains should contribute to the Algopedia repository via the Algopedia UI. With the Algopedia repository at hand, one can easily develop a workflow by making use of some custom nodes provided in the workflow designing tool. From the purview of an application developer in the context of a signal processing domain, an end-to-end working of the system is discussed here. A standard signal processing

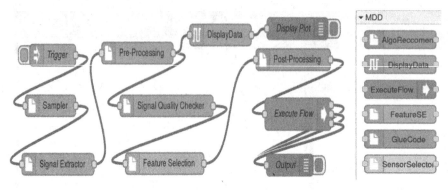

(a) Sample workflow for signal processing application   (b) MDD Custom Nodes

Fig. 4. Workflow designer tool

solution follows stages like: *Sampling* → *Signal Extractor* → *Preprocessing* → *Signal Quality Checker* → *Feature Selection and Modelling* → *Post Processing* → *Output*. Corresponding workflow may look like one shown in Fig. 4a. The above sequence of stages can be considered as a template workflow for a signal processing domain, which can be further modified by adding or deleting different nodes. Newly formed workflows can again be stored as template workflows and can be recommended to other users. In order to create this workflow, developer needs to use some (one or more) custom-nodes (Fig. 4b) like *SensorSelector, AlgorithmRecommender, FeatureSE, DisplayData* etc. from the list of custom-nodes provided in a separate palette called *MDD*, on the left hand pane of the designer tool. In **SensorSelector** node, user can semantically discover a sensor from a list of live sensors (capable of sending data) attached to the system and then collect data to pass on to next node in the workflow. A sensor ontology has been defined [12] at the backend to support the functionality of this node. **AlgorithmRecommender** node (refer Fig. 5a) enables developer to select a stage (like pre-processing, post-processing, signal quality checker etc.) of execution, the data type of the incoming signal (like periodic-stationary, aperiodic-nonstationary etc.) and the type of algorithm (from a list populated from ontology). On the basis of these three parameters, the node recommends a list of ranked algorithm instances from the Algopedia repository. Designer can select one such algorithm from this list which will be executed on the incoming data when the flow is triggered. Designer can also provide a name (like "My Pre-Processing") to identify this customised node.

The MDD palette provides another node named **FeatureSE** to apply feature extraction and selection on the data wherever required in the workflow (refer Fig. 5b). Feature selection can be done via a variety of methods such as SVM, PCA, MIC etc. Developers can make a choice among these options to decide how they want to train the model for their application. Each such machine learning technique requires a training data that can be uploaded by the developer to

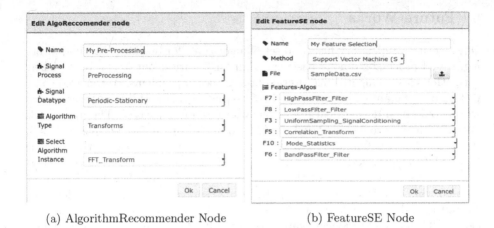

(a) AlgorithmRecommender Node   (b) FeatureSE Node

Fig. 5. Functionality of nodes

train and obtain a model corresponding to the feature selection method chosen. On the server end, the training data is used to find plausible features from the dataset and hence train the model in turn. Once the training is complete, the server returns a set of features extracted from the training dataset, along with the trained model exposed as a webservice to be used later during the execution of workflow. The set of features returned during this stage are listed along with a set of algorithms recommended by Algopedia for further processing. A combination of such *AlgorithmRecommender* and *FeatureSE* nodes are used to create the full workflow of algorithms to be executed. Along with these, **Gluecode** node can be used for tweaking the output of one node before entering another node as an input, or for incorporating some more computational code specific to user's need and for other similar purposes. **DisplayData** node is another useful node in MDD palette. This is used for visualizing data at any intermediate stage during workflow designing. This node supports plotting of data from various sources like URL, data file and previous node.

Each configured node in the workflow bundles the set of metadata information (like algorithm name and signature, dependent libraries, path of executable file etc.) in a form of JSON object and passes on to the next node in sequence. At the end, the whole JSON containing the sequence and metadata is forwarded to the **ExecuteFlow** node which parses it and executes them in sequence to obtain the final results. If the results seems to be satisfactory to the developer, they can register their workflow back into the algopedia repository, or else can reconfigure the algorithms and other nodes for better results. The job of the developer is to drag and drop the nodes of his/her choice to the worksheet, stitch them together in desired sequence, configure them and deploy and trigger the workflow.

5   Future Works

Our algorithm repository has good set of algorithms for machine learning, filtering, signal processing and a basic set of math libraries; but it can be enriched with other class of algorithms catering broader set of problems. Automated completion of a semantically correct and contextual workflow [13] is another aspect which could be a desired feature for our workflow designer tool. The framework described here is focussed at IoT problem domain, but it can be reused in different domains like banking, genetics, biochemistry etc. given that the domain knowledge can be modelled and incorporated into the system as envisaged in [15]. At present, execution of the workflow is done locally in a PC. Based on an algorithm requirement for computational resources the whole workflow can be partitioned into smaller units to be executed in a distributed manner across cloud, PC, handheld devices, gateways etc [14]. Works like Wings [11] which enables execution of semantic workflow in a condor based platform can guide us in this respect.

References

1. IBM   Bluemix.   www.ibm.com/software/bluemix/welcome/solutions2.html. Accessed 15 June 2015
2. OpenTox. http://www.opentox.org/dev/apis/api-1.1/Algorithms. Accessed 01 Sept 2015
3. PTC Axeda IoT Platform. http://www.ptc.com/axeda/product/iot-platform. Accessed 01 Sept 2015
4. Protege 4.0 (2006). http://protege.stanford.edu/. Accessed 01 Sept 2015
5. ThingWorx IoT Platform (2009). http://www.thingworx.com/. Accessed 01 Sept 2015
6. NodeRED (2013). http://nodered.org/. Accessed 01 Sept 2015
7. Gartner Says 4.9 Billion Connected Things Will Be in Use in 2015 (2014). http://www.gartner.com/newsroom/id/2905717. Accessed 01 Sept 2015
8. Algorithmia (2015). https://algorithmia.com/. Accessed 01 Sept 2015
9. Blackstock, M., Lea, R.: IoT mashups with the WoTKit. In: 2012 3rd International Conference on Internet of Things (IOT), pp. 159–166. IEEE (2012)
10. Blankenberg, D., Kuster, G.V., Coraor, N., Ananda, G., Lazarus, R., Mangan, M., Nekrutenko, A., Taylor, J.: Galaxy: a web-based genome analysis tool for experimentalists. Curr. Protoc. Mol. Biol. 19–10 (2010)
11. Deelman, E., Moody, J., Kim, J., Ratnakar, V., Gil, Y., González-Calero, P.A., Groth, P.: Wings: intelligent workflow-based design of computational experiments. IEEE Intell. Syst. 1, 62–72 (2011)
12. Dey, S., Jaiswal, D., Dasgupta, R., Misra, A.: A semantic sensor network (SSN) ontology based tool for semantic exploration of sensor. Semant. Web Chall. Compet. ISWC (2014)
13. Grambow, G., Oberhauser, R., Reichert, M.: Semantically-driven workflow generation using declarative modeling for processes in software engineering. In: 2011 15th IEEE International Enterprise Distributed Object Computing Conference Workshops (EDOCW), pp. 164–173. IEEE (2011)

14. Mukherjee, A., Paul, H., Dey, S., Banerjee, A.: Angels for distributed analytics in IoT. In: 2014 IEEE World Forum on Internet of Things (WF-IoT), pp. 565–570, March 2014

15. Pal, A., Mukherjee, A., Balamuralidhar, P.: Model driven development for internet of things: towards easing the concerns of application developers. In: International Conference on IoT as a Service, IoT360 Summit, Rome (2014)

16. Reyes-Aldasoro, C.C., Griffiths, M.K., Savas, D., Tozer, G.M.: Caiman: an online algorithm repository for cancer image analysis. Comput. Methods Prog. Biomed. **103**(2), 97–103 (2011)

17. Skiena, S.: Who is interested in algorithms and why? Lessons from the Stony Brook algorithms repository. ACM SIGACT News **30**(3), 65–74 (1999)

Biotelemetry System for Remote Monitoring of Cardiac Signals and Temperature Using Social Networks

Melissa Montalvo, Andrea García[✉], Julio Montesdeoca,
and René Ávila

Universidad Politécnica Salesiana, Cuenca, Ecuador
{mmontalvo11, agarciac1}@est.ups.edu.ec,
{jmontesdeoca, ravila}@ups.edu.ec

Abstract. Patients suffering from heart problems such as arrhythmia, failure and prone to heart attacks, need regularly monitoring of their vital signs. It is described in this article an inexpensive, free software based, easy-to use prototype of a telemetry system, applied for monitoring biomedical signals using a wifi module, a photoplethysmograph and an infrared temperature sensor; the measurements obtained by this sensors are transmitted on real time to an Android application and to an online platform that can be accessed anytime. The prototype also includes an alarm system that sends a message to the phone application, and by using social networks such as Twitter, timely notifies the treating doctor and respective relatives whenever a critical level on the patient's body signals is detected.

Keywords: Biotelemetry · Heart rate streaming · Remote monitoring · Social Networks

1 Introduction

In recent years, monitoring of body signals and activities represents an important resource in multiple fields that are focused on the development of new technologies to improve human's health. Biotelemetry helps this purpose by acquiring biosignals, avoiding to disturb the patients in their regular activities, and transmitting them from a remote spot to a location where is interpreted by a specialist [1, 2].

The development of this system will constitute a reliable constant monitoring of cardiac and temperature signals, target to people who are predisposed to seizures, cardiac arrhythmia or hypertension. Previous prototypes of cardiac monitoring use wireless communication and mobile network for signal transmission [3], as well as PC communication and data transfer to Arduino devices [4]; the described prototype explores new uses for Social Networks as health alarms and urgent notifications that can be easily read by attending physicians and relatives of the patient; it also implements a free software and Internet of Things technology to transmit the biosignals to an online platform, where the data is available at all times and from any device connected to the web. This information, and the body signals graphics, can help to learn more about the symptoms of the patient, signals evolution and health status [5].

© ICST Institute for Computer Sciences, Social Informatics and Telecommunications Engineering 2016
B. Mandler et al. (Eds.): IoT 360° 2015, Part II, LNICST 170, pp. 62–69, 2016.
DOI: 10.1007/978-3-319-47075-7_8

Three phases were established for the process of data acquisition; the first one consists on heart rate measuring to sense the patient's heart signals through a cardiac pulse sensor and determine critical levels on the collected data, the next phase involves sensing the patient's body temperature by the infrared temperature sensor Tmp006, finally takes place the transmission of the data via Wifi module, to further be sent to a cell phone with Android OS which will access to it by a develop APK. Additional to these procedures, the project also focuses on a code to provide alerts in the case that the patient presents critical heart rate or temperature levels.

2 Heart Rate and Temperature Acquisition

The Pulse Sensor essentially works as a photoplethysmograph, which is a well-known medical device used for non-invasive heart rate monitoring. Sometimes, photoplethysmography measure blood-oxygen levels (SpO_2), sometimes, as in this case, they don't [6]. The heart pulse, out signal of the photoplethysmograph, is a voltage analog fluctuation, and it has a predictable wave shape as shown in Fig. 1. The depiction of the pulse wave is called a photoplethysmogram, or PPG. The latest hardware version of the sensor used for this prototype, Pulse Sensor Amped, amplifies the raw signal of the previous Pulse Sensor, and normalizes the pulse wave around V/2 (midpoint in voltage) [7]. Pulse Sensor Amped responds to relative changes in light intensity, if the amount of incident light on the sensor remains constant, the signal value will remain at (or close to) 512 (midpoint of ADC range). In case of detecting more light, the signal goes up, and opposite with less light.

The temperature measures were taken using the TMP006 sensor which is characterized by the fact that uses a thermopile to measure the variable, it also captures the infrared energy being emitted for the surface of the object so it doesn't require any contact with it, making this kind of sensor desirable for not disturbing to the user.

A thermopile consists in a big amount of thermocouples aligned in parallel and wired in series, in a way that every microvolt-level signal proportional to the

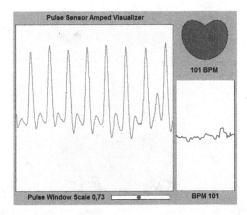

Fig. 1. Pulse sensor signal test using serial streaming and processing software.

temperature produced by each thermocouple will be part of the sum of these outputs [8]. The sensor has a better performance with non-reflective surface bodies which emissivity coefficient = 1, but due to the system is applied for body temperature the results of the sensor will be accurate given the emissivity coefficient of human skin has a value of 0.99 [9].

3   Methods and Materials

The primary code of the pulse sensor uses the Timer 2 of the ATmega328 to generate the interruption every 2 ms, this timer disables the PWM outputs number 3 and 11 of the Arduino Uno Board, which are used by the Wifi module, due to this inconvenient the Timer 1 of the sensor was used. Timer 1 disables PWM outputs 9 and 10, for this reason the Wifi module connection assigned to pin 10 was substituted by pin 6. Notice in the code and Fig. 2.

The best way to execute remote monitoring is through cloud web servers oriented to Internet of Things, based on the connection of physical devices to the web, allowing possible to access remote sensor data and remote controlling of physical world, this mash-up of captured data and the web, gives rise to new synergistic services that go beyond the services that can be provided by an isolated embedded system [10].

In order to plot the obtained data, it was proposed to work with different online platforms such as the case of Xively, ThingSpeak and Plotly Internet of Things Service; experimenting with each of them, various difficulties arose; for Xively, the access to their system requires to fill a form for a free developer account, therefore it was necessary to register as a company and request access to the servers.

In the case of ThingSpeak, a platform oriented to the Internet of Things streaming, its interface offers the creation of different channels and display charts. Using this tool the supposed real-time plotting was executed with a considerable delay producing a lack of determination and not trustable results, that leads to a disadvantage when

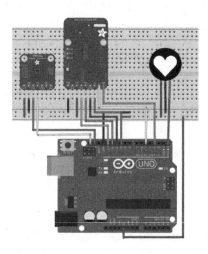

Fig. 2. Wifi module Adafruit CC3000, TMP006 sensor and pulse sensor wiring scheme.

improving human's health. Considering all this parameters, it was decided to work with Plotly platform, specialized on analytics and data visualization; this platform has a compatible library with the Wifi module Adafruit CC3000, which facilitated the process of streaming data and worked according to the objectives.

Although Plotly streaming was satisfactory, it was also explored the possibility of transmitting the data to our own Web Server. The data collected in the Arduino Board and its transmission to a server includes several steps; the main link of the data is performed by the statement aREST. The aREST framework was created to give RESTful interface to several embedded boards & platforms, in a nutshell, the library allows you to send commands to a given board running aREST, provoke an action (or just get some data), and send data back in a JSON container [11]. This requires running the code in a 1.5.7 Arduino IDE Version or higher.

The interface is develop in Javascript on the platform Express Jade, installation and code execution took place in Node.js Software. Express Jade tool was used to automatically generate code in html5, the variables exported to our website page were the magnitude value of the beats and BPM, and transmission status, as shown in Fig. 3.

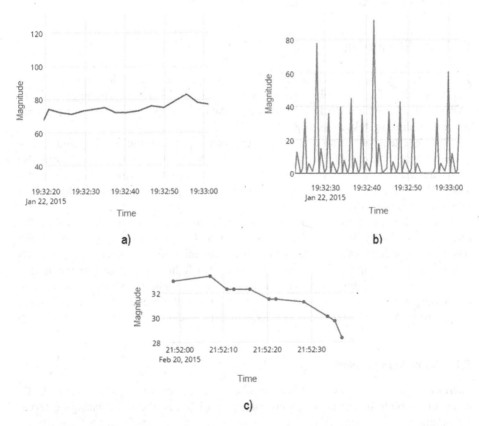

Fig. 3. BPM values (a), heart signal (b) and temperature values in (Celsius) (c) stream graph on Plotly web service.

The transmission and data displayed were achieved without inconvenience in the local computer IP address on port 3000. It has to be point out that in order to maintain the connection, the data refreshing should be done with a minimum delay of 250 ms, causing significant data loss in the heartbeat magnitude.

4 Connections and Wiring

Wifi Module. The order of the corresponding pins are shown as following VCC: 5v, GND: GND, VBEN: Digital 5, IRQ: Digital 3 [12].

Temperature Sensor. The TMP006 communicates over I2C, it is needed 4 wires to connect it to the Arduino. The order of the pins corresponds as shown as following VCC: 3.3v or 5v, GND: GND, SDA: SDA, SCL: SCL [13].

Pulse Sensor. The connection of the three different wires, colored as red, black and purple follows the following order, respectively: RED: 5v, BLACK: GND, PURPLE: Analog pin of preference, in this case Analog pin 0. The connection of the different devices can be appreciated in Fig. 2.

5 Data Streaming

Plotly streaming library for CC3000 Wifi module was used to send the acquired data to Plotly Servers. The streaming library uses an Application Programming Interface (API) combined with a REST API to stream data arrays to a plot into your personal account by linking tokens to data objects.

The code use for the prototype must initialize the user name, api key and tokens instances, subsequently the connection to the Plotly servers is initiated to confirm the user data and start the stream heading to http://stream.plot.ly address, thus, the transmitted data matches with the data object that corresponds to each one of the desired fields to stream and plot.

The main commands used in the prototype code are graph.init(), that enables the connection to Plotly Serves, and graph.openStream() that sets the way to stream the data to the selected plot of the account. On the streaming plotly library several aspects can be set depending on the users requirements including the maximum points displayed on each plot, number of axis, private or public visibility and the possibility of overwrite on every new stream. In Fig. 3 it is shown the plotted data of transmitted signals of BPM, heart signal and temperature data, respectively.

5.1 Alert Management

Alert messages in case of critical heart levels, i.e., values over the 120 beats per minute or under the 60 beats per minute, were managed using a notifications managing server Pushingbox.

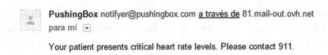

PushingBox notifyer@pushingbox.com <u>a través de</u> 81.mail-out.ovh.net
para mí ⊡

Your patient presents critical heart rate levels. Please contact 911.

🐾 **Biotelemetry** @biotelemetria · 15 de feb.
Emergency!! @AndreGarciaC your patient presents critical heart rate
levels. Please contact 911. (19:19:32)

↩   ⇄   ★   •••

Fig. 4. Email and Twitter emergency message.

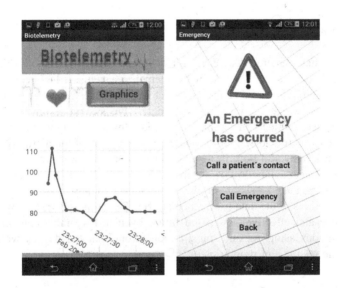

Fig. 5. Front screen (BPM streaming) and emergency screen of the APK.

Pushingbox it's an online service that allows to generate notifications through API calls. It is based on the creation of scenarios that are launched every time a Device ID calling is produced. Each scenario may have services as email send, twitter messages, MAC OS, iOS or Android OS notifications.

Each time a critical level is detected, the data stream is stopped and opens a connection to the Pushingbox servers through the Device ID linked to a scenario. The scenario starts a series of actions that include email send to the doctor's mail address, see Fig. 4, and a Twitter message, as shown in Fig. 5, indicating that the patient presents and emergency and that his/her assistance is needed.

6 Android APK

In order to create an Android OS application to display the stream data and manage alert messages in case of critical levels the MIT App Inventor 2 was used. App Inventor is based in a block diagram programming that allows to manage different cellphone aspects such as notifications, web access, calls and messaging.

The Biotelemetry App comprises a frontal page, indicated in Fig. 5, that displays in real time the graphic evolution concerning to the beat per minute values of the patient. On a secondary page, the BPM data can be visualized more detailed along with the pulse beat signal stream of the patient.

The application also contemplates the management of emergency notifications, this is possible due to the Twitter Developer App linked to the Biotelemetry App. When an emergency advise is published on a Twitter wall, the Biotelemetry app enables its own emergency management, this process includes the execution of a "talking message" and the display of emergency options, see Fig. 5, such as Call a Patient's relative, Contact the Emergency number 911 or ignore the message in case of false alarm.

7 Results and Discussion

This prototype has centered its efforts on developing an Internet of Things based technology and focused on the area of biotelemetry systems, it has been proposed a new type of transmission of biosignals as a first step to generate an online data base for patient's behavior and evolution. In order to test the system, extensive trials were conducted on three subjects in various conditions, their vital signs transmission was successful in each case and was notorious the effectiveness of the alarm system when simulated critical values in both heart rate variables and temperature.

Similar previous studies do not use free software on their systems, this characteristic has hindered the expansion of these researches in any field and restring the visualization features of the data from any platform. The proposed system may improve its performance and effectiveness in the future by using wearable sensors that will provide continuous sampling and transmission throughout the day as well as more accuracy in the results and graphics.

8 Conclusions

A Biotelemetry system consists on a necessary tool for any patient on treatment or under critical conditions whose biosignals must be monitored continuously. This prototype has been implemented for both patients and physician, constituting a system where the data is acquired by sensing the patient's signals and subsequently monitoring by a doctor anytime through access to any device connected to the web and the Biotelemetry Android APK.

The objectives of developing a free software based system and easy to use prototype were fully achieved. Recent developments on Internet of Things technologies allow to use on a optimal way the existing web platforms, open to free data stream and storage. This prototype approaches to the extended use of Social Networks in our media and repurposes them in order to extend their original functions into new fields of health information and real time alerts, nevertheless, it constitutes a new study sector that can take advantage of recent studies and developers work to improve the versatility of biosignal transmissions, increasing the overall health of the patient.

The implemented code in this prototype can be downloaded from the following link: https://onedrive.live.com/redir?resid=61BE7C7AD6CBB9C4%21156.

References

1. Güler, N.F., Übeyli, E.D.: Theory and applications of biotelemetry. J. Med. Syst. **26**, 159–178 (2002)
2. Karagozoglu, B.: Ambulatory monitoring, pp. 244–249 (2013)
3. Paradiso, R.: Wearable health care system for vital signs monitoring, pp. 283–286 (2003)
4. Hanady, A., Abdulkareem, A.: Wireless sensor network for medical applications. Iraqi J. Electr. Electron. Eng. **11**(1), 49–59 (2015)
5. Poblet, J.M.: Introducción a la Bioingeniería. Marcombo, Barcelona (1988)
6. Kirk, H.S.: Photoplethysmography: beyond the calculation of arterial oxygen saturation and heart rate. Anesth. Analg. **105**, S31–S36 (2007)
7. Pulse Sensor Datasheet: Technical Code Walk-through. PulseSensor (2012). http://pulsesensor.com/
8. Van Herwaarden, A.W., Van Duyn, D.C., Van Oudheusden, B.W., Sarro, P.M.: Integrated thermopile sensors. Sens. Actuators A: Phys. **22**, 621–630 (1990)
9. Optotherm Inc.: Emissivity in the Infrared. Optotherm Thermal Imaging (2014)
10. Kopetz, H.: Internet of things. In: Real-Time Systems: Design Principles for Distributed Embedded Applications, pp. 307–323. Springer Science & Business Media, Berlin (2011)
11. Jakl, M.: Representational State Transfer. Citeseer (2005)
12. Lesniak, R.: Adafruit CC3000 WiFi. Adafruit Industries, New York (2014)
13. Bill, E.: TMP006 Infrared Sensor Breakout. Adafruit Industries, New York (2013)

IoT Testing - The Big Challenge Why, What and How

Benny Sand[✉]

Jerusalem, Israel
benny.sand@gmail.com

Abstract. "Internet of Things" (IoT) is the network or associations between those Internets connected objects (smart Devices) that are able to exchange information by using an agreed method and data schema. The enormous amount of things, the communication protocols the combination between hardware and software, the Big Data impact, a verity of protocols, lack of standards and the high level of the required SLA by the end users set up new and challenging bars regarding QA in general and testing in particular in the IoT scene. This article will highlight the challenges as well as address potential strategies and solutions.

Keywords: IoT testing · Testing assurance · DevOps interoperability · Security · Validation · Protocols

1 Introduction

The Internet of Things (IoT) is a key enabling technology for digital and virtual technologies Apparently 3.5 Billion things were connected in 2014, and the figure is expected to rise to 25 Billion things by 2020.

The recent progress on Internet of Things deployments with the rise of Mobile culture have given a strong push to the IoT to be today's considered as one of the most promising emerging technologies. However the conceptual realization of Internet of Things is far from achieving a full deployment of converged IoT services and technology.

One of the key elements in the IoT go to market path is Interoperability. Interoperability can be generalized as the feature for providing seamless exchange of information to, for example, personalize services automatically or simply exchanging information in a way that other systems can use it for improving performance, enable and create services, control operations and information processing.

2 IoT Challenges

Internet of Things enables the things/objects in our environment to be active participants, i.e., they share information with other objects and/or communicate over the networks (wired/wireless) often using the Internet Protocol (IP). Processing the IoT data enables to recognize events and changes in the surrounding environments and "things" can act and react autonomously. However, all these require heterogeneous

© ICST Institute for Computer Sciences, Social Informatics and Telecommunications Engineering 2016
B. Mandler et al. (Eds.): IoT 360° 2015, Part II, LNICST 170, pp. 70–76, 2016.
DOI: 10.1007/978-3-319-47075-7_9

objects to exchange information in an interoperable way to make their data and services accessible and interpretable by other objects and services.

The IoT is an emerging area that not only requires development of infrastructure and technologies but also deployment of new services capable of supporting multiple, scalable (cloud-based) and interoperable (multi-domain) applications in a verity of telecommunication protocols. The significant IoT problem to be challenged is the interoperability of the information and services.

IoT refers to objects ("things") and the virtual representations of these objects on the Internet. It defines how the things will be connected through the Internet and how those things "talk" amongst other things and communicate with other systems in order to expose their capabilities and functionalities "services".

IoT is not only linking connected devices by using the Internet; it is also web-enabled data exchange in order to enable systems with more capacities to become "smart". In other words, IoT aims to integrate the physical world with the virtual world by using the Internet as the medium to communicate and exchange information.

IoT is mainly supported by continuous progress in wireless sensors and actuator diversified networks and by manufacturing low cost and energy efficient hardware for sensor and device communications. However, heterogeneity of underlying devices and communication technologies and interoperability in different layers, from communication and seamless integration of devices to interoperability of data generated by the IoT resources, is a challenge for expanding generic IoT solutions to a global scale.

Networking everyday objects to send and receive data has been received with as much hope and promise as it has worry and concern. Certainly, the day may come when your refrigerator automatically orders milk when you are running low, but a connected supply chain might just as likely be shut down by a security breach by malicious hackers.

3   IoT Testing Challenges and Vision

Software testing helps in finalizing the software application or service against business and user requirements. It is very important to have good test coverage in order to test the software application completely and make it sure that it's performing well and as per the specifications. While determining the coverage the test cases should be designed well with maximum possibilities of finding the errors or bugs.

Today's connected world unifies multiple company aspects, namely customer engagement channels, supply chains, interfacing devices and application touch points. Therefore Quality Assurance organizations need to assess their customer experience capabilities, as well as ensure the functionality of each individual application; introducing remarkable developments in quality, cost and agility.

Companies need to focus on the disruptive nature of digital technologies by paying close attention to customer experience-based testing. The key to successfully executing this new approach is to look for service offerings that feature an integrated test delivery platform, encompass omni-channel test automation frameworks, mobile testing strategies and crowd testing.

With the brilliance of a connected world, comes the necessary capability to provide more niche expertise closer to the customer and the realization that testing is a combination crowd testing in order to reflect real life conditions to ensure a delivery of top notch IoT services.

In a connected world, global companies realize that they need to organize their Quality Assurance and testing functions with a combination of centralized and decentralized approaches. A testing team tightly integrated into the product development process is vital for complex integrations and transformations pr in other words Agile will become the governing model and will implemented via DevOps platform. Moreover, companies need to ensure they define their own formula for success as one size does not fit all. It is vital that they look for a testing partner with a multi-layered test target operating approach, continuous delivery integration and outcome and output-based pricing models; all governed by a 24/7 real-time dashboard.

Companies need to stop the one-way upstream integration and align it with a downstream approach to create a new TestOps concept. In order to stay ahead of the game, companies need to drive efficiency through risk-based analysis techniques, risk-based testing, test-driven development, integrated test delivery, and service virtualization.

Understanding that security and performance testing is a top priority area; companies need to include multichannel and behavior driven testing models and approaches as well as focused platform migration testing. It is crucial to have strong links with test automation framework, connected world test strategies, end user performance analysis, and competition benchmarking capabilities.

In a connected world, it is vital for applications to be tested on numerous operating systems and devices in different geographies; such ample testing cannot be done on premise, it must be done in the cloud. This is why it is important to ensure your testing partner has access to the best possible testing environments that leverage all necessary services.

In a connected world, competition is rapidly increasing, so companies need to closely examine these trends and ensure they are following the right steps to enrich their test methodologies. Implementing the right testing practices will allow companies to seamlessly manage the complexity and scale that IoT presents.

4 The Interoperability Impact in IoT

4.1 The Interoperability ExFactor

Interoperability is a major theme in the IoT scene; hence it impacts the testing lifecycle of Internet of things strategic and operational wise. Interoperability in IoT is compound as well as influenced form several elements which impact in a direct and indirect way on the implementation process.

The Technical Interoperability is usually associated with hardware/software components, systems and platforms that enable machine-to-machine communication to take place. This kind of interoperability is often centered on verity of communication protocols.

The Organizational Interoperability, as the name implies, is the ability of organizations to effectively communicate and transfer (meaningful) data (information) even though they may be using a variety of different information systems over widely different infrastructures, possibly across different geographic regions and cultures. Organizational interoperability depends on successful technical, syntactical and semantic interoperability.

Needless to say those two things cannot interoperate if they do not implement the same set of services. Therefore when specifications are including a broad range of options, this aspect could lead to serious interoperability challenges. Solutions to overcome these aspects consist of definition clearly in clear requirements the full list options with all conditions. In the latter case, defining profile would help to truly check interoperability between two products in the same family or from different family if the feature checked belongs to the two groups.

4.2   Methodologies for Interoperability Testing in IoT

Interoperability testing involves testing whether a given software program or technology is compatible with others and promotes cross-use functionality. This kind of testing is now important as many different kinds of technology are being built into architectures made up of many diverse parts, where seamless operation is critical for developing a user base.

The factors in interoperability testing include syntax and data format compatibility, sufficient physical and logical connection methods, and ease of use features. Software programs need to be able to route data back and forth without causing operational issues, losing data, or otherwise losing functionality. In order to facilitate this, each software component needs to recognize incoming data from other programs, handle the stresses of its role in architecture, and provide accessible, useful results.

Interoperability testing can be addressed in two main approaches for testing:

The empiric approach of testing regroups several ways to do testing. Since this kind of testing is informal, they are generally carried out while coding. There is no set procedure for informal testing, and this is entirely up to the coder to implement without the need to submit the test reports. The coder feels confident that his code works as required and contains no obvious bugs.

Empiric approach for testing encompasses tests that are done while developing the product to identify bugs, as well as those that is done on the fly.

The main advantages of the empiric testing methodology are the following: Tests can be done very earlier while developing the products, allowing detecting errors/bugs in the earlier stage of the development, moreover the tests can be setup very quickly, without huge constraints such as having reports to prepare etc.

Having said that the above e advantages can be canceled by the following drawbacks:

No ideas regarding the test coverage since there is no real test plan, part of the properties to be tested cannot be measured. Thus, errors/bugs may not be detected.

Since these tests have been done informally, end users will have difficult to trust the final product so the marketing and business demerges can be rather significant.

The methodological approach for testing generally encompasses different steps leading to the execution step where test suites are generated against products. These products can be at different degree of their development.

Three main steps can be seen in this approach: Abstract Test Suite (ATS) specification, Derivation of executable test, and Test execution and results' analysis.

The advantages of the methodological approach are the following: Improved test coverage due to a real consist methodology that monitors the whole processes while maintaining KPI's, properties to be tested can be measured. Thus, it may help in determining more precisely how to cover important parts of the system and subsystems under test. By this way, it may reduce non-interoperability of the product at the end.

Moreover the methodological approach provides real added value to the market. As these tests have been done formally, end users will trust more easily the final product. In addition tests can be done very earlier in parallel with products' development, allowing detecting errors/bugs in the earlier stage of the development.

5   DevOps, TestOps and IoT

IoT implementation in intelligent corporate and residential IT networks poses unique challenges for DevOps as requirements apply well beyond the software development lifecycle and encompasses the complex quality assurance and robust back-end support phase.

Although IoT is largely consumer-driven, the technology is equally pervasive in corporate markets. In this context, DevOps engineers must address traceability and audit ability for all IoT firmware OS developments to ensure compliance success. Collaboration with hardware product specialists and vendors throughout the development process also ensures software robustness to enable streamlined integration with existing IT networks while avoiding vendor lock-in. The world's networking infrastructure with its finite capacity is reaching its limit as the number of IoT endpoints explodes. This in turn, drives interoperability, networking and connectivity issues impacting the wider IT network, whereas IoT development with a focus on network environments, protocols and standards can help eradicate these concerns. Given the scale of IoT production and deployment across the globe, maintaining a robust back-end architecture to automate testing and upgrades requires full visibility into the development cycle as well as a single repository to track changes that follow a device rollout.

Interoperability issues emerge naturally when billions of 'dumb' devices interact with each other. Developing for IoT with the API evolution in mind to expose unique functionalities of the hardware ensures easy rollout of upgrades in addressing integration, connectivity and interoperability issues that may arise down the line.

The performance and behavioral attributes of IoT hardware pose unique challenges for DevOps engineers who must test IoT software in complex real-world environments and use cases. For instance, weather conditions and durability of the hardware can impact software performance especially when the technology is designed for responding to environmental conditions, such as Web-connected automated fire alarms.

Quality assurance is inherently complex and specialized with the burden of architecture almost entirely falling on the back-end. With this service model, DevOps engineers can push updates frequently as the slow approval process of app stores doesn't hold for IoT software. The IoT ecosystem's vastness has also led to the unpredictability of application requirements for these devices. The understanding of IoT applications is therefore altered even after the launch, prompting significant updates regularly to incorporate the required changes. With the DevOps approach, these updates are directly pushed from the back-end with a continuous delivery service model.

6 Summary and Conclusions

The Internet of Things offers great potential for organizations and societies. A connected world where billions, or even trillions, of devices are connected to the Internet and as such can communicate with each other. If we manage to successfully develop the Internet of Things it will unlock a lot of value and the benefits of the Internet of Things are enormous for organizations and societies. However, there are still some major challenges for the Internet of Things.

Organizations will be able to track their assets in real time, improve utilization of the assets to meet demand. They will be able to predict required maintenance without visiting remote. Monetization of expensive assets becomes easier for organization as the Internet of Things will enable operating expenditure instead of capital expenditure; meaning that users of certain assets are billed based on their actual usage, engine hours, and fuel load etc. instead of having to purchase expensive assets. In addition, devices that are connected to the Internet can receive software updates regularly, instead of replacing the asset thereby prolonging the life of the asset.

The overall challenges in interoperability is first to stabilize the foundation of the real world data services, ensuring technical interoperability from technologies to deliver mass of information and then complementary challenges are for the information to be understood and processed.

The complexity and the diversification embedded in the IoT processes raises many challenges to the Testing organizations in many aspects such as: planning, monitoring, controlling and execution.

The huge amount of things, processes, the big data and complex processes requires a compressive centric testing strategy which will oversees the "Big Picture".

Interoperability testing is a key motive in IoT testing since it addresses the endless amounts of sub systems and its related interactions.

A crucial step for successful integration in a digital world is to reduce test cycle time through the adoption of swift practices and a dynamic test engineering platform. This means fast, responsive QA and testing solutions integrated with agile development.

Choosing the right testing partner can mean the difference between success and failure. Identifying the best practices ensures that products and applications are ready by deadlines and meet customer expectations; ensuring companies deliver defect-free products and services for a quantifiable return on investment.

Companies need to place a strong emphasis on specific cloud and virtualization solutions to create a solid test environment and to manage their cloud and virtualization strategies.

The DevOps approach should also address the disconnect between IT realities and management desires leading to interoperability and productivity concerns for enterprise customers.

The enormous amount of details demonstrated via the endless number of things, processes, sw, hw and SLA may lead to a comprehensive testing strategy which oversees and controls a unified testing life cycle.

Testing is a change agent in the IoT, it provides the natural link between Development and operation from the technological and cultural aspects.

References

1. Vermisan, O., Friess, P.: Building the Hyperconnected Society, IoT Research and Innovation Value Chains, EcoSystems and Markets. RiverSide Publisher, Aalborg (2015)
2. Serrano, M., Barnaghi, P., Carrez, F., Cousin, P., Vermesan, O., Friess, P.: Internet of Things IoT Semantic Interoperability: Research Challenges Best Practices, Recommendation and Next Steps. European Research Cluster on Internet of Things (2015)
3. Security Call in Action, Preparing to the Internet of Things Accenture (2015)
4. D4.1 – Framework for studying existing IoT testing solutions (2013)
5. Internet of Things a Developer's Mandate (2014)
6. TESDT Maturity Model Integration, TMMI Foundation (2012)
7. Certified Tester Foundation Level Extension Syllabus Agile Tester ISTQB (2014)
8. Tester Foundation Level Extension Syllabus Agile Tester ISTQB (2011)

Data-Centric Security for the IoT

Daniel Schreckling[1]([✉]), Juan David Parra[1], Charalampos Doukas[2],
and Joachim Posegga[1]

[1] IT-Security, University of Passau, Passau, Germany
ds@sec.uni-passau.de
[2] Future Media Area, CREATE-NET, Trento, Italy

Abstract. This work presents a paradigm shift and introduces a data-centric security architecture for the COMPOSE framework; a platform as a service and marketplace for the IoT. We distinguish our approach from classical device-centric approaches and outline architectural as well as infrastructural specifics of our platform. In particular, we describe how fine-granular and data-centric security requirements can be combined with static and dynamic enforcement to regain governance on devices and data without sacrificing the intrinsic openness of IoT platforms. We also highlight the power of our architecture, converting concepts such as data provenance and reputation into efficient, highly useful, and practically applicable complements.

Keywords: Internet of Things · Information flow control · System security · Reputation · Provenance · Identity management · Static analysis · Node-RED

1 Introduction

COMPOSE is an FP7 EU funded project targeting at the development of a full end-to-end solution for developing Internet of Things (IoT) applications and services: from mobile apps for users interaction, to connected objects that sense or interact smartly with the environment, to a scalable data streaming and processing infrastructure, to service discovery, composition and deployment of applications. The logical architecture of the COMPOSE platform is depicted in Fig. 1. Its main components are the COMPOSE Marketplace, the runtime engine, and the Ingestion layer.

The Marketplace is the front-end interface to developers for the publication, exchange, and access of reusable services. It consists of a graphical interface for creating application logic and offers mechanisms for the discovery of existing services, registration of new ones, and the deployment of applications.

Applications are executed on the second layer, the runtime, which is transparent to the developers and provides interfaces for monitoring and support for usage analytics. It is based on an enhanced version of CloudFoundry [3], an already established, open-source PaaS solution with a large community supporting its development. It provides the essential environment for hosting applications, in our case Node.js that we are using for workflow execution.

© ICST Institute for Computer Sciences, Social Informatics and Telecommunications Engineering 2016
B. Mandler et al. (Eds.): IoT 360° 2015, Part II, LNICST 170, pp. 77–86, 2016.
DOI: 10.1007/978-3-319-47075-7_10

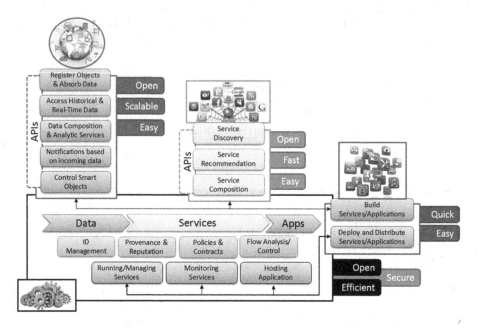

Fig. 1. Conceptional view of the COMPOSE architecture

The third layer, the Ingestion layer, is the interface to the connected objects. Bi-directional communication over different M2M and HTTP-based protocols allows the remote interaction with the devices (e.g., requesting status updates, performing actuations, reading sensor information etc.).

Connected objects play one of the most important roles in IoT systems since the core concept is data aggregation and interaction with smart devices [9]. Within this context, COMPOSE has developed servIoTicy, a data storing and streaming framework with support for device interaction [15].

To interact with real-world objects, users, and services, servIoTicy exposes both, RESTful Application Programming Interfaces (APIs) and M2M protocols (like MQTT, STOMP, and WebSockets). Through these interfaces, devices can store sensor information on the platform. Developers can be notified about updates or retrieve data based on special queries (e.g., time-series based analysis). For this purpose, servIoTicy integrates ElasticSearch [1]. For sensor data stream processing, the Apache Storm [16] component is used, in addition to CouchBase [4] for storing data. Through exposing device communication via REST protocols, servIoTicy also provides an important bridge between REST and MQTT/WebSockets/STOMP [6] as most of the M2M protocols cannot be utilised within a browser.

To simplify the creation and deployment of applications, COMPOSE provides glue.things (http://www.gluethings.com). It is a web-based application to register and access COMPOSE components. It mainly offers the following features: (1) Creating and configuring virtual smart objects in servIoTicy (allowing them to store sensor data, create subscriptions to events, and generate actuations), (2) testing the deployment of sensors by receiving sensor data in real time, and (3) creating IoT applications through a visual workflow editor.

The latter is based on the popular open-source tool Node-RED (http://www.nodered.org). This editor for the IoT allows the easy design of workflows based on components that communicate with devices or services. It is based on node.js and can be executed as a standalone or be integrated in a users application. Workflows (called *flows*) are created in a drag-n-drop fashion by selecting available processes (called *nodes*) that can communicate with external services COMPOSE services.

For the development of applications for connected objects, as well as for mobile or web applications, COMPOSE provides libraries and mobile SDKs as part of glue.things. Libraries for popular embedded platforms (like Arduino, Flyport, mBed, SparkCore, etc.) are provided to simplify the interaction with servIoTicy over the available protocols. In addition, JavaScript libraries are provided for web application development and mobile app development using cross-platform frameworks like the Titanium Appcelerator.

The freedom to interact with numerous devices and applications, the ability to process a new magnitude of data in completely novel ways, and the simplification of the development process comes with a burden: The provisioning of a security framework that supports the openness of IoT, ensures the governance over data, and supports non-security-experts in the development of secure applications.

This burden is particularly hard when considering the application of existing security frameworks. Instead of fixed architectures and pre- and well-defined application scenarios, we face unpredictable contexts in which data is processed and applications are executed. Data becomes easily reusable, may be processed by various types of applications with different functionalities and properties. Further, applications simply emerge from the combination of other services or applications. Their internal complexity may be completely hidden from the developer and their impact on data may be unknown or very hard to determine. Thus, static security perimeters around applications or devices are infeasible and the specification of their security policies is simply impossible.

2   Design Decisions

Our security framework addresses these issues by shrinking the security perimeter to the granularity of data. Instead of forcing developers to foresee which possible application scenarios he wants to cover and which security policies and enforcement technologies are required for that, we ask the entities generating data in the system to define security policies for this very data. This idea is inspired by the mechanisms designed to protect privacy by using the decentralised label model (DLM) [10] extending flow policies introduced by Denning and Denning [5]. Our approach mainly differs in the application of such techniques to highly dynamic architectures in which enforcement must be applied in an ad-hoc fashion and various computational entities. Even more important is the fact that we consider user-defined security policies. Users specify how, by whom, and in which context their data should be processed and which data should gain which kind of access.

Of course, fine-granular policies require complex evaluation and enforcement machineries. This particularly holds for the IoT where additional dimensions, such as spatial or temporal constraints need to be enforceable. Further, policies must not only be able to define the specific security requirements for data and entities but it must also be possible to evaluate them efficiently during static analysis of software and networks as well as during dynamic flow enforcement. Thus, a unified policy framework for our architecture is inevitable. Through the combination of this unified policy framework with an attribute based identity management (IDM) our security framework also simplifies the development of policy enforcement tailored to specific applications.

The IoT will also deploy user-defined code. Thus, devices may run legacy, vulnerable, or manipulated code changing their intentional functionality. They may be physically manipulated to generate new data reading or perform different actions. Further, services which process and consume IoT data may contain malicious or vulnerable code. As a consequence, it is essential that a security architecture for the IoT can detect misbehaving entities which do not allow direct security enforcement. Hence, our architecture provides a reputation system, monitoring devices, and security services. This also allows to use reputation values as policy dimensions.

Finally, our security architecture aims for the definition of novel data security policies by generating provenance information for individual data items. Through a complete history of data, users will be able to define security policies which can also prevent complex data harvesting attacks.

3   Architecture Overview

Centre of the security architecture (see Fig. 2) is the security core. It hosts essential components such as an attribute based IDM and the global policy decision (PDP) as well as policy information points (PIP). While our architecture also supports local instances of these components we use centralised servers to guarantee the consistency of security critical data. The same holds for additional components that extend the functionality of the security core: The reputation- and provenance manager, the static analysis, and the instrumentation component. Reduced to these components, the architecture resembles classical security architectures. Thus, the remainder of this section briefly outlines the functionality of the components relevant for our data-centric framework before going into more detail in the following sections.

To abstract from the complexity of servIoTicy we distinguish three main components: Data Store, Data Management, and Service Object Registry. The latter administrates virtual representations of devices, together with their security policies and reputation information. In particular, reputation information

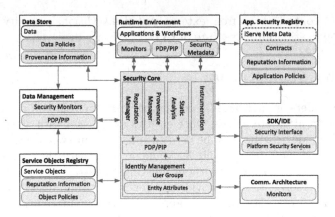

Fig. 2. Outline of the COMPOSE security architecture

is updated frequently according to the use of the associated devices. As soon as devices generate data, it is stored in the Data Store together with its appropriate flow policies derived from device policies. Every time data is used, provenance in the data store is updated based on the operations performed.

The data management which manages access to data and service objects, deploys a local PDP and PIP. In this way, appropriate security monitors can control access within the central data processing component of the overall architecture. The authorised usage of devices and data can be enforced and provenance and reputation information can be generated. Additionally, local security monitors can control data-centric flow-control policies.

servIoTicy can forward data to the runtime environment where it can be processed by applications. They are either provided by COMPOSE or implemented and/or composed by users of the platform. Similar to the data management layer, the execution of every application is secured by dynamic security monitors which can be either holistic, i.e., all components of an application are monitored, or selected in-lined reference monitors. In this way, our architecture enables the fine-granular flow tracking and enforcement of data and the monitoring of specific application properties. For efficient local enforcement and data accumulation, this architectural setup also requires a local PDP, PIP, and stores which allow the local accumulation of security metadata. System-wide security meta data about an application, i.e. reputation information, ownership, or access rules, are stored in the security registry.

The simplification of the creation and deployment of IoT applications is an essential functionality offered by COMPOSE. Hence, it is important to complement this functionality with mechanisms that allow non-experts to assess the compliance of their application with various security requirements. For this purpose, we provide features for editing policy settings, validating and re-configuring data flows within applications, for checking provenance, and for assessing the reputation of system entities.

Finally, to control access from external entities additional security monitors in the communication infrastructure of COMPOSE are deployed.

4   Identity Management

Our platform offers an attribute-based approach. Every user can tag himself or his entities with attribute values. Once entities are tagged with attributes, e.g. the brand of the device, they can be used to specify security policies, e.g. accept data only from devices from brand X. Main problem with this approach is to ensure trust in this information without creating a centralised authority.

Our platform solves this by providing a generic attribute-based IDM framework. This framework allows users to approve attribute information depending on the group where they belong [12]. More specifically, a group membership is defined as a tuple (u, r, g) where user u has role r in group g. But, before a membership is considered effective by the security framework, it has to be approved by two parties: the administrator/owner of g, and u. This mutual agreement policy ensures that users cannot be misplaced in a group against their will, and also that groups contain only users approved by administrators. As a result, users of the platform can rely on groups of their choosing, e.g. the group containing distributors of devices of brand X, to approve attributes used in their policies, e.g. brand of the device.

5   Flow Enforcement

Inputs and outputs of any COMPOSE entity which can process data are annotated with a data-centric flow policy. Apart from specifying the entities allowed to access, execute, or alter a component, flow policies also describe the security requirements of data entering a component and the security properties of data leaving it. Thus, each data item is annotated with security meta-data. Therefore, a unified policy framework is required to avoid additional evaluation overhead. The policy language used in COMPOSE is inspired by ParaLocks [2].

Their main idea is to logically specify with so called *parameterized locks* when a possibly polymorphic actor can retrieve information about a data item. Open locks represent fulfilled conditions under which information can flow. A set of such locks is interpreted as a conjunction of conditions. Combining those conjunctions by disjunctions yield a policy. We adopt this security specification as it is also based on the DLM, it is simple, evaluation is efficient, and it can be used to map against classical access control schema.

To obtain a specification language feasible for the IoT domain, we merge the Usage Control approach $UCON_{ABC}$ [11] with ParaLocks and obtain so called *UsageLocks*. It introduces typed actor and item locks which allow the checking of actor and item attributes, defined by IDM. These locks prevent a blow up of the set of required locks (each attribute could be modeled with another global lock) and they introduce a greater flexibility as pre-defined locks can be used to check user-defined attributes. Further, the new lock types also allow the definition of security contexts which depend on the data items themselves, their usage, and on temporal or spatial constraints. Finally, we also distinguish between flow-to- and flow-from-rules. While the first type of rule maps to the Horn clauses introduced by ParaLocks, flow-from-rules invert this formalism to also allow the specification of rules which describe conditions under which the modification of data or resources is allowed.

To maintain scalability and efficiency, the enforcement mechanisms for the policies described above, require techniques to avoid the dynamic and static analyses and evaluation of policies whenever possible. We partially achieve this through the generation of contracts which are also modeled using the lock-rule system. A static analysis generates an over-approximation of the behaviour of an entity and stores it in a JSON format which uses locks to specify how the programming logic of an entity impacts the flow of information, e.g. by indicating under which conditions (lock status) a flow from an input parameter to an output, such as a file, a socket, or to another COMPOSE entity takes place.

5.1 Dynamic Flow Enforcement

glue.things is based on node.js, i.e. the components used to build an application run on top of node.js and the interaction and flow of data between single nodes is managed by Node-RED. In order to support the enforcement of data-centric security policies even when facing user-defined JavaScript code in applications, we modified the execution environment for single nodes by integrating JSFlow [7]. It is a security-enhanced JavaScript interpreter which allows dynamic flow tracking. It covers the full non-strict JavaScript as specified by the ECMA-262 standard and allows the annotation of values with basic security labels. We extended these labels and the JSFlow infrastructure to support UsageLocks and their policies. Further, we extended JSFlow to support most language features and libraries of node.js and Node-RED.

To also track the information flow between nodes, we modified the basic node template of Node-RED. The primitives used for sending and receiving messages between nodes have been extended. The message exchange now ensures that security information for data, i.e. security policies and lock states, is available in the nodes processing them but protected from the user. To also support basic Node-RED node types, such as function nodes, we further modified the execution primitives to apply our modified JSFlow. To maintain scalability and decrease the performance impact, all other nodes, i.e. node templates deployed by the COMPOSE provider, only symbolically execute the contract of a node to propagate the security labels for data. This removes the need to apply JSFlow to the complete execution of a node but requires additional pre-processing as explained below.

5.2 Static Flow Enforcement

Evidently, contracts are an important pillar for the scalability of our architecture. They are generated by an over-approximating static analysis of the flows generated by an application. The analysis for basic nodes, i.e. nodes which do not represent another application composed, is based on TAJS [8]. Comparable to JSFlow, we extended this static analyser by important language features required to analyse Node-RED applications and to process policies based on UsageLocks. Results from this version of TAJS can be transformed into a contract indicating the flow-relevant behaviour of a COMPOSE entity.

To analyse and generate contracts for complete workflows, a simple model checker has been implemented. It exploits the flow description provided by Node-RED and extends it with contracts for applications which have already been analysed. Basic nodes without contracts are analysed by our TAJS derivate to generate and store their contract. Composed nodes, are forwarded to our model checker. On top of the model resulting from this analysis cascade, the checker identifies non-compliant data flows, i.e. it searches for traces which perform access to data items although locks specified in the security requirements for these items have not been opened.

These analysis results are also used in glue.things. As a consequence, developers with little or no security expertise are able to validate the compliance of applications with the security requirements of their data or the data of other COMPOSE users. This prevents the deployment of insecure applications which will then be subject to dynamic enforcement.

The use of contracts can tremendously simplify the analysis of complex software and support dynamic enforcement. We further exploits the precise information generated during the static analysis to allow code instrumentation. This does not only involve the instrumentation of JavaScript code in user-defined function or customised Node-RED nodes, but it also includes the instrumentation of workflows. Thus, we are able to further reduce the performance impact of the dynamic flow control and can integrate logging or enforcement mechanisms, e.g. prevent access to particular files, in security critical control flows of applications.

6   Reputation

The reputation manager (see Fig. 2), also called PopularIoTy [13,14], aims to cover scenarios when additional information collected during runtime, and users' feedback can help to assess whether a certain application or Service Object is providing a "good" service. Therefore, popularIoTy calculates reputation for entities based on three aspects: popularity, activity, and feedback.

Popularity reflects how often a certain Service Object or application is used, i.e. invoked by other entities. In the case of the data management, whenever data is generated, notifications are stored in the data storage. Likewise, the monitors placed in the runtime store notifications when an application is called. This information is processed to calculate a popularity score.

The *activity* score attempts to reflect whether an entity is behaving properly. In specific cases, data items, i.e. sensor updates, within the data management can be discarded due to several reasons: lack of security policy compliance, developer-provided source code interpretation errors, or developer-intended filtering. When sensor updates are discarded due to the previous reasons, a notification is stored in the data store. Afterwards, this information is used by popularIoTy to decrease the activity score for Service Objects that drop sensor updates, especially in the case of policy compliance and source code problems. To assess whether an application behaves as expected, security contracts are used. Security contracts for applications could be refined by developers when it is not feasible to determine certain flows, e.g. data is sent to a URL received as a parameter. This allows the reputation manager to leverage the monitors placed in the runtime to detect when the application behaves as promised by the developer in the contract refinement. In case the application complies, it will get a positive activity score reward.

PopularIoTy also encourages users to contribute to the reputation calculation through *feedback*. It is comprised of text, and a numerical value reflecting the user's perception about the Service Object or application.

7 Data Provenance

The data provenance manager tracks origins of data, the operations performed on it, and the time when operations took place. This empowers users to define policies based on data provenance, e.g. allow a Service Object to receive data only if it has been processed by a particular application. Further, visualising the provenance of data can help users to detect when certain errors occur; for example, if several data sources are combined, but one of them is malfunctioning, the developer could examine the sources of correct values, and compare them with wrong values to isolate the malfunctioning device. Also, provenance information has an interesting potential to help to protect the user's privacy. For instance, it could eventually help to detect when particular applications harvest and correlate information from specific entities, hinting to the possibility of user profiling.

8 Conclusion

The ability to simplify the development of applications for the IoT and mitigating the overhead for their deployment is essential for the emerging and wide-spread installation of smart devices. COMPOSE provides important tools to support this process and offers a platform for the design and implementation of both innovative and experimental as well as business application scenarios. We have shown how to accommodate this rapid development processes with data-centric security mechanisms. There are far simpler security technologies which could be implemented with less effort and a smaller performance impact. However, they require a clear security expertise at the developers side, concise and complete requirement collections, carefully selected security primitives at specific enforcement points and usually produce isolated silos of devices and services for specific application scenarios. The security paradigm chosen in COMPOSE removes this burden from the developer and delegates it to sophisticated security mechanisms.

They reconfigure and relocate security enforcement as needed and in accordance to the security requirements a user specifies for his data. In this way, our architecture presents the key to open closed silos and supports the most important but seemingly contradictory properties of the IoT: Openness, Simplicity, and Governance.

References

1. Bai, J.: Feasibility analysis of big log data real time search based on Hbase and elasticsearch. In: 9th International Conference on Natural Computation, ICNC 2013, Shenyang, China, pp. 1166–1170, 23–25 July 2013
2. Broberg, N., Sands, D.: Paralocks: role-based information flow control and beyond. In: Proceedings of the 37th Annual ACM SIGPLAN-SIGACT Symposium on Principles of Programming Languages, pp. 431–444. ACM, New York (2010)
3. Cloud Foundry (2015). https://storm.incubator.apache.org
4. Couchbase (2015). http://www.couchbase.com/
5. Denning, D.E., Denning, P.J.: Certification of programs for secure information flow. Commun. ACM **20**(7), 504–513 (1977)
6. Doukas, C., Pérez, J.L., Villalba, A., Carrera, D.: Bridging web technologies with M2M platforms. In: W3C Workshop on the Web of Things, Enablers and Services for an Open Web of Devices, Germany, Berlin, pp. 25–26, June 2014
7. Hedin, D., Birgisson, A., Bello, L., Sabelfeld, A.: JSFlow: tracking information flow in JavaScript and its apis. In: Symposium on Applied Computing, SAC 2014, Gyeongju, Republic of Korea, pp. 1663–1671, 24–28 March 2014
8. Jensen, S.H., Møller, A., Thiemann, P.: Type analysis for JavaScript. In: Palsberg, J., Su, Z. (eds.) SAS 2009. LNCS, vol. 5673, pp. 238–255. Springer, Heidelberg (2009)
9. Kortuem, G., Kawsar, F., Sundramoorthy, V., Fitton, D.: Smart objects as building blocks for the internet of things. IEEE Internet Comput. **14**(1), 44–51 (2010)
10. Myers, A.C., Liskov, B.: Protecting privacy using the decentralized label model. ACM Trans. Softw. Eng. Methodol. **9**(4), 410–442 (2000)
11. Park, J., Sandhu, R.: The UCON$_{ABC}$ usage control model. ACM Trans. Inf. Syst. Secur. **7**(1), 128–174 (2004)
12. Parra Rodriguez, J.D., Schreckling, D., Posegga, J.: Identity management in platforms offering IoT as a service. In: Jara, A.J., et al. (eds.) IoT 2014. LNICST, vol. 150, pp. 281–288. Springer, Heidelberg (2015). doi:10.1007/978-3-319-19656-5_40
13. Parra, J.D.: Popularioty (2014). http://github.com/nopbyte/popularioty-api/
14. Parra, J.D.: Popularioty Analytics (2014). http://github.com/nopbyte/popularioty-analytics/
15. servIoTicy: IoT streaming made easy (2015). http://www.servioticy.com/
16. The Apache Storm distributed real-time communication system (2015). https://storm.incubator.apache.org/

Privacy Aware on-Demand Resource Provisioning for IoT Data Processing

Tom Kirkham[1(⊠)], Arnab Sinha[2], Nikos Parlavantzas[2],
Bartosz Kryza[3], Paul Fremantle[4], Kyriakos Kritikos[5],
and Benjamin Aziz[4]

[1] STFC, Chilton, UK
tom.kirkham@stfc.ac.uk
[2] Inria, Rennes, France
arnab.sinha@inria.fr
[3] AGH, Krakow, Poland
[4] University of Portsmouth, Portsmouth, UK
{paul.fremantle,ben.aziz}@port.ac.uk
[5] FORTH Crete, Heraklion, Greece

Abstract. Edge processing in IoT networks offers the ability to enforce privacy at the point of data collection. However, such enforcement requires extra processing in terms of data filtering and the ability to configure the device with knowledge of policy. Supporting this processing with Cloud resources can reduce the burden this extra processing places on edge processing nodes and provide a route to enable user defined policy. Research from the PaaSage project [12] on Cloud modelling language is applied to IoT networks to support IoT and Cloud integration linking the worlds of Cloud and IoT in a privacy protecting way.

Keywords: Cloud computing · Scalability · Internet of Things · Models@run.time

1 Introduction

The vision of an Internet of Things (IoT) heralds a new dawn in how people and devices relate to each other. Within environments such as the Smart City personalised services can take into account a person's historical behaviour and their current location. Delivery of these services in the environment via personalised messaging or even public displays has the potential to change personal perceptions of space and privacy.

Emerging EU law is set on a course to require personal consent before IoT based services can interact with a person and their data. Without such consent the capture of this data would be illegal. Thus, in order to future proof emerging IoT services privacy assurance is needed and one such way of doing this is by the provision of data filtering at the edge of the IoT network.

Increased processing capability in low power chips used in IoT networks provide the possibility that data can be filtered at source with respect to specific privacy/security rules. This will enable the handling of most sensitive information to be taken out of the

© ICST Institute for Computer Sciences, Social Informatics and Telecommunications Engineering 2016
B. Mandler et al. (Eds.): IoT 360° 2015, Part II, LNICST 170, pp. 87–95, 2016.
DOI: 10.1007/978-3-319-47075-7_11

hands of the service provider and for such networks to comply with the law. However, such privacy filtering adds latency to the core operation of the sensor board and in data intensive applications can cause potential bottlenecks in relation to quality of service.

In order to counter this, hybrid IoT data processing solutions for both privacy and service provision are needed. Such solutions will enable IoT networks to embrace the benefits of both processing at the edge and extra capacity from the Cloud. Existing work in the model-driven Cloud community illustrates how data can be sent to specific cloud infrastructures based on requirements associated with it. Using Smart City requirements from Canary Wharf this paper illustrate how such an approach can be applied to IoT in the Smart City.

2   Adapting to Context

Personal interaction with devices and sensors in terms of both passive and interactive engagements are set to change human conceptions on how data is shared. For example, current data shared using traditional social networking technologies such as Facebook is largely reliant on personal input. Within IoT connected environments, data sourced from fixed and mobile sensors is often collected automatically. As privacy awareness in the online domain influences behaviour in terms of choice of websites and data shared, within IoT environments it could change the places people go and choices they make.

2.1   Consent

Emerging EU legislation for consent from data subjects prior to data processing in IoT environments is in-line with current approaches to privacy in the online data sharing domain. Within the online community this can be seen manifest in the notification panels asking for consent to track Cookies on most websites. Within the IoT community the approach to achieve this is yet to be defined.

A key challenge in gaining this consent is to determine when and where the consent is required. Personal data in IoT is often produced from multiple sources and varieties of contexts, it differs from web services where data sources are often fixed and application specific. Add to this supported processing on remote infrastructure and the extent to which and prior consent is valid becomes cloudy.

To manage this complexity consent can be better managed in models of deployment and use. In that way the application can investigate such models to ensure consent before the data is processed. Using user defined policy such as in [1] is one way of describing this complex consent as illustrated in Fig. 1.

Identity + Data / Policy

Fig. 1. Typical model for privacy provision in web service environments

Supporting these policies with deployment models can apply the context and is present in work developed in [2] as illustrated in Fig. 2.

$$Identity + (Data * Context) / Policy$$

Fig. 2. Model for privacy provision in IoT environments

Thus applying context to the equation can significantly enhance the sensitivity of the data. This is a particular concern with IoT devices, where the data collected may include significant amounts of meta-data and contextual data which can infringe on privacy. For example, it has been shown that sensors such as accelerometers have unique "fingerprints" that can be used to identify the device [8]. In a typical application data will consist of different privacy levels and how these levels are handled will be described in the model. Taking these concerns into account during processing proposes a problem of adaptation between the device and supporting cloud in both privacy and quality terms.

2.2 Adaptation

Edge processing at a significant level in IoT environments is a relatively new phe-nomenon and related directly to the increasing power in terms of processing and decreasing energy consumption of microchips [3]. From a security perspective, filtering data at the edge enables data marked as private by users to be discarded at source. In addition it can reduce the amount of metadata and contextual data that is published. This reduces both the volume of data to process and the threat of leaked private data. However, for data intensive applications that run complex data analysis, computation at the edge is not always suitable. Edge computation adds delays on data collection and processing and forms a potential bottleneck. A solution to this problem is to support this processing by using either local or remote computing power, one way is to present flexible and on-demand Cloud-based support. The provision of such resource can be realised using the PaaSage platform.

The PaaSage project delivers an open, integrated platform to support model-based lifecycle management of applications executing on multiple cloud infrastructures. Specifically, the PaaSage platform support the generation of application deployment models to best satisfies application owner requirements. When run-time events make the current deployment unsatisfactory (e.g., QoS constraints are violated, or application owner requirements are changed), the platform dynamically adapts this deployment in the most efficient and reliable way. Adaptation in PaaSage relies on the mod-els@run.time approach. Following this approach, the platform maintains models of the running deployment, requirements as well as environment properties. These models are continually updated through monitoring and form the basis of detecting deviations between the current deployment and requirements, of generating a target application deployment, and of transforming the current deployment into the target deployment.

In the context of IoT applications, the PaaSage platform can be used to optimally provide cloud resources when edge resources are insufficient. Specifically, the platform can monitor resource utilisation in the device and automatically trigger the deployment of additional data processing modules on cloud resources. The number and types of virtual machines and the associated cloud provider are selected in order to best satisfy the application's performance, security, energy consumption, and cost requirements. The selected application deployment can then be dynamically adapted when the platform identifies a better target deployment or when environment conditions change (e.g., workload variations, price changes of cloud providers).

PaaSage provides a set of interfaces to configure and monitor the Cloud. It not only enables non cloud specialists from the IoT domain to set specific deployment requirements such as security and quality of service but also to monitor how these requirements are respected during execution. Supporting the deployment and execution are Reasoning components that look to find optimal deployments based on user requirements and monitored metrics from the infrastructure (which can include the IoT network). From an IoT perspective this constant management of the Cloud environment ensures that security and quality can be maintained at the pace of change at the IoT platform.

3   Models

The PaaSage platform consists of various components that handle the life-cycle phases of configuration, deployment and execution of multi-cloud applications. Central to the operation of these components is the Cloud Application Modelling and Execution Language (CAMEL). This acts as a thread throughout each phase ensuring application deployment requirements are applied on multiple aspects of multi-cloud applications. These include operations such as provisioning and deployment topology, provisioning and deployment requirements, service-level requirements, metrics, scalability rules, providers, organisations, users, roles, security controls, execution contexts, and execution histories. Applying these models to link user requirements to the operation of IoT networks will enable the edge IoT processor to adopt privacy sensitive flexible Cloud based resource provisioning.

3.1   Handling Constraints Towards Privacy

The PaaSage platform can enforce data privacy in various ways through the CAMEL model. Firstly, it uses organisation models in the life-cycle phases of deployment and execution for representing organisations and users associated with a cloud-based application. For this purpose, the organisation package of the CAMEL metamodel is based on the organisation subset of CERIF [10], which is a modelling framework for specifying organisations, users and other entities in the research domain. It is an EU recommendation [11] for information systems related to research databases used for standardising research information and fostering research information exchange.

The CERIF model for an organisation contains blocks of information about the list of data centres offered by the organisation, the organisation itself, its users and user groups as well as the permissions and role assignments issued by the organisation. CERIF enables varied organisations to express user privileges in relation to data processing and mpa permissions in federated environments. This mapping of identity will provide the edge processor with the ability to handle data from multiple organisations.

Secondly, data privacy could be maintained by specifying location requirements, involving one or more locations. A location can be either a geographical-based location (e.g., region or country) or a cloud location (i.e., a location specific to a cloud provider). This type of requirement is attached in deployment models either at the global level or at the local VM level. In this way, the end-user can specify a set of locations which should hold either for all the specified VMs or for a specific VM.

It is the responsibility of the PaaSage *Upperware* component, and particularly of the *Reasoner* sub-component, to consider such requirements in order to guarantee that all instances of VMs to be generated are situated in the respective locations included in these requirements. This can ensure any constraints in relation to location of data processing can also be applied in the filtering at the IoT edge processing. This is particularly significant for mobile sensors where data collected in some locations could be processed in the Cloud or edge whilst other locations can be marked as private.

CAMEL has the ability to create a digital form of the specification of all possible security controls as they have been identified by Cloud Security Alliance (CSA) and store them. A security control is identified by a name, a particular domain and sub-Domain, a textual description and to a set of security properties and metrics that it links to. In this way, when security requirements will need to be defined, the end-user will have the opportunity to select the security controls that better satisfy his/her needs by either browsing the respective security control list or making focused searches.

Integrating IoT specific controls into this list would enhance the security of distributed IoT networks by ensuring that the Cloud fits to the IoT deployment. A key benefit of edge processing is the simplification of data processing at a local level to the sensor. As this can reduce risk of data propagation as opposed to when it is processed in the Cloud. In cases where data has to be taken from the edge to the Cloud (such as in the need for extra processing power) PaaSage can look to tailor specific Cloud deployments to suit data sensitivity.

This flexibility is of key importance as it is likely that data from the IoT network can be of various levels of sensitivity depending on sensors and context. The ability for a supportive Cloud to adapt to this when providing extra resource to the edge is a key motivation in using PaaSage to support IoT data processing.

3.2 Managing Adaptability

CAMEL supports monitoring and scalability information in the deployment model and this is used to trigger dynamic adaptation. Specifically, the platform detects specified events, such as violations of service-level objectives or component failures, and enacts adaptation actions, such as vertical scaling, horizontal scaling, relocating components to different clouds as well as application restructuring.

Within the IoT environment adaptation may also be triggered by monitoring on the device to trigger a Cloud burst or the availability of a deployment model that better satisfies user requirements and goals (e.g., taking into account updated cloud provider offerings). Importantly, the PaaSage platform continually seeks to optimise application operation by finding better deployment models and enacting them in a cost-efficient and safe manner. Deriving deployment models relies on a user-provided utility function that represents the extent to which a given deployment model satisfies user requirements and goals.

4   Use Cases and Implementation

The use case in which we have developing an initial deployment of our prototype is focused on the Smart City. Requirements for the platform in terms of business case and function were sourced from Canary Wharf as part of a Smart City Challenge [1].

4.1   Smart Cities

Smart Cities can be defined in a variety of ways. A common feature in all definitions is the use of connected devices within the urban environment. This includes connecting existing infrastructure and management systems with sensors in the environment to improve city management, including aspects such as traffic control, parking, air quality and lighting. However, more dynamic uses of technology within the Smart City are embracing increased processing power of devices both personal and at device level.

Such applications include features such as personalisation of retail environments and advanced crowd management. In these scenarios the demand on computing power of the sensors within the environment and data processing modules varies with the numbers of people and the data demands of the application.

Management of the performance of applications in the Smart City typically fall into the hands of various agencies with often different service demands. For example, traffic control systems are usually supplied by local authorities responsible for traffic management across wide areas and demanding high levels of application reliability. Within shopping centres typically the infrastructure is controlled by the owner of the built infrastructure. Here the service is less critical but relies on greater amounts of personal data.

Implementation of IoT within an environment such as Canary Wharf has to balance both the application goals and with support for the reputation of the Smart City brand. Central to reputation management is the control of how data is both used and secured particularly with respect to personal data privacy.

4.2   Data Processing

Data processing in our implementation is achieved using the Intel Edison device platform. Collection of data is achieved by the capture of Bluetooth association data from personal devices as they pass into range. In order to better associate identity with devices the project created a portal for device registration and association with users. During the device registration process personal privacy preferences can be set in relation to data yielded from the device and how it is used. In addition to these user-defined privacy policies, a set of core privacy policies were defined. These core policies implement the requirement to maintain the reputation of Canary Wharf within the Smart City domain.

These requirements captured in CAMEL initially sit at the middleware layer. Pushing them down to the device enables the management of sensed data with respect to privacy preference and identity. Example policies tested on the platform defined what types of data could be collected per user or identity. To implement this a data filtering module was created for the device that configured using policy and identity.

Identity is provided on the portal via user attributes submitted when signing onto the portal. This identity can be expressed using standards such as OAuth or SAML and transferred to the IoT platform. Policies defined by data subjects will enable association of specific context with certain users. DeviceID from sensed data is checked against identity and policy.

Using CAMEL to support the data filtering at the edge the prospect of data processing bottlenecks is reduced. Here, when the performance/processing levels of the core data processing module on the device reaches a pre-set threshold a notification is sent to Cloud burst. In this scenario, the message is sent to the PaaSage platform using the MQTT protocol.

5   Related Work

The platform presented in this paper offers a unique combination of data processing depending on the application/user specifications for computation in IoT networks. Significantly established areas for edge processing such as the routing of packets via Switches and Routers are now moving toward supported processing using Cloud based virtual networks and is the focus of newly funded research [2].

In terms of specific IoT and Cloud integration Aneka is an IoT application development Platform-as-a-Service (PaaS) that is capable of utilizing storage and compute resources of both public clouds [4]. It provides various services that allow users to control, auto-scale, reserve, monitor and bill users for the resources consumed by their applications. It also supports resource provisioning on public clouds such as Microsoft Azure, Amazon EC2 and GoGrid as well as on private clouds such as desktops and clusters. The resource provisioning is dynamic for a certain time and cost considering past execution history of applications and budget availability.

In comparison to our work, Aneka follows a similar approach. While on the one hand, the target vision is the same i.e. on-demand resource provisioning for IoT applications, on the other hand the approach for realization the ecosystem is different. PaaSage uses simple CAMEL model to specify the properties of the IoT application i.e. constraints and adaptability for data privacy, application performance and user preferences along with the IoT platform (which also serves for local data processing) and Aneka is itself a dedicated .NET-based application development PaaS.

In [9], the Webinos system pushes XACML policies out to devices to limit the spread of personal and contextual data. While the aims of this are broadly similar, there are two key differences. Firstly, the Webinos system is based around the core concept of devices being in the personal control of users and therefore having a "personal zone" to protect. By contrast, in a Smart City there are many devices that collect data on many different subjects, which is dealt with in our work. Secondly, in contrast with this work, the Webinos system does not implement automatic movement of processing based on load from edge devices into the cloud.

In [5], Aazam and Huh provides a model for Fog computing which provides a layer between IoTs and the cloud. Typically, their model performs resource management for the IoTs taking into account resource prediction, resource allocation, and pricing all in a realistically and dynamically; also considering customers' type, traits, and characteristics. The authors also mention that the Fog could provision for decisions concerning the security and privacy of data collected from the WSNs and IoTs using a Smart Gateway within the layer.

Contrasting with our work, this could be viewed as a different architecture where the Fog layer provides computation, privacy, security etc as services for IoTs. In fact, it overlaps with similar concepts like mobile cloud computing (MCC) and mobile-edge computing (MEC) [6]. Another notable difference as mentioned in Sect. 2.2, these kind of edge processing can add delays therefore leading to bottlenecks. Our PaaSage platform has the flexibility to adapt by using either local or remote processing, through flexible and on-demand Cloud based support. Another drawback as pointed out in [7], Fog devices are prone to greater threats like man-in-the-middle attack as they work at the edge of networks; we use a more tightly coupled architecture with the privacy module embedded within the IOT platform.

6 Future Work

This paper documents early stage research and investigations in combining IoT with existing work on the PaaSage project. Future work involves the broadening of the initial investigations to further define links between Cloud models and IoT. Configuration interfaces between the PaaSage platform and IoT devices also require further investigation. More efficient methods for device configuration taking into account combined IoT capability are interesting points of investigation.

7 Conclusion

Provision of edge processing in IoT networks can provide enhanced privacy provision and compliance in implementations processing personal data such as the Smart City. In order to support such provision at the edge extra provision for processing of non sensitive data can be provided via the Cloud. Using the PaaSage platform and Cloud modeling language CAMEL, Cloud computing infrastructure can be selected to suit the specific data processing needs and deployment characteristics of the IoT network.

Acknowledgement. This project has received funding from the European Community's Seventh Framework Programme (FP7/2007-2013) under Grant Agreement n° 317715".

References

1. Cognicity Smart City Challenge Canary Wharf. http://www.Cognicity.london
2. Becon Horizon 2020 project. www.beacon.eu
3. Spinnewyn, B., Latré, S.: Towards a fluid cloud: an extension of the cloud into the local network. In: Latré, S., Charalambides, M., François, J., Schmitt, C., Stiller, B. (eds.) AIMS 2015. LNCS, vol. 9122, pp. 61–65. Springer, Heidelberg (2015). doi:10.1007/978-3-319-20034-7
4. Gubbi, J., Buyya, R., Marusic, S., Palaniswami, M.: Internet of Things (IoT): a vision, architectural elements, and future directions. Future Gener. Comput. Syst. **29**(7), 1645–1660 (2013)
5. Aazam, M.; Huh, E.-N.: Fog computing micro datacenter based dynamic resource estimation and pricing model for IoT. In: 2015 IEEE 29th International Conference on Advanced Information Networking and Applications (AINA), pp. 687–694, 24–27 March 2015
6. Yi, S., Li, C., Li, Q.: A survey of fog computing: concepts, applications and issues. In: Proceedings of 2015 Workshop on Mobile Big Data (Mobidata 2015). ACM, New York, pp. 37–42 (2015)
7. Stojmenovic, I., Wen, S.: The fog computing paradigm: scenarios and security issues. In: 2014 Federated Conference on Computer Science and Information Systems (FedCSIS), pp. 1–8, 7–10 September 2014
8. Bojinov, H., Michalevsky, Y., Nakibly, G., Boneh, D.: Mobile device identification via sensor fingerprinting (2014). arXiv preprint arXiv:1408.1416
9. Desruelle, H., Lyle, J., Isenberg, S., Gielen, F.: On the challenges of building a web-based ubiquitous application platform. In: Proceedings of 2012 ACM Conference on Ubiquitous Computing, pp. 733–736. ACM (2012)
10. Jeffery, K., Houssos, N., Jörg, B., Asserson, A.: Research information management: the CERIF approach. IJMSO **9**(1), 5–14 (2014). doi:10.1504/IJMSO.2014.059142
11. CERIF Specification. http://cordis.europa.eu/cerif/
12. EU PaaSage project. www.paasage.eu

Mobility IoT

Internet of Things as Advanced Technology to Support Mobility and Intelligent Transport

Milan Dado[✉], Aleš Janota, Juraj Spalek, Peter Holečko,
Rastislav Pirník, and Karl E. Ambrosch

University of Žilina, Univerzitná 8215/1, 010 26 Žilina, Slovakia
{milan.dado, ales.janota, juraj.spalek,
peter.holecko, karl.ambrosch}@uniza.sk,
rastislav.pirnik@fel.uniza.sk

Abstract. This keynote paper creates the framework for the 2nd EAI International Conference on Mobility in the Internet of Things (IoT). The IoT offers advanced connectivity of devices, systems, and services that goes beyond machine-to-machine communications and covers a variety of domains and applications. The interconnection of embedded devices is expected in many fields including Mobility and Intelligent Transport. In the light of the latest knowledge and scientific projects findings the authors present actual R&D trends in the given field. New ideas, cutting-edge innovations and technologies for mobility agenda are needed together with a multidisciplinary perspective approach. The paper indicates most common recent aspects for future development of the IoT applications for support of Mobility and Intelligent Transport. Research and innovations projects including ERA Chair project in ITS at the University of Žilina are presented as examples of solutions for IoT applications for benefits of citizens (motorized and non-motorized public).

Keywords: Internet of Things · Mobility · Transport · Research · Application · Smart · Information and communication technology · Security and safety · Intelligent Transport Systems

1 Introduction

The Internet of Things (IoT) is an emerging technology that evolved from the convergence of Internet, wireless technologies and micro-electro-mechanical systems (MEMS). For the first time, the term "Internet of Things" was used by Kevin Ashton, founder of Auto-ID Center, in 1999. The 'thing' may be any natural or man-made object, assigned a unique identifier: a car with built-in sensors, a live organism (human or animal) with implanted devices (biochip, heart monitor), a home control system with detectors, etc. As defined in [1], the IoT can be realised in three paradigms – internet oriented (middleware), things oriented (sensors) and semantic-oriented (knowledge). The usefulness of IoT can be released only in an application domain where the three paradigms overlap. Therefore at the moment the prospective applications seem to be in health care, policy making, industry, defence sector, infrastructure monitoring, energy (smart grids), factories of future, retail, environment protection, business intelligence,

© ICST Institute for Computer Sciences, Social Informatics and Telecommunications Engineering 2016
B. Mandler et al. (Eds.): IoT 360° 2015, Part II, LNICST 170, pp. 99–106, 2016.
DOI: 10.1007/978-3-319-47075-7_12

smart metering, home management and many others. A very broad area for IoT deployment associated with mobility is transport and logistics, including parking, highway monitoring, emergency services and many other services. Machine-to-Machine (M2M) communication ability is a prerequisite of so called smartness.

Ubiquitous sensing by Wireless Sensor Networks (WSN) technologies offers in many areas new possibilities for the support of everyday life. One of the important areas for utilisation of ubiquitous sensing is mobility and transport in general. Variety of enabling technologies such as RFID tags, different types of embedded sensors and actuators are transforming the internet utilisation and create new services heading to a fully integrated Future Internet. The Digital Agenda for Europe - Europe 2020 Initiative in chapter "Future Internet" [2] has priorities in internet of services, things and infrastructure. This includes research into the Network Technologies of the Future, Cloud Computing, Internet of Things, Future Internet Research and Experimentation, Public-Private Partnership in Future Internet etc.

The OECD Technology Foresight Forum 2014 refers about the Internet of Things [3] as a term applied to the next 50 billion machines and devices that will go online in the next two decades. The number of connected devices in households in OECD countries is expected to be 14 billion by 2022 in comparison to around 1.4 billion in 2012. The large scale economic and societal influence of these developments will be influenced through the data collected in network with IoT implementation and machine learning can be an essential element for such data and the data they collect can be used to take action. Silver Spring Networks [4] refers that "a controlled plug every 30 m in each street" will be located for smart city solutions.

In accordance with Goldman Sachs [5] the Internet of Things is emerging as the next technology mega-trend, with effects across the business spectrum. By connecting to the Internet, billions of everyday devices – ranging from fitness bracelets to industrial equipment – the IoT merges the physical and online worlds, opening up a host of new opportunities and challenges for companies, governments and consumers. A very large number of embedded devices connected with IoT will generate a huge amount of data, even if individually each of them contributes only a limited amount. In mobility and intelligent transport systems (ITS), sensors and mobile devices (mobile phones, OBUs) generate it. The main role is to extract meaningful information from big data. For that the equivalent and corresponding computer software with optimal processing power and knowledge and skills of experts are needed.

It is assumed that the massive growth of M2M traffic based on IoT will require a more efficient and ubiquitous technology to carry the data traffic and the use of communication – especially wireless – technologies by humans and by machines. 5G technologies won't just be faster, it will bring new functionalities and applications with high social and economic value for mobility and intelligent transport too. The main current research directions were given at Globecom in December 2013. The capacity is to increase by a factor of 1,000. Data rates are to go up to 50 Gbps for low mobility, 5 Gbps for high mobility and 1 Gbps anywhere, i.e. this seems to be the minimum everyone should be able to enjoy also in remote areas. The latency should further decrease to less than 1 ms (it is 5–10 ms in LTE), and energy consumption should be reduced by a factor between 10 and 100. These targets will be achieved by enhancement of LTE which will include the deployment of dense, smaller cells and may include other general enhancements like the combined usage of higher and lower frequency bands and the substantial use of MIMO technologies and specification of completely new radio access technologies (11).

2 Innovation Cycle of the IoT

As any other new technology the IoT also follows a typical innovation cycle going through the usual phases: innovation trigger, inflated expectations, disillusionment, enlightenment and productivity. Seeing examples of the Gartner's hypo curve for emerging technologies published in recent years 2012–2015 it is apparent that since 2012 when the IoT was situated closely to the end the of the 1st phase this year the technology has reached the peak of inflated expectations.

Expectations are 5–10 years to reach plateau of productivity which means to have tools and products saturating the market. The promises are huge – the IoT seems to be the world's most massive device market in few years; however, estimations of exact size vary greatly. The Hype Cycle includes series of various emerging technologies; some of them being interconnected and/or interdependent. Each of them usually depends on one or more other sub-technologies that (if not quite ready) can limit the true potential and successful bringing to the life. For the IoT the right *balance of power consumption, cost and bandwidth* will have to be found for both industry or people needs. Otherwise the massive scale connection of things may come rather in the form of idle wishes than reality.

A *lack of standards* may turn out to be another troublesome barrier for rapid IoT development. Currently the IoT lacks a common set of standards and technologies that would allow for compatibility and ease-of-use. The war of IoT protocols has already started and hardly any winner can be identified at the moment. There are currently few standards/regulations for what is needed to run an IoT device. Instead of a single standard for connecting devices on the IoT there are several competing standards run by the following coalitions: The Thread Group (Qualcomm, The Linux Foundation, Microsoft, Panasonic), The Industrial Internet Consortium (Intel, Cisco, AT&T, IBM, Microsoft), Open Interconnect Consortium (Samsung, Intel, Dell), Physical Web (Google), AllSeen Alliance (Samsung, Intel, Dell) and huge number of smaller non-standardized protocols in use [6]. As far as the industrial IoT is concerned, the Industrial Internet Consortium (IIC) was founded in March 2014 to bring together the organizations and technologies necessary to accelerate growth of the Industrial Internet by identifying, assembling and promoting best practices [7].

A lot of potential applications will put increasing pressure on *security and safety issues*. Anything associated with the Web contains potential hazards, so more devices will have to be considered critical than nowadays. On one side data generated by the IoT has the potential to reveal far more about users than any technology in history. On the other side systems generating data could be (and surely will be) the subject of hacking with all negative consequences to the systems themselves, their users, environment, on local or even global scale. The industrial IoT opens the door of safety risks to industry and enterprises. Transportation may be a good example of potential vulnerability (web connected cars, communicating road-side infrastructure, railway SCADA systems, planes and airline systems).

The need to store and analyse big data in a secure way may require unexpectedly high demands on additional costs. Even at present, various countries and domains apply different privacy-related legislations that limit personal and other sensitive data processing [9]. Thus success and failure of IoT applications may be country specific. People do not use technology that they do not trust. Since in principle nothing may be 100 % secure or safe, the serious and open game with societal acceptance of risks must be played. After all, the benefits of privacy by design smart connected product should outweigh privacy and safety concerns.

At present it is hard to imagine all kinds of things potentially connected to the network in the future and their functionalities - from "dumb" objects such as light switches, toasters, fans up to "smarter" ones such as transport means, health monitoring stations, smart homes, etc. Even though it is clear that *natural interactions* will be highly preferred, i.e. using systems that understand gestures, expressions and/or movements and engage people in a dialogue, while allowing them to interact naturally with each other and the environment [8]. The aspect of intuitiveness may also become very important, with no need to wear any special device or to learn a set of instructions.

The idea of monitoring and controlling everything via wireless networks will bring a huge increase of data. ABI Research estimates [10] that the IoT communication in 2014 generated data traffic of 200 exabytes. At the end of the decade in 2020 the Internet of Things is expected to transmit 8 times of this data volume, i.e. 1 600 exabytes or 1,6 zettabytes. However, the real added value will be not in the data itself or technologies providing it but in the provided services.

We could foresee that IoT deployment will speed up customization trends and inevitably bring *changes to social and working patterns*. As an example the trend known as BYOD (Bring Your Own Device) is being often mentioned – enterprises allow their employees to bring their own personal devices into the work environment, to use them, share working data, etc. Gartner calls BYOD the "most radical change in the economics and the culture of client computing in decades" and expects that, by 2017, half of all companies will have mandatory BYOD policies.

Sometimes new technologies are adopted applying the so called M-U-D (Middle – Upper - Down) approach. The middle layer represented by managers in the field can see an added value of the new technology and convince the upper managers of benefits of adopting it by the lower layer employees. It is probable that IoT deployment initiatives may be operated in a similar approach. In any case, companies are expected to have sufficient level of maturity to manage their information and organization processes.

Filling the facts associated with IoT deployment is a big *challenge to semiconductor industry*. According to Dean Freeman, semiconductor manufacturing analyst at Gartner, Inc., perhaps by the end of this decade - the world may be home to a trillion sensors - eventually, a trillion sensors a year could be consumed [12].

3   ITS Projects Continuity at the UNIZA

The University of Žilina (UNIZA) uses its intellectual, technological, scientific, and research potential to solve problems of basic and applied research in the field of intelligent transport. At the turn of the century UNIZA became involved in the resolution of key transportation challenges on national and international level.

The titles of pinpointing university projects are shown in Fig. 1.

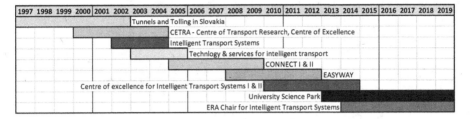

Fig. 1. ITS project continuity of UNIZA

These research directions are fully compatible with the European research heading formulated in the Strategic Research Agenda 2020 document, an EU frame programme for research and innovations Horizon 2020, as well as with the Long-term plan of state scientific and technical policy until 2015 (The Fénix strategy), National plan of research and development infrastructure – SK ROADMAP, and the Danube region strategy. On these foundations, a modern scientific-research infrastructure is further built, a cooperation with foreign research and educational institutions as well as with commercial sphere is being developed. New generation of experts has been formed focusing on intelligent transport technologies and services. The result of these activities was the acquirement of University Science Park.

UNIZA demarcated 2 long-term strategic development directions – "intelligent transport" and "digital enterprise". In line with this heading, in 2014 the construction of University Science Park (USP) and University Science Centre (USC) started. The initial conception of USP structure in the area of intelligent transport, as defined at the beginning of the USP project proposition, is shown in Fig. 2.

Its centre is constituted by a computer system in the position of a monitoring and control system (Virtual Smart City - ViSC), which enables to build the concept of "smart city" with emphasis on control of processes primarily related with monitoring of traffic state in a selected geographically defined area. The conceptual scheme of intelligent city virtual platform is based on traffic models using data gained from sensor networks. Using manually entered or generated input data, it will enable to model the operation of city, thereby serving as a source of virtual sensor information for the superordinate monitoring and control system. The superordinate system can subsequently, based on the acquired sensor data and analysis of the defined models, intervene the infrastructure control and optimize the traffic process.

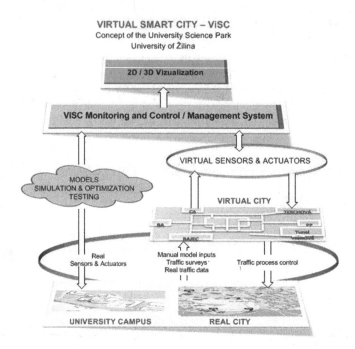

Fig. 2. The Virtual Smart City concept (ViSC) according to University Science Park

By the end of June 2014, UNIZA started a testing operation of IBM Intelligent Operations Center for Smarter Cities, specifically a transport oriented modification - IBM Intelligent Operations Center for Transportation (IOT) providing advanced analytical, optimisation and prediction tools. The basic idea of this concept is that the quality of life in city agglomerations is highly dependent on the quality of services provided to the residents, which is significantly affected by the perceived quality standard of transportation and many other services. This requires a considerable volume of information, real-time communication and cooperation of several subjects involved within the control of distinct city processes with the objective to counteract the emergent problems before they arise, if possible.

The current problem is that all critical data is typically stored in heterogeneous and mutually incompatible systems located within the premises of various administrators, thus disabling a single complex and integrated view on the events taking place. The system would enable a rapid sharing of information and a mutual coordination of all units and thereby to improve the effectiveness of the services provided.

The initial project phase will focus on the UNIZA campus at the Velky Diel, therefore this phase is referred to as Smarter Campus. In order to implement these strategic objectives, the Faculty of Electrical Engineering acquired in advance several new technologies which will provide a momentum for the development of so-far activities and enable to prepare their integration into the planned processes. The core of these technologies are the products of Libelium® (Meshlium® networks for Wapsmote® sensors).

4 ERA Chair

The EU-funded ERAdiate project [13] is promoting excellence of the University of Žilina and the Žilina convergence region in the field of Intelligent Transport Systems aiming for enhanced competitiveness in the European Research Area (ERA). The University Science Park (USP) of UNIZA is the home base of the ERA Chair Holder and his team. Using the research infrastructure the focus will be on ITS innovations such as cooperative ITS (connected vehicles and infrastructure, an already available and standardised pre-phase to IoT), decarbonisation of mobility (i.e. electro-mobility and its requirements), big and open data, interoperability, and human factors. These include acceptance, usability, data protection and privacy aspects, as well as liability aspects, where resilience and resistance to fraud, hacking, etc. are important.

5 Conclusions

Internet of Things is a crucial technology for the implementation of ICT into transportation in general. There are many areas which will be supported with this technology. IoT is a huge challenge and has urgent need to be standardised in many areas (information and communication networks and services, safety and security, etc.) for faster and more effective applications. IoT in general is always an innovative task for utilisation of the Interned networks and services and gives new requirements in many fields for it. New requirements are needed for collaboration among industries producing equipment, those who operate transport infrastructure, municipalities, academia, and citizens to answer on such challenges. Support from research and development agencies is very needed to speed up processes for developing smarter and greener solutions in transport and mobility.

Acknowledgments. This paper is the result of the project implementation: Centre of excellence for systems and services of intelligent transport, ITMS 26220120050 supported by the Research & Development Operational Program funded by the ERDF.

The paper was in part supported by the project ERAdiate – Enhancing Research and innovAtion dimensions of the University of Zilina in intelligent transport systems co-funded from European Union's Seventh Framework Programme for research, technological development and demonstration under grant agreement no. 621386.

References

1. Atzori, L., Iera, A., Morabito, G.: The internet of things: a survey. Comput. Netw. **54**, 2787–2805 (2010)
2. European Commission: Future Internet (2015). http://ec.europa.eu/digital-agenda/en/future-internet
3. OECD Technology Foresight Forum 2014 - The Internet of Things (2014). http://www.oecd.org/internet/ieconomy/technology-foresight-forum-2014.htm
4. Silver Spring Networks. http://www.silverspringnet.com
5. Sachs, G.: The Internet of Things: The Next Mega-Trend (2014). http://www.goldmansachs.com/our-thinking/pages/internet-of-things/
6. Engdahl, T.: IoT Trends for 2015 (2015). http://www.epanorama.net/newepa/2015/01/05/iot-trends-for-2015/comment-page-16/
7. Industrial Internet Consortium (2015). http://www.iiconsortium.org/
8. Valli, A.: Notes on Natural Interaction (2004). http://www.idemployee.id.tue.nl/g.w.m.rauterberg/lecturenotes/valli-2004.pdf
9. Miorandi, D., Sicari, S., De Pelegrini, F., Chlamtac, I.: Internet of things: vision, applications and research challenges. Ad Hoc Netw. **10**(7), 1497–1516 (2012)
10. ABI Research. https://www.abiresearch.com/market-research/service/automotive-infotainment/
11. Lammers, D.: Fabs in the internet of things era. Nanochip FAB Solut. **8**(2) (2013). http://www.appliedmaterials.com/files/nanochip-journals/nanochip-fab-solutions-december-2013-revised.pdf
12. Srotyr, M., Lokaj, Z., Zelinka, T.: Advanced VANET routing design. In: Smart Cities Symposium Prague (SCSP) (2015)
13. ERAdiate. http://www.erachair.uniza.sk/information-about-project/main-activities/

Multimodal Interactions: Embedding New Meanings to Known Forms and Objects

Predrag K. Nikolic[(⌧)]

Faculty of Digital Production, EDUCONS University, Vojvode Putnika 87,
21208 Sremska Kamenica, Serbia
Predrag.nikolic@educons.edu.rs

Abstract. The way we are experiencing and interacting with our everyday living environment define and anticipate our future behavior and actions. Today new digital technologies vastly diminish boundaries between virtual and physical world. Cross-reality design supported with recent mobile and context aware computing, gradually changed the concept of user interaction and moved it more toward usage of heterogeneous contexts, pervasive computing technologies, and multimodal spatial perception and transformed our living surroundings into smart environments, traditional living object into smart living objects. Ubiquitous computing vision implies more than ever to our lives. In order to make all these changes more human-centered in this paper we are investigated the cognitive and metaphorical aspects of future interface design strategies which could enhance user experience and ideas acceptance, communicated through multimodal interactions. In this paper we are presenting three tangible interfaces that we have developed for design and research purposes and results we collected during their public exposure. Hopefully, the results will give us sufficient insights for further investigations in the field of smart living environments and smart objects development. We believe that to fulfill these goals application and exploration of tangible interfaces frameworks and cognitive methods could be one of the crucial elements for the future research success.

Keywords: Multimodal interactions · Smart environments · Smart living objects · Ubiquitous computing · Interface design · Tangible interfaces · User experience design · Cross-reality design

1 Introduction

In this paper it has been explored how interactive user experience can be enhanced if human values and cognition directs the process of designing content and services for smart living environments [1]. The environments which are augmented with digital technology and widely spread mobile computing, could have a capability to enable automation, interactivity, ubiquity [2] while meeting user expectations and allowing interaction everywhere at almost a subconscious level [1]. Technologies itself are becoming increasingly invisible and personal; in practice this means that interaction is happening with minimal user distraction and with today user mobility at any time

© ICST Institute for Computer Sciences, Social Informatics and Telecommunications Engineering 2016
B. Mandler et al. (Eds.): IoT 360° 2015, Part II, LNICST 170, pp. 107–121, 2016.
DOI: 10.1007/978-3-319-47075-7_13

and everywhere. As pervasive computing technologies (mobile technologies, radio-frequency identification, sensors, microelectronics, wireless technologies, ambient displays, networked video-systems, context-aware systems, etc.) are becoming more reliable and cost efficient, researchers and industry show increasing interest in exploring ways to leverage them for new services design and in the development of multimodal experiential environments where users are enriched with multiple meanings and meta-phors. This could have a significant impact on the time-space aspect of user experience embedded into natural living surrounding and their mobility. In such fast environments people can interact any time at any place, in metaphorical way where meaning can be transferred between users and environments, an emotional way by which users will hold a long-term memory of experience, as well as a physical way in which the immediate conscious and unconscious impact takes place through the interaction with the applied technology [3]. Ubiquitous workspaces, augmented reality, online social interactions, wearable computers, mobile applications and multimodal environments, could become key contributors into innovative service development implemented into everyday living surrounding. The concept we be followed in our experiments, as relevant to achieve those ideas, is cross-reality design.

Cross-reality is an informational or media exchange between real- and virtual-world systems that closely conceptually correlates to idea of a smart living environments development [4]. For example, environments built upon cross-reality principles could serve as a bridge across sensor networks and Web-based virtual worlds, improving people's interactions with each other and with the physical world [5]. With the potential of bringing together two worlds that have been disjoint and of enriching user experiences, companies have started to change their service logic and are beginning to implement cross-reality ideas into widely used consumer devices such as: location and orientation in mobile phones (e.g. GPS in the mobile phones), biometrics in clothing (e.g. pedometers in Nike shoes), on-body gesture recognition in gaming controllers (e.g. accelerometers in the Nintendo Wii), off-body gesture recognition in gaming consoles (e.g. cameras in the Microsoft Xbox Kinect).

Together with the researches related to cross-reality as design concept (embraced with several major themes including augmented reality, mixed reality, ubiquitous computing, and wearable computing) interface design has become an important issue to deal with in realization of this concept and evolved toward exploration of the relationship between physical representation and digital information. Important first steps were done by Fitzmaurice, Buxton, and Ishii who described a new conceptual framework in their discussions about "graspable user interfaces" [6]. In further development Ullmer and Ishii extended the idea and proposed the term "tangible user interfaces" [7]. The framework supports concept where interface should not be just an input device but rather artefact which simultaneously integrated physical representation and control. Despite traditional graphical user interface approach where exists clear distinction between input (mouse, keyboard) and output devices (monitor), tangible interfaces tends to diminish this distinction.

2 Related Research

The researchers have been working for more than a decade on meaningful concepts for integration between real and virtual space. Followed by technology improvements, cross- reality ideas started widely to appear in projects ranging from interactive art installations, like Drew Harry's Stiff People's League installation (see http://labcast. media.mit.edu/?p=26) or The Parcer, an online interactive art installation based on the instrument capable to facilitate multiuser composition in a collaborative environment [4], to augmented reality in a Touring Machine project [8] or ubiquitous workspaces like the work by Gloria Mark [9] focusing on intensive design activities such as the design of NASA space missions or complicated software. Collaboration between participants, user-generated content together with intention to improve communication using 3D visualization were primary aspects to explore within the first experiments in cross-reality design [4]. Second Life, an online virtual world launched by Linden Lab in 2003, has been chosen by a group of researchers as the virtual platform for cross-reality experiments Shadowlab [10] with environments that supported user-generated content. A new approach to the visualization of information, which is one more considerable aspect of multimodal pervasive technology application, can be seen in projects such as Google Earth visualizations of the James Reserve done by the Center for Embedded Network Sensing [11]. Domain of data visualization was among the first to accept commercial implementations of cross-reality in the projects such as IBM's visualization of data center operation (see http://www.ugotrade.com/2008/02/21/the-wizard-of-ibms-3d-data-centers/) or VRcontext's Walkinside visualization software (www.vrcontext.com). Cross-reality systems also have the potential to reconfigure service environments into creative workspaces with high flexibility as a core design principle for certain collaborative projects [12]. Collaborative space made of sensate media [13], responsive furniture, paper-based interfaces and a mappable project space [14], could be a creative playground for future users of a living environments co-created by themselves.

Transformations we are experiencing continuously through new media have changed the way we are interacting, sensing and engaging with the objects in our everyday environmental space. What we can see from the examples above is that usage of cross-reality systems and concept of tangible interfaces could help us for example to extend collaborative tools into networked space, enrich user engagement in the experience of virtual space and move perception toward advanced levels. With such potential, we believe that cross-reality and interface design concepts based on usage of everyday objects and representations of known forms have a potential to radically affect the way we are experiencing services embedded in our living environment. This could lead to redefinition of existing interface and design communication practices and possibilities for application within the multimodal cross-reality smart living context: meaningful end user experience (collaborative, metaphorical, contemplative, creative, aesthetical).

3 Interaction and Communication

Merleau-Ponty's integrated view of action and perception makes an interesting starting point for a discussion of meaningful interactive experiences together with meaningful design. Based on his theory it is possible to lead users into interactions with the computer that are meaningful at a very basic level. With an application of Merleau-Ponty's philosophy to human-computer interaction, we get a new understanding of interaction as perception. We consider interaction as perceptual process which involves both human mind as well as human body, then distinction between tool and media disappears. Involvement of total body into perception transform it into active process and it is no longer the passive reception of information through a medium. When action in the same way is seen as an expression of our being-in-the-world, it no longer has meaning to see as a purely body activity.

From the other side, Activity Theory emphasizes the distinction between internal and external activities. The user experiences, raised on multimodal interactions, in three interactive installations (MindCatcher, Inner Body and Ciklosol) presented in this paper relate to internal processes such as perception, cognition and emotion and express them through external activities represented by participants' behavioral changes. The theory also highlights the importance of interface development for further mediation between internal and external human activities [15]. This opens the experimental space to usage of known objects and forms, with already embedded meanings, into development processes of contextually enriched environments, interaction and interface design. Hence, the importance of metaphors and aesthetic in design process could be pursued more comprehensively through Activity Theory [16]. According to Activity Theory human nature correspondence between the level of aesthetics and the activity level is driven by complex motives, of which the individual actors are seldom aware [17]. Engestrom also argues that the level of Activity is mediated by 'imaginative artefacts' that give identity and comprehensive perspective to human practice. Based on that theoretical foundations, we developed three experimental interactive installations where we investigated several different approaches to contextual and interface design applied in a meaningful and aesthetically conceptualized responsive environment.

4 The Floor, the Bicycle and the Heart

As mentioned previously, the term Tangible User Interfaces (TUIs) was presented by Ishii and Ullmer [7] in 1997 and defined as user interfaces that augment the real physical world by coupling digital information to everyday physical objects and environments. Terminology varied from within various researches, e.g. "passive real-world props" [18], "graspable" [6], "manipulative" [19], or "embodied" [20], till eventually Ullmer and Ishii [21] did suggest to adopt the most common phrase, tangible, to refer to them collectively. They all share the same basic paradigm of a user manipulation of some physical object(s) via physical gestures which are detected by computer system and gives feedback accordingly.

Furthermore, Ishii and Ullmer defined them as one that eliminates the distinction between input device and output device, although interesting interaction regimes are highlighted by relaxing these expectations [21]. According to Fishkin [22] broad scenario that characterizes TUIs would be:

1. *Some input event occurs.* This input event is typically a physical manipulation performed by users with their hands on some "everyday physical object," such as tilting, shaking, squeezing, pushing, or, most often, moving.
2. *A computer system senses this input event,* and alters its state.
3. *The system provides feedback.* This output event is via a change in the physical nature of some object – it alters its display surface, grows, shrinks, makes sound, gives haptic feedback, etc.

In case of three experiments with tangible interfaces and cross-reality, we are presenting in this paper, the different scenarios were used in the following manner:

The interactive installation MindCather was based on floor interface as input device and monitor as output device were input occurs when round colored circles enriched with sensors were pressed by foot (Fig. 1). As respond to that input, computer system played sound and generated colored circles on the screen, which were positioned according to contextual logic of the system. Multimodal interactions on the floor interface had two important manifestations, individual and collective in physical and virtual environment as participants were in position to collaborate between each other directly on the interface as well as joint generated digital content into one co-created artefact. The system direct feedbacks to the users during the interaction were light and sound indications which corresponded to user behavior on the floor interface. Aesthetically the floor interface represents completely authentic artefact without any reminiscence on surrounding everyday objects. So the way users perceived the interface was abstract and metaphorical, based on reaction on recognizable and sensory manifestations which forms through multimodal did not disturb desirable multimodal interactions offered by the responsive systems.

The interactive installation Ciklosol uses exercise bicycle as input device, and monitor as output device. The input occurs when users are starting with paddling the bike interface (Fig. 2). Speed of paddling correlated directly with the speed of projected sunflower rising. Multimodal interaction in this case consisted of sound effects

Fig. 1. The MindCatcher floor interface with colored circle switches (Color figure online)

Fig. 2. The Ciklosol bike interface where paddling is trigger to the system

which referred to sound of wind and birds in the field, interaction with the exercise bike interface through paddling and visual representation of the digital information generated from user inputs. Conceptual idea behind this interactive experiment was to connect body actions and movement based interaction with the metaphorical message of connection between people and the environment and how important is human role and invested energy in environmental preservation.

The interactive installation Inner Body had a model of human heart as input device, and the output device was wall projection. Users had to touch and grab by their hand the heart sculpture placed on the tube which was filed with the blood in same amount as it is in human body (Fig. 3). The system reacted on human touch and triggered audio-visual respond to the user. The interaction concept was based on simulated medical examination as the system made feedback on user gesture of grabbing the heart interface. Despite first two interface appearance, MindCatcher's abstract floor interface and Ciklosol's everyday living object (bike) interface, the Inner Body interface manipulated with a human heart as a symbolic representation of vitality, begging and end, living and dying, health and sickness.

Many researches today are directed toward realization of the ubiquitous computing vision which has in the core of its idea distribution of computing in everyday life. In order to fulfill such environmental concept transformation of traditional objects (known to us in meaningful and functional way) into so-called *smart living objects* which are augmented with digital technology and enhanced with additional functions affecting user experience with new interactions and multi-sensory perception. We could say that concept of tangible interfaces and tendencies to enrich living environments with *smart*

Fig. 3. The Inner Body Heart Interface, the output occurs when user grab it

living objects correlate closely between each other and lead us to sustainable design choices. Some questions has been raised from these choices such as in which direction we should extend functions (in correlation with their traditional features) or even more important perception and human understanding of new interactions we are capable of adding. Also important question to answer in this research was, to what extend user feels embodiment of the system feedback with physical environment where interaction is happening and how that depends on connection between input and output?

Fishkin [20] suggested four levels of tangible interfaces embodiment characteristics: *full* – is characterizing the output device which is at the same time the input device, *nearby* – characterizing the output that takes place near the input object, typically, directly proximate to it, *environmental* – is characterizing the output placed somewhere around the user, such as audio, light or heat levels, *distant* – is characterizing the output placed on another screen, or even another room. In all three experiments we are presenting in this paper we could say that the interface audio-visual attention is switched between the input (the floor interface, the bike interface, the heart interface) and the output (the wall or monitor projection), and as such the floor interface combines *distant* and *environmental* and the bike and the heart interfaces belong to *distant* type of tangible interfaces category.

Beside embodiment, metaphor represents highly important and powerful ingredient of any design and could help us give answers to question related to perception and human understanding of interactions embedded to objects and form users can recognize. Cognitive anthropologists argue that the ability to use metaphor is the ultimate characteristic that separates the minds of early humans from modern humans [23], philosophers of science believe that metaphor lies at the heart of how our theories of the world are created, explained, and communicated [24, 25]. All these studies together with rules of design and principle can be applied to user interface design and its implementation to smart environments, especially considering its physical tangibility. A designer can use a whole realm of physically afforded metaphors such as the shape, the size, the color, the weight, the smell, and the texture of the object to invoke any number of metaphorical links. Mithen [23] argues that the most powerful metaphors are those which cross domain boundaries, such as by associating a living entity with something that is inert or an idea with something that is tangible. If we take into account this statement, then tangible interfaces and cross-reality concepts possess all the required potentials to provide meaningful metaphors. That could lead into deeper immersion and user experience, which was of high importance to be achieved during the development of the three interfaces. In order to quantify the amount of metaphor, Fishkin [22] roughly group metaphor into two types: those which appeal to the shape of an object, which he termed metaphor of noun, and those which appeal to the motion of an object, which he termed metaphor of verb. The more any types of those metaphors are used, the higher would be placed the interface on this scale. He based this grouping on results from cognitive psychology [26], [27], which show that noun and verb are deeply natural and intuitive concepts arising even in deaf–mute children who are taught no linguistic grammatical structure. It is clear that in order to succeed with an application we must take care to raise metaphors as closest as possible to a level of understandable and meaningful end experience or else the power of metaphor can weaken the value of the application, or require an extra level of learning. Furthermore,

Fishkin [22] explains that promotion of metaphors as one of the key factors in interface development could take us to the great body of knowledge about metaphors and its use in other fields. He then refers to a five different fields we could involve and expand domain of this discourse, cultural anthropology – where metaphors vary from culture to culture which could be a crucial knowledge in improving TUI design, evolution of cognition – where research is focused on possibilities of giving additional meaning to the objects and explored the power of metaphor in that context, cognitive psychology – cognitive psychologists have found that nouns and verbs appear deeply ingrained in our consciousness, even for deaf–mute children who are taught no sign languages [26], [27], industrial design – if we are thinking of people who are constantly facing employment of metaphors in their work then industrial designers would belong to the most experienced in this matter. For example Gorbet [28] uses the investigation of "product semantics" in industrial design (examining the employment of metaphor in the design of everyday objects, such as toasters, TV sets, and answering machines), to illustrate the trade-offs of higher and lower levels of metaphor. Obviously there in no unified way we could use metaphor in design process of any tangible user interface such as the floor, bike or heart interfaces we investigated. But, by giving an attention to available choices, we will be able to create more effective design.

In case of the installation Mind Catcher the metaphor of the whole system should have been very clear in order to immerse participants deeply into the creative act. Thus, any unnecessary cognitive overheads could have disturb user experience through mismatch between the operations on the object and those of the analogized object. The floor interface was raised from the conceptual ideas rooted-in the installation Mind-Catcher overall research intention (measuring level of creativity in interactive act) and all the metaphors were designed to achieve specific experiential effect through created aesthetical environment. The metaphors were derived mainly from the shape and forms used for interface was construction, according to Fishkin [22] we could address it to metaphor of noun. Partly the metaphors were derived from body movements, during the interaction, performed by users and their personal attachment to it, metaphors of verb. Hence, during the period of exposure, through our personal observations and interviews with the users, we concluded that the floor interface itself could be re-used in some other applications and could cognitively lend to any number of situations such as stand-alone musical instrument, instructional dance platform or interactive theatre stage. However, by putting it in certain context, the metaphors attached become clear and can leverage the received meanings and ideas from many fields.

The Inner Body heart interface invoked metaphors based on shapes and forms recognition, and on correlation with our physiological and cognitive perception of the used object. Important role in case of the heart interface as well as the floor interface was given to the ambient in which the interaction was happening, together with multimodal perception and embedded metaphors which empowered user experience significantly. Upon this aesthetical foundation, the interactive installation Inner Body tended to induce, through interaction with the heart interface and virtual outputs projected on the wall, fear of dead and sickness through actions and responds participants' were getting from the digitally augmented responsive environment they entered. On a subconscious level the ideas of finality and focusing on real life values were tried to be communicated with the users.

Like in case of the MindCatcher floor interface, the Ciklosol bicycle interface belongs also to interfaces which combine metaphor of noun and verb type. The used traditional object itself was known to everybody as well as it functions, but in this case through cross-reality design and its augmentation with digital technology we tried to extend its original functions and enhance user experience and communicate ideas how important is human engagement in environmental protection initiatives. Through act of paddling, body movement based interaction had intention to deeply immerse participant in their role of saving and raising virtual sunflower projected on the screen.

In all of our three interfaces and installations environment conceptualization metaphors have had important role in our research goals fulfillment. As such, selection of shapes, forms, object, colors and textures we used to design interfaces was of a great importance and directly reflected on user actions and their understanding of embedded meanings. We believe this could be the direction to follow in use of multimodal interactions and cross-reality as a concept for future service design and human-relationships development integrated into everyday living environments.

5   Findings and Future Directions

With the experiments presented, our research goals were to investigate potentials of using tangible interfaces and known objects and forms in case we are extending their functions and embedding new meanings in future development of ubiquitous computing vision, design and innovate services within smart living environments. The idea of making environments enhanced with contemporary digital technologies in order to design more human-centered, emotionally and cognitively attached to everyday living surrounding, directed this research toward better understand of relation between physical world and the digital systems feedback, the way users feel that embodiment and how that could be applied in desired communication between users and devices, users and environments, and users and services. The data in the experiments were collected from the following sources:

- Personal observations (MindCather, Cklosol, Inner Body)
- Recorded user sessions with web camera (MindCatcher)
- User interviews (MindCather, Cklosol, Inner Body)
- Personal data delivered through login process (MindCatcher)
- Paths walked by users from the floor interface (MindCatcher)

The interviews were structured [29] so that the users were firstly indirectly observed during their trying of the installation. The interviews were done in the form of an informal, open conversation with participants. The goal of those interviews was to reveal the participants personalized qualitative impressions/opinions. The questions regarding their perception of the interfaces and the environment where interaction happened, were the following:

1. Describe your experience during interaction with the installation?
2. Describe meanings and metaphors which lead your actions?
3. Do you feel any connection between your inputs and generated outputs?

The MindCatcher research projects lasted for three years. During that period the installation had been exposed publicly three times and throughout that period 112 user sessions were recorded and 63 interview were done with the participants. Even the project was upgraded (in order to leverage user's multimodal interactions and engagement,) mostly in a sense of the system feedback and generated outputs, the floor interface, in all its original aesthetical and functional design, remained the core inter-action element of the installation. In this paper we will address only findings which correlate to the research topic of interface design and its application in user perception and cognition. The different visitors had different experiences with computer-enabled environments and as such, the major divergence in the group's answers to the ques-tionnaire were used as a critical measurement. For this research the answers on question regarding metaphors, analogies or resemblance they could attach to the floor visual appearance were interesting as the MindCather floor interface was the abstract artefact assembled from known forms and shapes but nor explicit like ones in the Ciklosol and the Inner Body experiment. The answers were different, based on personal preferences but also on social-cultural differences, so we concluded it reminded them of a big ray fish, solar system they could stand on, interactive garden they could produce music with, etc. This type of analogies directly refers to the potentials of interface design to involve different fields such as cultural anthropology, evolution of cognition, philos-ophy of science, cognitive psychology which could empower user interaction and increase experience. What was more important for us is how those analogies were affecting users interactions and were involved in dissemination of ideas embedded into context of generated audio-visual outputs. The majority of participants described their experience in the installation as playful, creative and exciting (73 %) or sometimes confusing but dynamic and pleasant (23 %), while only minority of them found it disturbing and pointless (4 %) (Fig. 4). The first two groups were very inspired to describe metaphors which motivated them to continue with interaction, enjoy the feedback they were getting from the interface and deeply immerse with the creation of virtual audio-visual artefact they were connecting with the meanings and metaphors gained from the interface itself. As such, most of them felt that they had good control over the installation, sound, projection and interactivity (58 %), had good control over the floor interface but did not understand how (or not interested) to control projected personal audio-visual creation with it (39 %), had bad control over the installation (3 %) (Fig. 5).

Through achieved embodiment characteristics which reside somewhere between the environmental and the distant type of interface and the metaphor which could be moved from metaphor of noun to metaphor of noun and verb, the system was capable to communicate different ideas, trigger related emotions and induce user actions. The way users mentally access and experience the interface and the ideas behind installation narrative were of high importance. However, for some of them the fact they were in the interactive responsive space was enough to please their expectancy and behaviour. In case of MindCatcher floor interface, as well as the other two experimental projects, the cross point between virtual reality and physical reality was its tangible designed interfaces. As such, user's interactive freedom and open space for new experiences depended a lot of shape, objects and forms used in their design.

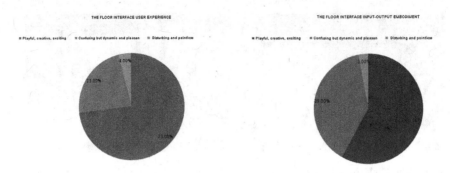

Fig. 4. TFI user experience

Fig. 5. TFI input-output embodiment

In our second experiment we created interface made of exercise bicycle. In comparison with the floor interface which was abstract this time the interface was made of traditional object we addressed certain functions and attached meanings based on our cognition. We used during the interface conceptualization and design that knowledge in order to maximize user engagement and immersion. The important issue was to extend existing functions and embed additional meanings to the used object. Additionally, to make possible effective transmission of ideas implemented in installation narrative and enhancement of user experience. Hence, we used paddling as a trigger for the system input-output communication. As the users were familiar with the used object we did not have any problems in their understanding of how to use the interface unlike in case of the Mind Catcher project. Participants enjoyed interaction from the start as we embedded it to pleasant physical activity. Second issue we explored by interviewing participants was connected with meaning and metaphors they experienced and how they perceived relationship between their inputs and audio-visual outputs they were getting from the system. From the answers collected we detected that participants were going through three different experiential phases during the interaction. The first phase, in which they were attracted with the traditional functions of the object and the physical environment which differentiate from the rest of the surrounding. In this phase they were enjoying paddling and introducing to the system. In the second phase, after they learned about connection between the inputs they were generating and outputs, they were involving themselves deeper into the responsive environments they were interacting with. They still had weak understanding of metaphors and meanings of the visually presented in outputs. For most of them moving of the virtual sunflower (up and down) according to energy they invested in paddling, was just visual representation of speed they achieved (the same way they were experiencing on the other sport machines). In the last phase, triggered with the multi-sensory perception and exposed to metaphors and meanings, they began to understand they developed emotional relationship (they fought now for life of their personal sunflower by giving it their own energy) with the virtual environment they communicated with during interactions (Fig. 6).

Even not all of them went through all of the three experiential phases, the fact we managed to induce them as part of user experience, showed the potentials of extending functionalities of traditional objects within smart responsive environments.

Fig. 6. The Ciklosol interface connection between user interaction and the system outputs

Third interface we investigate was The Inner Body interface which was stylized model of a human heart and cardio-vascular system. Design language used was metaphorical but not as abstract as in case of MindCatcher. The forms, objects and its representations were known to the participants even though they were not everyday life surrounding like in case of bicycle we used in the Ciklosol. Like in case of bike interface, participants were also familiar with the functions of heart and cardio-vascular system but unlike the Ciklosol humans were not addressing any interaction to the heart as it resides in our inner body. In conceptualization of the gesture which would trigger the system, the idea was to diminish psychological distance between Outside - Inner body and increase awareness of our "other" existences we cannot experience perceptually. That was the reason we instructed participants to grab the model of the heart (a bit bigger than the normal human heart size) in order to start with the so called "medical exam" and trigger the system (Fig. 7). With the intensive tactile gesture performed on the model of a human heart, together with the additional colors, shapes and objects which were part of the interface, we wanted to achieve only one state in desired user experience and that is contemplative. Hence, to provoke such fast and radical immersion of the users we paid a lot of attention to environment where interactions were happening so we used white textile, we used smell characteristic for the

Fig. 7. The Inner Body model of a human heart and cardio-vascular system interface

hospitals, played magnet resonance sound and loud beats of the heart during the fake examination, played video with real author's magnet resonance exams before entering the interaction space. People were frightened no matter they knew it was not real and that all was a part of directed performance. All of them understood the metaphors and the communication between them and the system was clear and easily understandable. What we used in this case to provoke desirable effects were deeply inherited fears in our consciousness we react on subconsciously. After interviewing the participants we concluded that even they were absolutely aware that it was fake exam, they were afraid of results and panicking during the session.

Presented experiments showed us several factors and circumstantial parameters we could use in service design concepts and strategies which are directed toward usage of interaction, cross-reality and smart environments. We are referring in that sense to the urban surroundings which are augmented, with contemporary digital technologies and everywhere computing. We also found that metaphors and meanings we embedded to surrounding objects and forms by using technology and interaction, could play crucial role in future service or social well-being ides acceptance. The way we add functions to the objects as well as the conceptualization of the environment where interactions will happen, has also high impact on user experience and engagement. Tangible user interfaces such as the MindCatcher floor, Cikolos bike and the Inner Body heart are abandoning the conventions of computer virtual world and taking steps into the physical world and reveals many interesting areas for future researches. By moving interfaces toward cross-reality technologies we are changing the whole design approach from philosophy computer–human interfaces into the realm of human interfaces in general. Our further research will be directed toward experimentation with the various objects as interfaces and the most sufficient way we can embed different metaphor types and appearances in user experience and in its understanding. This could lead us to better usage of everyday objects and forms within smart environments. Also it could become a key factor in shortening the learning curve throughout the process of accepting new technologies and ideas important for further society and community development.

References

1. Weiser, M., Brown, J.S.: The coming age of calm technology. In: Denning, P.J., Metcalfe, R. M. (eds.) Beyond Calculation: The Next Fifty Years of Computing. Copernicus, Göttingen (1998)
2. Muller, J., Alt, F., Michelis, D. (eds.): Pervasive Advertising, pp. 1–30. Springer, Berlin (2011)
3. Van Waart, P., Mulder, I., De Bont, C.: Meaningful advertising. In: Muller, J., Alt, F., Michelis, D. (eds.) Pervasive Advertising, pp. 57–79. Springer, Berlin (2011)
4. Coleman, B.: Using sensor inputs to affect virtual and real environments. IEEE Pervasive Comput. 8(3), 16–23 (2009)
5. Dindar, N., Balkesen, C., Kromwijk, K., Tatbul, N.: Event processing support for cross-reality environments. IEEE Pervasive Comput. Mag. 8(3), 34–41 (2009). Special Issue on Cross-Reality Environment

6. Fitzmaurice, G., Ishii, H., Buxton, W.: Bricks: laying the foundations for graspable user interfaces. In: Proceedings of the CHI 1995 Conference on Human Factors in Computing Systems, Denver, Colorado, pp. 442–449 (1995)

7. Ishii, H., Ullmer, B.: Tangible bits: towards seamless interfaces between people, bits, and atoms. In: Proceedings of the CHI 1997 Conference on Human Factors in Computing Systems, Atlanta, Georgia, pp. 234–241 (1997)

8. Feiner, S., MacIntyre, B., Hollerer, T.: A touring machine: prototyping 3D mobile augmented reality systems for exploring the urban environment. In: Proceedings of the 1st International Symposium Wearable Computers (ISWC 1997), pp. 74–81. IEEE, CS Press (1997)

9. Mark, G.: Extreme collaboration. Commun. ACM **45**(6), 89–93 (2002)

10. Lifton, J., Laibowitz, M., Harry, D., Gong, N., Mittal, M., Paradiso, J.: Metaphor and manifestation: cross reality with ubiquitous sensor/actuator networks. IEEE Pervasive Comput. Mag. **8**, 24–33 (2009)

11. Askay, S.: New visualization tools for environmental sensor networks: using Google earth as an interface to micro-climate and multimedia datasets. Master's thesis, Department Environmental Sciences, University of California, Riverside (2006)

12. Reilly, D., Voida, S., McKeon, M., Le Dantec, C., Edwards, W.K., Mynatt, E., Mazalek, A.: Space matters: physical-digital and physical-virtual co-design, in the inspace project. IEEE Pervasive Comput. **9**(3), 54–63 (2010)

13. Mistree, B.F.T., Paradiso, J.A.: ChainMail – a configurable multimodal lining to enable sensate surfaces and interactive objects. In: Proceedings of TEI 2010, pp. 65–72 (2010)

14. Reilly, D., Tang, A., Wu, A., Echenique, A., Massey, J., Mathiasen, N., Mazalek, A., Edwards, W.K.: Organic UIs and cross-reality spaces. In: 2nd International Workshop on Organic User Interfaces (OUI 2011), TEI 2011, Madeira, Portugal (2011)

15. Nardi, B. (ed.): Context and Consciousness: Activity Theory and Human-Computer Interaction. MIT Press, Cambridge (1996)

16. Leont'ev, A.N.: Activity, Consciousness, Personality. Prentice Hall, Englewood Cliffs (1978)

17. Engeström, Y.: Learning, Working and Imagining: Twelve Studies in Activity Theory. Orienta-Konsultit Oy, Helsinki (1990)

18. Hinckley, K., Pausch, R., Goble, J.C., Kassell, N.F.: Passive real-world interface props for neurosurgical visualization. In: Proceedings of the CHI 1994 Conference on Human Factors in Computing Systems, Boston, Massachusetts, pp. 452–458 (1994)

19. Harrison, B., Fishkin, K., Want, R., Gujar, A., Mochon, C.: Squeeze me, hold me, tilt me! An exploration of manipulative user interfaces. In: Proceedings of the CHI 1998 Conference on Human Factors in Computing Systems, Los Angeles, California, pp. 17–24 (1998)

20. Fishkin, K., Moran, T., Harrison, B.: Embodied user interfaces: towards invisible user interfaces. In: Chatty, S., Dewan, P. (eds.) Engineering for Human–Computer Interaction, pp. 1–18. Springer Science + Business Media, New York (1998)

21. Ullmer, B., Ishii, H.: Emerging frameworks for tangible user interfaces. In: Carroll, J.M. (ed.) Human–Computer Interaction in the New Millennium, pp. 579–601. Addison-Wesley, New York (2001)

22. Fishkin, K.P.: A taxonomy for and analysis of tangible interfaces. J. Pers. Ubiquit. Comput. **8**(5), 347–358 (2004)

23. Mithen, S.: The Prehistory of the Mind. Thames and Hudson, London (1996)

24. Brown, T.: Making Truth: Metaphor in Science. University of Illinois Press, Champaign (2003)

25. Kuhn, T.S.: Metaphor in science. In: Ortony, A. (ed.) Metaphor and Thought, 2nd edn, pp. 1–539. Cambridge University Press, Cambridge (1993)

26. Goldin-Meadow, S.: Structure in a manual communication system developed without a conventional language model: language without a helping hand. In: Whitaker, H., Whitaker, H.A. (eds.) Studies in Neurolinguistics, vol. 4, pp. 125–209. Academic Press, New York (1979)
27. Goldin-Meadow, S.: The representation of semantic relations in a manual language created by deaf children of hearing parents: a language you can't dismiss out of hand. Ph.D. thesis (1975)
28. Gorbet, M.: Beyond input devices: a new conceptual framework for the design of physical–digital objects. Masters thesis, MIT Media Laboratory, Cambridge, Massachusetts (1998)
29. Kuhn, D.: The Skills of Argument. Cambridge University Press, Cambridge (1991)

Mobility of 65 + Society – Needs and Expectations of Third Age University Students

Janusz Grabara[✉], Katarzyna Grondys, and Sebastian Kot

The Management Faculty, Czestochowa University of Technology,
Armii Krajowej 19B, 42-200 Częstochowa, Poland
janusz@grabara.eu, katarzyna_grondys@vp.pl,
sebacat@zim.pcz.czest.pl

Abstract. Evolution of information society, which arises mainly from the development of technology and information technology, causes that older people may be marginalized and their activity in society may be limited. One can avoid such a phenomenon by all initiatives of stimulating seniors towards intellectual and physical activity. The most popular initiatives are Universities of the Third Age. The first university in Poland was founded over thirty years ago. Universities of the Third Age are one of the most common forms of education for older people. Their main task is to increase the intellectual activity of older people and to meet the needs arising mainly from psychosocial changes. The aim of this paper is to characterize the education of retirement age people with particular regard to their expectations in the age of computerization and digitization of society.

Keywords: University of the third age · Education of older people · Implementation of IT solutions

1 Introduction

According to forecasts of the Central Statistical Office in year 2035 the number of people in the retirement age in Poland reached almost 9.6 million, while in year 2008 it was 6.2 million [1]. According to Eurostat's forecasts from year 2008, in year 2030 in Poland the ratio of the number of over sixty-five year old people to the number of people between fifteen and sixty-four year old will be 36 %, while in year 2050 this figure will reach 56 %. EU population projections for years 2010–2060 predict an increase in the number of elderly people in the total population of the EU-27.

The Fig. 1 shows that elderly people will constitute an increasing proportion of the total population in the next fifty years. The age structure of the elderly will change. Our population will include more and more sixty-four year old people. At the same time, the number of people between fifty and sixty-four year old will decrease. Demographic problems cause increase in the number of older people, digitization of information and the dynamic development of indirect communication and enforces European space to take some actions in creating various types of initiatives. Their goal is to educate

© ICST Institute for Computer Sciences, Social Informatics and Telecommunications Engineering 2016
B. Mandler et al. (Eds.): IoT 360° 2015, Part II, LNICST 170, pp. 122–128, 2016.
DOI: 10.1007/978-3-319-47075-7_14

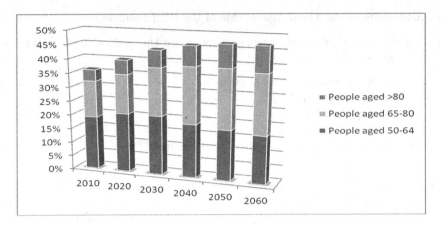

Fig. 1. The projected structure of the older population in the European Union divided into age group (% of total population) [2]

people between sixty and eighty year old, so that they will familiarize with changing conditions of human functioning as an individual in the society.

2 The Role of the European Union in the Education of Seniors

According to the Recommendations of the European Commission of 11th July 2011 [3] on initiatives in the field of joint research programming, EU countries should focus their efforts on fostering elderly people to be active in every field of social life, both at the regional and local level. Simultaneously, LifeLong Learning Program (LLL), which corresponds to the concept of learning throughout life is the result of the European Parliament and the Council's activities in year 2006, related to education and science development in years 2007–2013. Until now, 31 countries belonging to the EU, EFTA and EEA took part in this program [4].

The European Union supports the need for the use of modern information and communication technologies, which support older people. These technologies allow them to maintain social contacts, activity and independence. Since year 2008, the EU is also involved in the Modern technologies in Ambient Assisted Living project (Ambient Assisted Living, AAL), which the key objective was to introduce new solutions of information and communication technology (ICT) to facilitate the proper functioning of older people [5].

The positive impact of seniors education is confirmed by the results of Central Statistical Office in Warsaw [6]. It showed that elderly people, whose participate in UTA activities and have at least secondary education, are characterized by better mental and physical efficiency.

2.1   University of the Third Age as One of the EC Initiatives

One of the initiatives of elderly people education are Universities of the Third Age (UTA) created mainly at universities. UTA was created to:

- facilitate contacts with public institutions.
- promote educational initiatives.
- develop skills and knowledge.
- build and maintain social ties.
- improve interpersonal communication among seniors [7].

The number of functioning UTA in Poland until 2014 is shown in Fig. 2.

Currently, there are 187 Universities of the Third Age in Poland, including 145 of them in the Mazowieckie voivodship. In order to meet seniors' expectations and needs, UTA are intended to provide an adequate educational and activating program, which includes an auditorium, themed and open lectures, language courses, movement classes and computer courses.

Fig. 2. The number of Universities of the Third Age in year 2012 in Poland [8]

3   The Importance of Information Technology Among Seniors

Computer classes are very important in elderly people education, because we strive to a society based on knowledge and information. Teaching is also conditioned by an increasing access to the Internet, which gives not only the possibility of fast and efficient issues implementation, but it is also an opportunity for the development and

Table 1. The use of ICT in different age groups (%) [12]

Age group	Computer	Internet	Persons who do not use any technology	Persons using all new technologies
16–24	90.2	86.8	1.0	80.8
25–34	79.8	73.7	1.8	69
35–44	67.7	62	5.3	57.2
45–59	43.5	39.5	19.1	34.6
60–64	23.6	20.6	35.1	17.8
65 and more	7.5	5.8	66.2	4.6

active participation of older people in many areas of everyday life. Technology-assisted learning helps to develop interests and contributes to being creative and active in social life [9]. The possibility of using instant messaging or e-mail is also significant. Therefore, the Internet is an instrument of idea, which says that we should learn our whole life and which is a key factor in the implementation of the idea of creating a knowledge-based society [10] (Table 1).

Older people are usually learned how to use electronic and internet banking, Internet, how they can purchase through the Internet or use Internet communicators [11]. Older people, as a result of attending computer classes at UTA:

- develop basic skills in computer usage,
- use Internet sources of information and communication,
- improve their live by making online payment,
- deepen social relations.

The survey conducted in year 2009 showed that with age increase the number of people using computers and Internet significantly decreases. Young people and those under 45 years most frequently use new technologies. Every fifth person between 60 and 64 years use computer and Internet. The oldest part of the population (over 65 years) constitutes the smaller group participating in the computerized space.

This low participation of senior citizens in the use of modern technologies is mainly connected with emotional, psychical and material concerns. Therefore, seniors most often attend computer classes to expand their knowledge in the field of Information Technology, to maintain intellectual ability and to keep in contact with people from the same age group, what strongly emphasizes the importance of digital education for this social group [13–15].

3.1 University of the Third Age at the Technical University of Czestochowa

University of the Third Age at the Technical University of Czestochowa was created in year 2004. Currently, 800 people study there. Every year, the number of seniors on the UTA at the Technical University of Czestochowa is steadily increasing, what causes the demand exceeds supply (Fig. 3.) and forces organizers to restrict the number of

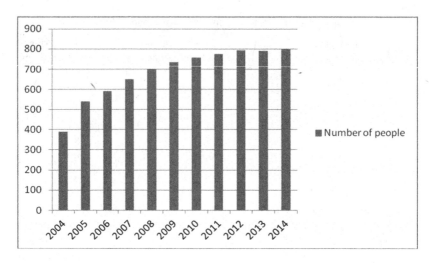

Fig. 3. The number of older people participating in UTA classes in the past few years

participants, especially in the area of subjects and issues related to IT, because the number of computer labs and instructors is limited.

The studies conducted among the participants of these courses showed that the need to use ICT (Information Communication Technology) results from current needs of 65+generation. The most common needs are: access to current information, especially information regarding the symptoms of diseases, ways and methods of prevention as well as information about available medicines and their prices. The next group of needs is communications (textual communications, emails "adu-Gadu" or video messenger such as Skype). What is interesting, conducted study shows that textual communicators are used mainly in order to exchange information with local government units, or to make an appointment in the medical health center. In contrast, in Poland video messengers such as Skype are mainly used for contacts with family.

Students at the University of the Third Age emphasize that it is mainly concerned with children and closer relatives living outside the place of residence of the contact person. Video conversation gives a semblance of real direct contact. Interestingly, respondents drew attention to the fact that during video conversation you can see the room where the caller is located and other people being in the room. Respondents argue that it allows them to assess caller's health status, mood or overall situation.

The third group using ITC is interested in organizing photos and documents, creating archives in electronic form, making presentations or modifying pictures and photos in order to print them. In addition, in this group, abilities to modify pictures and texts are used to create Christmas or note cards.

The study shows that there are three dominant groups but the Third Age University students want to be able to move freely in the areas of these three groups and do not reject decisively any of the group mentioned above. In addition, they claim (students 65+) that skills obtained in these three areas cause that they do not feel like socially rejected people.

The curriculum of the University is planned for the whole academic year and includes language classes, hobby classes, physical activities, but primarily classes which concern basic knowledge connected with computer usage and classes for advanced student. During the whole academic year, University also offers about thirty obligatory thematic lectures.

4 Summary

Economic and technology transformations resulting from rapid development of innovative technologies and globalization of market processes enforce process of continuous education [16] also in the case of older people. Development of ICT disrupts older people's lives. They need specific support in this increasingly mechanized environment, because otherwise they are cursed with marginalization.

Providing continuous education for older people, among others, through the creation of the Third Age Universities can improve their life's quality, support the process of social integration and thus facilitate an active participation in social life. In addition, from the perspective of people studying at the UTA, additional computer classes provide them greater security and independence of functioning in today's society, influence their personal development and stimulate creativity.

References

1. Smoląg, K.: Personalization of employee's knowledge in virtual labour space. Pol. J. Manag. Stud. **6**, 174–183 (2012)
2. Aktywność osób starszych i solidarność międzypokoleniowa. Statystyczny portret Unii Europejskiej. Eurostat Statistical Books, p. 34 (2012)
3. Dziennik Urzędowy Unii Europejskiej Nr L 18 z dnia 13 lipca 2011, Zalecenie nr 413 w sprawie inicjatywy w zakresie wspólnego planowania badań naukowych "Dł ugie lata, lepsze życie – potencjał i wyzwania zmian demograficznych" (2011)
4. Life Long Learning Programme. www.esn.pl/content/life-long-learning-programme
5. Ambient Assisted Living Joint Programme. http://www.aal-europe.eu/about/why-this-programme/. Accessed 28 Sept 2014
6. Kozieł, D., Trafiałek, E.: Kształcenie na Uniwersytetach Trzeciego Wieku a jakość życia seniorów. Gerontologia Polska **15**(3), 105 (2007)
7. Uniwersytety Trzeciego Wieku w Polsce. http://www.utw.pl/index.php?id=10. Accessed 28 Sept 2014
8. http://www.e-mentor.edu.pl/repozytorium-utw/. Accessed 28 Sept 2014
9. Dragolea, L.L.: Study regarding the most attractive domains in career management process for pre-university students. Pol. J. Manag. Stud. **11**(1), 39–46 (2015)
10. Batorski D., Korzystanie z technologii komunikacyjno-informacyjnych, [in:] J. Czapiński, T. Panek (red.), Diagnoza społ eczna. Warunki i jakość życia mieszkańców, Wyd. Rada Monitoringu Społ ecznego, p. 291, Warszawa (2009)
11. Stefko, R., Bacik, R., Fedorko, R.: Spendings on social media as part of marketing budgets. Pol. J. Manag. Stud. **8**, 243–250 (2013)

12. Pluta-Olearnik M.: Koncepcja Life Long Learning – wyzwanie dla kształ cenia na poziomie wyższym [in:] Goł ębiowski T., Dąbrowski M., Mierzejewska B. (ed.), Uczelnia oparta na wiedzy. Organizacja procesu dydaktycznego oraz zarządzanie wiedzą w ekonomicznym szkolnictwie wyższym, p. 61, Warsaw (2005)

13. Wrońska M., Od edukacji komputerowej do kultury medialnej seniorów – "Komfortowe starzenie się" w społ eczeństwie informacyjnym. Edukacja medialna seniorów, pp. 99. (file PDF http://www.pulib.sk/elpub2/FF/Balogova1/pdf_doc/11.pdf). Accessed 28 Sept 2014

14. Ferencova, M.: An analytical view of communication and managerial capabilities and their use in practice. Pol. J. Manag. Stud. **6**, 241–242 (2012)

15. Dima, I.C., Grabara, J., Vladutescu, S.: Comparative study on online education in Romania and Poland in terms of current globalization. Pol. J. Manag. Stud. **10**(1), 7–18 (2014)

16. Ślusarczyk, B., Herbuś, A.: Higher education as a crucial factor of staff development. Pol. J. Manag. Stud. **10**(2), 216–224 (2014)

The Use of E-communication in Promoting Selected Religious, Cultural and Historical Monuments in Presov in the East of Slovakia

Martina Ferencová[1(✉)], Beata Ślusarczyk[2], Sebastian Kot[2],
and Veronika Mišenčíková[3]

[1] Faculty of Public Administration, Pavol Jozef Šafárik University in Kosice,
Popradská 66, 040 00 Košice, Slovakia
mferencov@gmail.com

[2] Faculty of Management, Czestochowa University of Technology,
Armii Krajowej 19B, 42-200 Częstochowa, Poland
{jagoda, sebacat}@zim.pcz.czest.pl

[3] Roman Catholic Archbishopric Košice, Košice, Slovakia
veronika.misencikova@gmail.com

Abstract. Prešov, located in the east of Slovakia, is famous for religious, cultural and historical monuments, most of which are used by denominations for religious purposes and are of great importance to communities' religious life. Their promotion to target audiences in both domestic and global tourism market via modern promotional tools is of topical significance. This paper aims at examining the use of e-communication tools in promoting selected monuments with emphasis on social networks when addressing target audiences that include tourists (believers and unbelievers) from Slovakia and abroad.

Keywords: Communication · Social networks · Religious · Cultural and historical monuments

1 Introduction

Monuments present values of precious authentic and historical legacy. They are part of cultural and national identity and direct legacy left by ancestors and predecessors. Monument preservation primarily aims at preserving and promoting values reflected by those monuments. This is possible, however, only if those monuments are fully recognized and their value as well as responsibility for preserving this value and passing it to next generations are understood [1].

Informing the public and particular target groups is thus a priority when protecting monuments and raising awareness of their importance for the society and its development. In this sense, it is important to use marketing tools, especially tools of marketing communication when addressing the public and specific target audiences. This also applies to promoting religious, cultural, and historical monuments [2].

In this article we examine three religious, cultural and historical monuments and the use of e-communication tools for their promotion. These monuments are significant

© ICST Institute for Computer Sciences, Social Informatics and Telecommunications Engineering 2016
B. Mandler et al. (Eds.): IoT 360° 2015, Part II, LNICST 170, pp. 129–135, 2016.
DOI: 10.1007/978-3-319-47075-7_15

places of cultural and religious life of three religious congregations in Prešov in the east of Slovakia (representatives of the Roman Catholic Church, the Evangelical Church of Augsburg Confession and the Jewish community) and for tourists (domestic and foreign) they are a source of attractiveness and valuable information on religious, cultural and historical events in the Prešov region and in Prešov.

2 Marketing in Tourism – Theoretical Basic

Marketing is understood as a social and managing process in which individuals and groups gain what they need and want [3, 4] through production and exchange of products and values and/or the process of planning and implementing the concept, pricing, promoting and distributing ideas, goods and services aimed at the exchange that will satisfy the needs of individuals and organizations (American Marketing Association; AMA). It is also related to tourism where the exchange of services between providers and their customers, clients is primarily possible. Also when creating opportunities for leisure activities [5] and also in case of managing these marketing activities in relation to the target audiences [6].

In general, marketing includes 4 basic elements – the marketing mix tools: product (product/service), price, place (distribution) and promotion (advertising). Service marketing that includes also tourism contains three other elements: people, physical environment and process (process of providing services). Tourism falls into a specific category in the service sector thus the following elements typical for it may be mentioned: people, packaging – creating service packages (offers), partnership, programming – creating programs [7]. Marketing is based on the relationship to customers. In tourism marketing the customer is, more than anywhere else, "the alpha and omega of the business process" [8]. Thus it is necessary to provide him or her with quality, updated and attractive information concerning the offer.

Target audience is currently being informed about products and services of tourism mainly through e-marketing [9]. It helps tourism entities to undertake their business activities quickly, smoothly and accurately and well in advance.

This happens by means of several tools and means of e-marketing, e-communication such as on-line PR, viral marketing, microsites, buzz marketing, advergaming, marketing for the support of communities, advertisement in search engines (SEO, SEM, PPC), e-mail marketing, affiliate marketing, on-line customer competitions, social networks, profile websites (website sponsorship), banner advertisements, PageRank and others [10]. These tools of e-communication are the focus of our investigation in relation to religious tourism and religious, cultural and historical monuments.

3 Research Methodology

This paper aimed at analyzing a current state of the use of e-communication tools of selected religious, cultural and historical monuments situated in the Prešov region in Prešov.

The monuments were identified by selection using keywords, the Prešov region, Prešov and religious monuments in the Internet search engine. Subsequently, websites presenting monuments (preferably websites of monuments themselves, as well as websites of parishes, towns and others, for example tourist portals, projects, etc.) were searched for. Three monuments (Calvary – St. Cross Church, Evangelical College and the Synagogue, all in Presov) and their websites promoting were selected and analyzed for the purpose of this paper.

The analysis of the use of e-communication tools was carried out according to a designed model of e-communication (model elements set analysis criteria). Tools of descriptive statistics (bar and spider graphs) were used to process the collected data. E-communication model (of promotional tools on the Internet) comprised four elements:

- Applied e-communication tools: YouTube (the number of videos, updatedness), Facebook (updatedness, photographs, invitations, the number of fans, information, the number of shares), website, blog, Google+, PageRank, PPC, E-mailing, banners, external banners (160 points);
- Information (on a selected monument): history, photographs, opening hours and entrance fees, contact details (40 points);
- Services (services provided at the location of the monument and its vicinity): accommodation, catering services, hiking within 30 km, monuments within 30 km (40 points);
- Graphics (website providing information about the monument): a visual impact, content of the website, its layout, user-friendliness of the website (40 points).

Scores for particular criteria ranged from 0 to 10 points (10 being the highest awarded score and 0 the lowest). The maximum number of points that the promotion of the monument on the internet could gain was 208 points (Table 1).

Table 1. Categories according to scores

Category	Value	Description
1.	280–211	Above average use of promotional tools on the Internet
2.	210–140	Average use of promotional tools on the Internet
3.	140–70	Below average use of promotional tools on the Internet
4.	69–0	Insufficient use of promotional tools on the Internet

4   Results and Discussion

Selected monuments and their evaluation expressed by scores and percentages are shown in bar graphs, scoring for particular categories is presented in spider graphs.

Calvary – St Cross Church in Prešov [11]. It originated at the beginning of the 18th century and it consists of a complex of fourteen baroque chapels with the church at the top of the Calvary, Holy stairs chapel, catacombs and an adjacent cemetery. The complex was financed by a Lithuanian Prince Radziwill, who came to Prešov together with his court and personal guard in the autumn of 1764. He had the chapel built to express his gratitude to the town for granting him asylum after his forced fled from Poland.

From researches we found that the selected religious, cultural and historical monument – Prešov Calvary and/or its website scored 20 out of 160 points, that is 12.50 % for the use of Internet-based promotional tools. Criteria concerning providing information gained 0 out of 40 points. Graphics of the website gained 23 points out of 40 that is 57.50 %. Calvary – St Cross Church in Prešov exceeded the average only in the area of giving information on services (Graph 1).

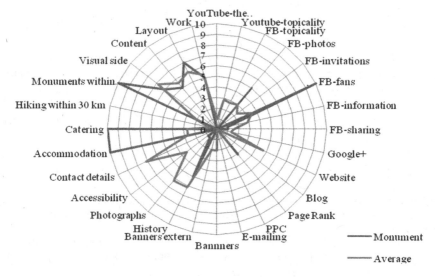

Graph 1. Criteria scoring– Calvary in Prešov

Evangelical College in Prešov [12]. The college was established in 1665 as a certain counterbalance to the Jesuit University in Trnava. The college building had been owned by various owners and four times it had been considered to gain the status of university, however social historical events prevented that. A lot of known people worked and studied at the college and their commemorating plaques can be found in the building even to this day. The research results showed that the use of Internet-based promotional tools by the website promoting this religious cultural heritage monument scored 3 out of 160 points that is 1.88 %. Criteria concerning providing information gained 16 out of 40 points, representing 40 %. Information about services in the nearby area scored 30 out of 40 points that is 75 %. Website graphics obtained 23 out of 40 points, 57.50 % (Graph 2).

The Synagogue in Prešov (A Museum) [13]. The orthodox synagogue in the Moorish style was built in the years 1897–1898 by the Kollacsek and Wirth construction company. The opening ceremony was held at Yom Kippur feast in 1898. The interior is decorated by rich frescoes in oriental fashion and the collection contains historical articles from the Jewish Museum, the first of its kind, which originated in 1928. Results pointed that the use of promotional opportunities on the Internet and Internet tools by the website promoting the monument was assigned 12 out of 160 points, making

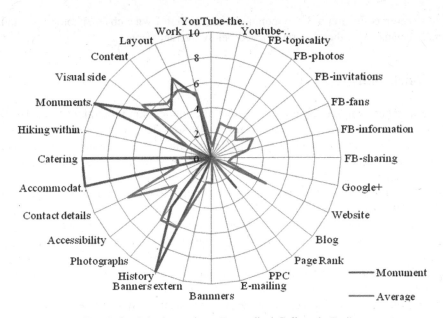

Graph 2. Criteria scoring –Evangelical College in Prešov

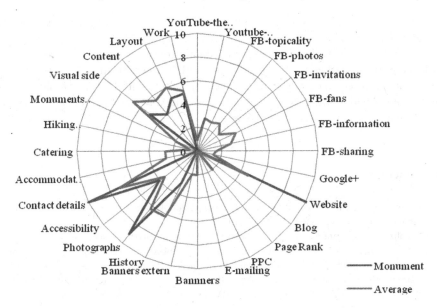

Graph 3. Criteria scoring – The Synagogue in Prešov

7.50 %. Criteria relating to providing information gained 26 out of 40 points that is 65 %. Giving information on services in the nearby area gained 0 out of 40 points. Website graphics scored 19 out or 40 points that makes 47.50 %. The Synagogue in Prešov exceeded the average only in providing information about the monument itself.

As presented in Graph 3, the monument excels in its own website, photographs and contact details. All other criteria reached below average score.

5   Conclusion

This article has analyzed the use of e-communication tools in promoting selected religious, cultural and historical monuments in Prešov. The findings of the analysis according to the scores assigned to particular criteria of the e-communication model used in this paper were unsatisfactory. They have shown the insufficient use of e-communication tools and below average use of on-line social media and special social networks considered to the latest and the most effective tools for addressing target audiences worldwide.

Business entities including tourism service providers are trying to achieve a synergic effect of using marketing tools over the Internet in their marketing strategy [14]. When promoting religious, cultural heritage monuments in Europe there are marketing objectives – informing, attracting an interest, arousing a desire for a visit and making potential and real visitors (believers and unbelievers) pay a visit. There are also cultural and religious aims – preserving cultural heritage, raising awareness about its significance (material and spiritual) and developing human and religious values during the crisis of values and humanity.

Although Slovakia is considered to be a strongly religious state, the awareness of the wealth of its religious, cultural and historical monuments by the young generation as well as other target audiences (believers and unbelievers) at home and abroad is at a low level. Active use of e-communication tools and their combination when promoting those monuments emphasizing social media may help to fulfill the given aims (marketing, cultural and religious) now and in the future as well as to increase awareness of those monuments in the east of Slovakia.

References

1. Pamiatkový úrad Slovenskej republiky. Ochrana pamiatok. http://www.pamiatky.sk/sk/page/ ochrana-pamiatok. Accessed 10 May 2014
2. Ali Taha, V.: Podpora a rozvoj kultúrneho a kreatívneho turizmu prostredníctvom využitia sociálnych médií. APVV Výskum súčasného stavu a možností marketingovej komunikácie významných kultúrnohistorických a pútnických miest v Prešovskom kraji a regióne Slaskie prostredníctvom internetových nástrojov s dôrazom na sociálne siete: zborník príspevkov vybraných štúdií výskumného grantu APVV SK-PL-0061-12. Štefko, R., S. Jenčová, E. Litavcová (eds.), pp. 51-57. Bookman, s.r.o., Prešov (2013)
3. Kotler, P., Amstrong, G.: Marketing Bratislava: Slovenské pedagogické nakladateľstvo (1992)
4. Kotler, P., Keller, K.: Marketing Management 14/E. Prentice Hall, Upper Saddle River (2012)
5. Stefko, R., Nowak, S.: Cooperation shrines of Europe in regional management and development. Pol. J. Manag. Stud. **10**(2), 209–215 (2014)

6. Grabara, J.: Employer's expectations towards the employees from the marketing and management department. Pol. J. Manag. Stud. **7**, 58–70 (2013)
7. Štefko, R., et al.: Marketing našej súčasnosti, pp. 4–99. Bookman, Prešov (2013)
8. Jakubíková, D.: Marketing v cestovním ruchu. Grada Publishing, a.s., Praha (2009)
9. Gúčik, M., et al.: Marketing cestovného ruchu. Slovak-SwissTourism, Banská Bystrica (2011)
10. Přikrylová, J., Jahodová, H.: Moderní marketingová komunikace. GradaPublishing, a.s., Praha (2010)
11. Mesto Prešov – Kalvária. http://www.presov.sk/portal/?c=12&id=3106. Accessed 10 May 2014
12. Mesto Prešov – Evanjelické kolégium. http://www.presov.sk/portal/?c=12&id=3087. Accessed 10 May 2014
13. Mesto Prešov – Synagóga. http://www.synagoga-presov.sk/. Accessed 10 Sept 2014
14. Smoląg, K.: IT solutions in the context of operation of virtual supply chain. Gospodarka Materiałowa i Logistyka **12**, 84–88 (2011)

The International New Ventures: Applicability of the Theory on the Slovak Innovative Start-Ups

Sonia Ferencikova Sr.[✉] and Sonia Ferencikova Jr.

School of Management, Panonska cesta 17, 851 04 Bratislava, Slovakia
sferencikova@vsm.sk, sonaferencikova@gmail.com

Abstract. The international new ventures literature focuses on the phenomenon of rapid internationalization of firms. Unlike the traditional theories focusing on MNCs, the new international ventures literature emphasizes the growing occurrence of firms becoming internationally active already from their inception. The fundamental focus of this concept lies within the firm's age, not the size when examining its ability to internationalize. Special attention is also paid to the aspect of entrepreneurial behavior and constantly changing international environment, including recent technological advances, increasing mobility of human capital, higher availability of financing options, and a growing number of internationally experienced staff. There is not enough literature on the internationalization of the start-ups from Central and Eastern Europe and therefore we try to test the applicability of this theory on the case of selected Slovak IT firms.

Keywords: International new ventures · Internationalization · Slovak start-ups

1 Introduction

The research in the international business faces the following questions: are existing internationalization theories relevant to the companies from CEE that have started the internationalization differently from the Western companies, with no experience, different resources, in different time and under different conditions? Or, is the CEE situation so unique that we can form some new theoretical perspective? These are major research questions we try to address.

We analyze one of the major internationalization theories at first. Secondly, we chose a sample of three Slovak start-ups in the IT sector and tested existing theory on them. We assume that the specific feature of the newly-born market economies are newly-born companies, and if we should bring some novelty to the existing theories, this sample is the most appropriate one since the IT companies are the most successful ones in the internationalization among the Slovak start-ups. They were all built from the scratch, and have a short and transparent history. On top of that, these companies have not been influenced by the past, neither in the positive (know-how from the foreign markets, existing network, etc.) nor in the negative sense (heritage of the socialist system, murky privatization, etc.).

We compare the existing theory with the selected cases of well-known Slovak companies from IT sector, as examples of successful foreign expansion. The case study

© ICST Institute for Computer Sciences, Social Informatics and Telecommunications Engineering 2016
B. Mandler et al. (Eds.): IoT 360° 2015, Part II, LNICST 170, pp. 136–141, 2016.
DOI: 10.1007/978-3-319-47075-7_16

design has been chosen in order to obtain the necessary information for answering the research questions. The depth of case study analysis should compensate for the limited representative sample. Focused interviews with the company representatives from January–April 2014, and the local economic press coverage are aimed to offer in depth analysis of the chosen Slovak firms in a qualitative way.

2   International New Ventures: Theoretical Background

The literature toward an International New Ventures (INV) theory introduced by Oviatt and McDougall in the 1990s focuses on the rapid internationalization of firms. Unlike the theories focusing on MNCs, the INV concept emphasizes the growing occurrence of firms becoming international already from their inception [8]. With this respect, the focus of this concept lies within the firm's age, not the size when examining its ability to internationalize. The authors [7] examine altogether 12 firms with US, UK, German, French and even Czech origin to offer a better understanding of the INV formation. As a result, these factors were identified in order to describe under what conditions start-ups are motivated to go global [7]: "The best human resources must be spread over different countries, foreign financing would be easier and more suitable, target customers require the venture to be international, rapid worldwide communications will lead to quick responses from competitors, worldwide sales are required to support the venture, domestic inertia will be crippling if internationalization is postponed."

The INV perspective may take multiple forms. The authors [8] identify four types of INVs; the global start up, often labeled as **born global**, being one of them. It is the most radical form as its operations are geographically unlimited and competitive advantage is achieved by extensive coordination among the firm's business activities [8]. A born global firm is a firm that internationalizes within three years after its formation, is less than 20 years old, and generates at least 25 % of its total output from its activities abroad [9]. The concept of INV lays special emphasis on the **entrepreneurial behavior** and its implications to the global start-up creation [7]. Entrepreneurs are believed to have superior market knowledge and thus be aware of resource combinations that could generate profits for firms [6]. The results of the study conducted by Oviatt and McDougall [7] confirm the importance the entrepreneurial behavior has on the new ventures creation, as their founders were people with superior education, international experience and well networked abroad.

Even though many researchers still try to identify reasons why firms internationalize rapidly, they all agree that each INV is highly specific, operates under different conditions, and thus, a single generalized explanation for this phenomenon cannot be applied in all cases [9].

2.1   International New Ventures and the Implications on CEE Countries

There are multiple factors that motivate firms from the CEE region to go global right from their inception. Firstly, better opportunity to raise the necessary financial capital abroad rather than in the home country is such an example. Another factor is the small customer base in the home countries. Furthermore, both the fear of potential domestic inertia and the recent technological advances support the decision of new ventures to operate globally right from the foundation. Even though, there is only limited number of studies associated with the INV creation and focusing on the CEE region available, few studies confirming the patterns of fast internationalization of local firms can be found: The study of Vissak et al. [13] which examines four Baltic firms does not only confirm the patterns of the Uppsala model, resource-based and network view, but also shows that the observed firms entered foreign markets rapidly, thus underlines the relevance of rapid internationalization modes.

The study of Cieslik and Kaciak [4] analyzes new ventures established in 1993–2003 in Poland and their speed: the authors identify three types of firms: instant, quick and late exporters [4]. While instant exporters engage in export activities right after their foundation, quick exporters start exporting within the second or third year after their formation and late exporters launch exports in the fourth year or later. This study also underlines the role of entrepreneurs on the creation of start-ups [4].

Even though various researchers identify reasons why firms internationalize rapidly and offer better understanding to the dynamics of the new international ventures, there is still very limited empirical research conducted with the focus on the CEE region. To prevent inconclusive findings, before applying commonly used theories on international new ventures and rapid internationalization on the CEE firms, it is crucial to take the local context and settings into consideration beforehand. It is important to understand the above mentioned internationalization theory in order to test the applicability on internationalization patterns of Slovak firms.

3   Case Studies of Selected Slovak IT Start-Ups

3.1   Quality Unit

Quality Unit, established in 2004, is a software development company focused on web-based products and information systems for middle-to-large sized enterprises. Its products are aimed at affiliate marketing systems, which consist of retailer, affiliate partner, network and customers. The annual growth of the company is 30–40 %. Quality Unit is focused rather on larger number of smaller clients than on several large customers. According to Zeman [14], the co-founder of the company, it was this strategy that has helped them to grow during the economic crisis. Quality Unit currently has more than 15,000 clients and roughly 20 employees.

The share of the company on the global market is less than 1 %, however, its annual sales are more than 1 million €. Quality Unit's results in particular countries are rather diversified: in Brazil and Turkey, the annual growth is more than 100 %. On the other hand, Slovakia represents less than 1 % of the sales. The company even offered one of its products, Life Agent, to several Slovak companies for free, however, they declined the offer because they "did not need such service".

Internationalization started immediately after the creation of the company. Zeman [14] thinks the main advantage is the size of the global market and the possibility of larger feedback. According to him, company should pursue foreign expansion even in the case the product has certain imperfections. Quality Unit has low costs of marketing and it does not use on-line marketing tools such as pay-per-click. Company prefers viral publicity, blogs and positive users' reviews. The company expanded abroad at the time when the affiliate-software market was not well developed. It was also one of the determinants of company's success. Furthermore, continuous work, product improvements immediate solution of problems and care of customers are their important competitive advantages [14].

3.2   Nicereply

Nicereply is an on-line service for the quality evaluation of the e-mail communication between companies and their customers. Cooperation with foreign companies as Zendesk, Desk, Helpscout, TeamSupport and others was a major step in the Nicereply internationalization. The cooperation can be explained on the example of Zendesk, which serves more than 30,000 other companies. It is a multi-channel customer-support system: the employee is notified via e-mail, telephone, chat or tweet about the customer's question. After receiving a reply, the customer is automatically given a unique link in order to rate how satisfied he or she is with it. The company is thus able to receive direct, relevant and immediate feedback about its customer services.

Nicereply does not conduct any market research, because – when it comes to startups – these companies usually do not have the needed time and finance. According to Truban [11], the founder of Nicereply, even though it is important to know the competitors while expanding abroad, Nicereply is focused rather on the improvement of its services, e.g. in the form of the forum about the proposed improvements. Nicereply has never been aimed primarily at the Slovak market, internationalization was its goal from the beginning. The reasons were the same as in the Quality Unit case: more potential clients and higher awareness of this kind of service abroad.

Nicereply is an example of the approach of many other start-ups creating solution to the problem they faced, with unavailability to find the proper product or service on the market. In order to raise the profitability of the project, Nicereply offered its services to other companies. On the present, it has more than 100,000 business clients.

3.3   Synopsi.tv

Synopsi has aimed at the personalized film recommendations since 2011. Public version was made available in April 2012. The company has reached an important milestone, 100,000 active users in the first three months of its existence. Subsequently, Synopsi launched also B2B service. In the beginning of 2013, the company gradually started its relocation from Slovakia to Silicon Valley, USA. Currently, Synopsi has more than 350,000 users and processes more than billion entries a day with less than 30 employees. The user enters the films he or she has watched and liked. Based on these data, the unique algorithm recommends other films the user might like. The company currently has 6 business clients, among them Followmy.tv (similar service as Synopsi, but aimed at TV series), XBMC (multimedia system enabling to play user's files on the TV set) or Netflix (provider of on-demand Internet streaming media).

Exports create 99 % of the company's profits. According to Turek [10], two main reasons for internationalization were the shortages of the Slovak business environment and insufficient state protection of businesses. Company's success was based on cheap labour force (R&D centre was still based in Slovakia at that time) and "hard work". The problems associated with the relocation were mainly the lack of contacts and initial distrust of investors, combined with marketing costs, which were ten-times higher than in Slovakia. The strengths of Synopsi are the relative simplicity of the service, low price, direct targeting of customers and unique algorithm [10].

4 Discussión and Conclusions

After the fall of the Iron Curtain the existing CEE firms that tried to penetrate foreign markets faced the scarcity of resources, know-how, networks, state support, and an established foreign competition. As the literature review [5] shows, the central element in the discussion is finding a comparative advantage on which the internationalization initiative can be built. Without it, it is difficult to overcome the scarcity of resources and the additional disadvantage of the negative country-of-origin effect. In order to be successful internationally, the firms need to be cheaper than competitors or have to offer unique products or service features. We assume that CEE firms found their competitive arenas by focusing on neighboring markets and by basing their competitive strategies on good value-for-money (price advantages vis-à-vis developed country firms) and specialization advantages – often combining both aspects. Due to the lack of financial and physical resources SMEs in CEE are using intangible resources as the many start-ups in the ICT underline. In the case of the software industry entry barriers are lower than in many other markets, which makes it attractive to newcomers. Also, many CEE countries are small, have relatively high-quality education and superior talents that can compete in the international ICT arena because this is the one where physical resources are relatively less important at the beginning, and even small and resource-scarce companies can successfully develop their business. All three cases that we studied are these types of the SMEs.

We have shown that existing theory explain the internationalization patterns well. In our case of the study of Slovak IT start-ups, we confirm the applicability of the INV theory. However, given our findings, we believe that one theory is not sufficient for the explanation of the internationalization of similar companies: combining the resource-based view (see e.g. [1–3]), with the INV theory seems to be a promising theoretical approach that can be further developed and used in the conditions of the small, former transitional economies.

All three companies in our sample internationalized very quickly, and their explanation was the nature of their products, their industry and surprisingly, bad institutional environment in Slovakia that "pushed" them to go abroad. Their founders had the vision and strong entrepreneurial behavior. Slovak companies in our sample had to rely on their most valuable resources – human resources, if they wanted to enter foreign markets. This is particularly important, as the companies had to counterweight their lack of finance and foreign market knowledge with unique and high-quality products, which served as their competitive advantage. Another important factor might be their narrow specialization, as they do not diversify their product portfolio into new categories, but rather they focus on improving the quality of their existing product or creating its new variations. What is more important, Slovakia has a large pool of highly-qualified IT talent.

Slovakia is an extremely open economy: however, Slovak export is based on large companies in the automotive and consumer electronics sectors. Therefore Slovakia also has a project aimed at helping the start-up companies: Connect Coworking in Bratislava is a space dedicated to start-ups. Its keywords are space, people and innovation, which describe also the idea of the project. Connect offers rental of offices and mentoring by the successful entrepreneurs. According to Vaculík [12], the founder of Connect, there are roughly ten start-ups on the present, while about 50 companies made use of the centre services during its existence.

In our future research we plan to study the relevance of all the theories of internationalization on a more representative sample of the Slovak companies including companies from different industries, companies of different size, ownership structure and history.

References

1. Andersen, O., Kheam, L.S.: Resource-based theory and international growth strategies: an exploratory study. Int. Bus. Rev. **7**(2), 163–184 (1998)
2. Antoncic, B., Konecnik, M., Ruzzier, M.: The resource-based approach to the internationalisation of SMEs: differences in resource bundles between internationalised and non-internationalised companies. Zagreb Int. Rev. Econ. Bus. **9**(2), 95–116 (2006)
3. Chadee, D., Roxas, H.: A resource-based view of small export firms' social capital in a Southeast Asian country. Asian Acad. Manag. J. **16**(2), 1–28 (2011)
4. Cieslik, J., Kaciak, E.: The speed of internationalization of entrepreneurial start-ups in a transition environment. J. Dev. Entrep. **14**, 375–392 (2009)
5. Ferencikova, S., Schuh, A.: The internationalization of firms from Central and Eastern Europe - a discussion of theoretical contributions. In: Springer, R., Chadraba, P. (eds.) Proceedings of the 20th Annual Conference on Marketing and Business Strategies for Central & Eastern Europe, pp. 39–55. WU Vienna, Vienna (2012)
6. Madsen, T.K., Knudsen, T.: International New Ventures: A New Organizational Form? (2003). http://www.sam.sdu.dk/globalfirms/pdf/inv.pdf
7. Oviatt, B.M., McDougall, P.P.: Global start-ups: entrepreneurs on a worldwide stage [and executive commentary]. Acad. Manag. Exec. **9**, 30–44 (1995)
8. Oviatt, B.M., McDougall, P.P.: Toward a theory of international new ventures. J. Int. Bus. Stud. **25**, 45–64 (1993)
9. Oviatt, B., McDougall, P.P.: Challenges for internationalization process theory: the case of international new ventures. Manag. Int. Rev. **37**, 85–99 (1997)
10. Turek, V.: Co-founder, Synopsi - interview, 11 March 2014
11. Truban, M.: Co-founder – WebSupport, Nicereply – interview, 10 February 2014
12. Vaculik, V.: Co-founder – Connect Coworking – interview, 20 March 2014
13. Vissak, T., Ibeh, K., Paliwoda, S.: Internationalising from the European periphery: triggers, processes and trajectories. J. Euromark. **17**, 35–48 (2007)
14. Zeman, V.: Co-founder, Quality Unit – interview, 10 March 2014

Smart Infrastructure in Bratislava

Julius Golej[(⊠)], Miroslav Panik, and Andrej Adamuscin

Institute of Management, Slovak University of Technology in Bratislava,
Bratislava, Slovakia
{julius.golej,miroslav_panik,
andrej.adamuscin}@stuba.sk

Abstract. After the fall of former political regime in Slovakia in 1989, Bratislava has undergone many dynamic developing changes that were not too positively influenced the appearance and functions of the city. Spontaneous and unsystematic development in this period seems to continue even after 25 years. Conversely, a significant decline is becoming increasingly marked in the urban infrastructure, of which insufficient attention is paid. This is because infrastructure for developers is often only enforced expenditure and the city does not have sufficient financial resources to meet requirements on its renewal. Moreover, the infrastructure requirements from before 30 years are now heavily modified and it is currently inadequate and capacity insufficient. Here we can mention for example a significant parking problems in many parts of Bratislava mainly caused by the substantial increase in the level of motorization to the period when the present transportation infrastructure was planned. Of course, in Bratislava there are also some positive examples, to which the authors of this paper focuses, that are currently considered significant by the fact that towards the Bratislava closer to the concept of Smart City. In these selected examples it is also important the implementation of existing ICT technologies that form an integral part of the modern Smart Cities. The Aim of the paper is also propose improvements to the current solutions.

Keywords: Urban infrastructure · Smart city · Bratislava · Urban mobility · Knowledge infrastructure

1 Introduction

In the urban context, the physical infrastructure is understood as an integral part of every urbanized area. It constitutes an important segment ensuring economic and social system functions as well as material and technical background of the city. Urban infrastructure may be compared to the human cardiovascular system, that is quite complicated vascular (network) system, which plays a crucial logistical tasks - allows movement and distribution of energy, services, capital, etc. in urban living organism.

Generally we can urban infrastructure subdivided on:

- Transport infrastructure, including private transport, urban public transport, cycling, pedestrian traffic, tram or other rail transport, air and water transport;
- Technical Infrastructure, which includes all utilities, i.e. electric, water, gas and sewerage networks, or further distribution of waste management; optionally

© ICST Institute for Computer Sciences, Social Informatics and Telecommunications Engineering 2016
B. Mandler et al. (Eds.): IoT 360° 2015, Part II, LNICST 170, pp. 142–149, 2016.
DOI: 10.1007/978-3-319-47075-7_17

telecommunications networks; including all structures related to the operation of these networks (e.g. water towers, transformer stations, substations or pipelines);

- Social infrastructure, which includes homes and housing stock, education, health, social welfare, culture, sports, recreation and services for the population;
- Public areas (all areas to be used in the public interest).

For the past 25 years Bratislava has undergone many dynamic changes. Disordered and uncontrollable urban development without comprehensive strategy or insufficient implementation of support system - both static and dynamic transport infrastructure [1] should be the main reasons such as these developing processes should be started to meet the highest requirements of contemporary modern European cities. The technical state of transport infrastructure is closely linked to the technical state of most of the technical infrastructure, which is often conducted in the corridors of roads.

The new millennium is marked by new technologies and ever increasing demands for comfort and enhanced quality of living. Every day of a human beings life is extremely valuable and to use it fully, it is necessary to accelerate and simplify the performance of routine activities by the deployment of central management systems, providing more efficient operation and reduce energy consumption and optimisation, which means concept by implementation of the newest smart technologies [2].

Bratislava in recent years has tendency to move towards the European modern smart city. It certainly can take as an example the nearby city Vienna that its programs and policies at least the last past five years is ranked among the most modern and most innovative cities in Europe. Right here, authors want on selected examples show how Bratislava in recent years is moving closer to achieve the Smart City concept.

2 Smart Urban Mobility

Urbanisation is accelerating at pace, placing new, intense pressures on city resources and infrastructure. Urban Mobility will be one of the toughest challenges for cities around the globe. In many cities, existing mobility systems are already inadequate, yet urbanisation and increasing populations will increase demand still further. Cities have traditionally sought to solve such challenges by adding new capacity to match demand. However, a capacity-building approach alone is neither efficient nor sustainable [3].

Mobility describes the ability of people and goods to move around an area, and in doing so to access the essential facilities, communities and other destinations that are required to support a decent quality of life and a buoyant economy. Mobility incorporates the transport infrastructure and services that facilitate these interactions [3].

There is a need for substantial changes in Europe's transport systems, as well as in the mobility behaviour of people and businesses in urban areas. Solutions concern the creation of an efficient and integrated mobility system that allows for organising and monitoring seamless transport across different modes; increasing the use of environmentally-friendly, alternative fuels; creating new opportunities for collective mobility. The proposed solutions lead to a decreased environmental impact [4].

At this point, authors' deals with selected aspects of urban mobility, which tend to shift Bratislava to achieve Smart City concept. The first area is so-called bike-sharing system as an important tool for alternative urban transport and reflects a growing pressure for green mobility. Another area of research is the use of Information and Communication Technologies (ICT) in public transport and in parking.

2.1 Bike-Sharing System

At the beginning it should be said that the city bike-sharing program does not exist. However, in Bratislava arose a community bike-sharing program called White Bikes - public bicycle rental system. The project is organized by the Association "Cyk-lokoalicia" and use is conditional upon completion of the training - how to use the bikes. Currently is available fifty white bikes (Fig. 1) and 70 registered users. All bikes come from the Netherlands from Park De Hoge Veluwe [5].

The main motivation is not sharing of bikes, but their presence in the city and even at night. The aim is to promote cycle transportation and thus get rid the roads of onslaught of cars. The entire system is set up via SMS and is based on the approval process. If someone wants to use a bicycle, it is necessary to always register and receive the training [6].

The whole system works so that the White Bikes can borrow only Bratislava citizens, the third sector, non-profit organizations, or anyone who works for the municipality of Bratislava. Bicycles are free to lend. It's a reward for active Bratislava citizens consider that they are doing something for their city. However, in the future it is planned the collection of fees due to the fact that bikes have been returned back. The aim of the bike-sharing project is that bikes were seen in the streets, so that they truly can benefit people. There is currently 25 positions, where bicycles can be stored in Bratislava.

Fig. 1. Bike-sharing program White Bikes [12]

The authors see the greatest negatives in:

- The need for registration and approval process,
- The need to undergo training,
- Lack of storage sites.

Authors Innovation: We suggest the automatic functioning of the system. It would be necessary to transform the SMS system to a system based on a smartphone application. The location information of the bicycle would be sent automatically based on the GPS and was marked to the dynamic map which will be available for all online users. So they know where they can take a bicycle. The user would be identified based on the IP address of the mobile device, which would they entered on the station store. Bicycles should be equipped with GPS devices to track the current location in order to prevent theft. Financing would be secured by the municipality of Bratislava, NGOs and by voluntary contributions.

2.2   SMS Parking System

Since 2010, drivers can on marked parking areas of the Bratislava centre pay parking fees via mobile phone - through SMS, without further registering. Electronic parking card driver immediately receives in a return SMS, while the price is currently set for 1 Euro per hour. Vehicles which have paid parking through SMS-Parking System are registered in a protected database system and when checking the paid parking by authorized persons, so there is no risk of any penalty.

Parking system in Bratislava by using SMS, after several years shows no significant problems. So we do not have thus any significantly complaints. At this point, we just advised the option to purchase parking at different time periods. Today, after the expiry of the time 90 min, it is necessary once again to extend the parking by sending a new SMS.

2.3   SMS Tickets for City Public Transport

Since 2008, in Bratislava it is possible to travel by public transport by using electronic SMS ticket. SMS ticket can be bought through Slovak mobile operators. The price of SMS ticket is € 1 per 70 min or € 4.50 per 24 h (including baggage). Discounted tickets or any other time alternative tickets are not provided via SMS.

It should be added that the SMS ticket has stagnated for years and it is not developing further.

Authors Innovation: Improving of this provided service authors see mainly in the fact that it could be possible to purchase all possible types of tickets, including discounted for students and for all time alternatives. Nowadays, of omnipresent Wi-Fi networks and of the mobile internet, we suggest other way of ticket buying which could be realized through internet applications, respectively by using of the QR code. The QR code is an open standard, two-dimensional barcode, which would be accessible on the bus stops. After capturing the code buyers would be redirected through the application on public transport website where they could simply buy tickets.

Inspectors in the vehicle should have a connection to the Internet through smartphone applications and by online real-time payment they could immediately found buying tickets based on the IP address of the devices. This would help to avoid the above problems which arise when tickets are paying through SMS.

3 Smart Knowledge Infrastructure

Edwards (2010) defined knowledge infrastructures as "robust networks of people, artefacts, and institutions that generate, share, and maintain specific knowledge about the human and natural worlds." [7] Under this definition, knowledge infrastructures include individuals, organizations, routines, shared norms, and practices [8].

But the essence of Knowledge Infrastructure are in particular information whether in the form of data, findings, experience or other forms. Smart solutions involve data gathering, real-time processing, data analytics and visualisation. Using data ultimately aims to support better decision and enable innovation. New technologies and availability of data, and the near-universal uptake of mobile devices, therefore offers an opportunity to innovate in order to make our urban areas more adaptive and resilient [9].

Among the selected aspects of Knowledge Infrastructure the authors chose an area that the essential nature is in dissemination of information.

3.1 Tourist Info-Points

Bratislava is visited each year approximately 500 000 tourists. From several surveys conducted on a sample of foreign tourists many times was indicated that one of the significant problems in Bratislava are currently limited possibilities of obtaining information about the city. Tourists' awareness in Bratislava is distributed through Tourist Information Centers (TIC). There are actually four centers in Bratislava.

Authors Innovation: The issue of obtaining tourist information in Bratislava authors see in strategically placed of Tourist Information panels – Info-points in the form of kiosks with the interaction touch screen monitors (Fig. 2) and Internet access. In addition to the Internet connection these Info-points could offers the possibility of free internet access through Wi-Fi. Info-points should be mobile, deployed in the most frequented tourists' sites, including all bigger business centers and major transport hubs and other frequented places.

3.2 Free Internet Connection

Signal coverage area for wireless ICT facilities are located in the building of Municipality of Bratislava; also in three large squares in the center and one is on the Danube embankment. Internet connection are free of charge and has no limits to the public. The public Wi-Fi could be used quite comfortably, because in the vicinity of these areas are benches.

Fig. 2. Example of Info-point panel in Gronau, Germany [13]

Internet kiosks are urban pilot project of introducing the Internet for the public in the city center. There are currently three terminals based on PCs that serve to the public for free of charge. Other possibilities are "hot spot areas" in cafes, shops, restaurants and bars that offer a limited time of free connection [10]. There are now more than 120 of such places throughout the city. Free Wi-Fi is also accessible in public transport in a fifty buses [11].

Authors Innovation: As an innovation we propose building of the so-called "Power boxes", designed for free charging of ICT facilities on public areas such as on squares, stations and other frequented places and important transport hubs.

Of course, the city should be striving to improve the Wi-Fi service in the form of quality improvement of the signal but also increasing places of coverage.

3.3   e-Governance

Municipality of Bratislava launches e-governance project in 2015. It is a project of electronic council, which contributes to saving the environment and optimize the work of the City Office. The official website of the city will be available invitations and materials for meetings, profiles of deputies and information about their individual vote, or resolution of the City Council. The new application will serve all - as citizens, as well as local authorities and the deputies.

4 Other Smart Infrastructure

4.1 Smart Public Lighting

It would be mainly on communication for pedestrians as well as joint public spaces that meet the assembly function like squares, parks; or parking lots. It is the concept of a public street lighting with modern LED lighting, which would use alternative solar energy with built-in twilight switches that turns on and off automatically; and with intelligent control and management of public lighting. Furthermore, this smart lighting would regulate the light intensity by means of motion sensors - if the pedestrian roads in the same time will be empty, then the light intensity will be automatically reduced to a minimum set limit. Once someone came to that communication, via motion sensors would be increased the light intensity.

5 Conclusion

Bratislava in recent years, striving to become smart modern metropolis. Unfortunately, initiative that develops toward this current global trend is far from sufficient state. Because of some elementary but very important deficiencies such as the city parking policy, or the creation of spatial plans at zonal levels, whether completion of the city core transport system, Bratislava cannot be classified among the European elite metropolis such as near partner city Vienna.

Of course we agree with several "minor" initiatives in the aforementioned examples. However, even here it is important to have a rather critical stance towards certain concepts. Providing of information and working with them is the typical Slovak long-term problem. Lack of information in the form of data (such as non-existent databases on static and dynamic traffic), or their non-transparent publishing often leads to a distorted view of the relatively important facts.

Therefore we think that the first step towards achieving the concept of Smart City might be just the creation of informational databases and their transparent disclosure from the municipality.

References

1. Spirkova, D., Golej, J., Panik, M.: The issue of urban static traffic on selected examples in Bratislava in the context of economic sustainability. In: 2014. International Conference on Traffic and Transport Engineering ICTTE 2014, 27th–28th November 2014, Belgrade, Serbia (2014). ISBN: 978-86-916153-1-4
2. Spirkova, D., Caganova, D.: Smart housing in sustainable development. In: Giaffreda, R., Cagáňová, D., Li, Y., Riggio, R., Voisard, A. (eds.) Internet of Things. IoT Infrastructures. LNICST, vol. 151, pp. 52–59. Springer, Heidelberg (2015). doi:10.1007/978-3-319-19743-2. ISBN 978-3-319-19742-5

3. Smart Cities Cornerstone Series: Urban Mobility in the Smart City Age. 2014. Arup, The Climate Group, Schneider Electric. http://digital.arup.com/wp-content/uploads/2014/06/Urban-Mobility.pdf

4. Sustainable Urban Mobility. Market Place of the European Innovation Partnership on Smart Cities and Communities. 2015 SMART CITIES, An initiative of the European Commission (2015). https://eu-smartcities.eu/sustainable-urban-mobility

5. Mikesova, M.: Mestské bicykle sú v Bratislave zatiaľ iba biele. Pravda.sk (2015). http://spravy.pravda.sk/regiony/clanok/364796-bratislava-stale-nema-mestsky-bikesharing-zachranuju-to-biele-bicykle/

6. Cyklokoalicia. http://cyklokoalicia.sk/biele-bicykle/

7. Edwards, P.N.: A Vast Machine: Computer Models, Climate Data, and the Politics of Global Warming. MIT Press, Cambridge (2010)

8. Edwards, P.N., et al.: Knowledge infrastructures: intellectual frameworks and research challenges. In: 2012 Report of a workshop sponsored by the National Science Foundation and the Sloan Foundation. University of Michigan School of Information, 25–28 May (2012). http://deepblue.lib.umich.edu/bitstream/handle/2027.42/97552/Edwards_etal_2013_Knowledge_Infrastructures.pdf?sequence=3&isAllowed=y

9. Morwen, J.: How data and smart city infrastructure can support transport planning. The Knowledge Exchange blog (2015). http://theknowledgeexchangeblog.com/2015/07/17/how-data-and-smart-city-infrastructure-can-support-transport-planning/

10. Wi-Fi internet zadarmo v Bratislave - miesta s pokrytím. www.BratislavaGuide.com. http://www.bratislavaguide.com/wifi-hotspoty-bratislava

11. Durdovansky, M.V.: Bratislave sú tisícky wifi sietí. Petit Press, SME Bratislava (2014). http://bratislava.sme.sk/c/7134469/v-bratislave-su-tisicky-wifi-sieti.html#ixzz3jaF4vgLG

12. http://bratislava.dnes24.sk/rozhovor-vsimli-ste-si-v-uliciach-bratislavy-biele-bicykle-komunitny-bikesharing-je-pre-aktivnych-bratislavcanov-192787

13. http://www.eyescreens.de/wo-steht-eyescreens/Infopoint.html

Economic Aspects of Land Grabbing
in the Connection with Development Projects

Daniela Spirkova[1,2(✉)], Dagmar Cagáňová[1,2], and Manan Bawa[1,2]

[1] Institute of Management,
Slovak University of Technology in Bratislava, Trnava, Slovakia
{daniela.spirkova,dagmar.caganova,
manan.bawa}@stuba.sk
[2] Institute of Industrial Engineering and Management,
Faculty of Materials Science and Technology in Trnava,
Slovak University of Technology in Bratislava, Trnava, Slovakia

Abstract. The long-term problem in Slovakia is the seizure of agricultural land for the purpose of implementation of development projects. Factors contributing to land grabbing and occupancy of land were and are mainly due to the need for new residential, industrial and commercial sites as well as transport infrastructure. The Slovak Republic is one of the transition countries, which since 1990 has transferred to a market economy. Subsequent positive legislative changes and the development of new economic instruments in Slovakia has increased interest of foreign companies in business development activities. The consequences of uncontrolled construction boom is reflected in seizure of quality agricultural land for the construction of development projects and the subsequent formation of negative externalities.

Keywords: Development projects · Land grabbing · Land management

1 Introduction

Land is one of the most important resources in any country. Since the land is a key factor in the investment project, it significantly influences its final price. All countries have to deal with the land management. They have to deal with the four functions of land tenure, land value, land use, and land development (see Fig. 1) in some way or another [1]. The management of land is a critical and essential requirement for sustainable development. Many of the issues that affect land development and management, impact ultimately on economic, financial and environmental sustainability and on the country's social development.

Land management is an economic-technical term that characterizes the process of managing land administration; conservation of land and routing of the relevant organizations through the deployment and manipulation of land resources. It is a land-use management in economic and environmental terms. From the functional point of view it represents processes dealing with adjustments, measurements and activities related to land and territory.

© ICST Institute for Computer Sciences, Social Informatics and Telecommunications Engineering 2016
B. Mandler et al. (Eds.): IoT 360° 2015, Part II, LNICST 170, pp. 150–157, 2016.
DOI: 10.1007/978-3-319-47075-7_18

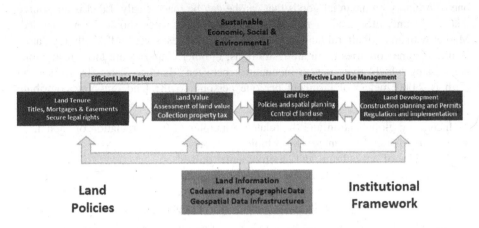

Fig. 1. A global land management perspective [1]

According to Enemark [1], land management is the process by which the resources of land are put into good effect. Land Management includes all activities associated with management of land and natural resources that are necessary to achieve sustainable development. Land Administration Systems can be considered as a institutional frameworks burdened with tasks they must be performed by means of national, cultural, political, legal environments and technologies [2]. It can be described by three components: land policy frameworks, land information infrastructures and land administrative functions in support of sustainable development [2]. This land management model is shown below in Fig. 2.

Land policy has also impact on a better use of existing land and space resources in most municipalities in the transitive countries. It is important to note that the land is not

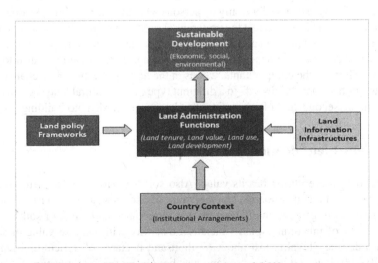

Fig. 2. Land management model [1]

one of ordinary commercial goods that can be can be made easily. Land is a resource that is not unlimited, and therefore the normal market rules should be not applied. Market with an agricultural land in the EU Member States is very differently regulated. While in some countries there are restrictions, in other countries are those restrictions are missing which gives rise to inequalities between Member States. In average on earth is 2,000 meters of farmland per one person. To the land grabbing contribute following factors:

- Increasing globalization and the related principles of free circulation of capital,
- growing demand for energy from biological sources,
- downsides of agricultural and environmental policies,
- effort of large investors to invest capital (released as a result of the financial crisis in 2008), into the agricultural land, which is safer investment,
- grabbing of the large agricultural land for development projects etc.

Interest in global soil is considerable. It is difficult to obtain reliable data on the extent of agricultural land grabbing, because not all transactions are registered and land transactions of mutual legal persons on the land are often not transparent, as in the case of land purchase through subsidiaries and partner companies. According to World Bank estimates were in the years 2008–2009 worldwide seized 45 million hectares of land, wherein the industrial and "transit" countries lose annually 2.9 million hectares of cultivated agricultural land in exchange for building land. Approximately 75 % of Europe's population currently live in urban areas and is estimated that by 2020 this will rise to 80 % [3]. European areas classified as suburban currently have equal size of built-up areas as urban areas, but their population density is only half size [4].

Within the negotiations with the inclusion of the Slovak Republic to the European Union (2000) Slovak Republic's accession process defined the land as the goods in contrast to Hungary or Poland. Land on Slovakia became a commodity which can be freely marketed with. Slovakia subsequently asked the European Commission for deferral from the free disposal of land. Since June, 2014, the law was modified in a way that acquisition of land can be done only by persons who are in agricultural production for at least three years. This means that the preferential right to purchase has collective farms, and farmers who are engaged in agricultural activity in the municipality where the land is situated. The Act aims to enhance the protection of agricultural land and also to avoid speculative efforts of the complainants, who is in the first step requesting a change of the type of agricultural land "vineyard" to a different type of agricultural land such as garden and then, in the second step of requesting the change of "garden" to building projects.

2 Problem Identification

In market society everything has its value. Also soil has. However, does it have only cost of money? The soil primarily has the value of life, permanent, constant, not just one, but also future generations. Therefore, the importance and value of soil grow and as the numbers of inhabitants planet increase, that way will increase value of soil. In less than a decade Slovakia lost about 67 thousand hectares of agricultural land and another 40–100 thousand hectares of land was bought by foreign investors. Change of the land owner also opens the door to ownership of water. Under the ground is located water, and the largest reservoir of drinking water is on the Rye Island (southern Slovakia), where are one of the best soils in Slovakia. Exactly on them is focused the interest of foreign investors. Land, but also clean water reserves in the world are gradually shrinking, thus both natural resources are becoming more valuable. Therefore, any sale of land, mainly to foreign development companies, gives rise to big debate, which is further exacerbated by the Act on land trading [5]. It is impossible to exist without land because it provides ecological stability of the country and its sustainability. European countries like France, the United Kingdom, but also the neighbouring Austria share the same understanding that land is not a commodity that is traded across borders and therefore land in their territory is diligently defended from strangers by different legal standards.

Long-term problem in the Slovak Republic is grabbing of farmland for the purpose of mainly large development - building industrial and residential projects. The Slovak Republic is one of the transition economies, which since 1990 has undergone major political and economic changes. Factors that contributed to the grabbing of land are primarily due to the need for new residential, industrial and commercial sites, as well as transport infrastructure. The continued urban growth in the Slovak Republic can be explained from several views. Many people reside in urban areas because there is higher quality housing with more living space per person. For the negative trend (negative externalities) can be considered extensive building - suburbanization, urban sprawl. Suburbanization and urban sprawl "consumes" parts of the country, which could be used for example as agricultural lands or forests [6]. With that the natural environment is losing its ecological function.

The question about construction of development projects, industrial parks, storage facilities and new production halls are also linked to the question of location and how they are implemented. In most cases, these complexes are built in the open and undeveloped spaces - on the "greenfields" All this is a consequence of distorted priorities of the public sector. The fact is that for the investor is building on a greenfield much more advantageous than brownfield revitalization. Cities and state leads to new networks to industrial zones, looking for investment propositions because of "greenfields" without environmental and other loads are quickly ready for construction. On the other hand, in the case of projects which revitalize brownfields means a crumbling demolition of buildings, removal of environmental loads and then build new premises. On the one hand it represents a high cost which the developer/investor does not want and on the other hand, such projects require financially strong and experienced developer.

Development of real estate market in the Slovak Republic and huge interest of foreign development companies to enter this market after 2000 affected mostly the growth of gross domestic product (GDP). This positive development mainly affected the industry, construction and agriculture, in which growth of GDP exceeded overall economic performance. Determinant which undoubtedly contributed to the positive image of Slovakia in the area of foreign investors and the real estate market has been re-granting investment rating of the world's largest rating agency Japan Credit Rating Agency, which reacted to previous rating improvement of Slovakia. The rating increase had consequences in terms of interest rates lowering, improvement in financing options and so on.

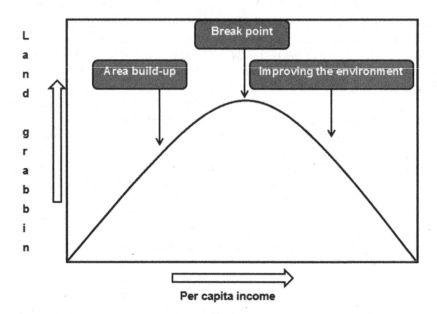

Fig. 3. Environmental Kuznets curves [7]

Building boom in the Slovak Republic in the last 15 years has caused several serious problems. This is particularly the failure of the State administration to manage development activities. Building authorities contribute to the existence of negative externalities, are under pressure from rich development company, causing great damage for violations of land use plan. An important problem that threatens the availability of good quality land is building-up new investment projects. Land management in the country becomes a limiting factor for sustainable development. General knowledge can be complemented by a relatively lower risk of environmental threats for the developed, rich countries. The growth of wealth from a certain point pollution levels decrease and demands for environmental protection increase (this expresses so called environmental Kuznets curve - see Fig. 3), which has its importance in the field of sustainable land management.

3 Model Examples

Slovakia is one of the most attractive European countries among residential markets with high profits. Unceasing demand attracted other developers, not only foreign but also those that were previously devoted to commercial real estate while apartments were not considered as very profitable activity. Construction of large investment projects (in Bratislava and its surroundings), which attracted foreign developers, has been implemented on a green meadow.

Bratislava, the capital city of Slovakia is a fast growing and dynamic city which is full of energy and rich history. It presents mainly Slovak centre of business, employment, development, tourism and education. It benefits from its excellent geographic position, especially from nearby Hungary on the south and Austria on the southwest and it is also located near the central European economic centres such as Prague, Budapest and Vienna. But in comparison with other European capitals it is still not sufficiently developed. This was one of the main reasons why Bratislava became the centre of foreign investors' attention. Developers' focus so far has been mainly in projects that build premises for offices, retail and luxury residential areas. Unsatisfied demand still largely exists in the middle class households, mainly in rental housing projects, respectively construction of small apartments for young people. The main criterion for any development must be a good accessibility by car, which is the main mode of transport because of lack of metro in Bratislava and limited connections for bus and tram to new build areas. However, on the plan are for example speed tram lines linking the southern and northern part of the city. In this paper we present two examples of large investment projects which construction was conditional upon the grabbing of agricultural land.

3.1   Investment Project "Sunflowers - South City" in Bratislava

Investment project "Sunflowers - South City" is a pilot project of Petrzalka - South City, which consists of two parts - residential and terraced houses with family houses.

The project (Fig. 4) plans construction of 200 apartments in three apartment houses and 71 houses are linked by central park with playgrounds and sport fields. The "South City" project with its territory and urban intention is of one of the biggest development projects in Bratislava. Petrzalka is a part of Bratislava with the largest population and one of the most densely populated areas in Slovakia and Central Europe, where in panel houses currently reside 98.5 % of the nearly 120,000 residents.

Fig. 4. Residential project "Sunflowers - South City" in Bratislava [8]

Fig. 5. PSA Peugeot Citroën Slovakia in Trnava [9]

3.2   Automobile Factory PSA Peugeot Citroën in Trnava

Automotive industry in Slovakia constitutes a significant component of the economy and also attracts foreign investors. It is the driving force of economic development of the country. Based on this automotive industry Slovakia gained adjective "European Detroit". Project PSA Peugeot Citroën Slovakia is an automotive plant of company PSA Peugeot Citroën in Slovakia near town Trnava. Factory complex was built on 193 hectares of agricultural land and its construction began in 2003 (Fig. 5). The automaker in Trnava belongs to the newest in terms of technology in the PSA Peugeot Citroën group. Strategic investment realized by the French group in 2007 reached approximately 1 billion EUR.

4   Conclusions

The reason for the growth of residential and other development projects in the last two decades since 1990 were several. Gradually were increased incomes of population, interest rates on construction loans (including mortgages) declined and number of apartments offers increased slowly. On the other hand, "hunger" for residential real estate triggered a boom in the construction mainly in Bratislava and western Slovakia. The demand for real estates has caused a rapid increase in property prices to staggering heights.

Developers had significant support in its loan financing from Slovak banks, which provided loan resources primarily for the construction of residential real estate and mortgage loans up to 120 % of the value of purchased property. Another determinant, which significantly influenced the construction boom in the Slovak Republic, was the fact that after 1990, the agricultural land was reattributed to its original owners. Their relationship to land, however, was greatly disrupted and in many cases completely "uprooted". Many owners decided to quickly capitalize land ownership to maximize profit by selling the land for construction purposes.

Significant demand for building land, especially in attractive locations with good transport connections and also the lack of coordination of construction through spatial planning contributed to strengthen the process of land sales. As a consequence of selling agricultural land in the past decade was that about 100 thousand hectares of agricultural land was bought by foreign investors, while the volume of agricultural land is decreasing.

References

1. Enemark, S.: Building land information policies. In: Proceedings of Special Forum on Building Land Information Policies in the Americas, Aquascalientes, Mexico (2004)
2. Golej, J.: Land and Development Process. Slovak University of Technology, Bratislava (2012)
3. EEA, The European environment — state and outlook 2010: Assessment of global megatrends, European Environment Agency (2010)
4. Piorr A., Ravetz J., Tosics I.: Peri-urbanisation in Europe: Towards a European Policy to sustain Urban-Rural Futures. University of Copenhagen/Academic Books Life (2011)
5. Sedlak, J.: The soil is not ordinary merchandise. J. Pravda (2014)
6. Spirkova, D., Ivanicka, K.: Transdisciplinary challenges of sustainable construction and real estate development in Visegrad countries. Eur. Sci. J. (2013). University of Azory, Portugal
7. Yandle, B., Madhusudan, B., Maya, V.: Environmental Kuznets curves: a review of findings, methods, and policy implications. Res. Study 2, 1–16 (2004)
8. Materials of CRESCO GROUP. http://www.slnecnice.sk
9. Materials of PSA PEUGEOT CITROËN Slovakia. www.psa-slovakia.sk
10. Prokop G., Jobstmann H., Schönbauer A.: Overview on best practices for limiting soilsealing and mitigating its effects in EU-27. Environment Agency Austria (2011). http://ec.europa.eu/environment/emas/index_en.htm
11. Postel, S.: Last Oasis - Facing Water Scarcity. W.W. Norton & Company, New York (1997)
12. Kulshreshtha, S.N.: World Water Resources and Regional Vulnerability: Impact of Future Changes, International Institute for Applied Systems Analysis. http://www.iiasa.ac.at/Admin/PUB/Documents/RR-93-010.pdf

An IoT Approach for the Connected Vehicle

Andrea Parodi[1(✉)], Massimo Maresca[2], Michele Provera[3],
and Pierpaolo Baglietto[2]

[1] M3S SrL, Genoa, Italy
a.parodi@m3s.it
[2] CIPI – University of Genoa, Genoa, Italy
p.baglietto@cipi.unige.it
[3] CRF – Centro Ricerche Fiat, Turin, Italy
michele.provera@crf.it

Abstract. This paper will showcase the iCore Project approach for instantiating an Internet of Things (IoT) Service Enabling Architecture to support the Connected Vehicles (Transportation in the Smart City).

Keywords: Connected vehicles · Internet of things · Virtual objects · Composite services · Context awareness · Connected infotainment systems

1 Introduction

In modern cities, roads and motorways an increasing amount of circulating vehicles are equipped with more and more sophisticated infotainment devices and systems, also capable of communicating through WAN 3G/4G connections, bringing the promise of an always-connected driving experience.

Nevertheless, a concrete ICT architecture is still lacking for enabling a safe and efficient connection of such equipment with the huge volume of information and services which could be potentially provided by many actors to the drivers while they are on trip.

Thanks to the efforts of the Industry and Academic Research in the field, the Internet of Things (hereon "IoT") paradigm and technologies are rapidly growing maturity, creating an ideal environment for enabling the concept of "Connected Vehicles". Like any other "thing" in the IoT, every vehicle will provide standard network interfaces and APIs towards in-the-cloud, service-enabling ICT platforms, realizing a vehicle "virtualization" which will allow service providers to reach different vehicles drivers through a uniform interface.

In the domain of Connected Vehicles, the service provider role could be potentially played by many actors like road infrastructure managers, city managers, tourist agencies and organizations, car insurance companies.

This short paper will showcase the iCore Project [1] approach for instantiating an IoT architecture to support the Connected Vehicle paradigm. In the following we will briefly introduce the key concepts and novelties of the iCore Project architecture for IoT, then the Smart City – Transportation Use Case will be described.

© ICST Institute for Computer Sciences, Social Informatics and Telecommunications Engineering 2016
B. Mandler et al. (Eds.): IoT 360° 2015, Part II, LNICST 170, pp. 158–161, 2016.
DOI: 10.1007/978-3-319-47075-7_19

2 The iCore Project

In the context of the IoT landscape, the iCore Project proposes a multi-level architecture based on cognitive technology, aiming at reducing the complexity of creating and deploying services in different IoT domains (transportation, logistics, healthcare, home and office automation). The iCore Architecture defines three levels for and IoT platforms: the Service Level, the Composite Virtual Object Level and the Virtual Object Level.

The **Service Level** lays at the topmost level of the iCore IoT architecture. The Service Level is responsible for processing the end user requests (in the context of this use case, the end user is the car driver) and detecting the best way to process the service request. This is accomplished exploiting techniques belonging to the Cognitive Science and Knowledge Based Reasoning, leveraging the big amount of data from the real world objects collected by the lower levels of the architecture, and it results in the selection of the most suitable Composite Virtual Object (hereon, "CVO") to be executed, according to the available Real World Knowledge.

The **Composite Virtual Object Level** is the "composition" layer of the iCore Architecture. This level provides the Execution Engine for processing the data coming from the virtualized objects/sensor and for controlling the virtualized objects/actuators, and the unit of work to be executed is defined as a Composite Virtual Object (CVO). In the context of this use case, the role of the Execution Engine has been played by a highly scalable event-based composition engine, which allows to define the CVO logic based on an "event/action" paradigm. The CVOs available for execution are published in a common CVO Repository.

The **Virtual Object Level** is the "virtualization" layer of the iCore Architecture. This level provides the Virtual Object Container which hosts the Virtual Objects and allows the exposure of a "virtual" and common interface from a real object (either a sensor or an actuator) towards the upper levels of the architecture. This approach has the great advantage of "decoupling" the real object from the other parts of the architecture, allowing the reuse of the same "virtual" interface whenever the "real" object hardware implementation is changed. The available Virtual Objects are registered in a common VO Registry, alongside with metadata (e.g. geographic location). The VO Registry provides query facilities based on RDF/SPARQL [2] in order to identify the VO that best suites a given context/situation.

3 The Smart-City Transportation Use Case

The iCore project Architecture for IoT has been instantiated to showcase the value of the architecture for deploying a Service Platform for the Connected Vehicles. The specific demonstrator, described in the following, has been called "Smart City - Transportation Use Case Demo".

3.1 The Storyboard

The Driver is driving her "Connected Car": the Connected Car is equipped with an advanced Infotainment System, exposed as a Virtual Object towards the iCore platform. The advanced infotainment system sends data to the platform (GPS position, speed), receives and displays messages/alerts about services availability, allows the driver to activate available services on demand and receives and displays informative messages sent by the services being executed.

While on trip, the driver is notified that the service "Parking Around Me" is available. As soon as he/she activates the service through the Infotainment System, the service provides to the Infotainment System an information message with the real-time availability of places in the parking lots nearby the current location of the driver.

While the driver proceeds, the platform is able to detect that he/she is driving towards a recurrent destination for such a user because the iCore system is increasing its own Real World Knowledge each time the user activates the service. In this case, the platform informs the Driver about the availability of the new service "Parking at Destination", and as soon as the Driver activates the new service the Infotainment display shows the availability of places in the parking lots nearby the final destination of the driver.

3.2 The iCore Architecture Instantiation

The following figures describes the instantiation of the iCore Architecture for the Smart City – Transportation Use Case.

3.3 Behind the Scenes: Playing the Storyboard

The Advanced Car Infotainment System is connected to the iCore Platform in two ways: (i) it interacts with the Service Management Unit shown in Fig. 1 for being notified of available services and request services and (ii) as a Virtual Object because it can send GPS/speed information messages and it can receive and display "generic" information messages and alerts from the services executed on the platform.

While driving the user activates his/her Infotainment System which interacts with the Service Management Unit to discover the available services. If no recurrent destination is recognized by the system, the Service Management Unit proposes to the Driver the "Parking Around Me" Service.

When the driver generates a new service request, the Service Management Unit creates a CVO execution request to the CVO Container; the requested CVO exploits the Parking System Virtual Object for interfacing an Open Data service made available by the City which provides real-time parking data.

It is worth noting that the CVO Container does not bind to a VO directly, but it is instructed to use a specific Parking System Virtual Object based on the location of the Driver (e.g. the Parking Open Data of a specific city). This feature allows the CVO to have a context-aware behavior.

While the Driver progresses on his/her trip, the Destination Learning and Detection system becomes aware that the Driver is on a recurrent trip, towards a recurrent

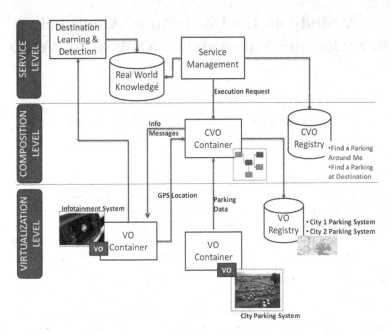

Fig. 1. The smart city transportation use case architecture

destination. This is achieved exploiting knowledge on user behavior obtained applying learning techniques to previously acquired data from the Car Virtual Object, and it allows the platform to identity a different CVO that can be executed. This CVO will provide a different parking suggestion, exploiting both the current position and the final destination, and possibly taking into account predicted traffic flows and situation.

Both the "Parking Around Me" as well as the "Parking at Destination" services will deliver the parking information to the Driver through the Car Display Virtual Object, and the Infotainment System will display it to the Driver. This architectural choice of having a Virtual Object Level allows (i) to decouple the Infotainment interface (Virtual Object) from the actual implementation (Real Object), and (ii) to retain the low level details of the Infotainment functions in the hand of the Car Maker/Car Maker Provide, who can be aware of specific constraints (e.g. avoid to show messages in particular conditions).

Acknowledgments. The work described in this paper has been carried on in the context of the iCore Project [1], partially funded by the European Commission in the context of the 7th Framework Program. Parts of this work (concepts, ideas, artifacts and architectural components) are due to the efforts of the partners belonging to the iCore Project Consortium

References

1. The iCore Project. http://www.iot-icore.eu
2. SPARQL. http://www.w3.org/TR/rdf-sparql-query

A Study on the Detection of Abnormal Behavior and Vulnerability Analysis in BYOD

Taeeun Kim[(⊠)]

Korea Internet & Security Agency, Seoul, South Korea
tekim31@kisa.or.kr

Abstract. When many companies recently introduced BYOD (Bring Your Own Device), i.e. allowing employees to use personal mobile devices at work, they also adopted the NAC and MDM system for prevention of confidential information leakage, access control and efficient user management. As the access control policy of the NAC and MDM system is uniformly applied to users, however, they cannot be aggressive in implementing BYOD since there are security threats due to the frequent loss and theft of devices and low security. Accordingly, it is necessary to be able to flexibly set up policies and detect and control abnormal users by collecting personalized context information. This paper proposes a behavior-based abnormality detection method that detects abnormal behavior by classifying vulnerabilities occurring in the BYOD environment and patterning various users' information use contexts.

Keywords: Mobile · BYOD · Security · Context information · Behavior pattern analysis

1 Introduction

As the use of employee-owned mobile devices is recently changing the working environment, the concept of BYOD (Bring Your Own Device) is drawing attention as a new corporate working environment. BYOD refers to the case of employees using their own mobile devices like notebooks, tablets and smartphones to access internal data and handle business. It can be expected to improve productivity and reduce costs.

As the appearance of new IT environments like BYOD increases convenience, there tends to be security problems like the leakage of enterprise data as personal devices are accessing the internal infrastructure of enterprises. A research found that personal devices can be easily attacked due to loss, theft and low security, and consequently the internal infrastructure of enterprises are accessed and attacked frequently [1].

For BYOD security, the NAC (Network Access Control) for network access control security and the MDM (Mobile Device Management) for mobile device control are proposed, but they certainly have limitations. The NAC controls users by authenticating users when they access the internal infrastructure of enterprises, but does not get involved in the user behavior after authentication [2]. As the MDM installs enterprise security programs in personal devices for monitoring and controlling, users may be repulsed by such programs. So it is thought to be far from the goal of BYOD [3]. Accordingly, it is necessary to detect and control abnormality by identifying the

© ICST Institute for Computer Sciences, Social Informatics and Telecommunications Engineering 2016
B. Mandler et al. (Eds.): IoT 360° 2015, Part II, LNICST 170, pp. 162–167, 2016.
DOI: 10.1007/978-3-319-47075-7_20

information generated by devices and users in order to respond to various contexts occurring in the BYOD environment [4].

This paper proposes a method of using the scenarios of abnormal behavior occurring in the BYOD work environment to classify vulnerabilities, and capitalizing on the characteristics of users and devices and various service use elements to generate pattern data and detect abnormal use behavior. In the BYOD environment various elements, such as diverse devices and access environments, exist, and these characteristics make it possible to analyze personal access/use through patterning. The proposed method patterns service-level use contexts identical to users' corporate business environments, and predicts the probability of new use behavior occurrence based on patterned past data. It compares the probability of users' past behavior and the one of present behavior to detect abnormal behavior. Chapter 2 analyzes the technological trends in protection of internal resources of enterprises in the BYOD environment and the methods of collecting context information. Chapter 3 proposes the method of patterning service use behavior and detecting abnormal use behavior in the BYOD environment. Chapter 4 is the conclusion which discusses how to apply the proposed method to the BYOD environment and the direction of future researches.

2 Related Work

The NAC security technology targeting the BYOD environment checks whether user devices comply with the security policy before accessing the network and controls network access.

The NAC blocks infected PCs' access to the network to prevent the diffusion of malware on the enterprise network. Currently it provides wired and wireless integrated security functions, such as IP-based access control, authentication of mobile terminals, terminal security and integrity validation. As the primary purposes of the NAC itself are user authentication and access control, however, it is lacking in the ability to detect and respond to the abnormal behavior of users or devices after network access. Also, as it focuses on authentication of registered users, it is lacking in the function to authenticate/manage devices [3, 4].

Accordingly, the BYOD environment has distinctive security requirements, i.e. protecting enterprise data by isolating users engaged in abnormal behavior, as well as the utilization of various personal devices and the guaranteeing of business continuity. Therefore, the NAC solution alone cannot handle security issues in the BYOD environment.

The MDM technology uses the OTA (Over The Air) to remotely registers/manages mobile devices that are powered on through the administrator authority regardless of time and place, stop the use of lost devices and track devices [5].

The MDM system-based access control method, which can directly control personal devices in the BYOD environment, has problems. As the MDM is an application, it is difficult to control and monitor the access to other applications. Also, it is impossible to analyze mobile devices' behavior with regard to network data. More than anything else, due to demands for protection of privacy, users are reluctant to install the

MDM agent in their personal devices. So it is difficult to popularize and diffuse it. Furthermore, the cost of continuously managing the versions of various terminal devices will increase.

3   Proposed Method

This proposed method selects access/use behavior elements occurring in the process of using business service and uses them as user behavior patterns in order to detect abnormal use behavior. It selects not only the network traffic characteristics, but also atypical data, such as the user's device type, access time (during business hours, outside of business hours, etc.), access location (in the company, outside of the company, etc.) and use time, and uses them to pattern users' access. It also patterns the information generated while using business service and compares it with the existing identical access patterns to detect abnormal use behavior.

3.1   Definition of Security Vulnerabilities and Abnormal Behavior Scenarios in the BYOD Environment

3.1.1   Normal Users' Malicious Information Leaks

Normal users refer to users authorized to access the service of the enterprise. The normal user can maliciously access/download important information of the enterprise and leak it to the outside after authentication.

As existing security systems, i.e. the NAC and MDM, perceive them as employees who were normally authenticated and conduct business, they cannot detect abnormal behavior. As corporate information and personal information are leaked by internal users frequently, and such leaks cannot be detected, it is impossible to control abnormal behavior.

3.1.2   Theft of Devices by Malicious Users

Many users do not lock their personal devices in most cases, and store the ID/PW for accessing business service often. However, it is difficult to force security measures on personal devices, e.g. locking and cancelation of automatic access.

In this context, malicious users can steal normal users' devices and access corporate service very easily, and existing security systems do not have any method of perceiving them as abnormal behavior (Fig. 1).

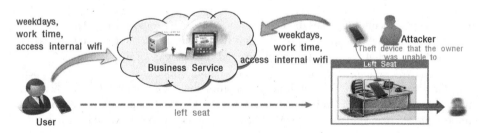

Fig. 1. Device theft scenario

3.1.3   Attackers Using Devices Infected with Malware to Access Internal Resources

The attacker may attempt to access internal service by infecting the devices of employees with malware. As the attacker tries to access the business service using the devices of normal users in case of this attack, it is difficult to detect abnormal behavior.

Recently enterprise agents are installed to prevent device problems, e.g. infection with malware, by checking if vaccines are installed when business service is provided, but since it is impossible to detect all malware, it is impossible to defend against such attacks all the time.

3.2   Configuration of the Experimental Environment and Definition of Context Information

The structure of the corporate business environment and system is illustrated in Fig. 2. The context information is collected through the network traffic, collected during users' Captive Portal connection and use of business service. This patterned information will be used to detect users' abnormal behavior, and abnormal users or devices will be controlled in real time.

Meanings as user behavior will be imparted to the data generated by various devices of users and the access/use context, and this data will be processed into context information. The context information is defined as one of the set of attribute ranges for patterning behavior, and this defined information is used for comparison to detect abnormal behavior.

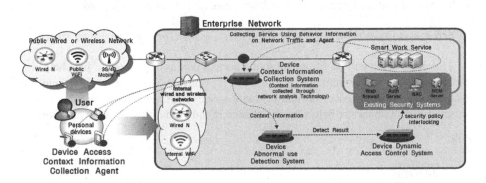

Fig. 2. BYOD and the structure and security system of the smart work environment

3.3   How to Pattern Service Use Information

In the BYOD environment, users use their own devices to access the enterprise network and use services. The corporate business services provide users with the business environment through fixed services (bulletin board, e-mail, schedule management, etc.). The context information, generated when users use such business services, will be used to constitute generalized behavior models that users' behavior can represent.

To pattern the behavior of use context information, existing business service pages will be analyzed and structuralized using the web crawler. Each node (page) of this structuralized service will be connected to the behavior information used by users. In the context information, generated when users use services, the URL information will be connected to the node information of the structuralized service data and accumulated as service use behavior data.

3.4   Use Behavior Analysis and Abnormal Behavior Detection Method

The use behavior throughout the access cycle will be analyzed using users' accumulated service use behavior information, and compared with past use patterns to detect abnormal behavior.

3.4.1   Analysis of Use Behavior Throughout the Access Cycle

The behavior occurrence of each node of business service will be analyzed by accumulating the behavior information occurring when individual users use services throughout the access cycle.

3.4.2   Detection of Abnormal Use Behavior

The behavior information, collected and analyzed throughout the access cycle of users, will be compared with the past use behavior information that has the same access context information, and the overall behavior occurrence probability and the occurrence probability of each node will be compared to detect abnormal behavior.

To detect changes in overall behavior occurrence, as illustrated in Fig. 3, the error of the present and past behavior occurrence probability will be calculated.

$$Error = sqrt((present\ \#1 - past\ \#1)2) + \ldots + sqrt((present\ \#n - past\ \#n)2)$$

This error value will be compared to the normal permissible range of past behavior information. To supplement the false positive occurring when only the change in overall behavior occurrence (normal behavior range: error value < permissible range) is used to detect abnormal behavior, the change in individual items will be additionally

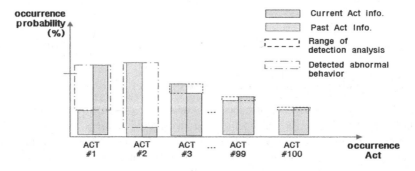

Fig. 3. Detection of abnormal behavior through analysis of use behavior

compared to the permissible range of normal behavior. (Normal behavior range: change in normal behavior of individual items is X% or lower).

4 Conclusions

Existing security systems, which manage access times, will have difficulties detecting users' abnormal use in the BYOD environment. Also, existing security technologies will have a hard time detecting the loss or theft of devices or theft of accounts, which is unknown to users, or normal users' malicious information leakage. This paper used various environmental factors to pattern and analyze user behavior in order to detect whether the behavior of business service users is abnormal. The authors will use stored user behavior to find additional methods of patterning user behavior, and minimize false positives by diversifying detection methods and applying commercial services.

Acknowledgments. This work was supported by the ICT R&D program of MSIP/IITP. [R0101-15-0026, The Development of Context-Awareness based Dynamic Access Control Technology for BYOD, Smartwork Environment].

References

1. Miller, K.W.: BYOD: security and privacy considerations. IT Prof. **14**(5), 53–55 (2012)
2. Singh, M., Patterh, M.S.: Formal specification of common criteria based access control policy model. Int. J. Netw. Secur. **10**(3), 232–241 (2010)
3. Singh, M., Patterh, M.S.: Formal specification of common criteria based access control policy model. Int. J. Netw. Secur. **10**(3), 232–241 (2010)
4. Singh, M., Patterh, M.S., Kim, T.-H.: A formal policy oriented access control model for secure enterprise network environment. Int. J. Secur. Appl. **3**(2), 1–14 (2009)
5. Rhee, K., Jeon, W., Won, D.: Security requirements of a mobile device management system. Int. J. Secur. Appl. **6**(2), 353–358 (2012)

Mobile App for Public Transport: A Usability and User Experience Perspective

Anaïs Luisa Habermann[(✉)], Kai Kasugai, and Martina Ziefle

Communication Science, Human-Computer Interaction Center (HCIC),
RWTH Aachen University, Aachen, Germany
{habermann,kasugai,ziefle}@comm.rwth-aachen.de

Abstract. The fast progress of smart devices and applications in the mobility sector open up a huge potential for mobility services that allow for an individualization of mobility patterns. In combination with an increasing infrastructure of public transport and diverse means of transportation, novel mobility concepts represent a promising solution to societal changes and mobility needs. However, the increasing functionality and multitude of options add to the complexity of using those services. The research is embedded into an interdisciplinary project – Mobility Broker – in which the central platform for planning and booking a journey using different public means of transport is developed. Different from other approaches, users are integrated in all stages of technical development. The paper reports on an empirical study in which the usability of the first prototype of the smart phone application was tested. Findings show that interface design and visual ergonomics are quite mature at this stage. Implications of findings are discussed and future research lines are explicated.

Keywords: Mobility services · Smart apps · Intermodal mobility · Usability · Interface design

1 Introduction

Mobility is a topic as old as mankind. Be it for leisure or business, people need to travel. Recent ICT developments promise to offer potent and ubiquitous mobility services [1]. Travel services delivered by small screen devices are highly developed [2], thus, travel and mobile services can be retrieved at any time, at any place, with travel information being wirelessly delivered, continuously updated, context-adaptive, and even targeted to user profiles [3]. Different people use different means of travel. Also, they use different methods to plan their journey, which reflect and affect the preferred means of transportation [4]. There are numerous services that help to find routes and offers for travelling by public transport, such as airplane, train, or bus or by individual transport by car. All means of transportation have certain limits and are more useful for certain distances. Except for long range travelling, for which the airplane stays unrivaled, the private car seems to be the most flexible and comfortable means of travel. In combination with an increasing infrastructure of public transport and diverse means of transportation, novel mobility concepts represent a promising solution to societal

B. Mandler et al. (Eds.): IoT 360° 2015, Part II, LNICST 170, pp. 168–174, 2016.
DOI: 10.1007/978-3-319-47075-7_21

changes and mobility needs [5]. Until now, it is rather cumbersome to plan a journey using a combination of different public transport services, let alone to book all parts of a so called mixed-mode journey, as it involves the consultation of numerous websites that offer planning and/or booking of one specific service only. This is where the project Mobility Broker comes into play [6].

The project aims at providing a central platform for both, planning and booking of a journey including all kinds of public means of transport, as well as semi public individual traffic, such as car sharing or e-bike rental. Barriers that result from the complexity of combining the results of several search engines and of using a variety of payment services could be overcome with such a service. Hopefully, this will contribute to an increased use of public transport compared to the use of private cars. The interdisciplinary project is lead by the local public transport provider, teaming up with IT service providers and research institutes from different disciplines to gain a holistic understanding. Both, a website offering mixed-mode routing and booking, and a smart phone application with a similar functional range are developed. As such, Mobility Broker is implemented resting on a well-designed server back end – current fundamental research regards the necessary system architecture to develop a single point of contact for travelers (see [7]). As a strong focus on end users' requirements regarding the front-end is a major aspect of the project, in all stages of technical development, feedback of potential users is integrated into future prototype variants.

2   Methodology

The evaluation of an initial prototype consisted of three parts. The first part referred to mobility requirements, which were assessed prior to the evaluation of the prototype. Then, participants were asked to interact with the prototype, carrying out typical tasks in the context of city mobility. Finally, participants were requested to evaluate the ease of navigation and the suitability of the interface design. Figure 1 pictures the schematic procedure of the approach.

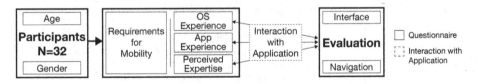

Fig. 1. Design of empirical approach.

2.1   Procedure and Experimental Design

Participants were asked to solve prototypic tasks by interacting with the application. For comparison reasons, each participant was given the same testing scenario in the same order. Figure 2 shows snapshots from the application screen, when tasks were solved. After participants had completed the tasks, they assessed the perceived ease of navigation and the perceived interface quality, each addressing different aspects (see next sections).

Fig. 2. Left: menu to select "Zuhause" (Home; Task 1). Center left: saving of a connection as a favorite (Task 2). Center right: menu to create a new mobility profile (Task 3). Right: map to find the closest bus stop near the current location (Task 4).

2.2 Measuring of Perceived Ease of Navigation

The perceived ease of navigation through the app's menu structure was evaluated through questions regarding the participants' perceived (dis)orientation when navigating through the menu [8]. Each one of four statements (Table 1) had to be (dis)-agreed to on a five-point Likert-scale. The items included "I knew where I was currently located in the menu", "I knew where to go next", "I did not feel lost in the menu" as well as "I knew how to reach a specific function".

Table 1. Items to evaluate interface quality.

	Items (1 = fully disagree; 5 = fully agree)
Use of colors	"The choice of colors is appealing to me." "In my opinion, the application is too colorful." (*) "The colors change too often." (*) "The choice of colors is adhered to consequently."
Relation of textual and graphical elements	"Overall, the application seems to be graphically overloaded." "In my opinion, the relation between text and graphical elements is well-balanced." "Overall, the application is too heavy on the text."
Visual ergonomics	"In general, the contrast between the elements/objects and the background is too low." (*) "I am able to identify all objects without difficulties." "Very often, the typing is too small." (*) "I can read all texts without difficulties." "I can identify some of the elements on the interface with difficulties only." (*)

2.3 Measuring of Perceived Interface Quality

To evaluate different facets of interface design, items were developed for "Use of colors", "Relation between textual and graphical elements" and "Visual ergonomics". The Likert scaling used for each item ranged from 1 = "I fully disagree" to 5 = "I fully agree". Scores of negatively formulated items were inversed (marked by (*) in Table 1). Items were summed up to a global score for "Use of colors" and "Visual ergonomics", all others were evaluated individually. All items are given in Table 1.

2.4 Participants

32 participants took part in the user test (50 % women). 18 were students and 16 (self-) employed. The average age was M = 29.6 years (SD = 8.6) on a range from 20 to 58 years. Participants were screened with respect to their mobility habits, their familiarity with mobility apps and their technical expertise.

Mobility Habits: 29 out of 32 users reported to go by foot on a daily basis. All participants used bus and car several times a week or even daily. A small group (N = 8) indicated to use the bicycle daily. 26 participants used trains more than monthly. Most of the participants (N = 27) reported to have used bike rental ever and 21 never used car sharing. 50 % of participants indicated not to have used ridesharing so far.

Experience with Mobility Applications: All participants were highly accustomed to international (Google Maps), nationwide (DB Navigator, Öffi, BlaBlaCar, qixxit, Pendel Panda, DriveNow, Mitfahrgelegenheit, moovel, allryder) and regional (ASEAG mobil, AVV connect, VRR App) trip assistant applications. Especially the DB Navigator was well known (78 %), but also Google Maps (78 %) and the local bus company's app - ASEAG mobil (56 %).

Technical Expertise: All participants had technical experience using smart small screen devices (26 out of 32 participants used the Android operating system that was also used in the experiment). Also, participants' self-reported technical self-confidence [9] yielded high scores. On a scale from 0 to 100 (very low to very high technical self-confidence), the participants reached 81.7 (SD = 14.4) on average. However, a gender effect was found: Women estimated their own technical self-confidence lower (M = 74.7, SD = 16.8) than men (M = 88.8, SD = 6.1, t = 3.1, p < .05).

3 Results

Data are assessed descriptively. We report on the perceived ease of navigation, followed by an outline of outcomes on the perceived interface quality.

3.1 Evaluation of Perceived Ease of Navigation

The acceptance of smart applications depends on a high usability. When looking at the perceived orientation in the menu, findings show promising results. Participants largely agreed to know where they were situated within the menu while solving the tasks (M = 4.4, SD = 0.9). When asked about the menu structure, on average, users stated to know where to go next (M = 3.8, SD = 1.2). They did not feel lost in the menu (M = 3.7, SD = 1.2). Furthermore, participants reported to know how to find specific functions (M = 3.4, SD = 1.2) (see Fig. 3, left).

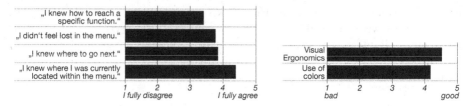

Fig. 3. Left: perceived quality of navigation. Right: perceived quality of visual ergonomics.

3.2 Evaluation of Perceived Interface Quality

On average, ratings show a high satisfaction with the given design. Visual ergonomics was rated with 4.5 out of 5 points maximum (SD = 0.5). Also the use of colors reached satisfying scores (M = 4.2, SD = 0.5) (see Fig. 3, right). When focusing on the relation between textual and graphical elements, ratings reveal a positive perception. On average, the relation

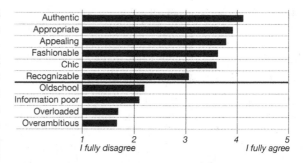

Fig. 4. Rating of the interface design with adjectives.

was judged with M = 4.2 (SD = 1.0), neither too much text (M = 1.7, SD = 0.8), nor too much graphics was used (M = 1.7, SD = 0.8). As many applications profit from an "appealing" overall design, participants were asked to describe the design with adjectives by rating the appropriateness of each adjective to the design, using a Likert scale (1 = "I fully disagree." to 5 = "I fully agree."). Figure 4 shows that adjectives associated with negative properties ("old school", "information poor", "overloaded", "over ambitiously colorful") had a much lower score than positive adjectives, such as "authentic", "appropriate" or "appealing". It is important to notice that the adjective "recognizable" had the lowest score of all positive adjectives.

4   Discussion and Future Work

This paper reports on the usability of a novel mobility app that provides a central platform to plan and book a journey using all kinds of public and semi public means of transport. In order to understand the usability in an early stage of development, ease of navigation and overall appearance of the visual design have been assessed, regarding interface quality, visual ergonomic, and the balance between textual and graphical elements. Results show that the current visual design and the perceived ease of interacting with the application receive a positive feedback by participants. However, in this research design a comparably small, quite educated, and technology affine group was examined. At this stage of research, the group is adequate in order to get insights from a benchmark approach. As travelers will be increasingly characterized by diversity, including less educated and less healthy users as well senior travelers, less familiarized with the usage of small screen devices in general and electronic mobility services in particular, we will have to replicate the findings in a broader user group. It will be of vital importance to collect data about navigation performance (effectiveness and efficiency). It is planned to assess the fit of the interface for persons with visual problems or otherwise physically impaired persons, to include their special needs in the development process [10]. Future research will address the role of navigation aids specifically designed for the use in cities [11], in order to enhance the overall experience with usage of electronic mobility services delivered by smart devices [12]. So far, the usability of the application was only tested in a static, quiet and thus, unrealistic experimental setting. A critical test of the real-world suitability will be carried out in the next six months. Participants will use the application during travelling and the usability of context sensitive information will be under study. Another question regards the social acceptance of using connected mobility services. Recent studies show that users are quite clairaudient regarding privacy [13] and safety issues [14] when using smart mobility services. A sensitive trade-off between mobility and travel assistance on the one hand and the disliked possibility to be tracked and monitored on the other hand has to be addressed.

Acknowledgment. This research was funded by the Federal Ministry of Economic Affairs and Energy. (Project Mobility Broker, grant reference no. 01 ME 12135A). Furthermore, thanks go to Christian Paul and Patric Dressia for research assistance.

References

1. Camacho, T.D., Foth, M., Rakotonirainy, A.: Pervasive technology and public transport: opportunities beyond telematics. Pervasive Comput. **12**(1), 18–25 (2013)
2. Emmanouilidis, C., Koutsiamanis, R.-A., Tasidou, A.: Mobile guides: taxanomy of architecture, context awareness, technologies and applications. J. Netw. Comput. Appl. **35**(1), 103–125 (2013)
3. Beul-Leusmann, S., Samsel, C., Wiederhold, M., Krempels, K.-H., Jakobs, E.-M., Ziefle, M.: Usability evaluation of mobile passenger information systems. In: Marcus, A. (ed.) DUXU 2014, Part I. LNCS, vol. 8517, pp. 217–228. Springer, Heidelberg (2014)
4. Zaunbrecher, B., Beul-Leusmann, S., Ziefle, M.: Laypeople's perspectives on electromobility: a focus group study. In: Giaffreda, R., Cagáňová, D., Li, Y., Riggio, R., Voisard, A. (eds.) Internet of Things. IoT Infrastructures. LNICST, vol. 151, pp. 144–149. Springer, Heidelberg (2014)
5. Ziefle, M., Wilkowska, W.: What makes people change their preferences in public transportation – opinions in different user groups. In: Giaffreda, R., Cagáňová, D., Li, Y., Riggio, R., Voisard, A. (eds.) Internet of Things. IoT Infrastructures. LNICST, vol. 151, pp. 137–143. Springer, Heidelberg (2014)
6. Beutel, M., Gokay, S., Kluth, W., Krempels, K.-H., Samsel, C., Terwelp, C.: Product oriented integration of heterogeneous mobility services. In: 17th ITSC, pp. 1529–1534 (2014)

7. Beutel, M., Gökay, S., Kluth, W., Krempels, K.-H., Samsel, C., Terwelp, C., Wiederhold, M.: Heterogeneous Travel Information Exchange (2015, unpublished)
8. Ziefle, M., Bay, S.: How to overcome disorientation in mobile phone menus: a comparison of two different types of navigation aids. Hum.-Comput. Interact. **21**(4), 393–433 (2006)
9. Beyer, G.: Kontrollüberzeugung im Umgang mit Technik. Rep. Psychol. **9**, 648–693 (1999)
10. Karim, N.A., Nwagboso, C.: Assistive technologies in public transport: meeting the needs of elderly and disabled passengers. In: ICICT, p. 69. IEEE Press, New York (2004)
11. Lyons, G.: The role of information in decision-making with regard to travel. Intell. Trans. Syst. **153**(2), 199–212 (2006)
12. Foth, M., Schroeter, R.: Enhancing the experience of public transport users with urban screens and mobile applications. In: 14th International Academic MindTrek Conference, pp. 33–40. ACM, New York (2010)
13. Schmidt, T., Philipsen, R., Ziefle, M.: From V2X to Control2Trust - why trust and control are major attributes in Vehicle2X technologies. In: Tryfonas, T., Askoxylakis, I. (eds.) HAS 2015. LNCS, vol. 9190, pp. 570–581. Springer, Heidelberg (2015)
14. van Heek, J., Arning, K., Ziefle, M.: Safety and privacy perceptions in public spaces: an empirical study on user requirements for city mobility. In: Giaffreda, R., Cagáňová, D., Li, Y., Riggio, R., Voisard, A. (eds.) Internet of Things. IoT Infrastructures. LNICST, vol. 151, pp. 97–103. Springer, Heidelberg (2014)

Open Platform Within the Smart Health Framework to Support the Development of Recreational Bike Path Applications

Smart Bike Path in the Context of the VAS Strategy in Colombia

Mónica Trujillo$^{(\boxtimes)}$ and Dario Correal

Departamento de Ingeniería de Sistemas y Computación,
Universidad de los Andes, Bogotá, Colombia
{m.trujillo10,dcorreal}@uniandes.com

Abstract. This article describes the design and development of an open data platform that was implemented as part of the Smart Health framework and aimed at supporting the development of Recreational Bike Path applications. Recreational Bike Path programs follow the guidelines of the World Health Organization and seek to reduce the appearance of Chronic Noncommunicable Diseases; these programs, although having great potential, do not have a source of data to investigate their impact or motivate public investment. This paper presents the design of a platform for integrating data through a service REST API by considering Smart Cities architectures as a reference. The final product features an extensible platform that supports basic functionalities, has the capability to integrate other APIs and has the ability to generate open data datasets while following the "Guidelines for the implementation of open data in Colombia".

Keywords: Smart Cities (S-Cities) · Smart Cities architecture · Smart Health (S-Health) · Mobile health (m-health) · Well being · Open data · REST API · Vías Activas y Saludables (VAS) · Ciclovía Recreativa (CR) · Open bike

1 Introduction

Smart Health (S-Health) is the tendency, within the concept of Smart Cities (S-Cities), which aims to improve health services by making them more secure, efficient, equitable and centered on patient comfort; through innovation in computer science, information science and engineering. This research addresses the development of an extensible platform, framed within the S-Health tendency, that provides various functionalities for Recreational Bike Path applications in the context of Colombia's Active and Healthy Paths. The latter are inexpensive public programs to encourage physical activity in a community in order to reduce Chronic Noncommunicable Diseases (NCDs) [1].

© ICST Institute for Computer Sciences, Social Informatics and Telecommunications Engineering 2016
B. Mandler et al. (Eds.): IoT 360° 2015, Part II, LNICST 170, pp. 175–180, 2016.
DOI: 10.1007/978-3-319-47075-7_22

1.1   Conceptual Framework

Smart Cities: The XXI century will be the century of smart cities; in this research, the concept of Smart City refers to the following: "A city that is instrumented, interconnected and people-oriented". Instrumentation enables the real time capture and integration of world data through the use of sensors, smartphones and the web. Interconnection involves the integration of data on a computer platform and the communication of such information among various city services. Intelligent refers to the inclusion of complex analysis, modeling, and the visualization of operational processes for making decisions. Although it is clear that a city's dynamic has its roots in the community, the concept of being people-oriented emphasizes that services should be provided in order to improve the living conditions of its inhabitants.

Smart Health: Medical and public health practice supported on smart mobile devices, with the ability to interconnect devices to applications and other emerging technologies, thus seeking that the health system and the synergy of its components behave more intelligently [2, 3].

Open Data: The philosophy of open data states that some data should be available without the restriction of copyright, patent rights, and other management mechanisms. These data are open to society and anyone can publish and freely use them for any purpose they want [4]. Open data are an opportunity to create value and enhance the creation of new services and economic and social opportunities, when the data and knowledge from all levels of government and business are integrated into applications [5]. In Colombia, the Ministry of Information Technologies and Communications defined the "Guidelines for the implementation of open data in Colombia" [6].

Vías Activas y Saludables (VAS): 63 % of deaths worldwide are caused by NCDs. The World Health Organization has defined a set of guidelines for nations to address this issue. In Colombia, a project called Vías Activas y Saludables [7]—Active and Healthy Paths in English—supports this initiative by temporarily closing some roads for vehicles so that citizens have a safe free space for the practice of physical activity, recreation and healthy use of leisure time. This event takes place on one or more fixed days a week and lasts four hours on average [8].

In the study carried out in [9], 38 bikeways from 11 countries were analyzed and the results showed that Bogotá-Colombia has the world's largest circuit, of 121 km, and a range of 600,000 to 1,400,000 participants per event. VAS are a beneficial cost because, for every dollar invested in Bogota's Ciclovía Recreativa program (CR)—Recreational Bike Paths in English—, US\$3 to US\$4 are saved on the direct costs of health care associated with physical activity. Furthermore, the study concludes that the VAS have other benefits such as the following: helping decrease pollution and noise levels, generating social capital, promoting equity and creating economic opportunities.

1.2   Problem Under Study

Some research highlights the importance of CR programs but indicates situations such as the following: "Although Ciclovía Recreativa programs are promising, the evidence of their effectiveness is limited to cross-sectional studies that have provided limited data to create a framework for future research and monitoring. ..." [9].

Regarding CR, the following was found: lack of data concerning the characteristics of participants; limited data available to other stakeholders interested in their dynamic such as the academic, governmental and business communities; outdated information on the mobile applications that promote them; and unarticulated data unknown by the managers of the program because it was gathered by third-party mobile applications.

As a solution, we proposed implementing an open support platform for health applications development in order to prevent NCDs in the context of CR.

2   Smart Bike Path Platform

2.1   Platform Architecture

The design of the Smart Bike Path platform architecture is based on the architecture proposed for S-Cities in [10, 11] because the scheme is aimed at data management. Figure 1 shows the layers that comprise this architecture. The application layer refers to the applications that consume support services; applications interact directly with citizens and offer them their expertise regarding intelligent cities. Inside this layer there is a sublayer of data acquisition which, in this platform, consists of the sensors of mobile devices such as the following: accelerometers, proximity sensor, GPS, etc.; the collected data are available to the other layers through the application layer.

The data layer comprises data networks and Internet infrastructure that enable communication between applications and the platform, and support the delivery of data to the storage layer. The layer of support services is responsible for arranging data for applications; in smart cities a variety of services must be provided to governments, businesses and citizens. The development of this project has been focused on this layer through the implementation of the API, which represents CR resources.

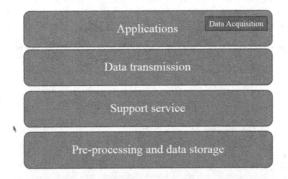

Fig. 1. Platform architecture for information integration.

In the layer of pre-processing and data storage, pre-processing helps detecting and correcting problems related to the quality of data while storage involves the ability to support large-scale complex data with high reliability and scalability; this is achieved through cloud services.

2.2   REST API Services

The REST API (Fig. 2) is a service that uses an HTTP request to provide and consume information from the CR. The pillars of its design were: usefulness, simplicity and value. Usefulness for the end user; simplicity given by the accessibility, ease, speed of implementation and functionality that it provides for developers; and value concerning the benefit generated to the management entities.

The API provides the following services: User represents anyone who attends and uses the spaces and services of the CR to practice recreational activities and sports; Service manages participant information such as age, gender, health risk, disability and activity; Location represents the whereabouts of the user at any given time.

Happen manages information about incidents or events of various types that occur simultaneously to the CR event, such as mobility, security, services or otherwise; events are reported to the platform by users. Via represents the stretch of road that is temporarily open. Place provides information about the location, name, description and pictures of sites that may be of interest to CR users such as parks, tourist sites, hospitals and police, among others; this information is categorized into different types such as art, Bike Path, security, etc.

Benefit includes additional services that can be found on the Bike Path; those offered by the managing entity or the community are included and categorized as art, Bike Path, culture, science, security, sports, technology, tourism and trade. Some CR services may include the following: aerobics, restrooms, bicycle, hydration spot, veterinary service, Physical Activity Recommendations spot—RAFI in Spanish—or bike-school.

Notification contains data from messages aimed at showing users an event, news, service or risk that happens in a path on which the participant is located; these data can be classified according to priority. Service Manager works as a proxy between API services and the services of other REST APIs that are registered on the platform; its purpose is to facilitate the integration of other functionalities.

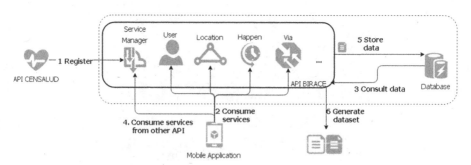

Fig. 2. REST API services and operation.

3 Validation

3.1 Validation Regarding Assessment Criteria of Recreational Bike Paths

In order to estimate the completeness and the value of the potential benefit generated from the platform for the entities responsible of managing the CR in Bogotá, such as the IDRD [12], the sufficiency of the platform regarding the calculation of the assessment measures defined in [13] is estimated. A sufficiency of 70.45 % was obtained in relation with the APIs coverage for calculating the evaluation criteria of bike paths, thus leading to the conclusion that the data collected by the API are relevant and are currently gathered in a non-automated manner by the entities running and investigating CR days.

3.2 Validation of a Case Study

To analyze the platform in terms of its usability for the developer interested in consuming REST API services, a software developer, who was not involved in the design of the platform and does not know the dynamics of bike paths, was selected; these conditions were intentionally sought assuming that other developers do not know these issues in depth. The developer was asked to design an application using the API to analyze the Bike Path Route that is enabled every Sunday from 7:00 a.m. to 2:00 p.m. on the 9th Avenue, between streets 117 and 147, in Bogotá; the simulation of the arrival of users takes a small Bike Path described in "A discrete event simulation model to estimate the number of participants in the ciclovía programs" [14] as a reference.

Figure 3 shows the resulting application. Statistics include: Total participants, Participants by activity, Average time spent on the route, Average time per activity and Participants by health risk. In addition, the following filters are included: age range, range of dates and times, activities, health risks and gender. The use of the API also shows that all the information collected from participants can be published in an open data repository to make it available for further analysis. Particularly, it is possible to use this open data to understand smart cities behavior based on the information obtained from the VAS.

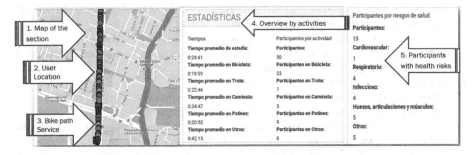

Fig. 3. Overview of the application including event reporting and general statistics.

4 Conclusions and Future Work

The design of the architecture for the information integration platform was developed taking architectures for S-Cities as reference, and is focused on data management and service integration. The module for generating open datasets enables the use of information collected by other parties interested in studying the dynamics of CRs. The platform is extensible in functionality, and experimentation leads to the conclusion that it abstracts the processes of the object of study. Furthermore, the adequacy of the data is evidenced by comparing the services regarding the evaluation criteria of the CR.

The possibilities for future work consider the following three areas: development of applications that use the services of the platform and extend its functionality through integration with other platforms. Integration and support for Internet of Things through the development of services that enable connection with and data collection from devices located on any object such as bicycles or pathways. And ultimately, the analysis of information to be performed using Big Data techniques on future datasets.

References

1. World Health Organization (WHO): Global status report on noncommunicable diseases (2010)
2. Chen, H.: Smart Health and Wellbeing (2011)
3. Ciriello, J.N., Kulatilaka, N., Act, R., Conundrum, T.C.: Smart health community: the hidden value of health information exchange. **16**, 31–37 (2010)
4. Governance, P.: Open Data, Crowdsourcing, and City Planning (2013)
5. Cowan, D., Alencar, P., Mcgarry, F.: Perspectives on open data : issues and opportunties, pp. 1–10 (2014)
6. Ministerio de Tecnologías de la Información y las Comunicaciones: Lineamientos para la implementación de Datos Abiertos en Colombia (2011)
7. Mitchell, A., Voon, T.: Implications of the world trade organization in combating non-communicable diseases. Public Health **125**(12), 832–839 (2011)
8. U. de los A. U. del R. Coldeportes: Manual Vias Activas y Saludables en Colombia (2014)
9. Sarmiento, O., Torres, A.: La ciclovía-recreativa: un programa masivo de recreación con potencial en salud pública. J. Phys. Act. **7**(Suppl. 2), S163–S180 (2010)
10. Wenge, R., Zhang, X., Dave, C., Chao, L.I., Hao, S.: Smart city architecture : a technology guide for implementation and design challenges. 56–69 (2014)
11. Anthopoulos, L., Fitsilis, P.: From digital to ubiquitous cities: defining a common architecture for urban development. In: 2010 Sixth International Conference on Intelligent Environments, pp. 301–306, July 2010
12. Instituto de Recreación y Deportes, IDRD (2015)
13. Sarmiento, O.L., Juliana Gómez, D.F., Medaglia, A., Southern, A., Jacoby, E.: Manual de criterios para la evaluación de las ciclovías recreativas (2012)
14. Andes, U.: A discrete event simulation model to estimate the number of participants in the ciclovia programs. Universidad de los Andes, EBSCO (2013)

Heterogeneous Travel Information Exchange

Markus C. Beutel, Sevket Gökay[✉], Wolfgang Kluth, Karl-Heinz Krempels,
Christian Samsel, Christoph Terwelp, and Maximilian Wiederhold

Information Systems, RWTH Aachen University,
Ahornstr. 55, 52074 Aachen, Germany
goekay@dbis.rwth-aachen.de

Abstract. Travel information brokers are complex systems, dealing
with a large amount of heterogeneous data from various sources. The
exchange and integration of such data is therefore demanding, particularly for small mobility service providers with few IT resources. To face
this problem, this work illustrates a key tool to support information and
service integration. On a conceptual level, we present a travel information broker system architecture and respective information flows. Additionally, we describe data exchange related to system components, e.g.,
intermodal routing, pricing and accounting. On this basis, we developed
and tested a communication adapter that enables and eases communication between the core system and second party service providers.
Furthermore we outline the method of extending public transportation
routing with information about sharing services. This enables travelers
to query combined information about public transport, bikesharing as
well as carsharing services using a single application.

Keywords: Bikesharing · Carsharing · e-mobility · Intermodal travel ·
Smart mobility · Travel information

1 Introduction

Combining diverse travel services (e.g., traditional public transport, parking services, carsharing, ridesharing) results in better offers and better service coverage
compared to individual services [1]. Eventually this leads to a higher acceptance
of alternative (compared to using a private car) services among travelers and
therefore better sustainability. Because of the complexity and amount of these
services, a supporting information system serving as single point of contact for
travelers is required. Unfortunately, integration of diverse travel information is
a demanding task. On the one hand, mobility modes differ significantly in structure, i.e., individual transport vs. train schedule, and payment model, i.e., single
ticket vs. subscriptions. On the other hand, travel information systems vary in
extent and functionalities. Either way, the respective data is heterogeneous and
has to be integrated effectively. Hence, this work focuses on the technological
data integration of different data sources and data types, to subsequently lower
the burden for mobility providers to join a collaborative service offering. For this

© ICST Institute for Computer Sciences, Social Informatics and Telecommunications Engineering 2016
B. Mandler et al. (Eds.): IoT 360° 2015, Part II, LNICST 170, pp. 181–187, 2016.
DOI: 10.1007/978-3-319-47075-7_23

purpose, we hereby refine the conceptual travel information broker architecture introduced in [2] and illustrate the workings and interaction of key components. We describe a communication adapter which enables optimized data exchange between mobility service providers and the core system. This solution allows second party providers to join the system and use its resources, e.g., intermodal routing and accounting, with little individual integration efforts.

2   Related Work

In general, travel information provision via information systems has been investigated and improved in several areas in the last years. Crucial for the success of these information systems are two main factors: (a) the quality of the provided information in terms of comprehensiveness and completeness and (b) the systems' usability. In [3] a technology acceptance model is applied to evaluate the usability of mobile passenger information systems. According to [4] travelers are highly frustrated when using public transportation because of lacking information provided whereas [5] also underline the importance of real time data provision. As a consequence, providing better information by integration of heterogeneous mobility services is a prominent research field.

Modern travel information applications like Transit App or Qixxit[1] differ in extend and functionalities. Above that, different research projects investigate issues related to travel information integration: For example the IMA System is an open agent based mobility platform, that combines heterogeneous mobility services, e.g. ridesharing [6]. The European research project SUPERHUB is another open platform for urban mobility, that enables multimodal journey planning. The system incorporates intermodal routing [7] and encourages sustainable travel behavior by a behavior management component [8]. Another example is the B2B platform OLYMPUS[2], which provides flexible multimodal transport solutions with focus on electric vehicle sharing [9] and the Integrated Mobility Platform (IMP)[3].

3   Use Cases

Using the integration method presented in Sect. 4, a platform is enabled to offer continuous intermodal travel in terms of planning, booking, ticketing and assisting. The following use cases exemplify the advantages of information exchange and integration.

---

[1] http://transitapp.com, http://www.qixxit.de (German).

[2] http://www.proeftuin-olympus.be/en.

[3] http://www.mobility.siemens.com/mobility/global/en/integrated-mobility/imp/pages/default.aspx.

Traditional Travel Without Data Integration. Adam has a business meeting with a project partner in St. Augustin (a suburb of Bonn), Germany in the afternoon. Currently he is planing his trip in his office in Aachen, Germany. He queries the website of Deutsche Bahn which returns an itinerary from Aachen Main Station to Bonn Main Station. To get to Aachen Main Station he asks a colleague which bus to take and to get from Bonn to St. Augustin he is thinking of taking a cab. Because the meeting is important and Adam knows neither the overall duration of the travel nor the price and also feels insecure about changing buses and trains, he opts for a rental car instead.

New Generation of Travel Supported by Data Integration. Bella is Adam's deputy and is in the same situation one day later. She queries a travel information system which integrates data of multiple mobility services. The system returns an itinerary involving a rental bike from the office to Aachen Main Station, trains from Aachen to Bonn and finally a reserved carsharing vehicle to St. Augustin. The system also shows the exact price and travel duration and allows to book the complete itinerary with a single click. After booking, the itinerary as well as tickets are transferred to her mobile device so she can check for train departure information easily and therefore feels secure to reach the destination in time.

Bella's travel costs less than half of Adam's and is almost as fast, while being more environment-friendly.

4   Heterogeneous Data Integration

This section outlines the technical infrastructure proposed for data integration and the required technology.

4.1   IT Architecture and System Components

Based on the general architecture presented in [2] we created a technical system infrastructure to support intermodal travel. The current architecture is depicted in Fig. 1. The traveler interacts with the system using a mobile application or a web portal which connects to the backend using the standardized APIs, URA2 and URA3. The URA interface family is widely used, i.e., by Transport for London[4].

The architecture of the backend resembles a distributed system consisting of different functional components and multiple internal and external endpoints. The following components represent existing functionality: The *Dispatcher* component serves as a single endpoint for all API calls from mobile applications and the web frontend. The dispatcher re-routes and combines requests, responses and push notifications to their respective receivers. The *Intermodal Router* serves exhaustive door to door routing queries and serves as a merger of the different routing

---

[4] http://www.tfl.gov.uk/info-for/open-data-users/.

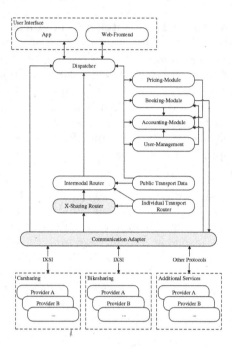

Fig. 1. Technical architecture.

techniques. It is invoked by the dispatcher. The Intermodal Router is based on the Raptor algorithm [10] for fast public transportation routing, using real time timetable data. The *Individual Transport Router* serves pedestrian and (private) bicycle routing queries. It uses established routing algorithms for finding shortest paths in networks. The *Pricing* module augments routing information supplied by the Intermodal Router with pricing information. The overall journey price is composed of a price per route segment which is handled individually. Prices for public transportation are modeled locally in the pricing module and can be calculated via stop numbers, distance, areas, daytime etc. Season tickets are also considered if specified in the request. For sharing service fees, the external sharing system is inquired via the communication adapter. This allows service providers to handle pricing corresponding to their individual tariff systems. The *Booking* module is responsible for forwarding booking requests to the respective mobility service and delivering the resulting ticket to the client. Price information is delivered to the billing module. The *Accounting / Billing* module collects all billing information from service providers to allow a real time cost check as well a monthly billing. The *User Management* component is responsible for creating and modifying user accounts and user authorization. If required, user data is also exchanged with external data using the Communication Adapter.

In addition, the Communication Adapter and X-Sharing Router are introduced in this work: *Communication Adapter* is responsible for all the communication with second party mobility providers. It supports communication via all noteworthy transport protocols: RESTful (using JSON or XML), SOAP and WebSocket (also using JSON or XML). The adapter exchanges travel information using a variety of open protocols i.e., IXSI (Interface for X-Sharing Information). IXSI [11] allows asynchronous exchange of vehicle sharing information, i.e. availability. The *X-Sharing Router* component extends the Intermodal Router with specific routing using sharing services. It employs real time vehicle availability data to calculate route segments. For faster query times, legs connecting sharing places are precalculated and cached. In order to calculate feasible path towards the destination using individual transport, several restrictions about a realistic routing alternative must be considered. Regular carsharing for example, usually requires the rented vehicle to be returned to exactly the same place it was taken from, which automatically prohibits this mode of transport from appearing in the middle of the journey.

4.2   Information Flow

To clarify how the components interact, consider the information/data flow of an intermodal travel query: Before the actual user interaction, the system has been initialized; all mobility service providers exchanged their availability as well as time table information and the user is registered. The user queries the system for an intermodal itinerary from location A to location B using a mobile app. The Dispatcher forwards the requests to the Intermodal Router which constructs multiple possible itineraries. Simplified, it does so by finding all stops and sharing places in the vicinity of both locations using the Individual Transport Router and finding the best connections between these places using both public transport and sharing service (calculated by the X-Sharing Router). In the next step, these itineraries are forwarded to the Pricing Module which calculates and annotates prices for every route segment. The list of itineraries, including prices, is then supplied to the app, respectively to the user. If the user opts to book a specific itinerary, he or she has to authenticate him or herself which is handled by the User Management (requests are again handled by the Dispatcher). Using the authentication token (supplied by User Management) and unique identifier for desired itinerary (supplied by the Routing), the booking commences: The Booking Module informs mobility services via the Communication Adapter to book the service and forwards the resulting billing information to the Accounting Module and the booking confirmation/ticket to the client. Now all preparation steps for the travel are complete and the user can conduct the travel. During the travel, he or she is notified about changes/updates in her subsequent route segments. Directly after the travel or alternatively at the end of the accounting period, the customer is billed by Accounting Module with the assistance of the User Management (for billing information).

5   Results and Discussion

We contributed a conceptual architecture and depicted the functional information exchange between system components. The solution allows system participation and service provision, based on standardized interface specifications.

We currently have a working instance of the architecture and most components presented in Sect. 4. Travelers are able to query time table information for public transport (buses and trains) and availability information for offered bikesharing pedelecs as well as carsharing vehicles and also book the services. This can be done via a single platform, respectively a single application. The information shown represents real world services/vehicles and by that demonstrate the functionality of the information exchange between systems. The respective services are provided by multiple independent mobility service providers, who operate their own business and IT infrastructure.

Main advantage of this solution is the technological accessibility of the core system towards second party providers with limited integration efforts. These providers can benefit from centralized user interfaces, intermodal routing and accounting functionalities without implementing them individually. Moreover, users benefit from a centralized information system that allows convenient and comprehensive intermodal travel information provision.

Some drawbacks might occur concerning the data management. Sensitive data, e.g., user information is located and aggregated at the centralized core system - instead of separated provider databases. Although standardized interfaces and architectures simplify data exchange, the implementation may be demanding for mobility service providers, especially if they are currently using old-fashioned IT systems.

Future Work and Outlook

The presented IT architecture was continuously refined during development and implementation and probably will be refined and possibly extended even more as required.

The implementation of the Communication Adapter is mature and ready for productive operation, only minor feature enhancements are anticipated. Such enhancements could include support for additional, potentially proprietary, protocols for even more mobility services. Specifically booked parking and/or charging of an electric vehicle appear worthwhile. The X-Sharing Router is currently being implemented. Depending on the initial results, further performance optimization to keep the whole system sufficiently interactive might be required. Besides performance, a specific route's feasibility from a user perspective might also be required to improve (i.e., avoiding slopes for rental bikes).

The overall system is currently partly working and operates in test mode with few test participators. After completion of pending functionalities, specifically full intermodal routing, a holistic field test will be conducted. This field test is supposed to, besides showing the technical feasibility, answer questions regarding the acceptance of such an intermodal travel information system, from providers as well as user perspective.

Acknowledgments. This work was funded by German Federal Ministry of Economic Affairs and Energy for project Mobility Broker (01ME12136).

References

1. Huwer, U.: Public transport and car-sharing - benefits and effects of combined services. Transp. Policy **11**, 77–87 (2004)
2. Beutel, M., Gokay, S., Kluth, W., Krempels, K.H., Samsel, C., Terwelp, C.: Product oriented integration of heterogeneous mobility services. In: IEEE 17th International Conference on Intelligent Transportation Systems, pp. 1529–1534 (2014)
3. Obermeier, M., et al.: Usability evaluation of mobile passenger information systems. In: Marcus, A. (ed.) DUXU 2014, Part I. LNCS, vol. 8517, pp. 217–228. Springer, Heidelberg (2014)
4. Papangelis, K., Sripada, S., Corsar, D., Velaga, N., Edwards, P., Nelson, J.D.: Developing a real time passenger information system for rural areas. In: Yamamoto, S. (ed.) HCI 2013, Part II. LNCS, vol. 8017, pp. 153–162. Springer, Heidelberg (2013)
5. Garcia, C.R., Candela, S., Ginory, J., Quesada-Arenciba, A., Alayon, F.: On route travel assistance for public transport based on android technology. In: 6th International Conference on Innovative Mobile and Internet Services in Ubiquitous Computing (2012)
6. Keiser, J., Masuch, N., Lutzenberger, M., Grunewald, D., Kern, M., Trollmann, F., Acar, E., Avci Salma, C., Dang, X.T., Kuster, C.: IMA-an adaptable and dynamic service platform for intermodal mobility assistance. In: IEEE 17th International Conference on Intelligent Transportation Systems (2014)
7. Hrncir, J., Jakob, M.: Generalised time-dependent graphs for fully multimodal journey planning. In: 16th International IEEE Conference on Intelligent Transportation Systems, pp. 2138–2145 (2013)
8. Wells, S., Forbes, P., Masthoff, J., Gabrielli, S., Jylha, A.: SUPERHUB: integrating digital behaviour management into a novel sustainable urban mobility system. In: 27th International BCS Human Computer Interaction Conference (2013)
9. Buchinger, U., Lindmark, S., Braet, O.: Business model scenarios for an open service platform for multi-modal electric vehicle sharing. In: The Second International Conference on Smart Systems, Devices and Technologies (SMART 2013), pp. 7–14 (2013)
10. Delling, D., Pajor, T.: Werneck, R.F.: Round-based public transit routing. Transp. Sci. 1–14 (2014)
11. Kluth, W., Beutel, M.C., Gökay, S., Krempels, K.H., Samsel, C., Terwelp, C.: IXSI - interface for X-sharing information. In: 11th International Conference on Web Information Systems and Technologies (2015)

S-CUBE

Strain Calibration of Substrate-Free FBG Sensors at Cryogenic Temperature

Venkataraman Narayanan Venkatesan[1,2], Klaus-Peter Weiss[1],
Ram Prakash Bharti[2], Holger Neumann[1],
and Rajinikumar Ramalingam[1(✉)]

[1] Institute for Technical Physics (ITEP),
Karlsruhe Institute of Technology (KIT),
76344 Eggenstein-Leopoldshafen, Germany
rajini-kumar.ramalingam@kit.edu
[2] Department of Chemical Engineering,
Indian Institute of Technology (IIT) Roorkee, Roorkee 247667, India

Abstract. Strain calibration measurements are performed for acrylate coated, substrate-free fiber Bragg grating (FBG) sensors at room temperature of 298 K and cryogenic temperature of 77 K. A 1550 nm Bragg wavelength (λ_B) FBG sensor, with its sensing part not being bonded to any surface, is subjected to axial strain using MTS25 tensile machine available at Cryogenic Material tests Karlsruhe (CryoMaK), KIT. The Bragg wavelength shift ($\Delta\lambda_B$) versus induced strain (ε) is regressed with a linear polynomial function and the strain sensitivity obtained is found to be 0.9 pm/$\mu\varepsilon$ at both the temperatures, verifying that the FBG strain sensitivity is independent of temperature.

Keywords: Fiber Bragg gratings (FBG) · Cryogenic applications · Strain sensitivity · Strain calibration

1 Introduction

Over the years, Fiber Bragg gratings (FBG) are being widely used as reliable sensors to monitor crucial parameters like temperature, strain, flowrate, concentration, etc., in various applications [1–3]. FBG sensors are a good replacement for most of the conventional sensors due to their miniature size, high sensitivity, multiplexing capabilities and immunity to electrical and magnetic fields [4, 5]. They have also been proven to be good candidates for accurate measurements at cryogenic temperatures [6–8]. As documented in many literatures [9–11], FBG is a short segment in the core of an optical fiber which has a periodic variation of refractive index. These gratings are inscribed into the optical fiber using UV interferometer [11]. Due to the varying refractive index of the FBG, one particular wavelength of the incident light is reflected and the others are transmitted, as depicted in Fig. 1. This reflected wavelength (central wavelength of the reflected band) is called the Bragg wavelength (λ_B) and it satisfies the following condition [12]:

© ICST Institute for Computer Sciences, Social Informatics and Telecommunications Engineering 2016
B. Mandler et al. (Eds.): IoT 360° 2015, Part II, LNICST 170, pp. 191–202, 2016.
DOI: 10.1007/978-3-319-47075-7_24

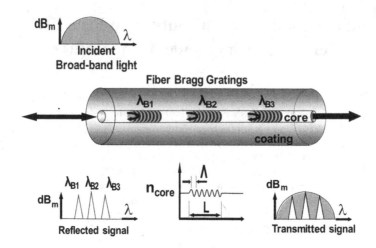

Fig. 1. Principle of fiber Bragg gratings.

$$\lambda_B = 2\Lambda n_{eff} \tag{1}$$

where Λ is the grating period and n_{eff} is the effective refractive index of the FBG.

FBG is sensitive to mechanical strain which causes linear expansion of the gratings, leading to a change in the grating period and refractive index due to photo-elastic effect. The gratings are also sensitive to temperature due to thermal expansion and the thermo-optic effect of the fiber material (usually Germanium doped Silica). Changes in strain (ε) or temperature (ΔT) causes a Bragg wavelength shift ($\Delta\lambda_B$), thus enabling its application in measurement technology. The Bragg wavelength shift can be expressed as [12]:

$$\frac{\Delta\lambda_B}{\lambda_B} = (\alpha_s + \alpha_e)\Delta T + (1 - p_e)\varepsilon \tag{2}$$

where α_s is the thermal expansion coefficient (0.55×10^{-6} for silica), α_e is the thermo-optic coefficient (8.6×10^{-6} for silica) and p_e is the effective strain-optic coefficient of the fiber which can be calculated using [12]:

$$p_e = \frac{n^2}{2}[p_{12} - v(p_{11} + p_{12})] \tag{3}$$

where p_{11} and p_{12} are the components of strain-optic tensor, n is the fiber core refractive index, and v is the Poisson's ratio. For a typical FBG sensor ($p_{11} = 0.113$, $p_{12} = 0.252$, $v = 0.16$ and $n = 1.482$), p_e is 0.22. For a Bragg wavelength ~ 1550 nm, the expected strain sensitivity is $1.2/\mu\varepsilon$, i.e., for an applied strain of 1 $\mu\varepsilon$, the change in Bragg wavelength will be 1.2 pm. The expected temperature sensitivity is 13.7 pm/K. The strain and temperature sensitivities of the FBG, however, differ from sensor to sensor, thus requiring a calibration of the sensor before using it for any measurement.

Both strain and temperature response of various types of FBG sensors are being investigated and reported regularly. Roths et al. [13] have reported the temperature sensitivity of a bare FBG and an FBG bonded to a poly (methyl methacrylate) substrate, at temperatures ranging from 4.2 K to 300 K. Strain response of FBG sensors at cryogenic temperatures have been reported by James et al. [14] where the FBG sensors were either attached to a stainless steel cantilever or invar sample. The reported strain sensitivities, however, vary depending on a lot of factors like the type of FBG sensor, strain transfer efficiency, gluing techniques used, etc., making it difficult for the comparison of these values. This leads to the importance of studying the strain response without attaching the FBG sensing part to any surface. Such an investigation was carried out by Roths et al. [15] where a 'free' FBG sensor was strained using weights-guided movable clamps attached to the non-sensing part of the fiber. Although this was one of the first reliable methods that can be used for FBG sensor standardization procedures, it was performed only at room temperature.

To the best of our knowledge, strain calibrations of un-bonded or substrate-free FBG sensors at cryogenic temperatures have not been reported so far. This paper discusses the strain response of a substrate-free FBG sensor whose sensing part is not attached to any surface for temperatures of 298 K and 77 K.

2   Experiment

A commercial polyamide coated single mode fiber (SMF 28) containing two FBG sensors is used in this study. Each sensor grating has different spatial period, thus having different Bragg wavelengths, namely, λ_{B1} and λ_{B2}. Of these two FBG sensors, one sensor's (FBG 1) ends are attached firmly to two stainless steel structures, making sure that the FBG sensing part is free and does not have any contact with any surface (Fig. 2). FBG 1 can sense both strain and temperature. The other sensor (FBG 2) is let to hang freely to ensure that there is no strain felt in it and is used to measure only temperature.

The ends of FBG 1 are glued to the metal structures using epoxy-phenol adhesive. This type of glue requires a heat treatment at about 160 °C for 2 h. The heating apparatus (Fig. 3) was supplied by Hochtemperaturöfen GmbH, Germany. The heating tube consists of an uncovered FeCrAl (Iron-Chromium-Aluminium) heating coil which is mounted on a ceramic fiber module. The low thermal conductivity of the ceramic fiber insulation guarantees low energy consumption and allows for high heating rates. The tube is wound with this wire and kept in the center of the furnace to provide

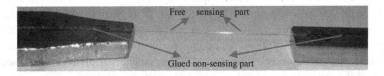

Fig. 2. FBG sensor glued to metal structures with the central sensing part not touching any surface.

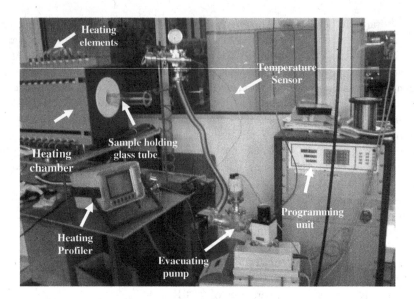

Fig. 3. GERO Hochtemperaturöfen apparatus for heat treatment.

uniform heating. High flexibility in the design of the temperature profile is a special characteristic of this type of furnace. The manual setting of homogenous temperature areas, temperature gradients, maximum temperature limits, heating duration, etc., is possible.

The metal structures with FBG sensors are placed in the glass tube and the maximum heating temperature is set at 160 °C which is well within the maximum limit of temperature the fiber can withstand. The furnace is then started by passing commands in the programming unit with the heating duration set to 2 h.

Once the temperature reaches 160 °C, it stays constant for 2 h and then the furnace gets turned off automatically. The heated sample is allowed to cool naturally till it reaches the room temperature. The spectra of FBG 1 before and after the heat treatment is plotted in Fig. 4. It can be seen that the spectral pattern is almost the same and there is no significant change in the initial Bragg wavelength. Thus, the chosen heat treatment has not affected the FBG sensor properties.

The sample is then transferred to the MTS25 tensile machine with cryostat available at Cryogenic Material tests Karlsruhe (CryoMaK) [16], ITeP, KIT. The tensile machine consists of an extensometer (also called top load cell) and a bottom load cell. An extensometer is a device that is used to measure the distance between two distinct points on the surface of the attached specimen [17, 18]. It is fixed on a Copper-Beryllium (CuBe) wire to measure the applied strain. Figure 5 shows a schematic of an extensometer and the connections that are required to measure the strain felt by the specimen. When there is any strain applied to the specimen (FBG with metal structures in this case), the extensometer attached with the specimen also gets strained. The resistance of the strain gauge glued in the arms of the extensometer vary according to the strain applied on the specimen. The change in the resistance is read out as a

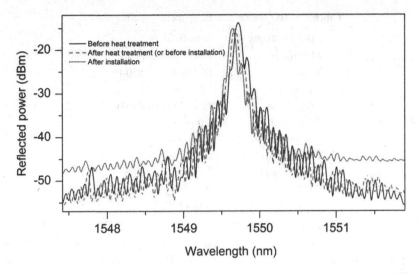

Fig. 4. Spectral comparison of FBG before heat treatment, after heat treatment (same for pre-installation) and after installation.

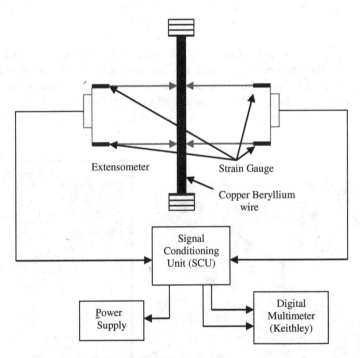

Fig. 5. Schematic of extensometer and its connections.

Table 1. FBG sensor and Braggmeter specifications

FBG Parameter	Specification
Manufacturer	FBGS technologies
Type	DTG®-LBL-1550-F
Diameter (coated)	195 μm
Braggmeter	FS22 Industrial (SI)
Resolution	1.0 pm
Absolute accuracy	±2.0 pm
Repeatability	±1.0 pm
Optical output power	10 dBm
Dynamic range	>50 dB
Optical detection	Logarithmic

millivolt (mV) change for applied strain. Such a contact type extensometer is calibrated by applying known strain and recording the output. The calibrated extensometer is used as a reference sensor for FBG strain calibration. Table 1 lists the parameters of the FBG sensor and Braggmeter considered with their respective specifications. The Braggmeter (FS22 Industrial BraggMETER SI) [19] has a very good resolution of 1.0 pm and absolute accuracy of ±2.0 pm. In other words, temperature can be measured with an accuracy of 0.2 K and strain with 1.7 με. The Braggmeter also has good repeatability of ±1.0 pm, showing that the error in measurement due to the measuring device is negligible.

The metal structures holding the fiber are installed by attaching to the load cells (Fig. 6) of the tensile machine, which has an accuracy of ±1 μm displacement. A pre-strain is given to the sensor to avoid errors in measurement due to bending of the sensor. To ensure that the installation has not affected the FBG properties, the spectral data before and after installation are also compared. Figure 4 shows that the Bragg

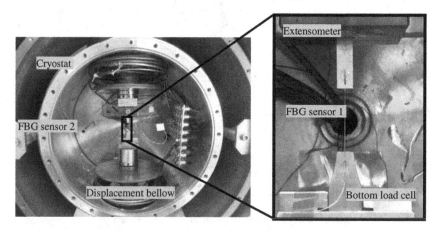

Fig. 6. The sample loaded in the calibration device MTS 25 in a cryostat (left) and the FBG sensor attached to the metal structures is zoomed in for a clear view.

wavelength of the sensor is almost equal before the installation (same as post-heat treatment) and after the installation of the sensor between the load cells.

Keeping the top load cell (extensometer) fixed, the bottom load cell is moved by the displacement bellow (works on hydraulic mechanism) under it for the given displacement values in the command. The given displacement is completely transferred to the FBG sensor, i.e., the change in length of the sensor is equal to the displacement. This induces a strain in the FBG sensor (FBG 1), which in turn causes a Bragg wavelength shift in it. Any temperature changes around it also adds to its Bragg shift ($\Delta\lambda_{B1}$). On the other hand, the Bragg wavelength shift of FBG 2 ($\Delta\lambda_{B2}$) which hangs freely in the cryostat is caused only due to the temperature changes.

After each displacement command it is necessary to wait for about five minutes for the bellow to settle down to the desired displacement. The calibration tests are first performed at room temperature for both straining (downward displacement of bottom load cell) and de-straining (upward movement of bottom load cell). The respective readings of the extensometer, FBG sensor and the displacement bellow are recorded for each given displacement. The test is performed 3 times to check the repeatability of the sensor.

For calibration tests at the desired cryogenic temperature (77 K), the test chamber (cryostat) is cooled down by the attached Liquid Nitrogen (LN_2) pipe up to 100 K. The temperature inside the chamber is monitored using a Si diode (Omega Inc., CYD 208 thermometer). To further cool the cryostat down to 77 K, compressed Helium (He) flow is started inside the pipe attached to the Cu-heat exchanger in the cryostat. Once the temperature reaches 77 K, the He flow is reduced to maintain the temperature constant.

As there are a lot of sources of heat transfer in the cryostat, the temperature might increase if He flow is stopped. Hence, it is important to make sure He flow is continuously regulated to maintain a constant temperature of 77 K. The pressure in the cryostat is maintained at 10^{-4} mbar during the cooling down process. The calibration procedure used at 298 K is repeated for measurements at 77 K. The values of Bragg wavelength shift, displacement, extensometer voltage and temperature are recorded for each given displacement for both room temperature and 77 K.

3 Results and Discussion

For the given displacement values, the response observed from extensometer and FBG sensors are depicted in Fig. 7. It can be seen that the response ($\Delta\lambda_{B1}$) of the strain sensor (FBG 1) has same pattern as that of the displacement. The probe is started at time = 500 s and the displacement is increased (straining) in steps of 4 μm up to 16 μm, with each step being held constant for 5 min. The sensor is then de-strained by decreasing the displacement in the steps of 4 μm back to 0 μm. Hysteresis of both tensile machine and FBG sensor response is evident from the plot as the de-straining phase does not show the same response as straining phase. Towards the end of de-straining a vast difference is seen in the pattern between displacement and Bragg shift. This is due to the hysteresis effect of the tensile machine which has gone below the initial displacement value, but the fiber cannot go below its initial Bragg shift value

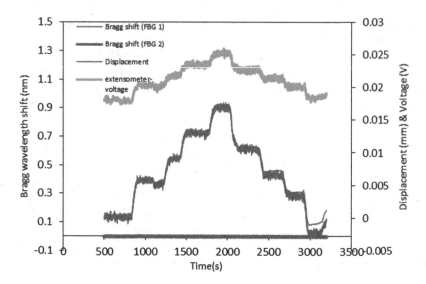

Fig. 7. Response of extensometer and Bragg wavelength for given displacement values.

as it gets completely de-strained at this stage. The figure also shows that the temperature remains constant as the Bragg wavelength shift ($\Delta\lambda_{B2}$) of FBG 2 is constant near zero.

As the given displacement is completely transferred to the sensor, the change in length of the sensor (ΔL) is equal to the given displacement. For each given displacement, the corresponding mechanical strain is calculated based on the attached length of the fiber (L) using the following expression:

$$\varepsilon = \frac{\Delta L}{L} \tag{4}$$

The initial length of the sensor and the corresponding initial Bragg wavelength ($\lambda_{B1,0}$) are taken after providing the sensor with some pre-strain, to ensure that there is no error in the length due to bending of the sensor. The purely strain-dependent Bragg wavelength shift ($\Delta\lambda_B$) is given by the difference of Bragg shift of FBG 1 and FBG 2 as follows:

$$\Delta\lambda_B = |\Delta\lambda_{B1} - \Delta\lambda_{B2}| \tag{5}$$

This Bragg wavelength shift is taken on the y-axis and the induced strain calculated from Eq. 4 is taken on the x-axis as shown Fig. 8. The repeatability test shows that the Bragg wavelength shifts of all the three runs are in good agreement with each other. It can also be observed that the FBG sensor has good repeatability irrespective of the temperature, i.e., the shifts agree with each other for both 298 K and 77 K.

Arithmetic average of the three runs are considered for the calibration plots for both the temperatures. Figure 9 shows the plot of Bragg wavelength shift versus induced strain. It can be observed that the plot is almost linear with little hysteresis effect, i.e.,

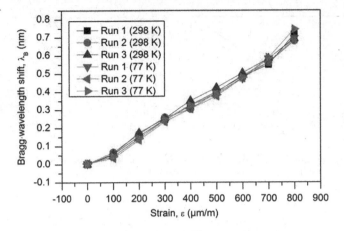

Fig. 8. Repeatability test of FBG strain sensor.

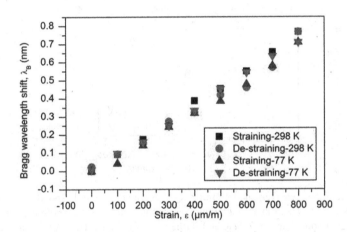

Fig. 9. Bragg wavelength shift (nm) of FBG corresponding to induced strain values at 298 K and 77 K. The legends "Straining" and "De-straining" refer to the measurements performed during straining and de-straining respectively.

for the same induced strain, the wavelength shifts during straining and de-straining phases are slightly different. This is expected out of any experiment and does not affect the calibration much. The hysteresis plots are showed in detail in Fig. 10.

Taking the average of straining and de-straining wavelength shifts for the corresponding strain values, a linear polynomial regression is performed as shown in Fig. 11. It can be observed that the Bragg wavelength shift as a function of induced strain is the same ($\Delta\lambda_B = 0.0009\varepsilon$) for both the cases of temperature with slightly different regression coefficient. In other words, the strain sensitivity of the FBG sensor is found to be 0.9 pm/$\mu\varepsilon$ at both 298 K and 77 K. Although the linearly regressed equations are the same, there is a visible difference in the individual wavelength shifts. This error could be due to a mild change in glue properties between these temperatures.

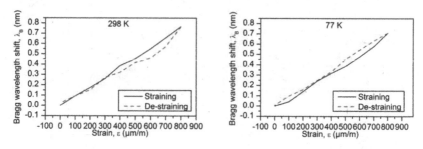

Fig. 10. Hysteresis plots of FBG sensor at 298 K and 77 K. The legends "Straining" and "De-straining" refer to the measurements performed during straining and de-straining of the sensor respectively.

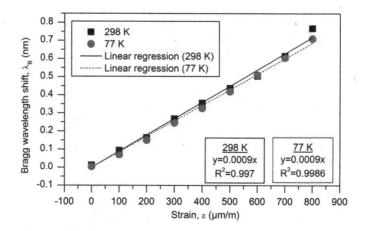

Fig. 11. Calibration measurements of Bragg wavelength shift for corresponding induced strain values at 298 K and 77 K. Linear polynomial regression is described for both the conditions and represented by a solid line for 298 K and dashed line for 77 K. The regression equations for Bragg wavelength shift (y in the graph) as a function of induced strain (x in the graph) are displayed.

The standard deviation between the obtained values and the regressed values is depicted in Fig. 12 in the form of error bars for both the temperatures. The FBG sensor shows less error at 77 K than at 298 K. This can be attributed to the material properties of the optical fiber. It is expected to be more rigid at cryogenic temperatures, hence there will be negligible vibrations in the sensor, which in turn reduces the error in measurements.

As the errors obtained are negligible, the linear equation obtained by regression can be reliably used for this particular sensor. The unknown strain values can be calculated for the observed Bragg wavelength shift and thus, the strain related measurands can be estimated.

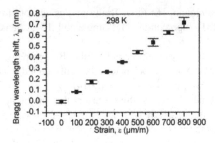 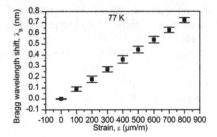

Fig. 12. Error plots of FBG strain sensor between fitted and obtained values of Bragg shift at 298 K and 77 K

4 Conclusions

An effective strain calibration method is implemented for an FBG sensor at room temperature (298 K) and Nitrogen's atmospheric boiling point (77 K). This is a unique and reliable method because the sensing part of the FBG sensor is not attached to any structure or surface. The strain sensitivity of a free, acrylate coated standard FBG sensor is found to be equal (0.9 pm/με) for both the temperatures. A couple of conclusions can be drawn based on the results obtained. As reported in earlier works [14], the strain sensitivity of the FBG sensor did not depend on the temperature. The obtained results also show that the error in measurement is much less at the cryogenic temperature when compared to room temperature. It can be concluded that this method of strain calibration of substrate-free FBG sensor is an effective method that can be used for FBG standardization procedures. Further investigations of strain response will be performed at lower cryogenic temperatures of 10 K and 4 K and analyzed with the results obtained at 298 K and 77 K.

References

1. Rao, Y.J.: Recent progress in applications of in-fibre Bragg grating sensors. Opt. Lasers Eng. **31**(4), 297–324 (1999)
2. Othonos, A., Kalli, K.: Fiber Bragg Gratings – Fundamentals and Application in Telecommunications and Sensing. Artech House Optoelectronics Library, Boston (1999)
3. Iniewski, K.: Smart Sensors for Industrial Applications. Taylor & Francis Group, Boca Raton (2013)
4. Wu, M.-C.: Simultaneous temperature and strain sensing for cryogenic applications using dual-wavelength fiber Bragg gratings. In: Proceedings of SPIE 5191, pp. 208–213 (2003)
5. Ramalingam, R.: Fiber Bragg grating sensors for localized strain measurements at low temperature and in high magnetic field. In: Proceedings of AIP Conference, vol. 1218, no. 1, pp. 1197–1204 (2010)
6. Ramalingam, R., Neumann, H.: Fiber Bragg grating-based temperature distribution evaluation of multilayer insulations between 300 K–77 K. IEEE Sens. J. **11**(4), 1095–1100 (2011)

7. Ramalingam, R., Kläser, M., Schneider, T., Neumann, H.: Fiber Bragg grating sensors for strain measurement at multiple points in an NbTi superconducting sample coil. IEEE Sens. J. **14**(3), 873–881 (2014)

8. Bharathwaj, V., Markan, A., Atrey, M., Neumann, H., Ramalingam, R.: Fiber Bragg gratings for distributed cryogenic temperature measurement in a tube in tube helically coiled heat exchanger. In: IEEE sensors 2014, Valencia, Spain, pp. 1535–1538 (2014)

9. Ramalingam, R., Nast, R., Neumann, H.: Fiber Bragg grating sensors for distributed torsional strain measurements in a (RE) BCO tape. IEEE Sens. J. **15**(4), 2023–2030 (2015)

10. Li, J., Neumann, H., Ramalingam, R.: Design, fabrication, and testing of fiber Bragg grating sensors for cryogenic long-range displacement measurement. Cryogenics **68**, 36–43 (2015). ISSN 0011-2275

11. Kashyap, R.: Fiber Bragg Gratings. Academic Press, San Diego (1999)

12. Othonos, A.: Fiber Bragg gratings. Rev. Sci. Instrum. **68**, 4309–4341 (1997)

13. Roths, J., Andrejevic, G., Kuttler, R., Süsser, M.: Calibration of fiber Bragg cryogenic temperature sensors. In: 18th International Optical Fiber Sensors Conference. Optical Society of America (2006)

14. James, S.W., Tatam, R.P., Twin, A., Morgan, M., Noonan, P.: Strain response of fibre Bragg grating sensors at cryogenic temperatures. Measur. Sci. Technol. **13**, 1535–1539 (2002)

15. Roths, J., Jülich, F.: Determination of strain sensitivity of free fiber Bragg gratings. In: Proceedings of SPIE 7003, p. 700308 (2008)

16. Bagrets, N., Weiss, E., Westenfelder, S., Weiss, K.-P.: Cryogenic test facility CryoMaK. IEEE Trans. Appl. Supercond. **22**(3), 9501204 (2012)

17. Nyilas, A.: Strain sensing systems tailored for tensile measurement of fragile wires. Supercond. Sci. Technol. **18**, S409–S415 (2005)

18. Nyilas, A.: Transducers for sub-micron displacement measurements at cryogenic temperatures. In: Advances in Cryogenic Engineering: Transactions of the Cryogenic Materials Conference – ICMC, vol. 52 (2006)

19. FS22 – Industrial BraggMETER SI. http://www.fibersensing.com/download/0b49e3852b 6452701f87b4a06fa4a90d439de5b1

Fabrication and Application of Low Cost Flexible Film-Based Sensors to Environmental and Biomedical Monitoring Scenarios

Vladimir Laukhin[1,2,3], Victor Lebedev[1], Elena Laukhina[1,2(✉)],
Andrey Somov[4], Alexander Baranov[5], Concepcio Rovira[1,2],
and Jaume Veciana[1,2]

[1] Institut de Ciencia de Materials de Barcelona (ICMAB-CSIC), Campus UAB,
Bellaterra 08193, Spain
laukhina@icmab.es
[2] CIBER de Bioingeniería, Biomateriales y Nanomedicina (CIBER-BBN),
Madrid, Spain
[3] Institució Catalana de Recerca i Estudis Avançats (ICREA), Barcelona, Spain
[4] CREATE-NET, Trento, Italy
[5] 'MATI'-Russian State Technological University, Moscow, Russia

Abstract. The paper describes the development of flexible lightweight highly sensitive film-based sensors capable of monitoring pressure, deformation, temperature and humidity. In particular, we present a family of the developed simple devices that successfully adopted polycarbonate films covered with organic molecular conductors as conductive sensing components. Proof-of-concept experiments with these prototypes demonstrate that such bi layer films are promising as sensing devices for the environment and biomedical monitoring. Besides, we present the interfacing of the flexible film-based sensor with a wireless sensor node and evaluate the sensing capability of this system in a real monitoring scenario.

Keywords: Flexible sensors · Organic molecular conductors · Wireless Sensor Network · Environmental monitoring · Biomedical monitoring

1 Introduction

The development of flexible, lightweight, conducting materials, whose electrical transport properties strongly respond to delicate strain, brings great opportunities in the field of strain, pressure, bending and temperature sensors for their applications in smart textiles, robotic interfaces and body sensing devices [1–3]. Here it should be noted that the modern working up wireless monitoring technologies take an active interest in using such conductive sensing materials. The wireless monitoring sensing systems based on the Wireless Sensor Network paradigm (WSN) enables a user to perform sensing measurements of a physical phenomena, process the data and send them to a user or machine over the network. WSNs have been already used in a large number of monitoring applications, including wildlife monitoring [4] and fire detection [5, 6], noise sensing in urban areas [7] and health monitoring [8].

© ICST Institute for Computer Sciences, Social Informatics and Telecommunications Engineering 2016
B. Mandler et al. (Eds.): IoT 360° 2015, Part II, LNICST 170, pp. 203–216, 2016.
DOI: 10.1007/978-3-319-47075-7_25

Until now the WSN nodes typically employ the off-the-shelf sensors. However, organic film sensors introduce a number of advantages over the off-the-shelf sensing devices [2]. Covering polymeric films with conventional metals and semiconductors is one of the traditional approaches to engineering flexible lightweight sensors [9]. Thus, Huang et al. [10] described a flexible thermistor fabricated by printing a square NiO thin film on a polyimide film. Such flexible Bi Layer (BL) sensors demonstrate a good sensitivity and fast response. Unfortunately, these flexible sensing materials demonstrate a common drawback: poor adhesion of conventional metals and their oxides to polymers. This disadvantage results in a low binding between inorganic sensing layers and plastic supports. With organic conductors one may overcome the problem. It was showed that conducting polymers can be successfully put to sensing technology [11]; the reported flexible capacitive-type humidity and temperature sensors - cellulose–polypyrrole nanocomposites – are ones of the promising examples of all-organic flexible sensors [12]. However, conducting polymers are not stable materials: their electronic properties are often unstable towards atmospheric moisture [13]. Moreover, they are expensive due to the high manufacturing costs. In this context, organic molecular conductors $(BEDT-TTF)_2X$, where $BEDT-TTF$ = bis(ethylenedithio) tetrathiafulvalen (Fig. 1) and 'X' is trihalide ions [14, 15] hold a great interest for sensor engineering due to important material properties, such as lightweight, stability, conductivity and high piezoresistivity.

It should be noted that the (001) oriented conducting layer of the highly piezoresistive $\beta-(BEDT-TTF)_2I_3$ metal can be formed on the surface of a polymeric film by a simple procedure carried out at moderated temperature [16–18]. This stimulated us to harness the BL films - polycarbonate/$(BEDT-TTF)_2X$ - for engineering sensing systems capable to detect ultra-small deformations or pressure. Recently, we have demonstrated that another BL film: polycarbonate/(001) oriented $\alpha-(BEDT-TTF)_2I_3$, can be reproducibly prepared as a temperature independent strain sensing material [19]. With the successful fabrication of the first prototype for a breathing control (Fig. 2, device 1) [18] the integration of developed conductive BL films as active components in flexible strain sensors is being evaluated. Recently, we have developed a BL thermistor: polycarbonate/$\alpha'-(BEDT-TTF)_2I_xBr_{3-x}$, were $\alpha'-(BEDT-TTF)_2I_xBr_{3-x}$ which is organic molecular semiconductor whose electrical resistance is highly sensitive to temperature [20]. In the body temperature range its temperature coefficient of resistance (TCR) is -1.4 %/degree. This value is four times larger than that reported for the platinum thermometer ($TCRPt_{111}$ = 0.3) [21].

In this work we present our recent advances in the development of flexible film-based sensors [18, 20, 22], demonstrate their sensing capabilities in wearable

Fig. 1. Skeletal formula of bis(ethylenedithio)tetrathiafulvalen (BEDT-TTF)

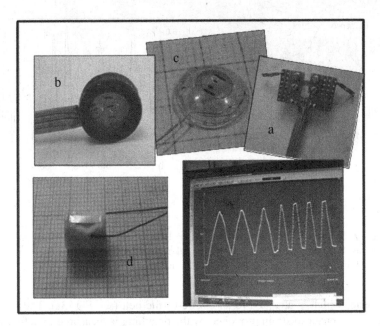

Fig. 2. Photos of some developed devices capable of monitoring the body tissue movements: (a) breathing sensor, (b) blood pulse sensor, (c) IOP sensing contact lens, and (d) pressure sensing element.

biomedical and environmental monitoring scenarios as well as their interfacing with a wireless sensing device to increase the number of potential autonomous monitoring applications.

The paper is organized as follows: in Sect. 2 we summarize the developed sensors and evaluate their performance. Next we explore the opportunity of the flexible film-based sensor interfacing with a wireless sensor node and apply this system in a real monitoring scenario in Sect. 3. Finally, we provide our conclusions and discuss our future work in Sect. 4.

2 Development of Sensing Devices

2.1 Flexible Piezoresistive Sensors Controlling the Body Tissue Movement

In this section, we discuss the development of the sensors as well as demonstrate and discuss their performance. Figure 2 presents the prototypes of sensing devices developed for the body tissue movement monitoring. In next sections we discuss each sensing device in details.

2.1.1 Breathing Sensor

The breathing sensor is shown in Fig. 2(a). This prototype contains the BL film: polycarbonate/β-(BEDT-TTF)$_2$I$_3$ as a tenzo-resistive diaphragm on springy plastic

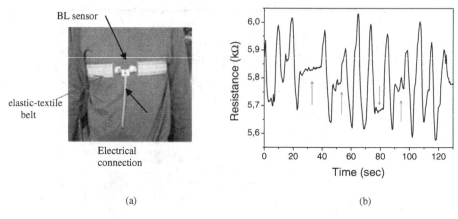

(a)   (b)

Fig. 3. (a) Photo images of the breathing sensor location on the breast of a volunteer for monitoring his breathing and (b) sensor electrical resistance response to the breathing of a volunteer (red arrows correspond to holding up his breathing) (Color figure online)

U-shape plate, which is attached to an elastic-textile belt (see Fig. 3a). The resistance response of the sensor to strain provoked by the breathing is measured by a four probes dc method. Data are gathered for different persons and time periods. Figure 3a shows that the breathing movement results in the oscillated resistance curve. A relatively long time periods between the oscillations, observed in Fig. 3a (left), correspond to holding up breathing.

2.1.2 Blood Pulse Sensor

Blood pulse sensor is presented in Fig. 2b. The membrane fabricated from the BL film: polycarbonate/β-(BEDT-TTF)$_2$I$_3$, is equipped with electrical contacts and fixed between two rigid plastic rings. To measure the pulse, the device is fixed on the body of a volunteer. The resistance response of the sensor to strain provoked by pulse movement is measured by a four probes dc method. Data are gathered from different persons and time periods (Table 1).

Figure 4 shows that the pulse movement, which resulted in an oscillated resistance curve, can be easily recorded and analyzed. Additionally Fig. 4 demonstrates that the sensor electrical responses for two persons – "$V.$" and "$L.$" show nonsymmetrical oscillations. Moreover, in the case of "$L.$" nonsymmetrical oscillations have irregular behavior. Interestingly, this test stimulated our colleague "$L.$" to visit a cardiologist

Table 1. Pulse per minute and signal structure indicated for four persons using the blood pulse sensor

Volunteer	Pulse/min	Signal structure
J.	66	Regular oscillations
V.	71	Regular oscillations
Vl.	62	Regular nonsymmetrical oscillations
L.	94	Irregular nonsymmetrical oscillations

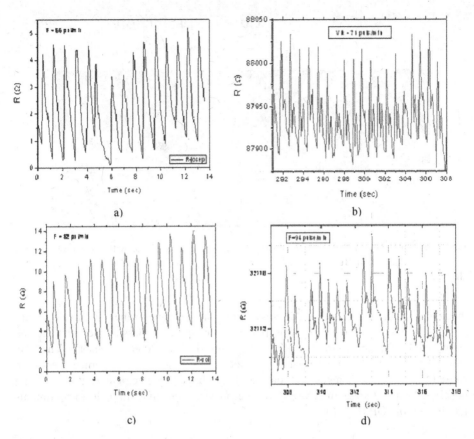

Fig. 4. Resistance response to the blood-pulse movement measured for 4 different persons: (a) volunteer "*J.*", men, 27 years old, (b) volunteer "*V.*", men, 27 years old, (c) volunteer "*Vl.*", men, 64 years old, and (d) volunteer "*L.*" men, 35 year old

who diagnosed that "*L.*" has ciliary arrhythmia. Therefore, our sensor assist the medical personnel in controlling blood pulse and revealing cardiologic problems by a simple procedure.

2.1.3 Intraocular Pressure Sensing Contact Lens

The contact lens capable of Intraocular Pressure (IOP) monitoring in noninvasive way is presented in Fig. 2c. Among numerous attempts to continuously monitor the IOP in a non-invasive way [23, 24] only Leonardi et al. have developed a marketable device [25]. The key element of the device is a soft contact lens with an embedded micro-fabricated strain gauge (platinum-titanium foil) allowing the measurement of changes in corneal curvature correlated to variations in IOP. We have developed the IOP sensing devices based on rigid and hybrid contact lenses equipped with flexible sensing membranes fabricated from polycarbonate/(BEDT-TTF)$_2$I$_3$ [26].

The developed devices (Fig. 5) use a different measure approach and, moreover, the gauge factor of the piezoresistor: polycarbonate/(BEDT-TTF)$_2$I$_3$ is five times larger

Cup-like protection

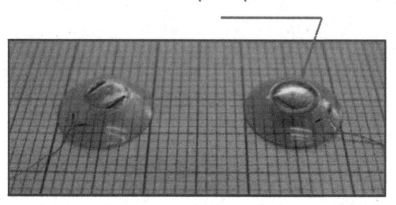

Fig. 5. Photo image of contact IOP sensing lenses without (left) and with (right) the top cap protection of the strain BL film based-sensor showing the wires for measuring the resistance changes

than the platinum gauge factor. All pressure tests are prepared using hand-made set-up. The contact lens based sensor was pasted over ring-like glass holder that can be connected by the tube to the Low-Pressure Controller CPC2000 ("Mensor"). The tests showed that our BL sensor is able to detect deformations in the corneal curvature caused by pressure changes as small as 1–2 mbar. The electrical response of the developed lenses to pressure changes reveals a proper sensitivity to perform continuous monitoring of IOP (Fig. 6).

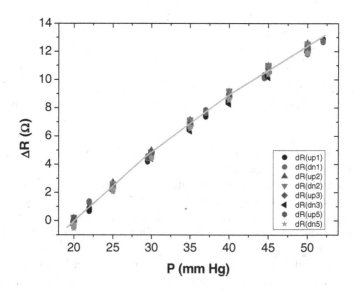

Fig. 6. Typical electrical response of the developed sensing lenses to IOP changes; data collected for four up-down sweeps

2.2   Temperature Sensing Device

Temperature is one of the crucial parameters to be measured in numerous monitoring applications. Healthcare, environment control, biomedical applications call for low cost, lightweight thermistors which might accurately measure temperature changes. This challenge prompted us to apply the BEDT-TTF-based conductors to engineering low cost, lightweight thermistor whose resistance will be able to respond to small temperature changes. For this purpose we propose to use the recently developed BL thermistor: polycarbonate/α'-(BEDT-TTF)$_2$I$_x$Br$_{3-x}$, where α'-(BEDT-TTF)$_2$I$_x$Br$_{3-x}$ is organic molecular semiconductor whose temperature coefficient of resistance (TCR) was found as -1.4 %/degree. A sample of the conductive BL film: polycarbonate/α'-(BEDT-TTF)$_2$I$_x$Br$_{3-x}$ with a sensing area around 2×3 mm^2 and thickness 10–30 μm (including temperature sensing layer: (0.5 to 1 μm) is located over a ridged support. Four Pt wires are connected to the sensing element using graphite paste as it shown in Fig. 7.

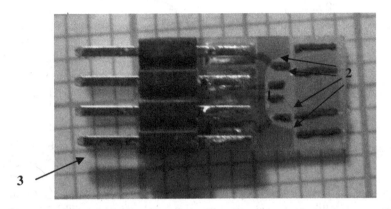

Fig. 7. Photo image of temperature sensing device: 1 - BL thermister: polycarbonate/α'-(BEDT-TTF)$_2$I$_x$Br$_{3-x}$, 2 - graphite contacts, 3 - connector

We note here that sensing area can be adjusted according to the sensing application requirements. Some important data on sensor testing are summarized in the following paragraph:

– range of ice point resistance: R = 10–20 kΩ for a sensing area 2×3 mm^2;
– temperature range: -50 °C to 80 °C; thermistor shows a weak semiconductor-like behavior;
– resolution is about: 0.001 °C;
– fundamental temperature interval: -10 °C to 40 °C;
– self heating: <0.1 °C/mW;
– thermal response: <0.1 s.
– the power needed for the measurement: 1–5 μW (current 10 μA).

Taking into account that temperature of water in ocean and others natural water reservoirs is very important characteristic, which is the major factor governing the

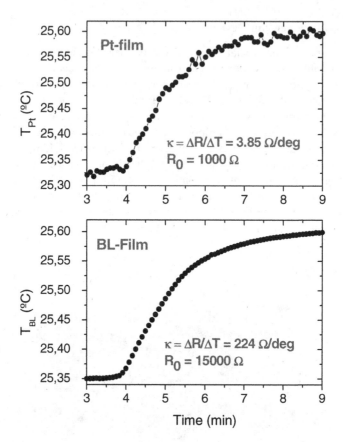

Fig. 8. Temperature control using (top) Pt Film Detector: Pt1000 (RS order code: 362-9907, Dimensions: 2.0×10 mm^2) and (bottom) developed detector with BL thermister: polycarbonate/α'-(BEDT-TTF)$_2$I$_x$Br$_{3-x}$

vertical movement of ocean waters [27], we studied the resistance temperature dependence of the fabricated device in water (Fig. 8, bottom).

For the sake of verification of obtained results, we experimentally evaluate them with respect to commonly used Pt-based thermometer (Fig. 8, top). According to this comparative study, the developed temperature sensing device far superior in sensitivity (*k*) the commercial Pt-based thermometer: for the developed sensing device the value of *k* was found as 224 Ω/degree while for Pt thermometer it is 3.85 Ω/degree.

3   Exploring Organic Film Sensors and Wireless Sensor Network Paradigm

As we noticed earlier, there is a growing interest in film based electronic components, e.g. sensors and storage [28], which can be deposited right on the surface of the embedded systems. The reason for this interest is grounded on newly available materials, which can ensure better performance, on full customization of printed/ deposited devices and, in most cases, on a simple fabrication process. However, there is still a gap between the printed devices and their integration with embedded electronics and, in particular, with WSNs. In fact the WSN paradigm is considered as a pillar technology in the forthcoming era of the Internet of Things (IoT) [29, 30]. The IoT paradigm aims at intelligent connecting devices, e.g. sensors and actuators [32], and services in a global network. This approach will help to resolve a number of problems including a remote medical assistance one which appears to be an important challenge in a growing urban areas. The IoT devices equipped with the wearable sensors presented in this work will enable the 'telemedicine' option. This approach will help the medical personnel to perform the remote assistance and consultation for a number of patients.

In this section we demonstrate how to interface a film sensor with a custom made wireless sensor node and conduct temperature measurement in real settings. We note that the sensor node is developed for the 'proof of concept' purpose only.

3.1   Interfacing of Sensing Device and Sensor Node

The architecture of the sensor node, shown in Fig. 9, includes four main blocks: processing, sensing, communication, and power management. The processing unit, based on an ATXmega128 Microprocessor Control Unit (MCU) with a precise 24-bit Analog-to-Digital Converter (ADC), manages the operation of the sensors and of the ETRX3 wireless modem capable of transmitting and receiving data. ETRX3 has a number of self-configuration options, e.g. network configuration, adjustment of transmit power, which ensure that the WSN can be deployed and debugged in short time. The sensing unit includes the temperature and humidity film sensors. The sensors advantages over off-the-shelf components are quick response time and high sensitivity. Power management provides the node with 3 V of supply voltage. As battery, a 3.6 V AA-size Li-ion cell can be used or two alkaline/NiMH 1.5 V each AA-size cells can be applied and wired in series (the first option is preferable due to higher energy density). In this work we use 3.6 V Li-ion AA-type battery with 3200 mAh capacity.

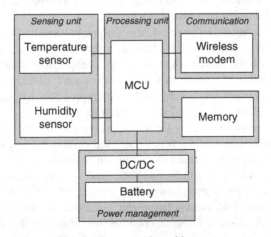

Fig. 9. Sensor node architecture

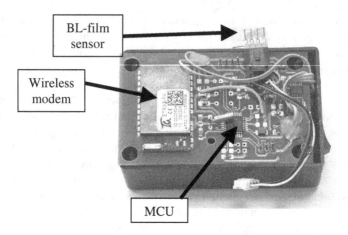

Fig. 10. Prototype of the wireless sensor node with the BL-film as a sensing element.

The prototype of the wireless sensor node with BL film is shown on Fig. 10. The node prototype is featured by a compact design (8 × 4.5 cm), the wireless communication capability and BL-film sensor.

Except for the sensors, which were fabricated in our laboratory the electronic components used in this design are off-the-shelf. These components were chosen with a special focus on their low power consumption which is highly important requirement for WSN devices [31]. The novel aspect of the sensor design is the use of "self-metallization" technology that allows the temperature and humidity sensors to be deposited in the empty spaces of the board. In the prototype, we have used an extra board for our testing convenience.

3.2   Experimental Results

In this section, we experimentally evaluate the film sensor performance in terms of response time and compare the result with a similar off-the-shelf component and present the sensor behavior in a real scenario.

The typical resistance response of the polycarbonate/$(BEDT-TTF)_2Br_x(H_2O)_n$ bilayer film to relative humidity (RH) changes is shown in Fig. 11. It shows how the internal resistance of the sensor changes as the temperature changes. The results indicate that the electrical response of the polycarbonate/α'-$(BEDT-TTF)_2I_xBr_{3-x}$ BL film to temperature changes is reversible and a well reproducible signal. Moreover, this response is as fast as the response of thermometer Pt110.

To calibrate the sensor we apply the supply voltage to the leftmost and rightmost contacts of the sample (see Fig. 7). It generates the current flowing across. The measurement of this current is performed by connecting a precise resistor of 1 Ω in series with the film and measuring its voltage by ADC. Next we measure the voltage between two central contacts of the sensor using ADC and calculate the resistance using the Ohm's law and taking into consideration the resistance of the contacts. Since the calibration is conducted in a climatic chamber we associate the temperature with

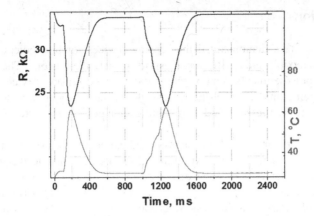

Fig. 11. Sensor performance: resistance of the polycarbonate/α'-(BEDT-TTF)$_2$I$_x$Br$_{3-x}$ BL film (black) and temperature (measured by reference thermometer Pt110) changes (red) *over* time (Color figure online)

resistance and program the table with these values in the memory of MCU. The film sensor resistance is a non linear function of temperature and humidity that is why we perform ten measurements of resistance at a know temperature, calculate the average value and, finally, associate this value with the temperature value.

Figure 12 demonstrates how the film resistance and ambient temperature change in an office environment during working hours. In this experiment we have used the wireless sensor node with the BL-film sensor for the evaluation of the ambient temperature. The sensor node conducts the measurements once per five minutes and sends the measured data to the coordinator once an hour for the sake of energy savings. The results demonstrate that even the temperature is kept at a particular temperature level in the building by a Heating, Ventilation and Air Conditioning (HVAC) system, the temperature in the office varies. We infer that the temperature grows in the beginning of working day (by 9:00) since the office workers arrive to their office place and gradually decreases by the lunch time (around 13:00). Then the temperature increase while people come back to the office and slows down by the end of the working day.

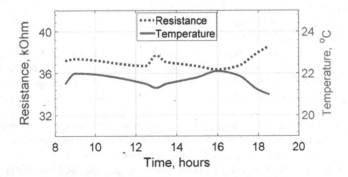

Fig. 12. Experiment showing how the film resistance and temperature change in an office environment during the working hours.

4 Conclusions

In this work we have demonstrated the sensing devices for biomedical applications equipped with flexible either BL piezoresitors or BL thermistors. The carried out proof-of-concept experiments demonstrate that developed sensing devices far superior in sensitivity their commercial off-the-shelf analogues and they are able to detect even negligible change in pressure and temperature changes by measuring the sensors' response signals.

Also we have demonstrated how the proposed temperature sensor can be interfaced with a wireless sensor node. The experimental results demonstrate that the obtained values of the temperature coefficient of resistance for the organic films is four times higher than the value of the platinum which results in better film performance. Apart from this, the films are characterised by cheap manufacturing process and film customization in terms of its shape and resistance which helps to use the unoccupied surfaces of the sensor node.

Our future work includes the investigation of sensor measurements stability and application of sensors in wearable scenarios.

Acknowledgments. The authors acknowledge the financial support from Instituto de Salud Carlos III, through "Acciones CIBER." The Networking Research Center on Bioengineering, Biomaterials and Nanomedicine (CIBER-BBN), an initiative funded by the VINational R&D&I Plan 2008–2011, Iniciativa Ingenio 2010, Consolider Program, CIBER Actions and financed by the Instituto de Salud Carlos III with assistance from the European Regional Development Fund. The authors also appreciate the financial support through the projects: BE-WELL (CTQ2013–40480-R) granted by DGI (Spain), and GenCat (2014-SGR-17) financed by DGR (Catalunya), the European Commission's Seventh Framework Programme for Research under contracts FP7-OCEAN-2013-614155, the Ministry of Education and Science of Russian Federation Grant RFMEFI57714X0133.

References

1. Lorussi, F., Rocchia, W., Scilingo, E.P., Tognetti, A., De Rossi, D.: Wearable, redundant fabric-based sensor arrays for reconstruction of body segment posture. IEEE Sens. J. **4**, 807–818 (2004)
2. Stoppa, M., Chiolerio, A.: Sensors wearable electronics and smart textiles: a critical review. Sensors **14**, 11957–11992 (2014)
3. Lumelsky, V.J., Shur, M.S., Wagner, S.: Sensitive skin. IEEE Sens. J. **1**, 41–51 (2001)
4. Dyo, V., Ellwood, S.A., Macdonald, D.W., Markham, A., Trigoni, N., Wohlers, R., Mascolo, C., Pásztor, B., Scellato, S., Yousef, K.: WILDSENSING: design and deployment of a sustainable sensor network for wildlife monitoring. ACM Trans. Sens. Netw. **8**(4), 1–33 (2012). Article 29
5. Somov, A., Spirjakin, D., Ivanov, M., Khromushin, I., Passerone, R., Baranov, A., Savkin, A.: Combustible gases and early fire detection: an autonomous system for wireless sensor networks. In: Proceeding of e-Energy, pp. 85–93 (2010)
6. Doolin, D.M., Sitar, N.: Wireless sensors for wildfire monitoring. In: Proceedings of Sensors and Smart Structures Technologies for Civil, Mechanical, and Aerospace Systems, San Diego, CA, USA, vol. 5765 (2005)

7. Segura-Garcia, J., Felici-Castell, S., Perez-Solano, J.J., Cobos, M., Navarro, J.M.: Low-cost alternatives for urban noise nuisance monitoring using wireless sensor networks. IEEE Sens. J. **15**, 836–844 (2015)

8. Dutta, T.: Medical data compression and transmission in wireless ad hoc networks. J. IEEE Sens. **15**, 778–786 (2015)

9. Mittal, K.L.: Preface in Metallized Plastics 7: Fundamental and Applied Aspects, p. vii. VSP BV, Utrecht (2001). Mittal, K.L. (ed.)

10. Huang, C.-C., Kao, Z.-K., Liao, Y.-C.: Flexible miniaturized nickel oxide thermistor arrays via inkjet printing technology. ACS Appl. Mater. Interfaces **5**(24), 12954–12959 (2013)

11. Waltman, R.J., Bargon, J.: Electrically conducting polymers: a review of the electropolymerization reaction, of the effects of chemical structure on polymer film properties, and of applications towards technology. Can. J. Chem. **64**, 76–95 (1986)

12. Mahadeva, S.K., Yun, S., Jaehwan, K.: Flexible humidity and temperature sensor based on cellulose–polypyrrole nanocomposite. Sens. Actuators A: Phys. **165**(2), 194–199 (2011)

13. Cardoso, M.J.R., Lima, M., Lenz, D.M.: Polyaniline synthesized with functionalized sulfonic acids for blends manufacture. Mater. Res. **10**(4), 425–429 (2007)

14. Shibaeva, R.P., Yagubskii, E.B.: Molecular conductors and superconductors based on trihalides of BEDT-TTF and some of its analogues. Chem. Rev. **104**, 5347–5378 (2004)

15. Saito, G.: Chap. 10. In: Jones, W. (ed.) Organic Molecular Solids. CRC, Boca Raton (1997)

16. Laukhina, E., Rovira, C., Ulanski, J.: Organic metals as active components in surface conducting semitransparent films. Synth. Met. **21**, 1407–1408 (2001)

17. Laukhina, E., Ulanski, J., Khomenko, A., Pesotskii, S., Tkacheva, V., Atovmyan, L., Yagubskii, E., Rovira, C., Veciana, J., Vidal-Gancedo, J., Laukhin, V.: Systematic study of the $(ET)_2I_3$ reticulate doped polycarbonate film: structure, ESR, transport properties and superconductivity. J. Phys. I Fr. **7**, 1665–1675 (1997)

18. Laukhina, E., Pfattner, R., Ferreras, L.R., Galli, S., Mas-Torrent, M., Masciocchi, N., Laukhin, V., Rovira, C., Veciana, J.: Ultrasensitive piezoresistive all-organic flexible thin films. Adv. Mater. **22**, 977–981 (2010)

19. Lebedev, V., Laukhina, E., Laukhin, V., Rovira, C., Veciana, J.: Tuning the electronic properties of piezoresistive bilayer films based on alpha-$(BEDT-TTF)_2I_3$. Eur. J. Inorg. Chem. **2014**, 3927–3932 (2014)

20. Laukhina, E., Tkacheva, V., Khasanov, S., Zorina, L., Gomez-Segura, J., Perezdel Pino, A., Veciana, J., Laukhin, V., Rovira, C.: Linked crystallites in the conducting topmost layer of polymer bilayer films controlled by temperature: from micro- to nanocrystallites. ChemPhysChem **7**, 920–923 (2006)

21. PT-100 Series Platinum RTDs. http://www.lakeshore.com/Documents/LSTC_Platinum_l.pdf

22. Lebedev, V., Laukhina, E., Rovira, C., Laukhin, V., Veciana, J.: All-organic humidity sensing films with electrical detection principle suitable to biomedical applications. Procedia Eng. **47**, 603–606 (2012)

23. Maurice, D.M.: A recording tonometer. Brit. J. Ophthal **42**, 321–335 (1958)

24. Svedbergh, B., Bäcklund, Y., Hök, B., Rosengren, L.: The IOP-IOL: a probe into the eye. Acta Ophthalmol. **70**(2), 266–268 (1992)

25. Leonardi, M., Pitchon, E.M., Bertsch, A., Renaud, P., Mermoud, A.: Wireless contact lens sensor for intraocular pressure monitoring: assessment on enucleated pig eyes. Acta Ophthalmol. **87**, 433–437 (2009)

26. Laukhin, V., Lebedev, V., Laukhina, E., Martin, R., Pastor, J.C., Villa, R., Aguilo, J., Rovira, C., Veciana, J.: Hybrid contact lens capable of intraocular pressure monitoring in noninvasive way. In: Solid-State Sensors, Actuators and Microsystems (Transducers and Eurosensors XXVII), pp. 1871–1874 (2013)

27. http://ocean.stanford.edu/courses/bomc/chem/lecture_03.pdf

28. Somov, A., Ho, C.C., Passerone, R., Evans, J.W., Wright, P.K.: Towards extending sensor node lifetime with printed supercapacitors. In: Picco, G.P., Heinzelman, W. (eds.) EWSN 2012. LNCS, vol. 7158, pp. 212–227. Springer, Heidelberg (2012)

29. Miorandi, D., Sicari, S., De Pellegrini, F., Chlamtac, I.: Internet of Things: vision, applications and research challenges. Ad Hoc Netw. **10**, 1497–1516 (2012)

30. Kelaidonis, D., Somov, A., Foteinos, V., Poulios, G., Stavroulaki, V., Vlacheas, P., Demestichas, P., Baranov, A., Biswas, A.R., Giaffreda, R.: Virtualization and cognitive management of real world objects in the Internet of Things. In: IEEE International Conference on Green Computing and Communications (GreenCom), pp. 187–194. IEEE Press (2012)

31. Somov, A., Minakov, I., Simalatsar, A., Fontana, G., Passerone, R.: A methodology for power consumption evaluation of wireless sensor networks. In: IEEE Conference on Emerging Technologies and Factory Automation (ETFA 2009), pp. 1–8. IEEE Press (2009)

32. Somov, A., Baranov, A., Spirjakin, D.: A wireless sensor-actuator system for hazardous gases detection and control. J. Sens. Actuators A: Phys. **210**, 157–164 (2014)

Hazardous Gases Sensing: Influence of Ionizing Radiation on Hydrogen Sensors

Boris Podlepetsky and Nikolay Samotaev[✉]

National Research Nuclear University MEPhI
(Moscow Engineering Physics Institute),
Kashirskoe Highway 31, 115409 Moscow, Russian Federation
nnsamotaev@mephi.ru

Abstract. The electron irradiation effect on characteristics of the hydrogen sensors based on metal-insulator-semiconductor transistor structures has been investigated by experiment. The models of hydrogen and radiation sensitivity were developed. Using these models the forecast of functional performance of the hydrogen sensors under ionizing radiation and the estimation of critical doses has been done.

Keywords: Hydrogen · Sensor · Irradiation · Sensitivity · Models · Monitoring

1 Introduction

The development of sensors with sensitive elements (SE) fabricated by means of microtechnology is a promising area for creation of small-sized gas-analysis devices and systems. Among the solid-state gas-sensitive SE, the elements based on metal-insulator-semiconductor transistors (MISFETs) possess the best compatibility with the standard elements of integrated circuits [1–3]. The hydrogen sensors based on MIS-FETs have been studied by many investigators [4–7]. The studies have shown that the sensor performance characteristics depend on many factors: technological processes of sensors, chip temperature, MISFET electrical modes and irradiation [2, 6, 7].

This paper deals with the integrated hydrogen sensors with MISFET sensing element based on Pd-Ta$_2$O$_5$-SiO$_2$-Si structure (named as TSE). These sensor characteristics have been already investigated at normal levels of radiation. However the gas analysis devices can be used for a long time at raised radiation levels.

Study of the effect of radiation on the characteristics of MISFET began in the 1960-ies and is still going on. It was found the common radiation effects in MISFETs: increase the concentration of trapping centers N_t, change charges in the dielectrics Q_t and on its border with the semiconductor Q_{ss}. As a consequence the threshold voltage V_T and transconductance b of MISFETs are changing [9]. The studies have shown that changes of electrical characteristics depend on technological factors, MISFET temperature and electrical modes, as well as on ionizing radiation absorption dose D and its rate P [7–9]. Since TSE has specific features that there are the unexplored issues. What the TSE characteristics and how much should be changed under irradiation? What

© ICST Institute for Computer Sciences, Social Informatics and Telecommunications Engineering 2016
B. Mandler et al. (Eds.): IoT 360° 2015, Part II, LNICST 170, pp. 217–222, 2016.
DOI: 10.1007/978-3-319-47075-7_26

models can be used for the radiation effect simulation on characteristics of the hydrogen sensitive devices and systems based on TSE? To get answers to these questions is the aim of this work.

2 Experiment

2.1 The Sensor Chip Structure and Initial Characteristics of TSE

The integrated sensor chip layout and TSE structure are shown in Fig. 1. This sensor has been fabricated by means of conventional MIS-technology. Technological processes details are presented in [2, 6]. The size of silicon chip is 2×2 mm^2. Structurally-technological and physical parameters TSE are the following: acceptors concentration $N_a = 5 \cdot 10^{15}$ cm^{-3}; length L and width z of the channel are 10 μm and 3.2 mm; dielectric capacitance $C_0 \approx 30$ nF/cm^2; transconductance $b \approx 2.0$ mA/V^2.

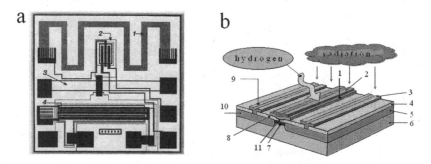

Fig. 1. (a) The sensor chip layout: 1 – Pd-resistor, 2 – test element and thermosensor, 3 – heater, 4 – TSE. (b) The TSE structure: *1* – the gas sensitive layer of a Pd gate ($\approx$70 nm); *2* – the outer part of a gate (Pd + PdO); *3* and *9* – drain and source Al connections; *4* and *8* – a thick (380–450 nm) Ta$_2$O$_5$-SiO$_2$ insulator; *5* and *10* – a drain and a source (n^+-Si); *6* – a substrate p-Si; *7* – a channel n-Si; *11* – a thin (150–200 nm) Ta$_2$O$_5$-SiO$_2$ gate insulator.

2.2 Experimental Technique

In the first stage of the experiment the transient current-voltage characteristic (the drain current I_D of the gate voltage V_G dependence) of the test TSE were measured. These characteristics were used to determine the initial values of the threshold voltage V_{T0}, the transconductance b_0, the charge in the oxide Q_{t0} and the charge Q_{ss0} at the interface SiO$_2$-Si.

In the second stage the threshold voltage of TSE as function of hydrogen concentration was determined. For this purpose the sensor hydrogen responses were measured with using special circuitry [7]. The measuring circuitry provides the constant $I_D \approx 0{,}1$ mA and source-drain voltage $V_D \approx 1$ V and the output voltage $V_{out} = V_G$. For this measuring circuitry the threshold voltage

$$V_T = V_{OUT} - \sqrt{2I_D/b} \tag{1}$$

The chip temperature 130 °C is supported by means of special temperature-stabilization circuitry with feedback loop using on-chip thermosensor and heater [6]. Each sensor was 3 times exposed to hydrogen pulses ($\tau_i \approx 20$–30 s with period $\tau \approx 60$ s) with concentrations (C): 0.005, 0.01, 0.05, 0.1 and 0.2 % vol. The computerized instrumentation with gas chamber was used for experiment. Typical hydrogen response (for $C \approx 0.05$ % vol.) and the response parameters are presented in Fig. 2.

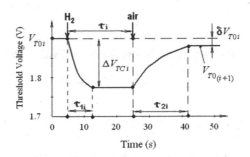

Fig. 2. The parameters of response for hydrogen concentration 0.05 % vol.

The following parameters of hydrogen responses were measured: initial threshold voltage V_{T0}, amplitude of response ΔV_{TCi}, residual value of response δV_{Ti}, response τ_{1i} and relaxation τ_{2i} times (i-ordinal number of hydrogen injection). Then average values of all the response parameters were determined as in [9, 10].

In the third stage of experiments the sensor radiation sensitivity was investigated. For this purpose 8 sensors with identical initial characteristics have been selected (dispersion V_{T0} was less than 10 %). The sensors were divided by two sorts: 3 – as the comparative samples (not be irradiated) and 5 samples have being irradiated. Before and after each irradiation all the sensors were 3 times exposed to hydrogen pulses with concentrations: 0.05 and 0.1 % vol. The sensors were 5 times exposed to electron radiation (6 MeV energy) with various doses in the linear accelerator U-28"MEPhI". The fluencies accepted the following values: 10^{11}; $2 \cdot 10^{11}$; $5 \cdot 10^{11}$; $2 \cdot 10^{12}$ and 10^{13} e/cm^2. These fluencies correspond to the accumulated absorption doses D(Si): $\approx$30, 90, 260, 920 Gy and 4,22 кGy. (1 Gy = 100 rad). The absorption dose rate P(Si) $\approx$2.0 Gy/s, during irradiations $V_G = V_D = 0$ V.

3   Results and Discussion

3.1   The Experimental Results

The average values and relative variation indices of V_{T0}, ΔV_{TC} and δV_T, as well as the time parameters of hydrogen responses (at $C = 0.1$ %) before and after irradiation are demonstrated in Table 1.

Table 1. Experimental results.

Quantities, parameters	Radiation absorbed dose D, Gy					
	0	30	90	260	920	4220
V_{T0}, V	1.89	1.83	1.78	1.57	1.13	0.277
ρ_1, %	1.3	1.3	1.4	1.45	1.45	1.6
ΔV_{TC}, mV	290	289	290	288	260	180
ρ_2, %	6–8	6–8	4–6	4–5	4–5	<4
δV_T, mV	7	6	5	4	4	<3
ρ_3, %	17.5	17.5	16	13	11	9
τ_1, s	9.5	9.5	8	6.5	6.5	6.5
τ_2, s	20	20	17.5	13.5	13.5	13.5

3.2   The Models of Hydrogen and Radiation Sensitivities TSE

The mathematic models of hydrogen and radiation sensitivity TSE were used as in [9, 10].

$$V_T(C,D) = V_{T0}(D) - \Delta V_C(C,D) \tag{2}$$

$$V_{T0}(D) = V_{T00} - \Delta V_t(D) + \Delta V_{ss}(D) \tag{3}$$

$$\Delta V_C = 0.5 \cdot [1 - \exp(-15 \cdot C)] \cdot \{1 - \exp[-k_3 \cdot (D_0 - D)]\} \tag{4}$$

$$\Delta V_t = [\Delta Q_{t0} + k_0 \cdot (V_G - V_T)] \cdot [1 - \exp(-k_1 \cdot D)]/C_0 \tag{5}$$

$$\Delta V_{ss} = \Delta V_{ssM} \cdot [1 - \exp(-k_2 \cdot D)] \tag{6}$$

Experimentally determined the model parameters: $V_{T00} \approx 1.9$ V; $\Delta V_{ssM} \approx 1.65$ V; $D_0 \approx 1.7 \cdot 10^4$ Gy; $k_0 \approx 25$ nC/V·cm^2; $k_1 \approx 10^{-4}$ Gy^{-1}; $k_2 \approx 3 \cdot 10^{-5}$ Gy^{-1}; $k_3 \approx 2 \cdot 10^{-4}$ Gy^{-1}; $\Delta Q_{t0} \approx 45$ nC/cm^2. The formulas are based on the classical physical models of MISFET by using the approximation and extrapolation of the experimental data for TSE.

3.3   Discussion on the Experimental Results

The threshold voltages of TSE as a function of hydrogen concentration were determined before and after irradiations (Fig. 3a). It is found that the transfer functions V_T (C,D) of irradiated samples are monotonically drifting up to 0.7 V under radiation doses $D \leq D_1 \approx 730$ Gy without changing of the hydrogen sensitivity $S_C = dV_T/dC$. That is only V_{T0} (D) were decreasing. For voltage error 1 mV the threshold values of dose $D_T \approx 3.8$ Gy and of dose rate $P_T \approx 0.4$ µGy/s. After following irradiations the hydrogen sensitivity S_C is steadily decreasing. The radiation sensitivity $S_D = dV_{T0}/dD$ gets the maximum values ~ 0.2 mV/Gy under doses ~ 10 Gy and $S_D \approx 0$ at doses ~ 20 kGy. The hydrogen sensitivity gets the maximum values ~ 4 V/% at $C \sim 0.002$ % and $S_C \approx 0$ at $C \sim 1$ % according to models (3) and (5).

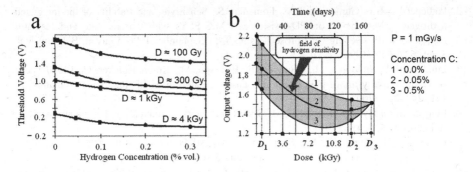

Fig. 3. (a) The threshold voltage V_T as a function of hydrogen concentration C before (1) and after irradiations. (b) Forecast dose and time dependences of output voltages of the hydrogen sensor based on TSE under ionizing radiation.

Using the models (2)–(6) the forecast of performance of the hydrogen sensors based on TSE under ionizing radiation has been done and is presented in Fig. 3b.

4   Conclusion

The electron irradiation influence on hydrogen sensitivity of the integrated sensors with palladium-gate MISFET has been studied. It was shown that the threshold voltage as a function of hydrogen concentration V_T (C) are monotonically drifting under radiation doses up to $D_1 \sim 730$ Gy without changing of the hydrogen sensitivity. After following irradiations the hydrogen sensitivity are decreasing in addition the V_{T0} (D) drift and decreasing parameter δV_T. The ionizing radiation doses less than 3.8 Gy and dose rate $P_T < 0.4$ µGy/s are not dangerous for the sensors.

According to used models the hydrogen sensitivity to diminish in 2 times under doses $D_2 \sim 10$ kGy and should be decreased to zero after irradiation by very high doses (more than 15 kGy). Such absorbed doses, for example, could be only under long time uninterrupted space irradiation ~ 200 days or ~ 1500 days into the upper atmosphere. For most applications of gas-analysis devices and systems based on TSE the irradiation is weak influencing factor.

In order to decrease the radiation sensitivity the sensors and monitoring systems TSE could be preliminary irradiated under dose ~ 50 Gy. In addition an irradiation can be used as technological means of improving sensor metrological characteristics [7].

References

1. Voronov, Y.A., Kovalenko, A.V., Nikiforova, M.Y., Podlepetsky, B.I., Samotaev, N.N., Vasiliev, A.A.: Elements of gas sensors based on micro-fabrication technology. Datch. Sist. **3**, 28–36 (2010)

2. Podlepetsky, B.I., Gumenjuk, S.V., Fomenko, S.: Sensitivity and stability of the integrated hydrogen sensors based on PD-resistor and MIS-FETs with various gate and insulator materials. In: Proceedings of Eurosensors X, 8–11 September 1996, Leuven, Belgium, vol. 3, pp. 637–640 (1996)
3. Lundström, I., Sundgren, H., Winquist, F., Eriksson, M., Krants-Rülcker, C., Lloyd-Spets, A.: Twenty-five years of field effect gas sensor research in Linköping. Sens. Actuators, B. **121**, 247–262 (2007)
4. Lundström, I.: Hydrogen sensitive MOS-structures, part I: principles and applications. Sens. Actuators **1**, 423–426 (1981)
5. Lundström, I., Armgarth, M., Spetz, A., Winquist, F.: Gas sensors based on catalytic metal-gate field-effect devices. Sens. Actuators **3–4**, 399–421 (1986)
6. Fomenko, S., Gumenjuk, S., Podlepetsky, B., Chuvashov, V., Safronkin, G.: The influence of technological factors on hydrogen sensitivity of MOSFET sensors. Sens. Actuators, B **10**, 7–10 (1992)
7. Podlepetsky, B.I.: Influence of ionizing radiation to characteristics of integral hydrogen sensors with MIS-transistor sensitive elements. Datch. Sist. **6**, 35–41 (2011)
8. Ma, T.P., Dressendorfer, P.V. (eds.): Ionizing Radiation Effects in MOS Devices and Circuits. Willey, New York (1989)
9. Podlepetsky, B., Kovalenko, A.: Influence of ionizing radiation on MISFET hydrogen sensors. In: 15th International Meeting on Chemical Sensors, IMCS2014, Buenos Aires, MPS-T8-3, p. 113, March 2014
10. Podlepetsky, B.I.: Integrated hydrogen sensors based on MIS transistor sensitive elements: modeling of characteristics. Autom. Remote Control **76**(3), 535–547 (2015). doi:10.1134/S0005117915030170

Approach to Engineering the Temperature Sensing E-textile: A Lightweight Thermistor as an Active Sensing Element

Victor Lebedev[1], Elena Laukhina[1,2(✉)], Vladimir Laukhin[1,2,3], Andrey Somov[4], Alexander Baranov[5], Concepcio Rovira[1,2], and Jaume Veciana[1,2]

[1] Institut de Ciencia de Materials de Barcelona (ICMAB-CSIC), Campus UAB, 08193 Bellaterra, Spain
laukhina@icmab.es
[2] CIBER de Bioingeniería, Biomateriales y Nanomedicina (CIBER-BBN), Madrid, Spain
[3] Institució Catalana de Recerca i Estudis Avançats (ICREA), Barcelona, Spain
[4] CREATE-NET, Trento, Italy
[5] 'MATI'-Russian State Technological University, Moscow, Russia

Abstract. In this paper, we describe an approach to fabricating conductive textiles with temperature sensing capability. The key point of our approach is in combining electronic properties of a molecular organic semiconductor with clothing. A polycarbonate film covered with organic molecular semiconductor was used as the temperature measurement element. To minimize the electrical response of the developed bi layer thermistor to deformations, the thermistor was attached to a rigid film-like platform specifically fabricated in the textile by its local melting. Our study shows that the developed platform enables engineering of the conductive fabric the electrical resistance of which exclusively responded to temperature changes. Such e-textiles may be easily prepared using a simple fabrication procedure and, therefore, they are compatible with conductive sensing fabrics prepared by printing techniques. The developed organic thermistor, being cheap, lightweight and biocompatible, is highly attractive for applications in wearable biomedical technology.

Keywords: E-textile · Bi layer sensing systems · Thermistors · Sensors for wearable technologies

1 Introduction

Temperature, deformation and pressure are among the crucial parameters to be measured in a number of sensing applications [1, 2] using the state-of-the-art sensing technologies, e.g. wireless sensor network (WSN) [3], wearable technology [4], e-textile [9]. Indeed, healthcare, environment control, biomedical applications call for low cost, lightweight thermistors and piezoresitors which are able to accurately measure temperature and pressure changes [5–10].

© ICST Institute for Computer Sciences, Social Informatics and Telecommunications Engineering 2016
B. Mandler et al. (Eds.): IoT 360° 2015, Part II, LNICST 170, pp. 223–234, 2016.
DOI: 10.1007/978-3-319-47075-7_27

With the emergence of above mentioned monitoring techniques the sensing technology on plastic substrates has become of especial research interest. It is expected that this technology will build up sensors introduced to new settings by significantly reducing their production cost and by adding new functionalities [5].

As the world population is ageing [11], the need in controlling the personal health status at and out-of home has been constantly increased. In this regard, there is also a particular interest in integrating lightweight conductive sensing materials in human wearable interfaces, such as fabrics, since wearable electronics could offer personalized healthcare, security and comfort [6, 8, 9]. These fabrics are able to sense and react to environmental conditions.

In this work, we present and discuss a new fabricating approach to processing the BL film-like thermistor into polyester textile which enables engineering of e-textiles being capable of controlling very small temperature changes with accuracy of 0.005 degree.

The paper is organized as follows: Sect. 2 will discuss related work in the field. Section 3 presents our approach and experimental results. Finally, we discuss our future work and provide conclusions in Sects. 4 and 5, respectively.

2   Related Work

The fabric-based sensing is a large field of research in the biomedicine. As M. Stoppa and A. Chiolerio have pointed in their recent review on e-textiles [9] the fabric sensors may be used for electrocardiogram (ECG) [9], electromyography (EMG) [12], and electroencephalography (EEG) [13, 14] sensing. Modern technologies developing for the sport, military and aerospace also call for sensing e-textiles. Many sensors and actuators have been developed, which are imparted to the fabric during finishing [5–8]. As measured elements they mainly utilize thin metallic wires being embedded in a fabric [9]. Electrically conductive fibers can also be prepared by coating the fibers with metals, galvanic substances or metallic salts. To fabricate electrically conductive textiles, the surface of a textile may also be coated with a thin layer of either metal or semiconductor. Developing metalized plastics [15] and conductive polymers [16] opens new opportunities for engineering e-textiles: coating textiles with conductive sensing plastics. It should be noted, however, that the major problems of metalized plastics are (i) poor adhesion of conventional metals to polymers that are chemical inertness [17, 18], (ii) significant difference in the Young's modules between soft plastics and rigid inorganic metals. These disadvantages result in low binding between the metallic and plastic layers [17, 18]. On the other hand, conducting polymers are not stable materials: their electronic properties are often unstable towards atmospheric moisture [19]. There are also others barriers to their applications, such as the high manufacturing costs, material inconsistencies, and poor solubility in solvents. In this context, one of the aims of our research was developing of the stable, flexible, composite materials that may be used as low cost, lightweight, conductive sensing components for their applications in wearable biomedical technology. We have recently

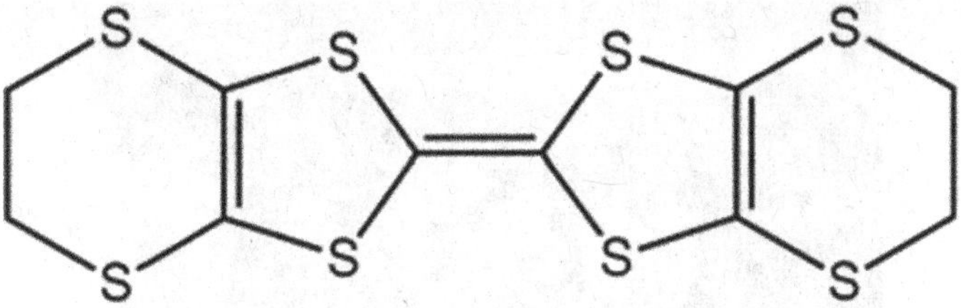

Fig. 1. Skeletal formula of bis(ethylenedithio)tetrathiafulvalen (BEDT-TTF)

developed an original approach to engineering such sensing materials which lies in preparing bi layer (BL) films polycarbonate/(001) oriented organic molecular conductor (BEDT-TTF)$_2$X, were BEDT-TTF = bis(ethylenedithio)tetrathiafulvalen (Fig. 1) and "X" is trihalide ions [20, 21].

These conductors are charge transfer salts with a 1/2 filled conducting band; they have very deformable layered crystal structures with strong electron–phonon coupling and due to this they demonstrate unique electronic properties that may be exploited in numerous sensing applications [22–24]. It has already been demonstrated that such BL films show a high piezo-resistive effect and could be successfully embedded in textiles as either strain or pressure sensors [25]. This result prompted us to apply the BEDT-TTF-based conductors to engineering conductive fabric whose resistance will be able to respond to small temperature changes.

3   Results and Discussion

The development of e-textiles at its first phase is reduced to engineering of sensing materials with electrical detection principle. It should be noted that modern wearable technologies are ideally suited for the electrical detection. In the second phase, it is to be considered how the developed sensing materials may be processed into textiles. In this context, we have developed a BL thermistor: polycarbonate/α'-(BEDT-TTF)$_2$I$_x$Br$_{3-x}$, were α'-(BEDT-TTF)$_2$I$_x$Br$_{3-x}$ is organic molecular semiconductor the electrical resistance of which is highly sensitive to temperature. In the body temperature range its temperature coefficient of resistance (TCR) is −1.4 %/deg. This value is 4 times greater than that reported for the platinum thermometer (TCRPt$_{111}$ = 0.3) [26]. We have recently pointed out [27] that this thermistor may be processed into textile using an impregnation procedure as it is shown in Figs. 2 and 3. However, our latest microscopic study revealed that this attaching approach provoked the formation of some cracks on the conductive sensing layer of the BL thermistor: polycarbonate/α'-(BEDT-TTF)$_2$I$_x$Br$_{3-x}$ (Fig. 4).

The SEM data stimulated us to look for another approach to the second phase. The experimental details of the developed fabricating method, as well as its advantages, will be presented in next sections.

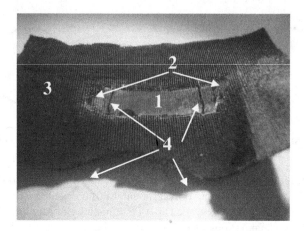

Fig. 2. Photo image of the fabricated e-textile: BL thermistor (1) is attached to the rigid impregnated part (2) of the polyester fabric (3); 4–electrical connections

Fig. 3. Photo image of the BL thermistor (1) that was attached to the rigid impregnated part of the polyester fabric (2)

3.1   Preparation and Characterization of the Flexible Lightweight BL Thermistor: Polycarbonate/α'-(BEDT-TTF)$_2$I$_x$Br$_{3-x}$

In line with the reported synthetic procedure the BL thermistor was fabricated as follows: first, a 25 μm thick polycarbonate (PC) film which contains a 2 wt% of BEDT-TTF was prepared. To do this, the film was cast on a glass support at 130 °C from a 1,2-dichlorobenzene solution of polycarbonate and BEDT-TTF. Second, to

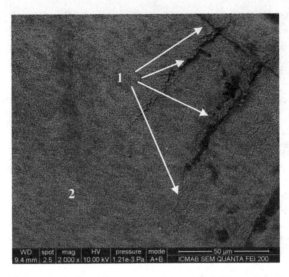

Fig. 4. The Scanning Electron Microscopy (SEM) image of the cracks (1) developed on the conductive sensing layer of the BL thermistor (2) attached to the rigid impregnated part of the polyester fabric

cover the film with the (001) oriented layer of α'-(BEDT-TTF)$_2$I$_x$Br$_{3-x}$, we exposed the film surface to the vapors of a dichloromethane solution of IBr. The surface of the film easily swells under this treatment, which facilitates the migration of BEDT-TTF molecules from the bulk of the film to the swollen film surface where they are oxidized by IBr. This redox process induces the rapid nucleation of the (BEDT-TTF)$_2$I$_x$Br$_{x-3}$ conductor with a consequent formation of the conductive polycrystalline covering layer. The resulting surface-modified film was fully characterized using Scanning Electron Microscopy (SEM) and X-ray diffraction techniques; its $R(T)$ dependence in the range of the human body temperatures was also investigated.

Figure 5 demonstrates that the sensing layer of the BL thermistor polycarbonate/α'-(BEDT-TTF)$_2$I$_x$Br$_{3-x}$ consists of submicro plate-like crystallites the crystal plans of which are oriented in parallel to the BL thermistor plan.

The powder X ray diffraction pattern (Fig. 6) shows only (00l) reflections of the α'-(BEDT-TTF)$_2$I$_x$Br$_{3-x}$ semiconductor. Therefore, the sensing layer of the thermistor has (001) orientation; it means that the layer is dominantly formed from c^*-oriented α'-(BEDT-TTF)$_2$I$_x$Br$_{3-x}$ crystallites. The direct current resistance measurements demonstrate that the value of the room temperature sheet resistance of the developed BL thermistor is $\cong 30$ kΩ/cm^2 and its conductance shows the linear temperature dependence in the temperature range from 28 to 50 °C; the sensitivity of the thermistor sheet resistance to temperature was as 250–300 Ω/cm^2 per degree.

In conclusion of this section, we would like to note that the above presented SEM and X-ray data, as well as the resistance temperature dependence, are in accordance with the early reported ones [21, 27].

Fig. 5. SEM image of the conductive sensing layer of the BL thermistor: polycarbonate/α'-(BEDT-TTF)$_2$I$_x$Br$_{3-x}$

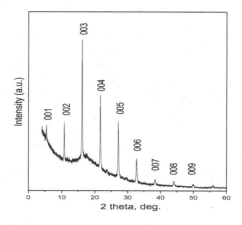

Fig. 6. X-ray diffraction pattern of the conductive sensing layer of the BL thermistor: polycarbonate/α'-(BEDT-TTF)$_2$I$_x$Br$_{3-x}$

3.2   Integration of BL Thermistor into Textile

To highlight the formation of the above described crack-like defects, we used a new approach to engineering of the polyester temperature sensing e-textile. We suggest that a rigid flat unit at the polyester textile to which the thermistor has to be attached may be prepared by locally melting of a small part of the textile being sandwiched between two plates. Under local melting the small part of the polyester textile has to lose its textile-like texture while becoming film-like. Due to such procedure, the melted part must become much more rigid as compared to the rest of the textile.

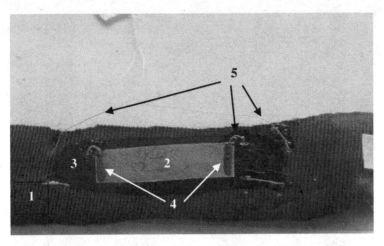

Fig. 7. Photo image of the new prototype of the temperature sensing textile: 1-polyester textile; 2- BL thermistor attached to the flat support (3) which was fabricated by textile melting; 4-electrical graphite contacts and 5- wire-based electrical contacts

In order to form the rigid support for the BL thermistors, the part of the textile was sandwiched between two glass slides and heated up to the textile melting point ($\cong$250 °C) using soldering iron; the textile plastification process was visually controlled. This procedure allowed us to prepare a smoother sensor support as compared to that fabricating by textile impregnation. The BL thermistor was attached to the rigid polyester-based support using the glue which was unable to destroy the polycarbonate layer of the polycabonate/α'-(BEDT-TTF)$_2$I$_x$Br$_{3-x}$ film.

At the final stage of the prototype fabrication, the electrical contacts were attached with graphite paste to the conductive temperature sensing layer of the thermistor (Fig. 7). In fact, the fabricated sensor can be easily interfaced with an embedded system, e.g. a wireless sensor node [28].

The surface of the temperature sensing layer of the BL thermistor was investigated using SEM. Figure 8 shows the sensing layer of the BL thermistor is attached to the rigid melted part of the polyester textile has no imperfectness which can be found in Fig. 4.

3.3   Temperature Testing of the E-textile Prototype

We test the e-textile prototype by connecting the sample to a wireless sensor node 'WaspMote'. In particular, we connect the sensor to the Analogue-to-Digital Converter (ADC) located in the Micro Controller Unit (MCU) of the sensor node. This simple testbed is prepared to ensure the proof of concept validation and performing the experiments associated with sensing.

The developed prototype was characterized as a temperature sensor in the temperature range from 23 to 50 °C. Figure 9 shows that the prototype electrical resistance almost linearly depends on temperature. As the resistance of the prototype decreases

Fig. 8. SEM image of the surface of the BL thermistor attached to the rigid film-like platform which was prepared using molding process.

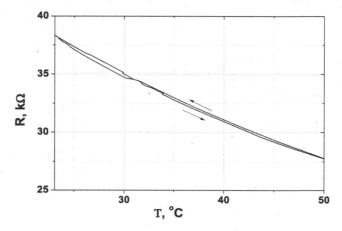

Fig. 9. Resistance temperature dependence of the e-textile equipped with lightweight BL termistor: polycarbonate/α'-(BEDT-TTF)$_2$I$_x$Br$_{3-x}$

from 38 kΩ at 23 °C to 27.6 kΩ at 50 °C, the sensitivity of the fabricated sample of the e-textile to temperature changes is 0.4 kΩ/degree. Therefore, the developed BL film is capable of controlling very small temperature changes (0.01–0.005 degree).

The prototype of the temperature sensing e-fabric was additionally subjected to several heating cycles from room temperature up to 60 °C (Fig. 10).

The data presented in Fig. 10 demonstrate that the electrical response of the fabricated prototype to temperature is reversible, repeatable and stable in time. The

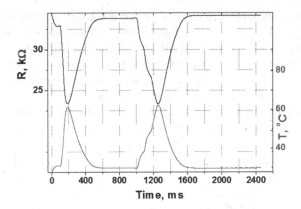

Fig. 10. Electrical response of the developed prototype of the e-textile to temperature cycles.

sensitivity of the conductive fabric to the temperature in the range of the human body temperatures is −1.2 %/deg; this well corresponds to the previously reported data [27]. This result shows that the developed organic BL film-like thermistor may successfully be used as temperature sensing components in smart wearable fabrics making it possible to measure very small temperature changes in the body temperature range. Additionally, it should be mentioned that biocompatibility testing of the thermistor is in progress.

4 Future Work

In our future work we plan a seamless integration of the developed sensing technology, as well as a processing unit and a wireless communication chip, in textile. To realize this idea into practice we are going to adopt the integration techniques developed in the EU Projects, e.g. PASTA (www.pasta-project.eu), Place-it (www.place-it-project.eu).

The integration of the developed sensing technology in textile has a high potential towards a number of monitoring application: environmental sensing (using the temperature and humidity sensors enables one to infer about the fire status), rehabilitation (ECG, EMG, temperature sensors). The application of a wireless technology makes the e-textile an autonomous monitoring system which has high potential in the forthcoming era of the internet of things [29, 30]. This activity requires further research, e.g. in communications [31] and power management [32], to guarantee autonomous operation of the system.

5 Conclusion

The BL thermistor: polycarbonate/α'-(BEDT-TTF)$_2$I$_x$Br$_{3-x}$ was fabricated and the texture, structure of its conductive sensing layer were investigated using SEM and X-ray analyses. The resistance temperature dependence of the thermistor was also measured. It was showed that all the investigated properties are in good agreement with the earlier reported data being indicative of the good reproducibly of the low cost synthetic procedure developed for the lightweight BL thermistor preparation.

A new approach to integrating the BL thermistor into textile was developed: the thermistor was attached to the smooth film-like rigid support prepared directly at the polyester textile by its local melting. It was found that the melted part of the textile is much more rigid as compared to the rest of the fabric.

The fabricated prototype was characterized as a temperature sensor in the temperature range from 23 to 50 °C. The temperature test revealed that the electrical response of the fabricated e-textile to temperature is reversible, repeatable and stable in time. The developed textiles are capable of controlling very small temperature changes with accuracy of 0.005 °C, which is significantly better than that reported for commonly used thermistors; for example, the measurement accuracy of a Pt-1000 detector is 0.01 °C. This kind of e-textile may find a number of applications in biomedical monitoring technologies usually reserved for lightweight highly sensitive temperature sensors with electrical detection principle.

Acknowledgments. The authors acknowledge the financial support from Instituto de Salud Carlos III, through "Acciones CIBER." The Networking Research Center on Bioengineering, Biomaterials and Nanomedicine (CIBER-BBN), an initiative funded by theVINational R&D&I Plan 2008–2011, Iniciativa Ingenio 2010, Consolider Program, CIBER Actions and financed by the Instituto de Salud Carlos IIIwith assistance from the European Regional Development Fund. The authors also appreciate the financial support through the projects: BE-WELL (CTQ2013–40480-R) granted by DGI (Spain), and GenCat (2014-SGR-17) financed by DGR (Catalunya), the European Commission's Seventh Framework Programme for Research under contracts FP7-OCEAN-2013-614155, the Ministry of Education and Science of Russian Federation Grant RFMEFI57714X0133.

References

1. Brunelli, D., Minakov, I., Passerone, R., Rossi, M.: Smart monitoring for sustainable and energy-efficient buildings: a case study. In: IEEE Workshop on Environmental, Energy and Structural Monitoring Systems (EESMS), pp. 186–191. IEEE Press (2015)
2. Wannenburg, J., Malekian, R.: Body sensor network for mobile health monitoring, a diagnosis and anticipating system. J. IEEE Sens. (2015). doi:10.1109/JSEN.2015.2464773
3. Somov, A., Baranov, A., Spirjakin, D.: A wireless sensor-actuator system for hazardous gases detection and control. J. Sens. Actuators A: Phys. **210**, 157–164 (2014)
4. Kalinauckas, A.: Wearable technology. Mag. Eng. Technol. **10**, 36–43 (2015)
5. Axisa, F., Schmitt, P.M., Gehin, C., Delhomme, G., McAdams, E., Dittmar, A.: Flexible technologies and smart clothing for citizen medicine, home healthcare, and disease prevention. IEEE Trans. Inf. Technol. Biomed. **9**, 325–336 (2005)
6. Lorussi, F., Rocchia, W., Scilingo, E.P., Tognetti, A., De Rossi, D.: Wearable, redundant fabric-based sensor arrays for reconstruction of body segment posture. IEEE Sens. J. **4**, 807–818 (2004)
7. Lumelsky, V.J., Shur, M.S., Wagner, S.: Sensitive skin. IEEE Sens. J. **1**, 41–51 (2001)
8. Ajmera, N., Priya Dash S., Meena, Ch.R.: Smart Textile. http://www.fibre2fashion.com

9. Stoppa, M., Chiolerio, A.: Sensors wearable electronics and smart textiles: a critical review. Sensors 14, 11957–11992 (2014)
10. Locher, I., Kirstein, T., Troster, G.: Conductive Textiles. http://www.wearable.ethz.ch/research/groups/textiles/ConductiveTextiles/ambience05_locher.pdf
11. United Nations, New York, Department of Economic and Social Affairs Population Division: World Population Ageing (2013). http://www.un.org/en/development/desa/population/publications/pdf/ageing/WorldPopulationAgeing2013.pdf
12. Linz, T., Gourmelon, L., Langereis, G.: Contactless EMG sensors embroidered onto textile. In: Leonhardt, S., Falck, T., Mähönen, P. (eds.) BSN 2007, vol. 13, pp. 29–34. Springer, Heidelberg (2007)
13. Löfhede, J., Seoane, F.: Thordstein: soft textile electrodes for EEG monitoring. In: 10th IEEE International Conference on Information Technology and Applications in Biomedicine (ITAB), pp. 1–4. IEEE Press, New York (2010)
14. Löfhede, J., Seoane, F., Thordstein, M.: Textile electrodes for EEG recording—a pilot study. Sensors 12, 16907–16919 (2012)
15. Mittal, K.L.: Preface in Metallized Plastics 7: Fundamental and Applied Aspects, Ed. K.L. Mittal, VSP BV, vii (2001)
16. Waltman, R.J., Bargon, J.: Electrically conducting polymers: a review of the electropolymerization reaction, of the effects of chemical structure on polymer film properties, and of applications towards technology. Can. J. Chem. 64(1), 76–95 (1986)
17. Pimanpang, P.-I., Wang, S., Wang, G.-C., Lu, T.-M.: Self-assembled monolayer growth on chemically modified polymer surfaces. Appl. Surf. Sci. 253, 3532–3540 (2006)
18. Joo, S., Baldwin D.F., Adhesion mechanisms of nanoparticle silver to substrate materials: identification. Nanotechnology, 21, 055204 8 (12 p) (2010)
19. Cardoso, M.J.R., Lima, M., Lenz, D.M.: Polyaniline synthesized with functionalized sulfonic acids for blends manufacture. Mater. Res. 10(4), 425–429 (2007)
20. Laukhina, E., Pfattner, R., Ferreras, L.R., Galli, S., Mas-Torrent, M., Masciocchi, N., Laukhin, V., Rovira, C., Veciana, J.: Ultrasensitive piezoresistive all-organic flexible thin films. Adv. Mater. 22, 977–981 (2010)
21. Laukhina, E., Tkacheva, V., Khasanov, S., Zorina, L., Gomez-Segura, J., Perezdel Pino, A., Veciana, J., Laukhin, V., Rovira, C.: Linked crystallites in the conducting topmost layer of polymer bilayer films controlled by temperature: from micro- to nanocrystallites. ChemPhysChem 7, 920–923 (2006)
22. Jerome, D.: Organic conductors: from charge density wave TTF − TCNQ to superconducting (TMTSF)2PF6. Chem. Rev. 104, 5565–5592 (2004)
23. Shibaeva, R.P., Yagubskii, E.B.: Molecular conductors and Superconductors based on Trihalides of BEDT-TTF and some of its analogues. Chem. Rev. 104, 5347–5378 (2004)
24. Saito G.: chap. 10. In: Organic Molecular Solids W. Jones (ed.), CRC, Boca Raton (1997)
25. Ferreras, L., Pfattner, R., Mas-Torrent, M., Laukhina, E., Lopez, L., Laukhin, V., Rovira, C., Veciana, J.: Highly piezoresistive textiles based on a soft conducting charge transfer salt. J. Mater. Chem. 21, 637–641 (2011)
26. PT-100 Series Platinum RTDs. http://www.lakeshore.com/Documents/LSTC_Platinum_l.pdf
27. Laukhina, E., Laukhin, V., Lebedev, V., Rovira, C., Veciana, J.: Conductive fabric responding to extremely small temperature changes. Procedia Eng. 87, 144–147 (2014). 28th European Conference on Solid-State Transducers
28. Somov, A., Lebedev, V., Baranov, A., Laukhina, E., Laukhin, V., Passerone, R., Rovira, C., Veciana, J.: Wireless sensor node with ultrasensitive film sensors for emergency applications. Procedia Eng. 87, 520–523 (2014). 28th European Conference on Solid-State Transducers

29. Kelaidonis, D., Somov, A., Foteinos, V., Poulios, G., Stavroulaki, V., Vlacheas, P., Demestichas, P., Baranov, A., Biswas, A.R., Giaffreda, R.: Virtualization and cognitive management of real world objects in the internet of things. In: IEEE International Conference on Green Computing and Communications (GreenCom), pp. 187–194. IEEE Press (2012)

30. Miorandi, D., Sicari, S., De Pellegrini, F., Chlamtac, I.: Internet of things: vision, applications and research challenges. J. Ad Hoc Netw. **10**, 1497–1516 (2012)

31. Baccour, N., Koubaa, A., Mottola, L., Zuniga, M., Youssef, H., Boano, C., Alves, M.: Radio link quality estimation in wireless sensor networks: a survey. ACM Trans. Sen. Netw. **8**, 34 (2012)

32. Somov, A., Baranov, A., Spirjakin, D., Passerone, R.: Circuit design and power consumption analysis of wireless gas sensor nodes: one-sensor versus two-sensor approach. IEEE Sens. J. **14**, 2056–2063 (2014)

exIMUs: An Experimental Inertial Measurement Unit for Shock and Impact Detection in Sport Applications

Ivan Minakov[(✉)] and Roberto Passerone

Dipartimento di Ingegneria e Scienza dell'Informazione,
Università degli Studi di Trento, Trento, Italy
{ivan.minakov,roberto.passerone}@unitn.it

Abstract. Wearable technology for physical activity recognition has emerged as one of the fastest growing research fields in recent years. A great variety of body-worn motion capture and tracking systems have been designed for a wide range of applications including medicine, health care, well-being, and gaming. In this paper we present an experimental inertial measurement system for physical impact analysis in sport-science applications. The presented system is a small cordless wearable device intended to track athletes physical activity during intensive workout sessions. The main distinctive feature of the system is its capability to detect and measure a wide range of shock intensities typical for many active sports, including martial arts, baseball, football, hockey, etc. Tracking of the sport specific irregular and fast movements is another important aspect addressed in the presented experimental system. In this paper we present the hardware-software architecture of the system and discuss preliminary in-field experimental results.

1 Introduction

Wearable computing systems for human motion tracking and physical activity recognition is a rapidly expanding field that is attracting a lot of attention from both academia and industry. Automatic human motion tracking facilitates the creation of new applications in a broad variety of domains, including human-computer interfaces, life care, wellness, sport, and gaming.

Over the past decade, various wearable motion capturing and gesture-posture recognition systems have been developed [1–3]. The integration into a single design of multiple sensors, such as triaxial MEMS accelerometers and gyroscopes, complemented with magneto and barometer sensors, has become a common practice in modern systems. In addition, recent advances made in MEMS and silicon technologies bring new a generation of miniature and low cost inertial sensors that provide high level of sensitivity, linearity, low noise level and high output data rate suitable for dynamic real time motion tracking applications. Existing motion tracking systems achieve a high level of accuracy when working either in a laboratory or when operated during very short execution time [1]. However,

© ICST Institute for Computer Sciences, Social Informatics and Telecommunications Engineering 2016
B. Mandler et al. (Eds.): IoT 360° 2015, Part II, LNICST 170, pp. 235–249, 2016.
DOI: 10.1007/978-3-319-47075-7_28

in real world scenarios, where various irregular motions and noisy background are present, the performance and accuracy of these systems might decrease dramatically [4]. How to achieve accurate and drift-free motion tracking, in terms of both hardware and software design, under real world conditions is therefore still an open research problem.

In this paper, we focus on Sport applications that are characterized in particular by strong physical impacts (shocks) and fast movements. The prime application domain for the presented system is the registration and tracking of *dynamic irregular movements*, such as boxing punches, baseball pitches, football kicks and volleyball hits. The main motivation behind of the presented system is to support a comprehensive analysis of the athletes performance by providing absolute values on the produced force, velocity and passed trajectory of the studied body segments. Such an analysis can provide a valuable feedback for athletes and objectively assess the individual's skills and techniques.

The main contribution of this paper is the exIMUs platform, an Experimental Inertial Measurement Unit for Sport applications. The exIMUs system is a single small wireless device designed to be worn on the studied body segments, including for instance the fist, ankle or head. The presented system consists of a full nine Degrees of Freedom (DoF) inertial sensors technology, including a triaxial acceleration sensor able to register high shocks (up to $\pm 400\,g$). A low-energy Bluetooth wireless transceiver is integrated in exIMUs for data communication with a host machine. On the software side, an Extended Kalman Filter based sensor data fusion algorithm [5,6] has been developed for motion tracking and velocity analysis. Preliminary in-field experiments have been run to verify the system functionality and collect an initial set of comprehensive data. The experimental setup was complemented with a high rate multi-camera visual analysis system in order to obtain ground truth data for accurate sensor calibration and to refine the tracking algorithms.

This paper is structured as follows. In Sect. 2 we overview mainstream motion capture and tracking technologies developed for various applications. Section 3 discusses the details of the exIMUs system architecture and the core hardware-software components. In Sect. 4 we present experimental results obtained in a real test case environment. Finally we conclude the paper in Sect. 5 with summary and future work discussion.

2   Related Work

Existing body-worn Inertial Measurement Unit (IMU) sensor systems for physical activity recognition vary in target applications, purposes, usage scenarios and final outputs. Visual analysis, traditionally, is the most popular method for human biomechanics analysis, and has been used in sport-science and sport medicine labs for years [7,8]. However, recently appeared MEMS sensor technology is able to complement and even replace traditional systems with equally accurate, and yet more flexible, personal and low cost solutions [9–11]. Ermes et al. [12] present a study on detection of both daily and sport activities in a real-life, non-laboratory environment. Two wearable acceleration sensors placed on the subject's hip and wrist were utilized to analyze actions such as cycling, playing football, exercising with a rowing machine, and running. A hybrid decision tree classification method was designed to recognize and classify different actions. Long et al. [13] present a single-sensor acceleration-based body worn system for computing daily energy expenditure in sportive activities such as soccer, volleyball, badminton and table tennis. This study compares a Bayesian classification method with the Decision Tree based approach. The results show a similar classification accuracy for both methods approximately equal to 80 %. Mitchell et al. [14] propose a framework for automatic classification of sporting activities using the embedded accelerometer found in modern smartphones. Three classification approaches were investigated: a Support Vector Machine (SVM) approach, an optimized classification model and a fusion of classifiers to recognize soccer and hockey activities. Recognition accuracy of 87 % was achieved using a fusion of classifiers, which was 6 % better than a single classifier model and 23 % better than a standard SVM approach [14]. IMU Arrays [15] introduced by Berkson are IMU-based systems designed for quantitative biomechanical analysis of baseball pitching. The system consists of a set of MEMS acceleration sensors placed on the chest, upper arm, forearm, and hand to allow independent measurements of each arm segment. The study shows general applicability, high level of accuracy and advantages of the presented system over traditional visual motion-tracking analysis.

Detection and analysis of motion sequences in martial arts is another popular application of wearable IMU systems. Motion sequences in combat and martial art sports are, typically, characterized by irregular and fast types of movements, that greatly complicate automatic recognition and limbs tracking. Heinz et al. [16] present an experimental work on real-time recognition of Kung Fu motion sequences using wearable sensors. The system contains a set of body-worn acceleration and gyro sensors for action detection. The tree-based classification algorithm was chosen for action recognition. The results confirmed feasibility of the task to automatically recognize movements in real time. Analysis of boxing punches using 3D gyro sensor was introduced by Morita et al. [17]. In this study, the authors discriminate different types of punches based on the angular velocity of the subject wrist measured by the gyro sensor.

Along with comprehensive motion, biomechanical analysis, detection and quantitative study of force (shock) is the subject of interest and research in many active sports, especially martial arts, baseball, football, and sport-medicine applications. Such an analysis has many applications in training and rehabilitation, assessment of individual physical conditions and techniques, as well as objective judgment and points scoring during competitions [18]. Traditionally, piezoelectric sensors and pressure transducers inserted under the target surface (punching bag, force plate, shoes) have been used as the major technology in this field [19]. In general, these systems provide an accurate measurement of static and dynamic pressures applied on the target object. However, traditional approaches have some critical drawbacks such as high cost, special setup, extensive calibration and large dimensions, making them only available for elite athletes in special sport medical labs. Modern market available MEMS accelerometers are able to tolerate and register high level of dynamic shocks (up to 10000 g and 400 g respectively) produced by any physical impact during sportive actions (throwing, kicking, jumping, punching, etc.). This, in turn, opens the possibility to complement and extend traditional human biomechanical analysis systems with force reporting facilities. However, due to the novelty of the technology and topic, there are only few scientific works available on this subject.

Walilko et al. [20] evaluated the punch of experienced amateur boxers to assess head impact responses and the risk of injury. Each boxer was instructed to strike a headform with a left hook or left jab. The headform was instrumented with MEMS accelerometers to determine the translational and rotational acceleration, and neck responses. The force impacts on the jaw region of the headform were measured using pressure sensor. High speed video recorded each blow and was used to determine punch velocity. Equilibrium was used to determine punch force, energy transfer, and power. The study showed strong correlation between pre-impact motion and post-impact shock.

In the field of force detection in martial art sports, several independent research [18,21] and many hobbyist projects were implemented. They all utilize similar technology by equipping punching bags or force plates with MEMS acceleration sensors to register geometrical inclination of the object after the impact. This, in turn, allows simple physics equations to be applied to compute force with known parameters of pendulum length and mass of the object.

The system presented in this paper improves on the above approaches in two ways. In the first place, unlike other body worn sensors, we aim to detect, classify and quantify *irregular* and *fast* movements, such as shocks, characterized by an extremely *wide range* of sensory values. While target mounted sensors are able to support these applications, as discussed above, our system is designed to be worn by the athlete on the body segment of interest. This extends the approach to those cases where no target is present, and provides critical data regarding the motion before and after a shock. On the other hand, a wearable approach raises certain issues and challenges in accurately measuring and quantifying the produced shock. To the best of our knowledge, however, there are no existing studies on this kind of approach.

3   System Design

The exIMUs system is an experimental inertial measurement unit designed specifically for sport-science applications. The main distinctive feature of the presented system is its capability to detect high level of shock (acceleration history) produced by any sportive actions such as punches, kicks and swings.

3.1   Hardware Architecture

Below we overview the implementation details of the exIMUs system focusing on its architecture and hardware details. The guiding requirements in designing

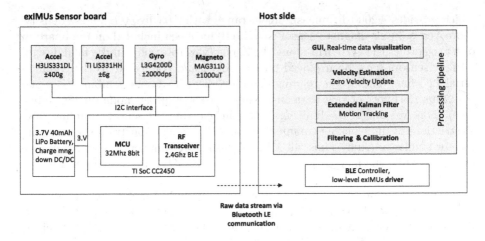

Fig. 1. exIMUs block diagram

wearable systems like exIMUs include real-time and accurate detection of motion series, weight and size constraints, wearable comfort, wireless communication capabilities and low power consumption. Additionally, due to our specific application scenarios, the physical reliability and damage tolerance after multiple shocks is another important aspect to be addressed in the design. Power consumption requirements determine the choice of low power hardware parts and system sleep-active scheduled operations.

The block diagram of exIMUs is presented on Fig. 1. It consists of a wearable sensor device, a wireless communication interface, and the host side processing that includes software analysis and visualization. A key component of our design consists of an appropriate and market available MEMS accelerometer whose sensitivity must span the entire range of all possible accelerations in the sports of interest. Based on the available information on the maximum level of shock and acceleration of ±80 g [19,20] measured during sport-medical experiments, we selected the newly introduced STMicroelectronics (STM) H3LIS331DL MEMS sensor. It provides 3-axis acceleration measurements with selectable range from ±100 up to ±400g with noise density of $15\,mg/\sqrt{Hz}$ for ±100 g range. Additional features of the selected sensor chip include a serial interface, several low power modes and small PCB foot print. However, during our first lab experiments we revealed that the level of noise of this sensor during stationary position was about ±1.2 g in magnitude, which would prevent us from performing any accurate motion analysis. We have therefore introduced an additional low-range, 3-axis acceleration sensor LIS331HH with high sensitivity ±0.07 g and low noise density $0.6\,mg/\sqrt{Hz}$ in the range of ±6 g, in order to complement the high-range sensor. Thus, two inertial acceleration sensors are used in our system: shocks and the pre-post impact phases of movements are detected by H3LIS331DL, while the relatively slow and medium actions (below ±6g) are sensed by LIS331HH. For angular rate detection we have selected the STM MEMS gyroscope L3G4200D which provides ± 2000 dps measurement range with $0.03\,\mathrm{dps}/\sqrt{Hz}$ noise density. Moreover, a 3-axis magneto sensor MAG3110 has been included on the board in order to correct the gyro drift along the Z axis (yaw rotation). In the final design, all four sensors have been placed on the board and connected to the common serial I2C line. The access reading time for all four sensors combined is equal to 2.1 ms (24 bytes of raw data in a burst packet reading mode on I2C interface). This was one of the limiting factors in selecting the sensor sampling rate. Restrictions of the blocking communication API [22] also constrain the sampling rate by similar amount. Thus, all MEMS sensors are sampled at a constant rate of 200 Hz while the magneto sensor is sampled at 80 Hz, the maximum rate for the selected magneto sensor.

On-board operations control, sensor sampling and RF operations are all handled by the Texas Instruments (TI) SoC CC2540 that combines a 32 MHz low power 8-bit microcontroller and a Bluetooth Low Energy (BLE) transceiver. The embedded application code is written in C and runs on top of the TI Operating System Abstraction Layer (OSAL) API. Communication operations are handled by TI's BLE Protocol stack [22], which provides a software interface to all BLE services including protocol configuration, devices and profiles discovery, and data transmission and reception. The power supply chain of the exIMUs board contains a 3.0 V step-down DC/DC converter, a battery charge management controller and a 3.7 V LiPo accumulator with a 40 mAh capacity. Although the relatively small capacity of the battery guarantees only about one hour of continuous operation, its limited size and weight are ideal to make our system unobtrusive. The peak power consumption measured during experiments was equal to 41 mA (all components are in active states). The current drawn in standby mode was measured at a level of 0.3 mA. The exIMUs sensor board with the attached battery is shown on Fig. 2. The complete and assembled system is

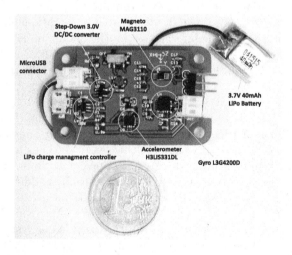

Fig. 2. exIMUs sensor board.

placed in a plastic enclosure with velcro strips for limb mounting. The size of the final system is 30 mm (W) × 60 mm (L) × 22 mm (H) and 40 g in weight.

3.2 Data Processing

Due to the limited processing capability of the on-board MCU, all the software data analysis on the raw sensor readings, including calibration, filtering, sensor data fusion and motion recognition algorithms, conducted on the host side, on a BLE enabled PC. The host consists of a built-in BLE controller, a set of custom developed exIMUs drivers, the core software algorithms and a front-end GUI. The SW processing part consists of calibration, filtering and motion tracking modules. The latter, in turn, includes a sensor data fusion algorithm based on the Extended Kalman Filter method.

The first software module in the processing pipeline is a low level driver that handles exIMUs ad-hoc service commands and delivers a stream of formatted raw sensor data from a built-in (or USB plugged) Bluetooth LE controller to the higher level application modules. Low-pass filtering operations are further applied on the acceleration and gyro signals in order to reduce the background sensor noise. The filtered data is then forwarded to the calibration module, which performs the offset calculation for the gyro and acceleration sensors. In stationary position, 256 samples are gathered to calculate the gyro mean bias from the zero level on each axis. Moreover, the magneto sensor is calibrated separately in order to cancel hard and soft iron effects. This operation is performed for each cold start of the sensor board.

Next, the filtered and calibrated data stream is fed into the sensor data fusion module, the heart of the entire processing pipeline. This part implements a quaternion based Extended Kalman Filter method [6,23] - a recursive algorithm that estimates the system state (state vector) and the state error covariance matrix from the acquired sensor measurements (two accelerometers, one gyroscope and magnetometer 3 axis each) and the known nonlinear system state transition dynamic model together with sensors measurement noise statistics. The quaternion representation provides a number of advantages over Euler angles including Gimbal lock-free representation, plain normalization and computation instead of complex trigonometry. The estimated state vector x contains an orientation quaternion q_0^b, angular velocity ω_0^b and low frequency gyro drift δ for in-line calibration:

$$x = \begin{bmatrix} q_0^b\ \omega_0^b\ \delta \end{bmatrix}^T \tag{1}$$

In the current implementation we use a non-variable measurement error covariance matrix, assuming white Gaussian noise in all sensor measurements. We also assume that the measurement errors are independent of previous states and perturbations.

The direction cosine matrix (DCM) in quaternion representation is given by the following equation as discussed in [6]:

$$C_0^b(q) = \begin{bmatrix} q_0^2 + q_1^2 - q_2^2 - q_3^2 & 2(q_1 q_2 + q_0 q_3) & 2(q_1 q_3 - q_0 q_2) \\ 2(q_1 q_2 - q_0 q_3) & q_0^2 - q_1^2 + q_2^2 - q_3^2 & 2(q_2 q_3 + q_0 q_1) \\ 2(q_1 q_3 + q_0 q_2) & 2(q_2 q_3 - q_0 q_4) & q_0^2 - q_1^2 - q_2^2 + q_0^2 \end{bmatrix} \qquad (2)$$

where quaternion q_0^b is given as $\begin{bmatrix} q_0 & q_1 & q_2 & q_3 \end{bmatrix}^T$.

The state transition matrix that represents quaternion transformation from body frame o to the global frame b, q_0^b is propagated according to the differential equation:

$$\dot{q}_0^b = 1/2 [\Omega_o^b] q_0^b \qquad (3)$$

where $\Omega_o^b = \begin{bmatrix} 0 & -\omega_x & -\omega_y & -\omega_z \\ \omega_x & 0 & \omega_z & -\omega_y \\ \omega_y & -\omega_z & 0 & \omega_x \\ \omega_z & \omega_y & -\omega_x & 0 \end{bmatrix}^T$ and $\omega_o^b = \begin{bmatrix} \omega_x & \omega_y & \omega_z \end{bmatrix}^T$.

The propagation of the rate gyro drift error defined in [23], δ, is determined prior to operation by static testing. The error propagates as:

$$\delta = \begin{bmatrix} 1/\tau_\delta & \cdot & \cdot \\ \cdot & 1/\tau_\delta & \cdot \\ \cdot & \cdot & 1/\tau_\delta \end{bmatrix} + w_\delta \qquad (4)$$

The measurements from the exIMUs board are given as a measurement vector that consists of acceleration, rate gyro and magnetometer triads:

$$z = \begin{bmatrix} f_{imu} & \omega_{imu} & h_{imu} \end{bmatrix}^T \qquad (5)$$

The accelerometer measurements for the EKF are modeled as the gravitational force complemented with a stochastic error vector $\triangledown_{ac}$ as defined in [23]. Using the quaternion representation to rotate the constant gravitational force, the accelerometers measure:

$$f_{imu} \simeq C_0^b(q) \begin{bmatrix} 0 \\ 0 \\ -\|g\| \end{bmatrix} + \triangledown_{ac} = \|g\| \begin{bmatrix} 2(q_0 q_2 - q_1 q_3) \\ -2(q_0 q_1 + q_2 q_3) \\ -q_0^2 + q_1^2 + q_2^2 - q_3^2 \end{bmatrix} + \triangledown_{ac} \qquad (6)$$

This equation for orientation estimation is only valid when the magnitude of the measured acceleration vector does not exceed gravitational level, $\pm 9.8\,\mathrm{m}^2/\mathrm{s}$. In our application, however, the range of measured accelerations is far above gravitational e.g., when the motion or physical impact are taking place, which will be shown in the next section. In such cases the presented sensor fusion algorithm relies only on the gyro and magnetometer measurements for the orientation estimation during active motions. As soon as the magnitude of the sensed acceleration signal on all 3 axes combined returns to the gravitational level the EKF module corrects the orientation with accelerometer measures.

The sensed gyro angular rate ω_{imu} does not depend on the gravitation force and is modeled as direct measurement of the corresponding EKF state in addition to the gyro drift error, δ, and stochastic error vector ϵ,

$$\omega_{imu} = \omega_o^b + \delta + \epsilon \qquad (7)$$

The sensed magnetic field is modeled as magnetometer measurement vector transformed into the body frame DCM quaternion representation complemented with a stochastic error vector ∇_{mag},

$$h_{imu} \simeq C_0^b(q) \left[h_x \ h_y \ h_z \right]^T + \nabla_{mag} \tag{8}$$

The orientation of the gravity vector obtained in the sensor fusion module is used for the consecutive velocity estimation module. The estimation of linear velocity is calculated by subtracting the estimated gravity vector from the acceleration signal, measured either by the low or the high range acceleration sensors, and the successive integration of obtained values. To reduce the integration accumulation error, we utilize the in-line zero velocity update (ZUPT) technique [24] to reset the instantaneous velocity to the initial zero state. The motion phases recognition module implements a heuristic state machine that breaks down any movement into acceleration, impact, deceleration and steady states. ZUPT takes place when the exIMUs device is recognized to be in the steady state and no motion is happening.

3.3 Force Detection

Each triad of recognized acceleration, impact and deceleration states is an input for the successive force analysis module. According to Newton's laws, the quantitative force analysis with established acceleration is only possible when the mass of a collided object, in our case a studied limp on which exIUMs is mounted on, is constant and known. But this is not always the case for many sportive actions, like a boxing punch or a football kick. In such movements, the effective mass of the limb is combined with the partial mass of the body torso, which is difficult to measure directly. For these cases, in our method we introduce a lookup table-based approach that establishes the correspondence between the measured acceleration history, pre- and post-impact time, and a verified reference force values. The reference force data is obtained during an initial calibration step by measuring the physical impact by means of external (not wearable) dedicated force-pressure sensors mounted on a target object.

4 Experiments

Multiple pilot experiments were conducted to verify whether the exIMUs system is capable of picking up all relevant details of sportive actions performed in real life conditions. Currently the motion tracking and recognition modules are under development an evaluation. Two in-field experiments with exIMUs were performed to study football and boxing actions. The main objective of these experiments was to evaluate the on-board hardware parts and their settings, including sensors sensitivity and ranges, the selected sample rates, latency and sensors noise statistics. Additionally, the utilized Bluetooth low energy transceiver was evaluated with respect to the data throughput and maximum communication range. The host side processing pipeline included filtering, calibration, visualization and the data logging module for subsequent post processing analysis. All studies were complemented with camera-based motion analysis. The experimental setup included three high rate cameras (GoPro Black Edition with 240 fps at 848×480 pixel resolution) placed at different locations in the experimental scene. High contrast markers were placed on top of the exIMUs device to facilitate accurate visual tracking. The results obtained form the visual system, including velocity and displacement, are used as ground truth data for inertial motion tracking and as a reference to verify the EKF module output.

In the first experiment we studied football kicks performed by an amateur middle weight (80 kg) athlete with a standard size ball. The sensor device was fixed on the lower part of the subject shin. After the sensor calibration procedure, the athlete was instructed to perform a series of direct kicks with maximum force. A sample of the obtained sensor results is presented on Fig. 3. In accordance to the hardware architecture, the low range acceleration signal (top right graph) is clipped at the level of ± 6 g. The maximum levels of the registered acceleration and rotational velocity were equal to 57 g and 1800 deg/sec, respectively. The average impact time with the ball was equal to 60 ms, while the pre-impact acceleration time registered for all performed kicks was in a range of 300 to 460 ms.

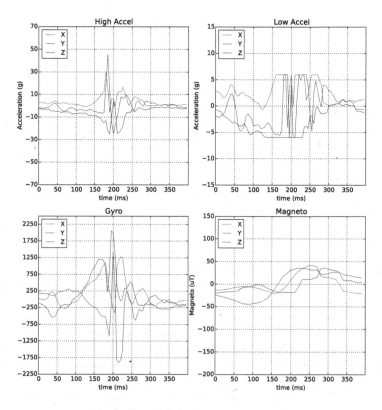

Fig. 3. Football kick sample example.

The Bluetooth LE communication range measured during this study (outdoor environment) was equal to 18 m at a −6 dBm output power setting, and 26 m at 0 dBm. However, communication was still possible at greater distances but this led to packet losses. Data latency from the remote sensor board to the host side logging system was on average equal to 40 ms.

The second experiment was intended to evaluate boxing striking techniques of two experienced amateur boxers. The weight of the athletes was 71 and 80 kg, respectively, that represented two different weight divisions. Certified 10 oz size gloves were used to perform two series of direct (cross punch) and rotational punches (right hook) with the maximum possible force and speed. A heavy punching bag with weight of 45 kg was used as a target object. The exIMUs device was placed on the athletes leading hand wrist. In order to increase fixation and minimize sliding effect during punch impact, the device was covered by the glove velcro strap. Figures 4 and 5 respectively present samples obtained for both kind of punching techniques for 80 kg athlete.

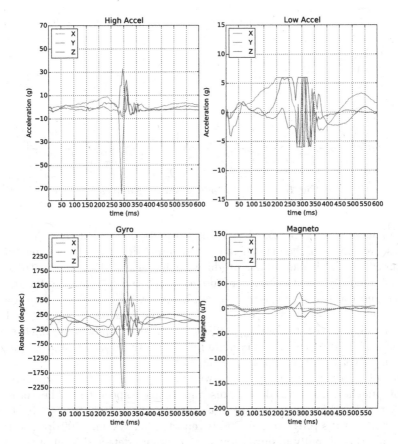

Fig. 4. Direct punch sensors samples.

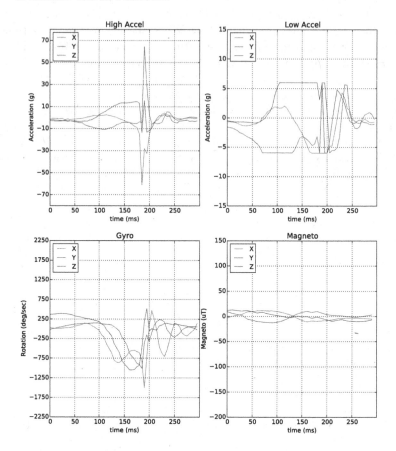

Fig. 5. Rotational punch sensors samples.

The analysis of the obtained inertial information revealed that the straight punches produce a higher shock impact of approximately 80 g in magnitude,· as opposed to the hooks which produce an impact of 65 g. Both athletes in our experiments showed similar pre-impact acceleration dynamics for straight (200 ms) and rotational punches (300 ms). However, pick shock acceleration was slightly higher for the heavier athlete (78 g max against 69 g for lighter). These values are aligned with previously published results [20] on boxing punches hand dynamics. This study reports maximum impact shock for direct punch registered at the 80 g level with pre-impact time at 330 ms.

The total impact time for hooks was longer than the time registered for straight punches, for a total of 25 ms and 15 ms respectively. The rotational velocity registered for hook punches was equal approximately to 1500 dps that is aligned with results presented in [20]. It reports a maximum 1700 dps rotational rate for punches. Finally in our study, the maximum detected level of rotational velocity for direct punches exceeded the threshold of 2000 deg/sec along the Y axis at the moment of impact, the maximum measurement range of the utilized gyroscope. This can be explained by the high acceleration magnitude of 80 g and the very short impact time of 15 ms that produced a very fast twist of the device along the Y axis at the moment of contact with the punching bag. This led us to the conclusion that the chosen gyroscope is not capable to completely cover the whole range of possible rotational velocities in sport. As an example, the maximum level of rotational rate reported for baseball pitch experiment [15] was equal to 2500 deg/sec.

5 Conclusion

In this paper, we presented a wearable inertial measurement system, exIMUs, for human biomechanical analysis in sport-science and sport-medical applications. The system consist of a set of cutting-edge triaxial MEMS and magneto sensors that support capturing motion in 9 DoF. The main distinguishing feature of exIMUs is the use of a high range acceleration sensor for registration and analysis of high level physical impacts and shocks produced by various sportive actions. The details on the exIMUs system hardware architecture and software processing pipeline have been presented.

Two proof-of-concept, in-field experiments on football and boxing techniques have been conducted in order to verify the sensor platform performance in real life conditions. The analysis of the obtained timing and inertial information shows their strong consistency with previously reported studies. However, the experiments have revealed certain limitations in terms of sensitivity range of the chosen gyroscope sensor. In spite of that, our experiments proved the general applicability of the presented system for biomechanical analysis in sport that might provide valuable information for athletes and coaches in related sports. Moreover, the presented sensor system and analysis might be applied also to other sports such as golf, tennis and volleyball, among others, where fast and strong movements constitute the main part of the performance.

Future developments on the exIMUs system includes a thorough evaluation and verification of the EKF algorithm using the reference values obtained from visual analysis, as well as further refinement of the sensor data fusion, motion recognition, and quantitative force measurement modules. Along with the software algorithms, our future work includes a revision of the hardware platform. For instance, the sensors sampling rate can be increased by improving the platform performance for an even more accurate and fine grained detection of physical actions. More compact and light weight platforms can be constructed for more comfortable usage. Finally, we are studying the feasibility of a complete onboard motion processing run on a separate ARM-based MCU, which would eliminate the need of continuous RF streaming to the host and allow the battery life to be considerably extended. For the energy-performance optimization of the ARM-based sensing platform we utilize a model-driven design approach supported by simulation environment presented in [25].

References

1. Chernbumroong, S., Atkins, A., Yu, H.: Activity classification using a single wrist-worn accelerometer. In: Proceedings of the 5th International Conference on Software, Knowledge Information, Industrial Management and Applications (SKIMA), pp. 1–6 (2011)
2. Khan, A., Lee, Y.K., Lee, S.: Accelerometer's position free human activity recognition using a hierarchical recognition model. In: Proceedings of the 12th IEEE International Conference on e-Health Networking Applications and Services (Healthcom), pp. 296–301 (2010)
3. Mantyjarvi, J., Himberg, J., Seppanen, T.: Recognizing human motion with multiple acceleration sensors. In: Proceedings of the IEEE International Conference Systems, Man, and Cybernetics, vol. 2, pp. 747–752 (2001)
4. Tsang, C.C., Leong, P., Zhang, G., Chung, C.F., Dong, Z., Shi, G., Li, W.: Handwriting tracking based on coupled IMU/electromagnetic resonance motion detection. In: Proceedings of the IEEE International Conference on Robotics and Biomimetics, pp. 377–381 (2007)
5. Willner, D., Chang, C., Dunn, K.P.: Kalman filter algorithms for a multi-sensor system. In: Proceedings of the 15th Symposium on Adaptive Processes, Decision and Control, vol. 15, pp. 570–574 (1976)
6. Sabatini, A.: Quaternion-based extended kalman filter for determining orientation by inertial and magnetic sensing. IEEE Trans. Biomed. Eng. 53(7), 1346–1356 (2006)
7. Tomita, A., Echigo, T., Knrokawa, M., Miyamori, H., Iisaku, S.: A visual tracking system for sports video annotation in unconstrained environments. In: Proceedings of the International Conference on Image Processing, vol. 3, pp. 242–245 (2000)
8. Wattanamongkhol, N., Kumhom, P., Chamnongthai, K.: A method of glove tracking for amateur boxing refereeing. In: Proceedings of the IEEE International Symposium on Communications and Information Technology, vol. 1, pp. 6–9 (2005)
9. Buonocunto, P., Marinoni, M.: Tracking limbs motion using a wireless network of inertial measurement units. In: 2014 9th IEEE International Symposium on Industrial Embedded Systems (SIES), pp. 66–76, June 2014
10. Bahillo, A., Angulo, I., Onieva, E., Perallos, A., Fernandez, P.: Low-cost bluetooth foot-mounted imu for pedestrian tracking in industrial environments. In: 2015 IEEE International Conference on Industrial Technology (ICIT), pp. 3430–3434, March 2015
11. Kagami, N., Murakami, T.: An approach to modeling and evaluation methods of human locomotion using IMU sensors. In: 2015 IEEE International Conference on Mechatronics (ICM), pp. 380–385, March 2015
12. Ermes, M., Parkka, J., Mantyjarvi, J., Korhonen, I.: Detection of daily activities and sports with wearable sensors in controlled and uncontrolled conditions. IEEE Trans. Inf. Technol. Biomed. 12(1), 20–26 (2008)
13. Long, X., Yin, B., Aarts, R.: Single-accelerometer-based daily physical activity classification. In: Engineering in Medicine and Biology Society (EMBC), Minnesota, USA, pp. 1–10, 2–6 September 2009
14. Mitchell, E., Monaghan, D., O'Connor, N.E.: Classification of sporting activities using smartphone accelerometers. Sensors 13(3), 5317–5337 (2013)
15. Berkson, E., Aylward, R., Zachazewski, J., Paradiso, J., Gill, T.: IMU arrays: the biomechanics of baseball pitching. Orthop. J. Harv. Med. Sch. 8, 90–94 (2006)

16. Heinz, E., Kunze, K., Gruber, M., Bannach, D., Lukowicz, P.: Using wearable sensors for real-time recognition tasks in games of martial arts - an initial experiment. In: IEEE Symposium on Computational Intelligence and Games, pp. 98–102 (2006)
17. Morita, M., Watanabe, K., Kobayashi, K., Kurihara, Y.: Boxing punch analysis using 3D gyro sensor. In: Proceedings of the SICE Annual Conference (SICE), Tokyo, Japan, pp. 1125–1127, 13–18 September 2011
18. Chi, E.H.: Introducing wearable force sensors in martial arts. IEEE Pervasive Comput. **4**(3), 47–53 (2005)
19. Smith, M., Dyson, R., Hale, T., Janaway, L.: Development of a boxing dynamometer and its punch force discrimination efficacy. J. Sports Sci. **18**(6), 445–450 (2000)
20. Walilko, T., Viano, D., Bir, C.: Biomechanics of the head for olympic boxer punches to the face. Br. J. Sports Med. **39**(10), 710–719 (2005)
21. Navas, V., Destefano, J., Koo, B.J., Doty, E., Westerfeld, D.: Smart glove. In: Systems, Applications and Technology Conference (LISAT), Farmingdale, NY, USA, pp. 1–4, May 2012
22. Texas Instruments CC254x Bluetooth Low Energy Software Developers Guide. Texas Instruments Inc., SWRU271D Version 1.3 (2013)
23. Kim, A., Golnaraghi, M.: A quaternion-based orientation estimation algorithm using an inertial measurement unit. In: Position Location and Navigation Symposium, PLANS 2004, pp. 268–272, April 2004
24. Harle, R.: A survey of indoor inertial positioning systems for pedestrians. IEEE Commun. Surv. Tutor. **15**(3), 1281–1293 (2013)
25. Minakov, I., Passerone, R.: PASES: an energy-aware design space exploration framework for wireless sensor networks. J. Syst. Archit. **59**(8), 626–642 (2013)

Towards Generic Intelligent WSN Platform for Hazardous Gases Detection

Nikolay Samotaev[1]([✉]), Anastasia Ivanova[1], Konstantin Oblov[1],
Pavel Laguzov[2], and Andrey Sokolov[2]

[1] National Research Nuclear University MEPhI (Moscow Engineering Physics Institute), Kashirskoe highway 31, 115409 Moscow, Russian Federation
nnsamotaev@mephi.ru
[2] Open Joint Stock Company "NPP "Delta",
Klara Zetkin Street 18, 127299 Moscow, Russian Federation

Abstract. The focus of this work is made on standardization and unification process during the design and production of a commercially available system for gas analytical instruments industry. The implementation of Wireless Sensor Network (WSN) platform for hazardous gases detection includes the development of software which relies on the digital data exchange protocol using National Standard of Russian Federation. The goal of software is to support hardware electronics for smart gas sensitive modules and Wi-Fi wireless digital platform. This idea allows the user to work with the web application available on most mobile device (tablet PC, smart phone, etc.) using widely available free internet browsers (Mozilla Firefox, Google Chrome, etc.) without necessity of downloading any additional service software.

Keywords: Gas detection · Wi-Fi · Digital data exchange · Electrochemical gas sensor · Metal oxide gas sensor

1 Introduction

Development of the gas control equipment for industrial safety and environmental atmosphere monitoring is based on the use of gas-sensitive sensors. Since the variety of physical principles is used to convert the chemical signal into electrical, different types of gas sensors significantly vary in their electrical parameters, design and sizes [1]. Modern microelectronic technologies allow producing sensors with small size and convenient dimensions. Universal digital bus provides reliable communication of the sensors with measuring electronics. Versatility is aimed, primarily, to the convenience of the user and operational feasibility of the standard unit – gas sensing module – replacing. Currently, dozens of companies offer their products on market of gas analytical instruments [1–4]. Each of them is trying to 'fix' the consumer to its products and introduce own standard for gas-sensitive sensors. Electronics and software of gas sensitive modules are usually designed for a specific standards and data exchange protocols typical for different industries, such as chemical industry [2], air quality monitoring [3], domestic alarm systems [4], automotive production [5], etc. It is not a secret that half of the firm's profits comes from the sale of spare parts and sensors to the

B. Mandler et al. (Eds.): IoT 360° 2015, Part II, LNICST 170, pp. 250–259, 2016.
DOI: 10.1007/978-3-319-47075-7_29

previously delivered equipment. From another side in many works, attention was paid to low power consuming sensors for wireless platforms and to cloud technology enabling the communication between each sensor under harsh industrial environments [6]. There are now commercial products, for example, Wasp Mote [7] which require frequent recalibration and may result in inaccurate gas measurement, because only one sensor can be used in sensing circuit and because of neglecting environmental effects [8]. Another similar example of wireless sensor – actuator system for gas leak detection with single catalytic sensor was demonstrated in [9, 10]. Upon detection of a dangerous gas in the environment, the sensor node communicates to a remote actuator in wireless way using ZigBee/IEEE802.15.4 standard and BACnet protocol. These examples show that the multisensory platform really rare because producers and developers mainly focused on energy consumption and increasing network complexity with elements of backup for data transmission channels. From the other hand, if we talk about wireless systems for domestic monitoring, various types of implementation could be observed: the data transfer in such systems is realized by the ZigBee [11], GSM [12] or Wi-Fi [13] technologies. But mostly there is a problem of system operating with restricted accessibility [14], as well as the need to use special algorithms to collect and store large data arrays [15].

2 The Concept of WSN Platform for Hazardous Gases Detection

Taking into account all of the advantages and disadvantages describing above, we decided in our work for developing a wireless sensor network platform (WSN Platform) work without special user software and frequent recalibrations. The WSN Platform should be also easily accessible for inexperienced users. The main commercial segment for this kind of WSN Platform is private households, farms, sewage manholes, heating systems using flammable substances, etc. with inaccessibility of dangerous gas sources location. From the one hand WSN Platform should have an open and easy access interface to the user, from the other hand signal should not be extended beyond 30 m from the place of the source (to avoid admission of any unauthorized person to the signal).

Based on the presented reasons we chose Wi-Fi as a wireless data transfer standard. This standard is supported by most modern mobile devices (laptop, smart phone, etc.). For data exchange between sensors and mother board of the wireless digital platform, we chose open digital protocol according to Russian National Standard "Digital intellectual gas sensitive modules" [16]. This choice enables the application of any type of gas sensors only limiting by sensor package dimension and value of sensor power supply (voltage and current).

The hardware concept WSN Platform in first is creating a series of sensors with digital modules, having unified digital interface, communication protocol and standardized set of commands as well as setup, calibration and verification methodic. The sensors should have the 'hot swap' (PnP) ability as well as identification and configuration in the system after connection. The second idea of concept is have a separate transmitter as a base for digital gas sensor modules.

3 Interface and Digital Data Exchange Protocol

Figure 1 shows the structure of system with several sensors. It consists of a controlling processor (MASTER) and a number of sensors (SLAVE) with digital modules. Controlling processor sends commands and receives from the sensor the result of commands execution. Digital interface is the SPI bus. It has several advantages over the I2C or 1-wire ones. It provides hardware destination choice by the SS (Slave Select) signal and duplex synchronous exchange, which allows reliable and quick work in a system with several sensors on a single bus.

For the I2C bus or 1-wire bus work it is necessary to pre-install the unique serial number of the device on the bus, which may require changes (reprogramming) during the device (sensor) replacement. It is not considered appropriate to multiplex different digital bus types in digital interface, as this leads to a complication of procedures for incorporation in sensors and eventually decreases the reliability of the sensor system identification. Sensors with digital modules must contain a microcontroller providing data exchange with SPI-bus, managing, converting the sensor signal from the sensing element, and storage of the settings and sensor calibration data. Communication protocol must be the same for all sensors without exception. It consists of the system controlling processor request and the response of the sensor. Request consists of a start byte, command byte, data bytes and checksum. Sensor response consists of a start byte, the sensor status byte, data bytes and checksum. The composition of the commands set may differ for different types of sensors, but it must be unified. If, for example, team number 0×10 instructs to read voltage value of the sensor, the command for all types of sensors should be numbered 0×10. System controlling processor constantly asks the system for new sensors connecting, manages the connection of new sensors and receives data from the already connected sensors.

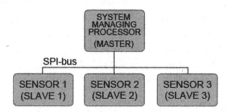

Fig. 1. The block diagram of the system working with several digital sensors.

3.1 Software and Programming for Gas Sensors Digital Modules

The digital sensor programmer is intended for programming, calibration and testing of sensors and consists of a programmer and control program for the PC. The program runs on Windows XP and Windows Vista. The programmer has 8 channels (ports) for digital sensor modules (Fig. 2). The programmer has the ability to operate as a separate sensor mounted on the selected channel, and a group of sensors located in different channels. In this case, the operation of the sensor configuration reading will still remain individual, and data write operation and calibration of the group are carried out with all installed digital sensor modules.

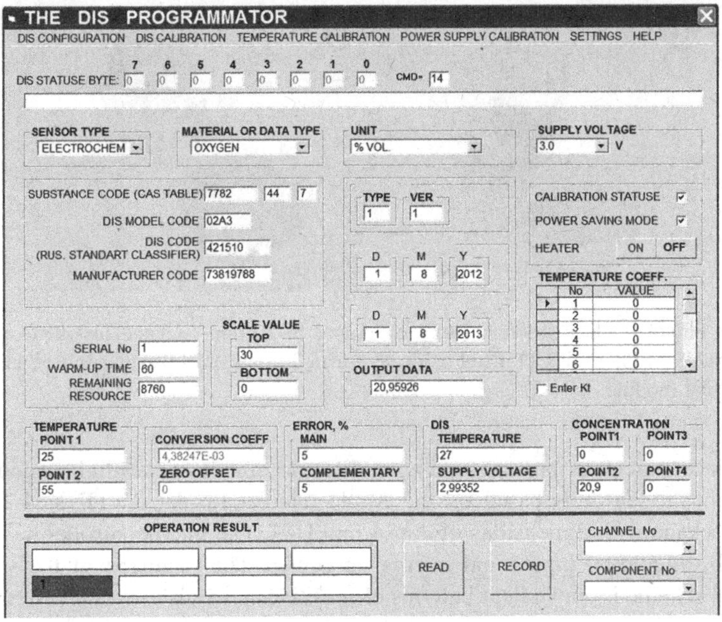

Fig. 2. The main program window contains a field for digital sensor configuration.

With the help of the digital sensor programmer could be performed the following operations: data reading from the digital sensors modules, the digital sensor modules configuration entry, working with the pre-installed table of chemical compounds CAS. Setting or status the configuration of the digital sensor modules can be saved in the database. After configuration recording the digital sensors modules can be calibrated. Sensors calibration always starts with the temperature calibration. It is important that this calibration has been performed at the very beginning, since precise data on the temperature required for proper calibration of the sensor to the measured value (component). In sensors with built-in heater the first calibration is conducted together with the heater calibration. Heater should be turned off and cooled before calibration. Absolute error of temperature measurement with one-point calibration is ± 10 °C; with two-point calibration is ± 3 °C in the temperature range from -40 °C to $+80$ °C. After the calibration of the temperature digital sensors modules can be calibrated by component (output value). Also during operation digital sensor modules constantly monitors the supply voltage. For its accurate measurement of the sensor must be calibrated to the supply voltage. Measurement error after calibration voltage is equal to 1 %.

3.2 Digital Module for Electrochemical Gas Sensor

One of the easiest in terms of technical implementation for digital modules is the oxygen gas sensor based on electrochemical sensing element O2-A3 [17] produced by Alphasense Ltd. Photo electrochemical oxygen sensor with digital module presented on

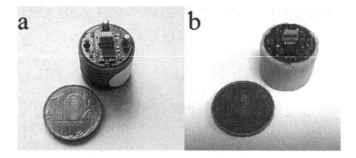

Fig. 3. (a) Photo of electrochemical oxygen sensor in 20 mm package installed on PCB of digital module; (a) Photo of CO metal oxide sensor in 20 mm ABS plastic package installed on PCB of digital module.

Fig. 3. Sensor circuit is present on Fig. 4. Electric circuit of the digital modules for electrochemical sensor is based on the Atmel microcontroller ATTINY84-20MU in QFN20 package with dimensions of 4 × 4 mm [18]. The microcontroller has a 10-bit ADC with differential inputs and internal amplifier. The inclusion of the sensor by differential scheme is convenient in terms of sensitive elements use with current output, because to produce an output by voltage, sensor output is shunted with small magnitude resistor (about 100 ohms). The microcontroller comprises a temperature sensor whose accuracy is low (±2 °C after calibration in the temperature range of 40…80 °C) but allows providing temperature correction of the electrochemical sensor response.

3.3   Digital Module for Metal Oxide Gas Sensor

More complicated example of technical implementation of digital gas sensor modules is carbon monoxide gas sensor based on semiconductor metal oxide sensing element fabrication of our past work [19]. The electric circuit of digital modules for metal oxide gas sensor and photo of semiconductor metal oxide sensor with digital module are presented on Figs. 5 and 3b respectively.

Main complication of sensor system development with semiconductor metal oxide sensor consists in relativity high temperatures necessary in sensors working conditions [17]. The heating process has two negative factors – power consumption and load to processing power of microcontroller responsible for temperature management. Power reduction could be done by pulse heating mode using, also in work [19] was investigated trade-off between sensitivity of such sensors type and power consumption during the heating. In the work [4] was shown that most energy efficient and reliable mode of system operation is at 70–80 % PWM, with maximum temperature heating up to 450 °C. Using this fact we developed electronic controller with PWM regime for semiconductor sensor heating.

Scheme of the digital module is based on the Atmel microcontroller ATTINY84-20MU in QFN20 package with dimensions of 4 × 4 mm (Figs. 3b and 5). The microcontroller has a 10-bit ADC with differential inputs and internal amplifier which using for measuring resistances of sensor's metal oxide gas sensitive layer and

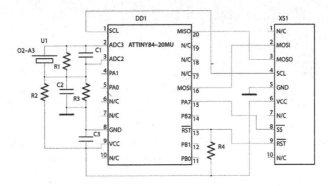

Fig. 4. Electric circuit of digital module for electrochemical O_2 sensor. GND - ground; VCC – voltage supply; RST - reset the sensor controller by low level; Trst > 10 ms; MISO, MOSI, SCL – SPI interface bus lines; N/C – not connected output.

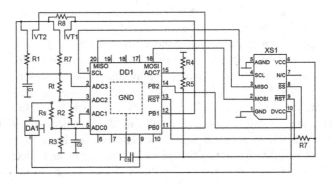

Fig. 5. Electric circuit of digital module for metal oxide CO sensor. GND - ground; VCC – voltage suplay; RST - reset the sensor controller by low level; Trst > 10 ms; MISO, MOSI, SCL – SPI interface bus lines; N/C – not connected output.

platinum heater each PWM cycle. Measurement resistance of the platinum heater plays an important role in the calibration of the metal oxide gas sensor. It is important to know in advance the temperature coefficient resistance for sensor's platinum heater by which the subsequent calculation is operating temperatures for measuring different gases (these temperatures can vary by tens and hundreds of °C for various gases and metal oxide gas sensitive layers).

4   WSN Platform for Hazardous Gases Detection

4.1   Software Implementation WSN Platform

The WSN Platform software consists of two major parts - built-in and client part. Built-in part was written in "C" programming language and uses functional

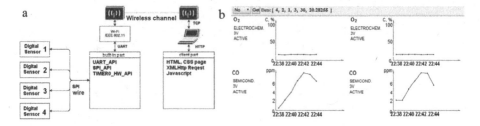

Fig. 6. (a) Software WSN Platform architecture; (b) The screen shot of the WSN Platform user software interface in internet browser during simultaneous measurement oxygen and carbon monoxide (CO) gases by two O_2 electrochemical and two CO metal oxide gas sensors.

programming techniques. The client part is implemented in object-oriented Javascript programming language. The WSN Platform software structure is shown in Fig. 6a. Client interface program runs via free internet browsers (Mozilla Firefox, Google Chrome and etc.). For lunch client-part interface program need in browser address bar need to indicate wireless network address for the WSN Platform - http://169.254.1.1. After this, network address of the WSN Platform client-side program is loaded and starts implementation. Code execution begins only after a complete download of source code of the program. The user interface of the WSN Platform is shown in Fig. 6b. The user interface has four plots showing real-time information obtained from four smart digital sensors. Near each plot small tables displays the name of measured gas, type of sensor, supplied voltage and sensor status. New points are added to the plot after each measurement and the plots shifts automatically, when the scale is full. In the upper area of the interface, there is information line displaying the last incoming JSON line and the test result of this line by a regular expression. The info line has also start key for the survey of sensors, selector that lets us choose the polling period and selector for change of alarm set up levels. An example of the JSON object: [4, 2, 1, 3, 30, 20.28255] present on Fig. 6b, where "4" is the digital sensor module number, corresponding to the position of the module on the device; "2" is the sensor type, according to the type of gas sensitive element in digital sensor module (electrochemical, catalytic, optical and etc.); "1" is the gas or another controlled parameter type; "3" is units of measurement (ppm, %, etc.); "30" is voltage supply of the digital sensor module, and the last value is the measurement result.

4.2   Hardware Implementation WSN Platform

During designing hardware for WSN Platform we focused on optimization of data transmission and neglected the minimization of power consumption. Therefore, we used the stationary power supply +12 V, although the system has an opportunity to apply the battery power supply, making the wireless digital platform independent from electrical power lines. Such approach gives possibility to use in experiments relatively powerful commercially available metal oxide sensors, consuming ~200 mW in continuous operation mode for detection of methane. However developed digital module for CO metal oxide sensors mentioned above allow to use in the future for the same purpose metal oxide or catalytic sensors with lower power consumption (about 1 mW) working in pulse heating mode describing in [20].

Strong attention was paid to the ergonomic design of the WSN platform. It was reached, for example by introducing the function of "hot swap" for digital sensors in the system. Attention was also paid not only to software implementation of this function, but also to the exclusion of mechanical errors during this operation. For these purposes, the holder was made to specifically prevent the destruction of electrical connector and to prevent a possibility of false installation of wrong type of sensor to the WSN platform. That is illustrated in Fig. 3, which shown on back side of PCB digital drivers, electrical connectors of oxygen liquid electrochemical and carbon monoxide semiconductor metal oxide sensors respectively. The holders preventing breakage of electrical connectors during "hot swap" of sensors to be installed in the WSN platform are shown in Fig. 7b.

Another ergonomic benefit realized into design is that WSN Platform does not require for work any additional software, other than widespread free Internet browsers (Mozilla Firefox, Google Chrome and etc.). However, in this approach there is a hidden conflict of price and quality of the product. The use of inexpensive 8-bit microcontroller with a small volume of RAM [18] leads to the limited capabilities of web design user software, and to the restricted number of measured point of gas concentrations and technical settings stored in memory. We plan to use more powerful microcontroller in subsequent upgrades of the WSN platform; this is justified from economic point of view, as currently the most expensive part of the device is a gas sensor, which is more expensive than microcontroller by more than one order of magnitude.

It is also possible to use the WSN platform as a standalone device. For that purpose, the WSN platform has LEDs displaying the operation status (on /off of sensors) and availability of power supply. As well, the wireless digital platform may give sound alarm using a piezoelectric sound element, depending on hazardous gases concentrations measured by digital sensors. To install the alarm levels for hazardous gases in the WSN Platform, it is possible to use internet browsers or using already present in memory default values for dangerous gas concentrations according to the maximum permissible concentration of hazardous gases substances in the working area by Russian State standard [21].

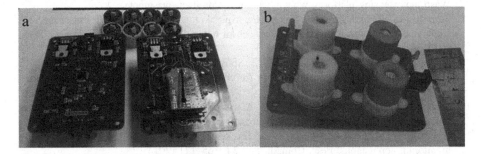

Fig. 7. (a) The bottom view of PCB of the WSN platform. The left PCB is without Wi-Fi transmitter and the right is with attached Wi-Fi transmitter; (b) The top view of WSN Platform with digital sensor modules. The attached holder preventing break of electrical connectors during "hot swap" (PnP) of digital sensors modules.

5 Conclusions

The wireless WSN Platform for hazardous gases detection with possibilities to work with up to four digital gas sensors modules was designed. The WSN Platform uses Wi-Fi standard for data transmission. Advantages of the WSN Platform are the following: opportunities to use any type of gas sensor with power consumption up to 200 mW; possibility of "hot swap" of sensors during work; standardization for 20 mm diameter typical of commercial electrochemical, catalytic and optical sensors; open digital standards for digital data exchange protocol giving chance to easily update the WSN Platform and create customer's own digital sensors. The WSN Platform does not require for visualization the transmitted data any additional software except widely available free internet browsers (Mozilla Firefox, Google Chrome and etc.).

Acknowledgments. This work was supported by grant of the Russian Federation President for young scientists №. 14.Y30.15.7910-MK from 16.02.2015.

References

1. Rock, F., Barsan, N., Weimar, U.: Electronic nose: current status and future trends. Chem. Rev. **108**(2), 705–725 (2008)
2. DrägerSensor EC - Electrochemical Sensors for Fixed Gas Detectors. http://www.draeger. com/sites/en_aunz/Pages/Chemical-Industry/DraegerSensor-EC-Electrochemical-Sensors.aspx
3. IAQ5000 Indoor Air Quality Sensor Module produced UST Sensor Technic Co., Ltd. http:// www.ustsensor.com//upload/File/20160627165754632.pdf
4. Spirjakin, D., Baranov, A.M., Somov, A., Sleptsov, V.: Investigation of heating profiles and optimization of power consumption of gas sensors for wireless sensor networks. Sens. Actuators, A: Phys. **247**, 247–253 (2016)
5. HPS-100 – Hydrogen Process Sensor produced by AMS AG. http://ams.com/eng/content/ download/686604/1787813/file/ams_HPS-100_Screen_Update.pdf
6. Mottola, L., Picco, G.P., Ceriotti, M., Guna, S., Murphy, A.L.: Not all wireless sensor networks are created equal: a comparative study on tunnels. ACM Trans. Sens. Netw. **7**, 1–33 (2010)
7. Wasp mote sensing platform. www.libelium.com/products/waspmote
8. Somov, A., Baranov, A., Spirjakin, D., Spirjakin, A., Sleptsov, V., Passerone, R.: Deployment and evaluation of a wireless sensor network for methane leak detection. Sens. Actuators A: Phys. **202**, 217–225 (2013)
9. Somov, A., Baranov, A., Savkin, A., Spirjakin, D., Spirjakin, A., Passerone, R.: Development of wireless sensor network for combustible gas monitoring. Sens. Actuators, B **171**, 398–405 (2011)
10. Somov, A., Baranov, A., Spirjakin, D.: A wireless sensor-actuator system for hazardous gases detection and control. Sens. Actuators, B **210**, 157–164 (2014)
11. Abraham, S., Li, X.: A cost-effective wireless sensor network system for indoor air quality monitoring applications. Proc. Comput. Sci. **34**, 165–171 (2014)
12. Zheng, Z.B.: Design of distributed indoor air quality remote monitoring network. Adv. Mater. Res. **850–851**, 500–503 (2014)

13. Lian, K.-Y., Hsiao, S.-J., Sung, W.-T., Chen, J.-H.: Mobile device monitoring system in the plant by an innovative approach. Appl. Mech. Mater. **418**, 104–107 (2014)
14. Kim, J.-J., Jung, S.K., Kim, J.T.: Wireless monitoring of indoor air quality by a sensor network. Indoor Built Environ. **19**(1), 145–150 (2010)
15. Abdulsalama, H.M., Alia, B.A., Al Yatamab, A., Al Roumia, E.S.: Deploying a LEACH data aggregation technique for air quality monitoring in wireless sensor network. Proc. Comput. Sci. **34**, 499–504 (2014)
16. Russian State standard: Hardware electronics for smart gas sensitive modules. http://www.internet-law.ru/gosts/gost/54487/
17. Electrochemical sensing element O2-A3. http://www.alphasense.com/WEB1213/wp-content/uploads/2015/09/O2A3.pdf
18. Datasheet for Microcontroller Attiny84-20mu. www.atmel.com/Images/8006s.pdf
19. Samotaev, N.N., Vasiliev, A.A., Podlepetsky, B.I., Sokolov, A.V., Pisliakov, A.V.: The mechanism of the formation of selective response of semiconductor gas sensor in mixture of $CH_4/H_2/CO$ with air. Sens. Actuators, B: Chem. **127**(1), 242–247 (2007)
20. Baranov, A., Spirjakin, D., Akbari, S., Somov, A.: Optimization of power consumption for gas sensor nodes: a survey. Sens. Actuators, A: Phys. **233**, 279–289 (2015). Article no. 9248
21. The Russian State Hygienic standard: Maximum permissible concentration (MPC) of hazardous substances in the working area. http://www.internet-law.ru/stroyka/text/4654/

Management of Ionization Source Based on a Pulsed Corona Discharge

Vladimir Belyakov, Anatoliy Golovin, Viacheslav Pershenkov,
Yulia Shaltaeva, Valeriy Vasilyev, Nikolay Samotaev[(✉)],
Evgeniy Malkin, Evgeniy Gromov, Vladimir Shurenkov, Igor Ivanov,
Maxim Matusko, and Dmitry Yakovlev

National Research Nuclear University MEPhI
(Moscow Engineering Physics Institute),
Kashirskoe Highway 31, 115409 Moscow, Russian Federation
nnsamotaev@mephi.ru

Abstract. It is developed igniting electrical circuit for pulsed corona discharge ionization to operate a source as part of an ion mobility spectrometer. The simulation circuit for forming a corona discharge allowed optimizing the parameters. The possibility of electronic switching of the primary winding and reverse polarity diodes in the high voltage part of the circuit provide operation of the corona discharge ion source for detection both positive and negative ions.

Keywords: Ion mobility spectrometry · Ionization source · Pulsed corona discharge

1 Introduction

Ion mobility spectrometers are widely used [1–5], particularly as environmental monitoring system [6–8]. Intense competition in the market for analytical equipment necessitates improving design methods. The most common sources of radioactive ionization based on 63Ni. Less popular sources of ionization by corona discharge, although they are quite stable and easy to operate [9–15]. In this article, it is developed the igniting electrical circuit for pulsed corona discharge ionization to operate a source as part of an ion mobility spectrometer.

1.1 The Circuit for Control of Ionization Source

The general structure of an ion mobility spectrometer control is shown in Fig. 1:

One of the circuits on the microcontroller generates the control signals for the ionization source, which are fed to an electrical circuit discharge formation. The discharge is produced in a mechanical structure consisting of four pairs of electrodes, the geometry of the tip edge, the ionization chamber placed in the spectrometer, which passes through the sample flow withdrawn from the subject.

In the case of usage of continually burning corona discharge it takes place problems with lifetime of source. As a result of the constant burning defects are formed needles,

© ICST Institute for Computer Sciences, Social Informatics and Telecommunications Engineering 2016
B. Mandler et al. (Eds.): IoT 360° 2015, Part II, LNICST 170, pp. 260–268, 2016.
DOI: 10.1007/978-3-319-47075-7_30

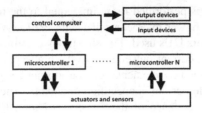

Fig. 1. The circuit of common control system architecture.

as a consequence - changing of their geometry and discharge parameters. Consequently, the ionization source should operate in a pulsed mode in order to prolong life and improve the stability characteristics. Ionization source on the basis of pulsed corona discharge must have a certain speed. It is determined by the requirements for ion mobility spectrometry. To ensure a timely response to the presence of target analyzable compounds in the sample spectrometer should hold at least 10 measurements per second. Generation and breakdown of the corona discharge must be for a period not exceeding 100 ms.

1.2 Corona Discharge Ionization Source

A development of a pulse generating circuit corona discharges includes the following tasks: the formation of the current pulse in the primary winding of the transformer, the accumulation of energy in the magnetic field of the transformer and the selection of this energy in the discharge gap. The circuit is shown in Fig. 2.

The primary winding of the transformer is connected to a power source via an electronic key Q1. A current increases and the energy accumulation is performed in a magnetic field of the transformer when applying the control pulse to the gate of the transistor in the primary winding. This energy is released in the secondary winding through a rectifier element D1 charging funded chain R1, when closing the transistor. Subsequently, tension from the chain is applied to the discharge gap. The circuit should provide a rapid accumulation of energy and it is subsequent discharge into the

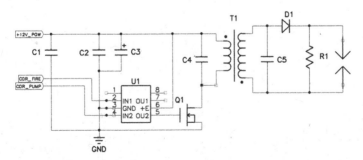

Fig. 2. The schematic diagram of pulse corona discharge ignition. The design of the ionization source, based on corona discharge.

discharge gap. The reset is performed for a time equal to the time constant. To match the signals from the low power microcontroller with the low-voltage transistor driver, high-speed MOS transistors U1is used. The circuit power is produced by capacitors C2 and C3. It is formed by a current pulse is fed to the high-voltage transformer forming T1. The parasitic capacitance elements of the discharge gap are dependent on arrangement of the needles of the connecting conductors. The geometry used for the value of the parasitic capacitance of the arrester is about 2pF. Therefore, the time constant of the RC-circuit arrester is 2mks. Experiments show that the shape of the discharge gap voltage ensures stable operation of the pulsed corona discharge.

2 Simulation of Pulse Corona Discharge Forming Circuit

To simulate the circuit it was chosen a simple case of Single negative polarity discharge. Model of corona discharge punch is based on a design of the discharge lamp. Circuit of formation of pulsed corona discharge is shown in Fig. 3. Below are presented the waveforms of the control points for different occasions. Point A is located at the output of the high voltage transformer. Point C is located on the discharger.

The Fig. 4. shows that the signal at the point C is relative to the delayed signal at the point A and has a smaller amplitude. The voltage at the Punches reaches the breakdown voltage of the discharge gap. The pulse at point C should have a larger amplitude or longer duration. This method is considering the option of increasing the amplitude of the signal at the arrester. Also the method includes increasing the amplitude of the output transformer. This method has limitations due to the technological characteristics of the components used. In forming the high-voltage pulse capacitor, C1 can quickly charge to a voltage corresponding to the breakdown of the transformer (maximum permissible voltage transformer used in the circuit is 5800 V). If the voltage reaches this value, there are technological limitations associated with the breakdown of the transformer. The breakdown will not happen in the spark gap, it will be through the element U1 in the secondary circuit, which simulates the electrical strength of the structure.

The results shown below were obtained by increasing the pulse duration to the primary winding of 15 %. Waveforms at points A and C is shown in Fig. 5.

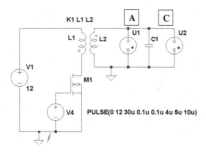

Fig. 3. The simulation of forming circuit pulse corona discharge.

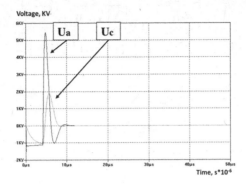

Fig. 4. The plot of voltage at the control points under conditions corresponding to the absence of discharge.

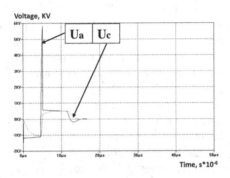

Fig. 5. The plot of voltage at the control points under conditions corresponding to the breakdown of the secondary winding of the transformer.

The voltage at point A is greater than the maximum allowed for the used transformer. Therefore breakdown occurs through the element U1. As a result, despite to the signal amplitude increase in at point A the voltage on the piercer doesn't reach the breakdown voltage of the discharge gap. Furthermore, the amplitude of the signal at the point C is reduced as compared with the case in Fig. 3. Thus, the goal is not achieved by only increasing the amplitude. This method has the technological limitations associated with the breakdown of the transformer.

Another option for solving the problem is to increase the pulse duration on piercer. Increases of the duration of pulse will lead to the fact that the amplitude of the signal exceed the voltage response of the punch (after the charge constructive capacity needles C1) and will occur electric discharge. In system added diode D1. A voltage pulse from the secondary winding charges the capacitor C2 via a diode D1. Voltage across the capacitor is held for long time, determined by the parameters of circuit C2. From this circuit a constructive capacity of needle C7 is charging, and when the discharge starts voltage breakdown and transfer of energy to the bit interval. The circuit is shown in Fig. 6.

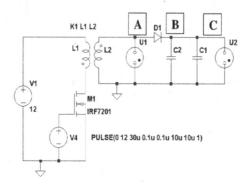

Fig. 6. The modeling circuit for forming a corona discharge with the extension of the high-voltage pulse.

The waveforms at the point B (after the diode D1) and at the point C are shown in Fig. 7. From the simulation can be seen that the developed ignition circuit with high-voltage pulse extension ensures the formation of the breakdown conditions of the discharge gap and the ionization source. Simulations performed with the technological limitations of the components is used no breakdowns in the secondary circuit of the transformer.

On the resulting chart, the following stages of the circuit: the accumulation of energy in the magnetic field of the transformer, increase of the voltage breakdown and burning of pulsed corona discharge, the zero voltage recovery across the discharge gap. The total duration of the process is 50mks. This speed allows to the source to operate more than one hundred times per second, which is much higher than the number of spectrum measurements for the same period.

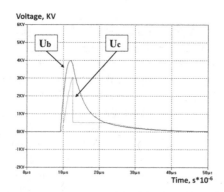

Fig. 7. Voltage at the control points under conditions corresponding to the breakdown of the discharge gap.

3   The Driving Source with Electronic Switching of Polarity

To solve the problem of functioning of the device in discoverable mode, both positive and negative ions is necessary to adapt the circuit developed by the ignition of pulse corona discharge in such a way that it allows you to create pulses of both positive and negative polarity. The previous sections described the essential work on the igniter of the pulse corona discharge, where the energy storage is carried out in a magnetic field of the transformer. The task of modifying the circuit is easier to solve in two stages: first, to change the circuit of energy storage and then design a switching circuit with the primary drive. The circuit is implemented with the possibility of mechanical switching of the primary winding and reverse polarity diodes in high-voltage part of the circuit (Fig. 8).

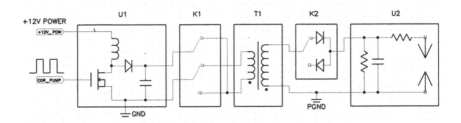

Fig. 8. The circuit of ion source with switching polarity.

The device includes a capacitive energy storage with an inductive circuit pump U1, switches K1 and K2 are input and output circuits of the pulse transformer T1, providing switching the polarity of the voltage at the arrester U2.

In the circuit the accumulation of energy is produced directly in the magnetic field of the transformer T1. The polarity switching is performed by mechanical switching of the primary winding. Simultaneously with the switching of the primary winding the diode of the high polarity part of circuit is switched.

In order to demonstrate compliance with the signal at the arrester Uc (in Fig. 6) it is simulated signal of corona discharge generating circuit with stored energy in the capacitor C3 (Fig. 9).

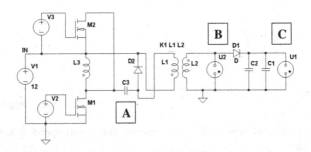

Fig. 9. The corona generating circuit is mechanically switching between modes.

Figure 10 shows the process of energy storage in the capacitor C3 and its discharge to the primary winding of transformer T1. The used circuit provides a much sharper edge of the signal on the primary winding, as compared with the case of directly accumulating energy in the magnetic field of the transformer.

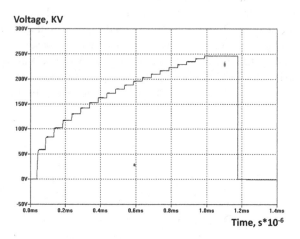

Fig. 10. The voltage at the test point A.

The signals at the control points B and C are shown in Fig. 11. The graph shows that the shape and the voltage across the discharge gap to form signals coincide in Fig. 7. Therefore, we can conclude that the correct operation of the circuit is forming a corona discharge with pre-stored energy.

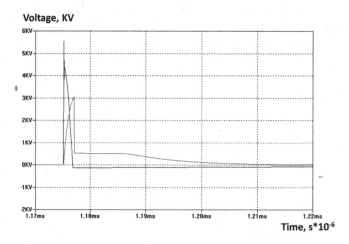

Fig. 11. Voltage at the control points B and C under conditions corresponding to the breakdown of the discharge gap.

In the practical realization of the device, it is managed to eliminate active electronic switch on the high voltage output of the pulse transformer and replace it with a diode-capacitor structure. A complexity of the structure of the corona discharge source control implemented microcontroller signals. In order to implement electronic switching polarity ionization source introduced four additional control signal. Two of them are submitted to the gates of the transistors, and allow for the accumulation of energy. Other control pulses supplied to another two gate keys, and allow to connect to a transformer capacitor corresponding to the selected polarity. The high-voltage circuit portion is modified so as to implement the passage of pulses of both polarities.

One of the criteria for the stability of the device is the stability of the current flowing through the needle when discharge corona is triggered. In the proposed circuit is made control the current flowing through a pulsed ionization source. The charge flowing through the discharge gap is transmitted across optocoupler to microcontroller for processing. Every act of tripping corona discharge leads to an equivalent change in the charge on the capacitor and the corresponding voltage.

Used diode optical pair is characterized by high speed and current coupling efficiency of about unity of the value of the input current. The photodetector type defines a linear transfer function of the optical pair. The resistor optocouplers is the most linear elements and thus suitable for use in analog devices, and then - optocouplers with foster photo-diode or with a single bipolar transistor. A separate connection to bias the photodiode improves speed by several orders of magnitude compared with conventional optical pairs by reducing the capacitance of arrival at the base-collector of the input transistor.

In the proposed circuit is implemented control voltage on the storage capacitor. The signal from the divider to the input of the analog-digital converter is controlled by a microcontroller. The voltage divider is parallel connected, which reduces the signal by a coefficient of 19: 1. The signal from the divider to the input of the analog-digital converter is controlled by a microcontroller.

In the proposed circuit, when switching polarity is not required to turn off the device and mechanical switching of ionization polarity. Polarity selection is done each time the ionization source via switching control signals corresponding drives. Thus, the achieved reduction of the time required to switch between the ion mobility spec-trometry modes between a few minutes (manual switching), up to one measurement cycle spectrogram, which is less than 100 ms. Given the technological limitations of the used components, the simulation circuit showed a substantial margin of the breakdown voltage in the secondary circuit of the pulse converter.

4 Conclusions

It is developed igniting electrical circuit for pulsed corona discharge ionization to operate a source as part of an ion mobility spectrometer. Modeling circuit is taking into account the technological limitations of the components used to optimize the circuit to prevent a breakdown in the secondary winding circuit of the transformer. The possi-bility of electronic switching of the primary winding and reverse polarity diodes in the high voltage part of the circuit provide operation of the corona discharge ion source for detection both positive and negative ions.

References

1. Eiceman, G.A., Karpas, Z.: Ion Mobility Spectrometry, 2nd edn. CRC Press, Boca Raton (2005)
2. Hill Jr., H.H., Siems, W.F., St. Louis, R.H., McMinn, D.G.: Ion mobility spectrometry. Anal. Chem. **62**(23), 1201A–1209A (1990)
3. Borsdorf, H., Eiceman, G.A.: Ion mobility spectrometry: principles and applications. Appl. Spectro. Rev. **41**(4), 323–375 (2006). doi:10.1080/05704920600663469
4. Samotaev, N., Golovin, A., Vasilyev, V., Malkin, E., Gromov, E., Shaltaeva, Y., Mironov, A., Lipatov, D.: IMS development at NRNU MEPhI. In: Natale, C., Ferrari, V., Ponzoni, A., Sberveglieri, G., Ferrari, M. (eds.) Sensors and Microsystems. Lecture Notes in Electrical Engineering, vol. 268, pp. 447–451. Springer, Heidelberg (2014)
5. Chua, B., Pak, J.J.: Miniaturized corona flow sensor operating in drift mobility increment mode for low flow velocity measurement. Sens. Actuators, A: Physical **224**, 65–71 (2015). doi:10.1016/j.sna.2015.01.022
6. Bottoni, P., Caroli, S.: Detection and quantification of residues and metabolites of medicinal products in environmental compartments, food commodities and workplaces. A review. J. Pharm. Biomed. Anal. **106**, 3–24 (2015)
7. Li, F., Xie, Z.-Y., Schmidt, H., Seiemann, S., Baumbach, J.I.: Ion mobility spectrometer (IMS): a novel online monitor of trace volatile organic compounds. Guang Pu Xue Yu Guang Pu Fen Xi/Spectrosc. Spectral Anal. **22**(6), 1027–1029 (2002)
8. Johnson, P.V., Beegle, L.W., Kim, H.I., Eiceman, G.A., Kanik, I.: Ion mobility spectrometry in space exploration. Int. J. Mass Spectrom. **262**(1–2), 1–15 (2007)
9. Goldman, M., Goldman, A., Sigmond, R.S.: Corona discharge, its properties and specific uses. Pure Appl. Chem. **57**(9), 1353–1362 (1985)
10. Hill, C.A., Thomas, C.L.: A pulsed corona discharge switchable high resolution ion mobility spectrometer-mass spectrometer. Analyst **128**(1), 55–60 (2003). doi:10.1039/b207558j
11. Tabrizchi, M., Khayamian, T., Taj, N.: Design and optimization of a corona discharge ionization source for ion mobility spectrometry. Rev. Sci. Instrum. **71**(6), 2321–2328 (2000)
12. Matsaev, V., Gumerov, M., Krasnobaev, L., Pershenkov, V., Belyakov, V., Chistyakov, A., Boudovitch, V.: IMS Spectrometers with radioactive, X-ray, UV and laser ionization. Int. J. Ion Mobility Spectrom. **5**(3), 112–114 (2002)
13. Chen, J., Davidson, J.H.: Ozone production in the positive DC corona discharge: model and comparison to experiments. Plasma Chem. Plasma Process. **22**(4), 495–522 (2002). doi:10.1023/A:1021315412208
14. Laakia, J., Pederson, C.S., Adamov, A., Viidanoja, J., Sysoev, A., Kotiaho, T.: Sterically hindered phenols in negative ion mobility spectrometry-mass spectrometry. Rapid Commun. Mass Spectrom. **23**, 3069–3076 (2009). doi:10.1002/rcm.4223
15. Adamov, A., Mauriala, T., Teplov, V., Laakia, J., Pederson, C.S., Kotiaho, T., Sysoev, A.A.: Characterization of a high resolution drift tube ion mobility spectrometer with a multi-ion source platform. Int. J. Mass Spectrom. **298**, 24–29 (2010). doi:10.1016/j.ijms.2010.02.008

Dynamic Reconfiguration of Network Protocols for Constrained Internet-of-Things Devices

Peter Ruckebusch[✉], Jo Van Damme, Eli De Poorter, and Ingrid Moerman

Ghent University, iGent Tower, Technologiepark 15 (Zwijnaarde),
9052 Ghent, Belgium
peter.ruckebusch@intec.ugent.be

Abstract. The Internet-of-Things paradigm shifts the focus of sensor networks from simple monitoring to more dynamic networking scenarios where the nodes need to adapt to changing requirements and conditions. For this purpose many configuration options are added to the network protocols. Today, however, they can only be modified at compile-time, which seriously limits the ability to adapt the behaviour of the network.

To overcome this, a solution is proposed that allows reconfiguring the entire network stack remotely using CoAP. The Contiki implementation shows that for a small memory overhead (1.2 kB) up to 57 configuration parameters can be reconfigured dynamically. The average latency for reconfiguring one parameter in a twenty node network is only three seconds. A simple case-study illustrates how the energy consumption of an application can be reduced with (50 %) by dynamically fine-tuning the MAC duty-cycle.

Keywords: Internet-of-things · CoAP · Contiki · Dynamic reconfiguration · Wireless sensor networks · Network management

1 Introduction

The Internet of Things (IoT) philosophy [4] announces the third wave of digitalisation. After the rise of the PC (a computer in every home) and the smartphone (a mobile computer for every person) also appliances (or things) will be equipped with a mini-computer and communication interface in the near future. When connected to the Internet, they become IoT devices and enable to further digitise certain aspects of modern day society. In first instance, these devices will automatise or optimise certain processes but there are endless new application possibilities in areas such as healthcare, surveillance, agriculture, personal fitness, home automation and many more.

The vast majority of IoT devices are constrained end-devices (a.k.a. sensors and actuators) with limited computing power and memory. For these type of devices, specialized software (e.g. operating systems (OS), network protocols, etc.) is required. Given the wide range of possible applications and the specific limitations, much effort was spent by a broad research community to develop this software. Custom OSs such as Contiki, RIOT and TinyOS were proposed

© ICST Institute for Computer Sciences, Social Informatics and Telecommunications Engineering 2016
B. Mandler et al. (Eds.): IoT 360° 2015, Part II, LNICST 170, pp. 269–281, 2016.
DOI: 10.1007/978-3-319-47075-7_31

that specifically target such devices. Also many standards emerged, providing answers to the specific challenges posed by these applications and devices.

Despite the societal and business potential, the uptake by industry of innovative large-scale sensor/actuator applications is slow. One of the major hurdles that retains innovation is the lack of built-in support for maintenance of such devices. Perhaps the most important aspect in maintainability is the possibility to dynamically reconfigure the network stack. Although the standards provide many options to configure network protocols, it is almost impossible to change the configuration settings at run-time. This implies that the entire network needs to reconfigured off-line if changes are required. In research this is not a major problem since experiments can be repeated using different settings. In real-life, however, application requirements and conditions change continuously. There is hence a clear need for enabling dynamic reconfiguration of the network protocols to adapt to changing situations.

In this work a light-weight approach is presented that enables to change configuration settings in the entire network stack using only a minimal amount of resources. Moreover, the presented solution is able to expose the configuration settings both locally, for a local controller, and remotely, for a network-wide controller. The core of the solution is completely agnostic to the access method (e.g. local or remote). The communication protocol for enabling remote access is also transparent. The proof-of-concept was implemented in Contiki and uses the REST-based ERBIUM Constrained Application Protocol (CoAP) supported by Contiki.

2   Background

This section gives an overview of the relevant protocol standards and operating systems targeted by the proposed control extensions. For each standard also the possible configuration settings, as described in the standard, are explored. Note that currently they can only be modified at compile time in the targeted OSs.

2.1   Operating Systems

TinyOS, RIOT and Contiki are operating systems specifically designed for constrained sensor devices in the IoT. They share three common features [3]: (1) platform and hardware abstraction for portability; (2) multi-tasking or multi-threading support; and (3) lightweight IPv6 compliant network stack.

Although these OSs also provide alternative network stacks, the IPv6 stack is chosen as default. This is because there is a continuous push towards standardization within the IoT ecosystem. Therefore, the protocols included in the default IPv6 stack are selected as primary candidates for the dynamic reconfiguration extensions.

The default IPv6-compliant network stack is illustrated on the left side (a) in Fig. 1. The following protocols and standards are included: an IEEE-802.15.4-2006 compliant PHY and MAC, 6LowPan header compression, IPv6 (addressing,

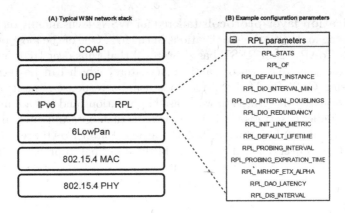

Fig. 1. (A) IPv6 compliant network stack available in TinyOS, Contiki and RIOT. (B) possible configuration parameters to fine-tune the RPL routing protocol.

headers and ICMP), Routing Protocol for Low-Power and Lossy Networks (RPL) routing, TCP/UDP transport and CoAP.

2.2 Network Protocols and Standards

This section briefly summarizes the main configuration settings in the standard IPv6 stack [13]. In total there are 57 available parameters. The possible configuration settings for the RPL routing protocol are illustrated, as example, on the right side (b) of Fig. 1.

The PHY and MAC protocols are based on the IEEE-802.15.4 standard [6]. PHY settings include channel, tx power and CCA threshold. Many custom implementations of MAC protocols exist. In Contiki, the default radio duty cycling MAC protocol is ContikiMAC [2]. It uses periodical wake-ups to listen for packet transmissions from neighbours. The wake-up interval can be modified as well as the number of listens (i.e. CCA checks) during each periodical wake-up or before packet transmission. On top of ContikiMAC, a CSMA based protocol controls the medium contention and packet retransmissions which can also be configured. Protocols with similar behaviour are also available in TinyOS and RIOT.

The network layer includes RPL [14], a proactive, distance-vector routing protocol specifically designed for Wireless Sensor Networks (WSN)s. RPL uses control packets (DIO, DAO and DIS) for building a tree like topology, called a Destination-Oriented Directed Acyclic Graph (DODAG). Many settings allow to fine-tune the various intervals that are used for maintaining the DODAG. Also the link estimation algorithms can be changed and configured. Next to RPL, various parameters controlling the IPv6 neighbour discovery [11] process can be configured. Also TCP/UDP implementations allow to configure the number of retransmissions and various time-out settings.

The application layer protocols tailored for WSNs focus mainly on integrating the sensing and actuating applications in the IoT. One of the most prominent examples is CoAP [12], a REST based protocol that runs over UDP and allows to define resources (e.g. sensors and/or actuators) which can be retrieved or changed using GET/POST/PUT methods using a response-request approach. CoAP can be easily integrated in web-based applications and has a limited overhead. The number of retransmissions and various time-outs and intervals used by the CoAP engine can be configured. Alternatives [10] for CoAP are MQTT and AMQP, both run over TCP and use a publish-subscriber approach managed by a message broker that allows nodes to publish and/or subscribe to topics. Compared to COAP they have a higher overhead and are less supported by operating systems for WSNs.

3   Design

This section discusses the design of the extensions required to support dynamic reconfiguration. First the requirements will be summarized, then the high-level architecture will be described and, subsequently, the communication flow. Finally, the most appropriate application layer protocol will be chosen.

3.1   Requirements

From a functional viewpoint the main requirement is to enable *updating configuration parameters of network protocols* after deploying the network. This functionality must be use-able by both a node-local and network-wide control engine.

In order to support remote control, the system must allow *automatic parameter discovery and bootstrapping* in the entire network. Moreover, *batch configuration* is required for enabling to change multiple parameters at once. From a user perspective, it must be possible to reconfigure the network via *web-based applications*.

From a non-functional viewpoint the main requirements is *resource efficiency*. The memory, CPU and network overhead must be as small as possible and scale with the number of parameters that can be changed at run-time.

Other important concerns are *modifiability, portability and compatibility*. To address them, the control engine must be (a) independent of the protocol used for providing remote access; (b) easily ported to existing operating systems; and (c) compatible with web-based applications.

From the aforementioned requirements, it can be deducted that a generic method for accessing configuration settings is required both on the node-local and network-wide level. For this purpose parameters are maintained in a repository and can be reconfigured using a generic interface implemented by a control engine. Different application layer protocols can be used for enabling remote access.

3.2   Architecture

Figure 2 illustrates the high-level design of the architecture. It includes the following entities: (a) *a sensor configuration server*, which offers a control API or UI for external users (human or software); (b) *a sensor gateway server* that maintains a network-wide view on the current configuration settings and acts as a border router for the WSN; and (c) *the actual sensor devices* that can be reconfigured.

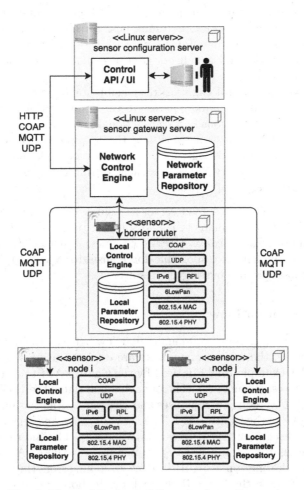

Fig. 2. The architecture of the reconfiguration system.

The sensor devices implement a *local parameter repository*, which maintains a local view on the current node configuration settings, and a *local control engine* implementing a remote configuration interface

The local control engine is responsible for (a) making parameters discoverable and participating in the bootstrapping phase; (b) implementing a generic interface that allows to get/set a specific parameter or a group of parameters; and (c) parsing remote configuration messages and performing the necessary interface calls for the get or set operation. To enable all these interactions, the local parameter repository stores references to each parameter. This reference contains function pointers to the getters and setters provided by the different protocols.

The sensor gateway server includes a sensor border router that acts as a gateway for the sensor network. The Linux host further implements a *network parameter repository*, which maintains a network-wide view on the current configuration of each node, and a *network control engine* implementing a remote configuration interface.

The network-wide control engine is responsible for (a) device discovery and bootstrapping; (b) enabling remote access to the configuration parameters; (c) performing batch configurations in a transactional manner; (d) translating messages between the local sensor network and the remote control API; (e) input validation when changing settings; and (f) authenticating remote access. The network parameter repository serves as a cache during get operations and facilitates roll-backs during set operations.

The sensor configuration server serves as a single entry point for reconfiguring the network both for humans (UI) and software processes (API). It consists of a single component, *the control API/UI* implementing an easy to use API and UI. This component is responsible for translating the API/UI calls into configuration messages and parsing the result.

3.3   Communication Flow

Figure 3 illustrates an example communication flow between the different entities in the architecture, the active components are depicted using white boxes and bold text. In this example HTTP is used by the Control API to configure sensor j. For this purposes, the network control engine translates the HTTP requests/responses into CoAP requests/responses and vice-versa. Another possibility is to directly use CoAP in the Control API. The network control engine will then serve as a proxy for delegating COAP requests/responses. The intermediate sensor nodes (e.g. border router and node i) do not process the CoAP message but forward it to the destination using RPL. Packets coming from the sensor network are injected directly in the Linux IPv6 stack by the border router.

3.4   Application Layer Protocol

Selecting the appropriate application layer protocol for exchanging configuration messages across the network is very important because this will have a high impact on the resource efficiency of the overall solution. Several candidates were

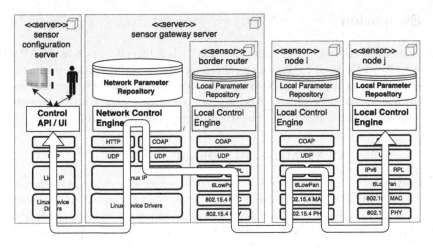

Fig. 3. The communication flow between the different entities in the architecture. The white boxes with bold text depict the active components in this example.

compared in [7] and evaluated based on the device memory requirements and message size overhead.

The most dominant application layer protocol for constrained IoT devices today is CoAP. It has built-in support for resource (e.g. parameter) discovery and block wise (e.g. batch configuration) transfers. From a functional viewpoint, all required features are present. Since CoAP is tailored for constrained devices, the memory and CPU requirements are limited. Moreover, the message overhead is also minimal because the CoAP header is very small and UDP is used as transport protocol. With portability and compatibility in mind, CoAP is also a logical choice because it is well supported by nearly all OSs and easily integrateable in web-based systems since it is REST based.

An alternative for CoAP is MQTT [5], a publish-subscriber system with a central MQTT broker that runs over TCP. MQTT clients can publish or subscribe to topics (e.g. parameters). For each parameter, two topics are required: (1) one published by the sensor node for supporting the get operation; and (2) one published by the configuration server for supporting the set operation. Because of this, MQTT will have a much higher device memory overhead. Also the message overhead will be bigger since it runs over TCP. Moreover, it is less supported, only a Contiki implementation is available. Other alternatives are AMQP and XMPP. Both also use TCP as transport protocol and have much higher device memory requirement and message overhead since they are not tailored for constrained devices.

To conclude, *CoAP is the most appropriate application layer protocol* to support dynamic reconfiguration, as also indicated in [13].

4   Evaluation

The evaluation consists of an analytical part, that investigates how CoAP can be most efficiently used for enabling remote access to configuration parameters, and an experimental part, in which the memory overhead and latency for changing parameters are determined. Also a proof-of-concept case study is presented emphasizing the practical use of the dynamic reconfiguration solution.

4.1   Analysing CoAP Memory Overhead

The CoAP memory requirements constitute of the fixed overhead for the CoAP engine (8.5 kB ROM/1.5 kB RAM [8]) and the variable amount of ROM occupied by the CoAP resources. The additional memory overhead for exposing configuration settings hence depends on the number of CoAP resources required to expose the parameters. Three granularity levels are considered: (1) a CoAP resource per configuration parameter; (2) a CoAP resource per protocol; and (3) one CoAP resource for the entire network stack.

In principal, CoAP is text based and resources are identified using unique string names encoded in the resource URI. Both need to be stored in the ROM memory of each sensor device. Depending on the granularity level, the string name of each parameter (1), protocol (2) or stack (3) is stored in memory causing extra ROM overhead. Moreover, when using granularity level (2) or (3), parameters still need to be identified. This can be done using either unique names, encoded in the URI query variable, or unique IDs, encoded in the payload.

In order to make well-founded decisions, the impact on the ROM memory usage for different granularities was analysed using stub resources in Contiki for CoAP. This allows to devise a mathematical model that can be applied on a real example network stack to estimate the overhead in each options. The total ROM overhead of an option is denoted by s_{rom}^{total} and comprises of S_{rom}^{res}, or the ROM required for the resource definition and the GET/POST/PUT handlers, and the *string_length* of the resource name. Note that S_{rom}^{res} will be different for each granularity because the GET/POST/PUT handlers are implemented differently

Also the parameter identification method in level (2) and (3) were investigated. For this purpose the auxiliary function $s_{rom}^{id}(param_i)$ is defined (Eq. 1) that returns the *string_len* when using unique names or $sizeof(int)$ when using unique IDs.

$$s_{rom}^{id}(param_i) = \begin{cases} string\_len(param_i) & \text{if } id \text{ is string} \\ sizeof(integer) & \text{if } id \text{ is integer} \end{cases} \quad (1)$$

A resource per parameter enables direct addressing of parameters without requiring any transformation. It is the most straightforward for integration in browsers using add-ons such as Copper [9]. The ROM overhead s_{rom}^{total}, on the other hand, will be high because for each parameter the string name must be stored and a resource must be defined (S_{rom}^{res}) as denoted in Eq. 2.

$$s_{rom}^{total} = \sum^{param_i} (string\_len(param_i) + S_{rom}^{res}) \tag{2}$$

where $S_{rom}^{res} = 157$

A resource per protocol groups parameters on a protocol level. They are addresses indirectly via the protocol resource implying that an if-else structure is required in the GET/POST/PUT handlers for identifying the correct parameter. Equation 3 defines the total ROM overhead s_{rom}^{total} as the sum over all $proto_i$ of the ROM memory required for storing the protocol name, the fixed CoAP resource overhead (S_{rom}^{res}) and, per parameter, the identification $(s_{rom}^{id}(param_j))$ and if-else (S_{rom}^{ifelse}) overhead.

$$s_{rom}^{total} = \sum^{proto_i} (S_{rom}^{res} + string\_length(proto_i) + s_{rom}^{param}(param_j \in proto_i)) \tag{3a}$$

$$s_{rom}^{param}(param_j \in proto_i) = \sum^{param_j} (s_{rom}^{id}(param_j) + S_{rom}^{ifelse}) \tag{3b}$$

where $S_{rom}^{res} = 280$ and $S_{rom}^{ifelse} = 40$

A resource for the entire stack has the advantage that there is looser coupling with the protocols, compared to the previous options. A tight coupling implies that a protocol update also require updating the CoAP resources(s). The third approach, however, requires an explicit implementation of a parameter repository that can be used by the generic resource to manipulate configuration settings and by the protocols to (de-)register parameters. Equation (4) expresses the ROM overhead s_{rom}^{total} when using a single resource for the entire stack. Now the fixed CoAP resource overhead (S_{rom}^{res}) also includes the resource name and the parameter repository implementation. For each parameter, a fixed amount of ROM S_{rom}^{param} is required for the parameter structure. The identification overhead $s_{rom}^{id}(param_i)$ depends on the chosen method.

$$s_{rom}^{total} = S_{rom}^{res} + \sum^{param_i} (s_{rom}^{id}(param_i) + S_{rom}^{param})) \tag{4a}$$

$$s_{rom}^{id}(param_i) = \begin{cases} name\_length(param_i) & \text{if } id \text{ is string} \\ 2 & \text{if } id \text{ is numeric} \end{cases} \tag{4b}$$

where $S_{rom}^{res} = 392$ and $S_{rom}^{param} = 12$

Conclusion: Figure 4 gives an overview of the ROM overhead estimated for the different resource granularities and identification methods. The results clearly show that a single generic resource requires 80 % less memory (1.2 kB) compared to a resource per parameter (11.6 kB) and 60 % less compared to a resource per protocol (4.5 kB). Using unique IDs instead of names also has a major impact. Given the size in ROM of the default Contiki IPv6 stack $(+ - 30 \text{ kB})$, using *a single generic CoAP resource and unique IDs is the preferred choice.*

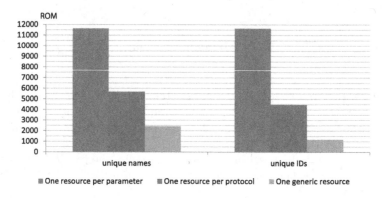

Fig. 4. Estimated ROM overhead for different resource granularities and identification methods.

4.2 Experimental Evaluation

Evaluation Set-Up: The sensor configuration and gateway server were implemented on a general purpose embedded PC running Linux. The sensor code was developed in Contiki 3.0 and executed on a Zolertia Z1 (16 MHz CPU, 92 KB ROM, 10 KB RAM and an IEEE-802.15.4 compliant transceiver). A single resource combined with a parameter repository is used for configuring the network stack. All communication between the different entities is CoAP based. On Linux libCoAP [1] is used while in Contiki the ERBIUM CoAP [8] engine is utilized.

Latency: The average latency for changing parameters depends on the number of PUT/POST requests needed to perform a batch configuration on all nodes. It is measured on the sensor gateway by calculating the delay between the first request and last response. The average latency is an important performance indicator because it defines the duration in which the network is in an inconsistent state. Figure 5 illustrates the average latency in seconds for one to twenty POST/PUT requests (e.g. number of nodes) in steps of four. Also the standard deviation over all experiments is indicated. The results clearly show that the average latency scales with the number of POST/PUT requests.

Case Study: Dynamically Reconfiguring the ContikiMAC Duty-Cycle: To illustrate the usefulness of dynamic reconfiguration, a simple case study is presented in which the duty-cycle of ContikiMAC is dynamically adapted based on the application load. It is applicable on use-cases such as a HVAC monitoring and control system which requires more traffic during the office hours. The duty-cycle of ContikiMAC [2], normally statically defined at compile time, is now dynamically configured using the *ChannelCheckRate* (*CCR*) parameter (e.g. the rate for checking RX activity). Figure 6 shows the energy consumed daily by the radio (RX/TX) and CPU (active/LPM) for three different CCR settings.

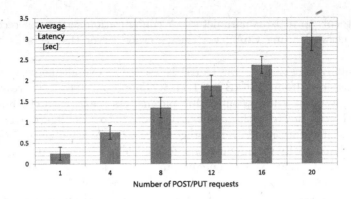

Fig. 5. Average latency for increasing number of POST/PUT requests (e.g. nodes). Also the standard deviation is denoted on the chart.

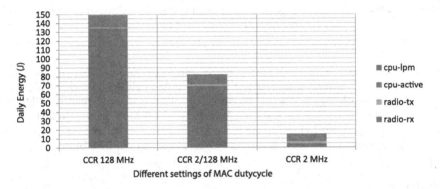

Fig. 6. The daily energy consumption for different settings of the channel check rate (CCR) in ContikiMAC.

A high duty-cyle (left) results in a high reliability at the cost of much energy spent in RX mode. On the other hand a low duty cycle (right) requires ten times less energy at the expense of reliability. When using a high-duty cycle during office hours and a low duty-cycle otherwise (middle), a high reliability can be achieved for half the amount of energy. The energy was mea

5   Conclusions

This paper presents a flexible approach for enabling dynamic reconfiguration of protocol settings in the entire network stack, either local or remote. The high level architecture is applicable on multiple OSs and compatible with different application layer protocols for providing remote access to the devices. The Contiki implementation uses CoAP for this purpose. A single CoAP resource is defined for the entire network stack combined with a parameter repository that allows protocols to register parameters. A configuration server can reconfigure the entire network using CoAP via the gateway server that acts as a CoAP proxy.

By carefully considering how CoAP is used, the overall memory overhead could be reduced from 11.6 kB to 1.2 kB. The proof-of-concept results also show that the latency for reconfiguring parameters scales with the number of POST/PUT requests (e.g. the number of nodes). To reconfigure a parameter in a network of twenty nodes, on average three seconds are required. The case-study that dynamically reconfigures the duty-cycle of ContikiMAC based on the traffic load, shows that 50 % of energy can be saved without sacrificing other performance indicators such as reliability and throughput.

Future work could built-up from this solution and develop more advanced case-studies where the effect of changing multiple parameters on the network performance can be investigated. To allow this, only limited modifications are required in the protocols to expose the parameters. The developed solution can hence be used by many experimenters for optimizing the network performance via parameter reconfiguration.

Acknowledgments. This work was partially supported by the Fund for Scientific Research-Flanders (FWO-V), project "ASN: wireless Acoustic Sensor Networks", grant #G.0763.12, and the agency for Innovation by Science and Technology Flanders (IWT-V), project "SAMURAI: Software Architecture and Modules for Unified RAdIo control", and the iMinds IoT Strategic Research program, and European Commission Horizon 2020 Programme under grant agreement n645274 (WiSHFUL).

References

1. Bergmann, O.: libcoap: C-implementation of CoAP (2015)
2. Dunkels, A.: The contikimac radio duty cycling protocol. Technical report, SICS (2011)
3. Farooq, M.O., Kunz, T.: Operating systems for wireless sensor networks: a survey. Sensors **11**(6), 5900–5930 (2011)
4. Gubbi, J., Buyya, R., Marusic, S., Palaniswami, M.: Internet of things: a vision, architectural elements, and future directions. Future Gener. Comput. Syst. **29**(7), 1645–1660 (2013)
5. Hunkeler, U., Truong, H.L., Stanford-Clark, A.: MQTT-S: a publish/subscribe protocol for wireless sensor networks. In: Communication Systems Software and Middleware and Workshops, COMSWARE (2008)
6. IEEE: IEEE standard for local and metropolitan area networks-part 15.4: low-rate wireless personal area networks (LR-WPANS). IEEE Std 802.15.4-2011 (2011)
7. Karagiannis, V., Chatzimisios, P., Vazquez-Gallego, F., Alonso-Zarate, J.: A survey on application layer protocols for the internet of things. Trans. IoT Cloud Comput. **3**(1), 11–17 (2015)
8. Kovatsch, M., Duquennoy, S., Dunkels, A.: A low-power CoAP for Contiki. In: Mobile Adhoc and Sensor Systems, MASS (2011)
9. Kovatsch, M.: Demo abstract: humanCoAP interaction with copper. In: Distributed Computing in Sensor Systems, DCOSS (2011)

10. Luzuriaga, J., Perez, M., Boronat, P., Cano, J., Calafate, C., Manzoni, P.: A comparative evaluation of AMQP and MQTT protocols over unstable and mobile networks. In: Consumer Communications and Networking Conference, CCNC (2015)
11. Narten, T., Nordmark, E., Simpson, W., Soliman, H.: Neighbor Discovery for IP version 6 (IPv6). RFC 4861 (2007)
12. Shelby, Z., Hartke, K., Bormann, C.: The Constrained Application Protocol (CoAP). RFC 7252 (2014)
13. Sheng, Z., Yang, S., Yu, Y., Vasilakos, A.V., McCann, J.A., Leung, K.K.: A survey on the ietf protocol suite for the internet of things: standards, challenges, and opportunities. IEEE Wirel. Commun. **20**(6), 91–98 (2013). doi:10.1109/MWC. 2013.6704479
14. Winter, T., Thubert, P., Brandt, A., Hui, J., Kelsey, R., Levis, P., Pister, K., Struik, R., Vasseur, J., Alexander, R.: RPL: IPv6 Routing Protocol for Low-Power and Lossy Networks. RFC 6550 (2012)

Surveying Indexing Methods
for the Internet of Things

Victor Kardeby$^{(\boxtimes)}$, Ulf Jennehag, and Mikael Gidlund

Department of Information and Communications Systems, Mid Sweden University,
851 70 Sundsvall, Sweden
{victor.kardeby,ulf.jennehag,mikael.gidlund}@miun.se

Abstract. The Internet of Things is expected to expand several magnitudes in the coming decade surpassing over 50 billion devices. In the Internet of Things there is a need to support complex queries on the massive amount of information that will be made available. The scalability of the indexes used to support the queries is therefore critical. This paper therefore investigate what type of index that could scale to the size required by the Internet of Things. We find that range query is an approach that support continuously changing information and fast updates with the lowest increase in signaling per participating device. We find that a Chord-based distributed hash table hosting a NUBL range query indexing scheme will scale to the required size while supporting multidimensional range queries.

Keywords: IoT · Internet of things · Survey · Indexing method · Distributed systems · Distributed hash table

1 Introduction

The Internet of Things (IoT) is defined in [1] as billions of devices having and sharing information with services in real-time. IoT promoters proclaim that there will be a torrent of new devices coming online to share information and provide new services within the next years. Some claim 50 or 100 billion devices by 2020 [2], while others are more modest, projecting 24 billion devices in the same period [3]. The need to quickly act upon acquired information requires devices to effectively find and acquire relevant sensor information. It becomes more difficult to acquire relevant information quickly as the amount of produced information increases; this is therefore one of several important research topics [4,5] in the IoT. However, other topics include for example device heterogeneity, privacy, and security. There are several viable approaches available for the current data volumes, but their fitness can be questioned [6] when there is both an information increase in the order of several magnitudes and an increased amount of dynamically changing information.

One approach to solve scalability issues is to increase the capacity of the current network infrastructure. However, increasing the capacity require either

© ICST Institute for Computer Sciences, Social Informatics and Telecommunications Engineering 2016
B. Mandler et al. (Eds.): IoT 360° 2015, Part II, LNICST 170, pp. 282–291, 2016.
DOI: 10.1007/978-3-319-47075-7_32

heavy investments in additional hardware, or the exchange of current hardware with more improved versions. Both would have already been done if they were economically feasible. Alternative approaches to sharing, finding, and acquiring information from sensors therefore look toward distributed peer-to-peer networks [7]. Where alternatives to brute force searches or complete data replication can be employed.

1.1   Related Work

Traditional approaches to peer-to-peer networks [8] are constructed to support an index method for exact matches through the use of a Distributed Hash Table (DHT). While such functionality is adequate for rapid resolution of locations for named information, it is unsatisfactory for more rich queries that the IoT will require. A typical IoT query is likely to be multidimensional with a varying amount of parameters which require a different type of index method. In the simpler end of the scale there are queries for certain specified types of sensors within a region, asking for example "All temperature sensors in Sundsvall, Sweden" or "Any temperature sensor that have a humidity sensor attached and is located outdoor near my location". More complex queries could request sensors with some specified values, past or present, e.g. "All temperature sensors that are submerged, have had a measurement above 30 °C within the last week, and that is located within 5 km of my cabin".

In [7] the origin of current peer to peer based multidimensional indexing methods is visualized. It is shown that current research typically examines the query types: window query, range query, or k nearest neighbor query. Their conclusion is that there are two performance related problems that are always considered and thoroughly discussed in the literature. They are load balancing problems and update strategy. Load balance and search performance in a family of index schemes that support wildcard searches is examined in [9]. The related work is divided into different categories based on the indexing complexity. The categories are: (a) exact matches, (b) categorized topics, (c) ranged query, and (d) full text indexing. All DHT support category (a) as part of their basic operation. Then the other categories are added either by mapping an indexing structure, such as a search tree, on top of the DHT (*over-DHT*), or by modifying the DHT algorithm (*in-DHT*). Category (b) indexing is commonly supported by either creating multiple DHTs, one per category, or by arranging the structure differently, such as in [10]. However, with the expected size of the IoT reduces the value of finding information based on categories. For example, requesting every sensor that have a location among millions of devices where most have a meaningful location will only overload the requester with replies. Others, for example [11], use technologies such as prefix based routing and order preserving hash functions to enable category (c) searches [7,10,12,13]. Others [9] focus on category (d), detailing how to enable full text indexing in a DHT.

1.2 Problem Motivation

The problem is to find a type of indexing that is suitable for sensor data stored in a DHT that originates from 50 billion sensors and that is continuously being updated with high sampling frequencies. A suitable indexing scheme should support complex queries such as the examples in Sect. 1.1 while keeping resource consumption as low as possible. In all situations involving small computers, such as the Raspberry Pi, Sensor motes, smartphones, or similar, it is less expensive in terms of hardware resources to perform local processing than communication [14,15], which mean that indexing schemes that favor local processing over network communication is preferable. The resource that is important to conserve is therefore communication. We therefore target a distributed topology where we measure communication by the discrete number of messages that is signaled as a part of routing requests between peers and performing maintenance of the indexing schemes. It is determined that the indexing category (a), exact matches, is supported by all options and cannot perform advanced queries. Category (a) is therefore of no interest to the problem. Category (b), categorical indexing, would include several categories that would contain every device and query results in these categories would then overload the requesting device and therefore be of little use to reduce the query. Full text indexing, category (d), would require extensive updates for continuously changing information and is therefore rejected as well. Therefore, this paper analytically investigates which algorithms for range queries (c) that could be supported by the IoT for dynamic information in a worst case scenario where large quantities of devices continuously insert new data and perform complex queries. Hence, an indexing scheme must support these following two requirements:

1. It must minimize the total number of signaled messages in a query.
2. It must reflect updated values quickly.

Our evaluation of requirement (1) focus on the total number of messages required for the query. Requirement (2) is evaluated by investigate the number of messages required to update the index in conjunction with a value update. The main scientific contribution of this paper is, (1) a survey of suitable indexing methods for continuously changing information for the volumes of information that is expected from the IoT, and (2), a recommendation of an indexing method that is indicated to scale well for the IoT.

1.3 Outline

The remainder of this paper is organized as follows. Section 2 details our approach to solve the problem. Section 3 examines several DHT to compare scalability of maintenance and lookup performance. Section 4 evaluates the listed DHTs, while Sect. 5 presents our conclusions.

2   Approach

In order to determine the scalability of range query indexing schemes we compare the number of messages that are required to route a request to the recipient and the number of messages that are transmitted during maintenance. The number of messages are compared to a typical well scaling DHT, Chord [16]. A number of different structures for both indexing and DHT are then selected to represent different topologies. Analytical expressions for the signaling are identified in the literature for every investigated indexing structure. *In-DHT* approaches are compared directly while *over-DHT* approaches are assumed to be used in conjunction with Chord if no alternative is given. All indexing schemes are then normalized to Chord and compared with each other. If an indexing scheme lacks analytical expressions for scalability then an extrapolation of presented measurements is used instead. An indexing scheme is determined to be scalable if its normalized values remain parallel to Chord. Any indexing scheme whose values remain less than Chord thus scale better and consequently any value above Chord scales worse. Intuitively we expect that well scaling complex indexing schemes remain parallel to Chord.

3   Indexing for the IoT

A number of DHT that support category (a), exact matches, are listed in Table 1 together with their individual routing and maintenance complexity. Chord [16] is selected as the base to compare other approaches to, since it is one of the most well-known DHT. It structures participating peers in a ring and maintain links, denoted fingers, to other peers and thus enable a distributed binary search to locate data logarithmically. CAN [17] is also a well-known DHT that form a Cartesian space that span the key space. Many researchers [18] have based their own approaches for supporting the other categories on these two DHT structures. Cycloid [19] and P-Grid [20] are examples of alternative topologies that contend with the performance of two previous DHTs. Cycloid distribute information over a hypercube with d dimensions where each vertex is a ring structure with 2^d identities. The total number of addressable peers is thus $n = d * 2^d$. Every peer in Cycloid maintains a list of 7 peers regardless of the number of participants. P-Grid is an example of a DHT that support more than index category (a). Every peer in P-Grid maintain a routing tree containing $O(\text{Log } N)$ peers and can route messages in $O(\text{Log } N)$ jumps.

3.1   In-DHT Approaches to Range Queries

In-DHT approaches modify the existing algorithms for routing and storage in a DHT to support new functionality. Table 2 displays a set of *in-DHT* approaches. The table presents the name, origin of the DHT, and the updated routing and maintenance cost. P-Grid support range queries in its basic operation and is therefore included here in addition to exemplifying a basic DHT. Chord# [12]

Table 1. Basic overlay networks

Name	Form	Routing	Maintenance
Chord [16]	Circle	$\frac{LogN}{2}$	$LogN$
CAN [17]	Multi-Torus	$\frac{d}{4} * N^{\frac{1}{d}}$	$d*2$
Cycloid [19]	Hypercube	$O(D)$	7
P-Grid [20]	Mesh	$\frac{LogN}{2}$	$LogN$

remove the hashing function, sorting keys lexicographically, modify the data placement algorithm to restore load balancing properties, and exchange finger table algorithm to adapt to lexicographical searches. Finally the binary search algorithm for finding data is modified to enable b-dimensional searches. This changes the lookup signaling from $O(Log_2 N)$ to $O(Log_b N)$ messages. SONAR [12] extends Chord# to enable multidimensional range queries. LORM exchange the algorithm that creates the identification for the data to use a data type category as one part of the two-dimensional identity. Where the other part is created using a locality-preserving hash algorithm [21].

Table 2. DHT with advanced indexes

Name	Origin	Routing	Maintenance
P-Grid [20]	P-Grid	$\frac{LogN}{2}$	$LogN$
Chord# [12]	Chord	$Log_b(N)$	$Log_b(N) * \frac{b-1}{2}$
SONAR [12]	Chord#	$-1.2 + 0.62 * log_2(N)$	$Log_2(N)$
LORM [10]	Cycloid	$Cycloid * d$	7

3.2   Over-DHT Approaches to Range Queries

An Over-DHT approach utilizes the existing structure established by the DHT to handle systemic issues, such as load balancing, churn handling, and routing by using the basic operations of the DHT. Table 3 show a representative set of *over-DHT* algorithms, their name, structure, maintenance overhead and signaling overhead. NUBL [22] is based on an earlier approach and construct a tree where leaf nodes are encoded and stored as object in the DHT. This enable peers to search through the tree to locate information within the desired range. The routing of a query is improved to $O(Log_2(D/4)/2)$ using Chord with only $O(D/2)$ in increased maintenance. DRing [13] constructs an additional overlay circle on top of the existing structure. This super-node structure consists of leaf nodes in a prefix based routing tree. The super-node structure reduce the tendency to overload the upper levels of the tree by traversing requests through caching. The DRing algorithm claim that optimal performance is achieved when queries greatly outnumber inserts.

Table 3. Over-DHT indexing algorithms

Name	Form	Routing	Maintenance
NUBL [22]	Tree	$\frac{Log_2(\frac{D}{4})}{2} * Chord$	$\frac{D}{2} + Chord$
DRing [13]	PHT	O(Log N)	O(Log N)

4   Results

The approaches are examined in a worst case scenario where up to 10^{10} devices continuously perform updates of their sensor data while performing complex queries in the DHT. Parameters, such as network topology, transmission delay, and query rate, are selected to be equal in each case and are therefore eliminated. All results are normalized to Chord, as it is determined to be well scaling for large number of devices. The figures will therefore show a message ratio where any solution that is parallel to 1 is determined to scale comparable to Chord. An approach that have a decreasing ratio that is <1 scales better than Chord, while having an increasing ratio that is >1 indicates that it scales worse.

In Fig. 1 the signaling is presented for the DHTs in Table 1, with the exception of CAN. Normalizing the routing and maintenance of CAN to Chord resulted in

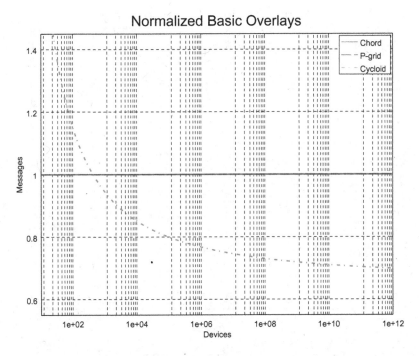

Fig. 1. Lin-Log plot of messages per node for basic overlay networks normalized to Chord for up to 10^{10} devices.

an exponential curve that ended at one thousand times the signaling in Chord for 10^{10} devices. Cycloid is shown to outperform Chord when the number of participating devices exceed 10^3. Since the maximum number of participants in Cycloid is determined as $n = d * 2^d$ where d is the dimension of the hypercube we opted for solving d for the current n along the x-axis. This simplification thus show the ideal solution at any given size and a practical implementation would require additional messages to be transmitted for each operation.

4.1   In-DHT Indexing Schemes

In Fig. 2 we examine the *in-DHT* approaches P-Grid, SONAR, and LORM. P-Grid follow Chord at 1. However, an analytic expression for SONAR routing were not found, and logarithmic coefficients were therefore found in [12] through logarithmic fitting. The discovered routing coefficients for SONAR are shown in Table 2. LORM is based on Cycloid and use the same equation as in Fig. 1. LORM is capable of maintaining multiple dimensions simultaneously but LORM is limited to a single dimension in this comparison since all other approaches would require multiple concurrent DHT to support the same. It is observed that there is an intersection between all three approaches in the vicinity of $5 * 10^2$ devices. After the intersection LORM outperform the other solutions. SONAR is

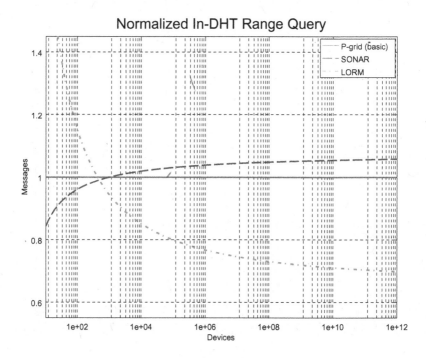

Fig. 2. Lin-Log plot of messages per node for *in-DHT* range queries normalized to Chord in peer-to-peer networks for up to 10^{10} devices.

performing better than the other approaches before the intersection and is then slightly more expensive than Chord. Since maintenance in LORM is constant, there is only one factor that scales logarithmic as opposed to two logarithmic scaling factors in Chord which implies that LORM will converge to 0.5 for very large numbers.

4.2 Over-DHT Indexing Schemes

Figure 3 display Chord and LORM which is compared with NUBL. Since NUBL is an *over-DHT* approach its routing is multiplied with that of Chord and its maintenance is added to the Chord maintenance. NUBL would perform better in conjunction with Chord than Chord by itself according to these calculations. Using only one dimension in NUBL yields a very low signaling when compared to Chord. Setting $d = 4$ make NUBL seems to converge with LORM for large networks with $>10^{10}$ devices. This behavior is caused by calculating logarithms for values less than one, making scalability estimations for $d < 4$ impossible using this method. The total routing term from Table 3 is less than one for $d < 8$ due to another division by 2.

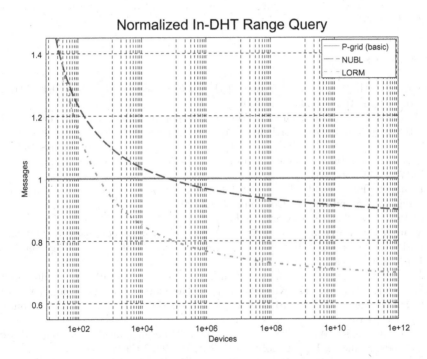

Fig. 3. Lin-Log plot of messages per node for *over-DHT* range queries normalized to Chord in peer-to-peer networks for up to 10^{10} devices.

5   Conclusions

The goal of this paper was to find what type of indexing the IoT would be capable of supporting for sensor information which is continuously changing. The focus was on distributed approaches that scale to billions of devices. The initial analysis of the literature concludes that range query indexing is the only indexing scheme in this survey that is viable for the scale that the IoT require. Several range query approaches are then investigated and evaluated based on two requirements. The indexing scheme must (1) transmit as few messages as possible in a query, and it must (2) reflect updates in information quickly. The approach was to compare the indexing schemes to a known scalable solution. Section 4 evaluated several indexing schemes that support range queries in terms of query length and maintenance. It is shown that LORM outperform the other alternatives, however the ideal parameters that were used in the evaluation of LORM are difficult to implement in practice. The second most effective algorithm is NUBL, which provide functionality for multidimensional range queries and still require less signaling than Chord. Both LORM and NUBL based approaches therefore require further investigation through both simulation and trial deployment in a testbed, to evaluate the possibility of selecting the parameters of LORM such that it is practical to implement and then compare that implementation to one of NUBL.

References

1. Xu, L.D., He, W., Li, S.: Internet of things in industries: a survey. IEEE Trans. Ind. Inform. **10**(4), 2233–2243 (2014)
2. Sundmaeker, H., Guillemin, P., Friess, P.: Vision and challenges for realising the Internet of Things. In: CERP-IoT, European, March 2010
3. Gubbi, J., Buyya, R., Marusic, S., Palaniswami, M.: Internet of Things (IoT): a vision, architectural elements, and future directions. Future Gener. Comput. Syst. **29**(7), 1645–1660 (2013)
4. Paganelli, F., Parlanti, D.: A DHT-based discovery service for the internet of things. J. Comput. Netw. Commun. **2012** (2012)
5. Perera, C., Zaslavsky, A., Christen, P., Compton, M., Georgakopoulos, D.: Context-aware sensor search, selection and ranking model for internet of things middleware. In: Proceedings - IEEE International Conference on Mobile Data Management, vol. 1, pp. 314–322, March 2013
6. Zhang, B., Mor, N., Kolb, J., Chan, D.S., Goyal, N., Lutz, K., Allman, E., Wawrzynek, J., Lee, E., Kubiatowicz, J.: The cloud is not enough: saving IoT from the cloud. In: 7th USENIX Workshop on Hot Topics in Cloud Computing (HotCloud 15). USENIX Association (2015)
7. Zhang, C., Xiao, W., Tang, D., Tang, J.: P2P-based multidimensional indexing methods: a survey. J. Syst. Softw. **84**(12), 2348–2362 (2011)
8. Lua, E.K., Crowcroft, J., Pias, M., Sharma, R., Lim, S.: A survey and comparison of peer-to-peer overlay network schemes. IEEE Commun. Surv. Tutorials **7**(2), 72–93 (2005)
9. Joung, Y.J., Yang, L.W.: On character-based index schemes for complex wildcard search in peer-to-peer networks. Inf. Sci. **272**, 209–222 (2014)

10. Shen, H., Xu, C.-Z.: Leveraging a compound graph-based DHT for multi-attribute range queries with performance analysis. IEEE Trans. Comput. **61**(4), 433–447 (2012)

11. Aberer, K., Cudré-Mauroux, P., Datta, A., Despotovic, Z., Hauswirth, M., Punceva, M., Schmidt, R.: P-Grid: a self-organizing structured P2P system. ACM SIGMOD Rec. **32**(3), 29–33 (2003)

12. Schütt, T., Schintke, F., Reinefeld, A.: Range queries on structured overlay networks. Comput. Commun. **31**(2), 280–291 (2008)

13. Hidalgo, N., Rosas, E., Arantes, L., Marin, O., Sens, P., Bonnairey, X.: DRing: a layered scheme for range queries over DHTs. In: Proceedings - 11th IEEE International Conference on Computer and Information Technology, CIT 2011, pp. 29–34 (2011)

14. Landsiedel, O., Wehrle, K., Gotz, S.: Accurate prediction of power consumption in sensor networks. In: The Second IEEE Workshop on Embedded Networked Sensors, EmNetS-II (2005)

15. Carroll, A., Heiser, G.: An analysis of power consumption in a smartphone. In: Proceedings of the USENIX Annual Technical Conference (2010)

16. Stoica, I., Morris, R., Liben-Nowell, D., Karger, D., Kaashoek, M., Dabek, F., Balakrishnan, H.: Chord: a scalable peer-to-peer lookup protocol for internet applications. IEEE/ACM Trans. Netw. **11**(1), 17–32 (2003)

17. Ratnasamy, S., Francis, P., Handley, M., Karp, R., Shenker, S.: A scalable content-addressable network. In: Proceedings of the 2001 Conference on Applications, Technologies, Architectures, and Protocols for Computer Communications, pp. 161–172 (2001)

18. Zhang, L., Mitton, N.: Advanced internet of things, pp. 1–8 (2011)

19. Shen, H., Xu, C.Z., Chen, G.: Cycloid: a constant-degree and lookup-efficient P2P overlay network. Perform. Eval. **63**(3), 195–216 (2006)

20. Schmidt, R.: The P-Grid System - Overview, pp. 1–11 (2007)

21. Bongers, E., Pouwelse, J.: A survey of P2P multidimensional indexing structures, arXiv preprint arXiv:1507.05501 (2015)

22. Fu, Y., Hu, R., Chen, J., Wang, Z., Tian, G.: An improved lookup algorithm on over-DHT paradigm based P2P network. In: Gong, Z., Luo, X., Chen, J., Lei, J., Wang, F.L. (eds.) WISM 2011, Part I. LNCS, vol. 6987, pp. 200–207. Springer, Heidelberg (2011)

Towards Precision Control in Constrained Wireless Cyber-Physical Systems

David Boyle$^{(\boxtimes)}$, Roman Kolcun, and Eric Yeatman

Department of Electrical and Electronic Engineering,
Imperial College London, London, UK
{david.boyle,roman.kolcun,e.yeatman}@imperial.ac.uk

Abstract. This paper introduces the problem of high precision control in constrained wireless cyber-physical systems. We argue that balancing conflicting performance objectives, namely energy efficiency, high reliability and low latency, whilst concurrently enabling data collection and targeted message dissemination, are critical to the success of future applications of constrained wireless cyber-physical systems. We describe the contemporary art in practical collection and dissemination techniques, and select the most appropriate for evaluation. A comprehensive simulation study is presented and experimentally validated, the results of which show that the current art falls significantly short of desirable performance when inter-packet intervals decrease to those required for precision control. It follows that there is a significant need for further study and new solutions to solve this emerging problem.

Keywords: Wireless sensor networks · Cyber-physical systems · Control · Communications protocols · Data collection · Dissemination · Routing · Reconfiguration · Structural monitoring · Fundamental limits · Performance

1 Introduction

Wireless sensor and actuator networks will be a key enabling technology in the next generation of cyber-physical systems (CPS). The CPS paradigm introduces new functional and associated design requirements that are not typically considered in the development of wireless sensor network (WSN) technologies. A key differentiator between WSN and CPS can be stated in terms of the evolution from sensor networks designed exclusively to collect sensor data to those with the ability to augment sensor data collection with physical control over the environment using one or more actuators. Thus, the notion of *control* becomes a significant factor, which raises a number of important questions. Furthermore, the potential to interact with and exert control over the physical environment presents an entirely new challenge to the research community, particularly in attempting to bring cheap and effective networked embedded systems to the fore in industrial monitoring, control and automation applications. Depending

© ICST Institute for Computer Sciences, Social Informatics and Telecommunications Engineering 2016
B. Mandler et al. (Eds.): IoT 360° 2015, Part II, LNICST 170, pp. 292–306, 2016.
DOI: 10.1007/978-3-319-47075-7_33

on the application, numerous potential control strategies may be applicable. This work considers the case where a central entity, man or machine, requires the ability to remotely control devices in a network. Notionally, this requirement may be to send a control message to a device equipped with an actuator to alter some physical state in the environment (e.g. adjusting a valve to achieve a desired rate of flow). This is not dissimilar to disseminating a message in a traditional WSN to change, for example, the rate at which a node samples a connected sensor, or its reporting interval (often referred to as *inter-packet interval* (IPI), i.e. the rate at which the application generates data packets to be transmitted towards a sink node) [7]. However, with the exception of RPL (Sect. 3), all contemporary approaches disseminate messages using network *flooding* mechanisms, irrespective of the intended recipient. We make the following assumptions:

- Applications of cyber-physical systems may include heterogeneous devices, i.e. numerous connected (or integrated) sensors and/or actuators [2], which participate in the same network
- Applications will to evolve from traditional networks collaboratively detecting distributed phenomena to targeted sensing of discrete, localised phenomena contributing to the monitoring and control of macro systems
- Applications will require the ability to exert fine-grained control over individual devices, which may include commands that can be generated autonomously or manually by *users*, i.e. human-in-the-loop

An important question is therefore raised: can (and if not, how can) we ensure effective, i.e. reliable and timely, transmission of *control* or *actuation* messages[1] to *specific* devices in a network? Furthermore, can this be done whilst respecting and adhering to traditional WSN design objectives, including energy efficiency, robustness and reliability? Similar questions have attracted increased attention in the recent literature, e.g. in [9,10][2] and [19]. Perhaps equally important are the questions: can both *collect* and *control* traffic types effectively coexist in a full network stack, what is the relationship between them, and what are the inherent trade-offs? There is a significant gap in the literature concerning how data collection, a standard function of most sensing systems, and fine-grained control, a *feature* that is increasingly required, can coexist in a fully integrated application stack in the context of CPS. In attempting to answer these questions, we present the following contributions in this paper:

- A rigorous evaluation of the performance of coexisting state-of-the-art *collect* and *control* protocols in a full network stack (Sect. 4), including quantified assessment of the trade-offs with regard to latency, energy efficiency and reliability performance under various operational loads. Our evaluation is predicated on a real application where WSN technology is used to monitor and

---

[1] The terms are hereinafter used interchangeably, and may apply to sending an actuation command or a reconfiguration command.

[2] *Downward routing* is a term also used to describe the traffic pattern for such messages, particularly in the standards community, e.g. [21].

control critical infrastructure, described in Sect. 2. We use selected state-of-the-art protocols described in Sect. 3.

– Evidence and subsequent examination, in Sects. 5 and 6, respectively, showing that the existing art does not sufficiently enable the level of high-fidelity control required for CPS without significant degradation in one or more performance metrics.

2   Background and Motivation

This work originates from efforts to apply wireless cyber-physical systems to the monitoring and control of critical infrastructures. Specifically, it stems from efforts to demonstrate the feasibility of WSN technology applied to structural health monitoring in an operational environment [1], i.e. that of a cable stayed bridge[3], during and post construction. Some interesting technical challenges were involved in the first instance, such as using heterogeneous sensors. Industrial, commercially available sensors were specified by collaborating geomonitoring specialists[4]. These included displacement, strain, inclination, acceleration, and pressure transducers, soil moisture probes, anemometers and precision temperature sensors. Each sensor type had varying electrical characteristics and communications interfaces [2]. They were connected to mote-class devices (below) in varying numbers and configurations, depending on the specified location on the structure and measurement of interest. This is representative of a new challenge in applied WSN research, whereby heterogeneous sensors, and their physical configuration, are used in combination to monitor a macro system whilst using a common wireless communication infrastructure. Traditional WSN implementations tend to use homogeneous devices across the network, collaboratively monitoring distributed phenomena, such as light and temperature. These features, coupled with highly localised sensing (e.g. using a displacement transducer, with a limited sensing range (i.e. centimetres), for crack detection), contributes to new challenges in terms of remote device interaction and control. The incorporation of hybrid energy harvesting and storage to effectively provide perpetual energy to the devices in the field was also required and demonstrated [1,17]. A simple system architecture was developed, where sensor data is periodically communicated over multiple hops towards a sink node, which in turn connects to a gateway and transfers data to networked servers, thus allowing analytics to be performed by domain experts.

Hardware. Bespoke sensor nodes, *mote*-class devices, were developed to satisfy monitoring and energy requirements, which include MSP430F5437[5] microcontrollers and TI CC2520[6] RFICs as key computational and communications components. We refer the interested reader to [1] and [17] for more on the hardware.

---

[3] http://www.fr.ch/poya/fr/pub/index.cfm.

[4] http://www.solexperts.com.

[5] http://www.ti.com/lit/ds/symlink/msp430f5419a.pdf.

[6] http://www.ti.com/lit/ds/symlink/cc2520.pdf.

Embedded Software and Communications. Original firmware was built using TinyOS [14], and used the available communications stack, i.e. CTP for data collection over BoX-MAC [18]. Remote management of the network was done using DRIP [20], with Deluge used for reprogramming [8] - both packaged with the TinyOS operating system. These are described in more detail in Sect. 3.

Energy Efficiency and Reliability. Energy efficiency is key to prolonged field operation. The hardware was designed to be as energy efficient as possible, achieving a quiescent current of $<10\,\mu A$ in the lowest power mode with sensors attached. Assuming inter-packet intervals of *hours* (suitable for long term monitoring), the system could be duty cycled aggressively ($\sim 1\,\%$). CTP has been shown to deliver $>90\,\%$ reliability under most conditions. For low-rate, i.e. large IPI, and low-density deployments, this approaches $100\,\%$ depending on the link layer. For long term monitoring tolerant of minor loss, it was sufficient to achieve $>95\,\%$ packet delivery, typically achievable using CTP over BoX-MAC [7].

2.1 Cyber-Physical Systems: Features and Design Objectives

The ability to remotely interact with individual devices in the network is a desirable feature that was not sufficiently implemented in our initial system. The end user requires control of individual devices during anomalous periods, e.g. to investigate a potentially dangerous situation detected by a device. This is achievable by changing the sampling rate or reporting interval of a particular sensor, connected to a particular port of a particular device. Theoretically, this also shifts focus towards high-fidelity control and actuation in CPS, where additional features and associated performance requirements are certain to emerge as applications become more complex. This work focuses on achieving high-precision control over devices, a required *feature* of both our original system and emerging CPS applications.

High-Precision Control. Where an actuator exists in the network, it is necessary to communicate with this device directly, with a high degree of reliability and low latency. Therefore, the ability to remotely exert fine grained control over each of these devices is of primary interest. There are some existing mechanisms to perform this task, assessed in more detail in the next section, where we later show and argue that they do not necessarily meet the following goals of an effective precision control mechanism for CPS. The main goals of a precise control scheme for wireless CPS are as follows:

- *Addressability:* each device should be individually addressable
- *Reliability:* control and actuation messages should achieve maximum delivery, i.e. approach $100\,\%$
- *Efficiency:* the system should retain the principles of minimising the resources required to deliver messages to target devices, i.e. minimum amount of transmissions, minimal state, energy, etc.
- *Low Latency:* control messages should exhibit low latency, approaching fundamental lower bounds

– *Robustness:* the system should continue to operate irrespective of dynamic communications conditions, topologies, loads, etc.

There are additional requirements, such as hardware independence and security, of equally significant importance. We retain the principle of ensuring hardware independence, but regard security as being beyond the scope of this contribution.

3   Data Collection and Dissemination Protocols

Most implementations of WSNs use a single point of data collection. This typically requires the creation of a tree routing structure, rooted in a sink node (or relatively fewer sink nodes to sensing nodes). This constitutes converge-cast network traffic (many-to-one), and has been the focus of the majority of research and development efforts to-date. Data dissemination requires transmitting messages in the opposite direction, either sending network-wide messages (one-to-many, or flooding), or one-to-one (sometimes referred to as point-to-point or any-to-any). The latter requires more complex routing information, which we consider in more detail in the following sections.

Data Collection Protocols. There are numerous popular solutions for data collection in WSNs, such as Collection Tree Protocol (CTP) [7] and RPL [21], both of which are based on converge-cast communication towards one or more sink nodes. In the standards community, these are often described as *destination oriented directed acyclic graphs.* We disregard early protocols, such as MulithopLQI[7] and MintRoute [22], which are obsoleted and improved upon by CTP. There have been recent efforts to enable any-to-any, e.g. [6,11], and multi-mode downward routing, e.g. [10], with similar objectives in mind, discussed later.

Dissemination Protocols. If we consider a multi-hop network - with *any* underlying communications infrastructure - controlling individual devices primarily requires finding a *route* to the device in question, and transmitting the necessary command to that node. There are solutions for disseminating data in WSNs, including DIP [16], DRIP [20] and RPL [21], many of which are closely related to and use the Trickle algorithm [15]. These differ from protocols like Deluge [8] and MNP [12], in that they are designed to deliver small values, whereas the latter are designed to deliver larger files such as binary code updates. The majority of traditional WSN research considered networks of homogeneous devices, where updates and configuration commands were disseminated to every device in the network, leveraging local neighbourhoods to advertise and agree upon *versions.* More complex dissemination is possible using the existing art, e.g. as described in TEP 118[8], performing predicate-based changes, implemented by layering interfaces above the existing low-level networking primitives. There are other proposed solutions that attempt to solve both simultaneously, such as Chaos [13]. As with many advances in WSNs, each solution is often well suited to different

---

[7] http://www.tinyos.net/tinyos-2.x/tos/lib/net/lqi/.

[8] http://www.tinyos.net/tinyos-2.1.0/doc/html/tep118.html.

scenarios, having been developed with different functionalities and performance metrics in mind. The function of a collection protocol is intuitive, however, the thinking behind dissemination requires more careful consideration, particularly as high-fidelity precision control is required over individual devices. For the purposes of our evaluation, we select CTP and Trickle as the most applicable protocols to evaluate as part of a full application. These are mature and well studied protocols that exemplify the current art in efficient and reliable wireless networking. Furthermore, their implementation does not require the accommodation of additional overheads associated with the standards under development. Finally, commercial protocols, including ZigBee and WirelessHART, are not considered. This is due to their implementation of the IEEE 802.15.4 MAC, which is founded on global time synchronisation[9]. This is significantly less energy efficient than asynchronous (or semi-synchronous) radio duty cycled MAC protocols, such as ContikiMAC and BoX-MAC.

4 Experimental Evaluation

To evaluate the performance of the selected coexisting collection and dissemination protocols, we implemented a full application using the Contiki operating system [3][10]. The application uses CTP for data collection, implemented as the Contiki collect protocol, and Trickle for the dissemination of messages using the Rime network stack [5], with ContikiMAC to manage the radio [4] using the default settings. ContikiMAC tends to provide better reliability and energy efficiency than BoX-MAC, and is therefore a natural design choice. We include a randomised destination address (of a node in our network) for each dissemination message in the payload of the packet (which in our case is less than the minimum Contiki packet size), and post-process the stored log files to compute results, thus allowing Trickle to be used without further modification.

4.1 Simulation

Cooja, the simulator/emulator packaged with the Contiki operating system, was used for this study. The Multi-path Ray-tracer Medium (MRM) radio model provided by Cooja was used to simulate a realistic radio environment. The noise floor was set to -90 dBm with a standard deviation of 2 dBm. These values were shown to be realistic for low noise environments in [9].

Topology. The topology used for simulation consists of a network of 45 nodes deployed in 3-dimensional space, guided by the bridge (see footnote 3) monitoring scenario described in Sect. 2. This corresponds to nodes placed 50 m apart, lining either side of the bridge (10 m separation) spanning 850 m. Nodes are

---

[9] The amended IEEE802.15.4e (TSCH) is insufficiently mature for consideration.
[10] We use the latest stable Contiki release, Contiki 2.7, available: http://www.contiki-os.org/download.html.

placed vertically perpendicular to the x- and y-axes on two pylons (325 m and 625 m from the sink, respectively) to a height of +150 m in the z-axis, using 3 nodes spaced 50 m apart. The sink node is placed 50 m from the node closest to the end of the bridge.

Parameter Selection and Evaluation Metrics. Inter-packet intervals (IPI) are swept from 5 to 45 s with 5 s interleaved, denoted IPI_D for dissemination and IPI_C for collect. IPI_C tends to vary depending on the application and the granularity of the sensor data required. It may be tuned towards saturation (i.e. $IPI_X \rightarrow 0$) during periods when additional data points are required to more thoroughly assess a situation[11]. The duration of the simulation was chosen so both protocols sent at least 250 messages, i.e. $t = 250 \times max(IPI_D, IPI_C)$, where *every* node must transmit the minimum number of collect messages. Therefore, the total number of simulated collect messages transmitted ranges from ∼11,250 to ∼101,250, and the number of control messages varies from a minimum of 250 to a maximum of ∼2250. This has a significant impact on the duration of each simulation run. At the beginning of the simulation, the network is afforded 120 s for the collect protocol to settle and obtain information about nodes' neighbourhoods. Thereafter, both protocols begin transmitting packets at the predefined rates. For the collect protocol, upon the expiration of the predefined interval, a secondary random timer is started, within a maximum length of 20 % of the main timer, to reduce congestion and increase the delivery rate. When the main timer expires on the base-station, a message is generated and sent to a node in the network, chosen at random. Because Trickle is initiated by one node only, there is no need for a secondary timer, as it would have no impact on the delivery rate. The evaluation focuses on following metrics: (*i*) reliability, (*ii*) latency, and (*iii*) energy efficiency. Reliability is calculated as percentage of messages that are successfully delivered to their destination. Latency is calculated as the time difference between the moment when the message was generated by the source node and the time the message is delivered to its destination. Timestamps are collected from the log file generated by Cooja. Energy efficiency is evaluated with the PowerTracker plugin, which tracks, for each node, how long the radio is turned on, transmitting or receiving.

5   Results and Evaluation

For each of the 81 $\{IPI_D, IPI_C\}$ pairs, we ran the experiment three times (i.e. 243 runs in total). For each run, average reliability, latency, and energy efficiency were computed. We discuss these metrics individually in the following subsections, where the results (i.e. each data point) is the computed average from three simulation runs. In addition to running the collect and dissemination protocols

---

[11] The literature suggests typical IPI_C values $\simeq$ 15 s. We include this interval, in addition to approaching saturation and selecting numerous divergent values. The same is done for IPI_D, where typical values for this frequency are relatively unknown.

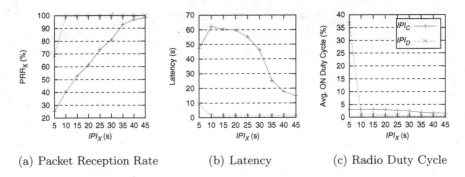

(a) Packet Reception Rate　　　(b) Latency　　　(c) Radio Duty Cycle

Fig. 1. Baseline figures for reliability (a), latency (b) and energy (c) performance for collect (red) and disseminate (green) protocols running independently (Color figure online)

in parallel, we also ran them separately to obtain baseline data. The results are illustrated in Fig. 1, which shows performance to be in line with expectation.

5.1 Reliability

Figure 2 shows that the collect protocol delivers less than 10 % of the messages when $IPI_D \leq 10$ s, regardless of the collect interval. For larger IPI_D, the reliability of the collect protocol increases, and stabilises at a certain value. This value differs, on average, by ~1.7 % from the baseline collect reliability, i.e. without the dissemination protocol running in parallel. This shows that significant performance degradation occurs in terms of data collection when dissemination intervals are below 25 s. Dissemination reliability is shown in Fig. 3. It is clear that for $IPI_D \leq 25$ s, the packet reception rate for disseminated messages (PRR_D) degrades significantly. There are two further interesting observations to be made. The first is that, for $IPI_D \geq 25$ s, PRR_D is consistently approaches 100 %. This demonstrates how successful dissemination is when compared to collection. This

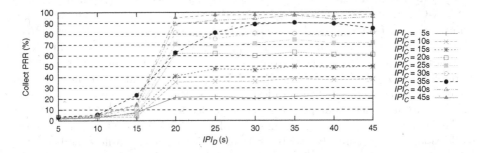

Fig. 2. Packet Reception Rate (PRR) for collect messages (PRR_C) for each inter-packet interval pair $\{IPI_D, IPI_C\}$.

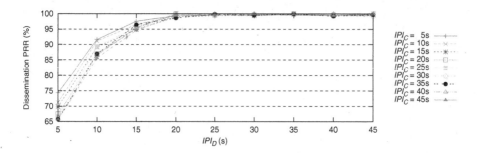

Fig. 3. Packet Reception Rate (PRR) for disseminate messages (PRR_D) for each inter-packet interval pair $\{IPI_D, IPI_C\}$.

is intuitive, as data collection via a tree rooted in a sink (many to one) is inherently more difficult than network-wide message dissemination (one to many). Secondly, there are some counter-intuitive data points in the graph. Looking at $IPI_C = 5\,$s, we can see that the average PRR_D is greater than that for larger IPI_C intervals. Owing to the random component used in the simulation and use of computed averages, the exact reason is difficult to pinpoint. High reliability is characteristic of the Trickle algorithm's dynamic tuning, and ability to rapidly propagate messages [15]. Practical evaluation of this phenomenon is inconclusive (Fig. 7(a)), and is worthy of further study. This does not detract from the overall result showing that for shorter IPI_D & IPI_C reliability performance is significantly degraded.

5.2   Latency

Figure 4 shows the time required for packets to be collected from the network. It follows the same trend as for reliability. It is worth remembering that the depth of the network is significant, where the number of hops can be as many as 15 to and from the sink[12]. This is a linear function of the delay experienced in end-to-end communication over multiple hops, and depends heavily on the *receive check interval* of the underlying MAC protocol in duty cycled asynchronous[13] CSMA-CA approaches. For $IPI_D \leq 10\,$s, it takes on average more than one minute for a message to be delivered to the sink, regardless the value of IPI_C. As IPI_D increases, the collect time stabilises at a certain value. This value does not differ by more than $\sim$10 % from the average collection time of the collect protocol baseline for that IPI_C. Figure 5 shows the time taken for messages to be disseminated to predetermined destination nodes in the network, on average. In this case it is clear that performance degrades for $IPI_D \leq 20\,$s for all IPI_C. In all cases, this is approximately an order of magnitude more efficient than data collection. This is similarly attributable to the fundamental difference between

---

[12] The average number of hops across all experiments is $\simeq 4.3$.

[13] We consider asynchronous MACs to be those without global or centrally coordinated time synchronisation.

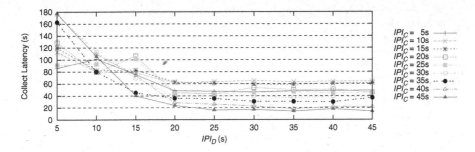

Fig. 4. End-to-end latency for collect messages for each inter-packet interval pair $\{IPI_D, IPI_C\}$.

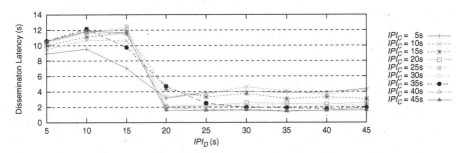

Fig. 5. End-to-end latency for disseminate messages for each inter-packet interval pair $\{IPI_D, IPI_C\}$.

collection towards a single point and dissemination throughout the network, and Trickle's ability to rapidly propagate messages.

5.3 Energy Efficiency

To estimate energy efficiency, we use the radio duty cycle (RDC) as a proxy. Although it is not a true approximation of the energy cost for our target system (where sampling the sensors is often significantly more energy intensive than radio communication [2]), we are interested in the impact of the protocols' coexistence on the system's energy efficiency, and thus it is sufficient for the purposes of this evaluation. Figure 6 shows the total time for which the radio is active for each $\{IPI_D, IPI_C\}$ pair. It shows that for $IPI_D < 20$ s the RDC ranges from 31–36%. The radio *ON* time in Fig. 6 is the sum of the TX and RX on times[14]. This is a significant energy cost, where total RDC for these types of systems would ideally be kept as close to ~1 % as possible. The ratio of time the radio spends in each of RX (i.e. *listen*) and TX (*transmit*) modes is approximately

---

[14] We disregard the total ON time. For *all* $IPI_D < 20$ s, ON is in the region 60–80%. We recalculate this as the sum of RX and TX active times, as they are reflective of the higher energy modes of the RFIC when listening and transmitting, respectively.

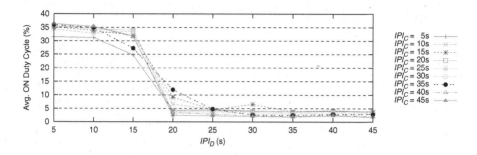

Fig. 6. Energy efficiency overhead estimation by proxy of radio duty cycle for each inter-packet interval pair $\{IPI_D, IPI_C\}$.

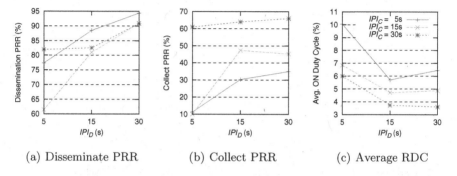

(a) Disseminate PRR   (b) Collect PRR   (c) Average RDC

Fig. 7. Practical results for a subset of $\{IPI_D, IPI_C\}$ pairs showing (a) disseminate Packet Reception Rate (PRR), (b) collect PRR, and (c) radio duty cycle

$10 : 1$, respectively. It is again noticeable that for $IPI_C = 5$ s, there is a counter-intuitive result. In this case, looking at Fig. 6, the radio consumes less energy. However, this does not detract from the overall result that there is a significant cost increase for all $IPI_D < 20$ s, and corroborates the preceding reliability and latency results. Compared with the baseline energy performance results for each protocol shown in Fig. 7(c), it can be seen that there is a significant overhead when the protocols coexist, most noticeably for $IPI_D \leq 20$ s.

6   Discussion

The results in Sect. 5 demonstrate that there are significant shortcomings in the performance of the best, i.e. most efficient, reliable and robust, communications protocols for data dissemination and collection when concurrently deployed in the context of emerging applications of CPS that may use constrained wireless networks. Our evaluation shows that energy requirements are significantly increased for small inter-packet intervals, and the reliability performance of the collection protocol is significantly affected by the presence of regular control messages in the network. PRRs $< 30\%$ for $IPI_D < 20$ s will hardly be acceptable for CPS. This is hugely problematic when considering the nature of control applications, where timely feedback, i.e. sensor data, is required to make control decisions. Furthermore, we show that latency with regard to sensor data collection is largely doubled for small IPI_D.

6.1 Caveats and Limitations

Our initial evaluation is based on simulation only, which is largely considered to be insufficient. There are justifiable reasons to adopt this approach. An evaluation *in the wild* for our use case would require uninterrupted access to approximately 1 km of operational civil infrastructure to conduct 81 individual experiments (243 to obtain similar averages). Gaining such access is almost impossible for the purposes of experimentation. Therefore, simulation is essential to conduct necessary pre-deployment validation and test. Accordingly, the simulation experiments in Sect. 4 considered a very specific application scenario, which tightly governs the network topology. Nevertheless, we conducted a smaller scale practical experiment on a subset of the $\{IPI_D, IPI_C\}$ pairs to assess and demonstrate the effects presented in Sect. 5, as follows.

Practical Evaluation. We built a reduced linear network, where 13 TelosB (clones) were distributed over three floors of the Electrical and Electronic Engineering building at Imperial College London. Experiments were conducted to generate data points for 9 $\{IPI_D, IPI_C\}$ pairs, governed in duration by IPI_D for 250 disseminated messages in each case. The average number of hops per message transmitted was $\simeq 3.8$; reasonably close to the 4.3 in the simulated networks. IEEE 802.15.4 channels 25 and 26 were used for each pair, in a typically noisy environment, and averages computed.

Figure 7 shows the results for PRR of dissemination and collect messages, and energy efficiency (by proxy of RDC, calculated by counting the clock ticks during active (i.e. TX and RX) modes of operation). Irrespective of the reduced scale of the experiment, the results show that performance degradation is in relative agreement with the simulation, thus validating the existence of the problem. It is likely that for different network topologies, depths and dynamic RF environments, the results will vary.

Interestingly, there is a marked improvement in the PRRs for $\{IPI_D, IPI_C\} = \{5\,s, 30\,s\}$. This is a fairer reflection, and attributable to both significantly fewer collect messages congesting the network and fewer overall nodes in the network (with respect to the simulation study). Nonetheless, the performance is still less than ideal for prospective wireless CPS applications, and the network is shown remain essentially non-functional for shorter IPI pairs. The energy performance of the nodes in the network relatively improved, but in larger networks, more messages in both directions will increase the active periods of the RFIC.

Finally, we neglect to propose a new solution that improves the *status quo*. This is because it is essential to completely understand the performance limitations of the state-of-the-art before proposing any new alternative. This constitutes essential knowledge for potential adopters of technologies using constrained wireless components. Methods to improve the situation are under development, but are left to future work. New methods to effectively store and manage routing information will be essential to overcome these performance limitations, and will exploit increasing on-chip memory, processing capability and energy efficiency.

7 Related Work

Stolikj *et al.* proposed improvements to the performance of Trickle by enhancing cross-layer interactions, showing how MAC layer implementations can lead to violations of Trickle's delicate timing requirements [19]. Isomin *et al.* show that current, and improved, versions of contemporary dissemination techniques fall short of the requirements for actuation in wireless CPS, and question of whether *P2P* traffic support is even necessary for CPS. They illustrate that Trickle outperforms an improved variant of RPL in terms of efficiency, a result that we leverage in the selection of Trickle in this work [9]. Furthermore, based on our evaluation, it is evident that there is cause to implement more complex downward routing information to improve overall network performance. Ko *et al.* propose DualMOP to solve the problem of heterogeneous modes of operation (i.e. storing and non-storing modes) of the RPL standard in overlapping networks [10]. Dunkels *et al.* proposed the Announcement Layer to coordinate beacons in the network to reduce overheads associated with concurrent collection and dissemination strategies. They extend Contiki Shell application through netcmd to demonstrate how a command may be run on *all* nodes in the network. They do not consider the requirement for direct addressability, or finding efficient methods that do not flood the entire network. They show how beacon coordination can contribute to improvements, e.g. reducing the overall number of beacons required by 9 % by exploiting coordinated announcements [4]. Dunkels *et al.*'s approach, if extended, would be similar to the explanation in TEP 118 on how to handle more complex dissemination, discussed in Sect. 3. However, none of the existing approaches directly address the problem of high precision control in wireless sensor and actuator networks where there exists the need for concurrent, highly reliable, timely and energy efficient data collection and (addressable) dissemination, which will be required for wireless CPS applications.

8 Conclusion

In this paper we describe the emerging problem of high precision control over cyber-physical systems with constrained wireless devices in the loop. We articulate the need for concurrent collection and dissemination strategies that satisfy conflicting objectives; namely energy efficiency, high reliability and low latency. We select two of the most established, studied and optimised protocols for each, CTP and Trickle, and evaluate them across a comprehensive range of inter-packet intervals in simulation. We demonstrate how these protocols, when implemented concurrently, do not achieve the performance requirements necessary for applications of cyber-physical systems. It follows that there is a significant need for additional study and new solutions to solve the problem of high precision control in constrained wireless cyber-physical systems.

References

1. Boyle, D., Magno, M., O'Flynn, B., Brunelli, D., Popovici, E., Benini, L.: Towards persistent structural health monitoring through sustainable wireless sensor networks. In: ISSNIP 2011, pp. 323–328 (2011)
2. Boyle, D., Srbinovski, B., Popovici, E., O'Flynn, B.: Energy analysis of industrial sensors in novel wireless SHM systems. In: 2012 IEEE Sensors, pp. 1–4, October 2012
3. Dunkels, A., Gronvall, B., Voigt, T.: Contiki - a lightweight and flexible operating system for tiny networked sensors. In: 29th Local Computer Networks, November 2004
4. Dunkels, A., Mottola, L., Tsiftes, N., Österlind, F., Eriksson, J., Finne, N.: The announcement layer: beacon coordination for the sensornet stack. In: Marrón, P.J., Whitehouse, K. (eds.) EWSN 2011. LNCS, vol. 6567, pp. 211–226. Springer, Heidelberg (2011). doi:10.1007/978-3-642-19186-2_14
5. Dunkels, A., Österlind, F., He, Z.: An adaptive communication architecture for wireless sensor networks. In: SenSys 2007, pp. 335–349 (2007)
6. Duquennoy, S., Landsiedel, O., Voigt, T.: Let the tree bloom: scalable opportunistic routing with ORPL. In: SenSys 2013
7. Gnawali, O., Fonseca, R., Jamieson, K., Moss, D., Levis, P.: Collection tree protocol. In: SenSys 2009
8. Hui, J.W., Culler, D.: The dynamic behavior of a data dissemination protocol for network programming at scale. In: SenSys 2004
9. Istomin, T., Kiraly, C., Picco, G.P.: Is RPL ready for actuation? A comparative evaluation in a smart city scenario. In: Abdelzaher, T., Pereira, N., Tovar, E. (eds.) EWSN 2015. LNCS, vol. 8965, pp. 291–299. Springer, Heidelberg (2015). doi:10.1007/978-3-319-15582-1_22
10. Ko, J., Jeong, J., Park, J., Jun, J.A., Gnawali, O., Paek, J.: DualMOP-RPL: supporting multiple modes of downward routing in a single rpl network. ACM Trans. Sen. Netw. **11**(2), 39:1–39:20 (2015)
11. Kolcun, R., McCann, J.: Dragon: data discovery and collection architecture for distributed IoT. In: Internet of Things (IOT) 2014, pp. 91–96, October 2014
12. Kulkarni, S., Wang, L.: MNP: multihop network reprogramming service for sensor networks. In: Proceedings of the Distributed Computing Systems, ICDCS 2005 (2005)
13. Landsiedel, O., Ferrari, F., Zimmerling, M.: Chaos: versatile and efficient all-to-all data sharing and in-network processing at scale. In: SenSys 2013, pp. 1:1–1:14. ACM
14. Levis, P., et al.: Tinyos: an operating system for sensor networks. In: Weber, W., Rabaey, J., Aarts, E. (eds.) Ambient Intelligence, pp. 115–148. Springer, Berlin (2005)
15. Levis, P., Patel, N., Culler, D., Shenker, S.: Trickle: a self-regulating algorithm for code propagation and maintenance in wireless sensor networks. In: NSDI 2004
16. Lin, K., Levis, P.: Data discovery and dissemination with DIP. In: IPSN 2008
17. Magno, M., Boyle, D., Brunelli, D., O'Flynn, B., Popovici, E., Benini, L.: Extended wireless monitoring through intelligent hybrid energy supply. IEEE Trans. Ind. Electron. **61**(4), 1871–1881 (2014)

18. Moss, D., Levis, P.: BoX-MACs: exploiting physical and link layer boundaries in low-power networking. Computer Systems Laboratory Stanford University (2008)
19. Stolikj, M., Meyfroyt, T.M.M., Cuijpers, P.J.L., Lukkien, J.J.: Improving the performance of trickle-based data dissemination in low-power networks. In: Abdelzaher, T., Pereira, N., Tovar, E. (eds.) EWSN 2015. LNCS, vol. 8965, pp. 186–201. Springer, Heidelberg (2015). doi:10.1007/978-3-319-15582-1_12
20. Tolle, G., Culler, D.: Design of an application-cooperative management system for wireless sensor networks. In: EWSN 2005
21. Winter, T., Thubert, P., Brandt, A., Hui, J., Kelsey, R., Levis, P., Pister, K., Struik, R., Vasseur, J., Alexander, R.: RPL: IPv6 routing protocol for low-power and lossy networks. RFC 6550 (Proposed Standard), March 2012
22. Woo, A., Tong, T., Culler, D.: Taming the underlying challenges of reliable multi-hop routing in sensor networks. In: SenSys 2003

DESAL$^\beta$: A Framework For Implementing Self-stabilizing Embedded Network Applications

Yangyang He$^{1(\boxtimes)}$, Yuheng Du^1, Shiree Hughes^2, Jiannan Zhai^2,
Jason O. Hallstrom^2, and Nigamanth Sridhar^3

^{1} School of Computing, Clemson University, Clemson, USA
{yyhe,yuhengd}@clemson.edu
^{2} I-SENSE, Florida Atlantic University, Boca Raton, USA
{shughes2015,jzhai,jhallstrom}@fau.edu
^{3} Electrical and Computer Engineering, Cleveland State University, Cleveland, USA
n.sridhar1@csuohio.edu

1 Introduction

The Dynamic Embedded Sensor-Actuator Language ($DESAL$) [2] is a rule-based programming language, without events, interrupts, or hidden control. Nodes have built-in access to their neighbors' state, with automatic node discovery and health monitoring. Applications communicate via shared variables, rather than explicit message passing. Shared variables naturally represent the state of self-stabilizing algorithms. $DESAL$ simplifies the construction of self-stabilizing embedded applications by eliminating network programming, while offering significant reliability improvements.

Contributions. This paper presents both incremental and fundamental contributions. First, we present $DESAL^\beta$, a significant improvement of the $DESAL^\alpha$ implementation reported in [1]. $DESAL^\beta$ includes a new, more complete compiler, with new support for C-based types and control flow constructs, as well as a new C/nesC code mixing feature. A comparative performance analysis between $DESAL^\alpha$ and $DESAL^\beta$ is presented. Second, and more fundamentally, we present an in-depth treatment of a self-stabilizing algorithm realized in $DESAL^\beta$ to assess the utility of the paradigm. The analysis centers not only on ease-of-use, but on fault-tolerance and convergence time, post-fault. Prior publications focused on grammar and architectural details.

2 Related Work

Prior work on programming approaches for embedded network systems span two paths. The first is focused on node-level programming. Representative solutions include Contiki [4], MANTIS [5], TinyOS [3], and others. Although the kernel of Contiki is event-driven, preemptive multi-threading is supported through a library. Contiki programs can be loaded dynamically and are C-based. Similarly, MANTIS provides users with a cross-platform, event-driven operating system

© ICST Institute for Computer Sciences, Social Informatics and Telecommunications Engineering 2016
B. Mandler et al. (Eds.): IoT 360° 2015, Part II, LNICST 170, pp. 307–312, 2016.
DOI: 10.1007/978-3-319-47075-7_34

that can be used to load programs dynamically. Programs for MANTIS are written in C, with slight changes to the basic program structure, such as requiring a `start` function instead of a `main` function, as well as other idioms. TinyOS is another platform for wireless sensor networks (WSNs). Programs are written in *nesC*, an event-driven language that derives from C [6].

The second path of prior work focuses on network-level macro programming, which hides the details of individual sensor nodes from programmers. TinyDB [7] and Cougar [8], for instance, abstract a WSN as a relational database and allow the use of declarative SQL-based queries to retrieve data from the network. Kairos [9] provides a shared memory abstraction to access one-hop neighbors and acquire their data. Regiment [10] is a functional language that enables *spatiotemporal* macroprogramming, which hides the direct manipulation of program states from the programmer. It divides a larger network into abstract regions and provides abstractions for querying the state across a region.

DESAL is introduced in [2]. It adopts five fundamental principles: (*i*) a state-based model of programming, which abandons event-driven logic in favor of state-based logic; (*ii*) shared variable communication, which enables the sharing of state variables across devices; (*iii*) a rule-based programming model, in which programs comprise a set of statements, where each statement is a guarded action dependent on a Boolean condition; (*iv*) dynamic binding, which allows for shared variable communication in the presence of changing wireless connectivity; and (*v*) synchronized, network-wide action timing. A preliminary implementation of a DESAL compiler is presented in [1]. SELFWISE [11] also supports state-based programming and offers a supporting runtime environment for self-stabilizing algorithms. However, it lacks support for coordinated, distributed actions, which is an important feature in many scenarios.

3   DESAL$^\beta$

DESAL$^\beta$ is a framework for implementing self-stabilizing embedded network applications. It provides a state-based programming language with support for C-based constructs, a runtime platform based on TinyOS and a Java user interface used to monitor and debug applications. We adapted the *DESAL* runtime to TinyOS 2.1.2, from TinyOS 1.x and replaced the time synchronization module with the Flooding Time Synchronization Protocol (FTSP) [15] to achieve better synchronization performance. *DESAL$^\beta$* code is translated to nesC code and compiled with the supporting runtime libraires. *DESAL$^\beta$* adapts the runtime design described in [1].

New *DESAL$^\beta$* language features include: (i) *C-based structs* to provide flexible data representation; (ii) *nesC/C code mixing* to accommodate situations where it is more convenient to use event-based semantics; (iii) *multi-hop binding* to enable variable sharing across multiple hops, and to simplify algorithms implemented based on the notion of a K-neighborhood; and (iv) *declarative link quality guarantees* to ensure network robustness.

4 Case Study: Spanning Tree

The case study involves creating a routing tree in the network. A key advantage of $DESAL^\beta$ is that complex logic for message exchange is hidden from the programmer. The self-stabilizing algorithm developed by Goddard et al. [18] is:

Rule 1:	Rule 2:	Rule 3:
$v.ID = 0 \rightarrow v.distance$ $= 0 \wedge v.parent = v;$	$v.ID \neq 0 \wedge \exists u \in N(v) : (u.distance =$ $minD) \rightarrow v.distance = minD + 1 \wedge$ $v.parent = u \wedge v.parentAlive = true;$	$v.ID \neq 0 \wedge v.parentAlive$ $= false \rightarrow v.distance$ $= \infty \wedge v.parent = v$

where $v.distance$ represents the distance of node v from the root of the tree, $v.parent$ points to the parent node of v, and $minD$ denotes the current shortest distance to the root, among all neighbors of a non-root node v. An ID value of zero is used to represent the root node, while non-zero values represent non-root nodes. $v.parentAlive$ indicates whether a node's parent is healthy. Rule 1 is responsible for declaring the root node of the tree. Rule 2 is responsible for searching for a parent. Rule 3 is responsible for recovering from a parent fault.

We translate the above rules to the $DESAL^\beta$ code shown in Listing 1. Line 2 shows that each node maintains a shared variable `distance` to represent its distance from the root. Initially, each node's `distance` is set to 255, indicating a disconnect from the tree. On line 3, local variable `parent` is similarly initialized to the host node's `ID`. Neighbors' distance information can be read from the multi-binding `nDistance`. The first subcomponent, on lines 9–23, implements rules 1 and 2. Every 3 s, the `foreach` loop on lines 11–17 finds the neighbor offering the shortest distance to the root. The `ID` of this node is acquired by `src()` and used to update `parent`. The `parentAlive` flag is set to *true*, and the host node's `distance` is set to 1 hop greater than the parent's distance, `minD`. The root node's `distance` is set to 0, as shown on lines 22–23. Rule 3 is implemented

```
1   component spanningTree
2     shared uint16 distance = 255
3     unshared uint16 parent = ID
4     unshared uint16 minD = 254
5     unshared bool parentAlive = false
6     binding uint16 nDistance <-
          *.spanningTree.distance[20]
7
8     // non-root node updates its parent
9     every 3\,s after 0s
10      (ID!=0 && parentAlive == false):
11        foreach d in nDistance {
12          if(d<minD){
13            minD = d
14            parent = src(d)
15            parentAlive = true
16          }
17        }
18      distance = minD+1
19      $Leds(distance)
20      []
21      // set root node's distance
22      ID == 0:
23        distance = 0
24
25      // check parent, recover if parent down
26      every 30\,s after 0s
27        (ID !=0 && parentAlive == true):
28          parentAlive = false
29          foreach d in nDistance {
30            // determine if parent is alive
31            if(parent == src(d)){
32              parentAlive = true
33            }
34          }
35      // if parent down, reset
36      if(parentAlive == false){
37        minD = 254
38        distance = 255
39        parent = ID
40        $Leds(distance)
41      }
```

Listing 1. Spanning Tree

on lines 26–41. The `src()` function is used to (implicitly) check whether the parent is still active. It returns the source ID of a binding. If it returns the parent ID in the `foreach` loop, it implies that the parent is still reachable, and `parentAlive` is set to *true*. When a non-root node detects a failed parent, it resets its distance (255) and gets ready to rejoin the tree, as shown on lines 9–19.

The $DESAL^\beta$ source code for the spanning tree algorithm is realized in only 35 lines of non-whitespace code. The conciseness of $DESAL^\beta$ makes the implementation of each rule a natural process and requires no understanding of the underlying nesC facilities.

To validate the application, we performed a simulation in Cooja with 35 randomly located nodes, each running the TinyOS image created from the $DESAL^\beta$ application. We specified a given node (node 35) to be the root node. Upon stabilization, the network organizes itself into a tree, and the parent of a given node (node 31) is node 9. Since distance is the only state variable shared within the network, we inject a parent fault by setting the distance of node 9 to 255. We see that after the next round of communication, node 31 has been accepted by node 12, its other neighbor, as its new child. This fault is corrected in 9.2 s, which is approximately the convergence time of the algorithm, as discussed later.

5   Evaluation

5.1   Space Overhead

We compare the space overhead for the spanning tree application using $DESAL^\alpha$ and $DESAL^\beta$. Nescc 1.3.4 [13] is used to collect the memory usage data. The $DESAL^\alpha$ program uses 17,516 bytes of ROM, and the $DESAL^\beta$ program uses 24,476 bytes. The difference in ROM usage is mainly due to the introduction of a more sophisticated time synchronization module. $DESAL^\beta$ uses TinyOS 2.x's TimeSync library, which introduces 5,128 bytes more ROM overhead than the TinyOS 1.x module used previously. ROM usage is also increased due to the new communication stack in TinyOS 2.x. Test results show that TinyOS 2.x introduces 2,768 bytes of ROM overhead when two parameterized AMSend interfaces are used. Since TinyOS 2.x uses more precise RAM allocation for timers [23], the RAM usage of the $DESAL^\beta$ program is smaller, at 214 bytes. Note that RAM is much more scarce than ROM on most embedded network platforms. Consequently, the decrease in RAM usage by $DESAL^\beta$, even at the expense of increased ROM usage, is a significant efficiency improvement.

5.2   Convergence Time

When a fault occurs in a self-stabilizing network, the system eventually converges to a legitimate state. A key performance measure for self-stabilizing algorithms is the time taken for convergence. Convergence is defined by a global predicate, which can often be expressed as a conjunction of local predicates. We measure the convergence time of the $DESAL^\beta$ application by tracking the local convergence time of each node. Network convergence time is expressed as the maximum local convergence time in the network.

To measure convergence time, we used the NESTBed [14], which consists of 80 Tmote Sky nodes arranged in a grid topology, as well as the Cooja simulator. We first use the testbed to test networks consisting of 20, 40, 50, and 80 nodes.

We then use Cooja to test networks of 100, 150, 200, and 250 nodes. In Cooja, each algorithm is simulated on 3 different topologies in a 100 m*100 m area. A random topology places the nodes randomly, a grid topology places the nodes evenly over the region in a matrix format, and an elliptical topology places the nodes in a circle over the region. Each simulation assumes a Unit Disc Graph Medium (UDGM), with a 100 % reception rate inside the disc, and 0 % outside. Collisions occur if two nodes transmit concurrently.

For the Spanning Tree algorithm, the local predicate is $(n.parent \neq n) \wedge (n.Distance = n.parent.Distance + 1)$. Figure 1 shows the convergence time of the algorithm. Figure 1a shows convergence time in terms of rounds, as a function of network size. Figure 1b shows convergence time in terms of wall clock time, again as a function of network size. Both metrics grow as expected with increased size.

From Fig. 1, we observe that the elliptical topology has the lowest convergence time of the three topologies. This is because this topology results in the least number of message collisions compared to the other topologies. Also, as network size increases, it becomes more difficult for the algorithm to stabilize. This is because our experiments are performed within a limited area (100 m*100 m); the probability of message collision significantly increases as network density increases. We also tried to enlarge the network to more than 300 nodes. However, the simulation became too slow due to the RAM consumption caused by the increase in Java threads in the Cooja application.

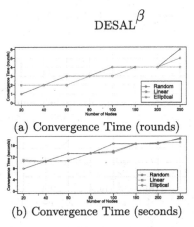

DESAL$^\beta$

(a) Convergence Time (rounds)

(b) Convergence Time (seconds)

Fig. 1. Spanning tree

6   Conclusions

In this paper, we presented $DESAL^\beta$, a framework for implementing self-stabilizing embedded network applications. A spanning tree algorithm was used to demonstrate that using $DESAL^\beta$ to develop self-stabilizing embedded network applications is significantly easier than using event-based programing languages, such as nesC. However, when it is more convenient to use event-based semantics, applications can also be written using a mixture of $DESAL^\beta$ and nesC/C. Experimental results show that the space overhead of $DESAL^\beta$ is acceptable and convergence time is low.

Acknowledgment. This work is supported by the NSF through award CNS-0746632.

References

1. Dalton, A.R., et al.: $Desal^\alpha$: an implementation of the dynamic embedded sensor-actuator language. In: Proceedings of the ICCCN 2008, vol. 8 (2008)
2. Arora, A., et al.: A state-based language for sensor-actuator networks. ACM SIGBED Rev. **4**(3), 25–30 (2007)
3. Hill, J., et al.: System architecture directions for networked sensors. In: Proceedings of the ASPLOS IX, pp. 93–104 (2000)
4. Dunkels, A., et al.: Contiki - a lightweight and flexible operating system for tiny networked sensors. In: Proceedings of the LCN 2004, pp. 455–462, November 2004
5. Bhatti, S., et al.: Mantis OS: an embedded multithreaded operating system for wireless micro sensor platforms. Mob. Netw. Appl. **10**(4), 563–579 (2005)
6. Gay, D., et al.: The nesC language: a holistic approach to networked embedded systems. In: Proceedings of the PLDI 2003, pp. 1–11 (2003)
7. Madden, S.R., et al.: TinyDB: an acquisitional query processing system for sensor networks. ACM Trans. Database Syst. **30**(1), 122–173 (2005)
8. Yao, Y., Gehrke, J.: The cougar approach to in-network query processing in sensor networks. SIGMOD Rec. **31**(3), 9–18 (2002)
9. Gummadi, R., Gnawali, O., Govindan, R.: Macro-programming wireless sensor networks using *Kairos*. In: Prasanna, V.K., Iyengar, S.S., Spirakis, P.G., Welsh, M. (eds.) DCOSS 2005. LNCS, vol. 3560, pp. 126–140. Springer, Heidelberg (2005)
10. Newton, R., et al.: The regiment macroprogramming system. In: Proceedings of the IPSN 2007, pp. 489–498. ACM, New York (2007)
11. Weyer, C., Turau, V.: SelfWISE: a framework for developing self-stabilizing algorithms. In: David, K., Geihs, K. (eds.) Kommunikation in Verteilten Systemen (KiVS), pp. 67–78. Springer, Heidelberg (2009)
12. Osterlind, F., et al.: Cross-level sensor network simulation with COOJA. In: Proceedings of the LCN 2006, pp. 641–648, November 2006
13. NESCC. linux.die.net/man/1/nescc
14. Dalton, A., et al.: A testbed for visualizing sensornet behavior. In: Proceedings of the ICCCN 2008, pp. 1–7, August 2008
15. Maróti, M., et al.: The flooding time synchronization protocol. In: Proceedings of the SenSys 2004, pp. 39–49. ACM (2004)
16. McPeak, S., Necula, G.C.: Elkhound: a fast, practical GLR parser generator. In: Duesterwald, E. (ed.) CC 2004. LNCS, vol. 2985, pp. 73–88. Springer, Heidelberg (2004)
17. Hedetniemi, S.M., et al.: Self-stabilizing algorithms for minimal dominating sets and maximal independent sets. Comput. Math. Appl. **46**(5–6), 805–811 (2003)
18. Goddard, W., et al.: Self-stabilizing protocols for maximal matching and maximal independent sets for ad hoc networks. In: Proceedings of the IPDPS 2003, p. 14. IEEE (2003)
19. Mahafzah, M.H.: An efficient graph-coloring algorithm for processor allocation. Int. J. Comput. Inf. Technol. **02**(1) (2013)
20. Johnson, D.S., Garey, M.R.: Computers and Intractability. Freeman, New York (1979)
21. Hedetniemi, S.T., et al.: Linear time self-stabilizaing colorings. Inf. Process. Lett. **87**, 251–255 (2003)
22. Moteiv. Tmote sky (2005). http://www.eecs.harvard.edu/~konrad/projects/shimmer/references/tmote-sky-datasheet.pdf
23. Levis, P.: Experiences from a decade of tinyos development. In: Proceedings of the OSDI 2012, pp. 207–220. USENIX, Berkeley (2012)

Automatically Quantitative Analysis and Code Generator for Sensor Systems: The Example of Great Lakes Water Quality Monitoring

Bojan Nokovic$^{(\boxtimes)}$ and Emil Sekerinski

Computing and Software Department, McMaster University, Hamilton, Canada
{nokovib,emil}@mcmaster.ca

Abstract. In model-driven development of embedded systems, one would ideally automate both the code generation from the model and the analysis of the model for functional correctness, liveness, timing guarantees, and quantitative properties. Characteristically for embedded systems, analyzing quantitative properties like resource consumption and performance requires a model of the environment as well. We use *pState* to analyze the power consumption of motes intended for water quality monitoring of recreational beaches in Lake Ontario. We show how system properties can be analyzed by model checking rather than by classical approach based on a functional breakdown and spreadsheet calculation. From the same model, it is possible to generate a framework of executable code to be run on the sensor's microcontroller. The goal of model checking approach is an improvement of engineering efficiency.

Keywords: Water quality monitoring · Probabilistic model checking · Validation · Verification

1 Introduction

In this work we build a model for and analyze the power consumption of water monitoring motes developed in the MacWater [1] project. The sensors are intended for water quality monitoring of beaches on Lake Ontario, to supplement and speed up the existing practice of manually taking water samples and analyzing them in a lab. For battery-powered motes, power consumption has the main impact on product usability. A shorter battery life requires more frequent battery replacements. As the motes are deployed in buoys (placed on a specific distance from the shore according to local regulations for testing water quality of beaches), there is a significant effort in battery replacements or any kind of maintenance.

There are two ways of power consumption evaluation (1) on the physical hardware, by periodically measuring the remaining battery, or (2) by modelling. In both cases, the interaction with the environment determines the power consumption. While in the measuring approach inputs are real, in the modelling approach they are simulated or *synthetic*. Modelling can be less accurate than

© ICST Institute for Computer Sciences, Social Informatics and Telecommunications Engineering 2016
B. Mandler et al. (Eds.): IoT 360° 2015, Part II, LNICST 170, pp. 313–319, 2016.
DOI: 10.1007/978-3-319-47075-7_35

measuring, but it can give designers flexibility and agility to evaluate complex power consumption scenarios [2]. The classical approach to power model design is based on a *functional breakdown*. First, power consumption is calculated following a design process similar to the one described in [3,4]. Next, all activities that are possible sources of power consumption or *logical activities* [5] are identified. Finally power consumption is calculated manually by standard mathematical operations or with the help of some tools, e.g. spreadsheet.

In our approach the system is first described by pCharts, a visual language for specifying reactive behaviour. Then, after specifying power consumption in relevant states, input code for a probabilistic model checker is automatically created and power consumption calculated as a *cost* over probabilistic computational tree logic (PCTL) formulae. On the example of Waspmotes, commercial Arduino-based motes by Libelium, we present the interaction between the environment and a device as a complex probabilistic timed automaton (PTA), on which it is still feasible to perform quantitative analysis by an off-the-shelf probabilistic model checker. In addition to the calculation of power consumption, we generate the framework of executable code to be run on a microcontroller. We model complex embedded systems, but the code is executed on 8-bit microcontrollers with restricted resources.

2   Related Work

For power consumption evaluation by analytical modelling there are two approaches: the evaluation of whole wireless sensor networks (WSN) [6,7], or the evaluation of WSN applications [2]. The difference is that the evaluation of whole wireless sensor networks includes an in-depth evaluation of communication protocols. This work is about evaluation of WSN application. It is already shown that models created by Coloured Petri Nets (CPNs) can be used to estimate power consumption of sensors [2]. We follow a similar approach but use pCharts, extended hierarchical state machines. The main difference in our approach is in the fact that power consumption on pCharts models is calculated by probabilistic model checker. The random nature of environments impact implies a need for a probabilistic evaluation of different power consumption scenarios. In addition to this, from pCharts it is possible to generate framework of mote's executable code.

The experimental validation of probabilistic systems needs a bigger number of tests to acquire credible results [8]. That may be a time-consuming task. A short-cut to this problem is modelling together the device and environment impact.

In our previous works we introduced the basic features of *pState* [9] and described timed transitions [10]. In [11] we explained how the tool is designed, and we show how a communication protocol for radio-frequency identification (RFID) tags can be analyzed. In [12] we show on few simple examples how properties are specified in an intuitive way such that they can be written without knowledge of temporal logic. In this paper we are focused on the methodological aspect and show that systems with tens of thousands states can be effectively analyzed.

3   Waspmote Sensor Power Consumption

We show how pCharts can be used to model the power consumption of the *end-unit* devices, and how to generate the framework for device-executable code. In a collaborative research effort MacWater [1], new sensor types for water quality indicators are developed. MacWater isa research project for mobile sensor devices that can analyze water samples for biological and chemical contaminants in real-time. The sensors and communication boards are connected to Waspmote, a type of Arduino board [13]. Collected data, includes water *pH* factor, temperature, and a current location of the sensor (longitude and latitude), is transmitted to a nearby base station by a low power wireless protocol. The base station is a multi-protocol router Meshlium [13] that sends data to the central server either by WiFi or GPRS. Collected data are updated on the site, and all system operates as soft real-time process.

For the purpose of this paper, we use commercially available sensors to measure pH of lake water, to read the geographic position of the sensor by GPS, and to transmit data via the ZigBee protocol. In our experiment we also use sensors to measure water conductivity, dissolved oxygen, and dissolved ions, which we leave out here for brevity. We show how to specify the impact of the environment on the working device, and how to quantitatively verify that impact. The model in Fig. 1 has three concurrent states *Device*, *Environmnet* and *Test*. The state *Device* has itself four concurrent composite states *Board*, *pH*, *ZigBee*, and *GPS*. The state *Device* represents behaviour of the Waspmote [13] water monitoring mote. State *Environment* represents the impact of the environment on GPS communication. We add state *Test* to specify queries to be quantitatively verified by the model checker.

Initially, the state *Board* is in *DeepSleep*, state *pH* is in *pHOff*, state *ZigBee* in *ZigBeeOff*, and state *GPS* in the *GPSOff*. Every 10 s, *Board* wakes up, and broadcasts the event *pHOn*. On this event *pH* state goes from *pHOff* to *pHSensorOn* and executes the command *pHTurnOn*. This command is a separately written external function. For model checking, it is ignored, but it is used for executable code generation.

In the state *pHSensorOn*, *pH* stays only 5 ms, to measure water acidity, and then goes back to *pHOff* state. During this process it broadcasts *pHRead* event and call *TurnpHOff* command. On the event *pHRead*, *Board* goes from *pHWarmUp* to *GpsWarmUp*, and broadcasts event *GpsOn*.

On the event *GpsOn*, state *GPS* goes from initial state *GpsOff* to *GpsCheck* and broadcasts event *Connect*. On this event, *Environment* moves form *GpsEnvIdle* to *InitialDelay*. The GPS is used to read a position of the device. In normal operation, based on our measurements, is takes between 1.8 s and 2.2 s for GPS to get connected. No connection is possible in less than 1.8 s, in 50 % of the time a connection is establishes between 1.8 s and 2 s, in 60 % of time between

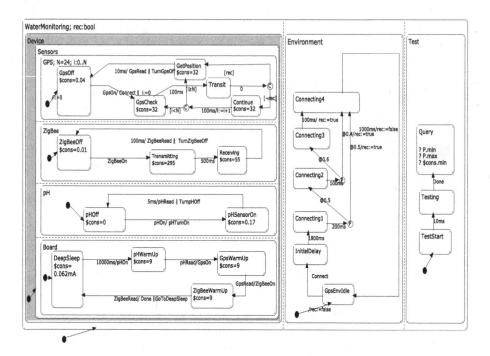

Fig. 1. Wireless sensor power model in pCharts

2 s and 2.1 s. By 2.2 s the connection is always established. This is modelled by probabilistic transitions between *GpsEvnIdle* state and *Connecting4*. When the connection is established, boolean variable *rec* is set to *true*. In our model GPS tries to acquire signal for 4.8 s, or every 200 ms for 24 times. Once the connection is established, GPS goes into *GetPosition* state. Consumption in GPS depends on how fast the connection is established, and that is modelled by probabilistic transitions in the *Environment* state. From state *GetPosition*, GPS goes back into *GPSOff*, broadcasts *GpsRead* event and executes the *TurnGpsOff* command. On broadcasted event *GpsRead*, *Board* goes from *GpsWarmUp* to *ZigBeeWarmUp* and broadcasts event *ZigBeeOn*.

ZigBee, a low-power secure networking protocol, is used to transmit the collected readings to a base station, from where data is further transmitted by a 3G connection to a database. We modelled the power consumption in the transmitting and receiving states, for data transmission and acknowledge reception. Once this process is finished *ZigBee* goes back to *ZigBeeOff*, broadcasts *ZigBeeRead* event and executes command *TurnZigBeeOff*. On the event *ZigBeeRead*, *Board* goes from *ZigBeeWarmUp* to *DeepSleep*, broadcast the event *Done* and executes the command *GoToDeepSleep*. The broadcasted event *Done* moves *Test* from *Testing* to *Query* state, where the queries

$$\text{``}?P.min\text{''} \qquad \text{``}?P.max\text{''} \qquad \text{``}?\$cons.min\text{''} \qquad (1)$$

for *min* and *max* probabilities (*P*), and *min* costs of the consumption ($*cons*) are specified 1. They are used for the calculation of the probability that the *Board* will go from initial *DeepSleep* back to *DeepSleep* mode, and to calculate the *consumption* in one cycle. Current consumption is specified in *mA* values according to the specification from Waspmote technical documentation [13]. From the pChart in Fig. 1, a PTA model is automatically generated by flattening the hierarchical structure and creating PRISM input code in the form of guarded commands.

The translation scheme of the pCharts model into input code for probabilistic model checker can be found in [10, 12].

Rewards. Properties based on *costs* are specified on states or transition. In our example, for each state of *Device*, the cost of consumption *cons* is specified. That is passed to PRISM in the module `rewards ... endrewards`; for instance when the *board* is in *DeepSleep*, the current is only 0.062 mA.

Results. The verification is done by the PRISM *Digital Clock* engine. The created model has 17221 states and 17232 transitions. The calculated minimal and maximal probabilities (*P.min* and *P.max*) to reach *Query* are the same and 1, which means that the test always terminates. There are no nondeterministic transitions, so the *min* and *max* probabilities are equal. The calculated expected minimal consumption (*cons.min*) is 248581.78 mAms, and it took 126.65 s to do calculation. The maximum time of one cycle is a simple sum of deep sleep time (10000 ms) and the times to read pH (5 ms), get position of GPS (2210 ms), and send data by ZigBee (600 ms) which is 12815 ms. So, the average current consumption is 248581.78 mAms/12815 ms = 19.39 mA. Waspmote devices are usually powered by the battery of 6600 mAh, so according to our calculation the battery can last for approximately 340 h, or 14.1 days. Thus we are able to predict automatically the battery life from the model. All properties are verified on Intel(R) Core(TM) i7-4770 CPU @ 3.40 GHz, 12.0 GB of RAM and on 64-bit Operating System.

4   Conclusions

This paper presents power consumption evaluation of motes used for water quality monitoring in the MacWater project. We show that hierarchical state machines modelling formalism pCharts is suitable for representing both the device and environment impact. Since input from the environment is of random nature, we use probabilistic transitions for environment specification. Assigned probabilities are based on the experimental evaluation of device to GPS signal connection probability. Analyzing together the device and environmental impact on the same model, allows different scenarios of the environmental impact to be validated. That can be used for optimization of the device's hardware and communication protocol used in a sensor network. Obtaining same measurement by experiment may give more accurate results, but would take more time, which makes modelling as a more convenient approach.

The generated model has about 17000 states and transitions, but the verification performed by PRISM model checker is done reasonably fast. The pState architecture allows in principle other probabilistic model checkers like MRMC [14], or some tool from the MoDeSt [15] toolset to be added. For bigger models, statistical model checkers like Ymer [16] or Vesta [17] can be used.

From the same pCharts model, it is possible to generate code for embedded microprocessors. The goal is to have a seamless and automated approach from modelling and analysis to code generation that can be used by engineers to evaluate design alternatives and to generate trustworthy code.

References

1. McMaster: MacWater, June 2015. http://macwater.org/
2. Damaso, A., Freitas, D., Rosa, N., Silva, B., Maciel, P.: Evaluating the power consumption of wireless sensor network applications using models. Sensors **13**(3), 3473 (2013). http://www.mdpi.com/1424-8220/13/3/3473
3. Negri, L., Sami, M., Tran, Q.D., Zanetti, D.: Flexible power modeling for wireless systems: power modeling and optimization of two bluetooth implementations. In: Cantarella, J. (ed.) Proceedings of 6th IEEE International Symposium on World of Wireless Mobile and Multimedia Networks, pp. 408–416. IEEE Computer Society (2005)
4. Negri, L., Chiarini, A.: Power simulation of communication protocols with StateC. In: Vachoux, A. (ed.) Applications of Specification and Design Languages for SoCs, pp. 277–294. Springer, Berlin (2006)
5. Mura, M., Paolieri, M., Fabbri, F., Negri, L., Sami, M.G.: Power modeling, power analysis for IEEE 802.15.4: a concurrent state machine approach. In: Consumer Communications and Networking Conference, pp. 660–664 (2007)
6. Rusli, M., Harris, R., Punchihewa, A.: Markov chain-based analytical model of opportunistic routing protocol for wireless sensor networks. In: TENCON 2010–2010 IEEE Region 10 Conference, pp. 257–262 (2010)
7. Cano, C., Sfairopoulou, A., Bellalta, B., Barceló, J., Oliver, M.: Analytical model of the LPL with wake up after transmissions MAC protocol for WSNs. In: International Symposium on Wireless Communication Systems (ISWCS 2009), Siena, Italy, September 2009
8. Leopold, M.: Sensor network motes: portability and performance. Ph.D. dissertation, Department of Computer Science, University of Copenhagen (2007)
9. Nokovic, B., Sekerinski, E.: pState: a probabilistic statecharts translator. In: 2013 2nd Mediterranean Conference on Embedded Computing (MECO), pp. 29–32 (2013)
10. Nokovic, B., Sekerinski, E.: Verification and code generation for timed transitions in pCharts. In: Proceedings of the International C* Conference on Computer Scienceand Software Engineering, Series, C3S2E 2014. ACM, New York (2014)
11. Nokovic, B., Sekerinski, E.: Analysis and implementation of embedded system models: example of tags in item management application. In: W01 1st Workshop on Model-Implementation Fidelity (MiFi), Grenoble, France, p. 10 (2015)
12. Nokovic, B., Sekerinski, E.: A holistic approach to embedded systems development. In: 2nd Workshop on Formal-IDE, Oslo, Norway, p. 14 (2015)
13. Libelium: Waspmote, July 2014. http://www.libelium.com/

14. Katoen, J.-P., Zapreev, I.S., Hahn, E.M., Hermanns, H., Jansen, D.N.: The ins and outs of the probabilistic model checker MRMC. Perform. Eval. **68**(2), 90–104 (2011)
15. Hartmanns, A.: Modest - a unified language for quantitative models. In: 2012 Forum on Specification and Design Languages (FDL), pp. 44–51, September 2012
16. Younes, H.L.S.: Ymer: a statistical model checker. In: Etessami, K., Rajamani, S.K. (eds.) CAV 2005. LNCS, vol. 3576, pp. 429–433. Springer, Heidelberg (2005)
17. Sen, K., Viswanathan, M., Agha, G.A.: VESTA: a statistical model-checker and analyzer for probabilistic systems. In: QEST, pp. 251–252 (2005)

Software Architecture for Remote Monitoring Systems of Surface Contamination by Alpha Radioactive Isotopes

Boris Gurkovskiy, Evgeny Onishchenko, Vladimir Miroshnichenko,
Andrey Simakov, and Nikolay Samotaev[(✉)]

National Research Nuclear University MEPhI (Moscow Engineering Physics
Institute), Kashirskoe Highway 31, 115409 Moscow, Russian Federation
nnsamotaev@mephi.ru

Abstract. In this paper, we present alpha-radiation monitoring system software. Detector works in accounting mode that adds some extra features. Possible detector applications such as pedestrian radiation portal monitor or portable alpha contamination dosimeter are presented. Detector is based on air ion method. In view of detector works in accounting mode, it shows high selectivity to alpha particles registration. Alpha selection principle is also shown. Control system and software system are considered in detail.

Keywords: Alpha radiation · Control system · Data processing system

1 Introduction

There is an urgent need for searching for alpha contamination sources, for example, at nuclear facilities. Well-known that alpha particle has a very short range in air. Air-ion method for alpha particles registration has been extensively studied. Method allows carrying out remote detecting alpha-particles on distance from a source of the radiation, essentially exceeding run particles in the air. Air ions are transferred to a trace of a particle in working volume of the detector with the help of a specially created air stream (see Figs. 1a, c). A close attention was paid to measuring of the current carried by the moving ions in the air-ion method by MacArthur et al. [1]. Whereas, in this study, detector works in accounting mode that provides sharp selectivity and accuracy of measurements [2, 5]. However, it has been found to be dependent on humidity [3]. Figures 1b, d provide experimental devices based on the detector.

For today, a lot of pedestrian portal monitors are commercially available. (companies Canberra, Mirion etc.). However, they work directly with alpha particles. Scheme of proposed pedestrian portal monitor (displayed in Fig. 1a) and its prototype (see Fig. 1b). Where (1) is a system for airflow directing, (2) – source of an ionizing radiation (α), (3) – doors, (4) – enlarged view of the detector, (5) – charge-sensitive amplifier and pulse shaper, (6) – air ions, (7) – wire netting and filter, (8) – fan, (9) – cathode, (10) – anode, (11) – data processing system, (12) – remote control computer.

© ICST Institute for Computer Sciences, Social Informatics and Telecommunications Engineering 2016
B. Mandler et al. (Eds.): IoT 360° 2015, Part II, LNICST 170, pp. 320–324, 2016.
DOI: 10.1007/978-3-319-47075-7_36

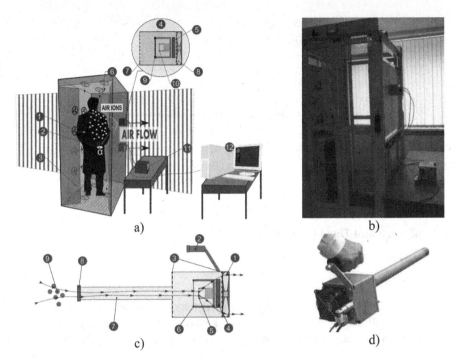

Fig. 1. Potential applications of the detector. Both devices use gas discharge detector. Description of numbered nodes is presented in the main text.

Diagram chart of the portable alpha dosimeter with a tube nozzle and its prototype can be found in Figs. 1c, d. Such nozzle is useful for monitoring places hard to reach. Apart from that, proposed detector can be applied to a wide range of nozzles. As listed in Fig. 1c, (1) – fan; (2) – handle; (3) – wire netting; (4) – amplifier and pulse shaper; (5) – anode; (6) – cathode; (7) – tube nozzle; (8) – filter; (9) – air ions.

1.1 Alpha Particle's Selection Principle

Figure 2 displays the principle of selecting alpha particles. This image suggests that there is a direct relationship between the number of pulses and presence of alpha particles.

Pulse shaper forms pulses acceptable for counter. Notwithstanding the control board can be used as a counter, external counter PIC16F628A was chosen. Unfortunately, the use of the user space counter and kernel module based counter was not successful in this task: not all pulses were accounted. And this counter is connected using serial interface to the control board.

Furthermore, when working in the Linux operating system at a frequency greater than 1 kHz, the number of counted pulses is dependent on duty cycle pulse sequence. At a certain value, it did not produce interrupts or they did not have time to be processed.

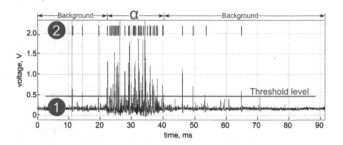

Fig. 2. The principle of alpha particles selecting. For the first stage there is a rejection of low noise pulses (1 – voltage on the discharge wire, 2 – selected pulses); for the second stage there is a detection of the time intervals with high pulse density.

1.2   Software and Hardware Scheme

In this section close attention is paid to the portal monitor control system and control program (see Figs. 3 and 4).

The control system of the portal is built on Atmel ARM9 microcontroller. uLCD panel of the 4D SYSTEMS company was used for data display (marked as "4" on Fig. 4a). This allows to use LCD panel as keyboard. For this device special core module, running under OS Linux, was written. That allows to operatively trigger events from the keyboard (marked as "3" and "5" on Fig. 4a), detector (marked as "8" on Fig. 4a) and counter (marked "9" on Fig. 4a). Using the control system of the portal combination of external computer and web-server interfaces (marked as "7" and "15" on Fig. 4a) is easy getting measurements dates, watching continuously current count and changing settings. When you need to make a backup for the data and settings, you just need to plug in the USB-flash drive (marked as "6" on Fig. 4a). All these options are controlled by standard Linux core modules (marked as "10" on Fig. 4a). The core of the control system program is the main control sub-program (marked as "1" on Fig. 4a) responsible for quality of measurement. That sub-program allows to control for the execution of main modes such as "Calibration" (in this mode device sets an operating voltage).

Control program (can be seen from Fig. 4a, item 1 and Fig. 4b) was made using Tcl/Expect [4]. Extension to the Tcl scripting language Expect, that is a program to automate interactions with programs that expose a text terminal interface.

Fig. 3. External and internal views of the control device.

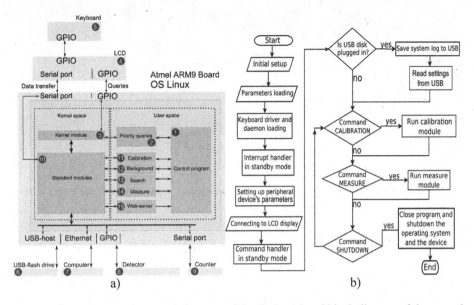

Fig. 4. Block-diagram of the control system of the device (a) and block-diagram of the control program (b). Description of numbered nodes is presented in the main text.

Keyboard software was made using 4DGL (high level graphic oriented language). The screen uLCD acts as an independent system. Hence images are drawn and stored in the display's memory. And it uses serial communication and bus interruptions to communicate to the control board. Little attention has been paid to it. To realize the interruptions, kernel module and corresponding daemon were made (as detailed in Fig. 5a). Figure 5b illustrates proposed transmission protocol for serial communication.

Figure 6 demonstrates the work of the device in calibration (a) and in search (b) modes. For a successful calibration, number of pulses should fall into the specified range certain number of times. As can be seen in Fig. 6a, calibration was successful. During the search mode, the Pu-239 source (760 Bq) was located on the chest. It is evident that number of counts significantly decreases when man leaves portal (see Fig. 6b).

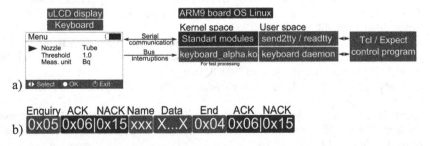

Fig. 5. The communication between control program and uLCD display connected to the keyboard (b). Transmission protocol (b)

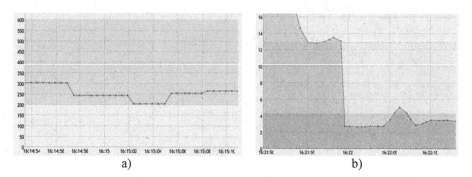

Fig. 6. Real-time calibration (a) and search (b) (web browser view). It is possible to use it from internet (using virtual private network).

2 Conclusion

This study provides insight into software architecture for remote monitoring systems of surface contamination by alpha radioactive isotopes based on air ion method. In this study, we present also different devices based on this principle. The detector works in accounting mode that is promising because selectivity can be increased. But, on the other hand, it depends on pulse shaper and counter characteristics.

As outlined in the introduction, it may be used at nuclear facilities. It also should be noted that it is economically important due to its relative cheapness because of its simplicity, while it gave satisfactory results.

Using alpha radiation monitoring device based on air ion method introduces some features to hardware and software. For precise counting external counter was used and connected via SPI interface.

Eventually, using multiple detectors and adjusting the fans' position, number, and strength, we can get rid of unwanted pedestrian portal monitor's dead zones.

References

1. MacArthur, D.W., Allander, K.S., Bounds, J.A., Butterfield, K.B.: Small long-range alpha detector (LRAD) with computer readout, United States (1991). doi:10.2172/5090469
2. Simakov, A.B.: A device for the remote detection of alpha emitters under field conditions. Instrum. Exp. Tech. **48**(3), 387–391 (2005)
3. Gurkovskiy, B.V., Miroshnichenko, V.P., Onishchenko, E.M., Simakov, A.B., Streil, T.G.: Long-distance detection of alpha-radioactivity: method and device. J. Environ. Radioact. **149**, 150–157 (2015). doi:10.1016/j.jenvrad.2015.07.019
4. Tcl.tk. Manpage of EXPECT. http://www.tcl.tk/man/expe-ct5.31/expect.1.html. Accessed 19 Aug 2015
5. Gurkovskiy, B., Miroshnichenko, V., Onishchenko, E., Simakov, A., Streil, T.: The Remote detection of alpha-radioactive nucleus decay. In: Advances in Radioactive Isotope Science, Tokyo, 1–6 June 2014

DriverGen: Automating the Generation of Serial Device Drivers

Jiannan Zhai[1]([⊠]), Yuheng Du[2], Shiree Hughes[1], and Jason O. Hallstrom[1]

[1] Institute for Sensing and Embedded Network Systems Engineering,
Florida Atlantic University, 777 Glades Road, Boca Raton, FL 33431, USA
{jzhai,shughes2015,jhallstrom}@fau.edu
[2] School of Computing, Clemson University, Clemson, SC 29634, USA
yuhengd@clemson.edu

Abstract. Microprocessors operate most serial devices in the same way, issuing commands and parsing corresponding responses. Writing the device drivers for these peripherals is a repetitive task. Moreover, measuring the response time of each command can be time-consuming and error prone. In this paper, we present DriverGen, a configuration-based tool developed to provide accurate response time measurement and automated serial device driver generation. DriverGen (i) simulates the command execution sequence of a microprocessor using a Java program running on a desktop, (ii) measures the response time of the target device to each command, and (iii) generates a device driver based on the received responses and measured response times. To evaluate DriverGen, three case studies are considered.

1 Introduction

Our work is motivated by the recurrent structure of most serial device drivers and the importance of accurate timing. The main contributions of our work are as follows: (i) We present a serial device driver configuration language that generalizes the specification of a serial device driver. (ii) We present an approach that measures response times with precision on the order of $10\,s$ of microseconds by monitoring data signals in the communication interface. (iii) We implement DriverGen, a configuration-based tool developed to accurately measure response times, and to automatically generate the specified serial device driver. (iv) Finally, we evaluate DriverGen, considering the performance of generated drivers for three serial devices.

2 Related Work

Automated driver synthesis is discussed in [8]. Ratter proposes synthesis as a method to ensure correct driver construction. A state machine is generated automatically using specifications for both the device and the (desktop) operating system, and ultimately supports the generation of a driver for the device in C. We similarly provide the ability to generate a microprocessor driver for device communication. When generating a driver for a microprocessor, we experience

© ICST Institute for Computer Sciences, Social Informatics and Telecommunications Engineering 2016
B. Mandler et al. (Eds.): IoT 360° 2015, Part II, LNICST 170, pp. 325–330, 2016.
DOI: 10.1007/978-3-319-47075-7_37

the added challenges of memory and power constraints, timing precision, and a single-threaded operating system. Our driver must be efficient with respect to both memory usage and power consumption.

Another method for automating device driver generation is Termite [9]. Termite acts as an interface between the OS and a target device. It uses a formal specification of the device to generate a set of OS-independent commands. It allows the device creator to focus on the device, and the OS expert to focus on the OS, and still create a communication link between the two. Similarly, we create a method to automatically generate drivers for serial devices, eliminating the need for developers to manually write the drivers.

In [6], O'Nils et al. show that by using synthesis, development time can be reduced by as much as 98%. Their method uses ProGram, a specification language, to model the behavior of a device based on sequences of permissible events. Three inputs are required to synthesize the device driver from its behavior: architecture independent protocols, a specification of the processor and bus interface, and a specification of the target operating system.

An important requirement of automatically generated code is that the quality must be equal to or surpass that of hand-written code. In [7], O'Nils et al. argue that their tool produces a quality driver (generated in C) that is comparable to handwritten code. This tool requires a protocol specification for both the device and the operating system.

3   System Design/Implementation

DriverGen is based on the observation that all serial device drivers work in almost the same way. Our system simulates the execution of each command and generates the target device driver based on the execution results. Each command sequence is implemented as a function in the driver. To match the response pattern and save the desired information, we implement regular expression libraries in Java and C, used by DriverGen and the generated drivers, respectively. To determine if the target device is responding, or the response is finished, timeouts are used, making accurate timing important. DriverGen monitors the UART communication signals to measure the response time of a device to each command (response time), and the time between bytes in the response (inter-byte times).

3.1   Hardware Setup

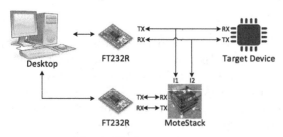

Fig. 1. Hardware setup

The DriverGen hardware, shown in Fig. 1, consists of a desktop running a Java program, two FT232R chips, and a MoteStack [3]. The FT232R chips are used by the desktop to communicate with the target device and a

MoteStack, respectively. The MoteStack is used to monitor the UART data signals to measure the response and inter-byte times.

3.2   Driver Configuration

DriverGen runs based on a driver configuration file that is used to configure UART communication, control execution of each command, and generate the target driver. The configuration parameters specify (i) basic driver information, such as driver name, version; (ii) global definitions, such as response timeout, which specifies the maximum time before the first response byte should be received; and (iii) function details, such as function names, the commands to be sent to the target device, the responses expected, and other information.

3.3   System Architecture

The DriverGen system consists of three modules. The *Parser* module is used to read, parse, and validate a driver configuration. The *Executor* module is used to execute the functions specified in the configuration, and to control the MoteStack to measure response times and inter-byte times. The *Generator* module is used to generate the driver source code based on the configuration parameters and execution results.

4   Evaluation

We now present our evaluation of the driver generation approach. We introduce three serial devices and corresponding applications previously developed to operate with functionally equivalent, time-tested, handwritten drivers. We validate the correctness of each generated driver via substitution within the corresponding application. Finally, we consider the relative performance of the drivers, both in terms of space and execution speed.

In our experiments, the drivers and applications are implemented based on the AVR platform. To evaluate the WiFi and cellular devices, a standard x86 server is used to collect data sent from the devices.

4.1   Test Devices and Applications

Three serial devices are used to evaluate our approach. The WH2004A is an LCD device that executes commands to display characters. The RN131 is a standalone embedded WiFi device with built-in TCP/IP support. The GM862 is a quad-band GSM/GPRS cellular modem with built-in TCP/IP, FTP, and SMTP support.

To evaluate the generated driver for the WH2004A, an application which detects a door trespassing event and displays the event counts on the LCD is used. Since the WH2004A does not respond to incoming commands, the evaluation is focused on correctness only. The generated driver displayed the event counts without any errors for 100 door trespassing events.

To evaluate the generated drivers for the RN131 and GM862, two test applications were used. The applications sense data from a group of sensors every 10 and 120 s, respectively, and record the execution time of each function. Sensor readings and execution times are then sent to a server. Each application is configured to perform 1000 transmission rounds in each test, and the average is used. Based on stored messages in the database, both drivers work as expected.

4.2   Performance Evaluation

We next evaluate the performance of the generated drivers relative to the handwritten drivers, both in terms of space and execution speed. We focus on the WiFi and cellular devices.

Execution Speed. We first evaluate the execution speed of the generated drivers by sending 1000 850-byte messages to the server and tracking the execution time of each associated function. Figures 2a and b summarize the speed of the generated driver functions for the RN131 and the GM862 compared to the handwritten drivers. The x-axis represents the driver functions, and the y-axis represents the average cumulative execution time, in seconds, in a single transmission round. The functions are ordered by execution time, in decreasing order from left to right. As the figures illustrate, the generated drivers run faster than the handwritten drivers across all functions. The speed-up is achieved by reducing the time spent waiting for each response. The cumulative speed-up is proportional to the number of executions of each function in a transmission round. For example, in each round, the `gm862_gsm_registered` function executes approximately 40 times before detecting a valid network registration. Therefore, it shows a high speed-up in Fig. 2b. For the GM862, the overall execution time in each round is 48.50 s for the generated driver, compared to 59.60 s for the handwritten driver. For the RN131, the overall execution time in each round is 11.99 s for the generated driver, and 14.68 s for the handwritten driver.

Memory Usage. We next evaluate the memory overhead introduced by the generated drivers. *Avr-size* is used to collect the memory data. Figure 3a summarizes the drivers' program memory (ROM) usage. The x-axis represents the drivers, and the y-axis represents size, in bytes. The hashed area represents ROM overhead introduced by the regular expression library. The ROM overhead is approximately 3400 bytes for both drivers. Figure 3b summarizes the drivers' data memory (RAM) usage. Again, the x-axis represents the drivers, and the y-axis represents size, in bytes. The hashed area represents RAM overhead introduced by the regular expressions used in the generated driver. The RAM overhead is closely related to the number of regular expressions used. Since the GM862 requires more regular expressions, the overhead for the GM862 is slightly larger than the WiFi chip, at 503 bytes.

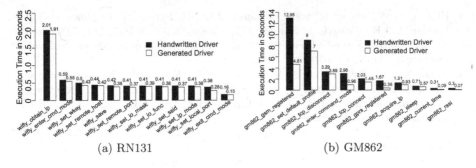

(a) RN131   (b) GM862

Fig. 2. Driver function execution time

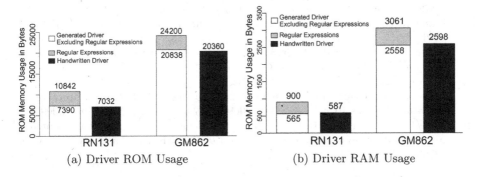

(a) Driver ROM Usage   (b) Driver RAM Usage

Fig. 3. Memory usage

5   Conclusion

We described a configuration-based system to automatically generate serial device drivers and accurately measure the timeout characteristics associated with each driver command. Results show that the generated drivers perform as expected, introducing modest memory overhead. Importantly, the execution time of each command is reduced compared to the handwritten drivers. As a result, driver performance is increased, and improved energy efficiency is achieved.

Acknowledgments. This work is supported by the NSF through awards CNS-1541917 and CNS-1545705.

References

1. CESANTA. SLRE: super light regular expression library, September 2013. slre.sourceforg.net/
2. Chou, P., Ortega, R., Borriello, G.: Synthesis fo the hardware/software interface in microcontroller-based systems. In: Proceedings of the 1992 IEEE/ACM International Conference on Computer-Aided Design, ICCAD 1992, pp. 488–495. IEEE Computer Society Press, Los Alamitos (1992)

3. Eidson, G.W., Esswein, S.T., Gemmill, J.B., Hallstrom, J.O., Howard, T.R., Lawrence, J.K., Post, C.J., Sawyer, C.B., Wang, K.C., White, D.L.: The south carolina digital watershed: end-to-end support forreal-time management of water resources. IJDSN, 1 (2010)
4. Li, J., Xie, F., Ball, T., Levin, V., McGravey, C.: Formalizing hardware/software interface specifications. In: Procceedings of the 2011 26th IEEE/ACM International Conference on Automated Software Engineering, ASE 2011, pp. 143–152. IEEE Computer Society, Washington (2011)
5. Locke, J.: Jakarta regexp Java regular expression package, April 2011. jakarta.apache.org/regexp/
6. O'Nils, M., Jantsch, A.: Operating system sensitive device driver synthesis from implementation independent protocol specification. In: Proceedings of the Design, Automation and Test in Europe Conference and Exhibition, pp. 562–567 (1999)
7. O'Nils, M., Jantsch, A.: Device driver and DMA controller synthesis from HW/SW communication protocol specifications. Des. Autom. Embed. Syst. **6**(2), 177–205 (2001)
8. Ratter, A.: Automatic device driver synthesis from device specifications. The University of New South Wales, November 2012
9. Ryzhyk, L., Chubb, P., Kuz, I., Le Sueur, E., Heiser, G.: Automatic device driver synthesis with termite. In: Proceedings of the ACM SIGOPS 22nd Symposium on Operating Systems Principles, SOSP 2009, pp. 73–86. ACM, New York (2009)
10. Shier, P., Garban, P.L., Oney, A.: System and method for validaitng communication specification conformance between a device driver and a hardware device. US2005246722 (2005)

Ultra-Low Power Context Recognition Fusing Sensor Data from an Energy-Neutral Smart Watch

Michele Magno[1,2(✉)], Lukas Cavigelli[1], Renzo Andri[1], and Luca Benini[1,2]

[1] ETH Zurich, Rämistrasse 101, 8092 Zurich, Switzerland
{magno, cavigelli, benini}@iis.ee.ethz.ch
[2] University of Bologna, Viale Risorgimento 2, 40136 Bologna, Italy

Abstract. Today sensors and wearable technologies are gaining popularity, with people increasingly surrounded by "smart" objects. Machine learning is used with great success in wearable devices and sensors in several real-world applications. In this paper we address the challenges of context recognition on low energy and self-sustainable wearable devices. We present an energy efficient multi-sensor context recognition system based on decision tree to classify 3 different indoor or outdoor contexts. An ultra-low power smart watch provided with a micro-power camera, microphone, accelerometer, and temperature sensors has been used to real field tests. Experimental results demonstrate both high mean accuracy of 81.5 % (up to 89 % peak) and low energy consumption (only 2.2 mJ for single classification) of the solution, and the possibility to achieve a self-sustainable system in combination with body worn energy harvesters.

Keywords: Ultra-low power · Smart watch · Context recognition · Machine learning · Sensor fusion · Energy neutral · Feature selection

1 Introduction

Today sensors and embedded technologies are gaining popularity, with people increasingly surrounded by embedded sensing devices. Smart, connected products are made possible by vast improvements in processing power and device miniaturization, and by the availability of ubiquitous wireless connectivity. Driven by Moore's Law these devices have become smaller and smaller and new applications are now possible. A fast growing class of such devices is "smart wearables", where electronics and sensors are tightly coupled with the human body [1]. The largest hi-tech companies, such as Google, Samsung, and Apple, have either already launched wearable consumer products, or are in the process of creating prototypes in an effort to fuel the next wave of exponential growth in the consumer market. Wearable technology is also very important for healthcare where electronic smart devices can continuously monitor patient health data and enable doctors to identify possible diseases earlier and to provide optimal treatment [2, 3].

© ICST Institute for Computer Sciences, Social Informatics and Telecommunications Engineering 2016
B. Mandler et al. (Eds.): IoT 360° 2015, Part II, LNICST 170, pp. 331–343, 2016.
DOI: 10.1007/978-3-319-47075-7_38

The clear trend is that wearables are becoming ubiquitous in our lives replacing classically non-electric items like shoes or clothes. Soon a trillion sensor-rich connected devices are going to produce a mind-boggling quantity of data and potentially useful information [4]. However, data alone do not provide value unless we can turn them into actionable, contextualized information. Big data and data visualization techniques allow us to gain new insights through batch-processing and off-line analysis. Real-time sensor data analysis and decision-making is often done manually, but to make it scalable, it should preferably be automated.

The major challenge for wearable systems is to be able to understand the world in a similar way humans do [5]. Perceptive low-power sensor devices should be able to interpret the context around their users and allow context-aware multi-agent interaction. In fact, human activity and context recognition is the key technology for achieving pervasive computing applications from home automation to healthcare, from sport and fitness to augmented reality. Machine learning technologies are used with great success in many application areas, solving real-world problems in entertainment systems, robotics, health care, and surveillance [6–10] and are becoming essential also to wearable applications [11, 12]. For example, helping athletes by providing motion sequence analysis, or detecting abnormal situations for elderly or patient care.

More and more researchers are tackling action and classification problems with algorithms which deal with feature extractors and classifiers with lots of parameters that are optimized using the unprecedented wealth of data that has recently become available. These techniques are achieving record-breaking results, and have started outperforming humans on very challenging problems and datasets, and surpass more mature ad-hoc approaches trying to model the specific problem at hand [7–17]. However, machine learning approaches are still a challenge for low power devices such as wearables, because, in their current embodiments, they still require massive amounts of computational power. Current wearable sensor technologies do not analyze data on-board and usually leverage smart-phones for computationally intensive activity (such as sitting, standing, walking, and running) monitoring. As opposed to conventional monitoring systems that send the sensor data to a datacenter or mobile phones to be stored and processed, embedded *smart systems* process the data partially, or fully, in situ. This can significantly reduce the amount of data to be transmitted and the required human intervention – the sources of the two most expensive aspects of distributed sensing.

A typical wearable device consists of a battery-powered computing unit, a wireless communication interface, sensors, and power supply packaged in a small and unobtrusive form factor suitable to be attached to the human body [12]. Thus, low power design and software optimization is even more challenging in wearable systems due to the limited energy availability of the battery and computational resources. In fact low power design alone is not enough to make these devices with battery lifetimes of months or years, instead of just mobile, with daily battery recharges, similar to today's smart phones. Power consumption reduction with power managed resources and low power software improves and extends the lifetime of battery-operated devices. Another method for re-charging the available energy stored in batteries or super capacitors is by using energy harvesters that collect energy from the environment is the most adopted technology. Researchers have been very active in this field and energy harvesting is today a well-understood technique. However most of the presented approaches usually imply an outdoor setting, using solar panels, wind turbines or high-frequency vibration as the energy source. Solar energy in particular has been demonstrated as optimal solution for achieving self-sustainability in many outdoor applications when the entire device is carefully dimensioned and designed. In the general case, where the device cannot be assumed to be continuously operating in an outdoor environment, energy harvesting still remains challenging. Energy harvesting for mobile/wearable devices is even more challenging due to the more stringent size/weight constraints, which limits the size of harvesters and energy storage devices [15].

This work focuses on low power smartwatch devices and on context recognition in our daily lives. The main contributions of this work are as follows: design and optimization of an energy efficient smart watch to perform context recognition with low power heterogeneous sensors; using an ultra-low power camera and microphone coupled with inertial and temperature sensors to improve the classification accuracy; investigation of a low power on board feature extraction and classification with a low power and limited computation resources microcontroller (MSP430 from Texas Instruments); evaluation of the energy efficiency and self-sustainability of the context recognition on a smart watch achieving an unobtrusive monitoring system. The key feature of the system is its low power algorithm as well as the heterogeneous system implemented allowing monitoring in diverse situations. The main goal is to explore the feasibility of low power multi-sensors classification algorithms with data fusion, and the benefits of a combination of hardware and software co-design to achieve a self-sustainability when the system works with energy harvesters (i.e. solar cells). This paper is organized as follows: Sect. 2 describes the existing work on using sound to monitor beehives; Sect. 3 describes the system architecture Sect. 4 outlines the low power context recognition; Sect. 5 shows experimental results of the in-field implementation of the demonstration system; and Sect. 6 concludes the paper.

2 Related Work

Research on mobile and wearable sensors systems has been very prolific in recent years with a variety of solutions in a wide range of application scenarios [3, 5]. Between them, there are many examples of implemented and deployed wearable devices that attempt to exploit intelligent sensing, wireless communication and computing abilities to monitor human activities [1]. Machine learning has been applied in a wide range of applications [7, 8], and in the field of embedded sensor devices has been very active in especially due to the Smartphone's increased computational power and the availability of on-board MEMS sensors (i.e. accelerometers, gyroscope) [9, 11, 12]. In fact, many recent works use Smartphone's and MEMS for activity recognition, crowd sensing, fall detection among many others [6, 12, 20]. For this reason, there are a huge number of classification algorithms from the machine learning area for smartphones, including decision trees, k-nearest neighbors, support vector machines (SVMs), naïve Bayes and more recently neural networks (NNs) [12–14]. A more detailed analysis is presented in [15] with accelerometers on both wrists, shoulder, legs, hip, and both ankles and different combinations of them. Accuracy with only one accelerometer on the left wrist was between 5 % and 95 % for 8 classes (sitting, standing, walking, upstairs, and downstairs, handshake, whiteboard and keyboard). Better results were achieved with accelerometer on the shoulder, wrist and elbow where accuracies between 40 % and 99 % has been achieved and 85 % in average when one sensor was placed on one leg. Another interesting study was done by Porzi et al. [17], where a system was built on the Sony ecosystem of Sony Xperia Z smartphone and Sony SmartWatch. The system was implemented using a smartphone for gesture recognition for use by the visually impaired. They presented an optimized kernel method (global alignment kernel) for discrete-time warping in SVMs. Discrete time warping allows to map similar gestures when moving at different speeds. Secondly, they implemented logo recognition like the "wet floor sign" where the camera of the smartphone was used. A recognition rate of 95.8 % was achieved.

Our works focuses on machine learning optimized for low power microcontrollers with limited resources, and on using sensor fusion, with camera and microphone, instead of a single low power sensor, such as a motion sensor. In the proposed work we investigate algorithms which can process the data close to the sensors instead of sending the data to a remote host or smartphone. Recently, many approaches tried to classify users' activities by deploying several heterogeneous sensors on the human body such as accelerometers, camera, acoustic, and temperature to capture characteristic repetitive motions, postures, and sounds of activities [16, 18]. However, the main challenges of wearable design are to prolong the operating lifetime and to enhance usability, maintenance, and mobility, while keeping a small and unobtrusive form factor. Low power embedded machine learning is still challenging due to the limited computational resources, limited power budget and the high requirements of the algorithms [21]. In this work we focus in low power heterogeneous sensors, optimizing the hardware and energy-efficient high accuracy machine learning algorithms to achieve a self-sustainable system.

3   System Architecture

Figure 1 shows the architectural overview of the smart watch whit different voltage domains and power switches to achieve energy efficiency. The core of the proposed hardware consists of the microcontroller TI MSP430FR5969. This 16-bit microcontroller has 2 kB of SRAM and 64 kB of non-volatile FRAM which uses less power than other non-volatile memories and reduces the gap in speed with the SRAM. The MSP430 also supports different low power modes which allows us to decide which components of the microcontroller are supplied. In low power mode LP4.5 it is praised to typically use 20 nA and in active mode 800 µA at a clock frequency of 8 MHz. The proposed system is equipped with a camera, a microphone, an accelerometer, and a temperature sensor. Furthermore the device can communicate using NFC and optionally by Bluetooth when the layer 2 board of the smart watch containing a Bluegiga WT12 module is attached. As an alternative, an external device can be attached to the UART pins by the main pin socket. Figure 2 shows the developed smart watch used to collect sensor data in real life indoor and outdoor scenarios. Additional memory is provided by a micro SD card holder with which a micro SD card can be

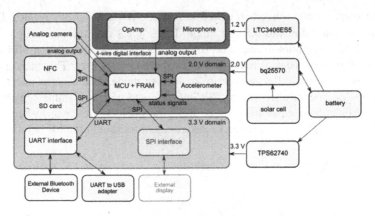

Fig. 1. Overview of the system architecture.

connected to the microcontroller using SPI. To minimize possible power consumption, each sensor can be completely switched off by a low-leakage load-switch with a quiescent current of 240 nA. The temperature sensor is directly supplied by an output pin from the microcontroller such that power is only consumed when temperature is measured and no additional load switch is needed. A load-switch for the accelerometer was resigned because leakage current in standby mode is only 10 nA.

Energy Harvesting and Voltage Suppliers. The device supports a power harvester chip TI BQ25570, which manages a LiPo rechargeable battery and solar cells. The internal DC-DC converter of the harvester chip can be set to a variable output voltage. This has been used to realize voltage scaling from 3.0 V down to 2.0 V, leading to much lower power consumption because dynamic power is related to the voltage squared:

$$P_{dyn} = \alpha C V^2 f,$$

where α is the switching rate, C is the load capacitance, V is the supply voltage and f is the operating frequency. The power harvester contains a highly efficient boost converter and supports maximum power point tracking.

In order to optimize the power consumption there are three different power domains. The peripherals are supplied with the buck converter TPS62740 from Texas Instruments which has an operating quiescent current of 460 nA and typically 70 nA in shutdown mode. The microphone is supplied separately with 1.2 V by the buck converter LTC3406ES5-1.2.

Camera. The camera is the ultra-low power 112×112 pixel gray-scale CMOS camera Centeye Stonyman, which has a focal plane size of 2.8 mm $\times$ 2.8 mm and a pixel pitch of 25 μm [22] that consumes only 2 mW@3.3 V. The camera comes on a pre-soldered PCB containing the image sensor and an objective lens and is connected to the smart watch by a socket connector. The camera provides an analog output which is connected with the internal ADC of the MSP430 [19].

Accelerometer. The accelerometer used is a ULP ADXL362 from Analog Devices with high resolution down to $9.8 \cdot 10^{-3} \mathrm{m/s}^2$. It needs 1.8 µA while sensing at 100 Hz and only 10 nA in standby mode and provides a burst mode including a FIFO buffer. This mode allows consecutive reading of the acquired sensor data. The microcontroller can do other jobs in parallel or enter a low-power mode. The accelerometer is connected to the microcontroller via the SPI interface and with two status signals. These status signals can be used to interrupt or wake the microcontroller up, when a predefined event happens like acceleration exceeds some threshold or the FIFO-buffer is full.

Fig. 2. Picture of the smart watch.

Microphone. The microphone which was used is the low-power microphone INMP801 which was mainly designed for hearing aids and consumes 17 µA at a supply voltage of 1.2 V and outputs a voltage of 570 ± 159 mV. The audio signal is amplified by a TI LMV951. Also this sensor is connected to the internal ADC of the MSP430.

Temperature Sensor. The temperature sensor is a Negative Temperature Coefficient Thermistor (NTC) thermistor from Epcos/TDK which is used in a voltage divider configuration and connected to the ADC.

4   Low-Power Context Recognition

Context awareness provides completely new use cases for a smart watch and makes it much more user-friendly. Figure 3 shows the software stack of the smart watch, where the close interaction between hardware and software directly on board can be seen. Our context recognition tries to classify the context of the action that is being performed by the wearer and the surroundings of the smart watch. It does so based on the data available from the many different sensors.

In order to train a classifier we need to collect and label a dataset. We chose 3 classes: public transport, office, and cafeteria, and acquired data from the temperature sensor, accelerometer, camera and microphone. Each data item lasts 5 s and contains 8 kHz audio data, 100 Hz 3-axis accelerometer measurements, one temperature read-out and one image of 112×112 grayscale pixel. Each of the classes has several hours of labeled data.

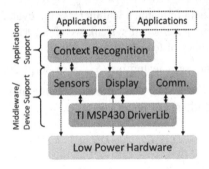

Fig. 3. Software stack of the smart watch

4.1   Feature Extraction and Selection

Performing classification on the acquired raw sensors data directly yields very poor results, because they usually represent the information in an unfavorable way, e.g. such that very little noise or small variations of the environment yield orthogonal representations. This is overcome by extracting features from this data. For the different types of sensors, there are different suitable features. For the sensors hosted by developed smart watch the possibility are as follow:

- For the audio data, we use the number of zero crossing with a 1 % hysteresis, the average energy of the signal, the maximum absolute value and dispersion. We also use features from the frequency domain, such as the spectral centroid, the bandwidth, and the well-known Mel-frequency cepstral coefficients (MFCCs).
- For the accelerometer data, we compute mean, variance, energy, covariance between the axes, the dynamic range and the frequency-domain entropy.
- For the temperature we calculate the average rate of change, mean, variance, and dynamic range.
- For the camera data we computed the mean (avg. brightness), variance and contrast.

Many of these features have an intuitive meaning, like the energy of a segment of the audio stream, which provides an indication of the loudness. In total we found 65 different features which are summarize in Table 1. There are 27 time domain feature, (4 for microphone, 16 for the accelerometer, 4 for the temperature sensor, 3 for the camera) and 38 features in frequency domain for microphone and accelerometer. Among the microphone feature there are 14 using Discrete Furier Transform (DFT) and 14 using Mel frequency.

Table 1. Total pool of features for different sensors.

Sensor	Time	Frequency	Total
Microphone	4	4 + 14(DFT) + 14(Mel)	36
Accelerometer	16	6	21
Temperature	4		4
Camera	3		3
Total	27	38	65

However, a large amount of features will increase the evaluation energy, and as our first goal is to have an energy-efficient system, we chose to perform feature selection, keeping only a fixed number of features.

Ideally we would choose a feature set $\hat{S} \subseteq \bar{S}$ of some fixed cardinality $\left|\hat{S}\right| = N$ among all features $\bar{S} = \bigcup_i \mathcal{F}_i$, such that we maximize the mutual information between the selected features and the set of target classes $\mathcal{C}$, i.e.

$$\hat{S} = \mathrm{argmax}_S D(S, \mathcal{C}), \qquad D(S, \mathcal{C}) = I(F_1, \ldots, F_N; C).$$

Solving this optimization problem is called *max-dependency* feature selection. However, with limited training data the estimated densities $p(x_1, \ldots, x_N)$ and $p(x_1, \ldots, x_N, c)$, where $x_1, \ldots, x_N$ are possible values for the various features and $c \in \mathcal{C}$ is the target class, are not very accurate. This makes it pointless to solve the above optimization problem, since the mutual information cannot be calculated with reasonable precision.

A simple approximation of the above problem is looking for the most relevant features, maximizing the mutual information individually with $D(S, \mathcal{C}) = \frac{1}{|S|} \sum_{i=1}^{N} I(F_i; C)$. Among the best features according to the solution of the maximum relevance problem, these are the mean of the temperature, the mean of the camera image, the spectral energy and entropy of the accelerometer axes, followed by a long list of audio features.

4.2 Classification

Input : Labeled training data $\left\{ (x^{(i)}, \ell^{(i)}) \right\}_{i \in \{1,2,\ldots,m\}},\ \ell^{(i)} \in \mathcal{C}$
Input : Maximum tree depth d_{max} and minimum number of items per node m_{min}
Output: Decision tree T
C45_MAKETREE($\{x^{(i)}, \ell^{(i)}\}_i, d = 1$) **begin**

    /* Stop descent if all samples are correctly classified, there are too few
        elements left, or we have reached that maximum depth: */
    if $\ell^{(i)} = \ell^{(j)}\ \forall i, j$ or $m < m_{min}$ or $d > d_{max}$ **then**
        | return leaf of class $\hat{c} = \arg\max_c p_c$ with $p_c = \frac{1}{m} \sum_i \mathbf{1}\{\ell^{(i)} = c\}$
    end
    /* Calculate entropy of current node: */
    $H_{root} \leftarrow -\sum_{c \in \mathcal{C}} p_c \log_2(p_c)$
    /* For each feature k find the threshold $\hat{t}_k$ maximizing inf. gain: */
    foreach *feature* k **do**
    | $\hat{t}_k \leftarrow \arg\max_{t_k} \left(H_{root} - p_{(x_k \le t_k)} H_{(x_k \le t_k)} - p_{(x_k > t_k)} H_{(x_k > t_k)}\right)$
    end
    /* Find feature with highest information gain: */
    $\hat{k} \leftarrow \arg\max_k \left(H_{root} - p_{(x_k \le \hat{t}_k)} H_{(x_k \le \hat{t}_k)} - p_{(x_k > \hat{t}_k)} H_{(x_k > \hat{t}_k)}\right)$
    /* Create two subtrees T_1 and T_2:   */
    $T_{left} \leftarrow$ C45_MAKETREE($\{x^{(i)}, \ell^{(i)}\}_{x^{(i)} \le \hat{t}}, d + 1$)
    $T_{right} \leftarrow$ C45_MAKETREE($\{x^{(i)}, \ell^{(i)}\}_{x^{(i)} > \hat{t}}, d + 1$)
    return $(\hat{k}, \hat{t}_{\hat{k}}, T_{left}, T_{right})$
end

Algorithm 1: Continuous C4.5 Algorithm

There are many well-known classification algorithms and concepts, ranging from simple decision trees to support-vector machines, nearest-neighbor algorithms and boosting to random forests, neural networks, naïve Bayes and complex graphical models, to name just a few. We perform the classification using a decision tree which is constructed using the continuous C4.5 algorithm (cf. Algorithm 1). The individual features of a data sample x are addressed by subscript, i.e. x_1 denotes the first feature. The decision tree was chosen because of its low computational complexity and consequential high energy efficiency during classification (as opposed to during learning) [1]. For performing the classification, there is only the decision tree, which has to be descended doing the corresponding comparisons until arriving at a leaf.

Decision trees are very susceptible to overfitting, so particularly with our continuous-valued and limited amount of training data this is an issue. It can be approached using bottom-up pruning, where leaves with only few samples (below some threshold) are combined to a single leaf of the most probable class. Pruning is also done offline and can only improve the time required for classification.

5   Measurement Results

In a first step, we tune the feature selection to choose the optimal number of features. The feature selection and construction of the decision tree were performed on the training set. The training set has been acquired using 7 subjects wearing the smart watch for 24 h and collecting data from all sensors. For each class a minimal number of 500 samples have been used for the training set. The results shown in Fig. 4 are the classification accuracy of the test set. The mean accuracy was best when selecting the 21 features of maximal relevance and minimal redundancy. With the low-complexity classification system presented here, we were able to achieve a mean accuracy of 81.5 % for all classes using 21 features.

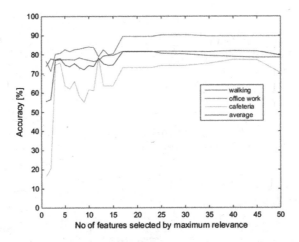

Fig. 4. Class-wise 1-vs-all accuracy depending on the number of features selected using the relevance evaluated with mutual information with data from all sensors.

Ø 81.5%	PT	Office	Cafetteria.
Publ. Transp.	**81.8**	13.6	4.6
Office	7.2	**89.5**	3.3
Cafeteria	17.2	9.6	**73.2**

Fig. 5. Confusion Matrix using 21 features.

To give more insight into the limitations, we present the confusion matrix in Fig. 5. The classes are very well identified from 73.2 % to 89.5 %, and we are expected to achieve even better performance when training the system with more subjects and data.

Energy vs. Accuracy. An important evaluation we measured is the link between energy used by the combination of sensors and the accuracy achieved. As the various sensors require a substantial amount of power, clearly, there is a trade-off between which sensors are used and what accuracy can be achieved. We visualize this trade-off in Fig. 6, considering only the data of some of the sensors mentioned. The energies presented here are based on the measurements during sensor data acquisition and estimates based on counts of the number of required operations for the feature extraction. As expected, utilizing all sensors achieves the best accuracy but also has high energy consumption. Another interesting result is the improved performance (in energy and accuracy) of the ultra-low power camera against the accelerometer which commonly is considered a low power high accuracy sensor. This demonstrates that the accelerometer is an ideal sensor for detecting motions (i.e. walking, running, gesture, etc.) but can be overcome in the context detection. In fact the camera needs less than 100 ms (so very small energy required) to acquire a frame but gives a lot of information while the accelerometer needs seconds (at least 1 in our classificatory) to acquire sufficient data for classification. Also it is interesting that the microphone over performs

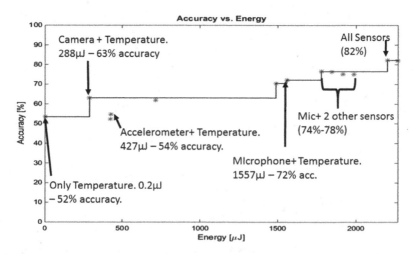

Fig. 6. Achieved accuracy by used sensors with annotated pareto-optimal points.

Activity	Run time [d]
Idle	661.38
Every day	660.92
Every hour	650.69
Every 30 minutes	640.34
Every minute	333.10
Every 10 seconds	95.67
Permanent	11.00

Activity	Run time [d]
Every 745 sec.	
Every 5 minutes	5617.52
Every minute	729.89
Every 10 seconds	113.37
Permanent	11.20

Fig. 7. Life time and self-sustainability analysis. This figure shows the life time based on one full battery charge without and with energy harvesting in the left and right table, respectively.

both the camera and accelerometer in accuracy but, of course, it is more expensive in terms of energy, as more energy is required by the sensor and frequency domain feature computation.

Lifetime Estimation. To evaluate the life time and self-sustainability of the proposed solution, we measured the energy for the acquisition of all sensors and feature calculation. The evaluation setup was preformed acquiring 1 picture for the camera, 1 data from the temperature sensor, 1 s of accelerometer data, and 1 s of microphone data, and we compute all 65 features for the classification algorithm to have a worst case. With this set up the energy needed for single classification is only 2.28 mJ. To evaluate the lifetime we assume that we use a small Li-Ion battery with 150 mAh capacity and 4.2 V. For the power harvester which we used an average value of the calculations are based on an average power generation of 40 µW. As we demonstrated in previous work [19] this is a pessimistic value that can be easily harvested from a wrist band with eight 1 × 4 cm solar cells. To evaluate the idle energy, when the smartwatch is not performing any classification, we measured the quiescent power of the developed version of smart watch (only 9 µW). Figure 7 shows the different lifetime according to the classification duty cycle. It can be observed that when there is no acquisition and no harvesting, the device can last for more than 661 days, which highlights the low quiescent energy. When the features are calculated continuously for all sensors, 11 days are possible. If a sensor acquisition is taken every 10 s, the device could last for more than 95 days. If this is further reduced to a periodicity of once per day, 660 days are possible. When considering the power harvester is plugged in, the device can do classifications every 10 s for more than 113 days. Self-sustainability is reached when a classification is performed every 745 s. But with a 5-min cycle more than 5,617.52 days are possible (15.5 years).

6   Conclusions and Future Work

We implemented a prototype of smart watch trained to recognize context directly on board and achieve self-sustainability. The smartwatch hosts an ultra-low power gray-scale camera, a MEMS microphone, a 3-axes accelerometer, and an analog temperature sensor. Moreover the device is equipped with a solar harvester and rechargeable Li-Ion battery to continuously recharge the battery even in indoor scenario. The implemented classifier is suitable for ultra-low power microcontrollers and this system demonstrates the recognition of various scenarios directly on board the existing smart watch, an accelerometer alone cannot achieve this without a smart phone. The experimental results confirmed both the benefits of the data fusion and the energy efficiency of the solution. Even if the dataset used for the training was not huge the preliminary results show a mean accuracy of 82.5 % when classifying 3 cases with peak of 89 %. In future work we are planning to improve the training dataset to have more labelled classes and that should increase the overall accuracy of the algorithm. Moreover, a full version of the context recognition algorithm will be implemented on the smart watch and tested in the field.

Acknowledgments. This work was supported by the SCOPES SNF project (IZ74Z0_160481).

References

1. Ghasemzadeh, H., Jafari, R.: Ultra low-power signal processing in wearable monitoring systems: a tiered screening architecture with optimal bit resolution. ACM Trans. Embed. Comput. Syst. (TECS) **13**, 9 (2013)
2. Kahn, J., Yuce, M.R., Bulger, G., Harding, B.: Wireless Body Area Network (WBAN) design techniques and performance evaluation. J. Med. Syst. **36**(3), 1441–1457 (2012)
3. Hung, K., et al.: Ubiquitous health monitoring: integration of wearable sensors, novel sensing techniques, and body sensor networks. In: Adibi, S. (ed.) Mobile Health, pp. 319–342. Springer, Heidelberg (2015)
4. Pejovic, V., Musolesi, M.: Anticipatory mobile computing: a survey of the state of the art and research challenges. ACM Comput. Surv. (CSUR) **47**(3), 47 (2015)
5. Perera, C., et al.: Context aware computing for the Internet of Things: a survey. IEEE Commun. Surv. Tutor. **16**(1), 414–454 (2014)
6. Anjum, A., Ilyas, M.U.: Activity recognition using smartphone sensors. In: IEEE Consumer Communications and Networking Conference (CCNC) (2013)
7. Sharma, S., et al.: Machine learning techniques for data mining: a survey. In: IEEE International Conference on Computational Intelligence and Computing Research (ICCIC) (2013)
8. Govindaraju, V., Rao, C.: Machine Learning: Theory and Applications. Elsevier, New York (2013)
9. Azizyan, M., et al.: SurroundSense: mobile phone localization via ambience fingerprinting. In: Mobicom, pp. 261–272 (2009)
10. Kerhet, A., et al.: Distributed video surveillance using hardware-friendly sparse large margin classifiers. In: IEEE Conference on Advanced Video and Signal Based Surveillance (AVSS), pp. 87–92 (2007)
11. Chon, Y., et al.: Mobility prediction-based smartphone energy optimization for everyday location monitoring. In: SenSys 2011, pp. 82–95 (2011)
12. Lara, O.D., Labrador, M.A.: A survey on human activity recognition using wearable sensors. IEEE Commun. Surv. Tutor. **15**(3), 1192–1209 (2013)
13. Gokgoz, E., Subasi, A.: Comparison of decision tree algorithms for EMG signal classification using DWT. Biomed. Signal Process. Control **18**, 138–144 (2015)

14. Silva, J., et al.: Human activity classification with inertial sensors. In: PHealth: International Conference on Wearable Micro and Nano Technologies for Personalized Health, vol. 200, p. 101 (2014)
15. Weddell, A.S., et al.: A survey of multi-source energy harvesting systems. In: Conference on Design, Automation and Test in Europe (DATE), pp. 905–908 (2013)
16. Maurer, U., et al.: eWatch: a wearable sensor and notification platform. In: International Workshop on Wearable and Implantable Body Sensor Networks (BSN), p. 145 (2006)
17. Porzi, L., et al.: A smart watch-based gesture recognition system for assisting people with visual impairments. In: ACM International Workshop on Interactive Multimedia on Mobile & Portable Devices (IMMPD), pp. 19–24 (2013)
18. Maekawa, T., Yanagisawa, Y., Kishino, Y., Ishiguro, K., Kamei, K., Sakurai, Y., Okadome, T.: Object-based activity recognition with heterogeneous sensors on wrist. In: Kay, J., Lukowicz, P., Tokuda, H., Olivier, P., Krüger, A. (eds.) Pervasive 2012. LNCS, vol. 7319, pp. 246–264. Springer, Heidelberg (2010). doi:10.1007/978-3-642-12654-3_15
19. Magno, M., et al.: InfiniTime: a multi-sensor energy neutral wearable bracelet. In: International Green Computing Conference (IGCC) (2014)
20. Seong, K.E., et al.: Self M2M based wearable watch platform for collecting personal activity in real-time. In: IEEE Conference on Big Data and Smart Computing (BIGCOMP), pp. 286–290 (2014)
21. Zhu, Z., et al.: Fusing on-body sensing with local and temporal cues for daily activity recognition. In: ICST International Conference on Body Area Networks, pp. 83–89 (2014)
22. Centeye, Inc., Centeye Stonyman/Haskbill silicon documentation (2013)

Adaptive Methods for Managing Heterogeneity in Smart Spaces

Mikko Asikainen[✉], Lauri Väätäinen, Aleksi Suomalainen,
Miika Toivanen, Keijo Haataja, and Pekka Toivanen

School of Computing Kuopio Campus, University of Eastern Finland,
P.O.Box 1627, 70211 Kuopio, Finland
{mikko.p.asikainen, lauri.vaatainen,
aleksi.suomalainen, miika.toivanen, keijo.haataja,
pekka.toivanen}@uef.fi

Abstract. In this paper we discuss our work to manage heterogeneity of devices, protocols and software in smart spaces by using adaptive methods to combat incompatibility issues. We present our experimental prototype which combines a telehealth system with the assisted living functionalities of a smart home, which we have developed to test our concepts. The result of this adaptivity study is a service repository which enables systems to match collections of sensors and actuators to loosely coupled services which are downloaded and activated in runtime without human interference.

Keywords: Adaptivity · Loose coupling · Middleware · Service repository · Smart spaces

1 Introduction

The proliferation of wireless technologies over the past decade has renewed commercial interest in all manner of applications for sensors and actuators for home automation. However, the majority of vendors usually offer their home automation solutions as closed, proprietary environments where the user must embrace a single hardware and software ecosystem. The promise of the "Internet of Things" is to have all devices within a ubiquitous computing environment connect and communicate with each other, sharing useful information and functionalities from a purely Machine-To-Machine standpoint. This promise is however far from reality as there are a lot of competing wireless technologies and communication standards with little incentive for industrial players to embrace a single suite of standards and technology. The success of the Internet owes much to an infrastructure that is both open and open ended. The communication interfaces that form the cornerstone technologies on the net such as e-mail, are open for anyone to make their own compliant implementations, and the layered model of TCP/IP allows for expanded services to be added on top of the stack without the need to re-implement the whole. Without this openness and flexibility, it would have been difficult for the Internet to grown from its humble beginnings into a thing that has made such a huge impact on human civilization. These same ideas should be adopted in home automation for the technology to become ubiquitous.

© ICST Institute for Computer Sciences, Social Informatics and Telecommunications Engineering 2016
B. Mandler et al. (Eds.): IoT 360° 2015, Part II, LNICST 170, pp. 344–348, 2016.
DOI: 10.1007/978-3-319-47075-7_39

In our study we asked ourselves, how can we enable meaningful interconnection of heterogeneous devices in a manner which enables hardware and software components to work together in a loosely coupled way? What are the aspects of building services in a wireless sensor network environment where dynamic interconnection is difficult to achieve? To answer these questions we have built an experimental prototype system to try out different adaptation strategies. Our prototype enables software components to be matched against the collection of sensors and actuators in the smart space, downloaded from an open service repository of service components and loosely coupled into the system. The use case for the system is to provide an assisted living environment for the elderly together with a telehealth system for caregivers. Many existing approaches to smart space adaptation focus more on runtime configuration of the system based on the behavior of the occupants. Approaches in studies such as [1–3] use learning algorithms to change the configuration of the smart home. Other approaches include ontology-based approaches (for example [4]) or context aware approaches such as [5]. In [6] a framework for a Java OSGi and middleware based approach using a different middleware layer. Our prime focus is on the establishment of services within the smart space. We want to learn how services can be obtained, built and reconfigured on-demand with minimal human interference.

2   System Overview

We have named our experimental prototype "Smart Environment for Assisted Living", henceforth "the SEAL system", the work for which was begun in [7] and continues here. The system consists of a top-level server, a smart home controller and the associated collection of sensors, actuators and mobile devices. At the core of the SEAL system is a smart home controller called the Local Reasoner, which is responsible for operating actuators, gathering data from sensors and executing automation and assisted living tasks ranging from simple HVAC control to intelligent activity monitoring and analysis. The Local Reasoner of our prototype runs on a Convergens smart hub [8] connected to the Internet. The Smart Hub is an embedded Linux computer with good connectivity options. The software running on the Hub is developed with Java and built on top of the DEMANES middleware [9]. It takes advantage of Java OSGi in handling the software components during runtime operation. The SEAL Server is an off-site server responsible for top-level administration and reasoning. Whereas the Local Reasoner is responsible for oversight on local sensors and actuators, the SEAL Server's reasoner is responsible for a number of smart spaces. The SEAL Server provides tools for caregivers to examine the occupants and to determine services and treatments to be executed using a careplan, which includes daily routines, automated tasks, home automation profiles and so on. The Local Reasoner polls changes in the careplan periodically and adapts its operation to fulfill these requests. In our prototype the SEAL Server runs on a Linux desktop computer connected to the Internet. The software is running on Java and MySQL with a HTML5 web interface on an Apache server. Android mobile phones and tablet computers are used to provide a user interface with the SEAL system for occupants and caregivers alike. We also take advantage of the onboard sensors on the Android devices as well as Bluetooth devices connected to it to gather data for analysis. To monitor the health status of the occupant, sensors that gather biosignals are required. In our prototype, we are using a Mega Electronics eMotion Faros sensor [10] for biosignal measurement and the Convergens Cognitive Node [8] for fall detection. Alerts and worrisome developments are detected by the Local Reasoner using these wireless nodes, relayed to the SEAL Server and relevant personnel are alerted to the situation [11]. The smart space requires various sensors and actuators to function such as light switches, temperature and lighting monitoring, heating control, door sensors, movement detection and so on. For this we use Z-wave devices [12] due to the easy off-the-shelf availability and the open source compatibility of the technology.

3 Adaptation of Services and the Careplan

The adaptivity in our prototype stems from the dynamic creation and modification of services. At the core of the system is a reasoner module running on the local controller and on the main server. The Local Reasoner is a software component responsible of data gathering and analysis within the scope of the smart space. Sensors and actuators associated with it form a collection of basic tools at the disposal of the system and are checked against a service directory to retrieve a higher level collection of services the Local Reasoner can utilize. The Local Reasoner is subservient to the Top-Level Reasoner on the SEAL Server, which is responsible for the top-level administration of a number of smart spaces. As mentioned, this Top-Level Reasoner is responsible for the maintenance of a "careplan" which acts as a stimulus to request new services and to modify existing ones in the smart spaces.

To aid development of the system, we include the Reasoning Engine module of the DEMANES Middleware [9]. This module is responsible for the inclusion/exclusion of sensors and actuators and the maintenance of the Observer Registry and Actuator Registry for access. It provides the Reasoner component (developed by the user) and Java interfaces to access the registries, poll sensor data, actuate devices and so on. The goal is to mask heterogeneity of hardware implementation from the designer of the Reasoner. The middleware provides classes for observers and actuators. These classes receive URN [13] requests from the middleware and it is up to the user (or hardware vendor) to implement the code to realize the requests. As a new component to the system, we must implement a Service Repository. This is a software component which would ideally be a common repository for services in the Internet. The idea is that once the Local Reasoner has a collection of sensors and actuators, it can when needed check them against the Repository for services that can be implemented using the collection of devices. This however is not the end of the story. Knowing which services you can implement is not useful in itself and the Reasoner cannot activate these arbitrarily. The Top-Level Reasoner is key in the management of services within the system. The careplan dictates which services should be implemented. The Top-Level Reasoner contacts the Local Reasoner and requests a certain service to be implemented. This triggers the following chain of events:

First, the Local Reasoner queries the Service Repository for the requested service. Then the Repository returns information on the sensors and actuators required for the implementation of the Service. The Local Reasoner checks its collection of sensors and actuators whether all dependencies are met. If yes, the Local Reasoner downloads the code of the service from the repository (much like installing software from a Linux repository) and activates the code using Java Classloader. The Local Reasoner then returns a successful activation response to the Top-Level Reasoner. If not, the Local Reasoner returns a failure to the Top-Level Reasoner, stating the cause of the failure. This can be used as a trigger on the system administrator to start a process to include the missing devices in the local smart space and to try again.

4   Experiments and Conclusions

We deployed the prototype system in a typical home environment. A selected portion of the house was instrumented with the smart home controller, fall detector, Android UI device and Z-wave devices enabling lighting control, controllable power sockets and sensors detecting movement, light levels and temperature.

The Service Repository was tested with two service cases. We implemented basic fall detection using the Convergens Cognitive Node. We also tested adding a service requiring controllable light switches and light level meters to activate a service which switches lights on when light levels are low. Both of these services were found to work using the Service Repository and calls based on URN words. With the Convergens Cognitive Node, we had an opportunity to test a node which communicated the URN associated with the functionality provided by the node directly. With the Z-wave light switches, we experimented using an adapter to allow the data sent by the legacy devices to be converted into URN's.

Both of the services were activated in the way described in Sect. 3, with the service requirement being added to the careplan, the Smart Home Controller checking the service repository for hardware dependencies and downloading the associated software package. The package was then activated and the services found working.

When it comes to singular devices which send their associated URN the hardware independence from the point of view of the Service Repository is strong. As long as the device driver works independently and the components using the DEMANES middleware can read the data the sensor is sending, a service such as the fall detection service described does not care which individual sensor is responsible for sending the alarm. A thorough dictionary for URN keywords must be maintained and the complete pairing of the service to its platform observed however. For example, if the fall detection service sends an alarm by passing an alarm URN to the middleware, the middleware must be ready to handle such and URN because the service component has no knowledge on the intended method of alarm delivery nor the destination.

With legacy devices, a platform agnostic service becomes more difficult to establish. A device specific adapter must be implemented to the system before it can interact with the middleware. This adapter should ideally be also available at the Service Repository, but implementing and testing that functionality is out of scope for this research.

In conclusion, the concept works and is ripe for further development. The next steps are develop this technology further and conduct more in-depth field research among the elderly who will be the users of the system. The research for this paper was made chiefly with the EU Artemis DEMANES project (Artemis-JU - Grant Agreement no. 269334) [12]. We use the middleware developed in the DEMANES project. Additional funding was provided from the ALMARVI (Artemis-JU – Grant Agreement no. 641439) project [14]. Our experimental prototype is a joint effort of the School of Computing of University of Eastern Finland, Convergens [8] and Mega Electronics [10].

References

1. Jihua, Y., Qi, X., Yaohong, X., Chunlan, W.: The research of an adaptive smart home system. In: 2012 7th International Conference on Computer Science and Education (ICCSE), pp. 882–887, 14–17 July 2012
2. Cook, D.J., et al.: Learning to control a smart home environment. Innovative Appl. Artif. Intell. (2003)
3. Sungjoon, C., Eunwoo, K., Songhwai, O.: Human behavior prediction for smart homes using deep learning. In: 2013 IEEE RO-MAN, pp. 173–179, 26–29 August 2013
4. El Kaed, C., Denneulin, Y., Ottogalli, F.: Dynamic service adaptation for plug and play device interoperability. In: 2011 7th International Conference on Network and Service Management (CNSM), pp. 1–9, 24–28 October 2011
5. Tinghuai, M., Yong-Deak, K., Qiang, M., Meili, T., Weican, Z.: Context-aware implementation based on CBR for smart home. In: 2005 IEEE International Conference on Wireless and Mobile Computing, Networking and Communications, (WiMob 2005), vol. 4, pp. 112–115, 22–24 August 2005
6. Papadopoulos, N., Meliones, A., Economou, D., Karras, I., Liverezas, I.: A connected home platform and development framework for smart home control applications. In: 2009 7th IEEE International Conference on Industrial Informatics, INDIN 2009, pp. 402–409, 23–26 June 2009
7. Väänänen, A., Haataja, K., Asikainen, M., Jantunen, I., Toivanen, P.: Mobile health applications: a comparative analysis and a novel mobile health platform. In: 5th International Conference on Sensor Systems and Software, S-CUBE 2014 (2014)
8. Convergens OY. http://www.convergens.fi/
9. Design, Monitoring and Operation of Adaptive Networked Embedded Systems (DEMANES). www.demanes.eu
10. Mega Electronics Ltd. http://www.megaemg.com
11. Demanes results video. https://www.youtube.com/watch?v=4gXT2AudV1U
12. Z-Wave Alliance. http://z-wavealliance.org/
13. Uniform Resource Names (URN) Namespace Definition Mechanisms, RFC3406. http://tools.ietf.org/html/rfc3406
14. Algorithms, Design Methods, and Many-core Execution Platform for Low-Power Massive Data-Rate Video and Image Processing (ALMARVI). http://www.almarvi.eu/

An Evaluation of Link Estimation Algorithms for RPL in Dynamic Wireless Sensor Networks

Peter Ruckebusch[(✉)], Jens Devloo, David Carels, Eli De Poorter,
and Ingrid Moerman

Department of Information Technology (INTEC),
Ghent University iMinds,
iGent Tower, Technologiepark 15 (Zwijnaarde), 9052 Ghent, Belgium
peter.ruckebusch@intec.ugent.be

Abstract. Link estimators are extremely important in dynamic wireless sensor networks for obtaining a good network performance because they drive the decisions made by the routing protocol. Many estimators exist but the quality of their estimation depends on the scenario at hand. In this paper, the impact of the estimator on the network performance is investigated in different networking scenarios. Also the influence of the underlying MAC protocol was evaluated. The evaluation was performed both in simulation and on a real-life testbed.

The results clearly show that there is no link estimator that is best in all scenario's. Another major finding indicates that the results obtained in simulator differ heavily from the testbed results. This illustrates that research findings cannot be solely based on simulation results but also requires real-world experiments. The influence off the underlying MAC protocol is limited on the choice of estimator.

Keywords: WSN · RPL · Dynamic wireless sensor networks · Routing · IoT · Mobility

1 Introduction

Link estimation is extremely important in dynamic Wireless Sensor Networks (WSN) since it drives the decisions made by the routing protocol. Selecting the best path towards the destination is crucial for increasing the overall network performance in terms of throughput, latency and reliability. Moreover, selecting the best links reduces the number of retransmissions and, consequently, the energy consumption.

For this reason, many link estimators for WSNs have been proposed [3]. While complex algorithms, taking asymmetrical links into account, perform better compared to simple estimators, they cause a higher overhead [10]. More intelligent algorithms, such as Four-bit [7], seem to obtain higher Packet Delivery Ratio (PDR) in networks with a high interference level [9]. In dense networks, however, these algorithms can encounter some scalability issues [5], due to variations in different sources of information causing constantly changing metrics [10].

© ICST Institute for Computer Sciences, Social Informatics and Telecommunications Engineering 2016
B. Mandler et al. (Eds.): IoT 360° 2015, Part II, LNICST 170, pp. 349–361, 2016.
DOI: 10.1007/978-3-319-47075-7_40

Given the numerous dynamic networking scenarios and applications envisaged for WSNs in the Internet-of-Things (IOT), it is to be expected that a single link estimator will not be able to provide the best estimation in all situations. Therefore it is important to know which link estimation algorithms delivers the best results in various scenario's.

To investigate this, several well-known link estimators were implemented for the Routing Protocol for Low-Power and Lossy Networks (RPL) and evaluated both in a simulator and on a real-life testbed, thereby also investigating if their exists a difference between simulations and real-life testbed experiments.

The main contributions of this paper are: (a) extending RPL with state-of-the art link estimators; (b) the analysis on the RPL network performance when using different link estimators in realistic scenario's; (c) a comparison between the results obtained via simulation and via a real-life testbed and; (d) a study on the influence of the underlying Medium Access Control (MAC) protocol and its settings on the performance obtained by the different link estimators.

2   Related Work

In this section, an overview is given of different routing protocols that rely on link estimation algorithms for making routing decisions. Next to this, different link estimation algorithms are also discussed.

2.1   Routing Protocols for WSNs

In this work, several link estimation algorithms were implemented into the routing process of RPL. It is a proactive, distance-vector routing protocol specifically designed for WSNs [17]. RPL uses control packets (DIO, DAO and DIS) for building a tree like topology, called a Destination-Oriented Directed Acyclic Graph (DODAG). As RPL routes a packet via the path which minimizes the sum of all link metrics, i.e. the path metric, it takes link quality into account when routing. In contiki RPL [16] only the objective function 0 and Estimated Transmission Count (ETX) methods were available.

Another well-known routing protocol for WSNs is the Collection Tree Protocol (CTP) [8]. CTP also is a pro-active distance-vector routing protocol. It optimizes for data collection applications towards a special node, the data sink. As its name suggests, CTP builds a tree topology with the sink as root using an adaptive beaconing technique. For this it relies on the four-bit (4B) link quality estimator [7] allowing each node to select the best parent.

In the broader field of wireless ad hoc networks, OLSR, BABEL and BATMAN are popular routing protocols [12]. OLSR is a proactive link-state protocol while BABEL and BATMAN are pro-active distance-vector protocols. They all use a variant of the ETX method for estimating the quality of each link.

2.2   Link Estimators

Link estimation algorithms take the lossy nature and time varying link quality of WSNs into account when determining the best neighbour to forward data to. As discussed in [3], link estimators can be classified in hardware- and software-based algorithms. The hardware based link estimators use quality indicators (i.e. RSSI and LQI) set by the radio driver after packet reception. Software based link estimators such as Four bit [7] and Fuzzy LQE [4], combine information from multiple network layers into a single metric. There are also very simple link estimators, such as the objective function 0, that select neighbours based on hop count. In this section a classification of the evaluated link estimators is given.

Hardware Based Link Estimation Algorithms. Hardware based link estimation algorithms use information provided by the radio (e.g. Received Signal Strength Indicator (RSSI) and Link Quality Indicator (LQI)) to calculate the link metric. Both link layer variables are highly correlated with the PDR [13] and can be used to model link quality. Due to the unstable nature of wireless communication, the raw values can be aggregated with an Exponential Weighted Moving Average (EWMA) filter [3] to improve the estimation. Because LQI and RSSI are only calculated after packet reception, packet-loss is not taken into account. For this reason the link quality of less reliable links can be overestimated.

Software Based Link Estimation Algorithms. The objective function 0 [15], also referred to as hop count, is a very simple software based link estimator that minimizes the number of hops from the source towards the destination resulting in a route where the preferred parent is the furthest reachable node in the direction of the sink. If the quality of the link with this node is poor, a lot of retransmissions and extra packet loss or energy consumption can occur. On the other hand, in stable networks the overhead is limited for maintaining link information.

More complex software based link estimation algorithms will tackle the aforementioned issue by using historical and/or cross-layer information to make more intelligent decisions when selecting the best links. ETX [11] based algorithms estimate the number of expected transmissions needed to successfully send a packet to each destination by counting the number of attempts needed in previous transmissions. ETX based algorithms select the path with minimal ETX. The Four bit algorithm [7] combines information from multiple OSI-layers to calculate link metrics. It uses LQI and RSSI values to account link quality and combines this with the ETX path metric. Fuzzy logic [4] combines multiple link metrics in a less deterministic way by using membership functions which assign a score in $[0, 1]$ for every link metric. These individual scores are combined with an aggregation function such as the Yagger operator. Multiple metrics are aggregated by calculating a weighted mean (β is typical 0.6) of the worst and average value of each metric. This results in a link score which can be inverted to obtain a link metric for routing purposes.

3   Evaluation Set-Up

The aforementioned link estimation algorithms have been implemented in Contiki RPL [16]. They were evaluated using the Cooja simulator and, experimentally, on the iMinds w-iLab.t office testbed [1]. Two metrics have been used to determine the performance. First, the PDR is defined as the number of received packets at the RPL sink to the total number of data packets sent in the network. Second, the energy consumption is modelled by the percentage radio-on time which dominates the power usage in sensor nodes.

The network stability was also determined by monitoring the control traffic overhead generated by RPL, e.g. the number of DIO messages and parent switches, and the required MAC retransmissions. These results show a clear correlation with the radio-on time, i.e. unstable networks suffer from a high packet loss and require regular DIO message exchanges and parent switches, resulting in a higher energy consumption. They are therefore not included in this paper.

All simulations and testbed experiments ran twice to determine the variance in results. The experiment and simulation settings can be found in Table 1.

Seven different real-life scenarios were investigated. First, a standard scenario was used where nodes are distributed evenly. The send interval was set to 30 s. The second scenario used a sparse topology where nodes are placed further from each-other. The third scenario investigates a dense node topology. The fourth scenario emphasizes the asymmetric behaviour of a real-life sensor node by changing the transmission and interference ranges dependent to the direction. In the fifth scenario, the influence of a bursty send pattern is investigated where each node sends a burst of 3 packets every 90 s. The impact of interference was analysed in the sixth scenario. The last scenario introduces mobility by adding two mobile nodes to the standard scenario. In each of the scenario's the sink is placed at the edge of the network to enforce a multi-hop topology.

Table 1. Experiment and simulation settings

Setting	Value
Contiki version	2.7
MAC protocol	CSMA
Radio duty cycling	ContikiMAC
Maximum number of retransmissions	5
Neighbor table size	16
Channel check rate (Hz)	16
CC2420 transmission power	-15 dBm
Cooja simulation time	10 min
w-iLab.t testbed simulation time	30 min
Network stabilization time	1 min
Mobile node speed	2 m/s (7.2 km/h)

3.1 Cooja Simulator

Cooja is a Java-based sensor network simulator for Contiki source code. Since Cooja is a software-based simulator, it doesn't take external interference into account and uses default values for radio driver variables such as LQI and RSSI. The Cooja Unit Disk Graph Medium (UDGM) channel model calculates the RSSI value based on the distance between the nodes and uses 37 as default for all LQI values [14]. The UDGM channel model degrades the signal quality based on the distance between nodes. Cooja allows to determine the average radio-on time with the Powertrace plug-in and to simulate mobile nodes with the Mobility plug-in.

Table 2 gives an overview of the different settings used in Cooja to construct the six scenario's.

Table 2. Specifications of the different scenarios in Cooja.

	Standard	Mobility	Asymmetric
Number of nodes	8x8 = 64	8x8 + 2 mobile = 66	8x8 = 64
Transmission range	45m	45m	Variable
Interference range	60m	60m	60m
Model of degeneration	UDGM	UDGM	DGRM
Send interval	1 packet/30s	1 packet/30s	1 packet/30s

	Dense	Sparse	Interference	Bursty
Number of nodes	12x12 = 144	8x8 = 64	8x8 = 64	8x8 = 64
Transmission range	45m	30m	45m	45m
Interference range	60m	40m	90m	60m
Model of degeneration	UDGM	UDGM	UDGM	UDGM
Send interval	1 packet/30s	1 packet/30s	1 packet/30s	3 packets/90s

The standard scenario uses an eight-by-eight grid with a transmission range of 45 m and an interference range of 60 m. The default UDGM channel model is used. Each node sends a packet every 30 s. The sparse scenario has the same configuration but with a limited transmission (30 m) and interference (40 m) range. To simulate a dense network, the standard scenario is extended to a twelve-by-twelve grid.

To investigate link asymmetry, the UDGM model used in the standard scenario is replaced with the Directed Graph Radio Medium (DGRM) channel model which allows to specify different delivery ratios for each directional link in the network. To determine the influence of the send pattern, the default send interval is changed to 90 s but now a burst of three packets is transmitted. The impact of interference was analysed by extending the interference range in the standard scenario to 90 m. The mobility scenario has exactly the same configuration as the standard scenario but with two additional mobile nodes.

3.2   iMinds w-iLab.t Testbed

Due to limitations of the Cooja simulator, a real-life testbed is needed to reliably evaluate all link estimation algorithms. The iMinds w-iLab.t [1] testbed contains 200 Tmote Sky sensor nodes in a real-life office environment (see Fig. 1). By varying the amount of nodes in the experiment a standard, sparse and dense networks can be created. Running these tests during daytime introduces extra external interference and varying the transmit power of the Tmote Sky CC2420 radio [2] allows to increase the asymmetry in the network. The mobile scenario could not be reproduced due to limitations of the iMinds w-iLab.t office testbed. It is important to note that a real-life office testbed always has an inherent level of asymmetry due to the use of real-life sensor nodes and the occurrence of walls and other obstacles. Next to the asymmetry, an office testbed always has a certain level of external interference from other wireless communication technologies.

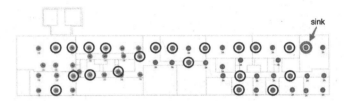

Fig. 1. iMinds w-iLab.t office testbed. Indicated nodes are used in the standard scenario while the sparse scenario only uses 10 nodes and the dense scenario uses all available nodes.

4   Evaluation Results

4.1   Cooja Simulator

Figure 2 illustrates the PDR obtained by the different link estimators in each scenario. In the standard network, Four bit and Fuzzy LQE algorithms obtain a 20 % higher packet delivery ratio compared to the other estimators. The PDR in the sparse scenario is nearly the same for all estimators but drops significantly (12 %) for Four bit and Fuzzy LQE compared to the standard scenario. This is because there are less paths towards the sink allowing less room for optimizations by the more complex algorithms. In dense networks lower PDR ratios are achieved overall, but especially using the RSSI-based and Four bit algorithms (a drop of 50 %). Algorithms based on ETX and Fuzzy LQE perform best in dense networks. The interference scenario only results in a small drop in PDR compared to the standard scenario except for the RSSI and Four bit estimators that show a decrease of 10 %. The PDR of all link estimators degrade in the asymmetric scenario and again the Four bit and Fuzzy LQE algorithms suffer the most with a drop of 30 %. Now the objective function 0 obtains the best

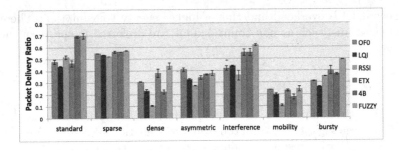

Fig. 2. Packet delivery ratio in the Cooja simulator.

results. The mobility scenario shows very low PDRs overall, especially the RSSI algorithm cannot establish a stable network. Again, the objective function 0 obtains the best results. In the bursty scenario, also a significant drop in PDR can be noted especially for the Four bit algorithm which is very sensitive for changes in the send behaviour, showing a decrease of 30 %. Fuzzy LQE performs best in this scenario.

The radio-on time, measured for the different link estimators in each scenario, is shown in Fig. 3. The results demonstrate that overall the RSSI algorithm has a much higher energy consumption. This is because the RSSI link estimation is highly fluctuating, resulting in more RPL parent switches and, consequently, a higher energy consumption. One exception is the sparse scenario where less parent switches are possible. The radio-on time in the sparse and bursty scenarios is nearly identical to the standard scenario. Dense networks on the other hand show an increase in energy consumption, especially for the ETX, Four bit and Fuzzy LQE algorithms. When considering asymmetric links, the results are again nearly identical to the standard scenario except for the Fuzzy LQE which shows a clear increase in radio-on time. In the interference scenario, each estimator consumes slightly more energy, albeit that the differences between them remain constant. In contrast, the scenario including mobility shows a lower energy consumption, but again the differences remain stable.

Overall, the simulation results show that combining information from multiple network layers improves the performance of link estimation at the cost of

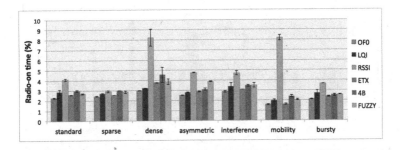

Fig. 3. Average radio-on time (in %) in the Cooja simulator.

an increased RPL overhead and thus a higher energy consumption. Therefore simple algorithms, such as hop count or LQI, are preferred in sparse or mobile scenarios.

4.2   iMinds w-iLab.t Testbed

Compared to the simulations, the results show a higher variance in the testbed experiments (see Figs. 4 and 5). In the standard scenario, the complex algorithms confirm the simulation results, although Fuzzy LQE performs slightly better with less energy consumption. The sparse scenario in the testbed also shows that the objective function 0 obtains a high PDR with a lower radio-on time. This is due to a low RPL-overhead and a small amount of retransmissions. In dense networks, the objective function 0, ETX and Fuzzy LQE algorithms obtain the best results. They even show an increase in PDR opposed to the decrease noticed in the simulator. The testbed results confirm that the Four bit algorithm has a degraded performance in dense networks.

Compared to the simulation results, the asymmetric scenario shows a decrease in performance for most simple algorithms, but an increase for the complex ones. This can be explained by the network configuration which gives certain nodes higher transmit power to increase asymmetry. The complex algorithms seem to benefit from this higher transmit power. The number of parent switches also decreases, due to larger difference in route qualities less path

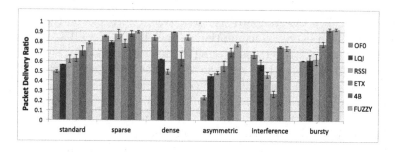

Fig. 4. Packet delivery ratio on the iMinds w-iLab.t testbed.

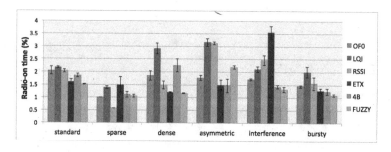

Fig. 5. Average radio-on time (in %) on the iMinds w-iLab.t testbed.

switches occur. The Four bit algorithm performs a lot better in the interference scenario compared to the simulation results, while ETX performs significantly less. These results clearly show the limitations on the LQI and RSSI values used in Cooja. The bursty scenario shows a performance increase compared to the standard scenario, contradictory to the results in the Cooja simulator.

5 Influence of RDC/MAC Protocol

Since several link estimators utilize information from received packets, the MAC protocol potentially has a significant influence on the choice of the optimal link estimator. This section investigates the effect of the RDC/MAC protocol and its settings on the PDR and radio-on time. In Contiki, the Radio Duty Cycling (RDC) driver is responsible for reducing the energy consumption by turning the radio on and off. The MAC driver is responsible for the CSMA/CA and for packet retransmissions in case of collisions. Both have a major impact on the PDR and radio-on time. ContikiMAC [6] and CSMA are the default RDC- and MAC-driver respectively. Other implementations of the RDC driver include X-MAC, CX-MAC and NullRDC. A dummy version of the MAC driver, i.e. nullMac, is also available.

As illustrated in Figs. 6 and 7, ContikiMAC outperforms other drivers with a higher PDR and low energy consumption. NullRDC obtains a slightly higher PDR compared to X-MAC, CX-MAC and NullMac, at the cost of a much higher energy consumption because NullRDC never turns the radio off. Despite this, NullRdc has much lower PDR then contikiMAC because it does not include

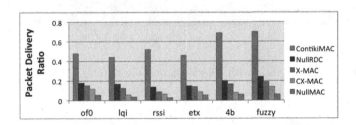

Fig. 6. Packet delivery ratio with several radio duty cycling protocols in the Cooja simulator.

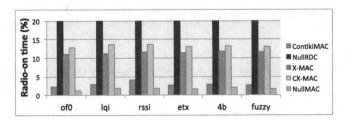

Fig. 7. Radio-on time of several radio duty cycling protocols in the Cooja simulator.

any retransmission. X-MAC and CX-MAC, have less strict timings to support more radio's and require 4 times more energy compared to ContikiMAC. They obtain a PDR close to NullRDC. NullMAC has the lowest energy consumption but also a very low PDR because no retransmission and CCA is performed. All MAC- and RDC-drivers seem to have an equal impact on all link estimation algorithms because the differences in performance between the estimators are retained. Contiki also allows us to specify a Channel Check Rate (CCR), which is the frequency the MAC- and RDC-driver use to turn on the radio and check the channel for possible transmissions. A higher CCR results in higher PDR (see Fig. 8), but requires more energy (see Fig. 9). Again, varying the CCR seems to has no impact on the type of estimator. The maximum amount of retransmissions can be freely chosen in ContikiRPL, which allows to limit excessive retransmissions and energy usage. The default value of 5 indicates there will be 6 attempts to send the packet before it gets dropped. Figure 10 indicates how much packets needed multiple retransmissions while performing the standard scenario on the w-iLab.t office testbed.

The results show that almost all packets that need two retransmissions, also required three or more retransmissions. This indicates that using more then two or three retransmission only has a minor impact on the packet delivery ratio, but causes a much higher energy consumption.

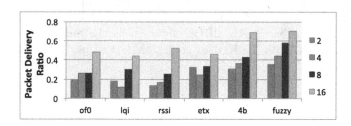

Fig. 8. Packet delivery ratio with several channel check rates in the Cooja simulator

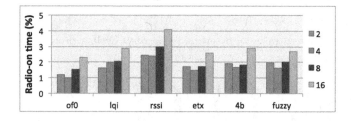

Fig. 9. Radio-on time of several channel check rates in the Cooja simulator.

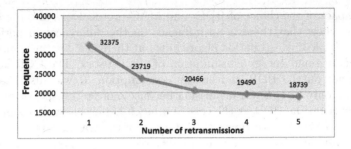

Fig. 10. Influence of maximum number of retransmissions in RPL.

6   Conclusions

Several link estimation algorithms were implemented for ContikiRPL. Next to ContikiRPL's standard objective function 0 and ETX algorithms two additional estimators based on the data link layer RSSI and LQI values and two more complex algorithms, i.e. Four bits and Fuzzy LQE, were added.

All link estimators were thoroughly evaluated in different dynamic network scenario's both in a simulation environment and in the real-life iMinds w-iLab.t office testbed. After evaluation using PDR and radio-on percentage as performance metrics, it can be concluded that there is no algorithm which performs best in all scenarios. In Table 3 an overview is given of the best performing algorithms for each scenario. Fuzzy LQE is the best choice in most scenario's while the Objective function 0 is better suited for the sparse and mobile scenarios. ETX is also a good choice in the dense and mobility scenario. The complex Four bit algorithm is only better in the asymmetric scenario at the cost of a higher energy consumption.

Table 3. Overview of the conclusions of this research.

Scenario	Best link estimation algorithm
Standard	Fuzzy LQE
Sparse	Objective function 0
Dense	Fuzzy LQE or ETX
Asymmetric	Four bit or Fuzzy LQE
Interference	Fuzzy LQE
Bursty	Fuzzy LQE
Mobility	ETX or objective function 0

The results obtained in the simulation environment show a high discrepancy with the results obtained in the iMinds w-iLab.t testbed. We can hence conclude that simulators are decent tools for algorithm development but lack capabilities to model real-life network characteristics and deliver reliable results.

The impact of the choice of RDC- and MAC-protocol was also investigated. The results show that there is no influence on the differences in performance between multiple link estimation algorithms but there is a difference in the overall performance and energy consumption of the network. The CCR also has a major impact on the PDR and energy consumption. It was also shown that there should only be two retransmission because more retransmissions only has a minor effect on the PDR at the cost of a much higher energy consumption.

Future work could investigate the influence of the transmit power, node distance or modulation scheme on the quality of a link. Moreover, since real-life networks are often a combination of multiple scenarios it can be interesting to combine different link estimation algorithms in a single network. The link estimators can also be further optimized. For instance, the mapping of LQI and RSSI values to a link metric can be varied, the thresholds in the Four bit algorithm can be changed and different membership and aggregation functions can be used in the Fuzzy LQE algorithm. An optimal link estimation algorithm would be self-adapting, changing the link estimator algorithm (settings) based on the observed network characteristics.

Acknowledgments. This work was partially supported by the Fund for Scientific Research-Flanders (FWO-V), project "ASN: wireless Acoustic Sensor Networks", grant #G.0763.12, and the agency for Innovation by Science and Technology Flanders (IWT-V), project "SAMURAI: Software Architecture and Modules for Unified RAdIo control", and the iMinds IoT Strategic Research program, and European Commission Horizon 2020 Programme under grant agreement n645274 (WiSHFUL).

References

1. iMinds w-iLab.t website. http://ilabt.iminds.be/iminds-wilabt-overview. Accessed 12 July 2015
2. Texas Instruments CC2420 Radio Datasheet. http://www.ti.com/lit/ds/symlink/cc2420.pdf. Accessed 12 July 2015
3. Baccour, N., Koubâa, A., Mottola, L., Zúñiga, M.A., Youssef, H., Boano, C.A., Alves, M.: Radio link quality estimation in wireless sensor networks: a survey. ACM Trans. Sens. Netw. **8**(4), 34:1–34:33 (2012)
4. Baccour, N., Koubâa, A., Youssef, H., Ben Jamâa, M., do Rosário, D., Alves, M., Becker, L.B.: F-LQE: a fuzzy link quality estimator for wireless sensor networks. In: Silva, J.S., Krishnamachari, B., Boavida, F. (eds.) EWSN 2010. LNCS, vol. 5970, pp. 240–255. Springer, Heidelberg (2010)
5. Dawans, S., Duquennoy, S., Bonaventure, O.: On link estimation in dense RPL deployments. In: 2012 IEEE 37th Conference on Local Computer Networks Workshops (LCN Workshops), pp. 952–955, October 2012
6. Dunkels, A.: The contikimac radio duty cycling protocol. Technical report, SICS (2011)
7. Fonseca, R., Gnawali, O., Jamieson, K., Philip, L.: Four bit wireless link estimation. In: Proceedings of the Sixth Workshop on Hot Topics in Networks (HotNets) (2007)
8. Gnawali, O., Fonseca, R., Jamieson, K., Kazandjieva, M., Moss, D., Levis, P.: CTP: an efficient, robust, and reliable collection tree protocol for wireless sensor networks. ACM Trans. Sens. Netw. **10**(1), 16:1–16:49 (2013)

9. Gungor, V.C., Korkmaz, M.K.: Wireless link-quality estimation in smart grid environments. Int. J. Distrib. Sens. Netw. **2012**, 10 p. (2012). Article ID 214068, doi:10. 1155/2012/214068

10. Iova, O., Theoleyre, F., Noel, T.: Stability and efficiency of RPL under realistic conditions in wireless sensor networks. In: 2013 IEEE 24th International Symposium on Personal Indoor and Mobile Radio Communications (PIMRC) (2013)

11. Javaid, N., Javaid, A., Khan, I., Djouani, K.: Performance study of ETX based wireless routing metrics. In: Computer, Control and Communication (IC4) (2009)

12. Klein, A., Braun, L., Oehlmann, F.: Performance study of the better approach to mobile adhoc networking (batman) protocol in the context of asymmetric links. In: World of Wireless, Mobile and Multimedia Networks (WoWMoM) (2012)

13. Meier, A., Rein, T., Beutel, J., Thiele, L.: Coping with unreliable channels: efficient link estimation for low-power wireless sensor networks. In: 5th International Conference on Networked Sensing Systems, INSS 2008, pp. 19–26, June 2008

14. Osterlind, F., Dunkels, A., Eriksson, J., Finne, N., Voigt, T.: Cross-level sensor network simulation with COOJA. In: Local Computer Networks (LCN) (2006)

15. Thubert, P.: Objective Function Zero for the Routing Protocol for Low-Power and Lossy Networks (RPL). RFC 6552 (Proposed Standard), March 2012

16. Tsiftes, N., Eriksson, J., Dunkels, A.: Low-power wireless IPv6 routing with ContikiRPL. In: International Conference on Information Processing in Sensor Networks, IPSN 2010. ACM (2010)

17. Winter, T., Thubert, P., Brandt, A., Hui, J., Kelsey, R., Levis, P., Pister, K., Struik, R., Vasseur, J., Alexander, R.: RPL: IPv6 Routing Protocol for Low-Power and Lossy Networks. RFC 6550 (Proposed Standard), March 2012

A Mobile Camera-Based Evaluation Method of Inertial Measurement Units on Smartphones

Lars Middendorf[1]([✉]), Rainer Dorsch[2], Rudolf Bichler[2], Christina Strohrmann[2], and Christian Haubelt[1]

[1] University of Rostock, Rostock, Germany
lars.middendorf@uni-rostock.de
[2] Bosch Sensortec GmbH, Reutlingen, Germany

Abstract. In order to support navigation, gesture detection, and augmented reality, modern smartphones contain inertial measurement units (IMU) consisting of accelerometers and gyroscopes. Although the accuracy of these sensors directly affects the soundness of mobile applications, no standardized tests exist to verify the correctness of the retrieved sensor data. For this purpose, we present a novel benchmark, which utilizes the camera of the phone as a reference to estimate the quality of its sensor data fusion. Our experiments do not require special equipment and reveal significant discrepancies between different phone models.

1 Introduction

A large number of mobile and ubiquitous applications for smartphones rely on a sound and stable orientation estimation. For example, a step counter [1] can improve the accuracy of indoor localization when the GPS signal becomes unavailable [2]. However, both the occurrence of a step and its direction must be measured precisely to track the relative movement of the user. Similarly, augmented reality applications [3] also require the exact orientation of the device to display context-dependent information on the screen, which should match the real environment as close as possible. For instance, the navigation application presented by [4] shows the direction to the destination as a perspective arrow within the camera image and counts the remaining number of steps. In addition, the detection of gestures for user authentication strongly depends on the accuracy of the IMU [5].

Inertial sensors are often built as micro-electro-mechanical systems (MEMS) to reduce size, power consumption, and production costs. According to [6], possible error sources are a constant bias, thermo-mechanical noise, bias instabilities due to flicker noise, temperature effects, and calibrations errors. Due to the integration, even small deviations can lead to significant differences. For example, a constant bias in the gyro causes a continuously growing angle error. As a result, the soundness of the sensor data at the application-level, is directly affected by the accuracy of the IMU.

As an introductory example for the relevance of an IMU benchmark, we show the results of a pedestrian tracking application running on three different but

© ICST Institute for Computer Sciences, Social Informatics and Telecommunications Engineering 2016
B. Mandler et al. (Eds.): IoT 360° 2015, Part II, LNICST 170, pp. 362–372, 2016.
DOI: 10.1007/978-3-319-47075-7_41

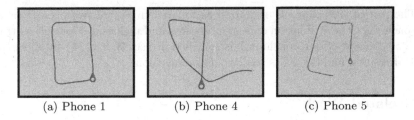

| (a) Phone 1 | (b) Phone 4 | (c) Phone 5 |

Fig. 1. Rectangular path measured on different phones.

anonymized phones (Fig. 1). Only *Phone 1* has correctly captured the rectangular shape, while the path of *Phone 5* is slightly deformed. On *Phone 4*, the second half of the path is flawed due to the integration of erroneous directions.

Consequently, the development of sensor-based applications requires extensive testing to deal with the large variations between different IMUs. As a possible solution, we present a benchmark for Android phones (Fig. 2), which measures both the static and dynamic accuracy of the sensor data fusion through the usage of the built-in camera and a specially developed reference pattern. For this purpose, the application simultaneously records sensor data and captures a video stream, which is then used to reconstruct the 3D orientation of the phone. Since the camera represents a potential error source, the latency between camera and sensor is compensated through a calibration procedure.

In particular, the innovations of our benchmark can be summarized as follows:

1. The camera of the smartphone is used to estimate a reference orientation. If the rotation vectors obtained from sensor and camera match, we can assume the correctness of the IMU.
2. Our benchmark computes an error metric, which permits the quantitative comparison of multiple test runs and different inertial sensors.
3. The test can be performed without additional equipment like an external camera system and requires only a sheet of paper containing the pattern.

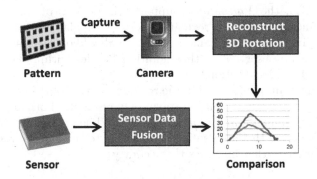

Fig. 2. Data flow model of our sensor benchmark.

The rest of this paper is organized as follows: In Sect. 2, we present related approaches for the evaluation of inertial sensors and techniques for optical tracking. The concept of our benchmark is specified in Sect. 3, Sect. 4 contains experimental results, and Sect. 5 is reserved for conclusion.

2 Related Work

Several methods for the calibration of IMUs through image processing already exist. For instance, the work presented in [7] utilizes an optical tracking system (*Optotrack*) consisting of three IR cameras and three LEDs, which are attached to the IMU in order to determine its absolute orientation. In addition, the relative orientation between a camera and an IMU can be estimated by capturing several images of a chessboard and correlating the vertical lines with the gravity vector [8]. Further, also the mirrored image of the camera is suitable for self-calibration of the sensor [9]. Our approach takes the opposite direction and assumes a fixed orientation between camera and IMU to evaluate its accuracy.

Determining the orientation of the device from a single camera image requires a set of *feature points* in screen space and their corresponding coordinates in world space. For this purpose, iterative algorithms like [10] provide a robust solution in case of inaccurate input data. Although four coplanar points are sufficient to compute the relative camera orientation [11], a larger number of features increase both the accuracy and the robustness of the result [12]. Our benchmark utilizes the algorithm presented by [13], which accepts a variable number of corresponding points for calculating the camera orientation and has been implemented in the *OpenCV* library [14].

The detection of feature points usually depends on distinct markers, which encode their world position in form of different shapes [15]. Alternatively, each marker can be uniquely identified by patterns of black and white blocks [16]. In comparison to a more regular chessboard [17], this technique permits extensive rotations of the camera because only a sub-set of the markers must be visible in each frame. However, for use cases like the video-based augmented reality conferencing system [18], six markers are adequate to locate a virtual shared whiteboard. Also, the *VideoMouse* supports six degrees of freedom [19] and contains a camera to record a regular pattern of circular markers. Due to the restricted viewing angle of the camera, only a small and quickly changing section of the grid can be observed, so that additional codes within the markers are necessary for global localization.

Since we are mainly interested in the relative rotation of the camera, we have chosen a regular pattern of uniform squares. It resembles both [13,19] but can be detected in a similar way to QR codes [20]. While one rectangle offers four feature points and is therefore sufficient to estimate the camera rotation, each additional marker further increases the accuracy.

3   Benchmark

The test procedure (Fig. 2) consists of an image processing step, which determines the relative rotation of the phone, the recording of sensor data, and the final evaluation. In particular, the reconstruction of the rotation and the analysis of the results represent the main contributions of this paper, which are discussed in the following sections.

3.1   Overview

In order to compute the rotation of the phone from a camera frame, a set of corresponding feature points must be found in the image. For this purpose, we have designed a reference pattern (Fig. 3a), according to the following requirements:

- The benchmark is performed in office environments under different lighting conditions and backgrounds.
- The benchmark runs on a mobile phone with memory restrictions and limited computational power.
- Since the phone is rotated during the test, a small part of the pattern must be sufficient to compute its orientation.

Our pattern contains a regular grid of uniforms squares, which are enclosed by a thick border. All elements are either black or white to reduce memory usage as well as the complexity of image processing. As a consequence, the contrast is increased so that the quality of the camera becomes less important. In addition, the thick border helps to distinguish the squares of the pattern from the background. Since the rotation of a single square is ambiguous for steps of 90°, we include an internal marker to determine its actual rotation. Further, the edge length of each square is three times larger than the width of the border and the padding, which is used for identification. As a result, the pattern can be printed in any size and can contain an arbitrary number of squares as long as its relative proportions remain constant.

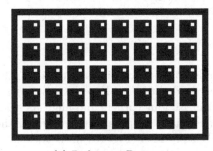

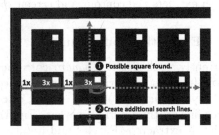

(a) Reference Pattern	(b) Detection of Squares

Fig. 3. Reference pattern developed for the purpose of the tracking; it is used for measuring the orientation of the camera. (Color figure online)

The image processing algorithm first looks for the pattern and collects screen space coordinates of each square. Although the four corners of a square are sufficient to compute the rotation of the camera [21], a larger number of squares significantly increases the accuracy. Due to the regularity of the pattern, already detected squares are used as hints to guide the further search. In a second step, the relation between squares is examined to assign world space coordinates, which are then used for 3D reconstruction. In the next sections, these two steps are described in more detail.

3.2   Detecting Possible Squares

The goal of this first step is to compute a list of *possible squares* from the 8-bit greyscale image. We start by applying a binary threshold for simplification, so that the resulting pixels are either set to 0 or 255. Experiments have shown that a threshold of 128 is sufficient to highlight the pattern. Due to the white balancing in the camera of modern phones, an adaptive filtering is not necessary.

The next step utilizes the unique proportion between squares and spacing to separate the pattern from the background. For this purpose, we trace a set of random lines through the image and look for alternating black and white segments. According to the design of the pattern (Fig. 3b), the characteristic ratio between these segments corresponds to $\approx 3:1$ if the camera is aligned in parallel to the raster. However, in order to improve the detected of squares at steep angles, the ratio of $\approx 3:1$ is automatically adapted by our algorithm.

If a run of at least four consecutive segments has been found, the current position might be located at the border of square region (red). Hence, the center of the square can be reached by stepping back half of the distance (blue).

Since only lines, which are more or less aligned to the pattern, satisfy these conditions, we can speed up the search by creating more appropriate lines (green). After a square has been found, additional search lines are constructed through the midpoints of opposing sides. Consequently, they are automatically aligned to the grid and intersect most likely several other squares. As a result, the entire pattern can be retrieved from a single square in two iterations. Finally, each region is flood-filled with a different color and passed to the next stage, which extracts the contour and screen space coordinates of the square.

3.3   Extracting Valid Squares

Currently, each *possible square* corresponds to a set of pixels with a specific color. In order to derive its screen space coordinates, we have to ensure that the region is actually a valid square, discover its four corners and align its sides according to the internal marker (Fig. 4). For this purpose, the contour of the region is extracted (Fig. 4a) and iteratively simplified (Fig. 4b) until it consists of exactly four points (Fig. 4c). Invalid regions either vanish during this process or converge to a polygon with a different number of corners.

To compensate for inaccuracies during the simplification step, the corners of the remaining squares are adapted to match the color gradient in the original

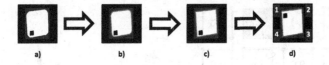

Fig. 4. Extraction and alignment of a square.

image (*cornerSubPix*). Since the 3D reconstruction requires consistent world space coordinates, the squares must be also aligned, so that the internal marker is located at the first point. Let $p_1, p_2, p_3, p_4 \in \mathbb{R}^2$ be the screen space coordinates of the square. Based on the construction of the pattern, the four possible locations of the marker $m_1, m_2, m_3, m_4 \in \mathbb{R}^2$ are given by the weighted sums:

$$m_1 := \tfrac{9}{16} \cdot p_1 + \tfrac{3}{16} \cdot p_2 + \tfrac{1}{16} \cdot p_3 + \tfrac{3}{16} \cdot p_4$$
$$m_2 := \tfrac{3}{16} \cdot p_1 + \tfrac{9}{16} \cdot p_2 + \tfrac{3}{16} \cdot p_3 + \tfrac{1}{16} \cdot p_4$$
$$m_3 := \tfrac{1}{16} \cdot p_1 + \tfrac{3}{16} \cdot p_2 + \tfrac{9}{16} \cdot p_3 + \tfrac{3}{16} \cdot p_4$$
$$m_4 := \tfrac{3}{16} \cdot p_1 + \tfrac{1}{16} \cdot p_2 + \tfrac{3}{16} \cdot p_3 + \tfrac{9}{16} \cdot p_4$$

Since the square is printed in black and the marker is printed in white, it can be identified by choosing the brightest of all four possible locations. Finally, the points of the square are rotated until p_1 corresponds to the corner of the marker.

3.4 Collecting Squares

While the four screen space coordinates of each square are known at this point, we also require corresponding world space coordinates to compute the orientation of the camera. Actually, the square can be placed anywhere on a XY-plane in world space because relative distances are sufficient to determine the current rotation vector. Hence, the four coordinates $w_1, w_2, w_3, w_4 \in \mathbb{R}^3$ of a single square are defined as follows:

$$w_1 := (0,0,0) \qquad w_2 := \left(\tfrac{3}{4},0,0\right) \qquad w_3 := \left(\tfrac{3}{4},\tfrac{3}{4},0\right) \qquad w_4 := \left(0,\tfrac{3}{4},0\right)$$

The size of $\tfrac{3}{4}$ is specified according to the ratio of $(3 : 1)$ between squares and spacing in the pattern, which becomes especially important when using multiple squares. In this case, their relation must be considered as well to construct a global coordinate system. In particular, two squares are either neighbours in one of the four directions (*left, right, up, down*) or not directly connected. Each direction is associated with an offset in world space, so that one of the two squares can be placed at the origin, while the other is shifted accordingly.

By iteratively assigning coordinates of adjacent squares, we can successively construct a world space coordinate system as shown in Fig. 5. In this example, some of the squares are missing (*dark*) and the initial square (*grey*) is placed at the origin $(0,0)$. The arrows (*green*) illustrate the incremental expansion, so that the square at the right of $(0,0)$ gets an offset of $(1,0)$. In order to determine the

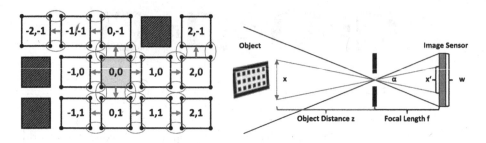

Fig. 5. Building the coordinate system.
(Color figure online)

Fig. 6. Pinhole camera model.

relation of two arbitrary squares, the distances between the four pairs of opposing edges (*red*) are calculated. Due to the layout of the pattern, two edges can be considered as adjacent if their average distance is shorter than their length. At the end of this iterative process, all squares either belong to the connected subset containing the origin or correspond to separated isles, which are removed from the set. Hence, in case of n valid squares, the result contains $4n$ pairs of screen space and world space coordinates.

3.5   Camera Model

Our camera model describes the relation between a point in homogeneous coordinates (x, y, z) and its projection (x', y', z') on the screen using the equation:

$$\begin{pmatrix} x' \\ y' \\ z' \end{pmatrix} := I \cdot R \cdot \begin{pmatrix} x \\ y \\ z \end{pmatrix} \tag{1}$$

In particular, the rotation matrix R is the unknown variable to be determined, while the intrinsic matrix I can be derived from the camera model (Fig. 6). We utilize a pinhole camera, which is characterized by the focal length f and the field-of-view α. According to the intercept theorem, the relation between the width x of an object and its projection x' is given by:

$$\frac{x}{x'} = \frac{z}{f} \Leftrightarrow x' = \frac{x \cdot f}{z}$$

This relation can be also expressed in homogeneous coordinates using a projection matrix P:

$$\begin{pmatrix} x' \\ y' \\ z' \end{pmatrix} := P \cdot \begin{pmatrix} x \\ y \\ z \end{pmatrix} \quad \text{width } P := \begin{pmatrix} f & 0 & 0 \\ 0 & f & 0 \\ 0 & 0 & 1 \end{pmatrix}$$

The coordinates are scaled according to the size $w \times h$ (matrix S) of the image sensor and its resolution $u \times v$:

$$I := S \cdot P = \begin{pmatrix} \frac{u}{w} & 0 & \frac{u}{2} \\ 0 & \frac{v}{h} & \frac{v}{2} \\ 0 & 0 & 1 \end{pmatrix} \begin{pmatrix} f & 0 & 0 \\ 0 & f & 0 \\ 0 & 0 & 1 \end{pmatrix} = \begin{pmatrix} \frac{f \cdot u}{w} & 0 & \frac{u}{2} \\ 0 & \frac{f \cdot v}{h} & \frac{v}{2} \\ 0 & 0 & 1 \end{pmatrix}$$

The width w of the image sensor is derived via trigonometry,

$$\tan\left(\tfrac{\alpha}{2}\right) = \tfrac{w}{2 \cdot f} \Leftrightarrow w = 2 \cdot f \cdot \tan\left(\tfrac{\alpha}{2}\right)$$

while the height h can be computed from the aspect ratio:

$$h = w \cdot \tfrac{v}{u}$$

Therefore, the intrinsic matrix I of the camera is given by:

$$I := \begin{pmatrix} \lambda & 0 & \tfrac{u}{2} \\ 0 & \lambda & \tfrac{v}{2} \\ 0 & 0 & 1 \end{pmatrix} \text{ with } \lambda := \tfrac{f \cdot u}{w}$$

Beside the rotation matrix R, all variables of Eq. (1) are known. As a result, we can insert the $4n$ pairs of world space and screen space coordinates to compute an approximation of R via [11–13] or the OpenCV method *solvePnP* [14].

3.6 Evaluation

Since the reference pattern (Fig. 3) can be placed anywhere for testing, it is impossible to determine the absolute orientation of the camera from the image. As a consequence, our benchmark compares relative rotations of camera and sensor with regard to a reference orientation, which is captured at the beginning of a test run.

Optimally, the relative rotation angles match at all times but since camera and sensor are usually implemented as separate hardware components, their time stamps are not synchronized. We have examined a latency of approximately one frame between camera and inertial sensor. Since the sensor usually produces a significant higher number of samples, both curves must be adjusted and cross-correlated to minimize this error.

For a test run of length l, the error $e(t)$ at time t is defined as the shorted rotation angle in degrees between camera and sensor. As a result, we can define an error score E as the weighted mean error over the time t of the test.

$$E := \frac{1}{t} \int_0^t e(x)dx \tag{2}$$

The unit of E is degrees and smaller values are better.

4   Results

Based on the concept of Sect. 3, we have developed a benchmarking application for *Android* phones, which records the video sequence of a reference gesture (Fig. 7) in order to compute the dynamic accuracy of the IMU. The error score is calculated in a post-processing step and defined by the integral of the mean deviation between camera and sensor angles (2). The application also shows a detailed presentation in form of graphs and statistics for every test run.

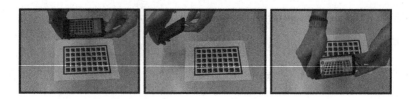

Fig. 7. Gestures performed for the rotation test.

Table 1. Results of the rotation test and the pedestrian tracker

Phone	Rotation vector		Game rotation vector		Pedestrian tracker
	$\overline{x}$	σ	$\overline{x}$	σ	Score $s \in [-1, 1]$
Phone 1	1.48	0.20	1.33	0.23	0.208
Phone 2	2.35	0.29	1.37	0.13	−0.278
Phone 3	4.67	3.89	1.75	0.61	0.083
Phone 4	6.79	3.58	7.89	0.96	−0.333
Phone 5	9.62	11.96	n/a	n/a	−0.125

Our benchmark has been evaluated using the *LG G3*, the *Samsung S5*, the *LG Nexus 5*, the *Moto G2*, and the *HTC One*, which are anonymized in a different order as *Phone 1* to *Phone 5*. During a test run, the phone is tilted $\approx 40°$ forwards, backwards, and to both sides, while the camera is pointed at the pattern (Fig. 7). As a possible error source, blurring artefacts might prevent the correct detection of the pattern, so that the speed of the gesture must be adapted according to the quality and exposure time of the camera. Therefore, smaller resolutions like 800×480 pixels usually provide more accurate results than HD recordings due to higher frame rates.

The rotation gesture is performed manually but repeated ten times per phone to improve the significance of the benchmark. Table 1 lists the mean error ($\overline{x}$) as well as the standard deviation (σ). We are using both the default rotation vector and the game rotation vector, which are acquired using the *SensorManager* API of Android. While the default rotation vector is automatically recalibrated by a compass, the game rotation vector is better suited for fast movements and cannot be disturbed by magnetic influences. The results show significant differences between the evaluated phones. In particular, the average error is less than 3° for *Phone 1* and *Phone 2* but reaches almost 10° for *Phone 5*. For the three best phones, the game rotation vector (not available on Phone 5) offers even better results with an error score of less than 2°.

Our benchmark assumes that the reconstructed rotation vector from the camera is more accurate than the rotation obtained directly from the IMU. Since both rotations are computed using entirely different algorithms, a correlation between camera and sensor is a strong indicator for the correctness of the measurement. The reproducibility of our test is further emphasized by the fact that accurate results coincide with a small standard deviation of less than 1°. However, in case of discrepancies like *Phone 5*, it remains ambiguous whether the camera, the IMU, or both provide erroneous data.

For comparison, we have also evaluated the pedestrian tracker application using various paths, which results in a score $s \in [-1, 1]$ for each phone (Table 1). Contrary to the rotation test, larger values are better in this case and we can detect a coincidence between precise results. For instance, *Phone 1* produces sound results in both tests, while *Phone 4* and *Phone 5* are much less reliable with $\bar{x} > 6$ and $\sigma > 3$.

5   Conclusion

This paper describes the concept of a mobile and camera-based benchmarking method for inertial sensors and sensor fusion on smartphones. As a result, we can identify significant discrepancies between the accuracy of different IMUs, which also affect their usability at the application-level. In contrast to existing methods, our benchmark does not require an expensive test environment but can be performed using a recent *Android* phone and the reference pattern printed on a single sheet of paper. Future work includes improving the reproducibility of the test, supporting a wider range of movements, and detecting external error sources like magnetic fields.

References

1. Mladenov, M., Mock, M.: A step counter service for Java-enabled devices using a built-in accelerometer. In: COMSWARE 2009. CAMS (2009)
2. Serra, A., Carboni, D., Marotto, V.: Indoor pedestrian navigation system using a modern smartphone. In: MobileHCI 2010 (2010)
3. Schmalstieg, D., Wagner, D.: Experiences with handheld augmented reality. In: Mixed and Augmented Reality, ISMAR 2007 (2007)
4. Mulloni, A., Seichter, H., Schmalstieg, D.: Handheld augmented reality indoor navigation with activity-based instructions. In: MobileHCI 2011 (2011)
5. Liu, J., Zhong, L., Wickramasuriya, J., Vasudevan, V.: uWave: accelerometer-based personalized gesture recognition and its applications. Pervasive Mob. Comput. **5**(6), 657–675 (2009)
6. Woodman, O.J.: An introduction to inertial navigation. University of Cambridge, Computer Laboratory, Technical report UCAMCL-TR-696, vol. 26(6), pp. 561–575 (2007)
7. Kim, A., Golnaraghi, M.: Initial calibration of an inertial measurement unit using an optical position tracking system. In: PLANS 2004 (2004)
8. Lobo, J., Dias, J.: Relative pose calibration between visual and inertial sensors. Int. J. Robot. Res. **26**(6), 561–575 (2007)
9. Panahandeh, G., Jansson, M.: IMU-camera self-calibration using planar mirror reflection. In: Indoor Positioning and Indoor Navigation (IPIN) (2011)
10. Oberkampf, D., DeMenthon, D., Davis, L.: Iterative pose estimation using coplanar points. In: Computer Vision and Pattern Recognition (1993)

11. Gao, X.S., Hou, X.-R., Tang, J., Cheng, H.-F.: Complete solutionclassification for the perspective-three-point problem. IEEE Trans. Pattern Anal. Mach. Intell. **25**(8), 930–943 (2003)

12. Lepetit, V., Moreno-Noguer, F., Fua, P.: EPnP: an accurate o(n) solution to the PnP problem. Int. J. Comput. Vis. **81**(2), 155–166 (2009)

13. Zhang, Z.: A flexible new technique for camera calibration. IEEE Trans. Pattern Anal. Mach. Intell. **22**(11), 1330–1334 (2000)

14. Bradski, G., Kaehler, A.: Learning OpenCV: Computer Vision with the OpenCV Library. O'Reilly Media Inc., Sebastopol (2008)

15. Zhang, X., Fronz, S., Navab, N.: Visual marker detection, decoding in AR systems: a comparative study. In: Mixed and Augmented Reality. ISMAR (2002)

16. Fiala, M., Shu, C.: Self-identifying patterns for plane-based camera calibration. Mach. Vis. Appl. **19**(4), 209–216 (2008)

17. Kelly, J., Sukhatme, G.S.: Visual-inertial sensor fusion: localization, mapping and sensor-to-sensor self-calibration. Int. J. Robot. Res. **30**, 56–79 (2011)

18. Kato, H., Billinghurst, M.: Marker tracking and HMD calibration for a video-based augmented reality conferencing system. In: IWAR 1999 (1999)

19. Hinckley, K., Sinclair, M., Hanson, E., Szeliski, R., Conway, M.: The videomouse: a camera-based multidegree-of-freedom input device. In: ACM UIST 1999 (1999)

20. Liu, Y., Yang, J., Liu, M.: Recognition of QR code with mobile phones. In: 2008 Chinese Control and Decision Conference, CCDC 2008, July 2008

21. Nister, D.: An efficient solution to the five-point relative pose problem. IEEE Trans. Pattern Anal. Mach. Intell. **26**(6), 756–770 (2004)

Fast Phase Analysis of SAW Delay Lines

Christian Gruber[(⊠)], Alfred Binder, and Martin Lenzhofer

Carinthian Tech Research AG, Europastrasse 4/1, 9524 Villach, Austria
{christian.gruber,martin.lenzhofer,
alfred.binder}@ctr.at

Abstract. Today continuous wave (CW) radar systems have been established as a standard method to interrogate surface acoustic wave (SAW) delay line sensors. They provide an ideal solution with high accuracy and reasonable reading distances for low dynamic measured quantities, which do not change fast in time. But their relatively long reading cycles [1] makes them unsuitable for high dynamic measurements. This paper illustrates a concept of an interrogation principle based on a pulse radar system which allows decreasing the reading cycle of a SAW delay line to a minimum of about 3 μs given by the physical dimension of the SAW delay line tag itself [2, 3].

Keywords: SAW · Surface Acoustic Wave Sensor · SAW sensor interrogation · Pulse radar · I/Q-demodulation

1 Introduction

Today surface acoustic wave (SAW) sensor technology is a state of the art technology to measure physical quantities like temperature, pressure and force. As a passive radio sensor technology don't need either any external power supply or additional electronic circuitry to operate, which enables them to operate almost without any limitations in their life time and makes them very robust against hazardous environmental conditions, e.g. high temperatures up to 400°C, hard radiation and strong electromagnetic interference [3].

A sensor system based on SAWs consists of a SAW tag and a reader unit (Fig. 1) which excites the sensor with a radio signal similar to the signals used in common radar systems. State of the art reader units, utilize continuous wave CW radar to interrogate the sensor. There are three different types of CW radars: Frequency modulated (FMCW), frequency stepped (FSCW) and switched frequency stepped (S-FSCW) continuous wave radar [4, 5]. All three radar types are using an RF ramp within the ISM band of 2.4 GHz. The duration of one sweep reaches from 100 μs (FMCW) to 125 ms (FSCW) and is limited by the used technology [1]. This results in one measurement per 100 μs (in FMCW), but usually, to improve the signal to noise ratio in order to increase accuracy and reading distance, the mean of several sweeps is taken. For measurements with low dynamic, i.e. which do not change fast in time, the used method is sufficient, but for high dynamic applications such as vibrations, accelerations or fast moving objects the applied method is not adequate and another interrogation principle is needed. In this paper we will present an interrogation principle, which uses

© ICST Institute for Computer Sciences, Social Informatics and Telecommunications Engineering 2016
B. Mandler et al. (Eds.): IoT 360° 2015, Part II, LNICST 170, pp. 373–382, 2016.
DOI: 10.1007/978-3-319-47075-7_42

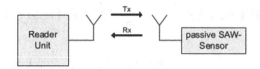

Fig. 1. Wireless transmission between reader unit and passive SAW sensor.

short pulses to interrogate a SAW delay line sensor, which enables to reduce the interrogation cycle to the limits of the sensor chip itself rather than to the limits of the reader technology.

2 SAW Sensor Delay Line Principle

SAW sensors use the propagation speed of SAWs on a plain polished piezoelectric substrate. The propagation speed depends on the material properties of the substrate which on the other hand are sensitive to environmental influences, for instance changing temperature of the substrate changes its elasticity constant which directly effects the wave propagation. The SAW is about 10^{-5} slower as the propagation of electromagnetic waves – therefore the name "SAW Delay Line Sensor".

The excitation occurs by metallic structures, the so called interdigital transducers (IDTs), arranged on the surface of the substrate. In the simplest case, the structure looks like two interlocking combs as shown in Fig. 2. If an alternating electrical signal is applied to the IDT, the piezoelectric substrate will expand and contract according to the applied electric field which generates a mechanical wave – surface acoustic wave – propagating across the substrate's surface. Vice versa a SAW passing the IDT generates an electric signal which can be measured on the connections of the IDT.

Delay line sensors use the propagation delay τ between two points on the substrate. Arranging two IDTs oppositely with a certain distance d according Fig. 3, a two port SAW delay line has been created. Applying a signal on the input IDT results in a time shifted and attenuated signal on the output IDT.

A big disadvantage of two port delay line SAW sensors is the fact that they have two ports which makes them not very suitable for wireless applications because additional radio frequency (RF) circuitry is needed directly on the SAW chip to separate the incoming and outgoing RF signals. Since SAW sensors are dealing with

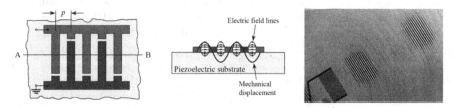

Fig. 2. Top view of an interdigital transducer on the left side, and its AB-cross section in the center. Propagating wave packages generated by an IDT on the left side [3].

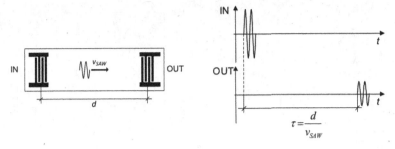

Fig. 3. IDT arrangement and input and output signals of a two port SAW delay line sensor.

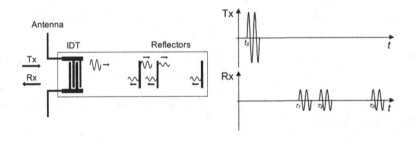

Fig. 4. IDT arrangement and input and output signals of a two port SAW delay line sensor.

waves, it is possible to use reflection to overcome this problem. In the simplest case we just take the second – or output – IDT and just let it open. The incoming wave front will see a not suitably matched interface which results in a reflection – or partial reflection – of the wave back to first – or input – IDT. This concept can be expanded to a one port multi reflective SAW delay line by arranging multiple reflectors on the substrate. Figure 4 illustrates a one port delay line sensor with three reflectors.

The reflectors are designed in a way that one portion of the SAW will be reflected while the other portion of the SAW will pass the reflector and propagate towards the next reflector where again a portion will be reflected and so on. Finally the received signal of a SAW delay line sensor is a sum of time shifted sinusoids.

3   Time Delay Measurement

The measurement of time delay between the transmitted and received signals can be done in different ways. One method is to measure the time duration of the envelope between transmitted and received pulses by a counter. Another method is evaluating the phase shift between the received pulses and a reference oscillation which is in-phase with the transmitted pulse as shown in Fig. 5a. Evaluating the phase shift may

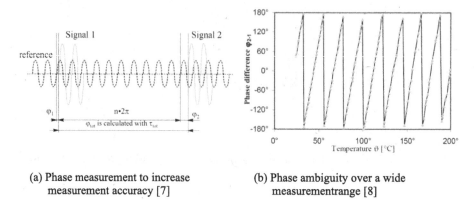

(a) Phase measurement to increase
measurement accuracy [7]

(b) Phase ambiguity over a wide
measurementrange [8]

Fig. 5. Evaluation of phase difference to increase measurement accuracy [3]

increase the resolution significantly by a factor of 100. For large measurement ranges, especially in the case of temperature measurement, the phase shift caused by the measured value can be larger than 2π, or even several multiple of 2π, so that a phase ambiguity, shown in Fig. 5b, occurs. To evaluate absolute values, at least three reflectors are needed [3, 7, 8].

4   Sensor Interrogation Principle with Cosine Bursts

As already stated, the fundamental principle of SAW delay line sensors is using, the variation of propagation speed of SAWs. Evaluating the signal delay allows to calculate the desired measurement quantity. The Signal delay can either be determined in the frequency domain, using CW radar, or in the time domain using pulse radar.

Instead of using a frequency modulated continuous wave, a sequence of pulsed cosine bursts (Fig. 7a) in the ISM-band at 2.4 GHz will be sent to the SAW sensor. Figure 6 shows an overview of the system with a minimal set of components to describe the theoretical aspects of the principle.

The impulse response of the SAW-sensors $h_{SAW}(t)$ can be assumed as a sequence of weighted Dirac impulses shown in Fig. 7b where each Dirac impulse corresponds to a reflector of the SAW-Sensor. It is well known that in the time domain the output signal of a system is the convolution of the input signal with the impulse response of the system. Therefore the received signal is a repeating sequence of the transmitted signal shown in Fig. 7c.

The transmitted signal $s_t(t)$ can be described as a cosine function with amplitude A, angular frequency ω and phase shift ϕ multiplied with a rectangular function:

$$s_t(t) = A \cdot \cos(\omega t + \phi) \cdot \sqcap (t). \tag{1}$$

As mentioned above the received signal $s_r(t)$ is a sequence of delayed bursts. It can be described as a sum of the transmitted signal shifted by τ_i and attenuated by α_i and α_p

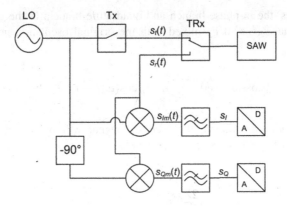

Fig. 6. IDT arrangement and input and output signals of a two port SAW delay line sensor.

where α_i is characterized by the impulse response of the SAW-Sensor and α_p is the overall attenuation of the transmission path

$$s_r(t) = \sum_{i=1}^{n} A\alpha_i\alpha_p \cos(\omega(t - \tau_i) + \phi) \cdot \sqcap(t - \tau_i). \tag{2}$$

After receiving the signal, it will be demodulated by an in-phase quadrature demodulator (I/Q-demodulator). In I/Q-demodulation the received signal $s_r(t)$ is split

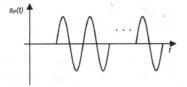

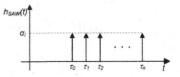

(a) Transmitted cosine burst

(b) Model of the impulse response of an ideal reflective delay line sensor

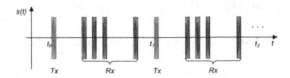

(c) Transmitted request sequence (Tx) and received response sequence (Rx) of a delay line SAW sensor

Fig. 7. Pulse radar sensor interrogation signal.

into two branches, the in-phase branch and quadrature branch. In the in-phase branch the received signal $s_r(t)$ will be mixed with the original oscillation generated by the local oscillator,

$$s_{Im}(t) = A\cos(\omega t + \phi) \cdot \sum_{i=1}^{n} A\alpha_i\alpha_p \cos(\omega(t - \tau_i) + \phi) \cdot \sqcap (t - \tau_i), \qquad (3)$$

while in the quadrature branch, the received signal will be mixed with the local oscillation shifted by $-90°$ or $-\pi/2$ respectively

$$s_{Qm}(t) = A\cos\left(\omega t + \phi - \frac{\pi}{2}\right) \cdot \sum_{i=1}^{n} A\alpha_i\alpha_p \cos(\omega(t - \tau_i) + \phi) \cdot \sqcap (t - \tau_i). \qquad (4)$$

For further considerations we will neglect that the received signal is a sum of bursts and look at each element of the sum separately. This is permitted because the single bursts are isolated in time and do not interfere with each other. This results for the in-phase sequence into

$$s_{Imi}(t) = A\cos(\omega t + \phi) \cdot A\alpha_i\alpha_p \cos(\omega(t - \tau_i) + \phi)$$
$$s_{Imi}(t) = A^2\alpha_i\alpha_p \cos(\omega t + \phi)\cos(\omega(t - \tau_i) + \phi) \qquad (5)$$

And for the quadrature sequence into

$$s_{Qmi}(t) = A\cos\left(\omega t + \phi - \frac{\pi}{2}\right) \cdot A\alpha_i\alpha_p \cos(\omega(t - \tau_i) + \phi)$$
$$s_{Qmi}(t) = A^2\alpha_i\alpha_p \cos\left(\omega t + \phi - \frac{\pi}{2}\right)\cos(\omega(t - \tau_i) + \phi) \qquad (6)$$

From the trigonometric product-to-sum identity [6] it is known that a product of two cosines can be expressed as a sum of two cosines where the argument of the two summands is the sum and the difference respectively, of the arguments of the two factors, divided by 2.

$$\cos(x) \cdot \cos(y) = \frac{1}{2}[\cos(x - y) + \cos(x + y)] \qquad (7)$$

Applying the trigonometric identity to the two signals $s_{Imi}(t)$ and $s_{Qmi}(t)$ results into

$$s_{Imi}(t) = A^2\alpha_i\alpha_p \frac{1}{2}[\cos(\omega\tau_i) + \cos(2\omega t - \omega\tau_i + 2\varphi)] \qquad (8)$$

and

$$s_{Qmi}(t) = A^2\alpha_i\alpha_p \frac{1}{2}[\sin(\omega\tau_i) + \sin(2\omega t - \omega\tau_i + 2\varphi)] \qquad (9)$$

Because the frequencies of both signals are equal, the time dependent component in the argument of the left cosine function vanishes and results in a DC-component. Due to the addition of the arguments in the right cosine function, a harmonic oscillation with twice the frequency of the original carrier signal is being obtained. In practice this term usually has no relevance and will be filtered out by a low pass filter. This finally results in the two expressions

$$s_{Ii}(\tau_i) = \frac{A^2 \alpha_i \alpha_p}{2} \cos(\omega \tau_i) \tag{10}$$

and

$$s_{Qi}(\tau_i) = \frac{A^2 \alpha_i \alpha_p}{2} \sin(\omega \tau_i) \tag{11}$$

Now there are the two signals s_{Ii} and s_{Qi}, both have the same amplitudes. By dividing them they will be canceled out which results in

$$\frac{s_{Qi}}{s_{Ii}} = \frac{\sin(\omega \tau_i)}{\cos(\omega \tau_i)} \tag{12}$$

Since the tangent of an angle φ_i is the ratio of the sine to the cosine, one can calculate the angle by taking the inverse tangent:

$$\tan(\varphi_i) = \frac{\sin(\varphi_i)}{\cos(\varphi_i)} = \frac{s_{Qi}}{s_{Ii}} \Rightarrow \varphi_i = \tan^{-1}\left(\frac{s_{Qi}}{s_{Ii}}\right) \tag{13}$$

The result represents a direct determination of the phase shift between reference oscillation and received bursts from the delay line by computing the inverse tangent of the quotient of the sampled and A/D-converted quadrature and in-phase signal levels.

5 Matlab/Simulink Simulation

The previously discussed interrogation concept has been verified by simulation in Matlab/Simulink. Since signal paths in Simulink are only unidirectional, i.e. signals can only propagate in one direction, the Simulink model differs slightly from the discussed model in Fig. 6. Especially a one port SAW delay line sensors is not able to model with only one port, so it has been realized as two port system but with the same behavior, Fig. 8 shows the modeling of the SAW delay line. Due to the fact that there transmitted and received signals do not share the same transmission paths, the TRx switch in Fig. 6 is obsolete as well and is therefore not modeled in the Simulink simulation. Figure 9 shows the simulation model, with burst generation, SAW delay line modeling, in-phase and quadrature mixing and low-pass filtering.

Running the simulation results in the following signals: The local oscillator generates a continuous cosine signal which is split into two branches. The first one feeds the switch, which generates the cosine bursts (yellow signal in Fig. 10a) sent to the SAW delay line. The output of the SAW delay line is a sequence of attenuated and delayed copy of the input signal (magenta signal in Fig. 10a). The output of the SAW delay line is then fed to the I/Q-demodulator where on one hand it is directly mixed with the signal of the local oscillator and on the other hand with the 90° phase shifted signal of the local oscillator which results in the two signals shown in Fig. 10b. After low pass filtering we get the DC-like signals in Fig. 10d and e, where the phase shift can be calculated by sampling the signal levels of the in-phase and quadrature channels.

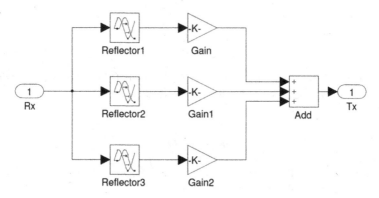

Fig. 8. Simulink sub system block.

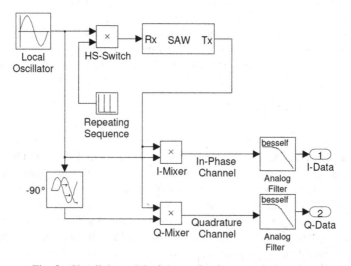

Fig. 9. Simulink model of the analog interrogation system.

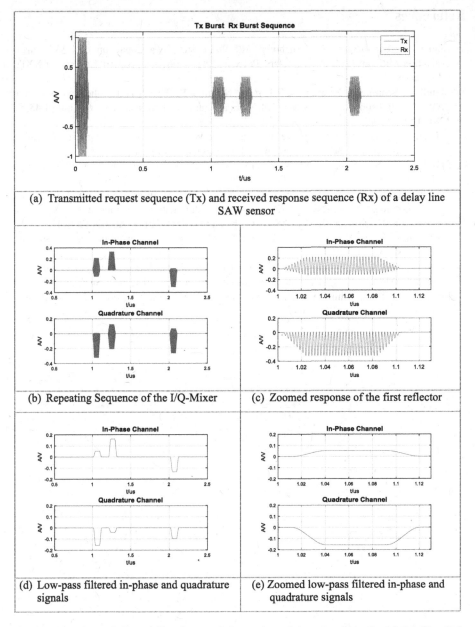

(a) Transmitted request sequence (Tx) and received response sequence (Rx) of a delay line SAW sensor

(b) Repeating Sequence of the I/Q-Mixer

(c) Zoomed response of the first reflector

(d) Low-pass filtered in-phase and quadrature signals

(e) Zoomed low-pass filtered in-phase and quadrature signals

Fig. 10. Signal processing chain of transmitting and receiving signals in the Matlab/Simulink simulation. (Color figure online)

References

1. Binder, A., Fachberger, R., Lenzhofer, M.: Phase stability comparison of SAW sensor evaluation with various CW type radars. Procedia Eng. **5**, 661–664 (2010). Eurosensor XXIV Conference
2. Reindl, L., Scholl, G., Ostertag, T., Scherr, H., Schmidt, F.: Theory and application of passive SAW radio transponders as sensors. IEEE Trans. Ultrason. Ferroelectr. Freq. Control **45**(5), 1281–1291 (1998)
3. Gruber, C.: Concept for fast phase analysis of SAW delay lines. Master thesis, Carinthia University of Applied Sciences/Carinthian Tech Research, Villach (2011)
4. Scheiblhofer, S.: Design und Realisierung von HF-Hardware zur Identifikation von Surface-Acoustic-Wave Sensoren. Diploma thesis, Johannes Kepler University of Linz
5. Scheiblhofer, S., Schuster, S., Stelzer, A., Hauser, R.: S-FSCW-radar based high resolution temperature measurement with SAW-sensors. In: International Symposium on Signals, Systems, and Electronics (ISSSE 2004), 10–13 August 2004, Linz, Austria (2004)
6. Bronstein, I.N., Semendjajew, K.A., Musiol, G., Muehlig, H.: Taschenbuch derMathematik. Harri Deutsch GmbH (2008)
7. Leonhard Reindl, M.: Wireless passive saw identification marks and sensors. Tutorial
8. Leonhard Reindl, M.: Wireless passive saw identification marks and sensors. In: Second International Symposium Acoustic Wave Devices for Future Mobile Communication Systems. Chiba University (2004)

InterIoT

Cross-Platform Scenario Module for Internet of Things Testing Architecture

Osama Abu Oun[✉], Christelle Bloch, and François Spies

FEMTO-ST Lab (CNRS) - University of Franche-Comte,
1 Cours Leprince-Ringuet, 25200 Montbéliard, France
{oabuoun,chirstelle.bloch,francois.spies}@femto-st.fr

Abstract. The Internet of Things (IoT) represents a vision in which the Internet extends into the real world embracing everyday objects [9]. Billions of objects are already connected to the Internet. These objects would intercommunicate without any human intervention and they would have different operating systems. Enterprises and developers should produce different versions of each application (same functionality) for each operating systems. For testing and evaluating all these versions, developers and testers should develop/redevelop the same scenario for all versions of this application. Cross-Platform Scenario Module is designed to solve this problem by separating the testing scenario (events and actions) from the application that will execute these events and actions on the object. Same scenario might be written using data serialization formats (such as, Extensible Markup Language (XML), JavaScript Object Notation (JSON) or Concise Binary Object Representation (CBOR)) for all versions of the application. As an example, the format used in this research is the XML.

Keywords: Internet of things · Testing IoT · Evaluating · Scenario module · IoTaaS

1 Introduction

According to Cisco Internet Business Solutions Group (IBSG), IoT is simply the point in time when more "things or objects" were connected to the Internet than people. Cisco projects that by 2020 there will be nearly 50 billion devices on the IoT [4]. Physical items are no longer disconnected from the virtual world. They can be controlled remotely and can act as physical access points to Internet services [6]. Within the IoT literally anything can be connected to a computer network, via an IP address like the one in your computer, and allowed to transfer data without the need for human-to-human or human-to-computer interaction. A "Thing" could be a car, an animal with a bio-chip transponder, a fitness band on your wrist, a refrigerator, the jet engine of an airplane, or your cat's collar. These objects, in addition to billions of others, could become connected to the Internet with the help of sensors and actuators [7].

© ICST Institute for Computer Sciences, Social Informatics and Telecommunications Engineering 2016
B. Mandler et al. (Eds.): IoT 360° 2015, Part II, LNICST 170, pp. 385–395, 2016.
DOI: 10.1007/978-3-319-47075-7_43

Designing an architecture for testing and evaluating IoT systems requires more than providing a server and several devices. It requires the ability to build/rebuild all the details of a real environment where the system will be deployed/run. Such environment could be built using a mix of the following items: real things (devices), simulators and emulators. One of the most important aspects in any testing environment is the ability to generate and regenerate several scenarios in order to test an application. Nowadays, each application has different versions, each of them works on different operating system or on different releases of the same operating system. In this paper, we will present a Cross-platform Scenario Module. This module is one of the components of our proposed architecture for building a cloud environment for offering IoT testing as a service. The remainder of this paper is organized as follows: Sect. 2 presents the state of the art of this work and we survey related work. Section 3 presents (briefly) the main architecture used to build an IoTaaS. Sections 4 elaborates designing our cross-platform scenario module for IoT testing architecture. The implementation and the results are discussed in Sect. 5. And finally, some concluding remarks and future work are mentioned in Sect. 6.

2   State of the Art

Many researches have been conducted in order to simplify application testing and evaluation. Most of these researches were targeting the desktop, web and mobile applications. One of the main differences between these applications and IoT applications is the human intervention. In IoT, a lot of objects and devices will be able to communicate directly without any human intervention. So any testing tools for the IoT should be able to automate testing scenarios in order to be executed without human intervention. To the best of our knowledge, cross-platform scenarios for testing IoT applications and devices yet to be introduced in the literature. Mobile application testing is the closest domain to the IoT testing. In mobile application testing, many companies have developed frameworks in order to help developers and testers to automate application testing. One of these projects is Appium [2]. Appium is an open-source tool for automating native, mobile web, and hybrid applications on iOS and Android platforms. It is based on Client/Server architecture. It allows tester to write tests against multiple platforms (iOS, Android), using the same API. This enables code reuse between iOS and Android test suites. There are client libraries (in Java, Ruby, Python, PHP, JavaScript, and C#) which support Appium's extensions to the WebDriver protocol. Robotium [8] is an open-source test framework for writing automatic gray box testing cases for Android applications. Each scenario needs new app to be generated. The new app can only send events to the application that has the same signature.

Our Cross-platform Scenario module depends on XML files, so testers don't have to write a new application for each scenario. It can work in both modes (client-server and standalone). It can be used in any operating system if it allows injecting event. The module is designed to permit the mix between static and dynamic scenarios.

3   IoTaaS Architecture

An IoT environment would consist of any device might be able to exchange data directly/indirectly with Internet/Intranet. In general, a simple IoT environment is formed of:

- **Sensor:** It is a device which can detect a physical state and convert it into data (readable by computer).
- **Actuator:** It is a device which can change a physical state.
- **Gateway:** It is a dedicated device or an application to read data from sensors, send data to actuators.
- **Network:** Many types of networks would exist in an IoT environment. Some networks would be traditional ones, such as Wi-Fi, while others would use technologies which have been developed for IoT.
- **Application:** It is the software which processes data. It could be hosted on any type of devices, such as: server, personal computer (PC), mobile, tablet, etc.

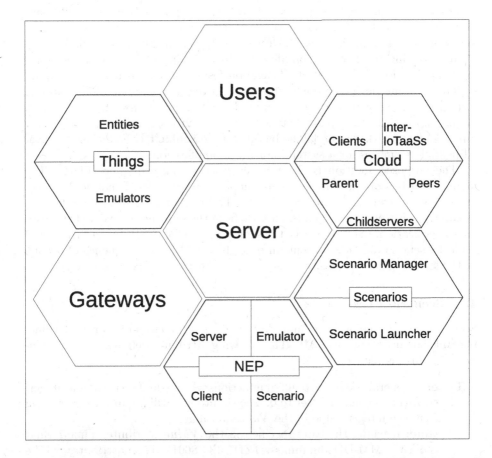

Fig. 1. IoTaaS architecture

The existence of these components could be realized by providing the devices (ex. sensors), or by using emulators. An IoTaaS might be used to test and evaluate any component of an IoT. For example, new sensors should be tested with certain IoT frameworks or with certain gateways, an updated IoT frameworks should be tested in order to test their compatibility with the old actuators, etc. The proposed IoTaaS architecture consists of 7 modules (components) (Fig. 1). These components are the following: Things, Gateways, Emulators, Network Emulation Protocol (NEP), Scenarios, Cloud and the Server.

4   Scenarios

A scenario is an outline or model of an expected or supposed sequence of events. For any application, there is a certain number of sequences of actions and events. This number varies depending on the application itself. For some applications, it could be infinite number of scenarios.

For standalone applications, it is possible to prepare a testing scenario in order to test some (or all) sequences of events. The same application could have different versions for same operating systems, or different versions for different operating systems. In this case, each version should have its own scenario.

It is getting much more complicated when talking about testing network-based applications, where events depend on results or actions from other applications on same device or different device. In nowadays applications, most of testing scenarios depend on user input. In IoT applications, the majority of events and actions take place between devices and applications directly (user input isn't needed). A standalone-based testing wouldn't be sufficient to cover all possible scenarios for a system, nor for an application.

The proposed solution is client-server-based scenario module (Fig. 2). The module consists of three main components: Scenario Files, Scenario Manager (Server) and Scenario Launcher (Client). The main idea of this module is to separate the actions on a given framework from the sequence of events (scenario) for an application. In other words, the same scenario file (XML file in this design) could be sent to different systems in order to run the same sequence of events. In the following subsections, we discuss in details these three components.

4.1   Scenario Files

Scenarios should be written and described using a cross-platform machine-readable language, such as XML. The following attributes define a general **Trigger** used in this file (repeatedly):

– **Type:** In general, there are 5 different actions which could be used as a trigger:
  1. **counter:** a counter is set to 0. The countdown will be initialized starting from the integer value in the **Value** attribute.
  2. **time:** reaching the time specified in the **Value** attribute. Time format is YYYY-MM-DDThh:mm:ss.sTZD (ISO 8601). Time attributes will be ignored on devices which have no internal clocks.

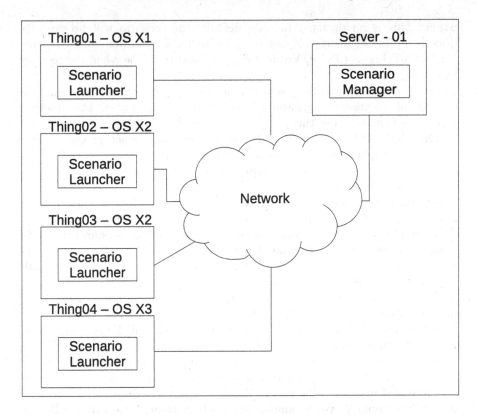

Fig. 2. IoTaaS - Scenario's general architecture

3. **action:** an action is triggered. The *Value* attribute should contain this action name or ID.
4. **delay:** a countdown timer has reached zero. The *Value* would have this time in the format PnYnMnDTnHnMnS (ISO 8601).
5. **never:** infinity.

- **Value:** This attribute could have different type of values depending on *Type*'s attribute.

In the following, we list the main tags and attributes in this file (Code 5.8.1):

- **Scenario:** It consists of the attributes which define the scenario in general. This is a mandatory tag. It has 5 main attributes:
  - **ID:** It is the scenario identifier. Each scenario should have a unique identifier. This identifier is used to collect the results and to prepare the statistics.
  - **Name:** It is human-readable name, it could be used to distinguish different scenarios.
  - **Type:** In case of having different categories of scenarios, this attribute could be used to indicate the type.

- **Start**: This is an optional tag. By default, the scenario will be executed directly unless of using this tag in order to fix a condition. It has a trigger **StartTrigger (Type/Value)** which is used to define when the scenario should be started.
- **Loop**: A scenario could be executed more than once. This is an optional tag (in case of its absence, scenario will be executed only once). The following attributes define loop settings:
    - **Enabled:** This is a boolean attribute determining whether the scenario will be applied once (=0), or it would be repeated (=1).
    - **StopLoopTrigger (Type/Value):** It is a trigger used to define when the scenario should be stopped.
- **End**: This is an optional tag. By default, the scenario will be stopped directly after the last action is applied (loop isn't defined). It has a trigger **StopTrigger (Type/Value)** which is used to define when the scenario should be stopped. In case of using this tag, the scenario will be stopped as soon as the trigger is hit, even in the middle of execution of the scenario. This tag should have a priority over all other events.
- **action**: Each scenario consists of a sequence of actions. Each action has 4 main attributes
    - **ID:** A unique identifier for each action is required. This ID is usually given by the framework.
    - **Name:** It could be the same as the ID. It could be a human-readable name.
    - **Command:** In case that the action isn't predefined, a command could be provided in order to be executed.

An action could have parameter(s). Each parameter has the following attributes:
    - **ID:** This is a local identifier. Each parameter of the same action should have its own ID.
    - **Name:** It is a human-readable name. It can have the same value of ID.
    - **Type:** It defines the type of the parameter. The type could be any simple type, such as: integer, short, float, string, etc. The complex types could be: file or server, which means that it should read the parameter from a file, or it should contact an external server.
    - **Value:** In case of simple types, this attribute contains the value of this parameter. Otherwise, this attribute will have file path or server URL. This attribute could be omitted in case of having an array of values.

A parameter could have an array of values. Each value is defined as follows:
    - **ID:** A unique identifier for each value is required.
    - **Name:** It is a human-readable name. It can have the same value of ID.
    - **Value:** In case of simple types, this attribute contains the value of this parameter. Otherwise, this attribute will have file path or server URL.

Other tags and attributes could be defined. It is important to mention that the same file should be used for all platforms.

```
Code 4.1 - Scenario File Architecture (XML)

<?xml version="1.0" encoding="UTF-8"?>
<scenario id="" name="" type="">
  <start startTriggerType="" startTriggerType=""/>
  <loop enabled="0/1" stopLoopTriggerType=""
                  stopLoopTriggerValue=""/>
  <end type="" value=""/>
  <actions>
      <action id="" name="" command="">
            <parameters>
                  <parameter id="" name="" type="" value=""/>
                  <parameter id="" name="" type="" >
                    <values>
                          <value id="" name="" value=""/>
                          <value id="" name="" value=""/>
                    </values>
                  </parameter>
            </parameters>
      </action>
  </actions>
</scenario>
```

4.2 Scenario Manager

This component preforms all functions on server side. Scenario Manager could be written in any programing language and it can run on any operating system. There are four main subcomponents which are responsible of performing server's functions (Fig. 3):

- **Dispatcher:** The principal function of this subcomponent is to maintain connections with scenario launchers (clients) in order to exchange data. The data exchanged is divided into four types:
  - **Scenario Files:** Dispatcher sends to launcher a scenario file (if exists). Scenario files could be stored directly on the server, separated database or on external storage server. Each scenario file should be categorized according to: the application, the scenario and the client.
  - **Parameters:** Scenario Launchers would need certain parameters from the scenario manager. Scenario Launchers send a request, the dispatcher send back the requested parameter.
  - **Dynamic Actions:** Dispatcher can send certain actions to certain clients. These actions would be obtained from the application analyzer.
  - **Results:** A Scenario Launcher sends the results of executing certain scenario (or certain dynamic actions) as soon as it has a connection with its own scenario manager. The results should be categorized according to: the application, the scenario and the client.

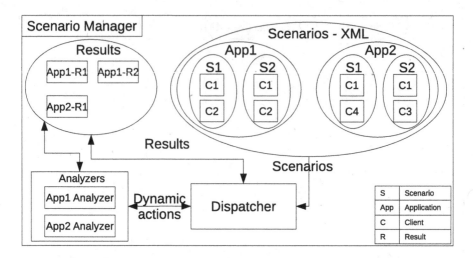

Fig. 3. IoTaaS - Scenario manager

Dispatcher and Scenario Launchers can communicate using a cross-platform distributed application protocol, such as: Web Services.

- **Results:** Results are all data received from Scenario Launchers as a result of executing a scenario or a dynamic action. Dispatcher receives these results and store them directly on the server, dedicated database or on an external server.
- **Analyzers:** Scenario Manager could have analyzers for certain application. An analyzer would analyze the results received from the Scenario Launchers. Depending on this analyze, it could send direct actions to certain clients through the Dispatcher. Analyzers can be a good tool in order to give dynamicity to a testing scenario. Analyzer output could be added as results.

Several Scenario Managers could be used in a given environment. Scenario Launchers could be configured to have a backup Scenario Manager. Other solutions could be provided using load-balancers techniques.

4.3 Scenario Launcher

Scenario Launcher is the component on the client device that perform testing end evaluating functions. This component varies depending on the device's framework. Each framework (or each version of framework) should have its own version of Scenario Launcher, it should be developed using a programing language supported by the framework, such as Java for Android and Objective C for OSX and iOS, etc.

There are four main subcomponents in any Scenario Launcher. In the following, we present these subcomponents (Fig. 4):

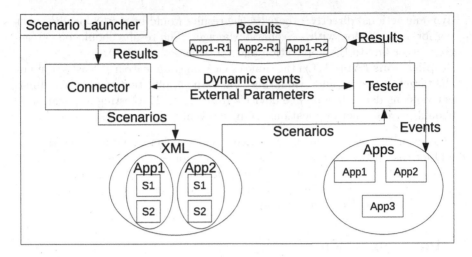

Fig. 4. IoTaaS - Scenario launcher

- **Connector:** This subcomponent is responsible of maintaining the connection with a Scenario Manager. This connection is used in order to exchange following types of data:
  - **Scenario Files:** Scenario Launcher receives the scenario file(s) from a Scenario Dispatcher. It stores Scenario File(s) locally. Each scenario file should be categorized according to: the application and the scenario.
  - **Parameters:** When Scenario Launcher needs certain parameters from the scenario manager. Scenario Launcher sends a request, the dispatcher sends back the requested parameter.
  - **Dynamic Actions:** When the Scenario Launcher receives a dynamic action from the Scenario Manager, this action will have a priority over all other actions.
  - **Results:** The results of scenario executed (or dynamic actions), they will be sent directly or from the local storage.

  Connector could be considered as the bridge that connects between the Scenario Manager and the other subcomponents in the Scenario Launcher.
- **Tester:** It is responsible of executing the scenarios which have been received from the Scenario Manager. The tester should have the permissions to:
  - inject events into other applications on the same device.
  - listen to events dispatched by other applications or by the operating system itself.
  - read/write files from/to the local storage.
  - set/get operating system parameters.

  Tester should be multi-threaded application in order to execute multiple scenarios at the same time.
- **Results:** In case of having a connection with the Scenario Manager, the Scenario Launcher sends the results of executing certain scenario (or certain

dynamic actions) directly, otherwise the results would be stored locally awaiting for a connection with a Scenario Manager. The results should be categorized according to the application and the scenario.

– **Applications (Apps):** On the same device, one application at least should be the target of testing and evaluating. The same application would have different versions depending on the device's framework. The testing application(s) should permit other applications to inject events.

For security reasons, and since the Scenario Launcher would have access to all the functions on the device, Scenario Launcher applications should run only in special mode (ex. debugging mode). This mode should be turned on/off manually by the user or the tester. This could protect normal devices from being hacked by using these privileges an permissions.

5   Implementation

Our experiments and scenarios aim at demonstrating the possibility to implement the cross-platform scenario module. We selected the following parameters for our testing environment:

– **Client:** The client used is a mobile phone working prepared with Android operating system.
– **Server:** The server's operating system is linux Ubuntu 14.04 server 64 bits.
– **application:** Notepad application.

This version consists of Java application (server) and an Android service (Scenario Launcher) on the client. The Android service has been developed in order to keep working in the background. As soon as it receives a scenario file from the server, it launches the target application on the mobile and start injecting the events into this application. The target application should have *inject_events* permission. Inject_events allows an application to inject user events (keys, touch, trackball) into the event stream and deliver them to ANY window [3]. The scenario launcher has to be signed with the system signature in order to be able to use this privilege. The Android service could read any scenario and inject its events into any application on the mobile phone. The performed experiment campaigns demonstrated the feasibility of this new testing and evaluation concept, and they showed, besides, that it is possible to change the scenario file in order to run the new scenario directly without changing the Android service.

6   Conclusion

The result of the implementation proves the possibility of separating the scenario files and the scenario application. Instead of wasting the time of testers and developers in developing different testing application for each scenario. The scenario launcher would be a general application capable of executing any scenario file by injecting the events into any application on the mobile phone. Our future work consists of developing the other functions, porting the application to the other operating systems used in IoT frameworks and building the client-server module using RESTful API [5] and representing scenarios using different languages (XML, JSON, CBOR) in order to handle implementation on constrained devices. Future work will focus on studying the impact of our design on performance of constrained devices. We are planning to exchange messages between the server and the clients using our protocol Connectionless Data Exchange (COLDE). COLDE utilizes Wi-Fi Management Frames to exchange data between devices without being connected to any network [1]. This will permit the clients to exchange data with the server as part of the management frames which keeps the primary network of the device available for the testing tasks.

References

1. Abu Oun, O., Abdou, W., Bloch, C., Spies, F.: Broadcasting information in variably dense environment using connectionless data exchange (CoLDE). In: Mellouk, A., Fowler, S., Hoceini, S., Daachi, B. (eds.) WWIC 2014. LNCS, vol. 8458, pp. 283–296. Springer, Heidelberg (2014). http://dx.doi.org/10.1007/978-3-319-13174-0_22
2. Appium: Automation for the apps. Technical report, Appium. http://appium.io. Accessed 2015
3. Developers, A.: Manifest-permission. Technical report, Android. http://developer.android.com/reference/android/Manifest.permission.html. Accessed 2015
4. Evans, D.: How the next evolution of the internet is changing everything. Technical report, Cisco (2011). https://www.cisco.com/web/about/ac79/docs/innov/IoT_IBSG_0411FINAL.pdf
5. Fielding, R.T.: Architectural styles and the design of network-based software architectures. Ph.D. thesis, aAI9980887 (2000)
6. Mattern, F., Floerkemeier, C.: From the internet of computers to the internet of things. In: Petrov, I., Guerrero, P., Sachs, K. (eds.) Buchmann Festschrift. LNCS, vol. 6462, pp. 242–259. Springer, Heidelberg (2010)
7. Morien, C.: Connectivity 101: the internet of things. Technical report, The University of Texas at Austin. https://identity.utexas.edu/id-perspectives/connectivity-101-the-internet-of-things. Accessed 2015
8. Robotium: robotium recorder. Technical report, Robotium. http://robotium.com/. Accessed 2015
9. Weiser, M.: The computer for the 21st century. Sci. Am. **265**(3), 94–104 (1991)

Semantic Metastandards Will Unlock IoT Interoperability

David P. Janes[(✉)]

Founder, IOTDB.Org, Toronto, ON, Canada
davidjanes@davidjanes.com

Abstract. Interoperability within the Internet of Things is mired in entrenched incompatible specifications, backed by industry giants and consortiums seemingly hoping to "win the stack". There is little hope that a common set of standards will be universally adopted that will allow all our Things to work together. However, by applying some of the core lessons of the Internet - use URIs for IDs, manipulate documents using the REST Model, and that documents should be "JSON-like" dictionary - we can create near seamless interoperability between Things independent of their standards stack.

Keywords: REST · Internet of Things · Interoperability · Semantics · Semantic web · Linked data · API · Semantic Metastandards · Standards

1 Introduction

1.1 The State of Play

The window of opportunity for a common, widely adopted TCP/HTTP/HTML-type stack of Internet of Things standards has passed. We now live in a world with a plethora of manufacturer and consortium based specifications, full of magic numbers, ID strings, and ad-hoc architectures. Like with Internet video in the 1990s, deliberate incompatibility is "baked in". Common amongst these specifications show little evidence of learning anything from the phenomenally successful Internet architectures of the last 25 years.

1.2 IOTDB/HomeStar

We have an Open Source reference implementation[1] which can be freely used to experiment with the ideas expressed in this paper.

---

[1] https://github.com/dpjanes/node-iotdb.

© ICST Institute for Computer Sciences, Social Informatics and Telecommunications Engineering 2016
B. Mandler et al. (Eds.): IoT 360° 2015, Part II, LNICST 170, pp. 396–402, 2016.
DOI: 10.1007/978-3-319-47075-7_44

2   Semantic Metastandards

2.1   Our Proposal

We propose a new approach for creating interoperability amongst Things, by describing what they do (or report) and providing a simple, well-understood method for relaying (or retrieving) these instructions to/from the Things. We call this approach "Semantic Metastandards".

The beauty of this approach is it's inherently independent of vendors and consortiums. A TV can be on or off, a lock can be open or closed, a stove burner can be set to a particular temperature: how this is done is out of our control, but the fact that they do it is not.

The trick is to discover this vocabulary and provide a programming model that developers can used to apply it to Things. Of course, something actually has to do the work, but this will be all invisible to end users.

2.2   Not in Our Proposal

Discovery, Security, Authentication, Authorization, ... Interoperability for the IoT is still a huge space with a lot of work to be done. This paper covers "once you connect, how do you talk?".

2.3   Architecture

Our Semantic Metastandard is built on top of the architecture that should be familiar to every Internet developer today:

- use dereferenceable URIs[2] as IDs;
- use the REST Model, that is, we manipulate and understand the state of Things by doing simple Atomic operations against documents found at URIs; and
- use JSON-like dictionary, that is, data hierarchically composed of a few simple types, arrays and dictionaries with strings for keys.

The first point is simply Linked Data[3], as outlined by Tim Berners-Lee. The second and third points are the architectural basis of most web APIs today.

Components. The core components of this system are as follows:

- ID: a unique identifier for a Thing
- Bands: JSON-like dictionaries of data associated with a Thing
- Vocabulary: URIs describing what are in bands.

---

[2] https://en.wikipedia.org/wiki/Dereferenceable_Uniform_Resource_Identifier.

[3] https://en.wikipedia.org/wiki/Linked_data.

The relationship between these points are simple:

- A Thing's ID will let you access it's Bands
- We change a Thing's state by writing to Bands
- We get a Thing's state by read and observing changes to its Bands
- We understand what the state means via its semantic description, also stored in a Band.

ID. An ID is a persistent unique identifier for a Thing. IDs are not usually assigned so much as systematically created. Ideally, this would be universally unique but unique within a given environment seems to work "good enough".

Our reference implementation creates IDs using a variety of methods, most notably by using unique identifiers expressed by the Things themselves.

Bands. The core insight here is that a "Thing" is not a single object that we manipulate. Instead we should view a Thing (as identified by some Thing ID) as a jumping off point to a cloud of related but independent bands of data.

These are, at a minimum:

- `istate` - the Input State: the actual state of thing
- `ostate` - the Output State: the state we want the thing to become. When this state is achieved, the corresponding values within the ostate are returned to null
- `meta` - the Thing's metadata (for example, it's name)
- `model` - the Thing's Model, which describes what it does
  What we're proposing is that Interoperability can be achieved in the IoT by reading and manipulating the data in these bands. This will be demonstrated further in this paper.

Vocabulary. Note that this entire vocabulary could potentially be swapped out and replaced with another vocabulary though more realistically, the vocabulary can be augmented as needed for certain specific applications. However, we think the current version of this covers certainly most home and small-business related IoT applications.

- `schema:` - the schema.org vocabulary, especially for things like name and description[4]
- `iot:` - core definitions, such as basic types, relationships, IDs etc.
- `iot-purpose:` - descriptions of manipulations, such as "turn this on", "set the color", "this is the sensor temperature", etc.

For completeness, we will mention two other sets of definitions:

- `iot-unit:` - weights and measures
- `iot-facet:` - the "purpose" of Things themselves, for example "Climate Control", "Lighting", "Security", etc.

---

[4] http://schema.org/Thing - not to be confused with a "Thing" in the IoT sense.

All the `iot-*:` types can be browsed at iotdb.org/pub. Forkable versions are also available on GitHub.

We use JSON-LD[5] to store the semantic descriptions in the model band.

3 Examples

3.1 Arduino Light

We will work through one of the simplest examples possible to demonstrate this idea.

Consider an Arduino with an LED light connected to Digital Pin 13. Turning the light on looks something like this in code:

```
digitalWrite(13, TRUE)
```

This clearly lends itself to a neater description as the manipulation of a JSON document.

```
{
    "D13": true
}
```

Because we're "reading the docs" we clearly know what this means, but it is hardly a scalable model for the IoT.

The "Model". What we need to do is describe what that JSON dictionary means. Here's one possibility (simplified for readability).

```
{
    "iot:model-id": "arduino-light",
    "iot:attribute:" : {
        "@id": "#D13",
        "iot:purpose": "iot-purpose:on",
        "iot:write": true
    }
}
```

There's a lot going on there, but most importantly, note that there's an attribute that:

- refers to "D13" in the dictionary
- has the purpose of `iot-purpose:on`, which is defined to mean "this turns something on and off"[6]

---

[5] http://json-ld.org/.

[6] https://iotdb.org/pub/iot-purpose.html#on.

Usage. How do we use this Model to turn on the light?

- we look for an attribute that has `iot:purpose` of `iot-purpose:on`
- when found, we look up the `@id`. This tells us what to manipulate in the JSON dictionary - D13
- we create the appropriate update dictionary `ostate: {D13: true }` and send it to thing's Bridge
- the Bridge does the actual work of turning the light on

Or to summarize, we say `state:on = true` but behind the scenes on the Arduino the code does `digitalWrite(13, TRUE)`. On a (e.g.) Philips Hue, an entirely different code path is executed, but both the initial command and the final result (the light turning on) are the same.

Programming. In our JavaScript reference implementation, this looks like:

```
thing.set(":on", true)
```

In IoTQL, this is done by

```
SET state:on = true;
```

Note. We will briefly note here that in a "real" Model, the pin number would be parameterized - otherwise we'd have to make a new Model for each different pin!

3.2   Interstitial State

The "interstitial state" of a Thing is the time period between when we ask a Thing to do a task to when it actually accomplishes that state. With traditional non-connected Things, when tend not to notice this: we flick a light switch and the light comes on. In a similar fashion, we do not see the concept with traditional APIs because we expect things to work or fail: we write to a database and it updates (or not). In the IoT, this is not tenable: we (e.g.) send a request to a WeMo Socket, and then 400 ms (or so) it changes state. This amount of lag is clearly noticeable to users and must be modeled correctly.

The solution we have come up with is to split the state into two parallel bands: an "istate" (input) for modeling the actual state of a Thing, and "ostate" (output) for modeling requests to change the Thing's state. The ostate transitions always its value to null once a command is executed.

Why do we not have one state, with different terms for input and output? As you start modeling 'real world' things is there's a lot of 'near duplication' of semantic terms.

For example, modeling Lights you might end up with something like this:

- `on`: turn the light on/off - `{write: true }`
- `is_on`: is this on or off - `{read: true }`

These have identically semantic definitions excepting that one is a command and one is reading. With more complicated Things you end up with large sets of near duplicate terms, which furthermore have to be correlate with each other to show interstitial state. Splitting the state into istate band and ostate band provides an elegant simplification.

Bands. Note in this case, the model indicates that we can both read and write to the "on" attribute.

```
model:
{
    "iot:model-id": "we-mo-socket",
    "iot:attribute:" : {
        "@id": "#powered",
        "iot:purpose": "iot-purpose:on",
        "iot:read": true,
        "iot:write": true
    }
}
```

The istate band is the current state of the Thing. In this case, the WeMo Socket is "off":

```
istate: {"powered": false }
```

(Note that we understand what `powered` means by looking at the model).

The ostate band only has data when it is actively doing an action. Thus initially, it has only `null` data.

```
ostate: {"powered": null }
```

We then send a request to turn the WeMo on by changing the ostate band

```
ostate: {"powered": true }
istate: {"powered": false }
```

Notice how we are now in the interstitial state - the ostate band has a value, and it differs from the istate. Finally, the command is executed, the WeMo turns on.

```
ostate: {"powered": null }
istate: {"powered": true}
```

One alternative is to keep the command value in the ostate band rather than transitioning to null; however we believe this makes what is happening more clear.

3.3 Type Units, Ranges, and More

This section is to illustrate that attributes can express more information than the "purpose"; they can also store the type of data expected (e.g. an integer, a Boolean), the units that the value is measured, ranges, enumerations, and so forth. Again, because we are using Semantic Web and Linked Data standards, what can be achieved is open-ended.

3.4   Type and Units Example

A WeMo Insight provides (amongst other things) a measurement of how much power is consumed in a day. This can be modeled as follows:

```
"iot:type": "iot:type.integer",
"iot:unit": "iot-unit:energy.si.joule"
```

3.5   Ranges

Here's how we would model a hypothetical light that has only ten levels of brightness (and off):

```
"iot:type": "iot:type.integer",
"iot:minumum": 0,
"iot:maximum": 10,
```

3.6   Enumerations

Here's an example of a TV band selector

```
"iot:purpose": "iot-purpose:band",

"iot:type": "iot:type.string",

"iot:enumeration": [

  "iot-purpose:band.tv",

  "iot-purpose:band.hdmi#1",

  "iot-purpose:band.hdmi#2",

  "iot-purpose:band.component",

]
```

4   Conclusions

This paper outlines a powerful, easily implemented method for creating interoperability amongst Things. The method is based on well-understood Internet technologies in use today. It has no dependency on the cooperation of Thing vendors and consortiums.

The method uses Semantic Web and Linked Data to describe how Things can be manipulated and what their state is. All data related to Things are stored in "bands", which are JSON-like dictionaries of data. The "model" is the Semantic Model of a Thing, the "meta" is Metadata associated with a Thing, this "istate" is the current state of a Thing, and the "ostate" describes changes we would like to make to its state. The "model" describes the data in the "ostate" and "istate", allowing users to understand what the data *means*. The "ostate" and "istate" are *bridged* to the actual Things to transfer actions and data; this bridging is essentially invisible to the end user, hence achieving Interoperability using Semantic Metastandards.

Internet of Things and Crowdsourcing – Towards a Multiple Integrating Model Based on the IoT Lab European Research Project

Sébastien Ziegler[(⊠)]

Mandat International, Geneva, Switzerland
sziegler@mandint.org

Abstract. This article presents an initial set of results from the IoT Lab European research project on crowdsourcing and Internet of Things (IoT). It presents the interoperability challenges faced by the project and how it solved them, in order to provide a fully integrated experimental platform for multi-disciplinary research combining the potential of the Internet of Things deployment together with richer end-user interactions. It gives an overview of its multiple integrations model, including with heterogeneous IoT, heterogeneous testbeds, crowdsourcing, virtual nodes, and other testbeds federations. It highlights the use of IPv6 as a global and strategic integration enabler.

Keywords: Internet of Things · Crowdsourcing · Interoperability · Crowd-sensing · Experiment · Testbed as a service · Pervasiveness · IPv6 · Interoperability · Multidisciplinary research · Virtual nodes · Testbed federation

1 Introduction and Project Presentation

There is a consensus on the fact that the Internet of Things will be massive and pervasive. It will play a growing role in many application domains, such as: environmental monitoring, transportation and mobility, waste management, energy efficiency and smart grid, water management, security, safety, assisted living, eHealth, etc.

Of course, developing and researching new IoT-related solutions requires addressing the usual technical requirements such as: scalability, reliability, Quality of Service, security, interoperability, portability, etc. Such requirements can be tested and validated in conventional research labs. However, an approach purely focused on technical requirements may lead to a missed target if the end-user perspective is not properly taken into account. In the IoT domain, end-user requirements are probably as much important as technical ones. Hence, understanding the end-user acceptance and satisfaction is critical.

IoT Lab (www.iotlab.eu) [1] is a European research project addressing this challenge, by developing a platform enabling researchers to work on both dimensions. It enables them to use IoT testbeds, including in public spaces, while collecting inputs from end-users through crowdsourcing and crowd-sensing.

IoT Lab is a 3 years FP7 European research project on the Internet of Things and crowdsourcing supported by the European Commission. IoT Lab is developing a research platform that combines Internet of Things (IoT) testbeds together with

© ICST Institute for Computer Sciences, Social Informatics and Telecommunications Engineering 2016
B. Mandler et al. (Eds.): IoT 360° 2015, Part II, LNICST 170, pp. 403–414, 2016.
DOI: 10.1007/978-3-319-47075-7_45

crowdsourcing and crowd-sensing capabilities. It enables researchers to exploit the potential of crowdsourcing and Internet of Things testbeds for multidisciplinary research with more end-user interactions.

On one side, IoT Lab approach puts the end-users at the centre of the research and innovation process. The crowd is at the core of the research cycle with an active role in research from its inception to the results' evaluation. It enables a better alignment of the research with the society and end-users needs and requirements. On the other side, IoT Lab aims at enhancing existing IoT testbeds, by integrating them together into a testbed as a service and by extending the platform with crowdsourcing and crowd-sensing capacities.

To achieve such aims, the IoT Lab focuses its research and development of the following objectives:

- Crowdsourcing and crowd-sensing mechanisms and tools;
- Integration of heterogeneous testbeds together;
- Virtualization of testbed components and integration into a Testbed as a Service;
- Testing and validating the platform with multidisciplinary experiments;
- Research end-user and societal value creation through crowdsourcing;
- "Crowd-driven research".

The project also follows a multidisciplinary approach and addresses issues such as privacy and personal data protection through 'Privacy by Design' approach and built-in anonymity.

The consortium is aiming at maintaining the platform beyond the duration of the project in order to serve the research community. A non-for-profit association has been established to jointly maintain the platform and make it available to the research community.

2 Interoperability Challenges

In order to build an integrated experimental platform, IoT Lab has to overcome several interoperability barriers. These various barriers can be summarized and categorized as follow:

A. Intra-tesbed Heterogeneity

Many IoT testbeds are combining and using more than one IoT technology. This heterogeneity needs to be resolved in order to enable the testbed to be integrated into a common experimental platform. Any IoT testbed can be split into three fundamental levels with their corresponding building blocks:

- **The Southbound** composed of physical IoT devices: sensors, actuators, etc. It gathers the end-nodes of the IoT deployment.
- **The Middleware** composed of gateways and a network infrastructure enabling the various end-nodes to be centrally connected and integrated. In the smallest config-uration, the middleware function will be provided by a simple gateway. In more complex cases, it can encompass hundreds of interconnected devices and equipment.

- **The Northbound** provides the API and interface enabling the applications and services to interact with the IoT testbed, including in our case the IoT Lab Testbed as a Service (TBaaS).

From the Northbound perspective, part of the communication protocol heterogeneity on the Southbound is usually hidden and ignored when the heterogeneity is limited to the lower layers of the protocol deicepile: when different physical layers are integrated into a common protocol stack, from the network layer upward. This is the case when combining wireless and wired technologies using a common protocol stack on top of the Internet Protocol network layer.

On the Southbound side, the issue emerges when the heterogeneity impacts the network layer and/or its upper layers. When it is the case, the heterogeneity may cause problem for the testbed integration. This heterogeneity can appear at various levels of the Open System Interconnection (OSI) model [2] and can be classified into three main categories:

- **Superficial heterogeneity:** The heterogeneity is limited to the application layer. Different systems are using the same protocol stacks up to the OSI presentation layer, but with distinct application layers and ontologies. In this case, the interoperability issue is often limited to data parsing on the gateway or server side.
- **IP-based heterogeneity:** The heterogeneity appears at a deeper level by combining different protocol stacks on a common IP layer. By impacting the session, transport and presentation layers, the interoperability becomes more complex than the Superficial heterogeneity.
- **Deep multi-protocol heterogeneity:** The heterogeneity impacts the complete protocol pile, including the network layer, by using and combining non-IP based standards and communication protocols such as EnOcean, X10, ZigBee or Z-Wave.

B. Inter-Testbed Heterogeneity

IoT Lab gathers several existing IoT testbeds, including:

- The smart campus of the University of Surrey, in the United Kingdom [3];
- A smart building and a smart office testbed run by Mandat International in Geneva, in Switzerland [4];
- A sensor network testbed from the University of Geneva, in Switzerland [5];
- A sensor and actuator testbed from the CTI in Patras, in Greece [6].

Moreover, Mandat International is interconnected with several distant testbeds, including the smart city of Santander in Spain [7].

Each testbed has its own genesis and will select a certain number of options in terms of architecture and configuration which will be specific and contextual. The natural consequence is a high heterogeneity in terms of architecture and technology deployment. One of the first challenges for IoT Lab has been to overcome this fragmentation by integrating the various resources together into a homogeneous and consistent addressing scheme and data plane.

Additionally, IoT testbeds being located in diverse regions may face diverse network connectivity profiles in terms of Quality of Service as well as in terms of Internet connectivity, including Internet Protocol version 6 (IPv6) availability from the Internet Service Providers (ISP).

C. Crowdsourcing-IoT Integration

Another axis of interoperability is related to the integration of IoT deployments with end-users interactions through their smart phones. In IoT Lab, the smartphone is used both as a source of human inputs (crowdsourcing) and embedded sensor data (crowd-sensing). Integrating both sources of data with IoT to enable direct interactions is another challenge.

D. Testbed Federation Interoperability

Finally, IoT Lab is designed to serve a research community, with a focus on the European FIRE research program [8]. In this context, it has to anticipate integration and interoperability requirements with other testbed federations, such as Fed4FIRE [9] and OneLab [10].

3 Technical Approach

IoT Lab has combined several approaches to overcome its multi cleaved environment.

A. Leveraging on IPv6 as an Integration Enabler

Since 1982, the Internet has benefited from the stable Internet Protocol version 4 (IPv4) [11]. Unfortunately, IPv4 only has a limited addressing capacity of about 4 billion theoretical public addresses (and fewer in practice). This corresponds to less than one public IP address per living adult on Earth, and less than one IP address per set of 10 IoT devices by 2020. The growing allocation of public Internet addresses started to cause concerns, leading to restricted public allocation policies and the introduction of Network Address Translation (NAT) mechanisms to provide end-users with private (and sometimes volatile) addresses. As a consequence, most users effectively became "Internet homeless", unaware that they were sharing potentially volatile public Internet addresses with others (Fig. 1).

The continuous growth of the Internet convinced the IETF to design a .new protocol with a larger addressing scheme, standardized in 1998 as the Internet Protocol version 6 (IPv6) [12]. IPv6 is based on an addressing scheme of 2^{128} addresses, split by default in two parts: 64 bits for the network address and 64 bits for the host ID. IPv6 is now globally deployed and a growing number of Internet Service Providers (ISP) is offering IPv6 connectivity.

Enabling an IoT mote to access the Internet through a NAT and a shared public addresses is still doable, but enabling the reverse connection where a service wants to access an IoT mote from the Internet is quite less efficient if the mote doesn't benefit from a unique public address. There is a rather large consensus in the IoT industry that we will reach over 50 Billion interconnected IoT devices by 2020 [13]. The exponential number of IoT devices to be connected highlights the inherent scalability limits of IPv4 as a global IoT addressing protocol.

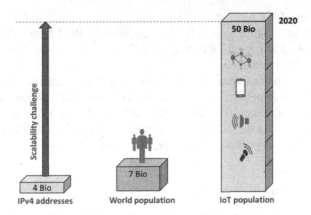

Fig. 1. IPv4 scalability challenge: highlighting the IPv4 addressing capacity gap.

UDG project [14] already demonstrated the ability to integrate all sorts of heterogeneous IoT protocols into an IPv6 addressing scheme. Online applications such as Turn It IPv6 enable IPv6-based control and addressing of non-IP devices [15].

Based on UDG results, the European research project IoT6 [16] designed a common IoT protocol stack based on IPv6 and 6LoWPAN for heterogeneous IoT integration [17–19]. In [20], the authors applied IoT6 model to testbeds and demonstrated multiple testbeds integration through IPv6. This integration was based on testbeds using similar technologies and directly integrated through IPv6.

In the case of IoT Lab, the problematic was more complex. The various testbeds were based on distinct technologies, with different levels of compliance with IPv6. Being distributed cross various countries, the corresponding ISP services offer was uneven too. We ended up with four distinct testbed profiles in terms of network configurations and connectivity,- all to be integrated together:

Case A - Local IPv6 integration, including with non-IP IoT devices:
In this case, the ISP constraints were avoided through a direct integration. However, the testbed included both IPv6 and non-IP IoT devices, using communication protocols such as KNX, ZigBee, EnOcean, BACnet and others. In order to integrate these heterogeneous devices, a UDG proxy has been used to generate consistent and scalable IPv6 addresses to the legacy devices.

Case B - Remote full end-to-end IPv6 compliance:
In this case (TB-B), the testbed integration was achieved through end-to-end IPv6 integration, including 6LoWPAN end nodes directly parsed into IPv6 addresses.

Case C - Remote IPv6 testbed through IPv4 ISP access:
In this case (TB-C), in order to overcome the lack of IPv6 connection at the ISP level, the testbed integration has been performed through v6 in v4 end-to-end tunneling, with a very limited latency impact.

Case D - Remote IPv4 testbed:
Finally, one of the testbed was fully and exclusively IPv4 based (TB-D). In this context, we decided to use a UDG proxy on the server side to map IPv6 addresses on top of the local IPv4 addresses.

The address definitions across the testbeds were maintained consistent by clearly separating the management of the Host ID on one side (IoT address) from the Network ID (Testbed address). This simple approach resulted in a consistent and highly scalable model, enabling the Testbed as a Service (TBaaS) to use a fully integrated and homogenized addressing scheme, including with mobile devices.

B. **Multi-protocol Interoperability**

In order to overcome the heterogeneity of communication protocols used in some of the testbeds, IoT Lab used the Universal Device Gateway (UDG) [21], a multi-protocol control and monitoring system developed by a research project initiated in Switzerland. It aimed at integrating heterogeneous communication protocols into IPv6. The UDG control and monitoring system enables cross protocol interoperability. It demonstrated the potential of IPv6 to support the integration among various communication protocols and devices, such as KNX, X10, ZigBee, GSM/GPRS, Bluetooth, and RFID tags. It provides connected device with a unique IPv6 address that serves as unique identifier for that object, regardless its native communication protocol. It has been used in several research projects, including by IoT6, where it has been used as an IPv6 and CoAP proxy for all kinds of devices.

In IoT Lab, the UDG platform has been used as a locally deployed proxy in the local testbed (TB-A in the Fig. 2) and as a cloud- based proxy in some other cases (TB-C and TB-D in the Fig. 2). However, for communication protocols which are non-compliant with the Internet Protocol, a local deployment was required.

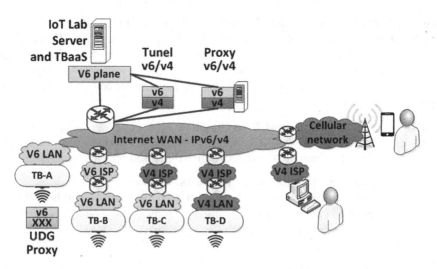

Fig. 2. IoT Lab IPv6-based network integration representing the four main testbed profiles.

C. Crowdsourcing and Crowd-sensing Tool

In the context of IoT Lab, the term "crowdsourcing" refers to direct interaction with participants from the crowd through surveys and other forms of interactions; "crowd-sensing" is understood as the interaction with the embedded sensors of the smart phones. In order to enable direct interactions with end-users, IoT Lab developed a dedicated smartphone application for crowdsourcing and crowd-sensing. This application enables end-users to share inputs and sensing data with researchers on a voluntary basis. The current version of the app is designed for Android environment and will be later extended to other smartphones. A public version of the application will be released in the last quarter of 2015 [22]. The question of IoT Lab application portability on other smart phone platforms is technically trivial and will be considered at a later stage.

D. Virtualizing Resources with a Testbed as a Service

In order to ease access and manageability, the IoT Lab resources are fully virtualized and integrated into a Testbed as a Service (TBaaS) represented in Fig. 3. This approach enables researchers to reserve resources for specific timeslots in order to perform their experiment. Beyond the conventional MySlice capacities, IoT Lab enables to select participants according to all sorts of criteria, including socio-economic profiles, ages and location.

The TBaaS is largely aligned with the Fed4FIRE architecture, including in terms of OML and Rspec specifications. This approach has been adopted for increased interoperability and for easier integration with other European testbeds in the future.

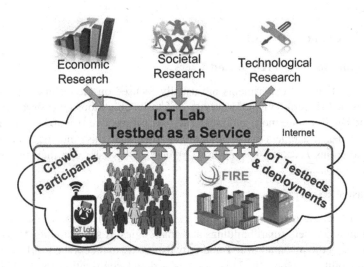

Fig. 3. IoT Lab 'testbed as a service' model combining crowdsourcing and IoT deployments into an online application enabling researchers to perform remote experiments.

E. Aligning on a de facto European Testbed Federation Standard

IoT Lab is closely linked to the FIRE programme of research supported by the European Commission aiming at supporting the research community with experimental infrastructure. In the context of the FIRE programme, several testbeds have been developed. One of the objectives of the European Commission is to interconnect and brings these various testbeds together. The lead project to support such federation is Fed4FIRE, which relied itself on previous research projects. Fed4FIRE has progressively selected and specified several open interfaces to enable such federations. In order to ease the integration with other testbeds, IoT Lab has decided to implement and provide Fed4FIRE compliant APIs.

F. Enabling Virtual and Physical Device Integration

One of the objectives of the IoT Lab project was to explore the potential of combining physical and virtual devices within the same platform. This objective has been implemented in the context of the project and enables researchers to emulate all sorts of nodes and to make them interact with real ones.

G. Privacy by Design Approach

Another key dimension of IoT Lab as a research project is its commitment to develop a fully privacy by design platform. It must find the right balance between the need for the researchers to access reliable and characterized resources, including socio economic profiles,- while ensuring a complete compliance with the European standards in terms of personal data protection. By following a holistic approach, this effort has enabled the consortium to develop a fully privacy-compliant platform by combining various methods, strategies and technology enablers.

4 Triple Paradigm Shift

A. Extending IoT Research to End-Users

Traditional IoT-related experiments are usually focused on the technical features and dimensions of IoT deployment. However, due to its ubiquitous and pervasive dimension, the IoT will require more and more end-user perspective to be taken into account. IoT Lab enables researchers to extend their experiments to this fundamental dimension: how are solutions accepted by end-users, where and what value they perceive in a given deployment, etc.

B. Pervasive Experiments

IoT Lab enables the researchers to perform experiments in all sorts of environments, including among others smart buildings and smart cities. A set of initial experiment has started to assess the potential of IoT and crowdsourcing to assess the level of smartness and sustainability of any city. This work is a direct contribution to the ITU Focus Group on Smart Sustainable Cities [23]. In other words, IoT Lab enables research to leak outside of traditional labs by exploring IoT deployments in real environment with real end-users providing real time feedbacks.

C. Crowd-Driven Research Model

Finally, IoT Lab is enabling and testing a new model of crowd-driven experiments. The key concept is to enable anonymous participants (the crowd) to suggest research topics and to rank them. According to the results, the favorite ideas will be proposed to researchers for selecting and implementing some of them. The results are expected to be shared with the participants (the crowd) in order to get their inputs and their assessment of the generated results. The idea is to explore the potential of a bottom-up research model on the IoT based on crowdsourcing and closer interactions between the researchers and potential end-users as illustrated in Fig. 4.

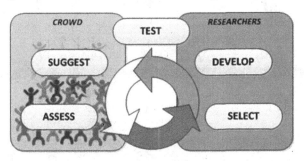

Fig. 4. Crowd-driven research model enabling anonymous end-users to trigger and drive experimentation process in cooperation with researchers.

5   Ongoing Experiments and Open Invitation

IoT Lab expects to support experimentally driven research, including multidisciplinary experiments. The initial version of the IoT Lab experimental platform is working and has been demonstrated at the World Summit on the Information Society (WSIS) [24].

At the present time, several experiments are in progress with targeted groups of end-users, including an experiment on energy efficiency in building, another one on a smart city deployment and the third one on the ITU Smart Sustainable Cities Key Performance Indicators (SSC KPI). Following an agile methodology, the first set of experiments enables the project to fine tune and to improve the designed tools.

In September 2015, the IoT Lab smart phone application will be released to the public. The objective will be twofold:

- Engaging the public (crowd) to join our community of participants to take art in experiments.
- Inviting researchers to use the IoT Lab platform for their own experiments. Any interested research team is welcome to contact us.

6   Conclusions – Towards a Quintuple Integration Model

In order to provide a completely integrated experimental platform combining IoT deployments with end-user interactions through crowdsourcing and crowd-sensing, IoT Lab had to overcome several interoperability barriers. Several IoT testbeds and a

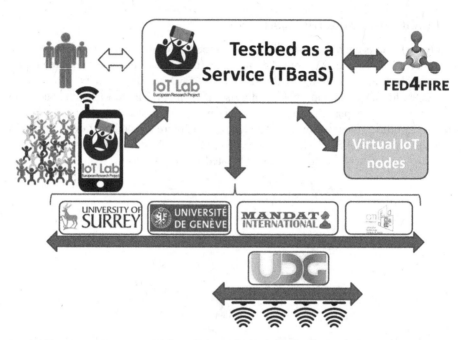

Fig. 5. IoT Lab six fold integration model represented by the blue arrows from the bottom and from left to right: heterogeneous IoT integration; heterogeneous testbeds integration through IPv6; crowdsourcing and crowd-sensing integration into the TBaaS; physical IoT testbeds integration into the TBaaS; virtual nodes integration; multiple testbed federations integration. (Color figure online)

potentially unlimited number of end-users are integrated together into a centralized and ubiquitously accessible Testbed as a Service (TBaaS).

As illustrated in Fig. 5, IoT Lab has applied and is further researching a six fold integration model by:

- Integrating heterogeneous IoT devices and communication protocols (including non-IP based protocols) integrated through the UDG technology;
- Integrating heterogeneous testbeds through IPv6 interconnection, proxy and aggregation;
- Integrating end-users through crowdsourcing and crowd-sensing capabilities enabled by the IoT Lab smart phone application;
- Integrating virtual IoT nodes with the physical ones for richer experiments;
- Integrating the IoT resources and testbeds into a Testbed as a Service in the Cloud, enabling all IoT Lab resources to be virtualized and to be accessible to researchers through remote access and control from anywhere.
- Integrating the platform with other testbed federations, such as Fed4FIRE, by using emerging de facto technologies for testbeds federation.

The IoT Lab platform is still in its improvement and fine tuning phase. It is open to partnerships with third parties research projects interested to test it and to join our effort for building a new experimental platform for the research community.

Acknowledgments. This article has been written in the context of the IoT Lab European research project of the 7th Framework Program supported by the European Commission. It is implemented by a consortium coordinated by Mandat International and gathering the Universities of Surrey, Geneva, Lulea, Southampton, as well as Dunavnet, Alexandra Institute, the Computer Technology Institute and Press "Diophantus", and the support of the Istituto Italiano per la Privacy. IoT Lab project work on interoperability also capitalized on other projects results, including IoT6 [16] and UDG [14].

References

1. IoT Lab is a European research project from the FP7 research programme. http://www.iotlab.eu
2. Open Systems Interconnection model developed by the International Standardization Orgaization: ISO/IEC 7498-1:1994. http://www.iso.org
3. University of Surrey. http://www.surrey.ac.uk
4. Mandat International. http://www.mandint.org
5. University of Geneva. http://www.unige.ch
6. CTI - Computer Technology Institute and Press "Diophantus". http://www.cti.gr
7. Smart Santanders. http://www.smartsantander.eu
8. Future Internet research in the ICT Programme. http://www.ict-fire.eu
9. Fed4FIRE is the main project aiming at federating European research testbeds. http://www.fed4fire.eu
10. OneLab. https://onelab.eu/
11. Postel, J.: Internet Protocol, RFC 791, Internet Engineering Task Force RFC 791, September 1981
12. Internet Protocol, Version 6 (IPv6), RFC 2460, IETF. https://www.ietf.org/rfc/rfc2460.txt
13. Ericson white paper 284 23-3149 Uen, More than 50 billion connected devices, February 2011. http://www.ericsson.com/res/docs/whitepapers/wp-50-billions.pdf
14. UDG is an IPv6-based multi-protocol control and monitoring system using IPv6 as a common identifier for devices using legacy protocols. It was developed by a Swiss research project and used by IoT6 for research purpose. More information on UDG ongoing developments. www.devicegateway.com
15. http://www.turnitipv6.com
16. IoT6 European research project. http://www.iot6.eu
17. Ziegler, S., et al.: IoT6 – moving to an IPv6-based future IoT. In: Winter, J., Ono, R. (eds.) The Future Internet. LNCS, vol. 17, pp. 161–172. Springer, Heidelberg (2013). doi:10.1007/978-3-642-38082-2_14
18. Ziegler, S., Thomas, I.: IPv6 as a global addressing scheme and integrator for the Internet of Things and the Cloud
19. Ziegler, S., Palattella, M.R., Ladid, L., Krco, S., Skarmeta, A.: Scalable integration framework for heterogeneous smart objects, applications and services. In: Internet of Things – From Research and Innovation to Market Deployment. River Publishers Series in Communication (2014)

20. Ziegler, S., Hazan, M., Xiaohong, H., Ladid, L.: IPv6-based test beds integration across Europe and China. In: Leung, V.C.M., Chen, M., Wan, J., Zhang, Y. (eds.) Testbeds and Research Infrastructure: Development of Networks and Communities. Springer, Heidelberg (2014)
21. UDG is maintained by the UDG Alliance managed by Device Gateway and has been used by several European rsearch projects, including Hobnet, IoT6, EAR-IT and currently by IoT Lab. http://www.devicegateway.com
22. The application will be made available on the IoT Lab website. http://www.iotlab.eu
23. ITU Focus Group on Smart Sustanable Cities. http://www.itu.int/en/ITU-T/focusgroups/ssc/Pages/default.aspx
24. World Summit on the Information Society 2015. http://www.itu.int/net4/wsis/forum/2015/

Lessons Learned from the 6TiSCH Plugtests

Maria Rita Palattella[1]([⊠]), Xavier Vilajosana[2], Tengfei Chang[3],
Miguel Angel Reina Ortega[4], and Thomas Watteyne[5]

[1] SnT, University of Luxembourg, Luxembourg, Luxembourg
maria-rita.palattella@uni.lu
[2] Universitat Oberta de Catalunya, Barcelona, Spain
xvilajosana@uoc.edu
[3] University of Science and Technology, Beijing, China
tengfei.chang@gmail.com
[4] ETSI, Sophia Antipolis, France
miguelangel.reinaortega@etsi.org
[5] Inria, EVA Team, Paris, France
thomas.watteyne@inria.fr

Abstract. The principal barrier to massive IoT technology adoption is
the lack of interoperability and the resulting segmented nature of the
IoT market. To cope with that the European Research Cluster on the
Internet of Things (IERC), the International Telecommunication Union
(ITU) and the European Telecommunication Standards Institute (ETSI)
promote the development of interoperability events to enforce real standard compliance and interoperability between vendors. In this paper, we
summarize the lessons learned during the first ETSI Plugtests event on
the technology developed by the IETF 6TiSCH working group. 6TiSCH
technology is cornerstone to the Industrial Internet of Things, enabling
operational technologies to converge to the Internet by providing seamless IP connectivity and standardized management. The event clearly
demonstrated the importance of such interoperability testing early on in
the standards development. Interoperability was tested between implementations of 6TiSCH technology from multiple vendors. A total of 221
tests were performed, with a 93.7 % success rate.

Keywords: Interoperability · 6TiSCH · Plugtests · OpenWSN

1 Introduction

The Internet of Things (IoT) allows a large number of heterogeneous devices
to interconnect, bringing new market opportunities and opening new technical
challenges. The Internet is expected to grow to up to 50 billion "things" by 2020,
according to a 2011 Cisco-IBSG prediction. The amount of data traffic they will
be injecting into the network will increase, up to an annual rate of 84 % for
machine-to-machine (M2M) communication, by 2018 [1]. Technology is developing on how to deal with huge numbers of smart things, how to make sense out

© ICST Institute for Computer Sciences, Social Informatics and Telecommunications Engineering 2016
B. Mandler et al. (Eds.): IoT 360° 2015, Part II, LNICST 170, pp. 415–426, 2016.
DOI: 10.1007/978-3-319-47075-7_46

of the amount of data they generate ("big data"), and how to efficiently use network resources to avoid the collapse of the network, and to allow the coexistence of flows with different Quality of Service (QoS) requirements. The first barrier to adoption is the lack of interoperability and the resulting segmented nature of the market. According to the European Research Cluster on the Internet of Things (IERC) and the International Telecommunication Union (ITU), lack of interoperability is one of the biggest obstacles to IoT market development [2].

The term "interoperability" was initially defined for Information Technology (IT) as "the ability of exchange data" [3]. A broader definition was proposed by the Network Centric Operations Industry Consortium (NCOIC), to take into account social, political and organizational factors that affect systems and system performance, when integrating them all together [4]. Interoperability issues arise when devices from different manufacturers interconnect.

Early IoT adoption was delayed because of the development of incompatible proprietary solutions that maintain the cost of goods and operations high. As is often the case, standardization bodies and industry consortia agreed on the need to develop standards that would guarantee inter-operation between devices from different vendors [5]. The Internet Engineering Task Force (IETF) is the body behind most standards used in today Internet. Various IETF Working Groups, such as 6lo[1], ROLL[2] and 6TiSCH[3] develop standards to allow seamless integration of low-power wireless networks into the Internet.

Standardization is only the first step to allow widespread adoption of a new technology. Once the standard is written, one has to make sure the different products that claim to implement it really work together. This is done by defining a set of "interop tests". Well-established test methodologies such as ETSI EG 202 237 [6] and ETSI EG 202 568 [7] distinguish two classes of tests: *Conformance* and *Interoperability*.

Conformance testing aims at checking whether a product correctly implements a particular standardized protocol. It determines whether or not the Implementation Under Test (IUT) meets the requirements specified for the protocol itself. This includes message format and message sequence. Conformance testing is done on a single device.

Interoperability testing is done between multiple devices from different vendors. Interoperability testing aims at verifying end-to-end functionality between at least two devices from different vendors. Conformance testing in conjunction with interoperability testing provide both the proof of conformance and the guarantee of inter-operation. ETSI EG 202 237 [6] and ETSI EG 202 568 [7] describe several approaches on how to combine these two methods. The most common approach consists in Interoperability Testing with Conformance Checks, where reference points between the devices under test are monitored to verify the appropriate sequence and contents of protocol messages, such as API calls and

---

[1] http://tools.ietf.org/wg/6lo/charters.

[2] http://tools.ietf.org/wg/roll/charters.

[3] http://tools.ietf.org/wg/6tisch/charters.

interface operations. Interoperability events are branded as "Plugtests^{TM}" when organized by the European Telecommunications Standards Institute (ETSI)[4].

The first ETSI "Plugtests" event took place in 1999. Since then, ETSI organizes an average of 12 Plugtests per year, covering diverse technologies. Such events provide essential feedback to technical committees, and help them improve standards and accelerate the standards-making process. They also enable engineers to get together and test the interoperability of their implementations, which reduces a product's time-to-market. ETSI organized the first Plugtests on the technology developed by the IETF 6TiSCH working group. 6TiSCH is emerging as a key enabler of industrial IoT (iIoT) [8].

6TiSCH aims at "gluing" together an IP-enabled upper stack developed by IETF (6LoWPAN, RPL, CoAP) with the IEEE802.15.4e Timeslotted Channel Hopping (TSCH) MAC protocol [9]. TSCH inherits from well-established industrial standards such as WirelessHART. The 6TiSCH protocol stack results in an IP-enabled and low-power protocol stack for Industrial applications, able to fulfill their stringent requirements in terms of reliability, latency, and power consumption [10, 11]. Because 6TiSCH federates different IoT standards developed by the IETF and the IEEE, testing interoperability between 6TiSCH implementations is challenging.

The first 6TiSCH Interop Plugtests event was organized by ETSI in Prague, Czech Republic on 17–19 July 2015. It was co-located with the IETF93 standardization meeting. The event was supported by OpenMote[5] and sponsored by the European Commission and Inria. 15 organizations – companies, opensource projects and academic partners – took part in the event. During the Plugtests, different vendors assessed the level of interoperability of their own implementation against others. They also checked whether their understanding of the implemented IEEE and IETF protocol specifications was correct. The scope of the event was on the "Minimal 6TiSCH Configuration" [12]. Interoperability tests included fundamental protocol operations such as synchronization and link-layer security.

The remainder of this paper is organized as follows. Section 2 summarizes the 6TiSCH minimal implementation, together with the configuration of parameters which were used during the Plugtests. Section 3 describes the golden device and the Wireshark dissector, two supporting tools developed for the event. Section 4 presents the detailed list of tests which were performed. Section 5 summarizes the lessons learned from the event. Section 6 concludes the paper.

2   Minimal 6TiSCH Configuration

The 6TiSCH "minimal" configuration [12] defines the basic set of rules for a 6TiSCH network to operate. Due to the wide and extensive configuration set enabled by the IEEE802.15.4e specification [9], it becomes mandatory to define a set of rules and requirements for vendors to inter-operate. The purpose of

---

[4] http://www.etsi.org/about/what-we-do/plugtests.

[5] http://www.openmote.com/.

the "minimal" document is twofold. First, include a fallback mode of operation, enabling all minimal-compliant networks to run using a common and basic configuration set and enabling it in case of network failure or lost of configuration. Second, support early interoperability events and guide early technology adopters to the integration of IETF standards on top of the TSCH MAC layer.

During the preparation of the Plugtests, and especially the writing of the Test Description, the minimal draft represented the main reference document, providing guidelines on how to make implementations compliant to the standard, from basic functionality, such as IEEE802.15.4e TSCH header configuration, use of Information Elements, to most advanced security settings (e.g. generation of the nonce, authentication and authorization keys).

The minimal specification also defines the network formation process, by indicating what is the period of the Enhanced Beacons and the specific Information Elements sent during the joining process. The layer 2 synchronization structure is defined as being the same as the routing topology, which is created by the RPL routing protocol [13].

All communication in a TSCH networks is orchestrated by a schedule. Time is sliced in timeslots, and timeslots are grouped in a slotframe which continuously repeats over time. The communication schedule indicates the use of each slot. In a minimal network, this schedule is the same for all nodes, and does not change over time. The schedule to use is announced by nodes already part of the network through Enhanced Beacons (EBs), a type of link-layer frames (see Fig. 1). In a minimal network, one active time slot is used in an "slotted Aloha" fashion, i.e. it is shared by all nodes. The IEEE802.15.4e TSCH default channel hopping template and timeslot timings are announced in the EBs, and time source neighbor selection is determined by the smallest join priority received by the node.

The minimal 6TiSCH configuration also defines how the Routing Protocol for Low Power and Lossy networks (RPL) [13] is configured to operate on top of a TSCH MAC Layer, and what the operation modes are. The Objective Function

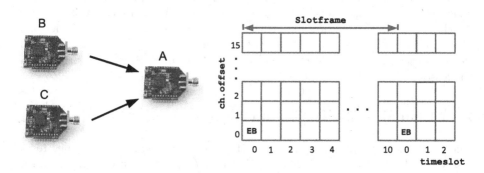

Fig. 1. The minimal schedule used during the interop event. We use a single 11-slot slotframe. The first slot in the slotframe is configured as an slotted Aloha slot, shared by all nodes in the network. Enhanced Beacons are also sent in that slot.

Zero (OF0) [14] is used to ensure the optimization of RPL routes within a RPL instance. According to the minimal draft, any compliant implementation must implement RPL and use the non-storing mode of operation when possible, and be able to use the storing mode of RPL when device characteristics permit. A policy to avoid parent selection hysteresis is used to avoid frequent parent changes due to slight rank differences.

Table 1 summarizes the configuration parameters as defined by the 6TiSCH minimal configuration, which were used during the plugtest event.

Table 1. 6TiSCH Plugtest minimal configuration.

Field	Value	Description
Slotframe length	11	11 slots per slotframe
Slotframe and link	1 active slot	Marked as shared, timekeeping, TX and RX
Timeslot template	Default	IEEE802.15.4e TSCH default slot template
Channel hopping template	Default	IEEE802.15.4e TSCH default channel hopping template
Security key K1	Well-known, as per [12]	Set to 6TiSCH minimal15
Security key K2	Randomly generated	Set to deadbeeffacecafe
RPL objective function	OF0 [14]	With Rf = 1, Sr = 0 and Sp = 2 * ETX [15]

3   Golden Device

To allow participants to do pre-testing, and get ready for the 6TiSCH Plugtests event, a *Golden Device* (GD) was developed. The *Golden Device* is pre-programmed with firmware that passed conformance tests, and is known to implement the 6TiSCH protocol stack correctly. Each vendor received a GD before the event, allowing them to test their implementation against it, and verify inter-operability by going through the test description (see Sect. 4).

The golden device uses an OpenMote-CC2538 [16], which features a Texas Instruments CC2538 micro-controller and radio. The CC2538xFnn is a wireless micro-controller System-on-Chip (SoC) for high-performance IoT applications. It combines an ARM Cortex-M3 micro-controller with an IEEE802.15.4 radio [17]. The OpenMote-CC2538 also features a serial port, which is used for outputting help information and verify interoperability.

Two different images were implemented on the GD, one acting as DAGroot (GD/root), and the other as packet sniffer (GD/sniffer). The source code of both golden images is based on the OpenWSN project[6]. In detail, the images contain the 6TiSCH configuration defined in the minimal draft [12]. On the GD/root, security can be enabled/disabled, through switches activated during compilation of the source code. In addition, both images have several configurable interfaces serving for the interoperability test during the Plugtests.

By interacting with a Python script over the serial interface, the vendor can configure the device, set the value of different parameters (e.g. frequency, slotframe size), or trigger the transmission of a given type of packet. Table 2 summarizes the different configuration which can be enabled on a device using that script.

Table 2. Golden device commands [18]

Command scope	Command ID	Length	Parameter	Range	Unit
Configure frequency	0	1 byte	Frequency number	0, 11 ~ 26	
Send EB	1	2 bytes	Sending period	0 ~ 65535	s
Send KA	2	2 bytes	Sending period	0 ~ 65535	ms
Send DIO	3	2 bytes	Sending period	0 ~ 65535	ms
Send DAO	4	2 bytes	Sending period	0 ~ 65535	ms
Set slotframe size	5	2 bytes	Slotframe length	0 ~ 65535	
Set rank value	6	2 bytes	Rank	0 ~ 65535	
Enable/disable ACK reply	6	1 byte	Option	True (enable) False (disable)	

The configuring commands, listed in Table 2, can be applied to GD/root. The *configure frequency* command is the only one which applies to the GD/sniffer, for activating it on a specific channel. By setting the frequency value to 0, channel hopping is enabled, and all the 16 available channels defined in [17] are used. Otherwise, the device can be forced to operate on a single channel (through 11 to 26).

The script also responds to output to assist in the tests. For example, by interacting with GD/root, the script shows the Absolutely Slot Number (ASN) and the time correction every time the golden device receives a packet from a different device. This is useful for tracking the clock drift between devices.

To help verify the format of packets during the interoperability test, the GD/sniffer listens on a specific frequency and injects the received packets into Wireshark. Wireshark is the de-facto tool for network protocol analysis. During the Plugtests, a Wireshark version with the dissector of IEEE802.15.4e/6TiSCH (Fig. 2), developed by Orange Labs, was used [19].

---

[6] http://www.openwsn.org/.

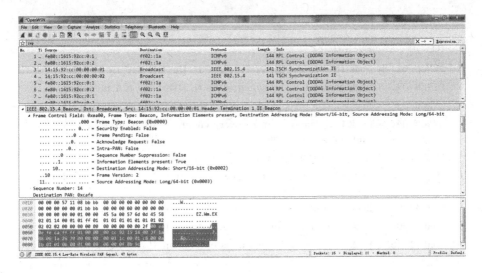

Fig. 2. Wireshark running the IEEE802.15.4e TSCH/6TiSCH dissector.

4 Tests Description

Prior to the Plugtests event, a group of four experts, together with ETSI support, prepared the 6TiSCH Plugtests Test Description (TD) [18]. The latter contains a set of test scenarios to be executed by vendors. The TD was distributed to participants some weeks before the event, allowing for comments and fine-tuning of the document itself. The TD document will be published in the future as an ETSI ISG IP6 group specification so maintenance and revisions can easily be performed for further 6TiSCH Plugtests.

The TD includes 18 tests, performed in two different configuration: *Single Hop*, with 1 DAGroot (DG) and 1 mote (6N), and *Multi Hop* with 1 DAGroot, and two motes, connected in a linear topology.

The tests are classified in four different groups, based on the type of features they aim to verify: Synchronization (SYNCH), Packet Format (FORMAT), RPL features (RPL), and Security (SEC). Each group contains several tests, summarized in Table 3.

4.1 SYNCH Tests

Synchronization is fundamental in TSCH-based networks, given the slotted nature of the communication. Devices *must* keep tight synchronization. Devices are equipped with clocks for keeping track of time. But, clocks in different devices drift with respect to one another. Therefore, they need to periodically resynchronize. The aim of the SYNCH tests is to check whether a device can synchronize with the DAGroot parent, by exchanging EB frames; keep synchronization by sending Keep Alive (KA) messages; and recover synchronization, after clocks

Table 3. List of 6TiSCH Tests performed during the Plugtests [18].

#	ID	Description
1	SYNCH-01	Check that a 6N can synchronize to the EB sent by the DR
2	SYNCH-02	Check that a 6N can synchronize to DR using KA messages
3	SYNCH-03	Check that a 6N's clock drifts if there is no re-synchronization
4	SYNCH-04	Check that the 6N can recover synchronization after de-synchronization
5	FORMAT-01	Check the format of the IEEE802.15.4e EB packet
6	FORMAT-02	Check the timing template of TSCH time slot defined in [12] is correctly implemented
7	FORMAT-03	Check channel hopping is correctly implemented according to [12]
8	FORMAT-04	Check the number of retransmissions is implemented following [12]
9	FORMAT-05	Check the minimal schedule is implemented according to [12]
10	FORMAT-06	Check the 6N sets its slotframe size correctly when joining the network
11	SEC-01	Check the 6N is correctly authenticated with K1, when it synchronizes to DR with EB
12	SEC-02	Check the data packet sent by 6N is correctly encrypted with K2
13	RPL-01	Check the value of EB join priority of a child 6N and a parent DR
14	RPL-02	Check the rank of 6N is computed correctly according to [12]
15	RPL-03	Check a 6N child changes its time source neighbor (parent) correctly
16	RPL-04	Check the format of RPL DIO message
17	RPL-05	Check the format of RPL DAO message
18	RPL-06	Check IP extension header in 6LoWPAN

drifts, applying the time correction specified in the ACK, sent after successful reception of the KA message.

4.2 FORMAT Tests

The set of FORMAT tests are mainly interoperability tests with conformance checks, aiming to check appropriate sequence and content of protocol messages. For instance, the format of the EB frame, and a set of Information Elements (IEs) is verified by printing out the different fields of the EB, with the Wireshark dissector. In detail, the format of the following IEs is verified: (i) the *synchronization IE* which contains the ASN and the Join Priority field, used to initially synchronize the nodes and establish the layer 2 topology; (ii) the *timeslot template IE* which announces the timeslot timing for nodes joining the network; (iii) the *channel hopping IE* which announces the channel sequence used to hop in frequencies; and finally (iv) the *frame and link IE* which advertises the initial network schedule used by joining nodes to communicate.

Some of the FORMAT tests checked conformance with IEEE802.15.4e [17] (related to EBs format and slotframe size), while others checked conformance with the minimal draft [12], for the implementation of timeslot template, channel hopping template, number of retransmissions, and minimal schedule. In test FORMAT-03, channel hopping is enabled. For all tests, the use of a packet sniffer and the Wireshark dissector were instrumental for checking the final outcomes of the tests.

4.3 SEC Tests

6TiSCH networks adopt link-layer security mechanisms, as defined by [17]. In the minimal draft, two security mechanisms are considered: authentication and encryption. Authentication applies to all packet content, while encryption applies to header IEs and MAC payload.

The minimal draft assumes the existence of two cryptographic keys, which can be pre-configured. One of the keys, K1, is used to authenticate EBs. For early interoperability tests, as the one performed during the Plugtests event, K1 is set to 36 54 69 53 43 48 20 6D 69 6E 69 6D 61 6C 31 35 ("6TiSCH minimal15"). To facilitate logical segregation of distinct networks, EBs are authenticated, with no payload encryption.

A second key, K2, is used to authenticate DATA, ACK, MAC COMMAND frame types and respective header IEs, with payload encryption. For the Plugtests event only, K2 is set to "deadbeeffacecafe".

The SEC tests aimed at checking both authentication of EBs (which are exchanged between the DAGroot and the device, only if they are sharing the same key K1), and encryption/decryption of DATA packets (Echo Request/Reply) with K2. The *Key Index*, advertised in the auxiliary security header of the packets allowed nodes to look up the right key (K1 or K2) before decrypting, during the SEC tests.

4.4 RPL Tests

Devices in a 6TiSCH network use the RPL routing protocol [13] and implement the RPL Objective Function Zero (OF0) [14]. Therefore, beyond checking features which are mainly related to the IEEE802.15.4 TSCH MAC [17], during the Plugtests event, other tests were performed for checking the RPL implementation into vendor devices was correctly done, according to the minimal specification [12]. In detail, tests RPL-01 and RPL-02 checks the value of the EB join priority of child and parent devices, and the value of the rank, which should be computed according to the RPL OF0 function [14]. The rank computation uses a *rank increment* that is added to the parents announced rank upon reception of a DIO. The *rank increment* is computed as a function of a metric: in the interop event $2 * ETX$ [15] was used.

The RPL tests group also includes conformance tests, to check the format of DIO and DAO messages is according to [13]. Finally, the use of extension headers was verified specially for the cases where IP tunneling (IP-in-IP encapsulation) was required. Mainly, when an IP packet needs to carry hop-by-hop extension headers, these headers are appended to an IP outer header avoiding the modification of the end-to-end scope of the inner header at each hop. The outer header is removed when crossing a border router leaving the inner header untouched. During the tests, IP tunneling was verified using the appropriate Wireshark dissector.

5 Lessons Learned

The overarching goal of the Plugtests event is to create better standards, resulting in better and interoperable products, larger and faster adoption of the technology, and a better end-user experience. This section summarizes the outcomes of the event in term of feedback to the standardization bodies, and lessons learned.

A first and important aspect to note is the importance of a close relationship between the interoperability event participants and the team of experts preparing the test specification. During that phase, the interaction and discussion between experts and participants accelerated the development and correction of standards under test as well as identified open issues in current standard implementations.

During the 6TiSCH Plugtests event, several issues arose from IEEE802.15.4e implementations brought by different participants. Those issues have been notified to the IEEE 802.15.4 task group. The main concern was related to Table 2a from IEEE802.15.4e-2012 [17] which contains inconsistencies. Table 2a specifies how the IEEE802.15.4 header bits in the Frame Control field are compressed (source and destination PANID compression, source and destination address compression). These inconsistencies have been discussed with the IEEE802.15.4 TG, who agreed that a problem exists. But it has been corrected by the IEEE, as indicated by internal IEEE documents. For the Plugtests event, however, only the published text from IEEE802.15.4e-2012 was used for implementations. We foresee that future Plugtests events, which will be based on future revisions of IEEE802.15.4, will hence fix the issue.

Regarding the minimal draft and it latest published version [12], several concerns arose.

One was related to RPL Mode of Operation (MOP). Some vendors implemented the RPL routing protocol in **storing mode**, others in **non-storing mode**. These modes are not interoperable, so these vendors could not build an interoperable multi-hop network during the event. Currently, the minimal draft does not specify the mode to implement. As follow up of the Plugtests, the issue was discussed during the IETF93 6TiSCH WG meeting. The WG agreed that there was a problem, and is discussing internally how to resolve this in a future revision of [12].

Analogously, some implementations were not using an IPv6 prefix information object in the RPL DIO messages to propagate the prefix of the network. Rather, they were using the prefix derived from the DODAGID. Based on this, in future revision of the 6TiSCH TD it would be recommendable to indicate the need of having this option in the DIO packets.

Finally, multihop tests required to filter packets or force the topology. The use of cables was problematic for MMCX and uFL antenna connectors while for SMA connectors it worked well. Therefore, it might be desirable to avoid forcing multihop topologies with coaxial cables and attenuators. We recommend for the next events one of the following approaches: (1) build/buy shield boxes to put nodes in or (2) ask vendors to add a functionality in their code that filters frames based on their source MAC address.

6   Conclusion

221 tests were performed during the 6TiSCH Pugtests event, and from these, 207 were PASS, resulting in a 93.7 % success rate. This high level of interoperability at the *first* 6TiSCH Plugtests event shows that 6TiSCH industrial IoT deployments will not run into big interoperability issues. The successful outcome can be attributed to the fact that each participant received a Golden Device prior to the event and could test their implementation against it before coming to the Plugtests event. Other 6TiSCH Plugtests will be organized in the future, to allow other vendors to take part, and perform new tests, checking more advanced features of the 6TiSCH technology.

References

1. Cisco-Systems: The Zettabyte Era Trends, Analysis (2014). http://www.cisco.com/c/en/us/solutions/collateral/service-provider/visual-networking-index-vni/VNI_Hyperconnectivity_WP.html
2. The Internet of Things: International Telecommunication Union (ITU), Technical report (2005)
3. IEEE: IEEE Standard Computer Dictionary: A Compilation of IEEE Standard Computer Glossaries. IEEE Std. (1990)
4. Slater, T.: What is Interoperability? Network Centric Operations Industry Consortium - NCOIC, Technical report (2012)
5. Palattella, M.R., Accettura, N., Vilajosana, X., Watteyne, T., Grieco, L.A., Boggia, G., Dohler, M.: Standardized protocol stack for the Internet of (important) Things. IEEE Commun. Surv. Tutor. **15**(3), 1389–1406 (2013)
6. ETSI: ETSI EG 202 237 V1.1.2 (2007-04). ETSI Guide. Methods for Testing and Specification (MTS), Internet Protocol Testing (IPT), Generic Approach to Interoperability Testing (2007)
7. ETSI: ETSI EG 202 568 V1.1.3 (2007-04). ETSI Guide. Methods for Testing, Specification (MTS). Internet Protocol Testing (IPT). Testing: Methodology and Framework (2007)
8. Dujovne, D., Watteyne, T., Vilajosana, X., Thubert, P.: 6TiSCH: deterministic IP-enabled industrial Internet (of Things). IEEE Commun. Mag. **52**(12), 36–41 (2014)
9. IEEE: IEEE802.15.4. Part. 15.4: Low-Rate Wireless Personal Area Networks (LR-WPANs) Amendment 1: MAC sublayer. IEEE Std., April 2012

10. Thubert, P., Watteyne, T., Palattella, M.R., Vilajosana, X., Wang, Q.: IETF 6TSCH: combining IPv6 connectivity with industrial performance. In: International Conference on Innovative Mobile and Internet Services in Ubiquitous Computing (IMIS), pp. 541–546. IEEE (2013)

11. Palattella, M.R., Thubert, P., Vilajosana, X., Watteyne, T., Wang, Q., Engel, T.: 6TiSCH Wireless industrial networks: determinism meets IPv6. In: Mukhopadhyay, S.C. (ed.) Internet of Things, pp. 111–141. Springer International Publishing, Switzerland (2014)

12. Vilajosana, X., Pister, K.: Minimal 6TiSCH Configuration. Internet Engineering Task Force Std., Rev. draft-ietf-6tisch-minimal-11 [work-in-progress], 6 July 2015

13. Winter, T., Thubert, P., Brandt, A., Hui, J., Kelsey, R., Levis, P., Pister, K., Struik, R., Vasseur, J., Alexander, R.: RPL: IPv6 Routing Protocol for Low-Power and Lossy Networks. Internet Engineering Task Force Std. RFC6550, March 2012

14. Thubert, P.: Objective Function Zero for the Routing Protocol for Low-Power and Lossy Networks (RPL). Internet Requests for Comments, Internet Engineering Task Force Std. RFC6552, March 2012

15. De Couto, D.S.J., Aguayo, D., Bicket, J., Morris, R.: A high-throughput path metric for multi-hop wireless routing. Wirel. Netw. 11(4), 419–434 (2005)

16. Vilajosana, X., Tuset, P., Watteyne, T., Pister, K.: OpenMote: open-source prototyping platform for the industrial IoT. In: 7th EAI International Conference on Ad Hoc Networks (AdHocNets). EAI (2015)

17. IEEE802.15.4. Part. 15.4: Wireless Medium Access Control (MAC) and Physical Layer (PHY) Specifications for Low-Rate Wireless Personal Area Networks (LR-WPANs). IEEE Std. (2011)

18. ETSI: ETSI 6TiSCH interoperability test descriptions, 1 26 v1.2 (2015-07) (2015)

19. Munoz, J., Gaillard, G., Barthel, D.: Example Packets for the Minimal 6TiSCH Configuration. Internet Engineering Task Force Std., Rev. draft-munoz-6tisch-minimal-examples-00 [work-in-progress], 6 July 2015

BLE and IEEE 802.15.4 in the IoT: Evaluation and Interoperability Considerations

PrithviRaj Narendra[1(✉)], Simon Duquennoy[1], and Thiemo Voigt[1,2]

[1] SICS Swedish ICT, Kista, Sweden
{prithvi,simonduq,thiemo}@sics.se
[2] Uppsala University, Uppsala, Sweden

Abstract. As the Internet of Things is gaining momentum, low-power communication technologies proliferate. In this paper, we focus on Bluetooth Low Energy (BLE) and IEEE 802.15.4 (CSMA, Low-power listening, and TSCH), and advocate low-power IPv6 for interoperability between the two. We perform a thorough experimental comparison of their link-layer performance, both in idle radio environment and when facing heavy (controlled) external interference. Our results suggest that both technologies can achieve interesting and complementary latency-energy trade-offs. Based on our results, we discuss possible interoperability between BLE and IEEE 802.15.4 and present related open issues.

Keywords: Interoperability · IoT · Link-layer · BLE · IEEE 802154 · IPv6

1 Introduction

Over the past few years, Internet of Things (IoT) applications have flourished, where everyday objects are made 'smart' by including sensors, processing units and low-power wireless communication means. Current applications, ranging from e-health, entertainment to smart buildings and energy, however, work in isolation. To enable them to interoperate and reach the full potential of the IoT, a practical approach is to run a low-power IPv6 stack in these devices. With this approach, the devices can access the Internet and benefit from network-layer compatibility. This enables interaction between devices running various applications and relying on heterogeneous technologies.

In this paper, we focus on two of the currently dominating technologies: Bluetooth Low Energy (BLE) and IEEE 802.15.4[1]. We review both technologies, evaluate their performance, and discuss their interoperability. An example application of BLE – 802.15.4 interoperability a smart health/fitness tracking band (BLE) that can communicate via IPv6 to the home thermostat (802.15.4) to regulate the temperature/humidity based on multiple users' pulse and body temperature. Because the application builds upon standards, it can be extended

---

[1] In this paper we use 'IEEE 802.15.4' and '802.15.4' interchangeably.

© ICST Institute for Computer Sciences, Social Informatics and Telecommunications Engineering 2016
B. Mandler et al. (Eds.): IoT 360° 2015, Part II, LNICST 170, pp. 427–438, 2016.
DOI: 10.1007/978-3-319-47075-7_47

easily, for example, with a cloud server used to store/process sensor data and make more complex decisions based on user preferences etc. The devices can also be accessed directly by the user via a smartphone or other means.

We port Contiki, a leading operating system for the IoT, to the nrf51822 System on Chip (SoC), a BLE platform. As our prototype does not support IPv6 yet, we focus our evaluation on the link-layer. We conduct an extensive experimental comparison of the BLE and IEEE 802.15.4 link layers (CSMA, Low-power listening and TSCH), and we challenge both technologies by exposing them to controlled external WiFi interference. We look at both request-response and bulk transmission schemes. Our focus is on reliability, energy consumption, latency and data rate. Overall, we find that both technologies are able to make different latency-energy trade-offs, which makes them suitable for a variety of applications. We believe there is room for both technologies in the IoT, which makes interoperability an even more important concern. We discuss practical issues and open research questions in making this interoperability happen.

The paper is organized as follows: Sect. 2 gives necessary background on BLE and 802.15.4. Sect. 3 describes the hardware platforms used for experimentation. Sect. 4 presents an experimental comparison of the BLE and 802.15.4 link layers. Sect. 5 discusses current trends and open issues in achieving full BLE-802.15.4 interoperability. We finally review related work in Sect. 6 and conclude in Sect. 7.

2 Background: BLE and 802.15.4

This section reviews BLE [5] and IEEE 802.15.4 [3] with a focus on the link layer, as this is the layer we evaluate experimentally. As illustrated in Fig. 1, both technologies share the 2.4 GHz ISM spectrum, but have their own modulation scheme, bit rate, channel map and channel spacing, and upper layers.

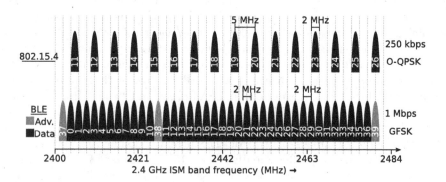

Fig. 1. The BLE and 802.15.4 channel maps share the 2.4 GHz ISM spectrum.

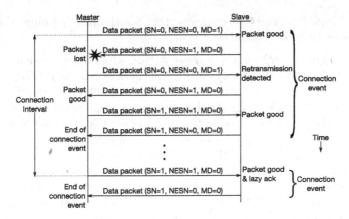

Fig. 2. Illustration of a connection event and connection interval (inspired from [14]). SN: Sequence Number. NESN: Next Expected Sequence Number. MD: More Data bit.

2.1   Bluetooth Low Energy (BLE)

BLE employs frequency hopping over 37 channels for (bidirectional) communication and 3 for (unidirectional) advertising, with a bitrate of 1 Mbps. In Bluetooth 4.0, the link-layer MTU is 27 bytes[2], protected with a 24-bit CRC.

At the link layer, BLE forms a star network, with a master orchestrating bidirectional communication with one or several slaves. Nodes have different link-layer states including advertising, scanning and connection. An advertising device (typically a low-power node) periodically broadcasts packets over channels 37, 38, 39 which are spread over the 2.4 GHz ISM spectrum such that they do not overlap the most common WiFi channels 1, 6 and 11. A scanning device (e.g. a smartphone) listens on these advertising channels, waiting for advertisement packets. Upon receiving an advertisement, the scanning device may initiate a connection with a 'connection request' packet. The advertising device becomes the slave and the scanning device the master.

After the connection is established, communication takes place in 'connection events', which occur at a period called 'connection interval'. At every connection event, the master transmits a packet to the slave, which may or may not respond. Several master-slave transmissions can occur in the same connection event, as driven by the 'More Data' bit (as illustrated by Fig. 2). Sequence numbers and acknowledgments ensure reliable, in-order delivery. We review a number of relevant connection parameters (set by the master during establishment).

Connection Interval. Interval between connection events. Can range from 7.5 ms to 4 s, and can be changed even after a connection is established.

Slave Latency. Slave devices can save further energy by skipping connection events. The slave latency tells how many such events can be skipped in a row.

---

[2] This has been increased to 251 bytes in Bluetooth 4.2 [6].

Channel Map. Specifies the channels used for channel hopping. Can be all 37 channels of BLE, or any subset.

Hop Increment. Every connection event BLE employs a frequency hopping mechanism to hop to a different frequency in the 2.4 GHz band. The hopping of the master is synchronized with the slave with the following equation: $f_{n+1} = (f_n + hop) \mod 37$. Where f_{n+1} is the next channel, f_n the current channel used and hop is the hop increment connection parameter. The process is iterated until reaching a channel that is part of the connection's channel map.

Above the link layer the BLE stack consists of the Logical Link Control and Adaptation Protocol (L2CAP), the Attribute Protocol (ATT), the Generic Attribute Profile (GATT), the Security Manager Protocol (SMP) and the Generic Access Profile (GAP) [12]. On top of them there are standardized profiles for various use cases that the application layer can use. Unlike 802.15.4, which is restricted to the physical and MAC layers, BLE is a full protocol stack. The adoption of 6LoWPAN, IPv6 and higher layers on top of BLE's L2CAP layers has been proposed in a currently active IETF Internet-Draft [19]. Hence, the lower layers are important indicator of the performance of a protocol.

2.2 IEEE 802.15.4

802.15.4 features a total of 27 non-overlapping channels, including 16 in the 2.4 GHz and 11 in the sub-GHz bands. We focus on the 2.4 GHz band, which has a bitrate of 250 kbps. The maximum transmission unit is 127 bytes, and frames are protected with a 16-bit CRC.

Unlike BLE, IEEE 802.15.4 can form various topologies, such as star network, cluster tree or mesh. 802.15.4 is widely used as a research platform and features many different MAC layers. Some of the latter are part of the standard, others research prototypes. In this paper, we focus on the three MAC protocols we selected for evaluation: CSMA, ContikiMAC and TSCH.

802.15.4 + CSMA. CSMA (non-persistent CSMA-CA) is one of the MAC layers defined in 802.15.4-2011 [3]. We use the Contiki implementation, which departs slightly from the standard configuration (non-standard back-off procedure) but follows the same overall operation.

With CSMA, nodes keep their radio always on, operate on a single channel, and access the medium through contention. Link-layer acknowledgments are used to confirm reception and enable retransmissions at the sender. Using the 'frame pending' bit of the 802.15.4 header, nodes can tell the receiver that they have more packets in their send queue. With this feature, nodes can send many consecutive packets, which is useful in high bandwidth applications.

802.15.4 + ContikiMAC. ContikiMAC is Contiki's default power-saving MAC layer [10]. It is an asynchronous low-power listening MAC, similar to BoX-MAC [18]. In ContikiMAC, nodes sleep most of the time, and wake up periodically (*e.g.*, every 125 ms) to sense the medium. Whenever detecting a signal, a node keeps the radio on for a few milliseconds, attempting a reception. At the sender side, the node transmits the data packet repeatedly until it receives an ACK from the receiver. ContikiMAC optimizes unicast using a so-called 'phase-lock' mechanism, where nodes stay loosely synchronized to minimize strobing time. ContikiMAC also supports the 'frame pending' bit for burst transmissions, but at a rate lower than with CSMA.

802.15.4 + TSCH. Time Slotted Channel Hopping (TSCH) is a MAC layer defined in the IEEE 802.15.4e [4] amendment. TSCH forms a mesh network where all nodes are globally synchronized. Communication is organizes in slots, with a typical duration of 10 or 15 ms (we use 15 ms in this paper). Every slot is long enough to accommodate the transmission of a frame and its acknowledgment. Slots are grouped in one or several slotframes, which repeat over time and form a schedule. At every slot, nodes know exactly whether they are supposed to sleep, transmit or receive. TSCH combats interference and link dynamics through channel hopping: at every slot, a channel is selected deterministically from a pseudo-random hopping sequence.

802.15.4: Upper Layers. There are many possible upper layers for 802.15.4, including ZigBee, 6LoWPAN, or custom network stacks. In interoperable low-power IP networks, the network stack is IPv6 along with the 6LoWPAN [17] adaptation layer. For mesh networking, a routing protocol such as RPL can be used, allowing low-power IPv6 nodes to be addressed over multiple hops. Upper layers typically employ UDP and CoAP. The IETF Working Group 6TiSCH [22] is currently proposing an architecture for 6LoWPAN/TSCH networks.

3   Platforms and Implementations

For this study, we work with two platforms: the nrf51822-based PCA10000 for BLE and the Tmote-Sky for 802.15.4. We ported the Contiki OS [1] to nrf51822 in order to use the same OS in both cases. Note that although Contiki supports a full-fledged low-power IPv6 stack, we run our experiments without it and focus on the performance at the link-layer, in part because we do not have yet all the mechanisms required to run IPv6 over BLE.

3.1   BLE: Contiki over nrf51822

As a BLE platform, we use the PCA1000 board, containing the nrf51822 SoC by Nordic Semiconductor. The nrf51822 SoC has a ARM Cortex M0 processor, BLE compliant radio and various on-chip peripherals. The BLE stack used is a precompiled and linked binary file called SoftDevice, S110 v6.0.0 for the slave role and S120 v1.0.0 for the master role. This stack provides an implementation of Bluetooth 4.0 specification. We perform all communication at the GATT layer because the binary from Nordic Semiconductor used in this project does not provide an API to access the lower layers in both master and slave devices. We enable the radio state change notification in the SoftDevice to enable logging the radio on-time, which we use for energy estimation.

3.2 IEEE 802.15.4: Contiki over Tmote-Sky

For 802.15.4, we use the Tmote-Sky platform, a widely used research platform that supports all Contiki features. The Tmote-Sky features an MSP430-F1611 MCU and CC2420 2.4 GHz transceiver. We use the Contiki energest module to log the radio on-time for energy estimation. Note that the CSMA experiments use the Contiki CSMA+NullRDC layers (*i.e.*, CSMA with no additional radio duty cycling protocol). As our experiments are without IPv6, we run Contiki with the Rime stack (a simple ad-hoc network layer).

4 Performance Comparison

This section compares the performance of BLE vs. 802.15.4 in terms of latency, data rate, reliability, and energy consumption. The goal is to gain a better understanding of the properties and trade-offs of each technology.

4.1 Setup

In order to assess both technologies in different scenarios, have run two different series of experiments: Request-Response (RR) and Bulk-Transmission (BT). Both experiments involve communication between two nodes: a master and a slave for BLE, a coordinator and simple node for 802.15.4. In all cases we use a transmission power of 0 dBm (the default of both the nrf51822 and Tmote Sky's cc2420 radios). We focus on the following metrics:

Latency. The latency is the time it takes to poll data in a request-response process. It is measured at the application layer as illustrated in Fig. 3.

Data Rate. The data rate is measured at the link-layer, i.e. the amount of link-layer payload (excluding link-layer header) per unit of time.

Energy. As a metric of energy, we measure the portion of time spent with the radio turned on, referred to as Radio Duty Cycle (RDC). The RDC is a commonly used metric which does not allow to derive exact consumption numbers,

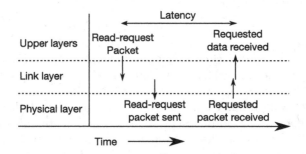

Fig. 3. Timeline of one request-response cycle. With both BLE and 802.15.4, we measure latency at the application layer.

but has the advantage of being completely platform-independent. RDC numbers can be fairly compared across protocols and platforms. We measure the RDC by logging, from the firmware, the total time spent with the radio turned on.

Reliability. We measure reliability at the link-layer as Packet Reception Ratio (PRR), i.e. the portion of packets received over sent. This does not account for retransmissions, i.e. the reception ratio at higher layers is typically higher than the PRR thanks to repeated attempts.

4.2 Request-Response (RR)

The RR experiment aims at determining the latency for reading data from another node. In the RR experiments we keep the nodes close to each other (10 cm) to reflect an almost error-free environment. We repeat the request-response cycle 1000 times for test case. The goal is to find the relation between energy consumption and latency based on different link layer configurations. Thus, the metrics evaluated in this experiment are **latency** and **energy**.

We run 802.15.4 with ContikiMAC, CSMA and TSCH. For TSCH, we use a slotframe of length 17 (repeats every 17×15 ms), with two dedicated unicast slots: one for the request and one for the response. We run BLE with a connection interval of 7.5 ms (denoted BLE 7.5) or 125 ms (BLE 125). We also evaluate the BLE slave latency mechanism, which allows the slave to skip a given number of connection intervals. With a 7.5 ms interval we use a slave latency of 65 (denoted BLE 7.5-65), while with a 125 ms we set the slave latency to 3 (BLE 125-3). This results in a maximum sleep time of 495 ms resp. 500 ms.

Figure 4 shows our results in latency and energy. The lowest latency is achieved with BLE with a short connection interval (BLE 7.5), but this leads to a high duty cycle of above 20 %. Next comes CSMA, with a duty cycle that is even higher (100 %). TSCH, ContikiMAC and BLE 125 strike an interesting

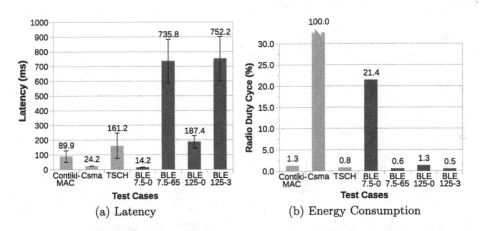

(a) Latency   (b) Energy Consumption

Fig. 4. Request-Response (RR) experiment. The various configurations of BLE and 802.15.4 offer complementary energy-latency trade-offs. 'BLE-x-y' denotes a connection interval 'x', and a slave latency 'y'.

latency-energy balance, with a duty cycle between 0.6 and 1.3 %, and a latency below 200 ms. Finally, BLE, using slave latency, achieves the lowest duty cycle, at the price of much a higher latency, in the 750 ms range. Overall, both 802.15.4 and BLE are able to achieve interesting latency-energy trade-offs, allowing to prioritize responsiveness and lifetime depending on application requirements.

4.3   Bulk Transmission (BT)

The BT experiment aims at measuring the maximum data rate of BLE and 802.15.4 CSMA and TSCH at the link layer with and without WiFi interference. In all cases, the link layer contains the maximum payload allowed, namely 27 bytes for BLE and 110 bytes for 802.15.4. For 802.15.4 TSCH, we run a simple schedule with a single unicast slot from source to destination, repeating every 15 ms. The nodes are kept 1 m apart and in case of environment with interference, a WiFi router is placed 2.5 m away from the two nodes. Each run of the experiment lasts one minute in order to measure a stable mean data rate. The metrics measured in this experiment are **data rate**, **energy**, and **reliability**.

To introduce external WiFi interference, we use the tool `iperf` running on a ThinkPad T420 to transmit UDP traffic at 3 MB/s to a WiFi router (Netgear N300). The WiFi devices use the 802.11b/g/n standard over channel 5. We run TSCH and BLE either over all channels, or the subset of channels that are WiFi-free. For CSMA we select channel 15 (overlapping WiFi channel 5) or 26 (not affected by WiFi). With CSMA we rely on the burst transmission mode and disable link-layer acknowledgments to reach the highest throughput. We evaluate CSMA both with and without CCA (test cases without CCA are denoted 'nC').

Figures 5a, 6a and 7a show the results without interference. 802.15.4 + CSMA achieves the highest data rate with 155 kbps, but with a higher energy consumption as it keeps the radio turned on nearly all the time. BLE is the most reliable, with 99.9 % PRR, which we attribute to channel hopping and short packet air time (high data rate, short frames).

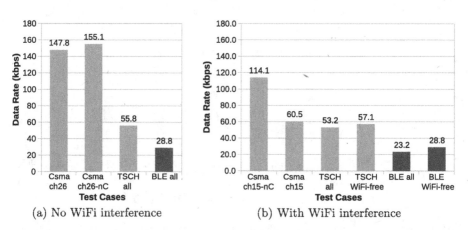

(a) No WiFi interference   (b) With WiFi interference

Fig. 5. Bulk Transmission (BT) experiment. 802.15.4 CSMA reaches higher throughput than BLE. BLE is less affected by interference thanks to channel hopping.

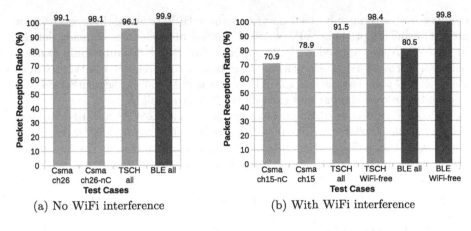

(a) No WiFi interference   (b) With WiFi interference

Fig. 6. BT experiment. Both protocols achieve similar link-layer reception ratios.

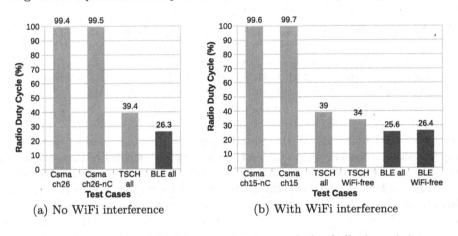

(a) No WiFi interference   (b) With WiFi interference

Fig. 7. BT experiment. BLE keeps saving energy during bulk transmission.

We show the results with external WiFi interference in Figs. 5b, 6b and 7b. Overall, we see the same trends as without WiFi, i.e. 802.15.4 has a higher data rate and consumes more energy. Disabling CCA helps CSMA to achieve a higher data rate, at the price of a PRR reduction from 80 to 70%. TSCH and BLE, through channel hopping, are less affected by interference than the single-channel CSMA. With the help of link-layer retransmissions, both BLE and TSCH achieved 100% reliability.

5 Discussion

5.1 IPv6 over BLE

The Internet Protocol Support Profile (IPSP) [7] defines how BLE devices running IPv6 discover each other and communicate at the L2CAP layer. With a focus on the layers above L2CAP, the IETF Working Group '6lo' is currently defining how to transmit IPv6 datagrams over BLE (Bluetooth version 4.1 or greater) using adapted 6LoWPAN [19]. A number of mechanisms already defined in 6LoWPAN are applied to BLE, among which: address auto-configuration, neighbor discovery (star network case) and header compression. 6LoWPAN fragmentation is not used, as the L2CAP layer can take care of segmentation and reassembly in case the payload exceeds the link layer MTU.

In a 6LoWPAN over BLE network, the master is a 6LoWPAN Border Routers (6LBR), while the slaves are 6LoWPAN nodes (6LN). This provides Internet connectivity to the nodes, and enables 6LN-to-6LN communication via the 6LBR. Multicast is implemented as individual unicast by the 6LBR to target 6LNs. Even though the specification is still in a draft state, Nordic Semiconductor has already released an IoT SDK based on it [2].

5.2   Dual-Protocol Devices

In the past years quite a few platforms have been released that can support both BLE and 802.15.4. As a module, Redpine Signal's RS9113 also supports 2.4 GHz/5 GHz 802.11b/g/n WiFi in addition to a dual mode Bluetooth 4.0 and 802.15.4-based ZigBee. CC2650, a SoC released by TI in 2015 has a low power 2.4 GHz radio compatible with both 802.15.4 and BLE. This SoC consists of an ARM Cortex-M3 for main application, ARM Cortex-M0 for radio operation and a low power 16 bit processor for simple periodic routines. Similarly KW40Z, a new SoC based on ARM Cortex M0+ also has a low power radio compatible with these two protocols. With the radio capable of changing its operation on the fly between the two protocols and availability of low level radio commands these SoCs can be good candidates in both commercial and research scenarios.

Since we foresee that both the protocols will have their role to play in the IoT, these platforms would be ideal as a bridge between the two technologies at a hardware level, similar to IPv6 at the network level. Since both these protocols need border routers to connect to the Internet, these platforms can provide a solution for both, while also enabling direct inter-technology communication.

5.3   BLE – 802.15.4 Co-existence

In joint BLE – 802.15.4 networks, spectrum sharing might become challenging. How to best handle co-existence between cross-technology (*e.g.*, BLE and TSCH) channel hopping networks is an open issue. Assuming coordination is possible through e.g. a home gateway, one could easily allocate disjoint parts of the spectrum to each network. In uncoordinated cases, possible directions include detecting external interference and restricting BLE to the subset of channels that does not overlap 802.15.4, or devising mechanisms for adaptive blacklisting in low-power channel hopping networks.

6   Related Work

We review previous work on comparing BLE vs. 802.15.4, and on IPv6 for both.

BLE – 802.15.4 Comparison. Several studies [9,11,15,21] compared BLE with 802.15.4 in simulation or experimentally, and under various application assumptions and protocol configurations. Siekkinen *et al.* [21] focused on the relation between throughput and energy, and found that BLE had a constant energy utility, while 802.15.4 got more energy-efficient as throughput increases. The paper also characterizes the overhead of both protocols at different payload sizes and runs experiment with external WiFi interference, but with BLE running in non-connected mode only. Other works [9,11,15] explored the energy-performance trade-off of both stacks for different configurations, and the found results aligned with ours in particular for BLE with 7.5 ms connection interval, and for 802.15.4 CSMA. To the best of our knowledge our paper is the first to explore 802.15.4 with low-power listening (ContikiMAC) in comparison with BLE at different connection intervals and under controlled interference.

Low-Power IPv6 for BLE and 802.15.4. IPv6 in low-power wireless is gaining more and more academic and industrial attention. While 6LoWPAN is being adapted to BLE by the IETF [19], there are already several implementations of IPv6 or 6LoWPAN stacks for BLE [13,20,23]. For instance, the Contiki low-power IPv6 stack was ported to CC2541 for BLE communication with a Linux system as a master [13]. Extending BLE to multi-hop, which could be useful in IPv6 IoT networks, is also currently under consideration [8,16]. As for 802.15.4, 6LoWPAN [17] was defined in 2007 and soon found its way to IoT OSes such as Contiki, TinyOS, OpenWSN, or RIOT. Several recent standardization efforts such as ZigBee IP, the Thread Group, and the IETF Working Groups Roll, 6lo, 6tisch (among others) demonstrate the rising interest in IPv6-based 802.15.4 and IPv6 in the IoT at large.

7   Conclusion

BLE and IEEE 802.15.4 have their own set of properties and performance, which makes them suitable to different applications. As a result, both technologies will likely continue to co-exist, making interoperability a central concern. This paper sheds the light on open interoperability issues, and presents experimental results on how each technology performs in a challenging environment.

References

1. Contiki: The Open Source Operating System for the Internet of Things
2. Nordic Semiconductor IPv6 over Bluetooth Smart Protocol Stack for nRF51 SoCs Enables Small, Low Cost, Ultra-low Power IoT Applications (2014)
3. 802.15.4 Task Group.802.15.4-2011: IEEE Standard for Local and metropolitan areanetworks–Part 15.4: Low-Rate Wireless Personal Area Networks (LR-WPANs), 6 September 2011
4. 802.15.4e Task Group.802.15.4e-2012: IEEE Standard for Local and Metropolitan Areanetworks–Part 15.4: Low-Rate Wireless Personal Area Networks (LR-WPANs) Amendment 1: MAC sublayer, 16 April 2012

5. Bluetooth SIG. Bluetooth Core Specification Version 4.0. Specification of the Bluetooth System (2010)
6. Bluetooth SIG. Bluetooth Core Specification Version 4.2. Specification of the Bluetooth System (2014)
7. Bluetooth SIG. Bluetooth Internet Protocol Support Profile Specification Version 1.0.0 (2014)
8. Decuir, J.: Bluetooth smart support for 6LoBTLE: applications and connection questions. IEEE Consum. Electron. Mag. 4(2), 67–70 (2015)
9. Dementyev, A., Hodges, S., Taylor, S., Smith, J.: Power consumption analysis of bluetooth low energy, ZigBee and ANT sensor nodes in a cyclic sleep scenario. In: IEEE International Wireless Symposium (IWS), pp. 1–4. IEEE, April 2013
10. Dunkels, A.: The ContikiMAC radio duty cycling protocol. Technical report T2011:13, Swedish Institute of Computer Science (2011)
11. Gomez, C., Demirkol, I., Paradells, J.: Modeling the maximum throughput of bluetooth low energy in an error-prone link. IEEE Commun. Lett. 15(11), 1187–1189 (2011)
12. Gomez, C., Oller, J., Paradells, J.: Overview and evaluation of bluetooth low energy: an emerging low-power wireless technology. Sensors (Basel, Switzerland) 12(9), 11734–11753 (2012)
13. Wang, H., Xi, M., Liu, J., Chen, C.: Transmitting IPv6 packets over Bluetooth low energy based on BlueZ. In: Advanced Communication Technology (ICACT), pp. 72–77 (2013)
14. Heydon, R., Energy, B.L.: The Developer's Handbook, 1st edn. Prentice Hall, Upper Saddle River (2012)
15. Mikhaylov, K., Plevritakis, N., Tervonen, J.: Performance analysis and comparison of Bluetooth low energy with IEEE 802.15.4 and SimpliciTI. J. Sens. Actuator Netw. 2(3), 589–613 (2013)
16. Mikhaylov, K., Tervonen, J.: Multihop data transfer service for Bluetooth low energy. In: 2013 13th International Conference on ITS Telecommunications (ITST), pp. 319–324. IEEE, November 2013
17. Montenegro, G., et al.: Transmission of IPv6 Packets over IEEE 802.15.4 Networks, RFC 4944, September 2007
18. Moss, D., Levis, P.: BoX-MACs: exploiting physical and link layer boundaries in low-powernetworking. Technical report SING-08-00, Stanford (2008)
19. Nieminen, J., Patil, B., Savolainen, T., Isomaki, M., Shelby, Z., Gomez, C.: Transmission of IPv6 Packets over Bluetooth Low Energy [Working Draft] (2015)
20. Shrestha, G.M., Imtiaz, J., Jasperneite, J.: An optimized OPC UA transport profile to bringing Bluetooth low energy device into IP networks. In: 2013 IEEE 18th Conference on Emerging Technologies & Factory Automation (ETFA), pp. 1–5. IEEE, September 2013
21. Siekkinen, M., Hiienkari, M., Nurminen, J.K., Nieminen, J.: How low energy is bluetooth low energy? Comparative measurements with ZigBee/802.15.4. In: 2012 IEEE Wireless Communications and Networking Conference Workshops (WCNCW), pp. 232–237. IEEE, April 2012
22. Thubert, X., Watteyne, T., Struik, R., Richardson, M.: An Architecture for IPv6 over the TSCH mode of IEEE 802.15.4e - draft-ietf-6tisch-architecture-06, IETF Draft, March 2015
23. Yoon, W., Ha, M., Kwon, K., Kim, D.: 6Lo Bluetooth low energy for patient-centric healthcare service on the internet of things. In: Proceedings of the International Conference on the Internet of Things (2014)

Visual Development Environment for Semantically Interoperable Smart Cities Applications

Aikaterini Roukounaki[1(✉)], John Soldatos[1], Riccardo Petrolo[2],
Valeria Loscri[2], Nathalie Mitton[2], and Martin Serrano[3,4]

[1] Athens Information Technology, Kifisias Ave. 44, 11525 Maroussi, Greece
{arou,jsol}@ait.edu.gr
[2] Inria Lille-Nord Europe, Avenue Halley 40, 59650 Villeneuve-d'Ascq, France
{riccardo.petrolo,valeria.loscri,
nathalie.mitton}@inria.fr
[3] National University of Ireland, Galway, Ireland
martin.serrano@insight-centre.org
[4] O'Brien Centre for Science, Science Centre East, Belfield, Dublin 04, Ireland

Abstract. This paper presents an IoT architecture for the semantic interoperability of diverse IoT systems and applications in smart cities. The architecture virtualizes diverse IoT systems and ensures their modelling and representation according to common standards-based IoT ontologies. Furthermore, based on this architecture, the paper introduces a first-of-a-kind visual development environment which eases the development of semantically interoperable applications in smart citites. The development environment comes with a range of visual tools, which enable the assembly of non-trivial data-driven applications in smart cities, including applications that leverage data streams from diverse IoT systems. Moreover, these tools allow developers to leverage the functionalities and building blocks of the presented architecture. Overall, the introduced visual environment advances the state of the art in IoT developments for smart cities towards the direction of semantic interoperability for data driven applications.

Keywords: Smart cities · Internet-of-Things · Semantic interoperability · Development tools

1 Introduction

1.1 IoT Application Silos in Smart Cities

The Internet-of-Things (IoT) [1] is a key enabler of software applications for smart cities, given that it deals with several integral elements of smart city applications such as the communication across heterogeneous devices, the dynamic discovery of sensors and data streams, the collection and filtering of information from multiple data streams, as well as the analysis of data stemming from multiple data sources within the city. As a result of the proliferating IoT deployments in smart cities in different sectors (such as energy, transport, e-government), most cities have nowadays to manage multiple smart

© ICST Institute for Computer Sciences, Social Informatics and Telecommunications Engineering 2016
B. Mandler et al. (Eds.): IoT 360° 2015, Part II, LNICST 170, pp. 439–449, 2016.
DOI: 10.1007/978-3-319-47075-7_48

city deployments and applications. In most cases these applications have been designed and developed independently from each other, even when they have been deployed as part of a unified strategic plan. Furthermore, the various applications tend to evolve independently of each other, given that updates and enhancements to existing smart city applications rely on heterogeneous platforms and architectures. Also, in most cases the various applications have been designed and purchased by different departments of the cities. Therefore, the interconnection of different smart city systems and applications is very difficult, which is a set-back to the integration of these applications towards pursuing city-wide (instead of application-specific) goals. Hence, smart cities are nowadays characterized by the presence of a set of disaggregated heterogeneous application silos [2].

Recent advances in IoT architectures and semantic web technologies enable the convergence of these silos and facilitate the development of added-value integrated cross-context applications. In particular, the advent of IoT ontologies that can represent IoT data streams and services in a semantically interoperable way provides the means for integrated semantically unified IoT applications. The later integrated applications refer typically to applications that combine data and/or services from different legacy deployments within the smart city. Along with IoT ontologies, platforms supporting IoT ontologies for semantically interoperable modelling data/services have emerged. Such platforms provide a foundation for the implementation and operation of semantically interoperable IoT applications in the smart cities. In this paper, we present an IoT architecture for semantically unified applications in smart cities, which leverages existing ontologies (such as W3C SSN ontology [3]) and middleware platforms that support them (such as OpenIoT) [10].

1.2   Development Environment and Tools

Based on the close affiliation of IoT with smart cities, tools and techniques for developing IoT applications can act as a catalyst for the development of smart cities applications. Early frameworks for programming IoT applications have focused on the areas of WSN (Wireless Sensor Networks) [4] and RFID applications [5]. Most of these frameworks provide the means for virtualizing sensors and actuators, thereby alleviating the heterogeneity of the various devices [6]. Recently, we have also witnessed the emergence of software engineering solutions for the integrated development of more general IoT applications (e.g., [7–9]). These solutions leverage semantic models that capture the main elements of IoT applications, including standard semantic models and ontologies, such as the W3C Semantic Sensor Networks (SSN) [11], which provides the means for abstracting/virtualising sensors. Such software engineering solutions are appropriate for supporting the development of applications that rely on the semantic unifications of the legacy disaggregated silos, which comprise the digital mature smart cities.

In addition to introducing an IoT architecture for semantic interoperability, the present paper presents also a development environments for integrated cross-silo applications in smart cities. This environment leverages the IoT architectures and its common IoT semantic models (ontologies) in order to provide the means for combining, aggregating and processing (in a unified way) data streams stemming from diverse IoT systems and application silos within a smart city. The environment comes with a range of visual drag-and-drop tools, which boosts developers' productivity. It also takes advantage of the IoT architecture towards providing added-value data processing functionalities such as data analytics.

1.3 Structure of the Paper

Following this introductory section, Sect. 2 introduces an IoT architecture for semantic interoperability, which provides a wide range of added-value data processing functionalities. The latter operates over multiple semantically unified systems, rather than over a single legacy IoT system. Section 3 is devoted to the presentation of the development environment and of the visual tools that it comprises. Section 4 illustrates a range of sample data processing applications, which demonstrated the added-value of the development tools. Finally, Sect. 5 concludes the paper.

2 IoT Architecture for Semantic Interoperability

An overview of the IoT architecture for semantic interoperability is provided in Fig. 1. It is structured according to the following layers:

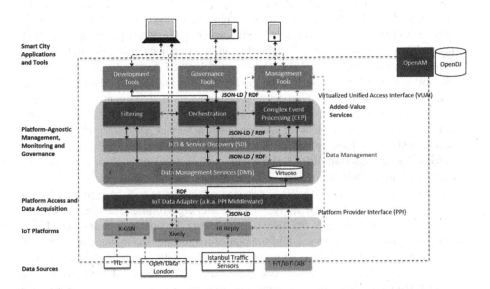

Fig. 1. Overview of IoT architecture for semantic interoperability

- **IoT Systems/Platforms and Data Sources Layer:** This is the lowest layer of the architecture, where various IoT systems (including IoT platforms, applications and data sources) reside. The architecture integrates and processes information from multiple IoT systems. Therefore, this layer comprises the various IoT systems that are virtualized and integrated as part of the architecture. In order to validate the architectural concept, we have integrated and processed data from several IoT platforms. However, the architecture is flexible in the integration of additional platforms and/or applications, as soon as these platforms (or applications) expose a well defined PPI (Platform Provider Interface).

- **Platforms Access and Data Acquisition Layer:** This layer enables access to data and services of the underlying platforms/systems in a secure and authenticated way. Its role is to access the low-level capabilities of the IoT systems (through the PPI) and accordingly to transform the acquired data and metadata into a common data model (i.e. expressed based on an IoT ontology comprising sensors, IoT and smart cities concept). Hence, the functionality of the layer involves translating the low-level semantics of the individual platforms to the high-level and richer semantics of the presented platform. At this layer we also specify the notion of the adapter module, which undertakes the transformation of the lower-level PPI semantics to the high-level ontology.

- **Platform Agnostic Data Management Layer:** This layer provides cloud-based functionalities for managing data and metadata that comply with the VITAL ontology. At this layer, the various data streams (and their metadata) are modelled and formatted according to the common ontology. The offered services include data and metadata persistence, creation of new data, discovery of data subject to various criteria and more. Access to the data of the platform will be based on semantic web technologies and techniques, given the modelling of the data according to the ontology. The platform agnostic data management layer offers a wide range of services to higher level applications, which reside in the added-value functionalities layer. These services will be accessible in a virtualized platform and location agnostic manner, through VUAIs (Virtualized Unified Access Interfaces). VUAIs are abstract interfaces residing at the top layer of the architecture, thereby enabling access to added-value data processing and process management functionalities, including CEP, service discovery, filtering, and other functionalities. The platform agnostic data management layer includes also a Service Discovery (SD) module, which enables the look-up and resolution of IoT resources.

- **Added Value Functionalities Layer:** This layer comprises a set of complete services and tools, which leverage data and services from the platform agnostic management layer. The virtualized services of this layer will be provided by the following modules (depicted in Fig. 1): (A) **Filtering Module**: The filtering module of the architecture provides the means for reducing the information associated with individual data streams persisted in the platform agnostic data management layer. It therefore reduces unwanted information, thereby optimizing processing performance and economizing on network bandwidth; (B) **Complex Event Processing (CEP) Module**: This module enables the processing of data streams for multiple sources in order to identify patterns and/or infer events; (C) **Orchestration Module**: This module combines and manages multiple services from the above-listed modules, in order to deliver new added-value services. The combination of the various services is based on a workflow of service oriented components and interactions, which may be specified on the basis of rules.

- **Smart City Applications and Tools Layer:** The architecture supports the development, integration, deployment and operation of smart city applications, notably applications leveraging data from multiple IoT platforms and applications (including legacy IoT applications in urban environments). All smart city applications are (during their operation) accessing data and services of the platform agnostic data management layer, including the discovery, filtering and CEP services. This layer includes management tools that enable the monitoring and configuration of IoT platforms, applications and services at various granularities. It also includes development tools enabling the development of smart city applications and services. The various applications and tools will be able to access data from the platform agnostic data management layer, as well as services offered from this layer.

In the scope of the FP7 VITAL project (www.vital-iot.eu) a prototype implementation of the presented architecture is provided. This prototype implementation constitutes a middleware platform (i.e. the VITAL platform) that enables the development, deployment and operation of semantically interoperable applications in smart cities. Due to the implementation of the VITAL platform in-line with the above-presented architecture, we also conveniently refer to the architecture as the VITAL project architecture.

3   Development and Deployment Environment

Based on the architecture described above we have implemented an environment enabling the assembly of IoT applications that take advantage of the functionalities of the architecture. The environment exploits the semantic modelling and added-value functionalities of the architecture towards enabling the development of semantically interoperable applications. It is built over the popular Node-RED open-source tool for wiring the Internet of Things [12]. Nodes and flows are the two fundamental concepts in Node-RED. A node is a well-defined piece of functionality. Based on the number of its input and output ports, a node can be of one of the following types: (A) An input node, which is a node that has one or more output ports; (B) An output node, which is a node that has one input port; (C) A function node, which is a node that has one input port and one or more output ports. Nodes can be wired together into what is called a flow. Input nodes sit at the start of a flow, output nodes sit at the end of a flow, and finally function nodes sit in the middle of a flow. Flows can be considered as programs, and nodes as the blocks that can be used to build them. The Node-RED platform comprises two components: (1) a browser-based editor that allows us to design flows (i.e. programs), and (2) a light-weight runtime where we can deploy and execute our flows. The browser-based flow editor is used for creating flows and deploying them on the Node-RED runtime. It comprises a palette, which can be extended with new nodes.

3.1   Development and Deployment Environment Overview

The development and deployment environment allows developers to access and compose the various capabilities offered by the architecture, in order to implement smart city applications. Part of the development and deployment environment is the VITAL development tool that serves as a single entry point to developers that want to build and deploy IoT applications that transcend multiple IoT platforms, architectures and business contexts by leveraging the capabilities provided by the VITAL framework. All these capabilities are exposed through VUAIs. All mechanisms to be integrated into that tool are exposed through VUAIs, which are implemented as RESTful web services, thus rendering Node-RED ideal as the basis for the implementation of the VITAL development tool.

The development tool has been also enhanced with a number of nodes relating to the architecture, as well as with functionalities provided by the R project [13], a programming language and an environment for statistical computing and graphics. The result is an easy-to-use tool that also enables its users to perform a number of task (e.g. retrieval of IoT system metadata) relating to the semantic interoperability architecture, along with data analysis (e.g. data value prediction or clustering) tasks.

Based on the above-mentioned nodes and extensions, the palette of the development tool, offers, apart from the nodes already present in Node-RED, one node for each piece of functionality offered by a VITAL component. For example, Fig. 2 depicts the node that corresponds to the sensor-resource discovery functionality. In a similar way developers can exploit any VITAL functionality by just adding the corresponding node in their flow and setting its properties. While the flow is running, the node interacts with the appropriate components of the VITAL platform in order to perform its tasks. Thus, VITAL nodes facilitate the use of VITAL capabilities by hiding (from the developers) low level implementation and formatting details.

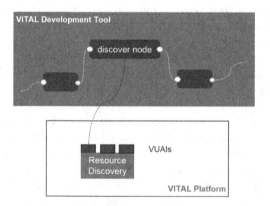

Fig. 2. Concept of VITAL resource discovery node within the development tool

3.2   Authentication and Multi-user Environment

In order to be able to direct each user to a dedicated Node-RED instance that has been created for him/her, a router component has been developed. The router component is a web application that is responsible for the user authentication, as well as for re-directing an authenticated user to the Node-RED instance that is associated with them. Hence, the VITAL platform users register to the router. Whenever a registered user wants to manage their workflows, they log into the router. Once the user has been successfully authenticated, the router looks up into its local repository (1) the host where the Node-RED instance that is dedicated to the user is running and (2) the port where the Node-RED editor of that instance can be accessed. In case there is no running instance for the user, the router creates one. This effectively means that the router creates a clone of the Node-RED codebase, sets all necessary settings (see below), and starts it. Once the new Node-RED instance has been successfully created, the router saves the new mapping into its local repository for future reference.

In order to allow only to the user that owns the Node-RED instance to access it, but without having to log in again (after they have been successfully authenticated by the router), we must (1) enable user authentication in all Node-RED instances and (2) define a user in each Node-RED instance that has the same username and password with the corresponding VITAL user, to whom this Node-RED instance belongs. Both these requirements can be satisfied by setting the appropriate values in the settings file of each Node-RED instance that the router creates.

Based on the above, before the router re-directs an authenticated user to the appropriate Node-RED editor, it needs to contact the Node-RED instance (i.e. perform an HTTP POST to/auth/token), and exchange the credentials of the user with an access token. Once the router has obtained the access token, it can finally re-direct the user to the Node-RED editor with the access token set in the Authorization header. The authentication process is depicted in Fig. 3. It is a process that overall alleviates the single-user nature of the Node-RED environment, thus enabling the VITAL platform to operate as a multi-user platform.

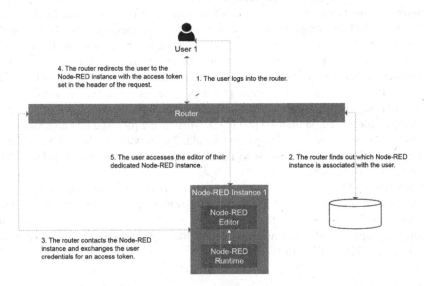

Fig. 3. User authentication in the scope of the VITAL multi-user Node-RED environment

3.3   VITAL Nodes

In following paragraphs we illustrate two of the new nodes that the VITAL platform has added to the core palette of Node-RED, notably nodes corresponding to PPI implementations and Resource Discovery.

3.3.1   Platform Provider Interface Implementation

The Platform Provider Interface (PPI) is defined as a set of primitives, marked as either mandatory or optional. All IoT systems that are compliant to the VITAL platform are expected to implement and expose (as RESTful web services) at least those primitives that are designated as mandatory. The following nodes have been specified and implemented:

- **PPI Nodes:** These are configuration nodes that store information about how to access the PPI implementation of a VITAL compliant IoT system (e.g. its base URL). Configuration nodes are a special category of nodes in Node-RED that can be used for sharing configuration among nodes. For example, PPI nodes can be used by system and services nodes (see below) in order to select the PPI implementation they want to access, without having to specify more than once details on how to access it. The properties of these nodes include the base URL of the PPI implementation, as well as whether basic authentication is required.
- **System Node:** System nodes can be used to retrieve metadata about a PPI compliant IoT system. When a system node receives a message, the node makes an HTTP POST request to BASE_URL/metadata, and then sends out a message that contains the response to that request. The properties of these nodes include the PPI implementation to retrieve metadata about.
- **Sensor Nodes:** Sensors nodes are function nodes that retrieve metadata about sensors that a VITAL compliant IoT system manages. The messages sent to these nodes can be used to filter the sensors to retrieve metadata for (based on their ID and type), whereas the messages sent by these nodes contain the retrieved sensor metadata.
- **Service Nodes:** Services nodes can be used to retrieve metadata about IoT services that a PPI compliant IoT system provides. The message that a services node receives may contain information, which can be used to filter the services to retrieve metadata for (based on their ID and type), whereas the message that a services node sends contains the retrieved service metadata. The services node is responsible for making an HTTP POST request to BASE_URL/sensor/metadata, in order to fetch the requested metadata
- **Data Nodes:** Data nodes are function nodes that pull observations made by sensors managed by a PPI compliant IoT system. Input messages may contain information, which can be used to filter the observations to fetch (based on the corresponding sensor, property and time), whereas output messages contain the retrieved observations in JSON-LD format.

3.3.2   Resource Discovery

The following extra nodes have been added to the node palette in order to enable access to Resource Discovery functionalities:

- **Resource Discovery:** Resource discovery nodes are configuration nodes that store information about how to access the Resource Discovery component of an instance of the VITAL platform. The properties of these nodes include the base URL of the component, as well as whether basic authentication is required (in which case a username and a password can also be provided).
- **Discover Sensors:** These are function nodes that can be used to discover sensors that reside within a certain radius from a certain point (latitude-longitude).The messages received by these nodes contain the radius, the latitude and the longitude. The messages sent by these nodes include metadata about the discovered sensors.

4   Sample Validating Applications

In this section we present a set of sample workflows which have been implemented using the VITAL development tool.

4.1   Sample Workflow #1: Find the Last Observation Made by a Specific Traffic Sensor

We have used the development tool to implement a web service that accepts HTTP GET requests, which contain the URI of a traffic sensor in a sensor parameter in the query string, and responds with the last observation made by that sensor. For the implementation of the web service, we make use of an implementation of the PPI specification provided for the traffic sensors in Istanbul. The flow consists of the following nodes: (A) An http in node that accepts HTTP GET requests at/last-observation; (B) A function node that extracts the sensor URI from the query string of the request, and uses http:// vital-iot.eu/ontology/ns/Speed as the property URI; (C) A data node that retrieves the last observation made by that sensor for that property; (D) An http response node that responds to the initial HTTP request with the observation value.

4.2   Sample Workflow #2: Show the Location of a Specific Traffic Sensor

This workflow implements a web service that accepts HTTP GET requests, which contain the URI of a traffic sensor in a sensor parameter in the query string, and responds with a static HTML page that contains a map with a marker set on the location of that sensor. For the purposes of this web service, we use again the PPI implementation for Istanbul traffic sensors. The result of using that flow is depicted in Fig. 4. The flow comprises six nodes: (A) An http in node that accepts HTTP GET requests at/locate-sensor; (B) A function node that extracts the sensor URI from the query string of the request; (C) A sensors node that retrieves metadata about the sensor with that URI; (D) A function node that extracts the name, the longitude and the latitude of the sensor from the retrieved metadata; (E) A template node that creates an HTML page with the name of the sensor in the title, and a map with a marker at the location of the sensor; (F) An http response node that responds to the initial HTTP request with the that HTML page.

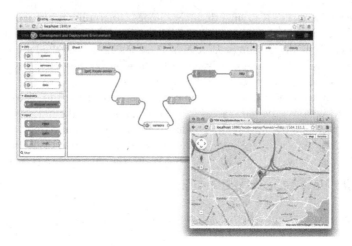

Fig. 4. Screenshot for sample workflow #2 - Show the location of a specific traffic sensor

4.3 Sample Workflow #3: Predict the Next Observation that a Specific Traffic Sensor Will Make

The implementation of this workflow is based on the rstats which is an interface to R project. In particular, the development tool and rstats are used in order to implement a web service that accepts HTTP GET requests, which contain the URI of a traffic sensor in a sensor parameter in the query string, and responds with a prediction for the next observation that that sensor will make. The flow contains five nodes: (A) An http in node that accepts HTTP GET requests at/predict-next-observation; (B) A function node that that extracts the sensor URI from the query string of the request, and uses http:// vital-iot.eu/ontology/ns/Speed as the property URI; (C) A data node that retrieves all observations made by that sensor for that property since a given (earlier) time instant; (C) A function node that retrieves the values from the returned observations, and uses R to predict the value of the next observation according to the best ARIMA model (using the forecast R package); (D) An http response node that responds to the initial HTTP request with that value.

5 Conclusions

Existing IoT ontologies and semantic models can serve as a basis for semantically unifying data sources and data streams from a variety of legacy IoT systems within a smart city. This paper has introduced an IoT architecture which collects and processes information from multiple IoT systems in a smart city environment. Based on this architecture it has also introduced a toolset for IoT application developers that: (A) Ensures virtualized access to diverse IoT systems, including the sensors they manage and the services they provide; and (B) Supports the functionalities provided by the VITAL platform as the latter are specified in the above-mentioned architecture. The toolset has been implemented on the basis of extensions to the popular Node-RED visual environment for IoT. The resulting tools provide the means for implementing semantically interoperable data driven applications in smart cities environment with only minimal programming effort, thus boosting IoT application developers' productivity.

Acknowledgements. This work was funded in part by the European Community in the framework of the VITAL FP7 project (Virtualized programmable InTerfAces for smart, secure and cost-effective IoT depLoyments in smart cities) under contract number FP7-SMARTCITIES-608662. The authors acknowledge help from all partners of the project.

References

1. Atzori, L., Iera, A., Morabito, G.: The internet of things: a survey. Comput. Netw. **54**(15), 2787–2805 (2010)
2. Schiele, G., Soldatos, J., Mitton, N.: Moving towards interoperable internet-of-things deployments in smart cities. ERCIM News, Special Theme: Smart Cities, 98 (2014)
3. Taylor, K.: Semantic sensor networks: the W3C SSN-XG ontology and how to semantically enable real time sensor feeds. In: Semantic Technology Conference, 5–9 June, San Francisco CA, USA (2011)
4. Chatzigiannakis, I., Mylonas, G., Nikoletseas, S.: 50 ways to build your application: a survey of middleware and systems for wireless sensor networks. In: ETFA, pp. 466–473 (2007)
5. Anagnostopoulos, A., Soldatos, J., Michalakos, S.: REFiLL: a lightweight programmable middleware platform for cost effective RFID application development. Pervasive Mob. Comput. **5**(1), 49–63 (2009)
6. Aberer, K., Hauswirth, M., Salehi, A.: Infrastructure for data processing in large-scale interconnected sensor networks. In: MDM, pp. 198–205 (2007)
7. Dimakis, N., Soldatos, J., Polymenakos, L., Fleury, P., Curín, J., Kleindienst, J.: Integrated development of context-aware applications in smart spaces. IEEE Pervasive Comput. **7**(4), 71–79 (2008)
8. Patel, P., Pathak, A., Cassou, D., Issarny, V.: Enabling high-level application development in the internet of things. Sens. Syst. Softw. **122**, 111–126 (2013). Lecture Notes of the Institute for Computer Sciences, Social Informatics and Telecommunications Engineering
9. Cassou, D., Bruneau, J., Mercadal, J., Enard, Q., Balland, E., Loriant, N., Consel, C.: Towards a tool-based development methodology for sense/compute/control applications. In: ACM International Conference Companion on Object Oriented Programming Systems Languages and Applications Companion, pp. 247–248 (2010)
10. Serrano, M., Quoc, H., Le Phuoc, D., Hauswirth, M., Soldatos, J., Kefalakis, N., Jayaraman, P., Zaslavsky, A.: Defining the stack for service delivery models and interoperability in the internet of things: a practical case with OpenIoT-VDK. IEEE J. Sel. Areas Commun. **33**(4), 676–689 (2015)
11. Compton, M., Barnaghi, P., Bermudez, L., Castro, R.G., Corcho, O., Cox, S., et al.: The SSN ontology of the semantic sensor networks incubator group. J. Web Semant. Sci. Serv. Agents World Wide Web **17**, 25–32 (2012)
12. Node-RED: A visual tool for wiring the Internet-of-Things. http://nodered.org/
13. R: The R Project for Statistical Computing. http://www.r-project.org/

Remote Management of a Large Set of Heterogeneous Devices Using Existing IoT Interoperability Platforms

Heleen Vandaele, Jelle Nelis[✉], Tim Verbelen, and Chris Develder

Department of Information Technology, Ghent University – iMinds,
Technologiepark 15, 9052 Ghent, Belgium
heleen.vandaele@ae.be,
{jelle.nelis,tim.verbelen,chris.develder}@ugent.be

Abstract. With the evolution of the Internet of Things, devices of many different technologies and manufacturers are being developed (e.g. for use cases ranging from home automation to smart cities). This creates challenges regarding interoperability between these heterogeneous devices, as well as integrating them to enable innovative applications. Currently, several integration platforms already exist to integrate technologies in a local gateway (e.g. OpenHAB, Zodianet, etc.). Yet, the local set-up and configuration still is overly complex, especially for non-technical users. In this paper, we present a remote management platform that focuses on ease of configuration and installation. It allows monitoring, configuration, diagnostics and service provisioning without manual intervention of a technical person. The platform reacts on local changes such as the installation of a new device or state changes of discovered services. This information can then be used to install required plugins, generate alarms or take problem-solving actions.

Keywords: Internet of Things · Integration · Remote management · DYAMAND · Interoperability

1 Introduction

Today, many devices in our environment are connected, and communicate with other entities to deliver a service to the user. The amount of connected devices will continue to grow over the next years [17]. At the same time the amount of technologies and standards interconnecting these devices is growing. Due to this rapid growth, the landscape of technologies is very scattered, making it difficult for end users and application developers to decide which technology to use or support. Also for non-technical users it becomes more difficult to choose one or more products, without getting locked in by a vendor. If the market does not converge to one single standard, which is unlikely to happen in the near future [7], interoperability platforms are required to overcome this problem.

While some technologies, like Qeo [19], LooCI [6], AllJoyn [1] or CoAP [18] push new standards for constrained device communication, attempting to

© ICST Institute for Computer Sciences, Social Informatics and Telecommunications Engineering 2016
B. Mandler et al. (Eds.): IoT 360° 2015, Part II, LNICST 170, pp. 450–461, 2016.
DOI: 10.1007/978-3-319-47075-7_49

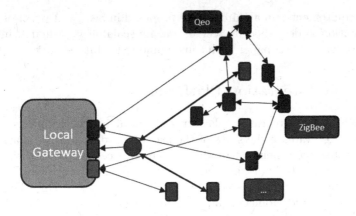

Fig. 1. Gateway centric integration

become the de facto standard in the future, other efforts are concentrating on integrating the huge amount of different technologies. These efforts result mostly in a gateway-centric approach, where an interoperability platform is located at the edge of the local network, providing the necessary abstraction for applications to communicate with devices, regardless of their technology.

The most used technology for implementing these gateway integration platforms is the Open Service Gateway Initiative (OSGi) because of its platform and application independence, service collaboration, security, support for multiple network technologies and its simplicity [11]. OSGi is chosen by [2,4,8,10,20,21] and many others to be the basis of their gateway implementation. There are alternative efforts as well, including HomeGate [20], Multimedia Home Platform (MHP) [4,10,21] or the Home Gateway Initiative [4]. However, many of these platforms are an installation and configuration nightmare. These platforms also tend to become very bloated in terms of storage and memory usage as they often try to support every technology out-of-the-box. Furthermore, a lot of manual configuration is required, and to manage all these platforms physical access to the device is needed. Especially in situations where multiple platforms are distributed across multiple locations, for example in home care or building management, the need for interventions needs to be kept to a minimum.

In this paper, we present a scalable architecture for a remote management platform that monitors and configures IoT gateways. This includes monitoring of information about the devices and services discovered by the gateway, data about their state and actuation of devices locally managed by the gateway as well as management of the local gateway itself. On the gateway, we also provide a technology discovery component, which enables to only install technology plugins that are present, resulting in a more lightweight gateway.

In the remainder of this paper, the existing solutions for local integration are discussed in Sect. 2. Based on the installation and configuration issues, the requirements for a remote management system are identified in Sect. 3. Based on these requirements, an architecture is proposed in Sect. 4. A proof-of-concept implementation is described in Sect. 5, and its scalability evaluated in Sect. 6. Section 7 concludes this paper with some pointers for future work.

2   Existing Integration Platforms

Today, quite a few integration platforms are available, both open source and commercial. To evaluate the state of the art, we have chosen five platforms for comparison, based on their availability to be used (free of charge), their supporting communication technologies and their underlying software platform. First, openHAB [15] is an OSGi based platform hosted by the Eclipse Foundation. Second we compared HomeOS [3], a Microsoft project to provide centralized control of devices in the home. A third platform is the ZiBase gateway for home control, manufactured by Zodianet [22]. Next we have OpenRemote [16], a software integration platform for residential and commercial building automation from OpenRemote Inc. Finally, DYAMAND [14] is a lightweight plugin based interoperability framework developed at Ghent University - iMinds.

We evaluated the procedure to integrate a new technology they all claim to support (i.e. EnOcean), by checking the steps required to plug in an EnOcean USB receiver to the gateway and connect a new EnOcean device. Table 1 gives the summarized results of this platform comparison. The most important conclusion is that most platforms require manual configuration, either using configuration files, or using a graphical user interface. Only DYAMAND and Zodianet automatically detect the EnOcean USB and DYAMAND is the only one to identify the EnOcean device automatically without any manual configuration. As DYAMAND is an academic project, it only has a developer API for supporting 3rd party applications, while the commercial products offer an App store to install new applications on the gateway.

Table 1. Existing integration platforms: conclusion

Platform	Platform installation	Add new technology	Detect new device	Install app
openHAB	Command line	Config Files + OSGi bundles	Config files	Config files
Open remote	Command line	Manual config in GUI	Manual in GUI	Manual config in GUI
Zodianet	App store, Sync with web server	Automated	Config via GUI, Partially automated	App store
HomeOS	Build from source	Manual config in GUI	Our device not detected	App store
DYAMAND	Start script	Automatic, at runtime	Automatic detection	Developer API

3   Requirements

Based on the results of the comparison of different integration platforms, we identified the main functional requirements for usable and configuration friendly interoperability platforms. One important aspect is the ability to remotely manage the integration platform, automating the configuration for the end user as much as possible.

This remote management entails that it should be possible to:

Monitor the interoperability platform and its environment: externalizing the local information so that it can be used for further analysis or improved diagnostics.

Configure the local interoperability platform.

Automatically install new software to support additional technologies (for example install a new driver on the platform) or additional applications without any physical interaction with the local gateway. This allows to ship a lightweight gateway platform and only install the required drivers.

Diagnose the system based on the externalized monitoring information: detect and solve problems without user intervention.

As interoperability platforms are meant to be used over a timespan of multiple years, and will change as the technologies evolve, modifiability is an important quality attribute for the remote management system. In addition to this, when the remote management system is responsible for managing multiple local gateways, the information externalized will require the application to be scalable. Furthermore, since the goal of this remote management is to take away much of the installation and configuration burden, usability is of key importance.

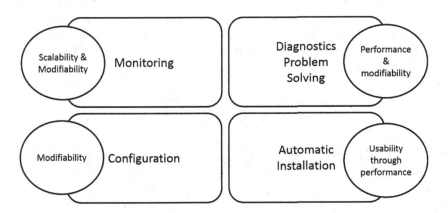

Fig. 2. Functional requirements and quality attributes

4   Architecture

The general decomposition of the system is shown in Fig. 3. We can make a distinction between the gateway plugin, located on the local interoperability gateway, and the remote management system. The gateway plugin is responsible for interacting with the interoperability platform installed on the gateway, for externalizing the information that is available on the gateway and executing commands that it receives from the remote management system. The remote management system (called Remote Manager in the figure), is responsible for analysing and acting upon the information it receives through both the plugin and the web client which provides a view on the monitored data for the end user, and can also be used by an administrator to manually trigger actions on the connected gateways.

4.1   Monitoring Information Generated by the Gateway Plugin

The gateway plugin is tightly coupled with the integration platform running on the gateway. Choosing a different integration platform (e.g. one from Table 1), will require changing the gateway plugin implementation. The plugin collects information about the status of the platform (whether it is still online, or for example how much of the gateway system resources are used), the devices in the environment of the gateway, installed software, or errors that occur. This information is sent to the remote management system over the public Internet. Based on the commands that are included in the response received from the remote management server, the plugin can execute appropriate actions, including control of local devices. For example, when an EnOcean USB dongle is plugged in at the local gateway, the gateway plugin will detect this device via the platform and notify the remote management system. In the response of the remote management system, an installation command for the EnOcean driver will be included. The plugin subsequently can execute the necessary steps to install that driver. The integration platform will be able to support EnOcean from then on.

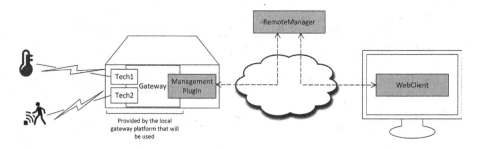

Fig. 3. High level deployment overview.

4.2   Scalability Through RESTful Design

The gateway plugin and the remote management system exchange REST messages. REST, which stands for Representational State Transfer [5], is a client-server model where the client and server are separated by a uniform interface and the messages are stateless. Each message should contain all the information that is needed by the remote management system to understand the request. To make this REST interface suitable for dynamic load balancing, when the amount of local gateways becomes larger than the amount of manageable gateways for one remote manager, the HATEOAS (hypermedia as the engine of application state [9]) principle is used. These principles state that the client must interact with the application entirely through the content provided by the server. This means that, for example when the local gateway is started and sends its first message to the remote management system, the response of the remote manager will contain the possible actions the client needs to proceed, as well as the web links to execute these actions. In further communication, the client will use the links that were provided in the previously received responses. This makes the client independent of where the server is located, and allows the server to dynamically redirect a client (based on e.g. the load of a particular instance of the remote management system, the profile assigned to a gateway, or even the type of request) or even migrate the remote management system to another location.

4.3   Decomposition of the Remote Management System

A more detailed decomposition of the Remote Management System is displayed in Fig. 4. A REST request arrives from the gateway plugin at the Remote Management System, in the Communicator module. To analyse the different messages that are received, various Management components can subscribe to receive the information they are interested in. However, to ensure that the response time remains acceptable (within 2 s, according to the study performed in [12]), the Communicator starts a coordination session to verify that the Management Plugins provide a response well within time. All Management components process the information asynchronously, log everything into the knowledge repository, and provide a response in the form of Commands that have to be executed at the gateway. When all subscribed Management components have their response ready, or when the maximum time-out has elapsed, the coordination ends and the Communicator will send a response containing all available Commands. When a management component fails to provide a Command on time, this Command will be included in the next response.

The Gateway Plugin is responsible to translate all information generated by the local gateway to the concepts understood by the Remote Management System. The Remote Management System can process information about the local gateway, e.g. resources used, plugins loaded and errors that occurred. Apart from that, information about devices and included services that are discovered by the local gateway can be sent. A technology-agnostic model is used to be able to

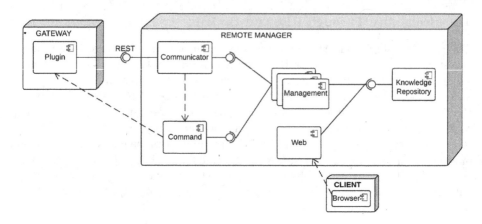

Fig. 4. Architectural decomposition of the remote management system.

represent all information about the discovered devices and services. This model is based on work done at Ghent University on the DYAMAND platform [14]. This model includes among others the concept of state variables that model the state of services in a generic way. Every time a state change is generated by a local device, the local gateway receives and translates it to the model used by the Remote Management System. Furthermore, services can contain Commands that can be executed locally. The Remote Management System will piggyback these commands using the next response sent to the gateway. This means that commands that are triggered by a local event can be executed immediately (given that the responsible Management component is loaded). In contrast, commands that are not the direct consequence of a local trigger must wait until the Gateway Plugin contacts the Remote Management System. Since the information mentioned before are sporadic events, a heartbeat is sent every 30 s. This enables monitoring of the local gateway in absence of other local events and ensures that commands will be executed within the heartbeat interval (as long as the gateway is online).

This architecture is extensible, as new Management components can be added to the system. Due to the asynchronous behaviour of these Management components, they can not only react quickly to incoming messages, but can also perform long-running analysis of data in the Knowledge Repository, which contains all information collected about the gateways that are managed by the remote management system. The Web component provides a view on the Knowledge Repository for making monitoring information available to the end user. An administrative user can also issue new Commands that will be sent to the gateway once the next coordination session ends, using the Web component.

5   Proof of Concept

As a proof of concept, we have built a prototype implementation of our architecture using the DYAMAND interoperability framework as local integration platform. DYAMAND enables flexible protocol support with zero user interaction, as mentioned in a case study in a professional environment in [13] in which the requirements for a remote management system are expressed based on real-life experiences. All concepts understood by the Remote Management System are supported by DYAMAND. However, in this prototype only a limited subset is used:

- **Heartbeat request** - periodically sent to indicate that the installation is online
- **Plugin request** - sent when a new DYAMAND plugin is installed (e.g. a device driver for a certain technology)
- **Device request** - sent when the DYAMAND framework had detected a new device

Using a different local gateway involves translating the concepts used by the local gateway implementation to the concepts of the Remote Management System. Depending on the different concepts supported by the local gateway, some functionality may not be available.

The REST interface is implemented using Jersey[1] and runs on a Glassfish[2] server. The Knowledge Repository uses JPA with a Hibernate[3] backend to access the database.

At the remote manager side, several management components wait to react to REST requests arriving at the interface: for each type of request a specific analyser is implemented. The Heartbeat Analyser checks whether the heartbeat it received originated from a new or existing installation and updates the Knowledge Repository with the timestamp of the last received heartbeat. The path through the architecture is displayed by the yellow line in Fig. 5. The Device Analyser handles information received with a device online request, adding new device information to the Knowledge Repository. The Plugin Analyser adds a new installed plugin to the list of plugins that are installed at the local gateway. This is the blue path displayed in Fig. 5.

We also implemented two Management components that analyse the Knowledge repository. The New Technology Analyser is responsible for checking whether newly detected devices, added to the Knowledge Repository by the Device Analyser, are indicators for unsupported technologies in the local gateway environment. For example, when plugging in an EnOcean USB, this is detected by the gateway plugin, which sends a device online request, resulting in the device being added to the Knowledge Repository by the Device Analyser. This is picked up by the New Technology Analyser that decides the EnOcean support

---

[1] https://jersey.java.net/.
[2] https://glassfish.java.net/.
[3] http://hibernate.org/.

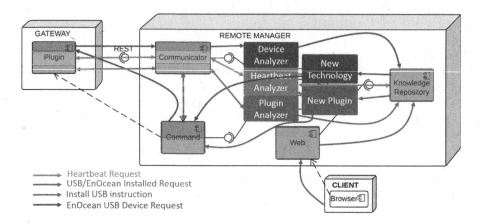

Fig. 5. Control flow path through the remote manager for the heartbeat, plugin and device requests. Each color represents a different scenario. (Color figure online)

plugin must be installed. This adds an installation command to the response that is sent back to the gateway. The red path in Fig. 5 displays this scenario. The New Plugin Analyser listens for new plugins that are added to the Knowledge Repository from the web user interface, and puts an installation command in the waiting line to be added to a response, as soon as the user adds a new (to be installed) plugin via the web interface. This is displayed in Fig. 5 by the green path.

6   Evaluation

Revisiting the scenario to compare the interoperability platforms in Sect. 2, we now have a complete automatic system for detecting and installing a new EnOcean device. Initially the gateway will only have a basic USB device driver installed. Once the EnOcean USB stick is plugged in, the EnOcean driver is automatically downloaded and installed, and new EnOcean devices are automatically detected and monitored. Using the web interface, one can also install additional application plugins on the local gateway.

The implemented prototype focused on installing support for a new technology. Other use cases include, but are not limited to, generating alarms whenever always-on devices are no longer discovered or when the state of a particular device is erroneous, executing commands on local devices based on state of devices located in the same or other installation sites, etc.

To evaluate the scalability of the system, we measured the response times for requests coming from multiple gateways sending various requests. Each simulated gateway sends a heartbeat every 30 s, a device online request every minute and one plugin request in a 3 min timespan as depicted on Fig. 6. When a new plugin is installed, this is followed by 10 new devices that come online, simulating

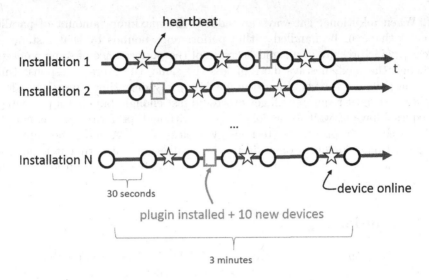

Fig. 6. Visualisation of the test scenario: each active gateway sends a heartbeat every 30 s, a device online request every minute and one plugin installed request.

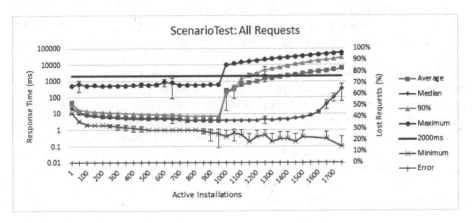

Fig. 7. Aggregated results for the test scenario, using JMeter to send data according to the scheme from Fig. 6

freshly installing support for a new technology. We use JMeter to send simultaneous requests for n gateways, n increasing from 1 to 1700.

We repeated the experiment 10 times and visualized the results in Fig. 7. The experiments were conducted on a server equipped with an Intel Xeon E5-2650 CPU clocked at 2.6 GHz and 48 GiB of RAM.

The left Y-axis shows the response time in milliseconds on a logarithmic scale for all graphs except *Error*, while the right axis' unit is the relative amount of lost requests in percentage for the *Error* graph. Up until 950 gateways using the same instance of the Remote Management System, the performance is up to par. When additional gateways are added, the maximum amount of parallel requests that can be handled within performance bounds by that instance is reached, which results in a rapid decrease of the performance of some requests. Although the median stays more or less the same, the average response time flirts with the 2-s threshold and the maximum response time skyrockets which implies that most requests still get processed fast enough, but that a percentage of requests have to wait for as long as 10 s. Although performance was not the main focus of the prototype (technology choices like JPA and Hibernate were inherited from a predecessor project), this evaluation learns that it is possible to implement the presented functionality in a scalable way if you leverage the benefits of HATEOAS.

7   Conclusion

The interoperability platforms providing a solution for the interoperability issues between heterogeneous devices, often are not designed for ease of installation and configuration that is important for the usability of these platforms. Key requirements therefore include monitoring, diagnostics, automated configuration and automatic software installation. For such usability, it is critical to avoid manual intervention and allow technically trained supervision of geographically distributed integration gateways. In this paper we have presented a scalable architecture for a remote management platform, aiming to reduce the configuration burden for the end user. New technologies are automatically detected at the local gateway, and the required drivers are automatically fetched and installed, resulting in a lightweight gateway installation. We built a proof of concept of our system, showing it can easily manage hundreds of installations on a single server. As future work, we aim to look into more complex management components, i.e., for automatic fault detection or other data analysis. We will also investigate how to better handle technologies that require manual configuration, such as device pairing in ZigBee, or cross-technology discovery, e.g. the Philips Hue bridge that can be discovered locally using UPnP.

Acknowledgements. Part of the work was supported by the iMinds IoT research program.

References

1. Alliance, A.: A Common Language for the Internet of Everything, November 2014
2. Arrizabalaga, S., Cabezas, P., Legarda, J., Salterain, A.: Multi-residential gateway: an innovative concept and a practical approach. IEEE Trans. Consum. Electron. **54**(2), 444–452 (2008)
3. Dixon, C., Mahajan, R., Sharad Agarwal, A.J., Brush, B.L., Saroiu, S., Bahl, P.: An operating system for the home. In: NSDI. USENIX, April 2012
4. Duenas, J.C., Ruiz, J.L., Santillan, M.: An end-to-end service provisioning scenario for the residential environment. IEEE Commun. Mag. **43**(9), 94–100 (2005)

5. Fielding, R.T.: Architectural styles and the design of network-based software architectures. PhD thesis, University of California, Irvine (2000)
6. Hughes, D., Thoelen, K., Maerien, J., Matthys, N., Del Cid, J., Horre, W., Huygens, C., Michiels, S., Joosen, W.: LooCI: the loosely-coupled component infrastructure. In: 2012 11th IEEE International Symposium on Network Computing and Applications (NCA), pp. 236–243. IEEE, August 2012
7. AutomotiveIT International. Gartner Laments Absence of Internet-of-Things Standards, February 2015
8. Choonhwa, L., Nordstedt, D., Helal, S.: Enabling smart spaces with OSGi. IEEE Pervasive Comput. 2(3), 89–94 (2003)
9. Lee, W.: Why HATEOAS a simple case study on the often ignored REST constraint, June 2009
10. Lo, S.-C., Ti-Hsin, Y., Tseng, C.-C.: A remote control and media-sharing system using smart devices. J. Syst. Archit. 60(8), 671–683 (2014)
11. Marples, D., Kriens, P.: The open services gateway initiative: an introductory overview. IEEE Commun. Mag. 39(12), 110–114 (2001)
12. Nah, F.F.: A study on tolerable waiting time: how long are web users willing to wait? Behav. Inf. Technol. 23(3), 153–163 (2004)
13. Nelis, J., Vandaele, H., Strobbe, M., Koning, A., De Turck, F., Develder, C.: Supporting development and management of smart office applications: a DYAMAND case study. In: 2015 IFIP/IEEE International Symposium on Integrated Network Management (IM), pp. 1053–1058, May 2015
14. Nelis, J., Verschueren, T., Verslype, D., Develder, C.: DYAMAND: dynamic, adaptive management of networks and devices. In: 2012 IEEE 37th Conference on Local Computer Networks (LCN), pp. 192–195. IEEE, October 2012
15. openHAB UG. openHAB, Empowering the Smart Home, September 2014
16. OpenRemote Inc., OpenRemote, Open Source Automation Platform, September 2014
17. Rivera, J., van der Meulen, R.: Gartner Says the Internet of Things Installed Base Will Grow to 26 Billion Units By 2020, December 2013
18. Shelby, Z., Hartke, K., Bormann, C.: The Constrained Application Protocol (CoAP). RFC 7252, June 2014
19. Technicolor. Discover Qeo, November 2014
20. Utton, P., Scharf, E.: A fault diagnosis system for the connected home. IEEE Commun. Mag. 42(11), 128–134 (2004)
21. Valtchev, D., Frankov, I.: Service gateway architecture for a smart home. Commun. Mag. 40(4), 126–132 (2002)
22. Zodianet. Zodianet, Home Robotics, September 2014

SDWNCT

Dynamic Monitoring Dashboards Through Composition of Web and Visualization Services

Sofie Van Hoecke[(✉)], Cynric Huys, Olivier Janssens, Ruben Verborgh,
and Rik Van de Walle

Data Science Lab, ELIS, Ghent University-iMinds, Ghent, Belgium
sofie.vanhoecke@ugent.be
http://datasciencelab.ugent.be

Abstract. In order to present and communicate the condition of monitored environments to supervising experts, a dashboard is needed to present the status of all sensors. The heterogeneity and vast amount of sensors, as well as the difficulty of creating interesting sensor data combinations, hinder the deployment of fixed structure dashboards as they are unable to cope with the accordingly vast amount of required mappings. Therefore, in this paper, the development of a dynamic dashboard is presented, able to visualize any particular and user defined data and sensor composition. By implementing the heterogeneous sensors as semantically annotated Web APIs, a dynamic sensor composition and visualization is enabled. The resulting condition monitoring dashboard provides a clear overview of the system KPIs in acceptable timing and provides helpful tools to detect anomalies in system behaviour.

Keywords: Web APIs · Semantic annotation · Monitoring environments · Dynamic composition and visualization · Dashboards

1 Introduction

Multi-sensor architectures, consisting of heterogeneous sensors, are becoming increasingly popular, despite the many challenges they face in terms of data heterogeneity and proprietary data representation standards and communication protocols. The sensors communicate their results through different protocols and represent their data in different formats, resulting in a huge heterogeneity in terms of sensor data representation. Nevertheless, monitoring applications expect a near real-time flow of up-to-date sensor data.

By adopting the Internet of Things vision and implementing the sensors as web-connected devices, sensors have a uniform Web API [1], solving most of the challenges listed above. By using RESTdesc to semantically describe the sensors, advanced sensor compositions and mash-ups can be dynamically generated with existing Semantic Web reasoners [1], enabling the detection of complex events that previously would have remained undetected.

In order to visualize the condition of monitored environments to supervising experts, a monitoring dashboard is needed to present the status of all sensors.

© ICST Institute for Computer Sciences, Social Informatics and Telecommunications Engineering 2016
B. Mandler et al. (Eds.): IoT 360° 2015, Part II, LNICST 170, pp. 465–474, 2016. ·
DOI: 10.1007/978-3-319-47075-7_50

Both the heterogeneity and amount of sensors, as well as the difficulty of creating interesting sensor data combinations, hinder the deployment of fixed structure dashboards as they are unable to cope with the accordingly vast amount of required mappings. Therefore, the development of a dynamic dashboard is required, able to visualize any particular and user defined data composition.

This paper introduces a system architecture in which dynamic sensor compositions and dynamic visualizations of these compositions are supported. The resulting visualization instantiation can be rendered in a widget on the dashboard. Both composition and visualization processes are feasible by semantically annotating the data and visualization services, and by providing these descriptions together with additional logic to a semantic reasoner.

The platform for dynamic visualization of multi-sensor architectures is implemented within an offshore wind farm use case where each of the wind turbines has several sensors by which the current condition of the turbine can be observed.

The remainder of this paper is as follows. Section 2 provides an overview on the current state-of-the-art of dynamic visualization techniques. Next, Sect. 3 describes the proposed platform architecture. In Sect. 4, an accompanying case study is performed, i.e. the monitoring of a (virtual) offshore wind farm. After presenting screenshots of the resulting dynamic dashboard, Sect. 5 evaluates the proposed platform in terms of usability, reliability and general performance. Finally, Sect. 6 formulates the major conclusions.

2   Related Work

Hoang et al. [3] propose a hypergraph-based Query-by-Example approach for developing a dashboard that satisfies a user query according to the current user requirements. Using this hypergraph, knowledge is mapped from heterogeneous and disparate data sources onto homogeneous ontological clusters. The hypergraph-guided data linkage supports interactive exploration, contextualization and aggregation of the data. Gitanjali et al. [2] adopt this Dashboard-by-Example framework to develop a dynamic dashboard that allows to identify semantically equivalent data in warehouses by modeling complex data as components and permitting users to link this data to detect structural dependencies.

Leida et al. [4] annotate both the data and the visualization services using a label and chart ontology using OWL DL and SWRL. The visualization process is initialized by a SPARQL query and generic types (labels) are assigned to each of its variables. A third ontology holds the instantiations of concepts that were defined in the two former ontologies. The semantic Pellet reasoner [5] is responsible for the actual creation of the visualizations.

In order to optimize and integrate global production processes, Mazumdar et al. [6] adopt Semantic Web and information extraction mechanisms to collect, structure and visualize document collections. The proposed methodology is domain independent, abstract and based on ontologies. The actual visualization process occurs in a similar way as the Dashboard-by-Example approach.

3   Dynamic Visualization of Multi-sensor Architectures

The vast amount and heterogeneity of data sources are two major obstacles for the dynamic and efficient composition of this data. In monitoring environments the data sources are sensors, having limited resources and storage. The automatic – and meaningful – composing of sensor data is essential in order to detect more complex events. It allows an early intervention and prevents permanent component damage. Furthermore, by linking sensor data with relevant ad hoc mash-up data, nontrivial associations can be exposed. From an analytical point of view, it is also crucial to have access to the evolution and history of the sensor data, enabling future failure detection and prevention. Sensors are typically not able to keep track of their previous values, so external storage is required.

Sensor and data compositions need to be dynamically visualized, hereby limiting the user input to selecting the preferred visualization method from a system-generated list of meaningful options, taking into account the preferences and characteristics of the current user profile. This results in a personalized and dynamically built monitoring dashboard that allows to correctly analyse and interpret the most critical functions of the monitored environment. Figure 1 presents the proposed system architecture, in which four major components can be distinguished. The central broker component contains the core functionality and connects (compositions of) data streams to an appropriate visualization service, enabling meaningful real-time visualization instantiations to be created and displayed on the dashboard widgets. The components are described below.

3.1   Data Services

Sensors can be implemented as Web APIs to cope with the heterogeneous (and possibly proprietary) data representation standards and communication protocols. By semantically annotating the obtained Web services and means of inference, a higher level coupling can be achieved without any additional configuration required. By considering each individual sensor as an abstract REST resource, the system will be less application specific. A resource requesting component needs to have access to the included semantic description, so (by means of *content negotiation*) sensor data can be correctly interpreted.

3.2   Visualization Services

The main responsibility of the visualization services is to visualize the submitted sensor data. Many satisfying and well performing visualization libraries exist, and it suffices to enclose one of them in a Web service, making it accessible by means of an API. This way, application specific functionality can be inserted. Data is submitted using query string parameters. The actual mapping of sensor data to these parameters is carried out in the central broker component, provided that data and visualization services are consistently and compatibly annotated. The visualization service interprets the submitted data using the query parameters, and subsequently processes it. Source code that visualizes the

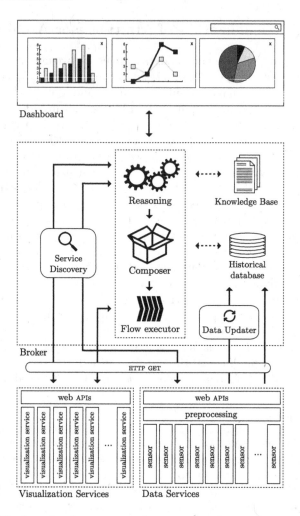

Fig. 1. Platform for dynamic visualization of multi-sensor architectures

data is generated, as well as an update function to which real-time data can be provided. This update function is called periodically, with a frequency specified by the current user. The ad hoc connection between visualization services and Web APIs allows the creation of a personalized monitoring dashboard, exposing formerly unknown relations between events and/or component behaviour.

3.3   Broker Component

Among the main tasks of the central broker component are (i) the discovery and management of data and visualization services, (ii) the execution of the three-phased reasoning process, (iii) the periodic retrieval and storage of up-to-date sensor data, and (iv) the presentation and updating of visualization instantiations on the dashboard. The broker component needs to have access to the data and visualization service URIs in order to involve the services in the reasoning process. Hard-coding these locations is not flexible. Therefore, the central component obtains the URIs autonomously using a discovery mechanism. This mechanism also actively monitors the statuses of discovered sensors by the use of pinging. Alternatively, sensor discovery can also be done passively by listening to a sensor's heartbeat. A sudden disconnection may indicate a component failure, so in this case all dashboard users are notified.

The semantic reasoner within the central broker component is responsible for, given a sensor combination, (i) suggesting appropriate visualization services, (ii) binding the sensor data with the selected visualization service (i.e. define a mapping between the sensor data and the query parameters) and (iii) proposing relevant sensors or sensor types that could be added to the composition. The execution times of each of these reasoning phases needs to be reasonable. The knowledge base (KB) contains the central logic that – along with semantic descriptions of the data and visualization services – is indispensable for the reasoning processes as it is the link between both service types.

The central component also maintains a historical database (HDB) that is responsible for the storage of historical data, as sensors generally have no or limited storage. The Semantic Web data model is closely connected to the relational database (RDB) model [7]. When the current visualization service is able to display historical data, the HDB has to be considered as a primary (pseudo) API. The *10 min mean* norm is a commonly applied measure for the frequency by which up-to-date data is fetched. When the historical data is extended with recent data that is collected with a higher frequency, the system allows the detection of particular patterns in the evolution. Moreover, by providing the evolution of the sensor values, future events can be predicted. The visualization service may assist the user by e.g. actively comparing data ranges and marking similarities or unexpected inconsistencies, hereby enabling anomaly detection.

Once the reasoner connects a given sensor (composition) with a selected visualization service, the composer fills in the data in the created HTTP GET request, along with historical data (if requested) and an identifier, by which the resulting visualization instantiation can be recognized. The flow executor executes this request, upon which the visualizer service generates the desired source code. This subcomponent also deals with potential visualization errors.

Once the connection between data and visualization services is established, it can be exploited unaltered in order to facilitate the stream of up-to-date sensor data. Accordingly, no reasoning is required for the update process.

As sensors and visualization services are already implemented as Web APIs and a platform independent – divergent user profiles usually come with divergent devices – application is desired, a web application implementation as dashboard is preferred. The dashboard in its most elementary shape has a search bar, allowing the user to browse the available entities and select the required sensors. Requested visualization instantiations are allocated to widgets on the dashboard.

4   Case Study: An Offshore Wind Farm

The monitoring of offshore wind farms is a complex task. Each of the turbines has multiple sensors by which the condition of the turbine can be observed. In order to correctly and promptly detect (partial) failures, the communicated data within this monitoring environment has to be reliable (i.e. both correct and timely). The main focus of this proof of concept case study is on composing meaningful sensor compositions, connecting them with a suited visualization service and identifying inconsistencies by exploiting the knowledge provided in the KB and acquired in the HDB.

All components are implemented using the Ruby on Rails (ROR) MVC framework. A ROR application offers a full web application stack, and follows a RESTful, resource-oriented approach. A proper web server is embedded, so apart from a working Ruby installation, no extra software is required. ROR provides a database by default and encourages the use of web standards (such as JSON) for data transfer and HTML, CSS and JavaScript for user interfacing.

4.1   Data Services

Because of the sensitivity of data from existing wind farms, a virtual offshore wind farm with 15 turbines (each turbine containing 9 sensors) is simulated. Three major sensor categories are created, each but one producing fictitious sensor values. In order to truthfully simulate the wind farm, the values are restricted and depend on the values of related sensors.

By semantically annotating the data these sensors produce, a machine is able to interpret it, hereby enabling spontaneous connections on a higher level, without requiring any additional configuration. JSON-LD semantically annotates the sensor data and offers mappings from JSON to the RDF model using the *context* concept, linking JSON object properties with ontology concepts [8].

4.2   Visualization Services

All visualization services employ the enclosed HighCharts JS library to visualize the submitted data. When required, additional parameters (restrictions) can be included to mark e.g. extreme values. The proof of concept contains eight different visualization services.

4.3   Broker Component

The reasoning phases are the most complex subtasks of the central broker component. Rather than a traditional service description, RESTdesc is used to describe the service functionality, enabling automated users and machines to use the service. RESTdesc is designed for compactness and elegance with modern Semantic Web technologies and tools, so existing vocabularies can be reused.

The KB contains all required logics (described in either RESTdesc or N3) to perform a successful sensor composition and visualization. In order to avoid duplicated source code and centralize knowledge, a hierarchy of data and visualization services is constructed. Using this KB and the annotated sensor data, the semantic EYE reasoner is able to perform the three-phased reasoning process.

As the HDB can expand very quickly, in future work, it can be advantageous to construct multiple databases, per sensor type, to reduce the search space reasonably without causing much overhead. The active monitoring of the statuses of the sensors is integrated in the periodic (*10 min mean*) data updating process – the sensors are approached by the latter process anyway. This way, the sensors are implicitly pinged when requesting their current value. Appropriate actions are taken according to the delivered HTTP status codes. The possible applications of the HDB are diverse and broader than covered. The HDB is *the* tool of choice when performing trend analysis and trend (or value) prediction.

The composer and flow executor interact with the visualization services and bundle, execute and process the composed requests. The resulting visualization instantiation is visualized on a dashboard widget.

As stated above, no reasoning is required when updating existing visualization instantiations. To update these instantiations, new data objects in which newly retrieved values are encapsulated, can be passed to their respective update function. The update frequency can be set for each widget individually. Users are often interested in some specific aspects of the monitored wind farm, requiring several minutes to build the corresponding dashboard. To solve this, the system provides *profiles* – predefined widget clusters that swiftly make specific functionality accessible – that can be instantiated in several seconds.

The connecting logic in the KB is located at the central broker component. In order to achieve a completely loosely coupled system, data and visualization services may only depend on their individual descriptions, which can also be stored in the KB. The location of the KB and whether or not it should be distributed is worth a discussion, and has to aim for maximized usability, maximized decoupling and knowledge centralization.

4.4   Resulting Dynamic Dashboard

Figure 2 presents a possible dashboard configuration for monitoring offshore wind farms. Widgets can be easily added and/or removed. Every widget holds the descriptions of the containing sensors and has a menu to adjust the visualisation and according options. Thanks to the semantic descriptions of all sensors and visualization services, related sensor data can also be easily selected from these widgets and added to the visualization.

5   Evaluation

The limited adaptability and static nature of traditional dashboards, as well as the automated detection of complex events and creation of advanced compositions, are the driving forces behind the design of the proposed platform. There

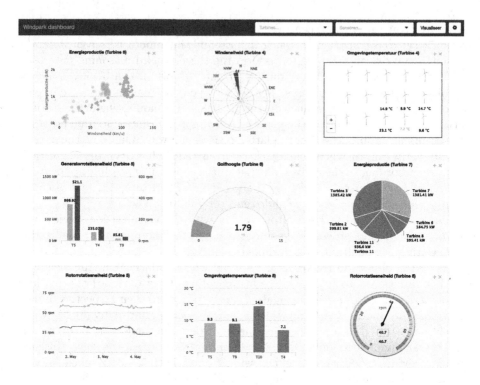

Fig. 2. Dynamic dashboard for monitoring offshore wind farms /

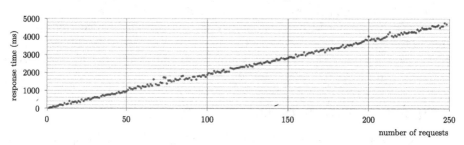

Fig. 3. Sensor data retrieval times

is a need for dashboards that satisfy current user needs, in a user-friendly way and with minimal configuration required.

New widgets are added in a straightforward way and the profile concept offers quick and easy access to vital system aspects. The interactive HighCharts library offers neat, accurate, well performing and user-friendly data charts.

Data needs to be fetched and visualized in *soft* real-time, so users can get no false sense of security. The reliable HTTP protocol transfers sensor data to the central component. Note that individual sensor requests are independent, and therefore are able to be executed in parallel. The prototype however executes

Table 1. Execution times of the three-phased reasoning process (ms)

Reasoning	Number of visualization services involved	Number of sensors involved									
		1	5	10	20	30	40	50	75	100	125
Phase 1	1	1	2	5	8	14	20	26	49	70	106
	2	2	3	6	14	17	22	32	54	81	114
	3	3	5	8	14	22	33	40	74	105	147
	4	3	4	8	17	24	34	43	69	105	150
	5	3	6	11	18	30	36	46	81	116	161
	6	3	6	11	19	27	41	54	88	132	186
	7	3	6	12	19	29	43	53	91	128	166
	8	3	6	9	17	28	41	60	86	126	170
Phase 2	1	26	962	3.719	13.263	27.269					
Phase 3		1	2	2	6	10	14	12	18	24	30

the update requests sequentially as the overhead would be too large considering the initial intention of the prototype (i.e. proving the concept). In this sequential case, retrieval times grow linearly with the number of sensors, but remain acceptable even for a larger number of sensors (see Fig. 3). As long as the total retrieval time does not exceed the user defined update interval, the user will not experience noticeable delays.

The three-phased reasoning process is the most time consuming. There is an acceptable initialization and networking overhead (in which the required semantic descriptions are collected), but the actual reasoning process, of which the execution times are presented in Table 1, is the most time-intensive. Although the reasoning procedures in the first and third phase generally have acceptable execution times, the second phase (in which the sensor data is mapped onto query parameters) is much more time consuming. Because of the (combinatorial) increasing number of possible mappings in this phase, the EYE reasoner may have a hard time connecting a visualizer service with multiple sensors.

Execution times could be reduced by providing the reasoner with additional directives and less generic linking logic. However, this undermines the dynamic nature of the system, which of course is its absolute strength. The creation times of *average* widget configurations are nevertheless acceptable, and creating new widgets only happens occasionally.

6   Conclusion

Dashboards present and communicate the condition of monitored environments to supervising experts. Contrary to current static solutions for monitoring dashboards, the proposed platform enables dynamic data visualization.

By adopting the Internet of Things vision and implementing sensors as Web connected devices, semantically annotated using RESTdesc, the presented platform allows to precisely visualize the data produced by sensors in multi-sensor environments by dynamically generating meaningful service compositions. Such a dynamic dashboard application, combined with advanced failure detection mechanisms – the HDB and reasoning component are excellent tools for this – proves to be a very powerful monitoring tool for complex, hardly accessible and/or critical environments. It enables its users to correctly monitor the condition of the environment and moreover, as a result of the meaningful sensor composition process, to detect complex events that used to remain undetected.

The platform only consists of existing technologies and Semantic Web concepts. Both the composition and visualization processes are fully dynamic, application independent and complete within acceptable time. Up-to-date data values – crucial for a monitoring application – are delivered in soft real-time.

Acknowledgement. This work was partly funded by the IWT VIS O&M Excellence project, and performed in the framework of Offshore Wind Infrastructure Application Lab.

References

1. Van Hoecke, S., Verborgh, R., Van Deursen, D., Van de Walle, R.: SAMuS: service-oriented architecture for multisensor surveillance in smart homes. Sci. World J. **2014**, 9 p. (2014). Article ID 150696, doi:10.1155/2014/150696
2. Gitanjali, J., Kuriakose, M., Kuruba, R.: Ontology and hyper graph based dashboards in data warehousing systems. Asian J. Inf. Technol. **13**(8), 412–415 (2014)
3. Duong, T.A.H., Thanh, B.N., Tjoa, A.M.: Dashboard by-example: a hypergraph-based approach to on-demand data warehousing systems. In: Proceedings of International Conference on Systems, Man, and Cybernetics (2012)
4. Leida, M., Du, X., Taylor, P., Majeed, B.: Toward automatic generation of SPARQL result set visualizations: a use case in service monitoring. In: Proceedings of the International Conference on e-Business (ICE-B), July 2011
5. Parsia, B., Sirin, E.: Pellet: an OWL DL reasoner. In: Third International Semantic Web Conference-Poster, vol. 18 (2004)
6. Mazumdar, S., Varga, A., Lanfranchi, V., Petrelli, D., Ciravegna, F.: A knowledge dashboard for manufacturing industries. In: García-Castro, R., Fensel, D., Antoniou, G. (eds.) ESWC 2011. LNCS, vol. 7117, pp. 112–124. Springer, Heidelberg (2012)
7. Berners-Lee, T.: Web Design Issues; What the Semantic Web can Represent. http://www.w3.org/DesignIssues/RDFnot.html
8. Lanthaler, M., Gütl, C.: On using JSON-LD to create evolvable restful services. In: Proceedings of the Third International Workshop on RESTful Design, pp. 25–32 (2012)

Real-Time Tracking Management System

Jose C. Almeida[1] and Artur M. Arsenio[2(✉)]

[1] Instituto Superior Tecnico/Lisbon University, Lisbon, Portugal
[2] Universidade da Beira Interior & IST-ID, Covilhã, Portugal
arsenio@alum.mit.edu

Abstract. Over the latest years many commercial Real-Time Tracking management systems (RTMS) were introduced into the market. The solutions started to be designed for single tracking purposes, but vendors soon realized that valuable tracking benefits would result by the appropriate design of a service layer. From the many RTMS solutions currently on market, it was not found a specific or suitable solution for general Law Enforcement Agencies (LEAs). A list of requirements was gathered from one of the Portuguese LEAs, GNR (Guarda Nacional Republicana) to fully understand the generic daily challenges. Main requirements raised by GNR strive with that address issues like cost, data exchange security, bi-directional communication services, performance, network fault tolerance and user-friendly interfaces. This paper presents a RTMS solution and a service layer specifically conceived for LEAs. It will be shown that learning over risk assessment mappings may bring additional benefits to LEAs. Experimental tests were performed to quantitatively measure the solution behavior.

Keywords: Real-Time tracking management system · Law enforcement agencies · Location based services · Security · Mobile

1 Introduction

Law enforcement agencies (LEAs) have primary responsibility for the maintenance of public order, prevention and detection of crimes. They fight on a daily basis for the indispensable order of society, but incidents are becoming day-after-day more complex, and LEAs human resources are limited. Therefore, it is required to maximize the efficiency of these organizations. Good coordination and support levels requires high availability of information on a real-time basis, not only directly to the field workforce but also for the ones in charge of the corresponding decision support. Furthermore, it is necessary to provide services to the workforce, such as monitoring agents' health status and providing them rapid support in medical urgencies.

Informal meetings with a Portuguese LEA' officers were held to understand the operational and management challenges of an LEA. The most relevant challenge is the use of radio (voice) as single tool of communication between agents. Despite radio network coverage and voice quality have been improved over the last 5 years, it was concluded that the single use of radio is far to fulfill the level of information on real-time basis nowadays required. From a management perspective, there is a significant lack of efficiency to get a clear (mind) picture of the fleet location using a single

© ICST Institute for Computer Sciences, Social Informatics and Telecommunications Engineering 2016
B. Mandler et al. (Eds.): IoT 360° 2015, Part II, LNICST 170, pp. 475–483, 2016.
DOI: 10.1007/978-3-319-47075-7_51

voice channel (radio). This issue leads to the adoption of a Real-Time Tracking Management System (RTMS), a system that provides the location of the fleet against a geographical map on a real time basis. The inefficient process of enquiry the fleet location, vehicle by vehicle, using voice, would in contrast be replaced by a system that provides instantaneously a clear picture of the fleet location. However, the location information is not the only issue raised.

The adoption of an RTMS opens the doors for delivery of a new level of services. This service layer enables for instance a fleet to receive a job/mission with specific geographic coordinates and respective navigation support to easily and time efficiently get on site, or the issuing of an SOS signal with respective coordinates requesting assistance from nearby agents or for medical support. Furthermore, it enables learning common patterns of risks by geographical areas according to past history.

Many RTMS solutions were designed to meet large market segments like transport of goods, public transportation, or utilities (e.g. big fleet workforce spread by the territory) [1]. This paper proposes a simple, efficient, secure, low cost solution. It is open to the integration of new specific LEA services and features, which can distinctively enhance the LEAs activity management and consequent citizen's safety.

2 State of the Art

A RTMS is a system capable to monitor in real-time an asset motion and corresponding valuable data (e.g. temperature, average speed, fuel consumption, etc.) This system is fed by a timely ordered sequence of data, fetched from many possible data sources (e.g. GPS receiver for geospatial information purposes). RTMSs can have a bi-directional communication, enabling the transmission of data/control commands from/to data sources, respectively. RTMSs manage multiple streams of data originated by those sources, and display it to the end-user using a suitable representational model (e.g. geospatial data against a geographical map). Despite the wide usage scenarios for RTMSs, they are mainly composed by 3 major components:

(a) Tracking unit (data source), which captures the location information at specific time intervals, and reports (push/pull) it to a tracking server. Location information may be coupled with data from other sensors/modules. In case of bi-directional communication, the tracking unit has the (additional) responsibility of receiving data/control commands from the tracking server. Smartphones, as well as other daily-life gadgets (e.g. tablets with GPS built-in), can be easily turned into a tracking unit device, simply running a GPS tracking software. This is suitable for human related tracking applications [2].

(b) Tracking server: It has 3 responsibilities: receive data from the tracking unit, securely store it, and serve this information on demand to the user front-end. In case of bi-directional communication, tracking server has the (additional) responsibility to transmit data/control commands to tracking units.

(c) RTMS Front-end: The user interface determines how to access information, or view asset valuable information such as location. In case of bi-directional communication, end-user might use front-end interface to transmit data/control commands to tracking units (through tracking server).

Communication between tracking units and tracking server is critical: the lost or even delay of data over the network might turn impossible to use an RTMS. For instance, the use of LEA RTMS on a criminal car chase requires an efficient communication system to provide details of the fleet location (along with other information) in near real time. Otherwise, LEA criminal intersection plan implementation might not succeed due to the latency/disparity of the fleet location on the RTMS (LEA decision point) and real location on the field.

Since LEAs exchanged data may contain valuable information to criminals, such as the real-time location of LEA workforce, data encryption plays an important role. The power consumption of encryption operations (computationally expensive) must be taken into account, since tracking units have a limited energy source.

Muruganandham [3] proposed Real Time Web based Vehicle Tracking using GPS. Tracking units report over GSM the vehicle information to a tracking server, storing reports in a database. They followed the classic (most used) approach of design/build a customized unit, in contrast to our approach of using a Mobile market device (Tablet or Smartphone) with all built-in. The design of a customized unit allows for better performance and efficiency. However it has disadvantages such as the effort/time cost to prototype a hardware solution, and the final price. Some requirements identified by the authors, such as the information of the vehicle ignition (on/off) and door status (open/closed), adds additional complexity to the Mobile device solution. Nevertheless, it could be solved with a simple CAN-BUS to Bluetooth device, assuming CAN-BUS is deployed in the vehicle.

Hasan et al. [4] have proposed a cost effective method of object tracking using GPS and GPRS technology. The user can view the present location of the object as well as the past history of its movement using Google Map and Internet. They take advantage of the IMEI number uniqueness to be used on the authentication of the device. Hence, the Tracking server drops all the messages that do not have a valid IMEI stored in the database. This is a simple security approach that resides in the secrecy of the IMEI, which can be easily exploited by man in the middle attacks and spoofing. Another important characteristic of this work is the use of HTTP POST method to transmit data between the tracking units and server. In that way, the implementation (e.g. validation, data manipulation, etc.) of the tracking server is developed in PHP, which is not the best solution in terms of performance. This choice represents a high cost of CPU and memory per vehicle. A shared tracking service business model shall be definitively more cost-efficient than the tricky shared web hosting proposed. Shared tracking services follow the growth of cloud computing usage and optimized elasticity of resources (e.g. GPSgate and GPS-Trace).

3   Solution

The overall solution is composed by a mobile app running on a tablet in each vehicle, and a tracking server along with a database and web server. The vehicles share a secret key with the tracking server, and exchange data securely through mobile operator network and (eventual) third party networks. The Central station(s) manage the fleet through a web based solution, as shown in Fig. 1.

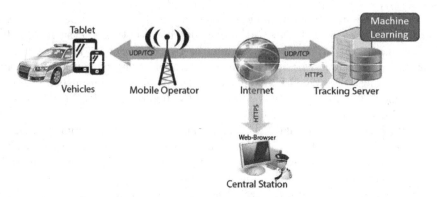

Fig. 1. High-level solution architecture.

Our solution strive to enhance the LEAs daily operational requirements through offering the following features:

- **Real-Time Monitoring:** Central Station can monitor fleet status (e.g. location) in real time (up to the second).
- **Alarm:** Vehicles can trigger an SOS alarm in Central Station. Central Station can send multiple POI to Vehicles.
- **Job Dispatcher:** Central Station can dispatch a job containing specific location to vehicles.
- **File exchange:** File transmission between vehicles and Central-Station.
- **Report:** Vehicles can report geo-referenced events.
- **Photo:** Vehicles can take photo directly to Central Station.
- **LEA data:** Vehicle terminal have local access to synchronized list of Person (suspects and lost) and Vehicles (suspects and robbed).
- **Risk Map:** Vehicles can easily see a risk representation over the map (layer). The layer is dynamic; it changes accordingly to the date and time of the day.
- **History:** All information is stored on the database, so the LEA is capable of representing previous fleet locations, and corresponding events, on map.
- **Security:** All data exchanged is confidential, authenticated and incorruptible.
- **Network:** Tolerant to networks faults through retransmission of data lost.

3.1   Central Station (Tracking Server)

The tracking server is coded in Java for high code portability, since existing technological infrastructures may widely differ between LEAs. The server architecture solution is designed according to Fig. 2-a.

DB Manager: Module responsible for all operations in the server database.

File Manager: Module responsible for all the local file system operations. In addition, features a simple versioning of files, enabling proper file synchronization.

Operation Handler: Module responsible to perform operations requested by the vehicles applications.

Application Manager: First module loaded by the server. It is responsible to load all the required data at start (e.g. server configuration). User credentials are also loaded, and it is kept on memory, since it will be accessed very often (e.g. anytime a message arrives). Once all data required by the server is loaded, Application Manager loads the Operation Handler module. Nevertheless, Application Manager remains on active cycle collecting and storing (via DB Manager) periodically all RTMS relevant data. The data storage is prioritized by the period of verification and thread priority. For instance, real-time status messages are updated on database with minimum delay comparing to the status history update (checked every second, and only stores 1 value every 10 s, using the minimum priority thread). It is responsible for management of allocated resources that each vehicle app demands from server.

Security: Module responsible for the encryption, decryption and validation of data (e.g. anytime a message arrives) using the open-source "Bouncy Castle" lightweight cryptography library on Android OS.

Message Handler: Module responsible to receive live status messages from vehicles apps, and to send control messages to the corresponding vehicle app (e.g. Dispatch a job). The communication is preferably done through UDP, but TCP is also supported. Both work in concurrency on the server and the logic of decision is implemented on the client side (mobile app).

The Database (depicted on Fig. 2-b) was designed for easy management. No security measures are applied by the tracking server solution to the database content, since database encryption is a feature supported natively by most popular DBMSs.

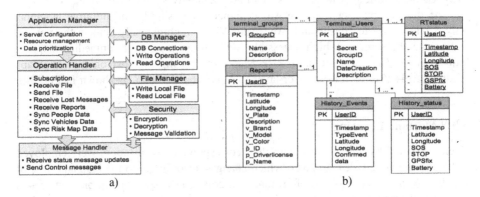

Fig. 2. (a) High-level architecture of tracking server. (b) UML Database model.

3.2   Vehicle

The mobile app is coded in Java for Android (API 17) and can also run on other OS through an emulator (e.g. Bluestacks). The overall design is shown in Fig. 3-a.

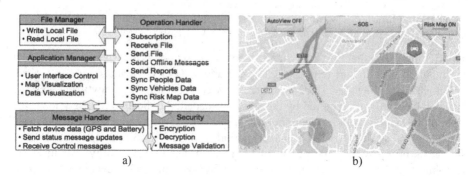

Fig. 3. (a) High-level architecture of mobile app; (b) Representation of risk map feature.

Operation Handler: Module responsible to perform operations. All the operations start with a TCP socket connection originated by the mobile app to the tracking server (e.g. File transmission).

Application Manager: Module responsible for all the user interface of the mobile app. It enables the user to trigger events through the mobile app (e.g. SOS alarm, Report), visualize current location and LAE data (e.g. missing persons). The first operation performed by this module is the subscription.

Message Handler: Module responsible to fetch data from devices modules (e.g. GPS), and send it as status messages updates to the tracking server (each second). The module also receives control messages, which are commands originated by the tracking server (e.g. Job dispatch). The communication is preferably done through UDP, but TCP is also supported (when the device is behind a NAT/firewall [5]). The detection of NAT/Firewall happens when a local IP is assigned to the network device. If the assigned IP is no longer local, the system automatically switches to UDP.

The mobile app user interface was designed to be simple and intuitive: contains only 3 buttons on the dashboard. An "Auto View" automatically centers the vehicle position in the screen. A high accessible SOS button triggers an immediate support request at the Central Station. A Risk Map feature (implemented on Google Maps Android APIv26) provides an over-layer (the risk) on the map, as shown in Fig. 3-b.

3.3   Machine Learning

Events reported by the vehicles, with their correspondent localization, were employed to build a dynamic risk map layer, which changes accordingly to the date and time of the day. Appropriate learning of criminal patterns may allow the exploitation of this feature with important data, from criminal investigation analysis perspective to crime prevention. Indeed, current work is exploiting two learning techniques to gather more information from risk maps: back-propagation neural networks, a supervised learning approach, and an unsupervised learning technique, k-means clustering. The inputs for training such networks are the time of the day, month of the year, location, and the type of criminal report. The goal is to allow LEAs to predict where, and at what time, a specific criminal activity has high probability of occurring.

4 Experimental Evaluation

Experimental tests were realized to measure and quantify the solution according to specific metrics. For each experiment 5 tests were executed for statistical analysis. The following metrics were chosen:

- **CPUconsumption** (Percentage): Percentage of CPU used by the overall tracking server solution.
- **Memory consumption** (Kilobytes): Numeric value of computer memory used by the overall tracking server.
- **Message lost rate** (Percentage): Percentage of messages not acknowledged (lost) by tracking server.
- **Maximum status delay measured** (Milliseconds): Maximum measured time a status message takes, from the mobile app status fetching process, to the successful introduction of data into the tracking server database. It is measured using the status message timestamp against the current database timestamp.
- **Network Traffic** (Kilobytes): Total sum of Bytes in and out of tracking server network interface.

4.1 Testbed

Mobile Network coverage and GPS signal strength are two uncontrollable variables with critical impact on testing. In order to eliminate these dependencies, the tests are run in a controllable local area network (LAN), and the GPS coordinates are generated internally by the App code. The mobile device app core (without user interface) was migrated to a single application that can manage multiple instances of mobile apps. The tracking server machine CPU has 2 cores at 2.0 GHz and 4 GB of RAM. It is connected to tracking units machine by a 100Mbps Ethernet link, with a measured latency lower than 1 ms. Enabling the clock synch (through Network Time Protocol, NTP) between machines with a much higher accuracy [6], measured offset is lower than 50 ms.

Every test starts by rebooting the tracking server machine, following a clock synch. A script that measures all metrics, launched on background, writes periodically (5 s) the corresponding values. The same script is also responsible to create the database table to store values, along with the generation of 100 users. Once the tracking server solution is launched, a new client is created and consequently connected to tracking server every 30 s. The evaluation is performed over the following scenarios: (1) TCP, no security; (2) UDP, no security; (3) UDP, with encryption (DES); (4) UDP, Encryption (DES) and MAC.

4.2 Experimental Results

The results are organized by metric. As shown in Fig. 4-a, not only the average CPU usage increases with the number of clients, but also the value of the CPU spikes. As expected, the addition of security functions originates additional CPU consumption.

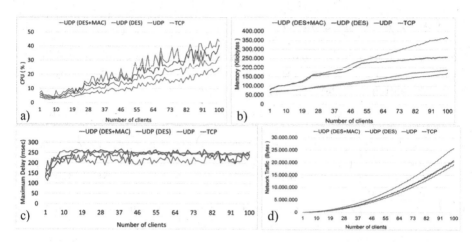

Fig. 4. (a) CPU consumption; (b) Memory consumption; (c) Maximum status delay; (d) Network traffic.

CPU average use increases 4.7 % whenever encryption (DES) is added to UDP, and 6.9 % with the addition of encryption along with MAC. Memory usage (Fig. 4-b) increases with the number of clients. The addition of security functions corresponds to additional memory consumption. Average memory in use increases 54 % when encryption (DES) is added to UDP, and 75 % with the addition of encryption along with MAC. Nevertheless, these values do not represent real memory in use, but memory allocated to the server application. The release of memory allocated but not in use, is managed by JVM (garbage collector) and machine OS.

Maximum status delay, as shown in Fig. 4-c, has similar values for all the tests (assuming a minimum of 50 ms offset). The values converge into 250 ms, which is the tracking server storage frequency of the received live status messages.

As shown in Fig. 4-d, TCP is the top traffic generator. This is mostly justified by the additional header size comparing to the UDP, since the combination of the test bed network and tracking server overload is relatively low turning the probability of a network segment to be retransmitted very low. Another fact that pushes TCP to generate more traffic is the overhead introduced by a connection oriented protocol. All together, makes TCP generate more 36 % traffic than UDP. Single encryption, and encryption with MAC, have similar values.

5 Conclusions and Future Work

The adoption of a RTMS specifically designed for LEAs has impact on daily performance of the organizations. However, it represents a large investment in tailor-made solutions, and eventual dedicated communication infrastructures (e.g. TETRA) for that purposes. This is an unfeasible alternative for a majority of countries with tight budgets. This work proposes a cost-effective RTMS that meets LEAs daily requirements with an extremely low budget, constituting an affordable solution that benefits from the higher trend for the improvement of the existing mobile network coverage and corresponding terminal devices (e.g. Tablets). Our solution shows that it is feasible to trade computational resources for enhanced security on third-party networks such as mobile operators, in contrast to the creation of dedicated secure communication infra-structures such as TETRA, which come out to be too expensive and inadequate to meet the LEAs requirements pace (e.g. data throughput).

The proposed solution allows for the integration of more disruptive LEAs services and features on top of it. The embracement of specific LAE accessories, such as automatic license plate recognition, unmanned aerial vehicles, or even wearables like augmented reality glasses and smart wristbands, is also very promising for the evolution of the solution.

Machine learning services have shown to provide many benefits for adding intelligence to the Internet of Things [7]. These services, on top of the risk map feature, will enable vehicles to perform an optimized patrol, with better coverage of critical zones at the right time and weekday.

References

1. Qayyum, E., Mohsin, Z., Malik, J.: Real-Time Vehicle Tracking System Using GPS & GSM. Lap Lambert Academic Publishing, Saarbrücken (2013)
2. Varandas, L., Vaidya, B., Rodrigues, J.: mTracker: a mobile tracking application for pervasive environment. In: IEEE 24th International Conference on Advanced Information Networking and Applications Workshops (2010)
3. Muruganandham, P.: Real Time Web based Vehicle Tracking using GPS. World Academy of Science Engineering and Technology, Los Angeles (2010). 37
4. Hasan, K., Rahman, M., Haque, A., Rahman, A., Rahman, T., Rasheed, M.: Cost effective GPS-GPRS based object tracking system. Lecture Notes in Engineering and Computer Science, vol. 2174, no. (1) (2009)
5. Chen, Y., Jia, W.: Challenge and solutions of NAT traversal for ubiquitous and pervasive applications on the Internet. J. Syst. Softw. **82**, 1620–1626 (2009)
6. Tomaciello, L., Vito, L., Rapuano, S.: One-way delay measurement: state of art. In: Proceedings of the IEEE Instrumentation and Measurement Technology Conference (2006)
7. Arsenio, A.: On the application of artificial intelligence techniques to create network intelligence. In: Laalaoui, Y., Bouguila, N. (eds.) Artificial Intelligence Applications in Information and Communication Technologies, vol. 607, pp. 71–97. Springer, Heidelberg (2015)

Distributed Neural Networks for Internet of Things: The Big-Little Approach

Elias De Coninck[✉], Tim Verbelen, Bert Vankeirsbilck, Steven Bohez,
Pieter Simoens, Piet Demeester, and Bart Dhoedt

Department of Information Technology, Ghent University – iMinds,
Gaston Crommenlaan 8/201, 9050 Gent, Belgium
elias.deconinck@intec.ugent.be

Abstract. Nowadays deep neural networks are widely used to accurately classify input data. An interesting application area is the Internet of Things (IoT), where a massive amount of sensor data has to be classified. The processing power of the cloud is attractive, however the variable latency imposes a major drawback in situations where near real-time classification is required. In order to exploit the apparent trade-off between utilizing the stable but limited embedded computing power of IoT devices and the seemingly unlimited computing power of Cloud computing at the cost of higher and variable latency, we propose a Big-Little architecture for deep neural networks. A small neural network trained to a subset of prioritized output classes is running on the embedded device, while a more specific classification is calculated when required by a large neural network in the cloud. We show the applicability of this concept in the IoT domain by evaluating our approach for state of the art neural network classification problems on popular embedded devices such as the Raspberry Pi and Intel Edison.

Keywords: Deep neural networks · Distributed intelligence · Internet of things

1 Introduction

Currently, the Internet of Things (IoT) is a popular paradigm that envisions a world in which all kinds of physical objects or "things" are connected to the Internet, interact with each other and cooperate to reach common goals [1]. This idea goes beyond machine-to-machine communications (M2M), as it covers not only communication protocols, but also the application domains and the services running on top of these connected things. By providing easy access to a myriad of devices such as sensors, surveillance cameras, home appliances, cars, actuators etc., the IoT will enable a new range of applications and use cases in the field of domotics, assisted living, logistics, smart environments, manufacturing, and many more.

© ICST Institute for Computer Sciences, Social Informatics and Telecommunications Engineering 2016
B. Mandler et al. (Eds.): IoT 360° 2015, Part II, LNICST 170, pp. 484–492, 2016.
DOI: 10.1007/978-3-319-47075-7_52

In order to create truly smart applications for the IoT, massive amounts of data coming from all connected things will have to be processed and analysed into actionable and contextualized information [8]. Currently, the Cloud is most often the natural choice to perform this data processing, benefiting from the huge computing power and scalability [15]. However, the Cloud is not a silver bullet solution, as a network connection to a Cloud datacenter often suffers from high and variable latency, as well as limited upload bandwidth [2]. Moreover, extensive Cloud processing incurs considerable cost for renting infrastructure. Therefore, our goal is to first use local computing power in the various embedded devices and gateways for data processing, before turning to the Cloud. This addresses the problem associated with network connectivity (latency and bandwidth) while also reducing operation cost.

A very important processing step in IoT applications is classification, i.e., determining the system "state" and its subsequent actions based on (sequences of) sensory data. A promising state-of-the-art technique in this field is the use of a Deep Neural Network (DNN), which offers a biologically inspired trainable architecture that can learn various invariant features [18]. As a neural network is trained by iteratively evaluating input samples and updating the neural network weights, one often relies on efficient GPU implementations that can exploit the parallelism and speedup neural network evaluation. However, the CPU power and internal memory available on an embedded IoT device imposes an upper limit on the size of neural networks that can be evaluated with sufficiently high throughput.

The contributions presented in the current paper is a Big-Little architecture for neural networks, that is tailored to the specific characteristics of IoT environments. The idea is to take a large trained neural network for a certain classification problem, and from that distil a smaller neural network that only classifies a well chosen subset of the output space. The little neural network is suited to be executed locally on the embedded devices, whether the input is also sent to the Cloud, for evaluation with the big neural network, is upto the application specific demands.

The rationale for this idea is the following. Consider a smart home environment that is monitored by a large number of sensors and some actuators to trigger an alarm, start the heating system, detect fire or leaks, etc. Some situations are critical to detect fast while others need a reliable response before taking a direct action. For example stop the robot before bumping into a domestic cat that popped up before it, or close off the water supply when a leak is detected. One can clearly distinguish between critical situations, in which you want a fast or a reliable response, versus non-critical ones, as well as the granularity of the response (a person versus which specific person). By carefully selecting the critical outputs and the granularity of the outputs, we can craft a little local neural network that offers fast response. This local neural network also acts as a filter to limit the number of inputs sent to the big neural network in the cloud. For example, only when a person is detected and one requires a more fine grained classification of the person, the input is evaluated in the Cloud.

The remainder of this paper is organized as follows. Section 2 presents related work in scope of distributed neural networks. Section 3 explains the proposed Big-Little architecture for neural networks in the scope of IoT. In Sect. 4 we show some preliminary results that validate our idea using a frequently used neural network evaluation dataset. Section 5 summarizes our conclusions and presents plans for future work.

2 Related Work

In a highly distributed IoT environment one could try to speed up neural network evaluation by distributing parts of the neural network among all the available devices. However, related work in distributing neural networks shows that the communication overhead quickly becomes the limiting factor [7], hence this approach is mainly used to speed up the training phase on a cluster of nodes connected through a high speed network. Krizhevsky et al. [12] showed how a larger neural network can be trained by spreading the net across two GPUs. This way the communication overhead remains limited, as the GPUs are able to read and write to each other's memory directly. In [10], the authors show that scaling up further to 8 GPUs can lead to a speed up factor of 6.16. Dean et al. [9] presented the DistBelief framework for parallel distributed training of deep neural networks. By adopting new training algorithms they can distribute the training procedure on a large number of CPU nodes, for example achieving a speed up of more than 12x using 81 machines.

As these methods all focus on the training phase and require high end server infrastructure, these are not applicable for speeding up small neural networks in an IoT use case. One approach to optimize distributed neural network execution with parts distributed across embedded devices is simplifying multi-class classification problems to one-vs-all (OVA) or one-vs-one classifiers (OVO). These methods are straightforward and often used to construct a multi-class classifier using binary-class classification [16]. One multi-class classification is split into a set of binary-class classifications for each class and later combine them to the original multi-class classifier.

Another optimization approach in which one part is deployed on an embedded device, and a second part is running in the Cloud, uses a cascade of neural network layers as depicted in [14]. The presented solution exists in augmenting the structure of the neural network to obtain intermediate evaluation output. Then, the evaluation with the remaining neural network layers is pre-empted if the quality of the intermediate output exceeds a given threshold. By deploying only first layers of the net on an embedded device, calls to the Cloud can be limited to the input samples that do not yet result in a good output after these first layers. Our paper proposes a similar approach, but instead of training intermediate layers that classify all outputs with a lower accuracy, we introduce a smaller neural network that is trained to only a subset of the outputs.

3   Big-Little Neural Network Architecture

A typical feed-forward neural network is composed of an input layer, one or more hidden layers and one output layer. The output layer has one output for each classification class, resulting in a value between 0 and 1, depicting the probability that the input can be classified as such. In order to process as much as possible locally on embedded IoT devices, and limiting communication to the Cloud, we designed a little neural network that can be processed with limited CPU power, which classifies only a subset of the output classes. This results in a Big-Little neural network architecture as depicted in Fig. 1.

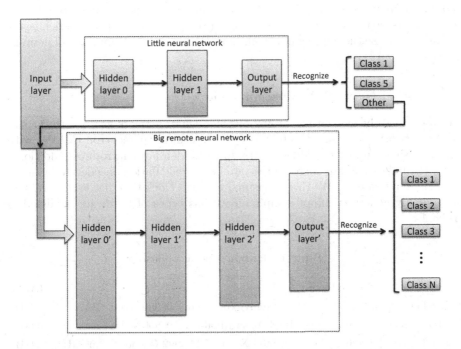

Fig. 1. Architecture of Big-Little feed-forward neural network: In this example, the little neural network only classifies a subset (2) of the N output classes, and can be executed locally with limited CPU power. When the little neural network cannot classify the input sample, a big neural network running in the Cloud can be queried.

The hypothesis of this paper is that by limiting the number of output classes, we can also limit the size and amount of hidden layers of the neural network, while maintaining the desired classification accuracy. By crafting the little neural network to classify high priority classes only, a local response is obtained very fast in these critical cases, while retaining the availability of the complete classification set by relaying to the cloud, that executes the big neural network. The application developer may decide to directly send the raw input data to the large neural network in the cloud, or only send the input after evaluation by the little network. Directly sending it to the cloud allows for a better classification but consumes more bandwidth, while waiting for completion of the little network takes some time.

Because the big and little neural network only share the input layer, these two networks can be trained independently from each other using state-of-the-art training techniques in an offline training phase.

4   Evaluation

To train and execute our neural networks, we used Theano [3,4], a Python module compatible with GPU/CPU and many computer architectures. In our experiments we use multilayer perceptrons (MLP) with one or more hidden layers to easily increase the number of calculations by increasing the number of neurons in each hidden layer.

4.1   Neural Network Evaluation Time

To assess how the evaluation throughput of a neural network varies with the size of the network, we created fully connected multilayer perceptron (MLP)s with an increasing number of hidden layers. Each hidden layer introduces additional weighted links and thus increase the number of calculations needed to evaluate a single input sample. We then measured the wall clock time needed to evaluate a randomly generated input sample on various types of hardware, as listed in Table 1.

Table 1. Hardware specifications.

Name	Architecture	CPU	RAM
Raspberry Pi 2	ARM	Cortex-A7 (quad-core @ 900 MHz)	1 GB
Intel Edison	x86	Intel Atom (dual-core @ 500 MHz)	1 GB
iLab.t server [5]	x86	2x Intel Xeon E5-2650v2 (8-core @ 2.60 GHz)	48 GB

Figure 2 shows how the execution time linearly scales with the number of weights in the neural network. In Fig. 2, we also included experimental results on server-grade hardware from our testbet iLab.t [5] (Table 1). Given a maximum response time of 40 ms, on a Raspberry Pi 2 we can run neural networks of sizes below 2×10^6 weights. The size of the large network in the cloud depends on the link delay between the nodes. With a link delay of for example 15 ms, the large neural network evaluated on our server hardware can spend at most $40ms - 2 * 15ms = 10ms$ on neural network processing, which corresponds with up to 6.5×10^6 weights.

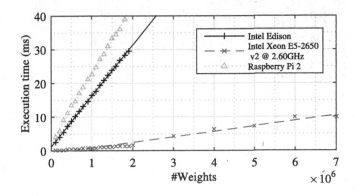

Fig. 2. Evaluation time of a single input sample for fully connected neural networks of different sizes. Extra cores do not improve performance.

4.2   Classification Accuracy vs. Network Size

In our second set of experiments, we want to measure the inevitable loss of accuracy when evaluating a little one-vs-all neural network compared to a big multi-class neural network. By increasing the number of weights in the hidden layer of both networks we can evaluate the difference in reliability. To fairly compare these networks we use the F_1-score of one priority class:

$$F_1\text{-score} = \frac{2 * \text{true positives}}{2 * \text{true positives} + \text{false positives} + \text{false negatives}}$$

This F_1-score is the harmonic mean of precision and recall and is independent of the total number of samples. Using the error rate as measure of comparison would yield misleading results because the one-vs-all classifier was trained with an unbalanced set, containing fewer samples for the 'one' class than for the 'all' class. The F_1-score of a multi-class neural network can be calculated for each class, but here we only look at the priority class of the little network.

To validate our neural networks, the popular MNIST dataset [13] was used. This dataset consists of a training, validation and test set of handwritten digits with a total of 70000 examples evenly distributed over the classification classes. Starting with the state of the art neural network of Ciresan et al. [6] as the big network that is executed on the cloud, we have distilled a small network by prioritizing some output classes and aggregating the others into one category, thus limiting the number of output classes. For this latter situation, a neural network structure was created that achieves the same accuracy for the prioritized output classes with a much lower neural network size.

Figure 3 shows a comparison between a big and a little fully connected neural network. A more detailed output is given in Tables 2 and 3. Neural networks with more output layers need more weights to reach the same accuracy. Our one-vs-all network outperforms the big neural network for a low number of neural network connections and more or less reaches the same quality of larger networks.

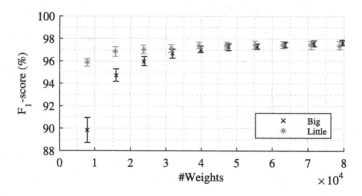

Fig. 3. F_1-score of big and little fully connected neural networks for MNIST classification. The graph shows the F_1-scores for classifying a '5' character on the big network (ID 3 - Table 2) and the little network (ID 1 - Table 2).

Table 2. Execution time of big and little neural networks on the server from Table 1. Each number in the architecture represents the number of neurons in that layer, starting with an input layer of $28 * 28$ neurons for MNIST. The last layer represents a binary or multi-class classifier layer.

ID	Architecture (number of neurons in each layer)	Weights	Process time for one sample [ms]
1	784, 1 000, 500, 2	1 250 502	0.98
2	784, 1 000, 500, 10	1 254 510	1.00
3	784, 2 500, 2 000, 1 500, 1 000, 500, 10 [6]	11 972 510	16.42

Table 3. F_1-score comparison of a big (ID 3) and a little (ID 1) neural network for two classification classes (1 and 8) of MNIST. Structure of these networks are shown in Table 2. The test error is not applicable for little networks with a unbalanced validation sample set.

ID	Priority class	Test error for best validation [%]	Priority class [%]			
			Recall	Specificity	Precision	F_1-score
1	1	NA	98.94	99.92	99.38	99.16
	8	NA	96.41	99.76	97.71	97.05
3	1	2.11	99.12	99.90	99.21	99.16
	8	2.11	96.82	99.70	97.22	97.02

Deploying the little network (ID 1 from Table 2) with 1 250 502 weights on a Raspberry Pi 2 roughly gives an execution time of 30 ms (from Fig. 2). This little network trained for classifying the priority class '8' has a F_1-score of 97.05 % which is 0.03 % better than the remote big neural network (ID 3). The overall performance of this little network is better for this specific class. Other classes yield similar results.

Forwarding the same sample input to the big network gives an execution time of 16.42 ms (from Table 2). From the moment the response time is more than 46.42 ms (sum of execution time of big and little neural network) we can get a faster and equivalent response from the little neural network executed on a Raspberry Pi 2. In most cases this will not make a big difference but in highly critical situations a fast response makes all the difference.

5 Conclusion and Future Work

In this paper we investigated the potential of Big-Little neural network architectures, to reduce response time of the overall network, maintaining a comparable accuracy. The results show that prioritizing one class can lower the calculations required to reach the same classification performance for that class. This can benefit use cases where reliability and response time are preferred.

Important points for future work are to deduce little networks and their weights from a pretrained big network and to test the same hypothesis for convolutional neural networks on Cifar [11] and/or ImageNet [17]. In the future we will distribute neural networks on multiple IoT devices in an environment to decrease the cloud usage and increase the independence of this environment.

Acknowledgements. Part of the work was supported by the iMinds IoT research program. Steven Bohez is funded by Ph.D. grant of the Agency for Innovation by Science and Technology in Flanders (IWT).

References

1. Atzori, L., Iera, A., Morabito, G.: The internet of things: a survey. Comput. Netw. **54**(15), 2787–2805 (2010)
2. Barker, S.K., Shenoy, P.: Empirical evaluation of latency-sensitive application performance in the cloud. In: Proceedings of the First Annual ACM SIGMM Conference on Multimedia Systems, MMSys 2010, pp. 35–46. ACM, New York (2010)
3. Bastien, F., Lamblin, P., Pascanu, R., Bergstra, J., Goodfellow, I.J., Bergeron, A., Bouchard, N., Bengio, Y.: Theano: new features and speed improvements. In: Deep Learning and Unsupervised Feature Learning NIPS 2012 Workshop (2012)
4. Bergstra, J., Breuleux, O., Bastien, F., Lamblin, P., Pascanu, R., Desjardins, G., Turian, J., Warde-Farley, D., Bengio, Y.: Theano: a CPU and GPU math expression compiler. In: Proceedings of the Python for Scientific Computing Conference (SciPy), vol. 4, p. 3, June 2010. Oral Presentation
5. Bouckaert, S., Becue, P., Vermeulen, B., Jooris, B., Moerman, I., Demeester, P.: Federating wired and wireless test facilities through emulab and OMF: the iLab.t use case. In: Proceedings of the 8th International ICST Conference on Testbeds and Research Infrastructures for the Development of Networks and Communities, pp. 1–16. Department of Information technology, Ghent University (2012)

6. Dan C.C., Meier, U., Gambardella, L.M., Schmidhuber, J.: Deep big simple neural nets excel on handwritten digit recognition. arXiv preprint arXiv:1003.0358 22(12) (2010)

7. Coates, A., Huval, B., Wang, T., Wu, D., Catanzaro, B., Andrew, N.: Deep learning with COTS HPC systems. In: Proceedings of the 30th International Conference on Machine Learning, pp. 1337–1345 (2013)

8. Da Li, X., He, W., Li, S.: Internet of things in industries: a survey. IEEE Trans. Ind. Inform. 10(4), 2233–2243 (2014)

9. Dean, J., Corrado, G., Monga, R., Chen, K., Devin, M., Mao, M., Senior, A., Tucker, P., Yang, K., Le, Q.V., et al.: Large scale distributed deep networks. In: Advances in Neural Information Processing Systems, pp. 1223–1231 (2012)

10. Krizhevsky, A.: One weird trick for parallelizing convolutional neural networks. arXiv preprint arXiv:1404.5997 (2014)

11. Krizhevsky, A., Hinton, G.: Learning multiple layers of features from tiny images. Technical report, Computer Science Department, University of Toronto (2009)

12. Krizhevsky, A., Sutskever, I., Hinton, G.E.: Imagenet classification with deep convolutional neural networks. In: Advances in Neural Information Processing Systems, pp. 1097–1105 (2012)

13. LeCun, Y., Cortes, C.: The MNIST database of handwritten digits (1998)

14. Leroux, S., Bohez, S., Verbelen, T., Vankeirsbilck, B., Simoens, P., Dhoedt, B.: Resource-constrained classification using a cascade of neural network layers. In: International Joint Conference on Neural Networks (2015)

15. Parwekar, P.: From internet of things towards cloud of things. In: 2011 2nd International Conference on Computer and Communication Technology (ICCCT), pp. 329–333, September 2011

16. Rifkin, R., Klautau, A.: In defense of one-vs-all classification. J. Mach. Learn. Res. 5, 101–141 (2004)

17. Russakovsky, O., Deng, J., Su, H., Krause, J., Satheesh, S., Ma, S., Huang, Z., Karpathy, A., Khosla, A., Bernstein, M., Berg, A.C., Fei-Fei, L.: Imagenet large scale visual recognition challenge. Int. J. Comput. Vis. 115(3), 211–252 (2015). doi:10.1007/s11263-015-0816-y

18. Schmidhuber, J.: Deep learning in neural networks: an overview. Neural Netw. 61, 85–117 (2015)

Learning About Animals and Their Social Behaviors for Smart Livestock Monitoring

João Ambrosio[1,2], Artur M. Arsenio[3(✉)], and Orlando Remédios[2]

[1] Instituto Superior Tecnico/Lisbon University, Lisbon, Portugal
[2] Sensefinity, Rio de Mouro, Portugal
[3] Universidade da Beira Interior, IST-ID & InstinctRobotics, Covilhã, Portugal
arsenio@alum.mit.edu

Abstract. Things are increasingly getting connected. Emerging with the Internet of Things, new applications are requiring more intelligence on these things, for them to be able to learn about their environment or other connected objects. One such domain of application is for livestock monitoring, in which farmers need to learn about animals, such as percentage of time they spend feeding, the occurrence of diseases, or the percentage of fat on their milk. Furthermore, it is also important to learn about group patterns, such as flocking behaviors, and individual deviations to group dynamics. This paper addresses this problem, by collection and processing each animal location and selecting appropriate metrics on the data, so that behaviors can be learned afterwards using machine learning techniques running on the cloud.

Keywords: Cloud computing · Learning · Internet of intelligent things · Smart livestock management · Social behaviors · Wireless sensor networks

1 Introduction

In the past, Livestock Management (LM) was based on farmer's observation, judgment and experience. Indeed, farms usually had people watching animals, which is a time consuming and expensive approach. However, due to the increasing scale of farms and the high number of animals that compose it, it is infeasible to continuously monitor the animals through visual observation during twenty four hours a day [1]. Furthermore, empirical evaluation from historical data is purely based on a human observer's experience, who cannot continuously track a single sheep 24 h a day, much less all animals on a flock of sheep.

Precision Livestock Farming (PLF) addresses such challenge, by continuously and remotely capturing measurements (e.g. position, head movement, bio-signals of animal) related with the condition of individual or groups of animals, as well as reporting this extracted data to a farm manager [2]. This paper proposes adding learning on top of it, so that livestock monitoring can be more effective than using human observation alone. Smart Livestock Monitoring (SLM) adds an extra dimension to the problem, enabling a LM system to learn from the history of such acquired data to provide added value information to a farmer.

© ICST Institute for Computer Sciences, Social Informatics and Telecommunications Engineering 2016
B. Mandler et al. (Eds.): IoT 360° 2015, Part II, LNICST 170, pp. 493–503, 2016.
DOI: 10.1007/978-3-319-47075-7_53

Animal's collars have been employed for real-time tracking of free-grazing animals' location, useful for various applications. For instance, it could be possible to deduce automatically the grazing habits of free ranging animals, which can be very useful to the farmer for making better decisions on the efficient usage of land. Additionally, it allows determining the path of the animals in a certain time, and consequently the utilized grazing area.

The real-time location of each animal may also be very useful whenever the farmer wants to fetch free-grazing animals at the end of a season, avoiding searching for them in a certain region. This is also true for animals' carcasses, since insurance companies in some countries reimburse the farmer for animal death if its body is found. Additionally, the cost of building and maintaining fences is one of the most expensive costs associated with Livestock grazing [3]. Geo-fences can be used to minimize these costs, since they do not rely on a physical fence. Furthermore, machine learning approaches can be employed to learn the geographic areas preferred by animals along different dimensions, such as weather, day time, month of the year, etc. Collecting the location of each animal can be also very interesting for detecting animals' diseases (which may affect the animals' walking pattern or behavior) employing learning strategies. This is especially important for infectious diseases, since it also enables the isolation of only those animals that had direct or indirect contact with the affected animal, avoiding the slaughtering of healthy animals.

1.1 Farm Producers: Motivation and Requirements

A requirement analysis included surveying several cattle producers, involving interviews with various experts at each location, working directly with the animals (dairy sheep) or who are directly involved on the business' management activities. Hence, requirements were gathered from three different producers:

- Queijaria Ribeira de Alpreade's offices, under the scope of Fundão's Terras do Xisto LivingLab
- Quinta do Pisão, Cascais City Council
- One of the largest farms in Portugal, with cattle and sheep, near the city of Setubal

In these farms, the dairy sheep graze freely in a large dimension pasture (tens of hectares) partially or totally covered by cellular mobile communications. They spend most of their time alternating between grazing and resting/ruminating, presenting slow movements (except during short stress periods). Sheep graze in cohesive groups and isolation is a source of stress to them. They are social animals and create strong social hierarchies between them. Typically, at the top of the hierarchy there are some leading sheep that influence the other animals, particularly their grazing movements. Therefore the other sheep tend to follow the leaders. Farmers usually tag these leading sheep with a bell on their collars to easily locate them.

Staff interviews revealed the need for learning different pieces of information based on sheep motion, behavior, or other features, according to priority requirements to be complied by the system prototype, which are illustrated in Fig. 1:

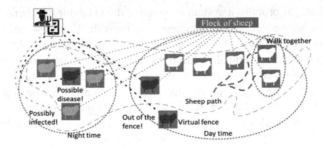

Fig. 1. Learning requirements for smart livestock management.

1. Alterations in the normal bustle of an animal may indicate to the farmer valuable information, therefore the farmers want to be informed when an individual animal presents movement values that are significantly different than the average, taking into account the history of that specific animal (based on distance travelled, velocities, erratic behavior, or any other relevant feature;

2. Whenever an animal picks an infectious disease, it is often necessary to slaughter the whole flock of sheep. Therefore it is crucial to infer the direct or indirect interactions between the various animals, based on the historical contact distances between them, to isolate solely the infected sheep, thereby avoiding slaughtering healthy ones that were not in danger of contagious;

3. Learning geographic patterns from sheep locomotion (e.g. relative to weather, hour of the day, month of the year, etc.). Learning common routes taken by a sheep or flock of sheep, to clearly identify sheep grazing habits, the used pastures, as well as the ones with better quality. Because sheep freely grazing sometimes surpass the farm limits, need also to implement a geo-fencing functionality that sends an alarm to the farmer staff indicating such occurrence;

4. Learn to detect a collar cut, indicating a possible theft;

5. Learning the percentage of fat on a sheep's milk based on previous history, such as the sheep grazing times and regions, weather conditions, time of the year, as well as using history data from other sheep.

Although these functionalities are specific to this pilot farm, some of them are transversal to the branch of the farm animals monitoring and even common to other sectors of our society. This paper will address mainly requirement 1, although compliance with some other requirements, such as 2 and 3, are also briefly discussed). Several metrics are considered aiming at the identification of the most relevant ones.

2 Related Work

Hereafter it is reviewed the most relevant previous work in the application of learning techniques for smart livestock monitoring using WSNs systems. A more extensive survey was presented by Sheikh [4], which reviewed machine learning techniques for WSN based livestock monitoring.

Nadimi et al. [5] propose a system to monitor the behavior of a herd in Denmark, capable of monitoring behavioral parameters of individual animals and transforming them into the corresponding behavioral mode, using for that an Artificial Neural Network (ANN). Farm animal's behavior and physiological responses provide important information about their health status and welfare. The behavior mode varies within five types: grazing, lying down, standing, walking and other modes. This animal behavior classification can be very useful to the farm's management.

Sikka et al. [6] deployed a large WSAN on a farm (a cattle breeding station at Belmont, in Australia) to understand the animals' behavior, improve the farms management as well as to maximize the farm production. Besides tracking animals, they also considered haptic and audio feedback to the animals. Based on the animal position, the system applies various stimuli (such as sound, vibration as well as low-level controllable electric shock) to the animal in order to change his behavior. This autonomous farm management system will automatically determine the areas more suitable for grazing based on soil moisture sensors. Such information is used to build accordingly the virtual fences, which will contain the animals that are automatically guided to these locations through stimuli.

In a related field, namely forest fire detection, Yu et al. [7] proposed a WSN solution employing a neural network for data processing. System evaluation was however through simulations.

3   Smart Livestock Management

The proposed architecture was developed for learning useful information for farm management, based on collected data from monitoring livestock animals (e.g., horses, cows, sheep, etc.), especially when they are freely grazing. Low energy consumption, storage and processing resources scalability is achieved using the cloud. Intelligent data processing makes use of machine learning and statistical methods for inferring additional valuable information. The monitoring is centered in the collection of the animal's geographical information through WSN nodes, to be fed into the learning services. Using this information, the system should make relevant deductions about the actual status of each animal, and of the entire flock, based on historical data.

This architecture is divided into three relevant components (see Fig. 2): the WSN infrastructure, the Cloud Computing platform responsible for event detection and data processing (including animal tracking, geofence and the learning services), and a Web application for the farmer to visualize the status of the system as well as to interact with it. This way, the heavy processing occurs on the Cloud Computing platform where learning should take place.

The leader sheep will correspond to the sink nodes of the WSN as they tend to have more sheep close to them. The other sheep will correspond to mesh nodes that will send its data through multi-hop to the sink nodes, using for that a short-range radio.

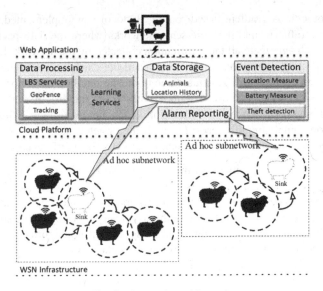

Fig. 2. System's architecture.

3.1   WSN Infrastructure

Each node of the WSN infrastructure corresponds to an animal that is equipped with a device providing sensing, computation as well as communication capabilities. Therefore, each animal will correspond to a mobile node that communicates wirelessly with the other system nodes.

Sensor Nodes. Sensor nodes are based on the eZ430-RF2500 module from Texas Instruments combined with Sensefinity's Butterfinger. The Butterfinger combines the MSP430F5419A MCU with a SIM908 module from SIMCom Wireless Solutions. It includes a GPS unit for collecting location data and a GPRS module for data transmission. In addition, it is possible to acquire as well its current battery status. As the Butterfinger has not a short-range radio (for communications within the WSN), it was necessary to combine it with an eZ430-RF2500 module, which provides the CC2500 transceiver. The sensor node (Fig. 3) is attached on the animals' collars.

Fig. 3. The final version of the hardware, its protective case, and installation on a sheep collar.

Network Protocol. A gradient-based routing protocol was implemented, appropriate for convergent traffic in mobile large-scale networks where the data packets flow to sink nodes, which aggregate all the information collected by the network. It was chosen a single-path routing approach in order to forward the data packets to the sink nodes, sending them through the most adequate neighbor (the one-hop neighbor that is closer in hops to a sink node, i.e. the neighbor with lower height). It was also used a point-to-point message delivery confirmation. Each network node adjusts its radio communication signal strength according with the targeted neighbor for communication, allowing to saving energy and reducing the network interference.

Routing. The monitored animals form a Mobile Ad-Hoc Network (MANET), providing high scalability and robustness to the network. For instance, in the cows' monitoring field, some authors [6] support this model by showing evidence that the animals on a cattle remain close to each other (typically herd together), so that overall connectivity between them was maintained using a multi-hop approach.

It is used a convergent protocol to route the data to the back-end infrastructure using a multi-hop approach. All system nodes use the short-range radio with low power consumption to communicate with the other animals inside the WSN. Due to this system's natural mobility constraints, some nodes eventually may become disconnected from each other, therefore forming independent and isolated ad hoc networks [8]. Our SML solution addresses this challenge by following a modified Full Cloud Connectivity model, employing data buffering and opportunistic routing of information in cases whether cellular coverage is inexistent.

3.2   Cloud Platform Services

The Machinates Cloud Computing platform provides the back-end infrastructure that supports the WSN, offering: data processing, data storage, event detection as well as alarm reporting. The Cloud Computing resources can be easily and automatically adjusted according to new application's demands, or as the application's requirements grow, without the farmer having to invest more in back-end infrastructure. The Cloud Computing platform is also in charge of sending digests to the end-user (via email) containing a monitoring summary during a period of analysis (day, week, month, etc.)

Location Tracking. A sensor node acquires its current geographic location, through GPS or other localization method, following a time-driven data reporting model. All this sensed information is aggregated in a sink node and then uploaded to a back-end infrastructure to be later processed. To accomplish these functionalities, each animal uses a technological device robust to the surrounding environmental conditions.

Geofence. Each time a position message is delivered to the Machinates® back-end, the geo-fencing algorithm will compare the new received animal's location with the existing virtual fence coordinates. Therefore, it is possible to determine if an animal is inside or outside the virtual fence, and erase or trigger accordingly an alarm. A simple geo-fencing algorithm was therefore implemented based on the Jordan Curve Theorem,

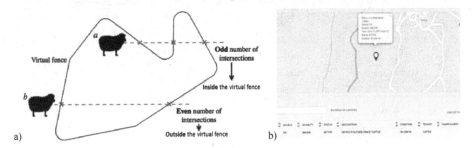

Fig. 4. (a) Example of the Jordan Curve Theorem; (b) Geo-fencing alarm on the Web application.

as follows. It is first necessary to draw a straight line from a given point (i.e., the sheep's location) to the outside of the whole drawing (i.e., outside the virtual fence). If the line meets the curve (i.e., the virtual fence) an odd number of times, that point (i.e., the sheep) is on the interior, otherwise if the line meets the curve an even number of times, that point is on the exterior. Figure 4a illustrates the application of the Jordan Curve Theorem. The line that intersects sheep a meets the virtual fence line 3 times (i.e., an odd number of times), therefore this sheep is on the interior of the virtual fence. The line that intersects sheep b meets the virtual fence line 2 times (i.e., an even number of times), therefore this sheep is on the exterior of the virtual fence.

Alarm Reporting, Storage and Event Detection. The farmer can use a Web app to visualize the last reported system (and its nodes) states, consult historical information that have been saved, access the events detected by the platform (see Fig. 4b), as well as interact with the system.

3.3   Pattern Learning Services

Machine learning approaches can be employed to add intelligence to the Internet of Things [9]. Running on the cloud, pattern learning aims at identifying healthy from non-healthy animals based on individual and group metrics (see Fig. 5a).

It was considered statistical and machine learning functionalities given by MATLAB tool (and libraries) in order to implement the two components of this module. The first component consists of feature extraction from geo-location data. It comprises, for each day of data, the extraction of statistical features, such as average and standard deviation values, and signal entropy, to feed such data into a learning algorithm (also employing matlab toolboxes). According to Fig. 5b, it was initially considered both supervised and non-supervised learning, namely clustering and neural networks, respectively. For supervised learning, the learning algorithm is first trained with inputs, for which the desired outputs for such data are known in advance (e.g. using data from known healthy and non-healthy animals). After the training process, and once the algorithm were fed with the inputs, it estimates the appropriate output. For unsupervised approaches, only the classification process takes place.

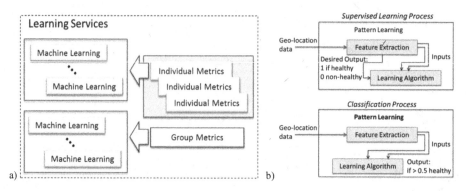

Fig. 5. (a) Metrics acquisition over acquired data for machine learning services; (b) Pattern learning strategies.

4   Pattern Learning Experiments

Experimental evaluation was performed at a large farm on the city of Setubal. Data concerning locations for two sheep is available for a two day period. A similar pair of sheep used collars, but one of them was injured. The results hereafter discussed are on (latitude, longitude) coordinates (see Fig. 6), distances and total velocities in degrees, over an equal period of nearly 6 h during daytime. Although different sheep were tracked during different day time periods, this 6 h period correspond to identical monitoring time intervals.

For each experiment, in each day and for each sheep, it was determined the velocity between two consecutive measured points. Thereafter, several features were extracted, namely average and standard deviation values, total sum of velocities (represented as d total on Table 1), and two entropy measures (corresponds to the two entropy values determined for the maximum scale according to Costa et al. [10]). In Table 1, velocities are given by $(\Delta x^2 + \Delta y^2)^{1/2}$, where $\Delta x_i = (\text{Latitude}_i - \text{Latitude}_{i-1})/\Delta T_i$ and $\Delta y_i = (\text{Longitude}_i - \text{Longitude}_{i-1})/\Delta T_i$, and $\Delta T_i = \text{timestamp}_i - \text{timestamp}_{i-1}$.

The results are shown in Fig. 7. Notice that the entropy value is smaller for the limp sheep during the two days of experiments. This may give some initial hint for a mechanism (e.g. clustering) to identify healthy from non-healthy sheep.

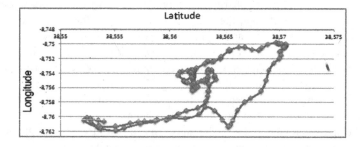

Fig. 6. Experiments in Setubal farm - Latitude/Longitude of limp sheep, day 2.

Table 1. Statistical measures for both normal and limp sheep during each day of experiments.

Sheep	Day 1					Day 2				
	avg vel	std vel	d total	Entropy 1	Entropy 2	avg vel	std vel	d total	Entropy 1	Entropy 2
Normal	0,211	0,149	23,9	1,56	1,63	0,221	0,157	22,3	2,44	1,87
Limp	0,176	0,168	19,9	1,42	1,12	0,213	0,241	21,6	1,8	1,34

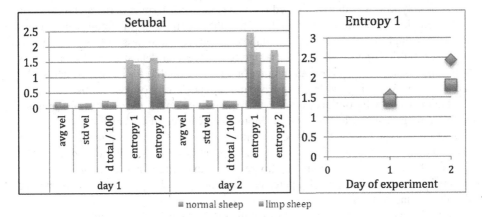

Fig. 7. Empirical results for the two monitored sheep at Setubal, for each of the two days of experiment. Several statistics are shown: average velocity and its standard deviation, two entropy values according to Costa et al. [10], and total distance during one day (scaled by 0.01).

The hypothesis concerning learning animal's health remains however to be tested upon the future availability of more training data to infer statistically relevant metrics (just two collars were available for experimental evaluation). It concerns the variation of the entropy value over several days, namely if for non-healthy individuals the entropy value over several days gets consistently lower than for healthy individuals. On a neural network, the inputs could be the entropy values of an animal over several days, and the output a value giving the probability of an animal being healthy, or not.

However, given the extremely small dataset available, no meaningful conclusions can yet be extracted concerning (i) the best features to extract from the data in order to feed a learning mechanism, either for clustering of a neural network approach; and (ii) the capability, or not, of identifying healthy animals from non-healthy ones using their patterns of motion. Concerning this last point, Costa et al. [10] have shown that the fractal property of organisms, such as given by a multi-scale entropy measure, gives a measure of an organism healthy, and have shown this strategy applied to ECG signals, as well as motion data. However, on their experiments the sampling frequency is significantly higher than 5,55 MHz (corresponding to 3 min in our system), and windows of analysis contain thousands of points (compared to nearly 100–200 data points for 6–8 h collection of sheep location data). Hence it is arguable if such approach could contribute in the future for the problem at hand.

5 Conclusions and Future Work

This paper proposed a learning architecture for a WSN system based on a Cloud Computing platform specifically designed for Livestock monitoring and management, centered on the periodical reporting of the animals' geographical location, and correspondent extraction of useful information for farm management from statistics and patterns detected on historical data.

A prototype was elaborated based on interviews with farm experts, and tested in a real scenario application, in particular for the monitoring of free-ranging dairy sheep. Although experimental evaluation evidenced the usefulness of this solution to a producer, further improvements will be pursued since real data statistical relevance is still rather weak, due to the small number of collars available for the experiments. We are however evaluating the learning system with sheep at two other farms.

Future work will continue to address the identification of the relevant features for each learning problem and algorithm. Moreover, features that were not completed in this first prototype system should be implemented (such as detect and report cuts in the sheep's collars). According to requests by experts at Queijaria Ribeira de Alpreade, the system should be upgraded in the future for monitoring other components of the business, namely predicting the percentage of fat on a sheep's milk, for aiding the farm's milking system.

Finally, experiments should be made with a higher number of monitored animals in different health conditions for a longer period of time in order to test the solution's effectiveness in detecting and distinguishing between healthy and non-healthy sheep. We are currently working on applying machine learning strategies to detect certain abnormal behavioral patterns that may suggest possible animal diseases.

Acknowledgments. Artur Arsenio work partly supported by CMU-Portuguese program through Fundação para Ciência e Tecnologia, AHA-Augmented Human Assistance project, AHA, CMUP-ERI/HCI/0046/2013CMU/2009.

References

1. Berckmans, D.: Automatic on-line monitoring of animals by precision livestock farming. In: International Society for Animal Hygiene, pp. 27–30 (2004)
2. Kwong, K., Wu, T., Goh, H., Sasloglou, K., Stephen, B., Glover, I., Shen, C., Du, W., Michie, C., Andonovic, I.: Practical considerations for wireless sensor networks in cattle monitoring applications. Comput. Electron. Agric. **81**, 33–44 (2012)
3. Edwards, W., Chamra, A., Mayer, R., Olsen, T.: Estimated costs for livestock fencing. In: Iowa State University Extension and Outreach, pp. 1–4, February 2012
4. Sheikh, S.: A survey on machine learning techniques used in tracking livestock in rural areas using wireless sensor networks. Int. J. Electron. Commun. Comput. Technol. **5**(1) (2015). ISSN: 2249-7838
5. Nadimi, E., Jrgensen, R., Blanes-Vidal, V., Christensen, S.: Monitoring and classifying animal behavior using Zigbee-based mobile ad hoc wireless sensor networks and artificial neural networks. Comput. Electron. Agric. **82**, 44–54 (2012)

6. Sikka, P., Corke, P., Valencia, P., Crossman, C., Swain, D., Bishop-Hurley, G.: Wireless ad hoc sensor and actuator networks on the farm. In: Information Processing in Sensor Networks, pp. 492–499, April 2006

7. Yu, L., Wang, N., Meng, X.: Real-time forest fire detection with wireless sensor networks. In: 2005 International Conference on Wireless Communications, Networking and Mobile Computing Proceedings, 1–2, Wuhan, China, pp. 1214–1217 (2005)

8. Wietrzyk, B., Radenkovic, M., Kostadinov, I.: Practical manets for pervasive cattle monitoring. In: 7th International Conference on Networking (ICN), pp. 14–23, April 2008

9. Arsenio, A.: On the application of artificial intelligence techniques to create network intelligence. In: Laalaoui, Y., Bouguila, N. (eds.) Artificial Intelligence Applications in Information and Communication Technologies. Studies in Computational Intelligence, vol. 607, pp. 71–97. Springer, Heidelberg (2015)

10. Costa, M., Goldberger, A.L., Peng, C.-K.: Multiscale entropy analysis of biological signals. Phys. Rev. E **71**, 021906 (2005)

Personal and Sensitive Data
in the e-Health-IoT Universe

Fiorella Guadagni[1], Noemi Scarpato[1(✉)], Ferroni Patrizia[1],
Grazia D'Ottavi[2], Fernando Boavida[3], Mario Roselli[4],
Graziano Garrisi[5], and Andrea Lisi[5]

[1] San Raffaele Rome University, Via di Val Cannuta, 247, Rome, Italy
{fiorella.guadagni,noemi.scarpato,patrizia.ferroni}
@unisanraffaele.gov.it
[2] San Raffaele S.p.A., Via Androne 81, Catania, Italy
grazia.dottavi@sanraffaele.it
[3] University of Coimbra, Coimbra, Portugal
boavida@dei.uc.pt
[4] University of Rome "Tor Vergata", Viale Oxford 81, Rome, Italy
mario.roselli@uniroma2.it
[5] ANORC - National Association for Digital Preservation Officers and
Operators, Via Stampacchia 21, Lecce, Italy
{grazianogarrisi,andrealisi}@studiolegalelisi.it

Abstract. Internet of Things (IoT), smart objects, are today part of our life and used in almost every industry and human activity: from e-health to e-learning not forgetting home automation and wearable technology. IoT promises to change our lives to make them easier, more efficient and "smart", however, we are now facing major challenges: security, data protection and privacy.

Keywords: IoT · Privacy · Informed consent · Security · Jurisdiction

1 Introduction

The market of IoT is exploding and many studies have deeply analyzed and defined the IoT architecture [1–3]. IoT promises to change our lives to make them easier, more efficient and "smart", however, we are now facing major challenges: security, data protection and privacy.

Article 29 of Directive 95/46/EC set up a Working Party (WP), an independent European advisory body on data protection and privacy. Its tasks are described in Article 30 of Directive 95/46/EC and Article 15 of Directive 2002/58/EC. In September 2014, the WP has issued the present opinion: "Opinion 8/2014 on the Recent Developments on the IoT" (WP223, adopted on 16 September, 2014) which focuses on three IoT developments: wearable technology, quantified self and home automation. This because, as stated by the WP in the Scope of the opinion, at the present time it is impossible to predict "*with certainty*" the extent of future IoT development due to fact that it is still an open question how all the data collected with IoT could be transformed.

© ICST Institute for Computer Sciences, Social Informatics and Telecommunications Engineering 2016
B. Mandler et al. (Eds.): IoT 360° 2015, Part II, LNICST 170, pp. 504–514, 2016.
DOI: 10.1007/978-3-319-47075-7_54

WP223 [4] should be read in connection with previous opinions adopted by the Working Party "on the application of the concepts of necessity and proportionality and data protection in law enforcement" (WP211), and "on surveillance" (WP 215), as well as "on apps on smart devices" (WP202, 2013), Opinion 4/2007 "on the concept of personal data" (WP 136, 2007) [5] Opinion 01/2010 "on the concepts of controller and processor" adopted on 16 February 2010 (WP 169) [6], Opinion 05/2014 "on Anonymisation Techniques" adopted on 10 April 2014 (WP 216) [7], Opinion 5/2009 "on online social networking" adopted on 12 June 2009 (WP 163) [8], Opinion 13/2011 "on Geolocation services on smart mobile devices" adopted on 16 May 2011 (WP185) [9], Opinion 15/2011 "on the definition of consent" adopted on 3 July 2011 (WP187) [10].

The first sentence of the WP223Summary states: *"The Internet of Things (IoT) is on the threshold of integration into the lives of European citizens. The viability of many projects in the IoT still remains to be confirmed but "smart things" are being made available which monitor and communicate with our homes, cars, work environment and physical activities."*

A succeeding statement stresses a crucial point: *"Many questions arise around the vulnerability of these devices, often deployed outside a traditional IT structure and lacking sufficient security built into them. Data losses, infection by malware, but also unauthorized access to personal data, intrusive use of wearable devices, or unlawful surveillance are as many risks that stakeholders in the IoT must address to attract prospective end-users of their products or services."*

The WP highlights that *"users must remain in complete control of their personal data throughout the product lifecycle, and when organizations rely on consent as a basis for processing, the consent should be fully informed, freely given and specific"* and continues stating that *"Indeed, empowering individuals by keeping them informed, free and safe is the key to support trust and innovation, hence to success on these markets."*

The WP has identified six *"significant privacy and data protection challenges related to the Internet of Things: Lack of control and information asymmetry; Low-quality consent; Extrapolation of inferences from data and repurposing of original processing; Intrusive identification of behavior patterns and user profiling; Limitations on the possibility of remaining anonymous whilst using services; Security risks"*.

Data exchanged through the IoT infrastructures could be private. For this reason, it is mandatory the platform must ensure privacy and security. It is important to note that privacy is not only a technical property but is an aggregation of a legal, socio-ethical and technical viewpoints. The legal regulation on privacy, especially when dealing with relevant health data (as in e-health), presupposes the application and respect not only of the legislation that is the main reference "Directive 95/46/EC" of the European Parliament and of the Council of 24 October 1995 "on the protection of individuals with regard to the processing of personal data and on the free movement of such data" (also called "Data Protection Directive (95/46/EEC)", but also a series of specific measures and guidelines (all linked together, due to the often absence of specific legislation) issued by the Authority for the protection of personal data.

Moreover, we should also consider the "European Parliament legislative resolution of 12 March 2014, on the proposal for a regulation of the European Parliament and of the Council on the protection of individuals with regard to the processing of personal data and on the free movement of such data (General Data Protection Regulation) (COM (2012)0011–C7-0025/2012–2012/0011(COD)-(Ordinary legislative procedure: first reading). This new European legislative resolution contains some important principles and rules of proper treatment and will replace all the individual national legislations of the EU member countries. A consolidated version of the first reading of this new European regulation can be found linking to [11]. At the time of this paper edition, the European Parliament is proposing 207 amendments, some of them crucial for IoT projects (e.g., amendment #95).

Although some security [12] and privacy [13] approaches have been proposed, IoT still raises several security and privacy challenges that must be addressed. In this paper we will analyze some critical issues related to privacy aspects in IoT architecture and consequent main legal requirements considering as a paradigmatic example the Italian Privacy Code.

2   Legal Scenario

Due to the sensitivity of data that may be processed, the regulatory perimeter within which it is possible to proceed with the development of IoT systems and the classification of information and documents that can be treated in different contexts (e-health, cloud, etc.) should be defined, through a phase of analysis of the main legal requirements concerning privacy. Preliminarily, therefore, it is necessary to evaluate:

– the requirements and the stakes imposed by the regulations;
– the compliance with the general principles and organizational measures and safety (according to the principles of privacy by design and privacy by default, further specified);
– the conformity of the treatment performed with new tools compared to current regulation;
– the severity of any discrepancies and the consequent urgent resolution,
– the possible sanctions in case of non-compliance with the requirements of legislation and with the measures of the Data Protection Authority (DPA).

The legal regulation on privacy, especially when dealing with relevant health data (as in e-health), presupposes the application and respect not only of the legislation that is the main Italian reference, Legislative Decree no. 196, 30 June 2003, "Code regarding the protection of personal data" (so-called Privacy Law) and its Annex B (Technical regulations regarding minimum security), but also a series of specific measures and guidelines (all linked together, due to the often absence of specific legislation) issued by the Authority for the protection of personal data.

In fact, the special attention given by the Lawmaker to the proper handling of personal data, especially sensitive ones, necessarily implies the performance of a whole series of requirements both organizational and technical security measures. From this legislation comes down a series of requirements, all of which occur in the management and treatment of personal data and that can be divided into:

- **General requirements** (disclosure ex Art. 13, right of access ex Art. 7 and eventual acquisition of consent to data processing in accordance with art. 23);
- **Special requirements** (notification to the DPA in cases specifically indicated in art. 37 and questioning or preliminary verification pursuant to Article 17, if the processing of some data might represent a specific risk for the person concerned);
- **Organizational requirements** (minimum security measures, necessary and appropriate, regulated by Articles 31 and the following, and by specific provisions of the DPA, especially with regard to the processing of data in health setting).

Compliance with these requirements is considered necessary in the development of a IoT architecture and in subsequent use in reference to identified or identifiable individuals. Nevertheless, privacy protection should not disregard defense instruments that not only prevent accidental loss of data, or the external non-authorized access, but also preserve the digital memory in time of the scanned documents.

In general, there are four main requirements that must be put in place in order to properly proceed with the processing of personal data: (i) notification to the DPA (if necessary); (ii) communication of the information to the individual; (iii) acquisition of the consent to treatment; (iv) establishment of minimum, necessary and appropriate security measures for the processing of personal data.

These concern, in particular, technological and organizational measures aimed at avoiding a treatment of data by unauthorized persons and the loss, destruction or dispersion of data stored in their databases. For this reasons, privacy protections in IoT devices *"should be built-in from the very outset, in application of the "Privacy by Design" principle"* (WP223) and before they are released in the market, a Privacy Impact Assessment should be performed, as detailed in Sect. 2.3.

2.1 Principle of Necessity

The main principle of the entire Italian Privacy Code (Legislative Decree no. 196/2003), which should inspire all treatments within the IoT (and, therefore, also regarding the processing of data concerning health) and must be kept in mind in the implementation of technology solutions in these areas, it is the "principle of necessity" (art. 3), which is considered an extension of the old principles of relevance and of no data surplus, compared to the treatment aim and certainly plays the role of general interpretative key for all items of the Italian Privacy Code. Under this principle, anyone dealing with personal data will have to do so to ensure that the personal data themselves can only be used and to the extent that is strictly necessary for the achievement of specific objectives, which in turn will have to be identified and disclosed to the person (disclosure ex Art. 13 Legislative Decree no. 196/2003). As repeatedly stated by the DPA, in the treatment of medical data, for example, all medical devices should be developed and programmed in such a way that this principle is respected from the beginning, also in accordance with the Community framework which sees the application the so called principle of "privacy by design" (i.e., the provision of measures to protect the data already at the design stage of a product or software).

Closely linked to the principle of necessity is the art. 11 of the Code, which develops the basic guidelines to follow during any processing of personal data. According to this article, the basic personal data undergoing processing shall be:

(a) processed lawfully and fairly;
(b) collected and recorded for specific, explicit and legitimate purposes and used in other processing operations in terms compatible with those purposes;
(c) accurate and, where necessary, updated;
(d) adequate, relevant and not excessive in relation to the purposes for which they were collected or subsequently processed;
(e) kept in a form which permits identification of data for a period of time not exceeding that necessary for the purposes for which they were collected or subsequently processed.

2.2   New Principles: Privacy by Design and Privacy by Default

In order to protect individuals, therefore, it is necessary to operate in accordance with the new principles of "Privacy by Design" and "Privacy by default", even considering to make a real "Privacy Impact Assessment" in relation to each instrument used. This means that:

– privacy must be incorporated in the design and architecture of IoT systems ("Privacy by design");
– there must be attention to the centrality of the interests of individuals (treat only the necessary data);
– the amount of data collected and the duration of their conservation should not go beyond the minimum necessary to achieve the aims pursued (principle of relevance and limits);
– these mechanisms must ensure that - by default - no personal data are made accessible to an indefinite number of people;
– personal data must be automatically protected in any IT system (taking account of technological and implementation costs);
– if the treatment has risks (by nature, scope or their purposes) the administrator must perform an impact assessment (Privacy Impact Assessment).

2.2.1   Privacy by Design

Because privacy must be incorporated in the design and architecture of IT systems, already in the design phase of an information management system, solutions ensuring that they are treated only the personal information necessary for each specific purpose of the treatment, must be provided. Privacy, therefore, becomes an essential and integrated component of the system (without reducing its functionality). To achieve this, the designers and operators should be asked to consider the priority interests of individuals by providing effective privacy default interventions, appropriate information and enhanced user-friendly options to the user.

2.2.2 Privacy by Default

Every IT system should ensure that only the personal information necessary for each specific purpose of the processing are treated, by default, and that the amount of data collected and the duration of their preservation does not go beyond the minimum necessary for the purposes sought. In particular, personal data should not be accessible to an indefinite number of people and those involved must be able to control the distribution of their personal data.

2.3 Privacy Impact Assessment (PIA)

This activity postulates a series of operations which identifies treatments presenting specific risks (e.g. profiling, special categories of data, data accessible to a vast number of people, large amounts of data or data combined with other data). In this case, the PIA must consider:

- the confidentiality of the individual data;
- the confidentiality of the person (physical integrity, biometrics, body checks, etc.);
- the confidentiality of personal behavior (video surveillance, sexual preference, political, etc.);
- the confidentiality of personal communications (interception, monitoring, email);
- identify the impacts that the project has on an individual privacy and identify less intrusive alternatives;
- assess the impact from the point of view of all stakeholders;
- understand the level of acceptance of the project and its characteristics;
- clarify the needs of the project that have negative effects on privacy and are not avoidable (acceptance of residual risk);
- document and publish results (PIA reports).

PIA, therefore, involves:

- a systematic description of the proposed treatment, its necessity and proportionality in relation to the objective pursued;
- an assessment of the risks to the rights and freedoms of data subjects;
- measures to address the risks and minimize the volume of personal data;
- safeguards, security measures to ensure the protection of personal data and demonstrate compliance with current legislation, taking into account the rights and legitimate interests of the data subjects.

All this can be also realized by means of a Privacy Impact Assessment, which focusing on risk management and securing compliance with the requirements of the legislation on data protection and privacy, will give us back a specific assessment of the privacy implications of developed programs or new activities to be undertaken.

2.4 Data Subject's Consent

The data subject's consent is one of the legal basis for the processing of personal/sensitive data. This aspect is becoming more and more relevant considering that in a few years, IoT devices will be a major generator of "big data" at a very high velocity. We are at a stage where data generated by IoT meet the 5 V's: Volume, Variety, Velocity, Variability and Value [14]. In this perspective, data subject should be aware of it and should be able to completely control the all lifecycle processing of her/his personal data.

The definition of Consent was set by the Council Common Position10 in 1995, as *"any freely given specific and informed indication of his wishes by which the data subject signifies his agreement to personal data relating to him being processed"*.

When consent is requested to processing personal data health-related in electronic health records (EHR) a specific consent must be obtained, as stated in WP131 - Working Document on the processing of personal data relating to EHR: *"Specific" consent must relate to a well-defined, concrete situation in which the processing of medical data is envisaged. Therefore a "general agreement" of the data subject - e.g. to the collection of his medical data for an EHR and to any future transfers of these medical data to health professionals involved in treatment - would not constitute consent in the terms of Article 2(h) of the Directive.*

Moreover, WP 131 highlights that *"consent by the data subject (must be) based upon an appreciation and understanding of the facts and implications of an action. The individual concerned must be given, in a clear and understandable manner, accurate and full information of all relevant issues, in particular those specified in Articles 10 and 11 of the Directive, such as the nature of the data processed, purposes of the processing, the recipients of possible transfers, and the rights of the data subject. This includes also an awareness of the consequences of not consenting to the processing in question"*.

The WP 187 "Opinion 15/2011 on the definition of consent", Adopted on 13 July 2011, reports that *"The more complex data processing is, the more can be expected from the data controller. The more difficult it becomes for an average citizen to oversee and understand all the elements of the data processing, the larger the efforts should become for the data controller to demonstrate that consent was obtained based on specific, understandable information."*

The Working Party stated that *"This Opinion is partly issued in response to a request from the Commission in the context of the ongoing review of the Data Protection Directive. It therefore contains recommendations for consideration in the review. Those recommendations include:"*

(i)   clarifying the meaning of "unambiguous" consent and explaining that only consent that is based on statements or actions to signify agreement constitutes valid consent;

(ii)   requiring data controllers to put in place mechanisms to demonstrate consent (within a general accountability obligation);

(iii)   adding an explicit requirement regarding the quality and accessibility of the information forming the basis for consent, and

(iv)   a number of suggestions regarding minors and others lacking legal capacity

Furthermore, WP 223, states that *"users must remain in complete control of their personal data throughout the product lifecycle, and when organisations rely on consent as a basis for processing, the consent should be fully informed, freely given and specific"* and continues stating that *"Indeed, empowering individuals by keeping them informed, free and safe is the key to support trust and innovation, hence to success on these markets."*

An example cited by WP on WP223 is the following:

"A health-related device uses a small light to monitor how blood flows in veins, and to derive heartbeat information. The device includes another sensor that measures blood oxygen level but no information is available on this collection of data neither on the device nor on the user interface. Even if the blood oxygen sensor is fully functional, it should not be enabled without first informing the user. Explicit consent will be required to enable this sensor."

Taken into account all the considerations above reported, it is understandable the need of requirements clearly defined that will support data subjects and e-health professionals.

2.4.1 Issues Related to the "Consent"

Consent to process personal/sensitive data should be informed. However, this is sometimes very difficult because many IoT devices are not designed to facilitate information to interested users. There is therefore:

- The need to obtain prior and informed consent, unless the treatment is objectively necessary, i.e., for the execution of a contract to which the data subject is party. The notice must state the identity of all those involved in various ways in the processing of personal data and specify that *"data subjects must have a possibility to revoke any prior consent given to a specific data processing and to object to the processing of data relating to them"* (WP223) at any time.
- The need to store and process only data collected on the data subject *"strictly necessary for the specific purpose previously determined by the data controller (the "data minimisation" principle)"* (WP223).

2.5 Jurisdiction

The exclusive problem with Internet jurisdiction in IoT might be the presence of numerous parties in several parts of the world. Then, if one party wants to sue the other, where can he sue? Traditional requirements generally comprise two areas:

1. the Place where the defendant resides, or
2. where the cause of action arises.

At large, in the context of the Internet, considering the lack of physical boundaries, both these are difficult to establish with any certainty. For example, a single transaction (e.g. data processing) can involve the laws of three jurisdictions:

1. the laws of the state/nation in which the user resides,
2. the laws of the state/nation that apply where the server hosting the transaction (e.g. data processing) is located, and
3. the laws of the state/nation which apply to the person or business with whom the transaction (e.g. data processing) takes place.

So, a user in one of the Indian States conducting a transaction (e.g. data processing) with another user in Britain through a server in Canada could theoretically be subject to the laws of all three countries as they relate to the transaction at hand.

In any case, in the privacy context it's necessary to refer to the European regulation (Directive 95/46/CE) to find out which is the correct regulation to apply to the specific case.

3 Security and Privacy in a Real Scenario

Medical devices connected to the network may be beneficial in many ways (time and money saving, rapidity of intervention), but may also be over shadowed by several critical issues: the theft of personal information, intentional and malicious tampering devices, deterioration and accidental failures. Medical devices in the network, therefore, are vulnerable as any other related technology. When, through a device connected and plugged into a person, a computer crime is committed, it is not always easy to identify the person held responsible for the custody and preservation of data staff treated (also in terms of omission in the adoption of security measures and/or organizational measures for the protection of personal data).

Moreover, we should also consider attacks aimed at people with the intent to cause physical harm. This is the case of, for instance, implantable cardioverter defibrillators (ICD), pacemakers or even insulin pumps. The first two devices, so important to the health of millions of people suffering from heart disease, are not designed to withstand attacks. Indeed, both defibrillators and pacemakers can be reprogrammed, forcing them to shut down or send a potentially fatal electric shock, or even infect other pacemaker or ICD. Moreover, the use of wireless control systems, in fact, exposes at least a theoretical risk of intrusion, sabotage and even theft of sensitive information. The researchers have succeeded to collect personal data of some patients by capturing signals emitted by radio systems implanted.

It is essential, therefore, that the safety of these medical devices is integrated from the moment of their design, and not reconsidered at a later time, thus ensuring an approach secure by design (and, therefore, also privacy by design). The IoT, in fact, allows the creation of tools to detect and continuously monitor parameters essential to health, to be included in the "wearable technology": bracelets, clothing, sensors with functions related to health that operate even through smart phones. This allows a great development of telemedicine and home care, which are becoming increasingly innovative fields.

4 Conclusions

One of the main issues relating to security and privacy is the analysis of the data flow in a IoT architecture that should be designed in accordance with the new principles of "Privacy by Design" and "Privacy by default", and verified by PIA. Although the IoT implementation of security mechanisms and privacy has been widely debated [15], there is still the open question of who should be in charge of informing users about the management of their personal/sensitive data and to collect and store all consents. In particular, the "lack of control" on the data is one of the main issues to wonder about. In fact, the sharing of personal data among physicians, device manufacturers, software developers, suppliers of computing power, clouds providers and analysts, entails for the people whose data are processed, extremely difficult to exercise proper control over these data, the method of their transmission by IoT devices, shared between third parties and, above all, on the objectives pursued different from those associated with the device (so-called "secondary use"). As above reported, WP 223 states that *"users must remain in complete control of their personal data throughout the product life-cycle"*. Thus, it remains to be clearly identified the role of all the actors in IoT (e.g. physicians, developers, IoT producers, etc.) in the management and storage of the collected data.

At the end of this analysis, we cannot provide a final answer to all poised questions, however, we may suggest technological and procedural efforts.

Standardizing requirements represent a mandatory issue that should ensure both uniformity in design research protocols and in strengthening digital privacy and security. This will be ensured one the one hand by providing the constructor with definite rules as to how to "maximize" the efforts to ensure adequate data protection and privacy ("Privacy by Design") and on the other by refining and reinforcing the regulations governing privacy and security. This point is of outmost interest when considering the perception that a general IT tool end-user has of the technology he/she is facing. Indeed, most people consider information stored on their mobile phones to be as or more protected than that stored in their personal computers (Urban et al. 2012), although it is virtually impossible to keep track of where data are being held, by whom, and for which purpose. Similarly, people consider data stored in institutions (such as online banks) to be safe and no one describes the potential dangers related to data breaches. This altered perception of privacy should hint new efforts at enhancing technological literacy of the population and at increasing public's knowledge of privacy and security in order to exercise a proper control over their data.

Likewise, in health research data protection depends on institutions, investigators and sponsors, although it appears unrealistic to think that ethical obligations can be fully met without guidance and resources. Also in this case, the governments should promote the development of education, certification, and accreditation systems that apply to all researchers, rather than mandating that privacy and confidentiality be "maximized" [The National Institutes of Health Guidelines for the Conduct of Research Involving Human Subjects (2004)]. In this way, the ethical obligation to protect participants, which lies first with researchers, can be more easily met, as requested by National Bioethics Advisory Commission (NBAC) (2001).

Acknowledgements. Partially supported by the ESF - Italian Ministry of Education, University & Research PON03PE_00146_1/10 BIBIOFAR (CUP B88F12000730005).

References

1. Gershenfeld, N., Krikorian, R., Cohen, D.: The Internet of Things. Sci. Am. **291**, 76–81 (2004)
2. Granjal, J., Monteiro, E., Silva, J.: Security for the Internet of Things: a survey of existing protocols and open research issues. IEEE Commun. Surv. Tutor. **17**, 1294–1312 (2015)
3. Medaglia, C.M., Serbanati, A.: An overview of privacy and security issues in the Internet of Things. In: Giusto, D., Iera, A., Morabito, G., Atzori, L. (eds.) the Internet of Things. Springer, New York (2010). doi:10.1007/978-1-4419-1674-7_38
4. http://ec.europa.eu/justice/data-protection/article-29/documentation/opinionrecommendation/files/2014/wp223_en.pdf
5. http://ec.europa.eu/justice/policies/privacy/docs/wpdocs/2007/wp136_en.pdf
6. http://ec.europa.eu/justice/policies/privacy/docs/wpdocs/2010/wp169_en.pdf
7. http://ec.europa.eu/justice/data-protection/article-29/documentation/opinionrecommendation/files/2014/wp216_en.pdf
8. http://ec.europa.eu/justice/policies/privacy/docs/wpdocs/2009/wp163_en.pdf
9. http://ec.europa.eu/justice/data-protection/article-29/documentation/opinion-recommendation/files/2011/wp185_en.pdf
10. http://ec.europa.eu/justice/data-protection/article-29/documentation/opinionrecommendation/files/2011/wp187_en.pdf
11. http://ec.europa.eu/justice/data-protection/index_en.htm
12. http://www.europarl.europa.eu/sides/getDoc.do?pubRef=-//EP//TEXT+TA+P7-TA-2014-0212+0+DOC+XML+V0//IT
13. Dong, C., Guiran, C., Lizhong, J., Xiaodong, R., Jiajia, L., Fengyun, L.: A novel secure architecture for the Internet of Things. In: Proceedings of 2011 Fifth International Conference on Genetic and Evolutionary Computing (ICGEC) (2011)
14. Alcaide, A., Palomar, E., Montero-Castillo, J., Ribagorda, A.: Anonymous authentication for privacy-preserving IoT target-driven applications. Comput. Secur. **37**, 111–123 (2013)
15. Fan, W., Bifet, A.: Mining big data: current status, and forecast to the future. SIGKDD Explor. Newsl. **14**, 1–5 (2013)
16. Steele, R., Clarke, A.: The Internet of Things and next-generation public health information systems. Commun. Netw. **5**(03), 4 (2013)

A Software Defined Network Solution
for Spontaneous Wireless Access Extension

Gianluca Aloi, Giancarlo Fortino, and Pasquale Pace[✉]

DIMES, University of Calabria, Rende, Italy
{aloi,fortino,ppace}@dimes.unical.it

Abstract. Spontaneous wireless networks enabled by mobile end-user devices (e.g. smartphones) are receiving considerable interest due the possibility to offer a wide range of novel, highly pervasive and user-centric network services and applications. Novel and extremely flexible network deployment strategies are required in order to cope with the user mobility, the limited communication capabilities of wireless devices, and the intrinsic dynamism of traffic loads and QoS requirements. In this paper, we want to trace the path, and related challenges, that lead toward a *Community Owned Wireless Access Network* (COWAN) to pro-vide Internet and Cloud-based services through the sharing of resources owned by the end-user devices. In such way, Software-Defined Network-ing (SDN) solutions could play a central role in order to make easier the network creation and management and to deliver performance guaran-tees to end users. However, the extension of the SDN paradigm to mobile devices requires facing the challenge of moving some network control on end-user devices to support network interaction capabilities and services.

Keywords: Wireless access networks · Software defined networks · Self-organizing and spontaneous networks

1 Introduction

Recent advances in telecommunications have led to the proliferations of wireless devices able to access the Internet through a multitude of wireless technologies. At the same time, we register an increasing research interest towards sponta-neous networks composed by mobile end-user devices which share their network resources in order to extend Internet coverage and services availability.

The interest is encouraged by the availability of several wireless interfaces (e.g. WiFi, Bluetooth, LTE) through which spontaneous networks can be dynam-ically established. A new communication paradigm, characterized by the fact that the access network has a strong spontaneous nature and is primarily made up of users owned devices, is emerging.

Several authors conducted previous works in such direction. In [1] a new generation of network nodes able to provide intelligent and city-wide services for citizens, city authorities and utilities was proposed. The proposed STEM-Net was conceived as an evolutionary solution for deployment, extension and

© ICST Institute for Computer Sciences, Social Informatics and Telecommunications Engineering 2016
B. Mandler et al. (Eds.): IoT 360° 2015, Part II, LNICST 170, pp. 515–520, 2016.
DOI: 10.1007/978-3-319-47075-7_55

management of the network infrastructure in a smart city. The proposed solution was capable to face the heterogeneity of devices and network technologies and the fragmentation of coverage and connectivity in urban areas. The STEM-Net paradigm foresees the realization of a new generation of wireless devices, called Stem Nodes (SNs), that are able to self-configure at multiple layers of the stack on the basis of their hardware configurations, and thus to assume multiple network roles (i.e. gateway, relays, etc.). Such a multi-purpose nature justifies the parallelism with the biological counterpart. Similar with a stem cell, a stem node can undergo mutation in order to fulfil a given task. Mutation is driven by both built-in node capabilities and additional capabilities that are dynamically learnt by cooperating with other nodes.

In [2] authors focused their attention on emergency-related scenarios and investigated the potential of spontaneous networks for providing connectivity over the emergency area through the sharing of resources owned by the end-user devices. A novel approach toward the deployment of spontaneous networks composed by wireless SNs was proposed to emphasize their ability to cover multiple network roles (e.g. gateway, router). The self-organization of the spontaneous network was achieved through the local reconfiguration of each SN.

In [3], a special case of User-Centric Networks (UCNs) named Spontaneous Smartphones-based Networks (SSNs), has been treated where the role of the end-user devices is played by smartphones that are, "*evolutionary*" and more active in supporting communication services. SSNs present key features like spontaneity in the creation of the network and redefinition of the device role in order to make them continuously adaptive to both network and users requirements. The work was devoted to identify the potential advantages of SSNs, by also providing a clear definition of the challenges and the issues that need to be faced in order to make this emerging paradigm effective and practically deployable.

As a natural evolution of these previous works, in this paper, we want to trace the path that leads toward a *Community Owned Wireless Access Network* (COWAN) to provide Internet and Cloud-based services through the sharing of resources owned by the end-user devices. This new approach offers great advantages in terms of *(i)* lower costs required to set up the network access, *(ii)* reduced or no maintenance at all for network management, and *(iii)* possibility to set-up a network even on scenarios where the infrastructure is poorly available (i.e., disaster scenarios, rural areas, least developed countries, etc.).

Despite the enormous potentials, a COWAN based on smartphones or similar devices (e.g., phablet, tablet), is still a challenge [3]. Usually, the network creation and management requires a massive intervention from the users that, however, would prefer being agnostic about technological issues. This requirement constitutes a unique challenge of COWAN compared to traditional self-organizing systems and generic multi-hop ad hoc networks [4,5]. Hence, a framework able to limit the human intervention, with the aim of making the network management as much spontaneous as possible, is mandatory for the success of the COWAN approach. In such way, Software-Defined Networking (SDN) contribution could play a central role in order to make easier the network creation and management and to deliver performance QoS guarantees to end users.

The rest of the paper is organized as follows. In Sect. 2 we introduce the concept of Community Owned Wireless Access Network. In Sect. 3 we motivate the benefits of a SDN contribution introducing open issues and challenges and then conclusions follow in Sect. 4.

2   Community Owned Wireless Access Network Scheme

Community Owned Wireless Access Network (COWAN) are based on smartphones or similar devices. The deployment of such kind of network is particularly suited on scenarios where the infrastructure is poorly available (Fig. 1). An extended pervasive wireless Internet access can be obtained by naturally extending the coverage of wide areas using the huge density of smartphones located in all daily life environments. When natural catastrophes disrupt traditional network infrastructures, a COWAN can support communications between survivals and rescue teams. Moreover, when special events (e.g., concerts, trade fairs, Olympic games) involve huge numbers of people with risks of overloading the communication infrastructure, COWAN can be used to offload mobile data traffic from cellular networks.

The logical architecture of a generic end-user smartphone is illustrated in Fig. 2. In our design, a network node is defined as a special case of Stem Node [2] and, in particular, we use the term Community Smart Node (CSN) to indicate novel family of software enhanced smartphones. We further note that in our view, a CSN may be like a simplified variant of Stem Phones (SPs) defined in [3], so a

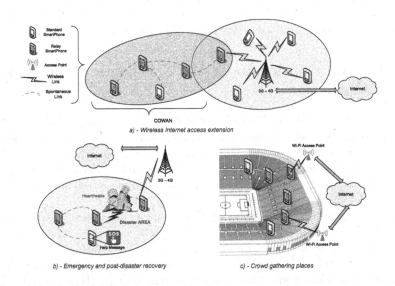

Fig. 1. COWAN communication scenarios.

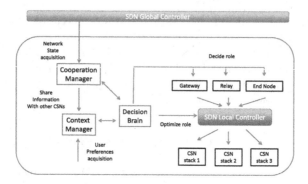

Fig. 2. Community Smart Node architecture.

limited fraction of the existing smartphones that can still provide useful services to the neighboring legacy phones.

Each CSN, participating to the COWAN setup, can play a given set of roles according to the network capabilities/functionalities supported by the specific device. The basic set of roles of each CSN include the ability *(i)* to produce/receive data (i.e. End Node role), *(ii)* to forward the traffic of other terminals (i.e. Relay role) and *(iii)* to act as a gateway (i.e. Gateway role) providing access to global network resources to other terminals.

The set of roles played by each CSN can vary in accordance of its own built-in characteristics (i.e., hardware features or user preferences). For example, the gateway role could require the simultaneous use of different communication technologies to connect other nodes (e.g., Wi-Fi, Bluetooth, IEEE 802.15.4) and to access to global network resources (e.g., LTE). Moreover, each role is mapped to a stack configuration and it is foreseen the possibility, for a CSN, to change its configuration over time for self-optimization purposes.

3   SDN Contribution to COWAN Scheme: Open Issues and Challenges

To make really feasible a COWAN solution the big challenge is to limit, or reduce to zero, the user intervention in the network creation and management. Such processes should be as much spontaneous and transparent as possible. In such way, Software-Defined Networking (SDN) contribution could play a central role in order to make easier the network creation and management and to deliver performance QoS guarantees to end users [6,7].

The main benefit of SDN is the separation of the data and the control plane to provide a global view of network and allow an easier way to configure and manage it. In SDN, user devices are substantially responsible only for packet forwarding. Existing mobile phones are generally equipped with multiple network interfaces, complicating the process of selecting the best access technology at each moment (e.g. WiFi hotspots, WiFi access to fixed residential home gateways, LTE cells). A generic mobile node may decide to use the available access network options sequentially (i.e., move all traffic from one technology to another) or simultaneously (i.e., move selected flows from one access to another).

In our vision, we suppose that telecom operators, which already offer both residential fixed and mobile connectivity services, can also offer to external parties (e.g., service providers) a set of SDN API to make available SDN services at the edge of the network. This particular condition influence the decision of which access technology should be used to deliver a certain type of traffic to a specific mobile terminal or group of users. In such a context, it can be assumed that each mobile node can easily join to a Software Defined Wireless Network (SDWN) [8].

These strong assumptions are away from the scope of our proposal and we are aware of the presence of several challenges, not yet overcome, which make such scenario extremely difficult to achieve. However, the main contribution that we want to provide is another step forward, the creation of a multi-hop extension of a SDWN, namely the COWAN.

To meet this challenge, we propose to export SDN software modules in the architecture of a Community Smart Node (CSN). The design of SDN is based on centralized control functionality for simplicity and flexibility (i.e. OpenFlow, NOX). However, they did not adequately address scalability and reliability requirements of a COWAN architecture. Some alternative distributed and/or hierarchical solution could be compliant with our purposes [9–11].

The Kandoo scheme [10] appears to be the most suitable because it is a hierarchical implementation of SDN controller for OpenFlow. Kandoo creates a two-level hierarchical SDN controlling system that distinguishes local controllers and management applications from global ones. The local controllers manage a subset of nodes and execute applications which do not need network-wide views, whereas the global controller is responsible for managing all the local controllers and implementing global policies. In such a way, the SDN integration is provided introducing a hierarchical implementation in CSNs architecture. The consequent introduction of a SDN Local Controller block allows each node to be able to select the most appropriate protocol stack, SDN compliant, related to the specific role to play.

4   Conclusions

In this work we have presented the potential of COWAN, motivating the need to integrate the functionalities of SDWN to minimize users' involvements in network set-up and maintenance. We believe that the implementation of SDN modules in each smartphone architecture, could favor the diffusion of research activities focused on Community Owned Wireless Access Network.

References

1. Aloi, G., Bedogni, L., Felice, M.D., Loscrí, V., Molinaro, A., Natalizio, E., Zema, N.R.: STEMNet: an evolutionary network architecture for smart and sustainable cities. Trans. Emerg. Telecommun. Technol. **25**(1), 21–40 (2014)
2. Aloi, G., Bedogni, L., Bononi, L., Briante, O., Di Felice, M., Loscrí, V., Trotta, A.: STEM-NET: how to deploy a self-organizing network of mobile end-user devices for emergency communication. Comput. Commun. **60**, 12–27 (2015)
3. Aloi, G., Di Felice, M., Loscrí, V., Pace, P., Ruggeri, G.: Spontaneous smartphone networks as a user-centric solution for the future internet. IEEE Commun. Mag. **52**(12), 26–33 (2014)
4. Boccia, L., Pace, P., Amendola, G., Di Massa, G.: Low multipath antennas for GNSS-based attitude determination systems applied to high-altitude platforms. GPS Solutions **12**(3), 163–171 (2008)
5. Gungor, V.C. , Pace, P., Natalizio, E.: AR-TP: an adaptive and responsive transport protocol for wireless mesh networks. In: IEEE International Conference on Communications (ICC), Glasgow Scotland, pp. 3740–3745 (2007)
6. Nunes, B., Mendonca, M., Nguyen, X.N., Obraczka, K., Turletti, T.: A survey of software-defined networking: past, present, and future of programmable networks. IEEE Commun. Surv. Tutorials **16**(3), 1617–1634 (2014)
7. Costanzo, S., Galluccio, L., Morabito, G., Palazzo, S.: Software defined wireless networks: unbridling SDNs. In: IEEE European Workshop on Software Defined Networking (EWSDN), pp. 1–6 (2012)
8. Ferrer Riera, J., Bock, C., Escalona, E., Parker, M.C., Walker, S., Quinlan, T., Jungnickel, V., Habel, K., Marques, V., Levi, D.: Software-defined wired-wireless access network convergence: the SODALES approach. In: IEEE Globecom Workshops (GC Wkshps), pp. 1522–1527 (2014)
9. Tootoonchian, A., Ganjali, Y.: HyperFlow: a distributed control plane for OpenFlow. In: Proceedings of the Internet Network Management Conference on Research on Enterprise Networking, p. 3. USENIX Association (2010)
10. Hassas Yeganeh, S., Ganjali, Y.: Kandoo: a framework for efficient and scalable offloading of control applications. In: Proceedings of the First Workshop on Hot Topics in Software Defined Networks, pp. 19–24. ACM (2012)
11. Koponen, T., Casado, M., Gude, N., Stribling, J., Poutievski, L., Zhu, M., Shenker, S.: Onix: a distributed control platform for large-scale production networks. In: OSDI, vol. 10, pp. 1–6 (2010)

Towards Adoption of Software Defined Wireless Backhaul Networks

Osianoh Glenn Aliu[1,2], Senka Hadzic[1], Christian Niephaus[2],
and Mathias Kretschmer[1,2(✉)]

[1] Network Research Department, Fraunhofer FOKUS, Sankt Augustin, Germany
mathias@defutech.de
[2] DeFuTech, Hennef, Germany

Abstract. The flexibility of future wireless network architectures is aimed at allowing more innovation, reducing complexity and improving service offerings. Software Defined Networking (SDN) has been identified as an enabler for this adoption. From an implementation perspective, we provide a description of use cases and a framework overview for its implementation. This framework and the future work identified serve as pointers for further research projects in Software Defined Wireless Network (SDWN).

Keywords: Backhaul · Software defined · Flexibility · Bootstrap · Auto-configuration

1 Introduction

Immersed in various marketing and research activities on breakthrough data download speeds as the basis of the Future Internet and 5th Generation (5G) wireless networks, the real game changers will be technologies that focus on being enablers to ensure future networks are self organised, flexible and programmable. Vertical system architectures where a single manufacturer is responsible for developing the hardware, software and applications will gradually be phased out by a separation of the application layer, control layer and the data layer. One of the main drivers for this new phase in communication networks is SDN.

Network operators are eager to embrace new services and revenue opportunities, but not necessarily new technologies that require overhauling their physical network. It is thus pertinent to give operators the freedom and flexibility to innovate and create new service offerings by providing them with a more flexible network architecture. This is the main driver for the evolution of today's communication networks towards being software based. With the introduction of OpenFlow in [1], and collaboration between all major stakeholders at the Open Networking Foundation (ONF), SDN has witnessed wide scale adoption.

This paper highlights three use cases and a corresponding architectural framework that can be adopted for implementing SDWN. The final section further highlights three areas which must be considered in future implementation projects.

© ICST Institute for Computer Sciences, Social Informatics and Telecommunications Engineering 2016
B. Mandler et al. (Eds.): IoT 360° 2015, Part II, LNICST 170, pp. 521–529, 2016.
DOI: 10.1007/978-3-319-47075-7_56

2 Use Cases and Applications

The possible benefits that the introduction of programmable, flexible software defined networking will have across all types of wireless networks is varied. The authors in [2] present a comprehensive survey on SDWN and virtualization. We discuss only three use cases and applications in which the introduction of SDWN will lead developers to rethink the design of future wireless network architectures.

2.1 Flexible Wireless Backhaul

One of the candidate technologies for meeting 5G cellular network performance targets is improving interference coordination schemes in very large scale Coordinated Multipoint (CoMP) transmission. Combining signals from multiple antennas requires creating a single logical cell with multiple low cost radio nodes (forwarding devices). Furthermore, the mass deployment of small cells and use of millimeter wave (with its inherent high speed but short distance) results in the necessity for flexible wireless backhaul. Implementing flexible wireless backhaul via conventional traffic engineering schemes will not suffice due to current protocol specific implementations. However, SDWN can introduce a separation of data plane from the control plane allowing compatibility with multiple traffic forwarding protocols in the control plane with MAC adaptors for simplified forwarding on the data plane.

2.2 Flexible Traffic Steering via Heterogeneous Radios

SDWN enables the possibility for smarter load balancing and flexible wireless backhauls with QoS based routing. This is achieved due to the support for media independent handover and protocol independent forwarding. Using information of location specific capacity requirements, flexible traffic steering schemes can be implemented to achieve various operator objectives. Having the knowledge of the network state, the controller can steer the traffic and thus optimize bandwidth utilization taking radio resources into account. Flow optimization within the backhaul can also be implemented with the flexibility SDWN provides. It also enables differentiated processing of flows based on the flow information (type of service, src port, dst port, etc.) for different service types. The network PHY and MAC can thus adapt its resources based on the class of service and QoS requirements of flows. This results in more flexibility and options to meet users QoS requirements by provisioning. This application is key as validity of Selected IP Traffic Offload (SIPTO) in cellular networks becomes established.

2.3 Integrating Heterogeneous Wireless Networks

SDWN defines open interfaces to manage and configure heterogeneous access networks, through coordinated efforts between ONF, OpenDaylight and the IEEE 802 OmniRAN groups. Furthermore, by abstracting multiple heterogeneous access technologies into a single access infrastructure, it is irrelevant which actual RAN technology the end user is connected to as this remains transparent. SDWN based architectures enable infrastructure sharing among multiple service providers. The end user is also able to utilize multiple radio interfaces for mobile traffic offload, where data originally targeted for cellular networks are offloaded to Wi-Fi or other complementary technologies but abstracted as a single network and technology to the user. This use case when applied to roaming scenarios between WiFi hotspots and eNodeB drastically ensures service continuity for critical applications envisaged in next generation wireless networks.

In spite of the aforementioned use cases, it must be understood that SDWN is not the magic wand that will provide solutions to all challenges in wireless communications. SDWN should be viewed as a tool that empowers us with the much needed flexibility as well as removing constraints in todays network architectures in order to innovate new solutions for existing problems and future challenges in wireless networks. Furthermore, we have encountered multiple implementation challenges which include:

1. Meeting strict QoS requirements to support provisioning of triple-play services over multi-hop, sometimes heterogeneous links
2. design tradeoff between architecture flexibility and optimal performance
3. support for heterogeneous networks with a set of technology agnostic, vendor independent primitives which are required for managing the forwarding devices

3   Unified Software Defined Wireless Networking Framework

During the course of the FP7 CARMEN project on carrier-grade wireless mesh networks', we began to investigate the programmability of simple, but heterogeneous wireless nodes and studied decentralized and centralized approaches [3]. We concluded that only a centralized controller would be able to make coherent spectrum allocation and traffic forwarding decisions in an environment potentially as volatile as the unlicensed U-NII band. Next, a technology independent messaging and addressing service was required. Extending the concept behind IEEE 8021.21 was found to be a viable solution, while the data plane required a means to enforce centrally computed data path across a multi-hop network. Multiprotocol Label Switching (MPLS) was considered a suitable and technology independent solution, among others. During the course of the SolarMesh projects [4] we developed this concept further with a strong focus on energy-efficient wireless back-hauling and arrived at a generic architecture with support for programming heterogeneous wireless interfaces. These architectures serve as the basis for what is explained in the following sections.

Figure 1 shows our proposed SDWN logical framework directly inspired from the framework used in SDN. A description of the key modules is provided as follows:

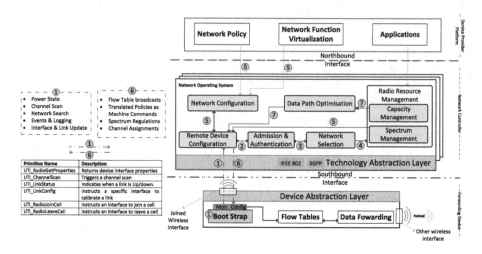

Fig. 1. SDWN logical framework

3.1   Control Plane

In wireless networks, the control plane consists of more than just a single physical controller or network entity. This is the core of the network architecture that serves as a platform for the network operating system. It orchestrates the traffic forwarding and signalling behavior of the network via its interface to the lower layers. Provisioning of network services, defining forwarding rules, traffic routes and radio resource management is enforced on the network at this layer. The control plane is responsible for enforcing polices defined in the service plane. As regards topology of the underlying infrastructure, this plane also incorporates functionalities for load balancing and Network Function Virtualization (NFV). In wireless networks, topology management is key due to new nodes joining and leaving the network on varying time scales. In addition, mobility management is required especially for infrastructure-less wireless networks.

Depending on the type of technology used in the wireless network, the control plane would consist of different network elements. For example in cellular networks its main network elements will be located in the core network, in IEEE 802 wireless[1] networks as a master node or controller managing a set of wireless access points. The framework shown in Fig. 1 is a logical representation. In practice, it is expected to utilize physically distributed instances of controllers managing different slices of the network while synchronization of all functionalities remains at a centralized point in this plane. The key modules which are technology agnostic which should be implemented on this plane include network selection, network configuration for managing forwarding devices on the data plane, and traffic routing for path computation and enforcing routing policies.

---

[1] WiFi, WLAN, WiMAX, etc.

3.2   Technology Abstraction Layer

An important module of the control plane is the technology abstraction layer as shown in Fig. 1. Abstraction helps reduce complexity in network design, implementation and supports interoperability. We strongly believe future wireless networks will be flexible to deliver services whereby the underlying technology (e.g. LTE, WiFi, etc.) remains transparent to the end user. This ensures support for operation over heterogeneous technologies and is achieved by having a common set of message primitives in which the control layer can seamlessly configure and manage the underlying network. Since multiple protocols can be used to implement this, an open southbound interface is defined between this layer and forwarding devices in the data plane. More information about the technology abstraction layer and device abstraction layer simply a generic abstract interface in [5] and further developed as a single universal technology interface in [6].

3.3   Southbound Interface

To ensure interoperability between vendors as well as to support heterogeneous networks, a standardized interface is specified to describe communication between devices on the data plane and network elements in the control plane. This communication is done over a secure channel and the main objective is to manage the forwarding devices or nodes, including device configuration. Various protocols can be used to achieve this, such as Forwarding and Control Element Separation (ForCES), Network Configuration Protocol (NETCONF), SNMP4SDN (an extension of SNMP), Interface to Routing System (I2RS) and Path Computation Element Communication Protocol (PCEP). Protocols used for secure control-data plane communications vary based on the type of network and use case being considered. OpenFlow is currently the most widely adopted but as it is just one protocol on the southbound interface, it is important to ensure the southbound interface remains "Open" for other protocols (existing and new) in a non-proprietary way.

3.4   Device Abstraction Layer

This layer is responsible for providing information on the type of device and capabilities of its forwarding interfaces to the control layer. A Universal Technology Interface (UTI) can be implemented both in the control and data planes as a technology abstraction layer and/or device abstraction layer, respectively as shown in Fig. 1. Depending on the type of technology and use case considered, implementation of this abstraction layer can be done in the physical controller or in the forwarding devices. One of the major proponents for its implementation in the controller is to ensure compatibility with generic forwarding devices for easier adoption. Similarly, implementation in the forwarding devices would help equipment vendors make device specific translations based on device agnostic, generic message primitives in order to improve device performance.

3.5   Data Plane

The final layer responsible for data forwarding and connecting to the end user device is the data plane. SDN concept advocates for devices that are simplified, low cost, minimal processing but specialized for forwarding packets. In essence, the devices here should primarily receive forwarding rules from the control plane and take actions based on a set of preconfigured traffic routes stored in its flow tables. Statistics of the network are periodically sent back to the control plane for optimising forwarding rules.

The peculiarity of the data plane in wireless networks requires configuration of the wireless links between forwarding devices, as well as the wireless link to their controller. It is thus pertinent to include a link configuration module in forwarding devices specifically for link monitoring and configuration. This includes simple localized functions, particularly for modules that cannot be performed efficiently from a physically centralized point. In essence, a boot strap phase will be used for initial setup connection and configuration of the device. An example is channel scan for outdoor Wireless Local Area Network (WLAN) to determine interference free channels, determining active links to neighbouring nodes, channel state information, etc.

Consider an example when a wireless node with plug and play functionality tries to connect to an already live network. The messaging flows indicated in Fig. 1 are described as follows:

1. At Bootstrap phase, the forwarding device does a self-discovery process to identify its interfaces and capabilities. A power-spectrum scan is initiated to identify free channels on its interfaces. This is done along with a network search. The scan results are encoded in a messaging format and sent out to the controller or master.
2. When the controller receives this encoded messages, it executes a security check for authentication and authorization.
3. Network selection module is responsible for selecting the type of physical network (assuming a heterogeneous network) and to which network slices this new node will be associated to.
4. Radio Resource Management (RRM) will aid in spectrum allocation based on a global view of the network, neighboring nodes and determine channel to be used on other interfaces (excluding the joined interface). This module is also responsible for DFS in networks operating on the UN-II bands, TVWS external database or licensing policies in event of operation on a licensed band as in mobile cellular networks.
5. Optimum allocations are signalled to the Remote Device Configuration (RDC) module. Simultaneously, network policies and virtualisation instances from the service provider platform aid the network configuration module to signal the RDC.
6. The RDC which translates the information via the Technology abstraction layer as simple machine language commands/instruction set to the forwarding device. Examples of 6 message primitives and their description are

summarized in Fig. 1. We have implemented these primitives and used to control the wireless nodes (see [5,6] for more details).

7. Based on statistical analysis on the types of applications and QoS requirements, the capacity management updates the data path optimisation. Updated flow tables and channel assignments for all interfaces are thus signalled to the RDC and sent as multicast.

There exists a fundamental tradeoff between achieving flexibility in the network and optimum performance, which leads to the consideration of different architectures. The key design principle however is choosing the right level of abstraction in separation of the control plane form the dataplane. The choice of these primitives highlighted in Fig. 1 was in no way trivial but based on ongoing in house development and testing which started in 2008 [3], feedback from service providers and performance benchmarking. A subset of the modules, required messaging primitives and the flow sequence have been made public in [5,7,8] by the same authors. Nevertheless, a full listing of all the primitives required, their descriptions and effect when generated will be provided in the SDN4wireless project [9]. Details of this framework for third party validation will also be made available in the project [9].

4   Future Research Directions

We present existing challenges in the form of questions that need to be addressed in order for full adoption of SDWN paradigms in the wireless domain.

Definition of Interfaces. Wireless heterogeneous networks deal with more compatibility issues from multiple technology specific protocols as compared to wired networks. The choice of a common descriptive language and command primitives set for all 'event-action'. By further defining specifications for open generic interfaces, what specialized networks functionalities may be lost? Do such heterogenous networks with common set of primitives have higher performance than existing proprietary implementations? To address these questions, more activity is expected to focus on interface description and published set of command primitives for network interface cards and to ensure protocols on these interfaces remain open and not closed to members of consortiums. There are also concerns on the level of information in the APIs provided by hardware manufacturers for third party developers.

Software Defined MACs. In order to achieve a general purpose but context aware MAC protocol, programmability of the network interface cards is required. Motivated by the attempt to program abstractions for wireless terminals, some research directions suggest MAC be made context-dependent, yielding simple programming models yet providing enough flexibility to support most customization needs. As wireless card manufacturers gradually make available their wireless MAC processor architecture to developers, more research activity and new innovations are expected on software defined MAC.

What Is the Role of Data Analytics? With the huge benefits SON had on mobile networks [10], future wireless networks in general are envisaged to incorporate more intelligence to ensure programmability from a logical central point, utilize real-time data analytics as well as incorporating Artificial Intelligence (AI) schemes. Such schemes will enable smart cities utilizing infrastructure from wireless networks. However, a lot of data will be required and statistics gathered from the forwarding layer in order to be analyzed at the service layer. This feedback enables the network to constantly self-optimize its performance, also creating personalized services for users. Further work should focus on stability of AI schemes, data analytic tools to serve as input for rule creation as well as legal issues surrounding user profiling and data gathering.

Our future work will include evaluation results which provides a comparison of our software defined wireless backhaul network with existing wireless backhaul networks. This will follow a 3 step approach listing functional module description to hardware implementation and quantitative performance evaluation.

5   Conclusion

In this paper, we have presented a logical framework for software defined wireless networks. The main impact is addressing the general question of how centralized decision making modules have to be for wireless networks. We realized that certain controller functions have to remain at the forwarding devices, i.e. initial channel scan, link status neighbor sensing. This is especially important during the bootstrap phase. Further description of a technology abstraction layer and device abstraction layer were described with references for more detailed technical description. This technology abstraction is pertinent for future heterogeneous networks, including satellite networks for ubiquitous backhaul connectivity in remote and rural areas. To support technology agnostic data forwarding devices, multilink CPE prototypes are also being investigated in [11].

We believe that the open issues, solutions and framework that have been identified and summarized in this paper, will trigger new ideas and further act as pointers to developing solutions. Software defined wireless networks will certainly create the required enablers for the next generation of wireless networks.

Acknowledgment. This work has been supported by the BATS research project which is funded by the European Union Seventh Framework Program under contract n317533. The views and conclusions contained here are those of the authors and should not be interpreted as necessarily representing the official policies or endorsements, either expressed or implied, of the BATS project or the European Commission.

References

1. McKeown, N., Anderson, T., Balakrishnan, H., Parulkar, G., Peterson, L., Rexford, J., Shenker, S., Turner, J.: Openflow: enabling innovation in campus networks. SIGCOMM Comput. Commun. Rev. **38**(2), 69–74 (2008)

2. Liang, C., Yu, F.: Wireless network virtualization: a survey, some research issues and challenges. IEEE Commun. Surv. Tutorials **17**(1), 358–380 (2015). Firstquarter

3. Banchs, A., Bayer, N., Chieng, D., de la Oliva, A., Gloss, B., Kretschme, M., Murphy, S., Natkaniec, M., Zdarsky, F.: CARMEN: delivering carrier grade services over wireless mesh networks. In: IEEE 19th International Symposium on Personal, Indoor and Mobile Radio Communications, PIMRC 2008, pp. 1–6, September 2008

4. Horstmann, T., Kretschmer, M., Modeker, J., Niephaus, C., Sauer, S.: Development framework for prototyping heterogeneous multi-radio wireless networks. In: 2011 Proceedings of 20th International Conference on Computer Communications and Networks (ICCCN), pp. 1–5, July 2011

5. Kretschmer, M., Batroff, P., Ghinea, G.: Topology forming and optimization framework for heterogeneous wireless back-haul networks supporting unidirectional technologies. J. Netw. Comput. Appl. **36**(2), 698–710 (2013)

6. Niephaus, C., Aliu, O., Hadzic, S., Kretschmer, M., Ghinea, G.: WiBACK: a backhaul network architecture for 5G networks, In: IET International Conference on Frontiers of Communications, Networks and Applications (IET ICFCNA) (2014)

7. Niephaus, C., Kretschmer, M., Jonas, K.: QoS-aware wireless back-haul network for rural areas in practice. In: 2012 IEEE Globecom Workshops (GC Wkshps), pp. 24–29, December 2012

8. Niephaus, C., Aliu, O.G., Kretschmer, M., Hadzic, S., Ghinea, G.: Wireless backhaul: a software defined network enabled wireless back-haul network architecture for future 5G networks. In: IET Networks, September 2015. http://digital-library. theiet.org/content/journals/10.1049/iet-net.2015.0009

9. SDN4Wireless, Project deliverables, 2015–2017. www.sdn4wireless.org

10. Aliu, O., Imran, A., Imran, M., Evans, B.: A survey of self organisation in future cellular networks. IEEE Commun. Surv. Tutorials **15**(1), 336–361 (2013)

11. BATS, Project deliverables 2012–2015. http://www.batsproject.eu/

USD: A User-Centric Software Defined Platform for 5G Mobile Devices

Kien Nguyen(✉), Kentaro Ishizu, and Fumihide Kojima

National Institute of Information and Communications Technology,
3-4 Hikarinooka, Yokosuka, Kanagawa 239-084, Japan
{kienng,ishidu,f-kojima}@nict.go.jp

Abstract. This paper introduces USD, a novel User-centric Software Defined platform for 5G mobile devices, which supports a wide range of users with the diversity of technical experience. Respecting user preferences, USD is able to exploit multiple wireless networks, as well as, to differentiate application traffic. The advantages of USD are realized by using a set of network virtualization (NW) and Software Defined Networking (SDN) technologies. Similar to the state-of-the-art works, USD leverages SDN in the exploitation of multiple networks. However, USD uniquely uses network namespace to isolate an application traffic at a granularity as fine as a process (i.e., each process's traffic belong to one networking stack). Moreover, USD relaxes the dependence on radio hardware by using wireless virtualization. The relaxation aims not only to efficiently utilize 5G networking resources but also to add an user-centric interface. As a proof of concept, we implement a prototype of USD using the Wi-Fi, Open vSwitch, and the network virtualization technologies. We evaluate the performance of USD in a comparison with a legacy platform in an assuming 5G scenario. The evaluation results show that the USD prototype achieves comparable performances to the legacy platform while it introduces the advanced user-centric features.

Keywords: 5G · User-centric · Device · NW · SDN

1 Introduction

It is widely recognized that the functional 5G system will be available by the year 2020. Generally, the 5G system has been designed toward the technical key performance indicators (KPIs) such as peak data rate > 1 Gbps, end-to-end latency < 1 ms, etc. [1]. The 5G infrastructure is expected to provide extremely high bandwidth, low latency, reliable connection, which aims to significantly enhance the quality of user experience (i.e., the final goal). Therefore, among the most important issues, the 5G design is shifted from system-centric to user-centric [2]. That means the users will play an active role in networking functions in the 5G era. The users, who have different technical backgrounds, experience many evolving and novel applications (e.g., Big Data applications). The applications, each of which has different KPI requirements, should satisfy user expectation.

© ICST Institute for Computer Sciences, Social Informatics and Telecommunications Engineering 2016
B. Mandler et al. (Eds.): IoT 360° 2015, Part II, LNICST 170, pp. 530–538, 2016.
DOI: 10.1007/978-3-319-47075-7_57

The 5G device hence should well support the traffic differentiation and user diversity.

The 5G device is commonly envisioned to have multiple wireless technologies, which operate under the dense deployments of multiple types of cells (e.g., small cell, micro cell, pico cell, etc.) [3]. The first important function on a 5G device is concurrent exploiting multiple wireless networks (same or different technologies) for applications. The benefit of exploitation is intuitive since a 5G application could aggregate different network's bandwidth or achieve seamless handover. On the other hand, many 5G wireless technologies promisingly provide sufficient 5G KPIs as shown in the standard committees' goals for releasing the 5G versions (e.g., Wi-Fi in [4]). Moreover, the switching cost between different technologies on device is not negligible (e.g., energy consumption, reconfiguration, etc.). Therefore, the 5G devices should avoid the switching as much as possible.

Addressing the aforementioned issues, this paper proposes a novel User-centric Software Defined platform (namely 'USD) for 5G mobile devices. USD leverages the advantages of network virtualization (NW) and software defined networking (SDN) technologies in the user-centric 5G design. Specifically, the NW in a form of wireless virtualization relaxes the dependent of hardware radio for the aims of enhancing resource utilization and creating an user-centric interface. The interface, which is SDN-based and open, allows the USD device to interact with a SDN control component through a well-defined API (i.e., OpenFlow). Hence, USD supports a wide range of users, who determines policies provided from a control component located on a device, from an operator, or a third party partner. Another advantage of USD is that it utilizes the NW in the form of network namespace in creating multiple networking stacks for application process isolation. As a result, a USD user is able to select networks for an application at the granularity as fine as a process. Similar to the state-of-the-art works, a SDN switch that attaches multiple radio interfaces is also used to exploit multiple networks in USD.

As a proof-of-concept, we build a prototype of USD with the Wi-Fi, Open vSwitch, and the network virtualization technologies. The wireless virtualization is adopted to create virtual Wi-Fi interfaces, which assumingly exploit the huge capability of 5G Wi-Fi links. Open vSwitch [5] attaches one or several wireless interfaces, each of which is programmed to direct the application flows to a different network. Open vSwitch could be programmed by a local controller or a remote controller (i.e., via the user-centric interface). Moreover, the USD prototype uses two network namespaces, which create independent networking stacks for determined application processes. We evaluate the USD prototype in an assuming 5G scenario in a comparison with a legacy platform (i.e., Ubuntu networking stack). The results show that the USD prototype effectively exploits nearby Wi-Fi networks, introduces the user-centric feature while it still achieves a comparable performance to the legacy one.

The rest of paper is organized as follow. In Sect. 2, we describe the design of USD. Then, Sect. 3 includes USD evaluation results. In Sect. 4, we present the related works. Finally, we conclude the paper in Sect. 5.

2   USD Design and Implementation

2.1   Problem Description

In the 5G era, the advanced technologies on both the 5G infrastructures and devices are capable of providing sufficient capacity in terms of bandwidth, latency, reliability. The 5G users will experience a plethora of applications, which are evolved from the existing applications and totally novel ones (e.g., Internet of Things (IoT) and Big Data applications). Generally, the 5G applications will have various requirements and generate a diversity of traffic types and traffic load. However, they should satisfy, or at least, avoid to degrade the quality of user experience. Many existing problems on the current legacy devices should be also solved in 5G. For example, network selection is following the user's criteria. That requires an important demand from the 5G user, that is controlling the application traffic with a fine granularity through user-expected networks.

On the other hand, the 5G network supports various types of users, who have different experience and technical levels. Therefore, the supported controlling level should be wide enough in order to support all of them. In this work, we consider an example of user classification, in which the 5G users are divided into expert, normal, novice categories. The expert user, who has good technical knowledge, should be able to build her/his own traffic control policies. The policy assigns a fine granularity of application to a network following her/his expectation. On the other end of controlling spectrum, the novice user with the limited technical experience simply relies on service providers (i.e., similar to in the current network). The normal 5G user, who has an average experience and technical knowledge, could define some simple policies his/herself. However, the normal user may refer for advanced policies from a third party (e.g., via a downloadable application). In order to support the users, it is highly required that a 5G mobile device should have an open interface to interact with the controlling components.

2.2   USD Design

In the user-centric software defined (USD) platform, we mainly leverage the power of software in controlling application traffic and radio access in a device (i.e., so-called software defined). The conceptual design of USD is presented in Fig. 1. In USD, an application process interacts with the module named *user preference*, which determines the process's destination networks. After assigning a user preference value, the process may directly follow either a private networking stack or an SDN-based one, which exploits one or several networks. In the case of using the private stack, the application works in a similar way as in the legacy one (i.e., Linux stack). Otherwise, it traverses through an SDN-based switch, which attaches one or several radios. The switch is controlled by a local or remote controller depending on the user expectation.

The advantage of using multiple networking stacks is that the service differentiation on the 5G device significantly improved. It allows the user to personalize

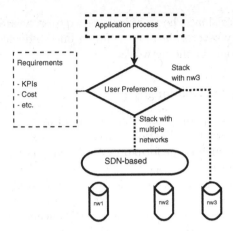

Fig. 1. User-centric Software Defined (USD) platform on a 5G device with two networking stacks and three networks (nw1, nw2, nw3)

the traffic flows with a fine granularity (i.e., the process level). For example, two identical traffic flows, which belong to different processes, could travel through different networks. Moreover, the stacks are created and controlled by software, hence they are efficient and flexible. In the SDN-based stack, USD also provides other SDN-based methods of traffic differentiation. The methods follow matching and forwarding based on various header fields of incoming packets (i.e., defined by the SDN/OpenFlow standard). The flexibility of SDN matching and forwarding is also inherited to handle the coexistence of multiple wireless networks. USD allows the SDN switch to associate both the virtual and physical wireless interface. The usage of virtual interface is two-fold: efficiently exploit the surrounding networks (e.g., several Wi-Fi APs) and to adding the user-centric interface. USD features the additional importance of the single networking stack since it is necessary in bypassing the limitations of the state-of-the-art SDN technology when the controller is remotely located from the devices. In the such scenario, the control traffic will be conveyed via that networking stack.

2.3   User-Centric Function

In USD, the user preference is one of the most important modules, which requires interactions from users. The module could be configured proactively or reactively depending the user experience. For example, the novice user may prefer to use the proactive configuration provided by an expert (i.e., operators or third party) hence the technical task is transparent to the user. On the other hand, the expert user may require a reactive action per one application process. In USD, the simplest form of the user preference module is a user's decision (e.g., from an expert user). However, it is commonly expected that the user is suggested the required KPIs of application. Moreover, the networks information such as bandwidth, cost, end-to-end delay, or another context-aware values are available for the user before making the decision. The technical and context-aware information could be provided either by several daemons running on the device or by suggestions from a controlling point in the networks.

2.4   Implementation Challenges

We implement USD on the open operating system Linux. One of the major challenges is isolating different application processes. We solve that challenge by the network namespace, which is one form of NW. When a network namespace is created, it includes a networking stack that could directly interacts with the application layer on a Linux host. The networking stack in each network namespace operates as a normal networking stack and provides sufficient functions for applications (such as routing tables, association, ARP caches, etc.). A different network namespace has a distinct set of kernel structures for networking, hence the two processes in two different network namespaces could be isolated. The network namespace is well-known for creating the widely-used emulator mininet [6]. In this work we introduce a novel use case in wireless environments.

Another challenge in USD is how to exploit multiple wireless networks efficiently. Besides the network namespace's isolation, the multiple networks should benefit the application on 5G devices. We follow the state-of-the-art approach in SDN, which bridges several wireless interfaces in a programmable switch. There are several options for the implementation of the switch such as Linux bridge, Open vSwitch, etc. However, we select Open vSwitch USD since it well supports design features. First, Open vSwitch not only can attach wireless interfaces but also provides open APIs for implementing controlling policies (i.e., OpenFlow). Second, the Open vSwitch's new versions have been proven to provide high performance. Note that, we don't attach all the wireless interfaces on a devices to Open vSwitch since it will isolate the switch with the network infrastructure. In order to interact with Open vSwitch, we use virtual Ethernet (veth) interfaces. The virtual Ethernets are special interfaces that always appear in pairs. They work like a tube, in which the traffic is in at one side and out in other side. We attach one side of the tube to the Open vSwitch while the other behaves as a normal network interface in the Linux networking stack.

3   Evaluation

This section presents evaluations of a USD prototype in an assuming 5G scenario, where the link capacity is sufficient. We built the USD prototype on Ubuntu 13.10, which includes Open vSwitch version 2.3.1, wireless virtualization, network namespace, and Wi-Fi technologies. The USD interfaces with the user preference module via a virtual Ethernet interface. Note that, the virtual Ethernet includes a pair of interfaces (i.e., veth0 and veth1). Moreover, the traffic, which is an input of veth0, will be output of veth1 and vice versa. To efficiently utilize the 5G wireless link capacity, the wireless virtualization creates the two virtual wireless interfaces (i.e., vwlan1 and vwlan2) on the Wi-Fi card. The card

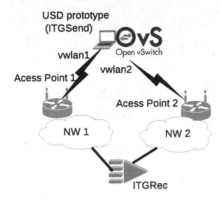

Fig. 2. Evaluation scenario

is Intel wireless card named Centrino Advanced-N 6250 (supporting IEEE 802.11 abgn) with the iwilwifi driver. We attach vwlan1 and veth0 to the Open vSwitch (OVS) with appropriate forwarding rules. In the evaluation, vwlan1 operates as one port of OVS, which routes the traffic via network one (NW1). vwlan2 is associated with the access point 2; then it forms a path to the network two (NW2). The connection diagram is shown in Fig. 2. The USD prototype is able to concurrently exploit the two Wi-Fi networks, to isolate application process, and to provide an user-centric interface. All the listed features are not supported on the legacy networking stack on Ubuntu. We then investigate the performance in order to evaluate the USD efficiency. In the evaluations, we use the simplest form of user preference; and compare the USD to the legacy networking stack (LEG). LEG includes the physical Wi-Fi card and the default network manager. The considered performance metrics include bandwidth, round trip time (RTT), and jitter. We use the distributed Internet traffic generator (DITG) [7] in this work. DITG is the traffic generator that accurately provides many traffic patterns such as the inter departure time between packets (IDT) and the packet size (PS) stochastic processes. In the operation, the ITGSend module of DITG is activated on the traffic generation machine, while the ITGRecv module is listening on the destination of the packets.

In the first evaluation, the ITGSend on the device sends UDP flows to a ITGRecv server (i.e., another Ubuntu 13.10). We assume that the user selects NW1 for the traffic flows. As a result, the UDP flows follows a network namespace's communication stack. We vary the sending rate from 8 Mbps to 12 Mbps with the step of 0.5 Mbps. With each value of sending rate, the constant rate remains in a period of 30 s. Moreover, each experiment at a rate step is repeated 10 times. The same process is experimented with LEG. We collect all the values of throughput, round trip time (RTT), and jitter and show them in Fig. 3. Note that, the RTT option of DITG is used to avoid the errors caused by clock synchronization between the machines of ITGSend and ITGRecv. In Fig. 3a, we plot the average, max, min values of throughput. We can observe

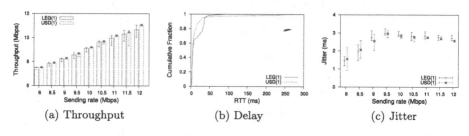

Fig. 3. Performance comparison between USD and LEG using NW1

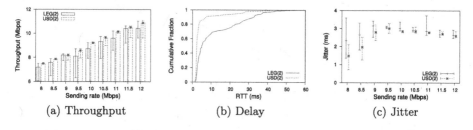

Fig. 4. Performance comparison between USD and LEG using NW2

that similar to LEG, USD intuitively increases the throughput when the rate increases. However, the USD throughput is slightly better than the other. In Fig. 3b, the cumulative distribution functions (CDFs) of all the RTT values are plotted. Most of the values of USD's RTT are better than the ones of LEG. However, there are several exceptional. The same observation could be drawn from the jitter value's figure (i.e., Fig. 3c). Therefore, we conclude that USD and LEG has the comparable performances in the case of using network one. In the second evaluation, we aim to use NW2. The USD machine is configured to send the UDP flows through the virtual Ethernet interface. The flows will be processed by the Open vSwitch, which is necessarily preconfigured a set of appropriate rules. In this work, the rules are local but they could be installed by a remote controller. We also compare the performance of USD with LEG using NW2. We plot the performance values of throughput, RTT, and jitter in Fig. 4a, b, and c, respectively. Even getting additional processing steps, USD still keeps comparable performances in all metrics with LEG.

4   Related Work

The researchers have thoroughly investigated potential technologies for 5G systems such as mmWave, massive MIMO, full-duplex communication, SDN, cloud RAN, [8], etc. The recent results show that the technologies promisingly reach the PKIs in the next few years. Since the major final goal of 5G is satisfying the user expectation, the 5G design should be shifted from system-centric (as in the existing networks) to user-centric. In the scope of this work, we focus on the user-centric issue on the 5G mobile device. We begin with the common agreement of the 5G device, in which there is a coexistence of multiple wireless on a mobile device [9]. The user-centric 5G device should effectively exploit its surrounding wireless networks for the quality of user experience.

In the mobile network research, there are several works related to exploiting multiple networks. In [10], the Delphi framework lets the application interface with the transport layer, which is specially designed for network selection (i.e., based on predetermined policies). The Delphi design is application-driven, which is different to the user-driven approach in our work. However, we can inherit the Delphi's advanced features to enrich the USD platform. Another approach is applying multipath transport control protocol in wireless networks [11,12]. However, it also shares the listed characteristic with Delphi. Regard using SDN for user-centric features, the work in [13] provides an interesting analysis although it is lack of implementations or evaluations. The real SDN-based implementation [14], in which the SDN technology is used to provide flexible ways for conveying application flows, inspires us to design USD. In that work, the rewriting header technique (i.e., address translation) is used to stitch bandwidths or to achieve handover between different networks. However, the technique causes overhead (e.g., lowering throughput); and its operation has to rely on a local controller. In our USD design, we inherit the method of exploiting multiple networks from [14]. However, USD can avoid the complicated network translation mechanisms (using single stack). Besides that, USD introduces an open, user-centric interface, which supports a wide range of user and controlling locations. Additionally, USD is able to route application flows at the process granularity.

5 Conclusion

This paper introduces the User-centric Software Defined (USD) platform, which is designed towards the service personalization demand of 5G users. USD relies on several software-based technologies (i.e., SDN and NW) in order to provide a rich set of networking policy. USD supports a wide range of users, who could determine the network policies generated by themselves, network providers, or even third party vendors. Additionally, USD is able to differentiate the application traffic at a process level, as well as, to concurrently exploit multiple wireless networks. To show the effectiveness of USD, we first build a USD prototype using the Open vSwitch, network virtualization, network namespace, and Wi-Fi technologies. We then evaluate the USD prototype in an assuming 5G scenario in a comparison with the Linux's legacy networking stack. The evaluation results show that USD achieves comparable performances with the legacy stack including the physical Wi-Fi card. However, USD introduces the user-centric and several advanced features, which could not be supported on the legacy stack.

Acknowledgement. This work was supported by JSPS KAKENHI Grant Number 26730055.

References

1. Monserrat, J.F., Mange, G., Braun, V., Tullberg, H.M., Zimmermann, G., Bulakci, O.: METIS research advances towards the 5G mobile and wireless system definition. EURASIP J. Wirel. Commun. Netw. **2015**, 53 (2015)
2. Liotou, E., Elshaer, H., Schatz, R., Irmer, R., Dohler, M., Passas, N., Merakos, L.: Shaping QoE in the 5G ecosystem. In: Proceedings of IEEE QoMEX 2015, pp. 1–6 (2015)
3. Bhushan, N., Li, J., Malladi, D., Gilmore, R., Brenner, D., Damnjanovic, A., Sukhavasi, R., Patel, C., Geirhofer, S.: Network densification the dominant theme for wireless evolution into 5G. IEEE Commun. Mag. **52**(2), 82–89 (2014)
4. Rayment, S.: The Role of Wi-Fi In 5G networks. http://johannesbergsummit.com /wp-content/uploads/sites/6/2013/11/Rayment-Johannesberg-Ericsson-Rayment-pA7.pdf
5. Open vSwitch. http://openvswitch.org
6. Handigol, N., Heller, B., Jeyakumar, V., Lantz, B., McKeown, N.: Reproducible network experiments using container-based emulation. In: Proceedings of ACM CoNEXT (2012)
7. Botta, A., Dainotti, A., Pescapè, A.: A tool for the generation of realistic network workload for emerging networking scenarios. Comput. Netw. **56**(15), 3531–3547 (2012)
8. Boccardi, F., Heath, R.W., Lozano, A., Marzetta, T.L., Popovski, P.: Five disruptive technology directions for 5G. IEEE Comm. Mag. **52**(2), 74–80 (2014)
9. Bangerter, B., Talwar, S., Arefi, R., Stewart, K.: Networks and devices for the 5G era. IEEE Comm. Mag. **52**(2), 90–96 (2014)
10. Deng, S., Sivaraman, A., Balakrishnan, H.: All your network are belong to us: a transport framework for mobile network selection. In: Proceedings of ACM Hot-Mobile 2014 (2014)
11. Raiciu, C., Paasch, C., Barr, S., Ford, A., Honda, M., Duchene, F., Bonaventure, O., Handley, M.: How hard can it be? Designing and implementing a deployable multipath TCP. In: Proceedings of USENIX NSDI (2012)
12. Nguyen, K., Ji, Y., Yamada, S.: A cross-layer approach for improving WiFi performance. In: Proceedings of IEEE IWCMC 2014, pp. 458–463 (2014)
13. Nunes, B.A.A., Santos, M.A.S., de Oliveira, B.T., Margi, C.B., Obraczka, K., Turletti, T.: Software-defined-networking-enabled capacity sharing in user-centric networks. IEEE Commun. Mag. **52**(9), 28–36 (2014)
14. Yap, K.-K., Huang, T.-Y., Kobayashi, M., Yiakoumis, Y., McKeown, N., Katti, S., Parulkar, G., Making use of all the networks around us: a case study in android. In: Proceedings of ACM SIGCOMM Cell Net, pp. 19–24 (2012)

Extending SDN Framework
for Communication Networks

M. Saravanan[(⊠)], Arud Selvan Sundaramurthy, Divya Sundar,
and K. Hiba Sadia

Ericsson India Global Services Pvt. Ltd., Tamarai Tech Park, Chennai, India
{m.saravanan, arud.selvan.sundaramurthy,
divya.sundar}@ericsson.com, hbsadia@gmail.com

Abstract. Software-Defined Networking (SDN) is an emerging new norm for networks which deals heavily on dynamic nature of higher bandwidth network applications to address the service velocity. SDN's features such as dynamic configuration of network elements, allowing appropriate open standards and centrally controllable tasks will make it suitable to introduce new applications for communication networks. In particular, by considering the voluminous telecom subscriber's transactions and supporting high performing applications in the event of network element failure, a manual Intervention is required for tuning of network elements. Even the recently introduced network resources for tuning could also fail due to unexpected flow of traffic without considering the exact load features dynamically. Any sudden failure in network functioning could bring huge revenue loss and also reduces considerable Quality of Experience of the service provider. In this paper, we have presented use cases relevant to Online Charging System (OCS) that highlight the integration of SDN with communication networks for managing optimized network utilization. Moreover, SDN with the use of machine learning techniques will take the proactive measure before the network node goes down. To support this feature of SDN, we have proposed Autonomous Resource Monitoring and Deployer application that monitors the continuous traffic flow in OCS, intelligently reroutes the traffic with the use of SDN controller by introducing new resources. Our approach handles specific network key performance indicators dynamically, which reduces maintenance and Operational Expenditure costs.

Keywords: Quality of Experience · SDN framework · Online Charging System (OCS) · Telecom applications

1 Introduction

Telecommunication service providers are witnessing a remarkable increase in volume, variety and velocity of subscriber's data due to technological advancements such as smart phones, social media, etc. This dynamic and rapid growth of today's telecommunication market demands new and innovative ways to compete and successfully introduce new technologies in the increasing competition. In the past decade, service providers with large networks and manpower ruled the telecom market. In the current scenario productive network administration and quick dispatch of new services is

B. Mandler et al. (Eds.): IoT 360° 2015, Part II, LNICST 170, pp. 539–550, 2016.
DOI: 10.1007/978-3-319-47075-7_58

expected rather than having sophisticated infrastructure. Thus the operators who know how to deal with their foundation and infrastructure all the more viably are considered to be more successful in business.

The recent big data projections which involve huge number of networking devices and humungous networking data traffic also demands smarter network management and control. The networking systems currently used consist of routers, switches, hubs etc., with limited software logic required to route the packets. Each and every router runs a distributed routing algorithm to enable packet forwarding. The present setup doesn't have the intelligence to reroute packets to an efficient path and maintain the heavy traffic due to large telecom transactions. One such application in telecom industry is the pre-paid charging system, which involves large volume of data transfer continuously taking place between Network Elements (NE). Due to high volume, the system is exposed to issues like network outage frequently which in turn degrades the overall (or specific location) network performance. These challenges have paved way for developing new norms for networking framework which is efficient and cost effective called Software Defined Networking (SDN). SDN allows network administrators to automatically and dynamically manage and control a large number of networking devices, service KPIs, topology, traffic paths and packet handling (i.e., Quality of Service) policies using high level language and APIs in a multitenant environment [1]. Thus by incorporating intelligence into this SDN controller with the use of machine learning techniques, the communication network can be made completely autonomous for future preemptive tasks.

SDN provides a dynamic enhancement to the current framework for the telecommunication industry. To meet the needs of exponentially growing network data scenario intelligently, integration of various IT technologies and virtualization techniques are needed. Telecom industries have to manage communications dynamically without any stoppage than any other industry. This data communication involves the location of customers, means of communication of the customers, handling Network Elements (NE) and methods of their business transactions. The data traffic involves bulk transfer of the network data, aggregation and partitioning of telecom subscribers data and control messages which are latency sensitive. SDN technology can be exploited to develop highly efficient applications. The features of SDN serve as a motivation to explore the design, architecture and framework details to build various applications in order to address typical network issues.

In the telecommunication industry, SDN has been trying to provide a flexible way of delivering quality in terms of bandwidth utilizations, efficient cloud based network optimizations and effectively handling subscriber's data [2]. In addition, SDN requires satisfying the core telecom demands in terms of providing proactive and optimized way of managing and handling network traffic thereby avoiding unnecessary traffic bursts [3]. In this paper, we have analyzed the capabilities of the enhancements of SDN in addressing packet loss due to network congestions and compared it with the capabilities of traditional networking systems. We have also provided an insight into integrating the Online Charging System (OCS) with SDN framework to identify the network variations in the flows and prevent failures occurring due to network outburst and congestions when similar flows are encountered. The failures in the charging system network elements or sudden deviations in the bandwidth utilizations of network will result in unnecessary spikes in CPU causing traffic congestion which results in loss of transactions in the network and reduces the operator's knowledge in Quality of Experience (QoE). This can be addressed by bringing up a new instance of network element and routing traffic to it in order to autonomously balance the load. In our experiment the threshold (i.e. No. of packets received on a particular port) is pre-fixed (i.e. already derived using machine learning), which are monitored by SDN controller. When the threshold is reached, a new host is added dynamically, which minimizes the packet loss when compared with early methods where network outage is detected by SDN and then new node is deployed. Implementation of the proposed idea on a real-time telecom environment straightaway is quite challenging considering the practical difficulties. Therefore, we have used the network emulator called MININET [4] to perform relevant experiments and to address similar network traffic issues. Hence, our paper focuses on the discussion in detail about the work flow of the proposed extension in SDN framework with machine learning, relevant use cases, and the experimental results. Finally we conclude with the merits and demerits of the proposed framework.

2   Related Studies

Telecommunication industry has moved from 3G to 4G mobile networks and it is progressing towards 5G to control and effectively handle the large volume transactions. The volume of data generated is increasing, thus industries which were earlier handling multiple terabytes of data are now handling data in petabytes. Moreover the advent of IPv6 would create enormous number of IP addresses which in turn would lead to the exponential growth of internet of connected devices [2]. This increased volume of data in the telecom sector demands new operational challenges. There are various kinds and format of data flooding into the telecom industry due to the advent of social media, cellular devices, location sensors, etc. It involves heterogeneous data which includes structured data in the form of traditional databases and unstructured data comprising of audio, video, text documents, stock ticker data, email and financial transactions. The most challenging task is to manage, merge and govern these data items, including the signaling data in OCS. In addition to this, the number of subscribers using mobile phones, especially smart phones is exponentially increasing, which in turn increases the stress in network elements due to high signaling data load in OCS. Signaling data in OCS systems are latency sensitive, which in turn are affected by high volume of data load. OCS signaling data delay degrades network performance and must be handled in a timely manner. Communication service providers have a tough time in handling data and service velocities in the present load. All these aspects together prevent the service providers to provide best service to their subscribers.

In comparison to the evolution of data systems to handle telecom service provider's data, network management and control systems should also be enhanced as the current systems are not efficient enough to transfer data which are real time and latency sensitive. It has also become extremely difficult to configure huge OCS networks, which might span in multiple locations in service providers' network. SDN is an evolving technology which can successfully address these issues. Wang et al. [5] provided an insight of incorporating SDN with telecom applications and have analyzed

SDN's architecture in a telecom operator's view. Ferrer et al. [6] have proposed an approach to address the complex Virtual Network Functions scheduling problem in the SDN domain. From another explorative study [7], we noted down the positional changes of SDN and NFV under a complementary and unified framework especially in future carrier networking domain. We also understood the capabilities of combining SDN controller with optical switching to explore tight integration of application and network control [8].

Open Networking Foundation (ONF) looks SDN as a new networking framework which originates or invents OPENFLOW protocol to simplify and generate new standard in networking [9]. It has been mainly developed in order to change routing policies on the fly, to have an easier programming framework and to serve as an operating system for networks. Figure 1 specifies the existing components of SDN framework.

The software defined networking which consists of OPENFLOW switches is controlled by the high powered centralized server called the SDN controller. SDN Applications can be developed by exploiting this framework and they interact with the controller using northbound APIs while the controller controls the underlying network using southbound APIs. SDN has the capability of creating a programmable network by considering both next generation systems and existing infrastructure making them more dynamic and flexible [10]. It is efficiently achieved by integrating essentially different systems and technologies together under a common monitoring and management. SDN is directly programmable, agile, centrally managed and open standards-based vendor

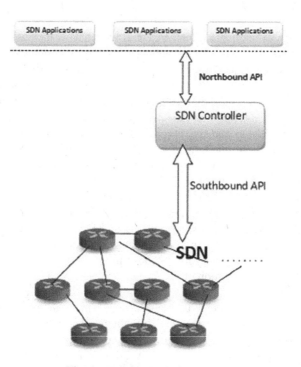

Fig. 1. Existing SDN framework

neutral architecture [11]. Certain benefits of SDN include virtualization, orchestration, dynamic scaling, automation, visibility, performance, multi-tenancy, openness and service integration [9]. In this paper, to utilize benefits of SDN usage, we developed a new application called ARMD to address unexpected traffic outbursts/congestions in OCS attached to SDN controller.

3 Telecom Domain Use Cases and Relevant Solutions

In this paper, we are providing an insight on the integration of SDN with OCS telecom network architecture to introduce two new practices specifically.

3.1 New Practices

First practice is to introduce network element monitoring to intelligently reroute the traffic and the second practice deals with the specific type of patterns and related intelligence incorporated in SDN to bring up a virtual instance of the network node dynamically during peak hours. To streamline the first practice, the traffic flow level and the network usage over a period of time needs to be monitored continuously. The changes with respect to the traffic disturbances should be alerted and handled proactively without causing service discontinuity and providing seamless service to the subscribers.

3.2 Execution Procedures

The traffic flowing through the charging system networking nodes could be continuously monitored by SDN controller. We would like to include all OCS network functions, which are monitored by SDN controller for network usages like bandwidth, load on NE, etc. SDN controller acts as an orchestration of OCS Network Function Virtualization (NFV). NFV uses software implementation of network functions called Virtual Network Functions (VNF) to deploy virtual network nodes into the underlying network [12]. SDN keeps monitoring load spikes in the OCS network functions. Usually, online charging traffic will increase during holidays or weekends or festival seasons due to many customers initiating enormous number of voice calls, text messages and MMS messages. This will create an operationally high volume of stress in OCS network nodes, which causes telecom service disruptions. To avoid this, an application can be developed to monitor the traffic load pattern in OCS network elements on a regular schedule. Based on the load pattern witnessed the application built over the controller instructs OCS network through the SDN controller, to deploy additional OCS network elements dynamically at the operator's site, thereby reducing the service outage during peak hours. Since the network elements are dynamically deployed on need basics, it will reduce online charging service unavailability and increase operator's revenue and also reduces OPEX cost. To introduce new practices, we have developed an Autonomous Resource Monitoring and Deployer (ARMD) application above (but connected to) the SDN controller which monitors the network and deploys new hosts into the network based on the requirements.

4 Workflow of SDN Controlled ARMD Application

This section describes the workflow of SDN controlled ARMD Application integrated with SDN. In Fig. 2 various stages of the application features are specified.

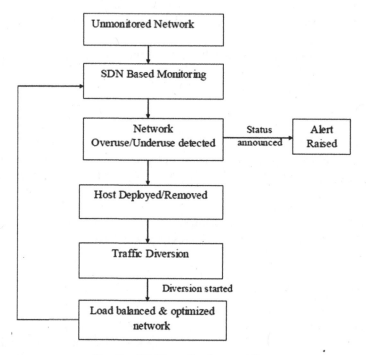

Fig. 2. ARMD application workflow

4.1 Unmonitored Network

The unmonitored network here refers to the network which is not controlled or monitored by the SDN controller. The network unless being changed manually, remains static. It is prone to packet loss and congestions. SDN based monitoring along with the incorporation of ARMD application will enable these capabilities and make the network intelligent enough to handle congestions.

4.2 SDN Controller Based Monitoring

SDN controller visualizes the global network view of the underlying network and understands the current scenario. The abstract view of the underlying network is presented to the ARMD application. The application is capable of capturing the packets received count on the ports of every switch present in the network.

4.3 Network Overuse/Underuse Detected

Every host present in the network is capable of handling only certain load after which the host may fail or will not be in a position to handle client requests. This scenario may result in packet loss which in turn might affect the operator's QoE. On the contrary, if the network is deployed with nodes greater than required, it makes the network underused which may result in unnecessary resource wastage. To avoid such discrepancies in the network, the ARMD application adds or removes hosts to or from the network based on certain threshold value (This value is learned based on the experiments). If the packets received count of a particular port exceeds the upper-bound, network overuse is detected and similarly if the packets received count of a port is found to be below the lower-bound, network underuse is detected. The alert is raised to explicitly intimate the internal counter-action taken by the application.

4.4 Host Deployed/Removed

After congestion or network overuse detection on a particular port, a virtual node/host is deployed dynamically through the controller to balance the load. In the same way if network underuse is detected, the corresponding host which has no traffic for a considerable amount of time will be removed from the network. Thus using ARMD application, hosts are being dynamically added to or removed from the network based on the network usage.

4.5 Traffic Diversion

Once the hosts are added to the network or removed from the network, traffic should be diverted. Traffic diversion is accomplished by reassigning the IP addresses of the hosts being removed or added. By enabling appropriate traffic diversion, there could hardly be any packet loss in the network.

4.6 Load Balanced and Optimized Network

The network always remains load balanced and optimized due to the use of ARMD application. Hosts are deployed dynamically when needed and removed if not required. In addition to load balancing, optimal use of resources is also ensured. Thus by using ARMD application with the SDN controller we can explore optimal, cost-effective and dynamic networks based on the operator requirement.

5 Developing Application in SDN Framework

To develop new application in SDN framework, we require OPENFLOW switches, Telecom nodes (hosts), an SDN controller, Southbound APIs and Northbound APIs. The SDN controller has the capability to monitor only the SDN aware OPENFLOW switches. Thus, building an application for the real-time SDN framework is challenging

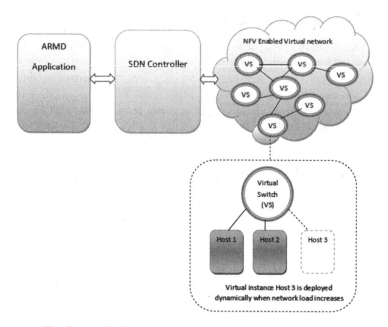

Fig. 3. ARMD for virtual network controlled SDN framework

and has some practical difficulties. Therefore, we have used a network emulator called MININET [4] for our experiments. Figure 3 depicts the virtual network created by MININET and controlled by SDN controller through the decisions made by the ARMD application.

5.1 ARMD Application

The ARMD *Application* is an intelligent module written to establish explicit, direct and programmatic communication with the SDN Controller via Northbound APIs (REST APIs). It communicates with the controller to provide awareness about the network requirements and to achieve desired network behavior. In addition, it requires an abstracted view of the network for its internal decision making purpose. It consists of telecom use case relevant logic along with one or more NBI Drivers.

5.2 SDN Controller

The SDN Controller is a logically centralized entity in charge of (i) translating the requirements from the SDN Application layer down to the SDN Data paths (logical network device) and (ii) providing the SDN Applications with an abstract view of the network which may include statistics and events. Control decisions are taken by the controller which includes dynamic deployment or removal of network nodes and traffic diversion through other nodes. An SDN Controller consists of more than one NBI

Agent, the SDN Control Logic, and the Control to Data-Plane Interface (CDPI) driver. The controller establishes connection with the underlying network via Southbound APIs such as OPENFLOW.

5.3   Virtual Network

The logical network devices referred to as Virtual Switches (VS) are being introduced and controlled by the SDN controller that can be emulated by MININET [4]. It has the capability to create realistic virtual network with simple commands. Users can also create custom topologies by running user-defined python scripts. MININET CLI enables the users to interact with the network. It creates virtual hosts with separate IP addresses. However it is possible to create desired number of hosts. It creates OPENFLOW software switch VS with ports. Different switch topologies can be created and these virtual switches created by MININET are capable of being monitored by the controller. Moreover, it connects the OPENFLOW switch with each virtual host via a virtual Ethernet cable and each host is assigned with a MAC address corresponding to its IP address. It also configures the OPENFLOW switch created, to connect to a remote controller. The inputs from the ARMD application makes the controller take dynamic decisions which are enforced on the virtual network. Figure 3 depicts OCS running on two hosts, Host 1 and Host 2. Whenever the threshold count is reached, the ARMD application observes and intimates it to the SDN controller which in turn dynamically deploys a new virtual instance Host 3 proactively. These decisions taken on the fly make the underlying network evolve gradually to handle network congestions autonomously.

6   Implementation of ARMD in SDN Framework

Due to practical difficulties in the implementation of our procedures in real-time network traffic, we have simulated the network congestion manually, by explicitly setting a valid threshold as per the experience gained. Once the threshold count is reached, the application gives instruction to the network emulator (MININET) to make changes to the current network via the SDN controller to minimize packet loss. The network changes are imposed by detecting the port that is overloaded (No. of packets received on a particular port increases the given threshold), addition of a new host to the network and reassigning the IP of the overloaded/failed host to the newly added host. We are explicitly making the host go down to illustrate the congestion in the network. In real-time setup the host will automatically fail due to high network traffic.

For this entire process to take place programmatically (with the help of SDN controller and the ARMD application developed above the controller), maximum of 3 packets are lost. However in certain cases there is lesser packet loss. But when this process is done manually, the packet loss is phenomenally high. On an average 40 to 45 packets are lost for these changes to take place even if congestion is detected immediately and this loss count may vary based on the factors like time taken to detect the congestion in the network, time taken to deploy a new host and re-assign IP and time

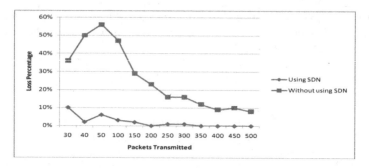

Fig. 4. Comparison of loss percentage in network with and without using SDN

taken to divert traffic flow to the newly added host. Figure 4 depicts the packet loss in the network in comparison with traditional system. It clearly shows the distinction of packet loss during the stages of packet transmission after extending the SDN framework with machine learning for this application.

After successful implementation of the proposed idea with MININET emulator, we would like to extend this setup to real-time networks by addressing the practical difficulties. Each and every virtual component created should be replaced by exactly same physical component. SDN controller is capable of monitoring only OPENFLOW switches, thus virtual switches should be replaced by real ones and they should be configured to address the procedures. After performing the physical setup, when MININET is initiated, SDN controller has a view of physical network of switches functioning in real-time.

One main limitation of using MININET is its inefficiency or lack of performance particularly at high loads. It is uncertain that a host that is prepared to send packets would be scheduled correctly and the rate at which the switches transmit would be the same. Currently, MININET has the capability to run only on a single machine. All the switches, hosts and Ethernet links are emulated on a single operating system. This limitation restricts all the network elements to share the same resources which turns out to be a great disadvantage to span the system on a large scale. Although not appropriate for substantially large scale simulations, MININET is a great network emulator for prototyping and testing network traffic.

7   Possible Extensions in Telecom Sector Using Machine Learning

SDN framework can be extended for various applications in the telecom domain. In this section, we have suggested an insight on how new applications could be built by extending the SDN framework with the use of Machine Learning techniques. We expect this possible extension can introduce more autonomous, security and intelligence in communications networks.

7.1 Suggesting the Use of Machine Learning Techniques

A learning agent could be built above the SDN controller which enables dynamic reconfiguration of network based on traffic estimates. The agent gets information about the underlying network, learns the network behavior and stores the details about the network congestions. Thus the agent contains the previous history of congestions. Machine Learning techniques could be employed to understand the dynamic nature of the networks and train the system accordingly. As a result, the learning agent gradually learns about network, stores all the learnt information and predicts discrepancies in the network before they occur based on the past learning experiences. The agent interacts with the SDN controller to dynamically configure the monitored network and also help to fix few needed thresholds.

Figure 5 describes about various modules of the learning agent which interact with each other to exert necessary changes to the network being controlled by the SDN controller. The knowledge base present in the learning agent has extracted knowledge about the current and previous network configuration states. Watchdog signal from the network elements represents various conditions of the network such as latency; link availability info etc., with this information the knowledge base provides feedback to the learning element. Considering the feedback and past learnt history, the learning element derives new interesting patterns or matches current pattern with the already learnt pattern. After pattern matching is performed it sets learning goals for the problem generator. Appropriate counter actions for the network congestion problems could be employed. The performance of the new decisions is evaluated by the performance element and the evaluated results are provided as a necessary base for new directions that will be considered in future. For example, in this application, a prediction-based technique is used to understand the exact threshold to introduce new host.

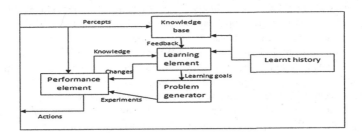

Fig. 5. Learning agent

8 Conclusion and Future Work

Our idea is an explorative work of integrating SDN framework in communication network by introducing new ARMD application. This will make the applications network aware rather than having traditional networking systems with application awareness. The telecom prepaid business models guarantee revenue assurance to operators, service assurance to subscribers and also quality of service for the products. Since the prepaid charging market is dynamic in nature, operators face a huge pressure in maintaining the QoS. It involves large OPEX cost to the operators. Hence the proposed enhancement in SDN framework with machine learning techniques introduces an automatic system to monitor the network elements and dynamically deploy additional nodes when the traffic is increased as well as remove the additional nodes in the network when the traffic decreases. The SDN controller in conjunction with the ARMD application helps in achieving this milestone by providing dynamic routing of traffic within network elements and reduces the packet loss significantly. Running the system in a completely parallelized architecture involving multiple controllers and streaming of data by the controller, data and service parallelization is also equally challenging. We are more interested to run the proposed framework in a real-time system by incorporating machine learning techniques to make the system completely autonomous and to achieve greater efficiency in handling high volume communication networks.

References

1. Humernbrum, T., Glinka, F., Gorlatch, S.: Using software- defined networking for real-time Internet applications. In: Proceedings of the International Multi-conference of Engineers and Computer Scientists, vol. I, IMECS 2014, Hong Kong, 12–14 March 2014
2. The real-time cloud. Ericsson White paper Uen 284 23-3219 Rev B, February 2014
3. http://www.radisys.com/solutions/telecom-solutions/telecom-cloud-sdn-nfv/
4. http://www.mininet.org
5. Wang, J.-Q., Fu, H., Cao, C.: Software defined networking for telecom operators: architecture and applications. In: 2013 8th International ICST Conference on Proceedings of the Communications and Networking in China (CHINACOM), pp. 828–833, 14–16 August 2013
6. Ferrer Riera, J., Escalona, E., Batalle, J., Grasa, E., Garcia-Espin, J.A.: Virtual network function scheduling: concept and challenges. In: 2014 International Conference on Smart Communications in Network Technologies (SaCoNeT), pp. 1–5, 18–20 June 2014
7. Haleplidis, E., Denazis, S., Koufopavlou, O., Lopez, D., Joachimpillai, D., Martin, J., Salim, J.H., Pentikousis, K.: ForCES applicability to SDN-enhanced NFV. In: 2014 Third European Workshop on Software Defined Networks (EWSDN), pp. 43–48, 1–3 September 2014
8. Software-Defined Networking: The New Norm for Networks. White paper, Open Networking Foundation, 13 April 2012
9. SDN Architecture Overview. Openetworking.org. Accessed 22 Nov 2014
10. Wang, G., Eugene Ngy, T.S., Shaikh, A.: Programming your network at run-time for big data applications. IBM T.J. Watson Research Center, Rice University, ACM, August 2012. 978-1-4503-1477-0
11. SDN and the Future of Service Provider Networks. White paper, Fujitsu Network Communications Inc. (2013)
12. Network Functions Virtualisation – Introductory White Paper. ETSI, 22 October 2012. Accessed 20 June 2013

Author Index

Printed in the United States
By Bookmasters